A People and a Nation

A History of the United States

Volume I: To 1877

FIFTH EDITION

Mary Beth Norton
Cornell University

David M. Katzman
University of Kansas

Paul D. Escott
Wake Forest University

Howard P. Chudacoff
Brown University

Thomas G. Paterson
University of Connecticut

William M. Tuttle, Jr.
University of Kansas

Houghton Mifflin Company   Boston   New Y

Senior sponsoring editor: Patricia A. Coryell
Senior associate editor: Jeffrey Greene
Basic book editor: Ann West
Senior project editor: Carol Newman
Senior production/design coordinator: Carol Merrigan
Manufacturing manager: Florence Cadran

Cover design: Henry Rachlin
Cover image: Miss Liberty, Barenholz Collection, Museum of American Folk Art.

About the Buttons

The icons used for the chapter title pages and headings within each chapter are photographs of buttons dating from the late nineteenth century. The button used in Volume I is a brass cutout of wheat over a wood background. The button for Volume II, known by collectors as "Brooklyn Bridge," is stamped brass. It may have been produced to commemorate the opening of the bridge in 1883. Picture buttons were popular in the late nineteenth century for women's clothing, often to celebrate major events, plays, and operas. Both buttons, despite their different appearance, were likely constructed from the same manufacturing technique—using a die to strike metal and then assembled into buttons with a wire shank at the back.

Printed in the U.S.A.

Library of Congress Catalog Card Number: 97-72527

ISBN: 0-395-78883-8

123456789-VH-01 00 99 98 97

Brief Contents

Keadey
1/98

Contents

14

Slavery and America's Future: The Road to War, 1845–1861 *375*

15

Transforming Fire: The Civil War, 1861–1865 *403*

16

Reconstruction: A Partial Revolution, 1865–1877 *443*

Appendix *A-1*

Index *I-1*

Charts

Maps

Preface

Some twenty years ago, when we first embarked on this textbook-writing adventure, most survey texts adequately covered American politics and diplomacy, important historical events, and the famous people at the top of the hierarchy of power, but something was missing: the stories of ordinary Americans. Our experience as teachers told us that, although a rich scholarship in social history had emerged, it was not yet being incorporated into survey texts. We set out to weave this significant dimension of American history into the traditional fabric of party politics, congressional legislation, wars, economic patterns, and local and state government. The response to our approach proved exceptionally gratifying.

As we wrote subsequent editions, always challenged by enriching scholarship, the task changed from "inserting" social history to integrating it fully into the historical narrative and treating social history not only as the study of the private lives of Americans but also as power relationships among competing groups that looked to the public sphere of politics and government to mediate their differences. In this new edition we especially worked to accomplish this new task. After all, like other teachers and students, we are always re-creating our past, restructuring our memory, rediscovering the personalities and events that have shaped us, inspired us, and bedeviled us. This book represents our rediscovery of America's history—its diverse people and the nation they created and have sustained. As this book demonstrates, there are many different Americans and many different memories. We have sought to present all of them, in both triumph and tragedy, in both division and unity.

After meeting in frank and searching planning sessions, critiquing one another's work, and reading numerous evaluations of the fourth edition of *A People and a Nation*, we developed a plan for this edition. Guided by up-to-date scholarship, we decided to place new emphasis on several themes and subjects that we had discussed in previous editions but believed needed more attention: the interaction of the private sphere of everyday life with the public sphere of politics

New Thematic Emphases

and government; grassroots movements; religion; the emerging cultural globalism of American foreign relations; the development of the American West; and the relationship of people to the land, including conflict over access to natural resources. By reexamining every sentence, editing every paragraph, and condensing, reconfiguring, and reconceptualizing chapters (see below), we accomplished a thorough revision (reducing the book by one chapter) while including a considerable amount of fresh material for new emphases, examples, and interpretations.

As before, we challenge students to think about the meaning of American history, not just to memorize facts. Through a readable narrative about all of the American people, we invite students to take themselves back in time to experience what it was like to live in—and to make life's choices in—a different era. Chapter-opening vignettes that dramatically recount stories of people contending with their times help define the key questions of a chapter (two-thirds of the vignettes are new to this edition). Succinct, focused introductions and conclusions frame each chapter. Illustrations, graphs, tables, and maps tied closely to text encourage visual and statistical explorations. We do not detail historiographical debates, but we acknowledge interpretations different from our own, and in the "Suggestions for Further Reading" sections at the end of each chapter we cite works with varying points of view to demonstrate that the writing of history is very much infused with debate.

Especially successful in the fourth edition, and strengthened here, is the "How Do Historians Know?" feature, which explains how historians go about using evidence to arrive at conclusions. In this highlighted section, our discussion—coupled with illustrations—explores how historians can draw conclusions from a variety of sources: crafts, political cartoons, maps, medical records, diaries, tape recordings, postcards, census data, telegrams, popular art, photographs, and more. This feature also helps students to understand how scholars can claim knowledge about historical events and trends. More than half of these discussions are new to this edition.

"How Do Historians Know?"

A People and a Nation is comprehensive in its treatment of the many ways in which Americans have defined themselves—by gender, race, class, region, ethnicity, religion, sexual orientation—and of the many subjects that have reflected Americans' multidimensional experiences: social, political, economic, diplomatic, military, environmental, intellectual, cultural, and more. We highlight the remarkably diverse everyday life of the American people—in cities and on farms and ranches, in factories and in corporate headquarters, in neighborhood meetings and in powerful political chambers, in love relationships and in hate groups, in recreation and in the workplace, in the classroom and in military uniform, in secret national security conferences and in public foreign relations debates, in church and in prison, in polluted environments and in conservation areas. We pay particular attention to lifestyles, diet and dress, family life and structure, labor conditions, gender roles, and childbearing and child rearing. By discussing music, sports, theater, print media, film, radio, television, graphic arts, and literature—in both "high" culture and "low" culture—we explore how Americans have entertained and informed themselves.

How We Study the Past

The private sphere of everyday life always interacts with the public sphere of politics and government. To understand how Americans have sought to protect their different ways of life and to work out solutions to thorny problems, we emphasize their expectations of government at the local, state, and federal levels; government's role in providing answers; the lobbying of interest groups; the campaigns and outcomes of elections; and the hierarchy of power in any period. Because the United States has long been a major participant in world affairs, we explore America's descent into wars, interventions in other nations, empire building, immigration patterns, images of foreign peoples, cross-national cultural ties, and international economic trends.

Major Changes in This Edition

Mary Beth Norton, who had primary responsibility for Chapters 1 through 8, further developed her comparative focus in Chapters 1 and 2, explaining the growth of contrasting American, African, and European societies in the colonial world, giving new attention to the Spanish borderlands. Chapter 3 includes new discussion of the introduction of slavery into English mainland colonies and comparisons with New France and the Spanish borderlands. Chapter 4 has been recast with new emphasis on intercultural interactions among Indians and Europeans and comparisons of families in New France, the Spanish borderlands, and the English colonies (including Indian and mixed-race families). Chapter 7 includes new material on economic/fiscal issues in the Confederation period.

David M. Katzman, who had primary responsibility for Chapters 9, 10, 12, and 13, rewrote to emphasize the role of the federal government and debates over centralized political authority. New emphases are found in his discussion of the conquering of the West (including a new vignette featuring Lewis and Clark in Chapter 9) and the growth of a Mexican-American culture in the Southwest (Chapter 12). He also widened his presentation of ethnic diversity, mental health reform, family and marriage (including divorce laws and women's property legislation), and manifest destiny.

Paul D. Escott, who had primary responsibility for Chapters 11, 14, 15, and 16, introduced new material on the westward movement of slaveholders and slaves and attitudes toward centralized government, African-American soldiers during the Civil War, and Confederate relations with Indians in the West. A new chart details the unprecedented losses of the Civil War, and several new and rarely seen photographs capture the drama of the Civil War period on many levels.

Howard P. Chudacoff, who had primary responsibility for Chapters 17 through 21 and 24, added new material on and gave new thematic emphasis to land (and water) control, conflict over access to natural resources, and environmental management in a newly titled Chapter 17, "The Development of the West and South, 1877–1892." Multiracial composition and racial tensions in the West are highlighted in Chapters 17 and 19, and new material is also presented on home life—indoor and family amusements and the impact of engineers and technology on household life—in Chapter 19. Chudacoff also reworked the section on agrarian protest and Populism, especially in the Rockies and Far West, and reconceptualized Gilded Age politics, adding the religio-cultural dimension (Chapter 20). To his discussion of Progressive reform (Chapter 21), he added coverage of women's clubs, the National Consumer's League, and federal policy on resource conservation. In his new account of the 1920s (Chapter 24), he emphasized the clash between "tried-and-true" and "modern" values and added new references to lobbying as a major influence in political decision making.

Thomas G. Paterson, who had primary responsibility for Chapters 22, 23, 26, 29, and 30, gave added emphasis to the theme of cultural relations and the conditioning of the foreign relations decision-making environment by ideology and images of foreign peoples. For Chapter 22, he included new material on relations with Africa, Canada, China, Chile, and Hawaii and on international environmental agreements. In Chapter 23, on the First World War, the role of women in the peace movement, African-American attitudes toward the war, the economic impact of the war, and treatment of the war dead also received added attention. In Chapter 26, newly titled "Peaceseekers and Warmakers: United States Foreign Relations, 1920–1941," Paterson integrated new material on the role of nongovernmental organizations such as the Rockefeller Foundation and the Americanization of Europe. As part of the restructuring of the post-1945 chapters in the text, Chapters 29 and 30 carry the foreign relations story to the present. These chapters, well cross-referenced, especially reflect the post–Cold War declassification of documents from foreign sources (Russian, Chinese, and German, for example). Here the reader will discover new examinations of the origins of the Korean War, the Cuban missile crisis, Japan's "economic miracle," covert activities of the Central Intelligence Agency, human rights, United States Information Agency propaganda, the Middle East peace process, Haiti, and the debate over foreign aid. In lengthy coverage of the Vietnam War, Paterson included new material on Ho Chi Minh's relationship with Americans in 1945, the Tonkin Gulf crisis, and the My Lai massacre.

William M. Tuttle, Jr., had primary responsibility for Chapters 25 and 27, and the post-1945 Chapters 28 and 31 through 33. In Chapter 25, he added new material on Social Security and the end of the New Deal. In Chapter 27 on the Second World War, readers will find new discussions of race and ethnic relations, women and children, and the decision to drop the atomic bomb. Tuttle substantially rewrote and reorganized the material on post-1945 domestic history, reducing the number of chapters covering this period by one. In a new Chapter 28 he interweaves the political, economic, social, and cultural history from 1945 to 1961, adding fresh material on Cold War politics, civil rights, and the baby boom. Chapter 31 takes the story from 1961 to 1974, shedding new light on the Equal Rights Amendment, women in the civil rights movement, *Roe v. Wade*, and Richard Nixon and the Watergate tapes. The next chapter incorporates recent studies on economic woes, the new immigration from Latin America and Asia, social polarization, and the rise of political and cultural conservatism in the 1970s and 1980s. Chapter 33, which concludes the book, is a new history of the 1990s, focusing on Americans' political disaffection and on their hopes and fears as they approach the twenty-first century.

The multidimensional Appendix, prepared by Thomas G. Paterson, includes a new, extensive table on the "Fifty States, the District of Columbia, and Puerto Rico." Here students will discover essential information on dates of admission with rank, capital cities, population with rank, racial/ethnic distribution, per capita personal income with rank, and total area in square miles. Once again, the Appendix begins with a guide to reference works on key subjects in American history. Students may wish to use this updated and enlarged list of encyclopedias, atlases, chronologies, and other books when they start to explore topics for research papers, when they seek precise definitions or dates, when they need biographical profiles, or when they chart territorial or demographic changes. The table of statistics on key features of the American people and nation also have been updated and expanded, as have the tables on presidential elections, the cabinet members of all administrations, party strength in Congress, and the justices of the Supreme Court.

Many instructors and students who have used this book in their courses have found its many learning and teaching aids very useful. The most exciting

Study and Teaching Aids

addition to our ancillary lineup is *@history: an interactive American history source*. This multimedia teaching/learning package combines a variety of material—primary sources (text and graphic), videos, audio, and links to Web sites—with activities that can be used to analyze, interpret, and discuss primary sources; to enhance collaborative learning; and to create multimedia presentations. *@history* provides instructors with an interactive multimedia tool that can improve the analytical skills of students and introduce them to historical sources.

The *Study Guide*, prepared by George Warren and Cynthia Ricketson of Central Piedmont Community College, includes an introductory chapter on studying history that focuses on interpreting historical facts, test-taking hints, and critical analysis. The guide also includes learning objectives, a thematic guide, lists of terms, multiple-choice and essay questions for each chapter, as well as map exercises and sections on organizing information for some chapters. An answer key alerts students to the correct response and also explains why the other choices are wrong.

A *Computerized Study Guide* is also available for students. It provides approximately 15 multiple-choice questions for each chapter and functions as a tutorial that gives students information on incorrect as well as correct answers. The computerized guide is available in Macintosh, IBM, and IBM-compatible formats.

A new *Instructor's Resource Manual*, prepared by Donald Frazier, Marvin Schultz, and Bruce Winders of Texas Christian University and Robert Pace of Longwood College, contains ten chronological resource units in addition to teaching ideas for each chapter of the textbook. Each chronological resource unit includes sections on geography, technology, physical and material culture (artifacts), historical sites, documentary films, popular films, and music. The manual also includes for each textbook chapter a content overview, a brief list of learning objectives, a comprehensive chapter outline, ideas for classroom activities, discussion questions, and ideas for paper topics.

A *Test Items* file, also prepared by George Warren, provides approximately 1,700 new multiple-choice questions, more than 1,000 identification terms, and approximately 500 essay questions.

A *Computerized Test Items File* for IBM and Macintosh computers is available to adopters. This computerized version of the printed *Test Items* file allows professors to create customized tests by editing and adding questions.

A set of full-color map transparencies is also available to instructors on adoption. A variety of videos—documentaries and docudramas by major film producers—is available for use with *A People and a Nation*.

At each stage of this project, historians read drafts of our chapters. Their suggestions, corrections, and pleas helped guide us through our revisions. We could not include all of their recommendations, but the book is better for our having heeded most of their advice.

Acknowledgments

We heartily thank

Diane Allen, *Columbia Gorge C*
David E. Conrad, *Southern Illinois*
Paige Cubbison, *Miami Dade Community College, Kendall*
Joseph A. Devine, Jr., *Stephen F. Austin State University*
Shirley M. Eoff, *Angelo State University*
Maurine Greenwald, *University of Pittsburgh*
Melanie Gustafson, *University of Vermont*
D. Harland Hagler, *University of North Texas*
Craig Hendricks, *Long Beach City College*
Robert Kenzer, *University of Richmond*
Timothy Koerner, *Oakland Community College*
Lisa M. Lane, *Miracosta College*
Larry MacLestch, *Mendocino College*
Jeff Ostler, *University of Oregon*
William Robbins, *Oregon State University*
Athan Theoharis, *Marquette University*
Lynn Weiner, *Roosevelt University*
Marianne S. Wokeck, *Indiana University–Purdue University of Indianapolis*
Gerald Wolff, *University of South Dakota*

Once again we thank the extraordinary Houghton Mifflin team who designed, edited, produced, and nourished this book. Their high standards and careful attention to both general structure and fine detail are unmatched in publishing. Many thanks to Jean Woy, editor-in-chief; Pat Coryell, senior sponsoring editor; Ann West, basic book editor; Jeffrey Greene, senior associate editor, Keith Mahoney, assistant editor; Carol Newman, senior project editor; Carol Merrigan, senior production/design coordinator; Charlotte Miller, art editor; and Florence Cadran, manufacturing manager.

For helping us in many essential ways, we also extend our thanks to Michael Donoghue, Jan D. Emerson, Steven Jacobson, Andrea Katzman, Eric Katzman, Sharyn Brooks Katzman, Walter D. Kamphoefner, G. Stanley Lemons, Pam Levitt, Shane J. Maddock, Jill Norgren, Aaron M. Paterson, Norman G. Radford, Zil-e-Rehman, Paul L. Silver, Peter Solonysznyi, Julee Stephens, Luci Tapahonso, Kathryn Nemeth Tuttle, Samuel Watkins Tuttle, and Daniel H. Usner, Jr. Some of these individuals sent us suggestions for improving *A People and a Nation*, and we took their recommendations seriously. We welcome comments from professors and students about this new edition, too.

For the authors, THOMAS G. PATERSON

The Authors

Mary Beth Norton

Born in Ann Arbor, Michigan, Mary Beth Norton received her B.A. from the University of Michigan (1964) and her Ph.D. from Harvard University (1969). She is now Mary Donlon Alger Professor of American History at Cornell University. Her dissertation won the Allan Nevins Prize. She has written *The British-Americans* (1972), *Liberty's Daughters* (1980), and *Founding Mothers and Fathers* (1996), which was one of three finalists for the Pulitzer Prize in 1997. She has coedited *To Toil the Livelong Day* (1987), *Women of America* (1979), and *Major Problems in American Women's History* (1995). Her articles have appeared in such journals as the *William and Mary Quarterly*, *Signs*, and the *American Historical Review*. Mary Beth has served on the National Council on the Humanities, as president of the Berkshire Conference of Women Historians, as vice president for research of the American Historical Association, and as general editor of the *AHA Guide to Historical Literature* (3rd edition, 1995). She has advised colleges on curriculum development in gender studies. The National Endowment for the Humanities, Guggenheim Foundation, and Rockefeller Foundation have assisted her scholarship.

David M. Katzman

Born in New York City and a graduate of Queens College (B.A., 1963) and the University of Michigan (Ph.D., 1969), David M. Katzman is professor of history and chair of American studies at the University of Kansas. He has written *Before the Ghetto* (1973) and *Seven Days a Week* (1978), which won the Philip Taft Labor History Prize. He has coedited *Plain Folk* (1982) and *Technical Knowledge in American Culture* (1996). He has also coauthored *Three Generations in Twentieth-Century America* (1982). David has been a visiting professor at University College, Dublin, Ireland, and at the University of Birmingham, England. He has also directed National Endowment for the Humanities Summer Seminars for College Teachers. He has sat on the Board of Directors of the National Commission on Social Studies and is coeditor of *American Studies*. At the University of Kansas, he is a former director of the College Honors Program. The Guggenheim Foundation, National Endowment for the Humanities, Ford Foundation, and Rockefeller Foundation have supported his research.

Paul D. Escott

Born and raised in the Midwest (St. Louis, Missouri), Paul D. Escott studied in New England (Harvard College, B.A., 1969) and the South (Duke University, Ph.D., 1974). He is Reynolds Professor of History and Dean of the College at Wake Forest University. He has written *After Secession* (1978), *Slavery Remembered* (1979), *Many Excellent People* (1985), and *A History of African Americans in North Carolina* (with Jeffrey J. Crow and Flora J. Hatley, 1992). Paul is the editor of *W. J. Cash and the Minds of the South* (1992) and coeditor of *Major Problems in the History of the American South* (with David R. Goldfield, 1990). His most recent publication is *North Carolina Yeoman* (1996). Paul's articles have appeared in *Civil War History*, *The Journal of Southern History*, and *The North Carolina Historical Review*. He was a member of the editorial board and a contributor to *The Encyclopedia of the Confederacy* (1993). The American Council of Learned Societies, Whitney M. Young, Jr., Foundation, and Rockefeller Foundation have assisted his research.

Howard P. Chudacoff

A professor of history at Brown University, Howard P. Chudacoff was born in Omaha, Nebraska. He earned his A.B. (1965) and Ph.D. (1969) degrees from the University of Chicago. He has written three books: *Mobile Americans* (1972), *The Evolution of American Urban Society* (with Judith Smith, 4th edition, 1993), and *How Old Are You?* (1989). He has also edited *Major Problems in American Urban History* (1993). His articles have appeared in such journals as the *Journal of Family History*, *Reviews in American History*, and *Journal of American History*. At Brown University, Howard has cochaired the American Civilization Program, chaired the department of history, and since 1990 has been faculty adviser to the women's basketball team. He has also served on the board of directors of the Urban History Association. The National Endowment for the Humanities, Ford Foundation, and Rockefeller Foundation have given him awards to advance his scholarship.

Thomas G. Paterson

Born in Oregon City, Oregon, and graduated from the University of New Hampshire (B.A., 1963) and the University of California, Berkeley (Ph.D., 1968), Thomas G. Paterson is professor of history at the University of Connecticut. He has written *Soviet-American Confrontation* (1973), *Meeting the Communist Threat* (1988), *On Every Front* (1992), *Contesting Castro* (1994), *American Foreign Relations* (with J. Garry Clifford and Kenneth J. Hagan, 1994), and *America Ascendant* (with Clifford, 1995). Tom has also edited *Kennedy's Quest for Victory* (1989), *Explaining the History of American Foreign Relations* (with Michael J. Hogan, 1991), and *Major Problems in American Foreign Relations* (with Dennis Merrill, 1994). With Bruce Jentleson he was senior editor for the four-volume *Encyclopedia of U.S. Foreign Relations* (1997). He has served on the editorial boards of the *Journal of American History* and *Diplomatic History*. He has been president of the Society for Historians of American Foreign Relations and has directed National Endowment for the Humanities Summer Seminars for College Teachers. His most recent award was a fellowship from the Guggenheim Foundation.

William M. Tuttle, Jr.

A native of Detroit, Michigan, William M. Tuttle, Jr., received his B.A. from Denison University (1959) and his Ph.D. from the University of Wisconsin (1967). A professor of history and American studies at the University of Kansas, Bill has written *Race Riot* (2nd edition, 1996) and *"Daddy's Gone to War"* (1993). He has also edited *W.E.B. DuBois* (1973) and coedited *Plain Folk* (1982). His articles have appeared in such journals as the *Journal of American History*, *American Studies*, and *Child Welfare*. He has been a research associate at the Institute of Human Development at the University of California, Berkeley. As a historical consultant, Bill has helped prepare several public television documentaries and docudramas, including *The Killing Floor*, which appeared on PBS's "American Playhouse." Bill's scholarly work has been assisted by the American Council of Learned Societies, Institute of Southern History at Johns Hopkins University, Charles Warren Center, Guggenheim Foundation, Stanford Humanities Center, Radcliffe College, and National Endowment for the Humanities. In 1995, Bill was awarded the Denison University Alumni Citation.

A
People
and a
Nation

1

Three Old Worlds Create a New
1492–1600

A t birth, she was called Malinalli. The Spaniards christened her Doña Marina. History knows her as Malinche, a name formed by adding the Aztec suffix *che*, a term of respect, to her original name. She has been celebrated as the symbolic mother of the modern Mexican people and maligned as a traitor to Mexico's ancient residents.

Born near the Gulf Coast of Mexico sometime between 1502 and 1505, Malinalli was the daughter of a cacique, or village chief, within the Aztec Empire. Her father died while she was young, and her mother soon remarried. To protect the inheritance of the son born to that second marriage, the mother sold her daughter into slavery. Eventually, Malinalli came to live with Mayan-speaking people in the province of Tabasco.

Along with nineteen other enslaved women, she was presented as a gift to the Spanish conquistador Hernán Cortés when he marched through Tabasco in 1519. Cortés, who first arrived in the Spanish West Indies in 1504, embarked for the mainland in search of wealthy cities rumored to exist there. Little did he know that the young woman whom the Spaniards baptized as a Christian and renamed Doña Marina would be one of the keys to his conquest of Mexico.

Doña Marina, who spoke both Nahuatl (the language of her birth and of the Aztecs) and Mayan (the language of her masters), and who soon learned Spanish, became Cortés's translator and mistress. She bore him a son, Martín—one of the first *mestizos*, or mixed-blood children. Accompanying Cortés on his travels in Mexico, she did more than simply interpret words for him: she explained the meanings that lay behind the language, opening the Aztec world to the Spaniards.

Bernal Diaz del Castillo, one of Cortés's lieutenants, greatly admired Doña Marina. In his *History of the Conquest of New Spain*, he observed that she was "a valuable instrument to us. . . . without her we never should have understood the Mexican language, and, upon the whole, have been unable to surmount many difficulties." The Aztecs even called Cortés "El Malinche," or "the captain of Marina," Bernal Diaz explained, because she "was always in his company, especially when ambassadors arrived and during talks with chiefs." The Aztecs and subsequent Mexican historians have blamed Malinche for betraying her own people. But who were her people? The Aztecs, in whose empire she had been born and who had sold her as a slave? The Mayas, among whom she was raised? Or the Europeans, who relied on her translations?

Malinche's life history, and her dual image as betrayer of ancient Mexico and symbolic mother of the modern mixed-race nation, encapsulate many of the ambiguities of the first encounter between Europeans and Americans. Sold into slavery by her Aztec-connected family, she owed that people little loyalty. The Spaniards gave her respect, yet she did not become Spanish: Cortés never married her, although she was the mother of his son. She did eventually marry one of Cortés's subordinates, but it is unclear whether she had any choice in the matter. Malinche may simply have been passed from one conquistador to another, much as her family sold her to slave traders or the Tabascans gave her to the Europeans.

Until she died around 1540, Malinche was caught between two worlds, part of both and of neither, alternately praised and blamed for her actions. Many people from both sides of the Atlantic were to meet the same fate as they attempted to cope with the rapidly changing world of the fifteenth and sixteenth centuries.

For thousands of years before 1492, human societies in the Americas had developed in isolation from the rest of the world. The era that began in the Christian fifteenth century brought that long-standing isolation to an end. As European explorers and colonizers sought to exploit the resources of the rest of the globe, peoples from different races and cultural traditions came into regular contact for the first time. All were profoundly changed by the resulting interaction. By the time Cortés and his troops invaded Mexico in 1519, the age of European expansion and colonization was already well under way. Over the next 350 years, Europeans would spread their influence across the globe. The history

of the tiny colonies in North America that became the first components of the United States must be seen in this broad context of European exploration and exploitation.

The continents that European sailors reached in the late fifteenth century had their own history, one the invaders largely ignored. The residents of the Americas were the world's most skillful plant breeders; they had developed vegetable crops more nutritious and productive than those grown in Europe, Asia, or Africa. They had invented systems of writing and mathematics and had created calendars fully as accurate as those used on the other side of the Atlantic. In the Americas, as in Europe, states rose and fell as leaders succeeded or failed at the goal of expanding their political and economic power. The Europeans' arrival in their world immeasurably altered the Americans' struggles with each other.

After 1400, European nations tried to improve their positions relative to neighboring countries not only by waging wars on their own continent but also by acquiring valuable colonies and trading posts elsewhere in the world. In response, nations in Asia, Africa, and the Americas attempted to use the alien intruders to their own advantage or, failing that, to adapt successfully to the Europeans' presence in their midst. All the participants in the resulting interaction of divergent cultures were indelibly affected by the process. The contest among Europeans for control of the Americas and Africa changed the course of history on four continents. Strategies selected by American and African leaders influenced the outcome of the Europeans' competition and determined the fates of their own societies. Although in the end Europeans emerged politically dominant, they did not control many aspects of the interactions among the divergent cultures of the Americas and Africa.

 American Societies

Human beings probably originated on the continent of Africa, where humanlike remains about 3 million years old have been found in what is now Ethiopia. Over many millennia, the growing human population slowly dispersed to the other continents. Because the climate was then far colder than it is now, much of the earth's water was concentrated in huge rivers of ice called glaciers. Sea levels were accordingly lower, and land masses covered a larger proportion of the earth's surface than they do today. About 30,000 years ago, a land bridge that scholars

• *Important Events* •

30,000–10,000 B.C.E.	Paleo-Indians began migrating from Asia to North American across the Beringia land bridge	1494	Treaty of Tordesillas divides land claims between Spain and Portugal in Africa, India, and South America
7000 B.C.E.	Cultivation of food crops begins in America	1496	Last of the Canary Islands falls to Spanish attack
c. 1000 B.C.E.	Olmec civilization appears	1497	John Cabot reaches North American coast
c. 300–600 C.E.	Height of influence of Teotihuacán	1513	Ponce de León explores Florida
c. 600–900 C.E.	Classic Mayan civilization	1518–30	Smallpox epidemic devastates Indian population of West Indies and Central and South America
1000 C.E.	Anasazi settlements in modern states of Arizona and New Mexico flourish as trading centers	1519	Hernán Cortés invades Mexico
1001	Norse establish settlement in "Vineland" (Newfoundland)	1521	Tenochtitlán surrenders to Cortés; Aztec Empire falls to Spaniards
1050–1250	Height of influence of Cahokia; prevalence of Mississippian culture in midwestern and southeastern United States	1534–35	Jacques Cartier explores St. Lawrence River
14th century	Aztec rise to power	1539–42	Hernando de Soto explores southeastern United States
1450s–80s	Portuguese explore and colonize islands in the Mediterranean Atlantic and São Tomé in Gulf of Guinea	1540–42	Francisco Vásquez de Coronado explores southwestern United States
1477	Publication of Marco Polo's *Travels*, describing China	1587–90	Sir Walter Raleigh's Roanoke colony vanishes
1492	Christopher Columbus reaches Bahama Islands	1588	Thomas Harriot publishes *A Briefe and True Report of the New Found Land of Virginia*

have called Beringia linked the Asian and North American continents at the site of the Bering Strait. Some of the peoples participating in the vast worldwide migration crossed this land bridge. When the climate warmed, the glaciers receded, and the sea levels rose about 10,000 years ago, those migrants were irrevocably separated from their fellow human beings who had remained on the connected continents of Asia, Africa, and Europe.

Those forerunners of the American population are known as Paleo-Indians. The earliest confirmed evidence of their presence in the Americas dates to approximately 28,000 years ago. The Paleo-Indians were nomadic hunters of game and gatherers of wild plants. Spreading throughout North and South America, they probably moved as extended families, or *bands*. By about 11,500 years ago the Paleo-Indians were mak-

Paleo-Indians

ing fine stone projectile points, which they attached to wooden spears and used to kill and butcher bison (buffalo), woolly mammoths, and other large mammals then living in the Americas. But as the Ice Age ended and the human population increased, all the large American mammals except the bison disappeared. Scholars cannot agree whether overhunting or the change in climate caused their demise. In either case, deprived of their primary source of meat, the Paleo-Indians had to find new ways of survival.

Consequently, by approximately 9,000 years ago, the residents of what is now central Mexico began to cultivate food crops, especially maize (corn), squash, beans, and peppers. In the Andes Mountains of South America, people started to grow potatoes. As knowledge of agricultural techniques improved and spread through the Americas, vegetables and

Importance of Agriculture

maize proved a more reliable source of food than hunting and gathering. Except for those living in the harshest climates, most Americans started to adopt a more sedentary style of life so they could tend fields regularly. Some established permanent settlements; others moved several times a year among fixed sites. They became adept at clearing forests through the use of controlled burning. All the American cultures emphasized producing sufficient food to support themselves. Although they traded goods, no society ever became dependent on another group for items vital to its survival.

Wherever agriculture dominated the economy, complex civilizations flourished. Such societies, assured of steady supplies of grains and vegetables, no longer had to devote all their energies to subsistence. Instead, they were able to accumulate wealth, produce ornamental objects, and create elaborate rituals and ceremonies. In North America, the successful cultivation of nutritious crops such as maize, beans, and squash seems to have led to the growth and development of all the major civilizations: first the large city-states of Mesoamerica (modern Mexico and Guatemala), then the urban clusters known collectively as the Mississippian culture and located in the present-day United States. Each of these societies, many historians and archaeologists now believe, reached its height of population and influence only after achieving success in agriculture. Each later declined and collapsed after reaching the limits of its food supply, with dire political and military consequences. Even the powerful Aztec Empire that the Spaniards encountered in 1519 is thought to have been approaching the point at which it could no longer sustain its population.

The Aztecs were the heirs of a series of Mesoamerican civilizations, the history of which stretched back to the Olmecs, who about 3,000 years ago lived near the Gulf of Mexico in large cities dominated by temple pyramids. More than 1,000 years later, the Mayan civilization developed on the Yucatán Peninsula. The Mayas built large urban centers containing tall pyramids and temples with brightly painted stuccoed and carved façades. They studied astronomy, created the first writing system in the Americas, and developed a richly symbolic religious life in which rituals of bloodletting played a major role. By the fifth century C.E. (Common Era), or about 1,500 years ago, the kings of the Mayan city-states started to war with each other, attempting

Mesoamerican Civilizations

conquest on a grand scale. But no king or city could win total victory. Eventually, the constant fighting combined with overpopulation and resulting environmental stress to cause the collapse of the most powerful cities, ending the classic era of Mayan civilization by 900 C.E. By the time the Spaniards arrived, only a few remnants of the once-mighty society remained intact.

The largest Mesoamerican metropolis was contemporary with, and a major trading partner of, the Mayas. Teotihuacán, founded about 300 B.C.E. (Before the Common Era)—some 2,300 years ago—in the Valley of Mexico, was one of the largest cities in the world in the fifth century C.E., with a population of over 100,000. (By contrast, Paris had only about 10,000 residents at that time.) The rulers of Teotihuacán gained their position chiefly through commerce; their trading network extended hundreds of miles in all directions. Thousands of craftspeople lived in the city, many of whom were especially skilled in working the green glass called obsidian, which was valued throughout the region as a source of fine knives and mirrors. Teotihuacán also served as a religious center; pilgrims must have come long distances to visit the impressive Pyramid of the Sun, Pyramid of the Moon, and the great temple of Quetzalcoatl—the feathered serpent, the primary god of central Mexico.

Teotihuacán's influence was felt so widely in Mesoamerica before its decline in the eighth century C.E. that some scholars have argued that this Mexican city-state also influenced societies farther north, in what is now the United States. The Moundbuilders of the Ohio River region, who flourished about two thousand years ago, just as Teotihuacán rose to prominence, constructed earthen mounds. But the Ohioan mounds were used as burial sites, not as bases for temple pyramids. Also, the Moundbuilders' economy, which was based on hunting and gathering, bore little resemblance to that of Mesoamerica. Trade goods from as far away as the Great Lakes and the Gulf of Mexico have been found in the mounds, but direct evidence of contact with Teotihuacán is lacking.

Moundbuilders, Anasazi, and Mississippians

The same is true for sites inhabited by the Anasazi peoples in the modern states of Arizona and New Mexico. Pueblo Bonito in Chaco Canyon, a city that by 1000 C.E. consisted of many large adobe buildings constructed along the sides of the canyon, sat at the juncture of over 400 miles of roads and

Pueblo Bonito in Chaco Canyon in what is now the state of New Mexico. More than six hundred buildings were present on the well-defended site. The circular structures were kivas, used for food storage and for religious rituals.   David Muench photography.

served as a major regional trading center. The Anasazi cultivated maize and other Mesoamerican crops, but they did not construct temple pyramids, nor did their towns resemble those built by their contemporaries in what is now Mexico. Accordingly, scholars have concluded that their contact with Mesoamerica was slight.

More likely, Teotihuacán and later Mesoamerican empires like that of the Aztecs had an impact on the development of the Mississippian culture, which flourished around 1000 C.E. in what is now the midwestern and southeastern United States. (Indeed, the historian Francis Jennings has recently argued that some of the Mississippians were "colonists" dispatched from Teotihuacán.) This civilization, like those to the south, was based on the cultivation of maize, beans, and squash. Not until about 700 to 900 C.E. were these crops grown successfully in the present-day United States; soon after their introduction, large cities with plazas and earthen pyramids first appeared in the region. The largest of the cities was Cahokia, near modern St. Louis. At its peak (in the twelfth century), Cahokia covered more than 5 square miles and had a population of at least 15,000—small by Mesoamerican standards but larger than any other northern community. Like

Teotihuacán, Cahokia was a religious and trading center. Its main pyramid, today called the Monk's Mound, was in 1492 the third largest structure in the Western Hemisphere. Although Cahokia's power declined after about 1250 C.E., Spanish explorers encountered Mississippian peoples in present-day South Carolina, Alabama, and Georgia in the mid-sixteenth century. The Natchez, a society characterized by temple mounds and autocratic priestly rulers, survived in the lower Mississippi River valley until the 1720s.

The Aztecs' histories tell of the long migration of their people (who called themselves Mexica) into the Valley of Mexico during the twelfth century.

Aztecs

The uninhabited ruins of Teotihuacán, which by then had been deserted for at least two hundred years, awed and mystified the migrants. The Aztecs' primary god, Huitzilopochtli, was a god of war represented by an eagle. Aztec chronicles record that Huitzilopochtli directed the Aztecs to establish their capital at the spot on an island where they saw an eagle eating a serpent (thus symbolizing Huitzilopochtli's triumph over the traditional deity, Quetzalcoatl). That island city became Tenochtitlán, the center of a rigidly

How do historians know that the ruins of Teotihuacán "awed and mystified" the Aztecs (see page 7) when they arrived in the Valley of Mexico at least two hundred years after that city had been abandoned by its inhabitants? One striking indication of the Aztecs' attitude toward the earlier civilization is this beautiful greenstone mask with polished obsidian eyes, which was created at Teotihuacán. Archaeologists found it not there but rather in the ruins of the Aztecs' Templo Mayor, constructed in Tenochtitlán (the site of modern Mexico City) about a thousand years after the mask was sculpted. The temple had two sides, one dedicated to the war god Huitzilopochtli, the other to the rain god Tlaloc. The place where the two sides met was at the heart of the Aztecs' most sacred site. There they buried this mask, which they must have found at Teotihuacán, about 20 miles from Tenochtitlán. Although we cannot know for certain what the Aztecs intended to accomplish by this gesture, it seems reasonable to conclude that they hoped to draw on the mysterious powers that the mask (and the civilization it represented) symbolized for them. Had they not been awed by it, they never would have buried the mask where they did. Michel Zabe-Thiriat.

stratified society composed of hereditary classes of warriors, merchants, priests, common folk, and slaves.

The Aztecs conquered their neighbors and forced them to pay tribute in luxury items, raw materials, and human beings who could be sacrificed to Huitzilopochtli. They also engaged in ritual combat, known as "flowery wars," to obtain further sacrificial victims. The war god's taste for blood was not easily quenched. In the Aztec year Ten Rabbit (1502) at the coronation of Motecuhzoma II (the Spaniards could not pronounce his name correctly, so they called him Montezuma), five thousand people are thought to have been sacrificed by having their still-beating hearts torn from their bodies.

The Aztecs believed that they lived in the age of the Fifth Sun. Four times previously, they wrote, the earth and all the people who lived on it had been destroyed. They predicted that their own world would end in earthquakes and hunger. In the Aztec year Thirteen Flint, volcanoes erupted, sickness and hunger spread, wild beasts attacked the Aztecs' children, and an eclipse of the sun darkened the sky. Did some priest wonder whether the Fifth Sun was approaching its end? Eventually, the Aztecs learned that their year Thirteen Flint was called 1492 by the Europeans.

 North America in 1492

Over the centuries, the Americans who lived north of Mexico had adapted their once-similar ways of life to very different geographical settings, thus creating the diverse cultures that the Europeans encountered when they first arrived (see map, page 9). Bands that lived in environments not well suited to agriculture—because of inadequate rainfall or poor soil, for example—followed a nomadic lifestyle similar to that of the Paleo-Indians. Within the area of the present-day United States, these groups included the Paiutes and Shoshones, who inhabited the Great Basin (now Nevada and Utah). Because of the difficulty of finding sufficient food for more than a few people, such hunter-gatherer bands were small. They usually were composed of one or more related families, with men hunting small animals and women gathering seeds and berries. Where large game was more plentiful and food supplies therefore more certain, as in present-day Canada and the Great Plains, bands of hunters were somewhat larger.

In more favorable environments, larger groups combined agriculture with gathering, hunting, and fishing. Those who lived near the seacoasts, like the Chinooks of present-day Washington and Oregon,

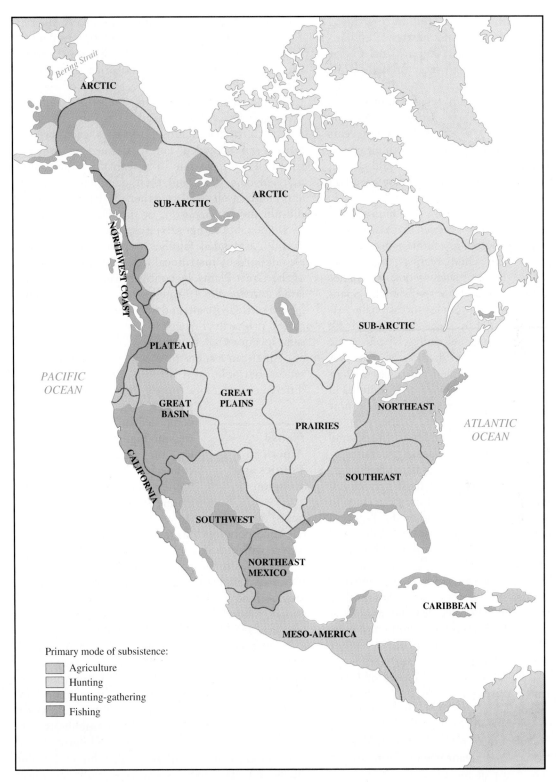

Native Cultures of North America *The natives of the North American continent effectively used the resources of the regions in which they lived. As this map shows, coastal groups relied on fishing, residents of fertile areas engaged in agriculture, and other peoples employed hunting (often combined with gathering) as a primary mode of subsistence.*

consumed fish and shellfish in addition to growing crops and gathering seeds and berries. Residents of the interior (for example, the Arikaras of the Missouri River valley) hunted large animals while also cultivating maize, squash, and beans. The Algonkian-speaking peoples of what is now eastern Canada and the northeastern United States also combined hunting and agriculture. Every few years they set fire to forests and underbrush to clear new fields, create open grasslands that would attract deer, and enrich the soil (the ashes made excellent fertilizer).

Societies that relied primarily on hunting large animals like deer and buffalo assigned that task to men and allotted food processing, clothing production, and child rearing to women.

Sexual Division of Labor in North America

Before such nomadic bands acquired horses from the Spaniards, women—occasionally assisted by dogs—also carried the family's belongings whenever the band relocated. Such a sexual division of labor was universal among hunting peoples, regardless of their location. Agricultural societies, by contrast, differed in their assignments of work to the sexes. In what is now the southwestern United States, the Pueblo peoples, who lived in sixty or seventy autonomous villages and spoke five different languages, defined agricultural labor as men's work. In the East, Algonkian, Iroquoian, and Muskogean peoples allocated most agricultural chores to women, although men cleared the land. In all the farming societies, women gathered wild foods, prepared food for consumption or storage, and cared for children, while men were responsible for hunting.

The southwestern and eastern agricultural peoples had similar social organizations. They lived in villages, sometimes sizable ones with a thousand or more inhabitants. The Pueblos, descendants of the Anasazi, lived in large, multistory buildings constructed on terraces along the sides of cliffs or other easily defended sites. Northern Iroquois villages (in modern New York State) were composed of large, rectangular, bark-covered structures, or long houses; the name Haudenosaunee (which the Iroquois called themselves) means "People of the Long House." In the present-day southeastern United States, Muskogeans and southern Algonkians lived in large houses made of thatch. Most of the eastern villages were surrounded by wood palisades and ditches to aid in fending off attackers. The defensive design of such villages and of the western pueblos discloses the sig-

nificance of warfare in pre-Columbian America. Long before the Europeans arrived, the residents of North America fought with each other for control of the best hunting and fishing territories, the most fertile agricultural lands, or the sources of essential items like salt (for preserving meat) and flint (for making knives and arrowheads).

In all these agricultural societies, each dwelling housed an extended family defined *matrilineally* (through a female line of descent). Mothers, their married daughters, and their daughters' husbands and children all lived together. Matrilineal descent did not imply *matriarchy*, or the wielding of power by women, but rather served as a means of reckoning kinship. Extended families were linked into *clans*, also defined by matrilineal ties. The nomadic bands of the Great Plains, by contrast, were most often related *patrilineally* (through the male line). They lacked settled villages and defended themselves from attack primarily through their ability to move to safer locations when necessary.

American leaders governed largely through consensus, but political structures in the various groups differed considerably. Among Pueblo and Muskogean peoples, the village council, composed of ten to thirty men, was the highest political authority; no government structure connected the villages. Nomadic hunters also lacked formal links among separate bands. The Iroquois, by contrast, had an elaborate political hierarchy incorporating villages into nations and nations into a widespread confederation. In all the North American cultures, political power was divided between civil and war leaders, who wielded authority only so long as they retained the confidence of the people. Autocratic rule of the sort common in Europe (see page 15) was foreign to these political systems.

Native American Politics and Religion

The political position of women varied. Women were more likely to assume leadership roles among agricultural peoples, especially those in which females were the primary cultivators, than among nomadic hunters. Squaw sachems (female rulers) led Algonkian villages in what is now Massachusetts, but women were never chosen as heads of hunting bands of the Great Plains. Iroquois women did not become chiefs, yet clan matrons exercised political power (see page 77). Probably the most powerful female chiefs were found in what is now the southeastern United States. In the mid-sixteenth century a female

Jacques Le Moyne, an artist accompanying the French settlement in Florida in the 1560s (see page 35), produced some of the first European images of North American peoples. His depiction of native agricultural practices shows the sexual division of labor: men breaking up the ground with fish-bone hoes before women drop seeds into the holes. But Le Moyne's version of the scene cannot be accepted uncritically: unable to abandon a European view of proper farming methods, he erroneously drew plowed furrows in the soil. John Carter Brown Library at Brown University.

ruler known as the Lady of Cofitachequi governed a large group of villages in present-day western South Carolina.

Americans' religious beliefs varied even more than did their political systems, but all the peoples were *polytheistic*, worshiping a multitude of gods. One common thread was their integration with nature. Thus each group's most important beliefs and rituals were closely tied to its economy. The major deities of agricultural peoples like the Pueblos and Muskogeans were associated with cultivation, and their chief festivals centered on planting and harvest. The most important gods of hunters (such as those living on the Great Plains) were associated with animals, and their major festivals were related to hunting. A band's economy and women's role in it helped to determine women's potential as religious leaders.

Women held the most prominent positions in those agricultural societies (like the Iroquois) in which they were also the chief food producers, whereas in hunting societies men took the lead in religious as well as political affairs.

A wide variety of cultures, comprising more than 5 million people, thus inhabited mainland North America when Europeans arrived. The hierarchical kingdoms of Mesoamerica bore little resemblance to the nomadic hunting societies of the Great Plains or to the agricultural societies that dominated a significant share of the continent. The diverse inhabitants of North America spoke well over one thousand different languages. For obvious reasons, they did not consider themselves one people, nor did they—for the most part—think of uniting to repel the European invaders. Instead, each village or band continued to try to better its circumstances relative to its neighbors, regardless of whether those neighbors were of American or European origin.

 African Societies

Fifteenth-century Africa, like fifteenth-century America, housed a variety of cultures adapted to different geographical settings (see map). Many of these cultures were of great antiquity. In the north, along the Mediterranean Sea, lived the Berbers, a Muslim people. (Muslims are adherents of Islam, founded by the prophet Mohammed in the seventh century C.E.) On the east coast of Africa, Muslim city-states engaged in extensive trade with India, the Moluccas (part of modern Indonesia), and China. In these ports, sustained contact and intermarriage among Arabs and Africans created the Swahili language and culture. Through the East African city-states passed a considerable share of the trade between the eastern Mediterranean and the Far East; the rest followed the long land route across Central Asia known as the Silk Road.

In the African interior, south of the Mediterranean coast, lie the great Sahara and Libyan deserts, vast expanses of nearly waterless terrain that served as a barrier to some types of travel yet also acted as a highway for transmitting religious and cultural ideas throughout the region. Below the deserts, much of the continent is divided between tropical rain forests (along the coasts) and grassy plains (in the interior). People speaking a variety of languages and pursuing different economic strategies lived in a wide belt south of the deserts. South of the Gulf of Guinea (see map, page 13), the grassy landscape came to be dominated by Bantu-speaking peoples, who left their homeland in modern Nigeria about two thousand years ago and slowly migrated south and east across the continent.

Most of the enslaved people carried to North America came from West Africa, which the Europeans called Guinea, a land of tropical forests, fishing, and agriculture that had been inhabited for at least ten thousand years before Europeans set foot there in the fifteenth century. The northern region of West Africa, or Upper Guinea, was heavily influenced by the Islamic culture of the Mediterranean. As early as the eleventh century C.E., many

West Africa (Guinea)

of the region's inhabitants had become Muslims. Trade between Upper Guinea and the Muslim Mediterranean was sub-Saharan Africa's major connection to Europe and the Middle East. In return for salt, dates, silk, and cotton cloth, Africans exchanged ivory, gold, and slaves with northern merchants.

Upper Guinea runs roughly north-south from Cape Verde to Cape Palmas. The people of its northernmost region, the so-called Rice Coast (present-day Gambia, Sénégal, and Guinea), fished and cultivated rice in coastal swamplands. The Grain Coast, the next region to the south, was thinly populated and not readily accessible from the sea because it had only one good harbor (modern Freetown, Sierra Leone). Its people concentrated on farming and raising livestock. Both the Rice and the Grain Coasts—especially the former—supplied slaves destined for sale in the Americas, but even more enslaved people came from Lower Guinea, to the east of Cape Palmas.

In the fifteenth century, most Africans in Lower Guinea practiced traditional religions, not the precepts of Islam. As in the religions of the agricultural peoples of the Americas, their beliefs revolved around rituals intended to ensure good harvests. Throughout the region, individual villages composed of groups of kin were linked into small, hierarchical kingdoms. At the time of initial contact with the Europeans, the region was characterized by decentralized political and social authority.

West African law did not permit individual ownership of land; instead, land belonged temporarily to anyone who cultivated it. Africans held in slavery on their own continent—primarily criminals, debtors, or wartime captives, and their descendants—were therefore essential components of the economy, because only the ownership of people allowed the accumulation of wealth. An African who possessed slaves also had a right to the products of their labor. Accordingly, an internal traffic in slaves thrived long before Europeans' ships arrived off the West African coast. The first slave voyages merely diverted some of that trade to Europe or the Americas.

Slavery in West Africa

Many of the first slaves destined for sale across the Atlantic came from the Gold Coast, composed of thirty little kingdoms known as the Akan States. By the eighteenth century, though, it was the area farther east, the modern nations of Togo and Benin, that supplied most of the slaves sold in the English

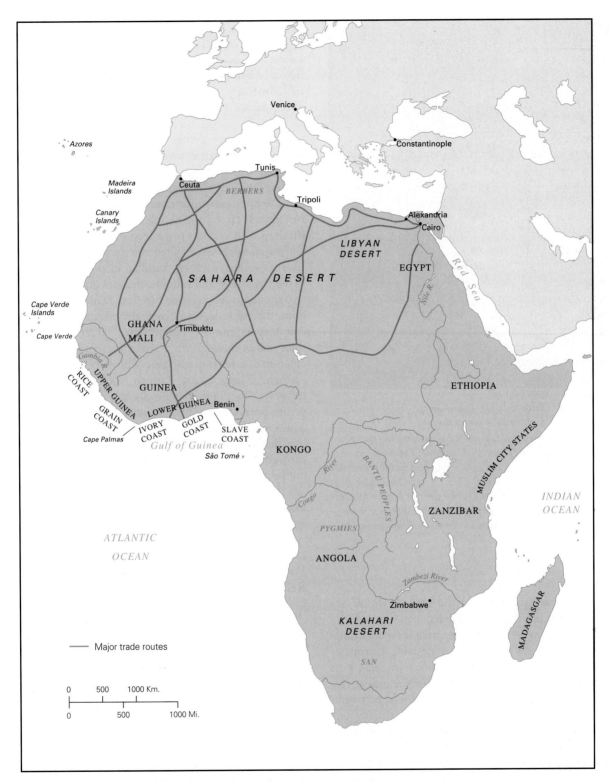

Africa and Its Peoples, c. 1400   *On the African continent resided many different peoples in a variety of eco-logical settings and political units. Even before Europeans began to explore Africa's coastlines, its northern regions were linked to the Mediterranean (and thus to Europe) by a network of trade routes.*

This decorative brass weight, created by the Asante peoples of Lower Guinea, was used for measuring gold dust. It depicts a family pounding fu-fu, a food made by mashing together plantains (a kind of banana), yams, and cassava. The paste was then shaped into balls to be eaten with soup. This weight, probably used in trading with Europeans, shows a scene combining foods of African origin (plantains and yams) with an import from the Americas (cassava), thus bringing the three continents together in ways both symbolic and real. Trustees of the British Museum. Photo by Michael Holford.

colonies. The Adja kings of the region, which became known as the Slave Coast, encouraged the founding of slave-trading posts and served as middlemen in the trade. Access to valuable European trade goods enhanced their positions in their own societies and improved their kingdoms' standing relative to their neighbors. Initially, those sent to the Americas came from the ranks of the already enslaved. By the early eighteenth century, however, after the demand for bondspeople in the American colonies had increased dramatically (see page 70), African rulers appear to have warred on other groups primarily to obtain slaves for sale.

The societies of West Africa, like those of the Americas, assigned different tasks to men and women. In general, the sexes shared agricultural duties. Men also hunted, managed livestock, and did most of the fishing. Women were responsible for childcare, food preparation, and cloth manufacture. Everywhere in West Africa women were the primary local traders. They managed the extensive local and regional networks through which goods were exchanged among the various families, villages, and small kingdoms.

Sexual Division of Labor in West Africa

Despite their different economies and the rivalries among states, the peoples of Lower Guinea had similar social systems organized on the basis of what anthropologists have called the *dual-sex principle*. In Lower Guinea, each sex handled its own affairs: just as male political and religious leaders governed men, so females ruled women. In the Dahomean kingdom, for example, every male official had his female counterpart; in the Akan States, chiefs inherited their status through the female line, and each male chief had a female assistant who supervised other women. Many West African societies practiced *polygyny* (one man having several wives, each of whom lived separately with her children). Thus few adults lived permanently in marital households, but the dual-sex system ensured that their actions were subject to scrutiny by members of their own sex, if not by a spouse.

Throughout Lower Guinea religious beliefs likewise stressed complementary male and female roles. Both women and men served as heads of the cults and secret societies that directed the spiritual life of the villages. Young women were initiated into the Sandé cult, young men into Poro. Neither cult was allowed to reveal its secrets to the opposite sex. Although West African women (unlike some of their Native American contemporaries) rarely held formal power over men, female religious leaders did govern other members of their sex within the Sandé cult, enforcing conformity to accepted norms of behavior and overseeing their spiritual well-being.

West African Religion

The West Africans brought to the Americas, then, were agricultural peoples, skilled at tending livestock, hunting, fishing, and manufacturing cloth from plant fibers and animal skins. Both men and women were accustomed to working communally, alongside other members of their own sex. They were also accustomed to a relatively egalitarian relationship between the sexes, especially within the context of religion. In the Americas, they entered societies that used their labor but had little respect for their cultural traditions.

 ## European Societies

In the fifteenth century, Europeans, too, were agricultural peoples. The daily lives of Europe's rural people had changed little for several hundred years. Split into numerous small, warring countries, Europe was divided linguistically, politically, and economically, yet in social terms Europeans' lives were more similar than different. European societies were hierarchical: a few families wielded arbitrary power over the majority of the people. English society in particular was organized as a series of interlocking hierarchies; each person (except those at the very top or bottom) was superior to some, inferior to others. Europe's kingdoms accordingly resembled those of Africa or Mesoamerica but differed greatly from the more egalitarian, consensus-based societies then established in America north of Mexico.

Most Europeans, like most Africans and Americans, lived in small villages. Only a few cities dotted the landscape, most of them political capitals.

Sexual Division of Labor in Europe

European farmers, who were called *peasants*, owned or leased separate landholdings, but they worked the fields communally. Because fields had to lie fallow (unplanted) every second or third year to regain fertility, a family could not have ensured itself a regular food supply had not the work and the crop been shared annually by all the villagers. Men did most of the fieldwork; women helped out chiefly at planting and harvest. In some areas men concentrated on herding livestock. Women's duties consisted primarily of childcare and household tasks, including preserving food, milking cows, and caring for poultry. If a woman's husband was an artisan or a storekeeper in a city, she might assist him in business. Since Europeans kept domesticated animals (pigs, goats, sheep, and cattle) for meat, hunting had little economic importance in their cultures. Instead, hunting was primarily a sport for male aristocrats.

Unlike African and American societies, in which women often played prominent roles in politics and religion, men dominated all areas of life in Europe. A few women—notably Queen Elizabeth I of England—achieved status or power, but the vast majority were excluded from positions of political authority. In the Roman Catholic Church and later in the new Protestant denominations, leadership roles were reserved for men. Husbands and fathers likewise expected to control their families. In short, European women generally held inferior social, economic, and political positions, yet within their own families they wielded power over children and servants.

When the fifteenth century began, European nations were slowly beginning to recover from the devastating epidemic of plague known as the Black Death, which first struck them in 1346. Bubonic plague, spread by rats and fleas as well as by human contact, arrived in Europe from China, traveling with long-distance traders along the Silk Road. The disease then recurred with particular severity in the 1360s and 1370s. Although no precise figures are available and the impact of the Black Death varied from region to region, the best estimate is that fully one-third of Europe's people died during those terrible years. That led to a precipitous economic decline—in some regions more than half of the workers were lost—and to severe social, political, and religious disruption because of the deaths of clergymen and other leading figures.

Black Death

As plague ravaged the population, England and France waged the Hundred Years War (1337–1453), initiated because the English monarchy claimed the French throne. The war interrupted overland trade routes through France that connected northern Europe to the Italian city-states and thence to Central Asia. Merchants in the eastern Mediterranean thus had to find new ways of reaching their northern markets. They solved that dilemma by forging a regular maritime link with the north to replace the overland route. The use of a triangular, or lateen, sail (rather than the then-standard square rigging) improved the maneuverability of ships, enabling them to sail out of the Mediterranean and into the North Sea. Also of key importance was the perfection of navigational instruments like the astrolabe and the quadrant, which allowed oceangoing sailors to estimate their position (latitude) by measuring the relationship of sun, moon, or stars to the horizon.

Political, Economic, and Technological Change

In the aftermath of the Hundred Years War, European monarchs relied on nationalistic feelings fostered by the conflict to consolidate their previously diffuse political power and to raise new revenues through increased taxation of an already hard-pressed peasantry. The long military struggle led to new pride in national identity (regional loyalties had previously held sway) and to heightened hostility toward foreigners. In England, Henry VII in 1485 founded the Tudor dynasty and began uniting a previously divided land. In France, the successors of Charles VII unified the kingdom and levied new taxes. Most successful of all were Ferdinand of Aragón and Isabella of Castile. In 1469 they married and combined their kingdoms, thereby creating the foundation of a strongly Catholic Spain. In 1492, they defeated the Muslims, who had lived in Spain and Portugal for centuries, thereafter expelling all Jews and Muslims from their domain.

The fifteenth century also brought technological change to Europe. Movable type and the printing press, invented in Germany in the 1450s, made information more accessible than ever before. Printing stimulated the Europeans' curiosity about fabled lands across the seas, lands they could now read about in books. The most important such work was Marco Polo's *Travels*, which recounted a Venetian merchant's adventures in thirteenth-century China and described that nation as bordered on the east by an ocean. Polo's account circulated widely among Europe's educated elites after it was printed in 1477. The book led many Europeans to believe that they could trade directly with China in oceangoing vessels instead of relying on the Silk Road or the trade route through East Africa. The transoceanic route, if it existed, would allow them to circumvent the Muslim and Mediterranean merchants who hitherto had controlled their access to Asian goods.

The European explorations of the fifteenth and sixteenth centuries were made possible by technological advances and by the growing strength of newly powerful national rulers.

Motives for Exploration

The primary motivation for exploratory voyages was each country's craving for easy access to desirable African and Asian goods—spices like pepper, cloves, cinnamon, and nutmeg (to season the bland European diet), silk, dyes, perfumes, jewels, and gold. Avoiding middlemen and acquiring such valuable products directly would improve a nation's income and its standing relative to other countries.

That economic motive was supported by a secondary concern about spreading Christianity around the world. The linking of materialist and spiritual goals might seem contradictory today, but fifteenth-century Europeans saw no necessary conflict between the two. Explorers and colonizers could honestly want to convert "heathen" peoples to Christianity. At the same time they could hope to increase their nation's wealth by establishing direct trade with Africa, China, India, and the Moluccas (also known as the Spice Islands).

 ## Early European Explorations and the Columbus Voyages

Before European mariners could discover new lands, they had to discover the oceans. To reach Asia, seafarers needed not just the maneuverable vessels and navigational aids increasingly used in the fourteenth century, but also knowledge of the sea, its currents, and especially its winds. Wind would power their ships. But how did the winds run? Where would Atlantic breezes carry their square-rigged ships, which, even with the addition of a triangular sail, needed to run before the wind (that is, to have the wind directly behind the vessel)?

Europeans learned the answers to these questions in the region that has been called the Mediterranean Atlantic, the expanse of the Atlantic that is south and west of Spain and is bounded by the island groups of the Azores (on the west) and the Canaries (on the south), with the Madeiras in their midst (see map, page 18). Europeans reached all three sets of islands during the fourteenth century. The Canaries proved a popular destination for mariners from Iberia (the peninsula that includes Spain and Portugal). Sailing to the Canaries from Europe was easy, because strong winds known as the Northeast Trades blow southward along the Iberian and African coastlines. The voyage took about a week, and the volcanic peaks on the islands made them difficult to miss even with navigational instruments that were less than precise.

Sailing in the Mediterranean Atlantic

The problem was getting back. The Iberian sailor attempting to return home faced a major obstacle: the very winds that had brought him so quickly to the Canaries now blew directly at him. Early travelers to the islands sometimes used galleys powered by oarsmen as well as by sails, but even oarsmen had a difficult time fighting the contrary winds and currents. Another alternative was similarly tedious: tacking back and forth to the east and west, attempting each time to make more headway north. The problem seemed intractable, and in earlier eras European sailors had been unable to solve it. When confronted with contrary winds, they simply waited for the wind to change. But for the most part, the Northeast Trades did not change. They blew steadily, never reversing course, though shifting slightly with the seasons.

What could be done? Some unknown seafarer figured out the answer: sailing "around the wind." If a mariner could not sail against the trade winds, he had to sail as close as possible to the direction from which the wind was coming without being forced to tack. In the Mediterranean Atlantic, that meant pointing his vessel northwest into the open ocean, away from land, until—weeks later—he reached the winds that would carry him home, the so-called Westerlies. Those winds blow (we now know, though the mariners at first did not) northward along the coast of North America before heading east toward Europe.

This solution must at first have seemed to defy common sense, but it proved to be the key to successful exploration of both the Atlantic and the Pacific Oceans. Once a sailor understood the winds and their allied currents, he no longer feared leaving Europe without being able to return. Faced with a contrary wind, all he had to do was sail around it until he found a wind to carry him in the proper direction. This strategy might seem to take him hundreds of miles out of the way, but in the long run it was safer and surer than attempting the monumental task of tacking against the wind.

During the fifteenth century, armed with knowledge of the winds and currents of the Mediterranean Atlantic, Iberian seamen regularly visited its islands, all of which they could reach in two weeks or less. The uninhabited Azores were soon settled by Portuguese migrants who raised wheat for sale in Europe and sold livestock to passing sailors. Madeira also had no native peoples, and by the 1450s Portuguese colonists were employing slaves (probably Jews and Muslims brought from Iberia) to grow large quantities of sugar for export to the mainland. Madeira thus developed by the 1470s into the world's first colonial plantation economy.

Islands of the Mediterranean Atlantic

One of the few surviving contemporary illustrations of a fifteenth-century European vessel, the caravel, is this engraving by the Flemish artist Peter Breughel. Notice the combination of square-rigged and lateen sails, the former for moving as efficiently as possible with a following breeze, the latter for maneuvering in unfavorable winds.   Private Collection.

The first islands the Europeans found—arriving as early as the 1330s—were the Canaries, inhabited by the Guanche people, who began trading animal skins and dyes with their European visitors. In 1402 the French attacked one of the islands; thereafter, Portuguese and Spanish expeditions continued the sporadic assaults. The Guanches resisted vigorously, but one by one the seven islands came under European control. The Guanches were then carried off as slaves to the Madeiras or the Iberian Peninsula. The last island fell to the Spanish in 1496, and the last known Guanche died in the middle of the next century. The Spanish conquerors then devoted the land of the Canary Islands to sugar cultivation. Collectively, the Canaries and Madeira became known as the Wine Islands because much of their sugar production was employed to make sweet wines.

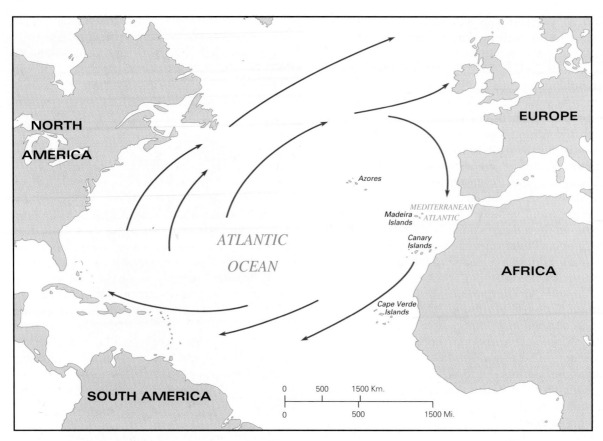

Atlantic Winds and Islands   *European mariners had to explore the oceans before they could find new lands. The first realm they discovered was that of Atlantic winds and islands.*

While some Europeans concentrated on exploiting the islands of the Mediterranean Atlantic, others used them as steppingstones to Africa. In 1415, Portugal seized control of Ceuta, a Muslim city in North Africa (see map, page 13).

Portuguese Trading Posts in Africa

Prince Henry the Navigator, son of King John I of Portugal, knew that vast wealth awaited the first European nation to tap the riches of Africa and Asia directly. Each year he dispatched ships southward along the African coast, attempting to discover an oceanic route to Asia. But not until after Prince Henry's death did Bartholomew Dias round the southern tip of Africa (1488) and Vasco da Gama finally reach India (1498).

Long before that, though, Portugal reaped the benefits of its seafarers' voyages. Although West African states successfully resisted European penetration of the interior, they allowed the Portuguese to establish trading posts along their coasts. Charging the traders rent and levying duties on the goods they imported, the African kingdoms set the terms of exchange and benefited considerably from their new, easier access to European manufactures. The Portuguese gained too, for they no longer had to rely on the long trans-Saharan trade route. They earned immense profits by swiftly transporting African gold to Europe. Another valuable cargo for the Portuguese traders was slaves. When they carried previously enslaved Africans back to the Iberian Peninsula, the Portuguese introduced black slavery into Europe.

An island off the African coast, previously uninhabited, proved critical to Portuguese success. São Tomé, located in the Gulf of Guinea (see map, page 13) was colonized in the 1480s. By that time Madeira had already reached the limit of its capacity to produce sugar. The soil of São Tomé proved ideal for raising that valuable crop, and plantation agriculture there expanded rapidly. Large numbers of slaves were imported from the mainland to work in the cane fields, thus creating the first economy based primarily on the bondage of black Africans.

By the 1490s, even before Christopher Columbus set sail to the west, Europeans had learned three key lessons of colonization from their experiences in the islands of the Mediterranean Atlantic and the African coast. First, they knew that they could transplant their crops and livestock successfully to exotic locations. Second, they learned that the native peoples of unknown lands could be either conquered (the Guanches) or exploited (the Africans) to European advantage. Third, they successfully developed a model of plantation slavery—an exploitative economy based on the labor of large numbers of people held in perpetual bondage—and a system for supplying nearly unlimited quantities of such workers. The stage was set for a critical moment in world history, and the man of the hour was a sailor named Christopher Columbus.

Lessons of Early Colonization

Columbus was well schooled in the lessons of the Mediterranean Atlantic. Born in 1451 in the Italian city-state of Genoa, Columbus, the largely self-educated son of a wool merchant, was by the 1490s an experienced sailor and mapmaker. Like many mariners of the day, he was drawn to Portugal and its islands, especially Madeira, where he commanded a merchant vessel. At least once he voyaged to the Portuguese outpost on the Gold Coast. There he acquired an obsession with gold, and there he came to understand the economic potential of the slave trade.

Christopher Columbus

Like all accomplished seafarers, Columbus knew the world was round. (So, indeed, did most educated people: the idea that his contemporaries believed the world to be flat is a myth dating from the nineteenth century.) But he differed from other cartographers in his estimate of the earth's size: he thought that Japan lay only 3,000 miles from the southern European coast. Thus, he argued, it would be easier to reach Asia by sailing west than by making a difficult voyage around the southern tip of Africa. Experts scoffed at this crackpot notion, accurately predicting that the two continents lay 12,000 miles apart. When Columbus in 1484 asked the Portuguese authorities to back his plan to sail west to Asia, they rejected the proposal. After all, why should they adopt such a crazy scheme just as their efforts to round the Cape of Good Hope promised success?

Ferdinand and Isabella of Spain, ruling a newly united kingdom and jealous of Portugal's successes in Africa, were more receptive to Columbus's ideas. Urged on by some Spanish noblemen and a group of Italian merchants residing in Castile, the monarchs agreed to finance the risky voyage, in part because they hoped the profits would pay for an expedition to conquer Muslim-held Jerusalem. And so, on August 3, 1492, in command of three ships—the *Pinta*, the *Niña*, and the *Santa Maria*—Columbus set sail from the southern Spanish port of Palos.

The first part of the journey must have been very familiar, for the ships steered down the Northeast Trades to the Canary Islands. There Columbus refitted his square-rigged ships, adding triangular sails to make them more maneuverable. On September 6, the ships weighed anchor and headed out into the unknown ocean.

Just over a month later, pushed by the favorable trade winds, the vessels found land approximately where Columbus had predicted (see map, page 18). On October 12, he and his men landed on an island in the Bahamas, which its inhabitants called Guanahaní but which he renamed San Salvador. (Because Columbus's sketchy description of his landfall can be variously interpreted, two different places—Watling Island and Samana Cay—are today proposed as possible contenders for Columbus's landing site.) Later he went on to explore the islands now known as Cuba and Hispaniola, which their residents, the Taíno people, called Colba and Bohío. Because he thought he had reached the Indies, Columbus referred to the inhabitants of the region as *Indians*.

Three themes predominate in Columbus's log, the major source of information on this first encounter. First, he insistently asked the Taínos where he could find gold, pearls, and valuable spices. Each time, his informants replied (largely via signs) that such products could be obtained on other islands, on the mainland, or in cities in the interior. Eventually he came to mistrust such answers, noting, "I am beginning to believe . . . they will tell me anything I want to hear."

Columbus's Observations

Second, Columbus wrote repeatedly of the strange and beautiful plants and animals. "Here the fishes are so unlike ours that it is amazing. . . . The colors are so bright that anyone would marvel," he noted, and again, "The song of the little birds

This map, produced in 1489 by Henricus Marcellus, represents the world as Christopher Columbus knew it, for it incorporates information obtained after Bartholomew Dias, a Portuguese sailor, rounded the Cape of Good Hope at the southern tip of Africa in 1488. Marcellus did not try to estimate the extent of the ocean separating the west coast of Europe from the east coast of Asia.   Trustees of the British Library.

might make a man wish never to leave here. I never tire from looking at such luxurious vegetation." Yet Columbus's interest was not only aesthetic. "I believe that there are many plants and trees here that could be worth a lot in Spain for use as dyes, spices, and medicines," he observed, adding that he was carrying home to Europe "a sample of everything I can," so that experts could examine them.

Third, Columbus also described the islands' human residents, and he seized some to take back to Spain. The Taínos were, he said, very handsome, gentle, and friendly, though they told him of fierce people who raided their villages and lived on other nearby islands. The Caniba (today called Caribs), from whose name the word *cannibal* is derived, were reported to eat their captives (today

The Taíno People

scholars disagree about whether the tales were true). Columbus believed the Taínos to be likely converts to Catholicism, remarking that "if devout religious persons knew the Indian language well, all these people would soon become Christians." But he had more in mind than conversion. The islanders "ought to make good and skilled servants," Columbus declared. It would be easy, he asserted, to "subject everyone and make them do what you wished."

Thus the very first encounter between Europeans and America and its residents revealed a theme that would be of enormous significance for centuries to come: the Europeans' desire to extract profits from North and South America by exploiting their natural resources, including plants, animals, and peoples alike.

Christopher Columbus made three more voyages to the west, exploring most of the major

In 1507 Martin Waldseemüller, a German mapmaker, was the first person to designate the newly discovered southern continent as "America." He named the continent after Amerigo Vespucci, the Italian explorer who realized that he had reached a "new world" rather than islands off the coast of Asia.   John Carter Brown Library at Brown University.

Caribbean islands and sailing along the coasts of Central and South America. Until the day he died in 1506 at the age of fifty-five, Columbus believed that he had reached Asia. Even before his death, others knew better. Because the Florentine Amerigo Vespucci, who explored the South American coast in 1499, was the first to publish the idea that a new continent had been discovered, Martin Waldseemüller in 1507 labeled the land "America," as is evident in his map (reproduced above). By then, Spain, Portugal, and Pope Alexander VI had signed the Treaty of Tordesillas (1494), confirming Portugal's dominance in Africa and Brazil in exchange for Spanish preeminence in the rest of the New World.

Naming of America

The first mariners to explore the region of North America that was to become the United States and Canada followed a very different route. Some historians argue that European sailors may have found the rich Newfoundland fishing grounds in the 1480s, even before Columbus's first voyage, but kept their discoveries a secret so that they alone could exploit the sea's bounty. Whether or not fishermen had crossed the entire width of the Atlantic, they had thoroughly explored its northern reaches. In the same way the Portuguese traveled regularly in the Mediterranean Atlantic, fifteenth-century English seafarers and others voyaged among the European continent, England, Ireland, and Iceland.

Northern Voyages

The winds these seafarers confronted posed problems on their outbound rather than homeward journeys. The same Westerlies that carried Colum-

Columbus received gold and this elaborate belt from a Taíno leader. In exchange, his log reveals, he presented the Taíno man with red shoes and an amber necklace.   Museum Für Völkerkunde, Vienna.

bus and other southern voyagers back to Europe blew in the faces of northerners looking west. But sailors soon learned that the strongest winds shifted southward during the winter and that, by departing from northern ports in the spring, they could make adequate headway if they steered northward to catch sporadic easterly breezes. Thus, whereas the first landfall of most sailors to the south was somewhere in the Caribbean, those taking the northern route usually reached America along the coast of what is now Maine or the Canadian maritime provinces.

Five hundred years before Columbus, in the year 1001, the Norseman Leif Ericsson and other explorers from Greenland briefly established a settlement at a western site they named Vineland. (In the 1960s, archaeologists determined that this encampment was located at what is now L'anse aux Meadows, Newfoundland.) Attacks by local residents forced them to depart hurriedly, the tale of their exploits subsequently being preserved in oral-history sagas. Therefore, the European generally credited with "discovering" North America is John Cabot. More precisely, it might be said that Cabot brought to Europe the first formal knowledge of the northern coastline of the continent.

Like Columbus, Cabot was a master mariner from the Italian city-state of Genoa. He is known to have been in Spain when Columbus returned from his first trip to America. Calculating that England—which traded with Asia only through a long series of middlemen stretching from Belgium to Venice to the Muslim world—would be eager to sponsor exploratory voyages, Cabot sought and won the support of King Henry VII. He set sail from Bristol in late May 1497 in the *Mathew*, reaching his destination on June 24. Scholars disagree about the location of his landfall (some say it was Cape Breton Island, others Newfoundland), but all recognize the importance of his month-long exploration of the coast. Having achieved his goal, Cabot rode the Westerlies back to England, arriving just fifteen days after he left North America.

The voyages of Columbus, Cabot, and their successors finally brought the Eastern and Western Hemispheres together. The Portuguese explorer Pedro Alvares Cabral reached Brazil in 1500; John Cabot's son Sebastian followed his father to North America in 1507; France financed Giovanni da Verrazzano in 1524 and Jacques Cartier in 1534; and in 1609 and 1610 Henry Hudson explored the North American coast for the Dutch West India Company (see map). All these men were primarily

John Cabot's Explorations

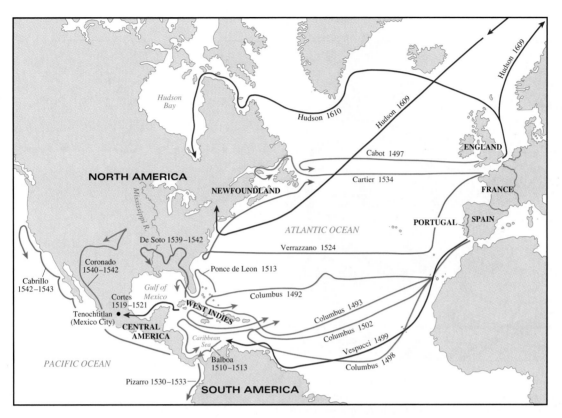

European Explorations in America *In the century following Columbus's voyages, European adventurers explored the coasts and parts of the interior of North and South America.*

searching for the legendary, nonexistent "Northwest Passage" through the Americas, hoping to find an easy route to the riches of Asia. Although they did not attempt to plant colonies in the Western Hemisphere, their discoveries interested European nations in exploring North and South America.

Spanish Colonization and the Exchange of Diseases, Plants, and Animals

The Europeans' greatest impact on the Americas was unintended. Diseases carried from Europe and Africa by the alien invaders killed millions of Indians, who had no immunity to germs that had infested the other continents for centuries. The statistics are staggering. When Columbus landed on Hispaniola in 1492, more than 1 million people

Smallpox and Other Diseases

probably resided there. Fifty years later, only 500 were still alive. Within thirty years of the first landfall at Guanahaní, not one Taíno survived in the Bahamas. The lethal combination of diseases and slave-raiding parties had wiped them out.

Although measles, influenza, and other illnesses severely afflicted the Native Americans, the greatest killer was smallpox, which was spread by direct human contact. A Spanish priest recorded the words of an old Aztec man who survived the first smallpox epidemic in Tenochtitlán, the Aztec capital. That epidemic began in Hispaniola in 1518 and was carried to the mainland by Cortés and his army of invaders. The epidemic peaked in 1520, during the Aztec month of Tepeilhuitl, and it fatally weakened Tenochtitlán's defenders. "It spread over the people as great destruction," the elderly Aztec remembered. "Some it quite covered [with pustules] on all parts—their faces, their heads, their breasts. . . . There was great havoc. Very many died of it. . . . Great was its destruction." In the Aztec year Three House, on the

The Codex Florentino, *which has the fullest Aztec account of the Spaniards' conquest of Mexico, contains this image of an Indian afflicted with the smallpox that ravaged Tenochtitlán during the Spanish siege of the city.*   Biblioteca Medicea Laurenziana, Florence.

day One Serpent (August 1521), Tenochtitlán surrendered. On the site of the Aztec capital, the Spaniards built what is now Mexico City.

Far to the north, where smaller American populations encountered only a few European explorers, missionaries, traders, and fishermen, disease also ravaged the countryside. A great epidemic, most likely chickenpox, swept through the villages along the coast north of Cape Cod from 1616 to 1618. The mortality rate may have been as high as 90 percent. An English traveler several years later commented that the people had "died on heapes, as they lay in their houses," and that bones and skulls covered the ruins of villages. Because of this dramatic depopulation of the area, just a few years later English colonists were able to establish settlements virtually unopposed.

The Americans, though, took a revenge of sorts. They gave the Europeans syphilis, a virulent venereal disease. The first recorded case of the new disease in Europe occurred in Barcelona, Spain, in 1493, shortly after Columbus's return from the Caribbean. Although less likely than smallpox to cause immediate death, syphilis was extremely dangerous and debilitating. Carried by soldiers, sailors, and prostitutes, it spread quickly through Europe and Asia, reaching as far as China by 1505.

The exchange of diseases was only part of a broader mutual transfer of plants and animals that resulted directly from European voyages. The two hemispheres had evolved separately for millions of years, developing widely different forms of life. Many large mammals like cattle and horses were native to the connected continents of Europe, Asia, and Africa, but the Americas contained no domesticated beasts larger than dogs and llamas. However, the vegetable crops of the Americas—particularly corn, beans, squash, cassava, and potatoes—were more nutritious and produced higher yields than those of the Old, like wheat and rye. In time, the Native Americans learned to raise and consume European livestock, and the Europeans and Africans became accustomed to planting and eating American crops. As a result, the diets of

Exchange of Plants and Animals

A European artist recorded this scene of a Carib war dance. The leaders in the middle of the circle blow tobacco smoke on the dancers to give them courage in the coming battles.   MAPes MONDe Ltd.

all three peoples were vastly enriched. One consequence was the doubling of the world's population over the next three hundred years.

The exchange of two other commodities significantly influenced European and American civilizations. In America, Europeans encountered tobacco, which was at first believed to have beneficial medicinal effects. Smoking and chewing the "Indian weed" became a fad in the Old World after it was planted in Turkey in the sixteenth century. Despite the efforts of such skeptics as King James I of England, who in 1604 pronounced smoking "loathsome to the eye, hatefull to the Nose, harmfull to the brain,

[and] dangerous to the Lungs," tobacco's popularity climbed. Its contribution to another disease, lung cancer, was discovered only in the twentieth century.

Also important was the impact of the horse on some Indian cultures. Horses brought to America by the Spaniards inevitably fell into the hands of Native Americans. Traded northward, they eventually became essential to the life of the nomadic buffalo hunters of the Great Plains. Sioux, Comanches, and Blackfeet, among others, used horses for transportation and hunting, calculated their wealth in the number of horses owned, and waged wars primarily from horseback. Women no longer had to carry the bands' belongings on their backs. Some groups that previously had cultivated crops abandoned agriculture altogether. Through the acquisition of horses, then, a mode of subsistence that had been based on hunting several different animals, in combination with gathering and agriculture, became one focused almost wholly on hunting buffalo.

The European and African invasion of the Americas therefore had a significant biological component, for the invaders carried plants and animals with them. Some creatures, such as livestock, they brought deliberately. Others, including rats (which infested their ships), weeds, and diseases, arrived unexpectedly. And the same process occurred in reverse. When the Europeans returned home, they deliberately took back such crops as corn, potatoes, and tobacco, along with that unanticipated hitchhiker, syphilis.

Only in the areas that Spain explored and claimed did formal colonization begin immediately. On his second voyage in 1493, Columbus brought to Hispaniola seventeen ships loaded with twelve hundred men, seeds, plants, livestock, chickens, and dogs—along with microbes and weeds. The settlement named Isabela (in the modern Dominican Republic) and its successors became the staging area for the Spanish invasion of America. On the islands of Cuba and Hispaniola the Europeans learned to adapt to the new environment, as did the horses, cattle, and hogs they imported. When the Spaniards explored the mainland, they rode island-bred horses and ate island-bred cattle and hogs. Everywhere the Spaniards went they carried with them what the historian Alfred Crosby has termed their "invasion team": European diseases and hooved animals. Those microorganisms and livestock ensured the Spaniards' success.

Spanish Colonization

At first, Spanish explorers fanned out around the Caribbean basin. In 1513, Juan Ponce de León reached Florida and Vasco Núñez de Balboa crossed the Isthmus of Panama to the Pacific Ocean. Eight years later, the Spaniards' dreams of wealth were realized when Cortés conquered the Aztec Empire, seizing a fabulous treasure of gold and silver. Venturing northward, conquistadors like Juan Rodriguez Cabrillo (who sailed along the California coast), Hernando de Soto (who journeyed to the Mississippi River), and Francisco Vásquez de Coronado (who explored the southwestern portion of what is now the United States) found few of the products the Spanish coveted. By contrast, Francisco Pizarro, who explored the western coast of South America, acquired the richest silver mines in the world by conquering and enslaving the Incas in 1535. Pizarro was able to defeat the Incas in part because many of their leaders had been wiped out by a smallpox epidemic shortly before his arrival. Just a half-century after Columbus's first voyage, the Spanish monarchs—who treated the American territories as their personal possessions—controlled the richest, most extensive empire Europe had known since ancient Rome.

Spain established the model of colonization that other countries later attempted to imitate, a model with three major elements. First, the Crown maintained tight control over the colonies, establishing a hierarchical government that allowed little autonomy to New World jurisdictions. That control included, for example, limiting the number of people permitted to emigrate to America and insisting that the colonies import all their manufactured goods from Spain. Roman Catholic priests were dispatched to ensure the colonists' conformity with orthodox religious views. Second, most of the colonists sent from Spain were male. They married Indian—and later African—women, thereby creating the racially mixed population that characterizes much of Latin America to the present day.

Third, the colonies' wealth was based on the exploitation of both the native population and slaves imported from Africa. The Mesoamerican peoples, many of whom lived in urban areas, were accustomed to autocratic rule. Spaniards simply took over roles once assumed by native leaders, who had also exacted labor and tribute from their subjects. The *encomienda* system, which granted tribute from Indian villages to individual conquistadors as a reward for their services to the Crown, in effect legalized Indian slavery. Yet in 1542 a new code of laws reformed the system, forbidding Spaniards from enslaving Indians while still allowing them to collect money and goods from their tributary villages. In response, the conquerors, familiar with slavery in Spain, began to import Africans in order to increase the labor force under their direct control. Indian and African workers were primarily employed on huge ranches, which raised horses, cattle, and sheep; in gold and silver mines; and on sugar plantations. Yet African slavery failed to be adopted on a large scale everywhere in New Spain: it was far more common in the Greater Antilles (the major Caribbean islands) than on the Mexican mainland.

In this early view of a Spanish gold mine in South America, enslaved Africans process gold—mining, washing, and drying the nuggets before giving them to a Spanish overseer.   Pierpont Morgan Library/Art Resource, NY.

The New World's gold and silver, initially a boon, ultimately brought about the decline of Spain as a major power. The influx of unprecedented wealth led to rapid inflation, which (among other adverse effects) caused Spanish products to be overpriced in international markets and imported goods to become cheaper in Spain. The once-profitable Spanish textile-manufacturing industry collapsed, as did scores of other businesses. The seemingly endless income from American colonies emboldened successive Spanish monarchs

Spain's Economy Crumbles

to spend lavishly on wars against the Dutch and the English. Several times in the late sixteenth and early seventeenth centuries the monarchs repudiated the state debt, thus wreaking havoc on the nation's finances. When the South American gold and silver mines started to give out in the mid-seventeenth century, Spain's economy crumbled and the nation lost its international importance.

Spanish wealth derived from American suffering. The Spaniards deliberately leveled American cities, building cathedrals and monasteries on sites once occupied by Aztec, Incan, and Mayan temples. Some conquistadors sought to erase all vestiges of the great Indian cultures by burning the written records they found. With traditional ways of life in disarray, devastated by disease, and compelled to labor for their conquerors, many demoralized residents of Mesoamerica accepted the Christian religion brought to New Spain by friars of the Franciscan and Dominican orders.

The friars devoted their energies to persuading Mesoamerican people to move into new towns and to build Roman Catholic churches. In such towns, they were exposed to European customs and to religious rituals newly elaborated in an attempt to assimilate Christianity and pagan beliefs. For example, the friars deliberately juxtaposed the cult of the Virgin Mary with that of the corn goddess. These conversion efforts met with remarkable success. Thousands of Indians residing in Spanish territory embraced Catholicism, at least partly because it was the religion of their new rulers and they were accustomed to obedience.

Christianity in New Spain

European Traders, Fishermen, and Early Settlements

Other European nations did not start at once to colonize the coasts their sailors had explored. The Portuguese finally turned their attention away from Africa and India to Brazil, founding a small colony there in 1532. Not until after the middle of the century, however, did Brazil begin to develop a booming economy based on large-scale sugar production for the European market. By 1600, Portuguese ships were annually carrying thousands of enslaved Africans from Lower Guinea to labor on Brazilian sugar plantations.

Northern Europeans, denied access to the wealth of Mesoamerica by the Spanish and beaten to South America by the Portuguese, were initially more interested in exploiting North America's abundant natural resources than in the difficult task of establishing colonies on the mainland. John Cabot reported that fish were so plentiful along the North American coastline that they could be caught merely by lowering baskets over the side of a vessel. Europeans rushed to take advantage of the abundance of fish, a product in great demand in their homelands as an inexpensive source of nourishment. By the

1570s, more than 350 ships were exploiting the bounty of the Newfoundland Banks each year.

European fishermen soon learned that they could supplement their profits by exchanging cloth and metal goods like pots and knives for the Native Americans' beaver pelts, which Europeans used to make fashionable hats. At first the Europeans conducted their trading from ships sailing along the coast, but later they established permanent outposts on the mainland to centralize and control the traffic in furs (see pages 36–37). All were inhabited primarily by male adventurers, whose chief aim was to send as many pelts as possible home to Europe.

Northern Traders

The Europeans' insatiable demand for furs, especially beaver, was matched by the Native Americans' desire for European goods that could make their lives easier and establish their superiority over their neighbors. Some bands began to concentrate so completely on trapping for the European market that they abandoned their traditional economies. The Abenakis of Maine, for example, became partially dependent on food supplied by their neighbors to the south, the Massachusett tribe, because they devoted most of their energies to catching beaver to sell to French traders. The Massachusetts, in turn, intensified their production of foodstuffs, which they traded to the Abenakis in exchange for the European metal tools they preferred to their own handmade stone implements. The intensive trade in pelts also had serious ecological consequences. In some regions, beavers were completely wiped out. The disappearance of their dams led to soil erosion, especially when combined with the extensive clearing of forests by later European settlers.

Although their nation reaped handsome profits from fishing, English merchants and political leaders watched enviously as Spain's American possessions enriched Spain immeasurably. In the mid-sixteenth century, English "sea dogs" like John Hawkins and Sir Francis Drake began to raid Spanish treasure fleets sailing home from the West Indies. Their actions caused friction between the two countries and helped to foment a war that in 1588 culminated in the defeat of a huge invasion force—the Spanish Armada—off the English coast. As a part of the contest with Spain, English leaders started to think about planting colonies in the Western Hemisphere, thereby gaining better access to valuable trade goods and simultaneously preventing their enemy from dominating the Americas.

The first English colonial planners took Spain's possessions as both a model and a challenge. They hoped to reproduce Spanish successes by dispatching to America men who would similarly exploit the native peoples for their own and their nation's benefit. In the 1580s, a group that included Sir Humphrey Gilbert and his younger half-brother Sir Walter Raleigh promoted a scheme to establish outposts that could trade with the Indians and provide bases for attacks on New Spain. Approving the idea, Queen Elizabeth I authorized Raleigh and Gilbert to colonize North America.

Sir Walter Raleigh's Roanoke Colony

Gilbert failed to plant a colony in Newfoundland, dying in the attempt, and Raleigh was only briefly more successful. After two preliminary expeditions, in 1587 he sent 117 colonists to the territory he named Virginia, after Elizabeth, the "Virgin Queen." They established a settlement on Roanoke Island, in what is now North Carolina, but in 1590 a resupply ship—delayed in leaving England because of the Spanish Armada—could not find them. The colonists had vanished, leaving only the word *Croatoan* (the name of a nearby island) carved on a tree.

Thus England's first attempt to plant a permanent settlement on the North American coast failed, as had earlier efforts by Portugal on Cape Breton Island (early 1520s) and France in northern Florida (mid-1560s). All three enterprises collapsed for the same reasons: inability to be self-sustaining with respect to food, and hostile neighbors, both American and European. Spanish soldiers wiped out the French colony in 1565 (see pages 34–35), and neither the Portuguese nor the English were able to maintain friendly relations with local Indians for very long.

The explanation for such failings becomes clear in Thomas Harriot's *A Briefe and True Report of the New Found Land of Virginia*, published in 1588 to publicize Raleigh's colony. Harriot, a noted scientist who sailed with the second of the preliminary voyages to Roanoke, was charged with describing the animals, plants, and people of the region for an English readership. His account revealed that although the explorers were almost wholly dependent on nearby villagers for food, they needlessly antagonized their neighbors by killing some of them for what Harriot himself admitted were unjustifiable reasons.

Thomas Harriot's *Briefe and True Report*

John White, an artist with Raleigh's 1585 expedition (and later the governor of the ill-fated 1587 colony), illustrated three different fishing techniques used by Carolina Indians: to the left, the construction of weirs and traps; in the background, spearfishing in shallow water; in the foreground, fishing from dugout canoes. The fish are accurately drawn and can be identified today.   Trustees of the British Museum.

The scientist concluded by advising later colonizers to deal with the native peoples of America more humanely than his comrades had done. But the content of his book suggested why that advice would rarely be followed. *A Briefe and True Report* examined the possibilities for economic development in America. Harriot stressed three points: the availability of commodities familiar to Europeans, like grapes, iron, copper, and fur-bearing animals; the potential profitability of exotic American products such as maize, cassava, and tobacco; and the relative ease of manipulating the native population to the Europeans' advantage. Should the Americans attempt to resist the English by force, Harriot asserted, the latter's advantages of disciplined soldiers and superior weaponry would quickly deliver victory.

Harriot's *Briefe and True Report* thus depicted for his English readers a bountiful land full of opportunities for a quick profit. The people already residing there would, he thought, "in a short time be brought to civilitie" through conversion to Christianity, admiration for European superiority, or conquest—if they did not die from disease, the ravages of which he witnessed. Thomas Harriot understood the key elements of the story, but his prediction was far off the mark. European dominance of North America was to be difficult to achieve. Indeed, some historians today argue that it never was fully achieved, in the sense Harriot and his compatriots intended, and that the societies that subsequently developed in North America owed as much to their native origins as to their immigrant ones.

 Conclusion

The process of initial contact between Europeans and Americans that ended with Thomas Harriot near the close of the sixteenth century had begun approximately 250 years earlier when Portuguese sailors first set out to explore the Mediterranean Atlantic and to settle on its islands. That region of the Atlantic so close to European and African shores nurtured the mariners who, like Christopher Columbus, ventured into previously unknown waters—those who sailed to India and Brazil as well as to the Caribbean and the North American coast. When Columbus first reached the Americas, he thought he had found Asia, his intended destination. Later explorers knew better but, except for the Spanish, regarded the Americas primarily as a barrier that prevented them from reaching their long-sought goal of an oceanic route to the riches of China and the Moluccas. Ordinary European fishermen were the first to realize that the northern coasts had valuable products to offer: fish and furs, both much in demand in their homelands.

The wealth of the north could not compare to that of Mesoamerica. The Aztec Empire, heir to the trading networks of Teotihuacán as well as to the intellectual sophistication of the Mayas, dazzled the conquistadors with the magnificence of its buildings and its seemingly unlimited wealth. As an old man, Bernal Diaz del Castillo recalled his first sight of

Tenochtitlán, situated in the midst of Lake Texcoco: "We were amazed and said that it was like the enchantments . . . on account of the great towers and cues [temples] and buildings rising from the water, and all built of masonry." Some soldiers asked, he remembered, "whether the things that we saw were not a dream."

The Aztecs had predicted that their Fifth Sun would end in earthquakes and hunger. Hunger they surely experienced after Cortés's invasion; and, if there were no earthquakes, the great temples tumbled to the ground nevertheless, as the Spaniards used their stones (and Indian laborers) to construct cathedrals honoring their God and his son Jesus rather than Huitzilopochtli. The conquerors employed first American and later enslaved African workers to till the fields, mine the precious metals, and herd the livestock that earned immense profits for themselves and their mother country.

The initial impact of Europeans on the Americas proved devastating. Flourishing civilizations were, if not entirely destroyed, markedly altered in just a few short decades. The Europeans' invasion team of diseases and livestock, along with a wide range of other imported plants and animals, irrevocably changed the American environment, affecting the lives of the Western Hemisphere's inhabitants. By the end of the sixteenth century, many fewer people resided in North America than had lived there before Columbus's arrival, even taking into account the arrival of many Europeans and Africans. And the people who did live there—Indian, African, and European—resided in a world that was literally new—a world engaged in the unprecedented process of combining foods, religions, economies, styles of life, and political systems that had developed separately for millennia. Understandably, conflict and dissension permeated that process.

Suggestions for Further Reading

General

Alfred W. Crosby, *The Columbian Exchange: Biological and Cultural Consequences of 1492* (1972); Alfred W. Crosby, *Ecological Imperialism: The Biological Expansion of Europe, 800–1900* (1986); Bernard Lewis, *Cultures in Conflict: Christians, Muslims, and Jews in the Age of Discovery* (1995); William H. McNeill, *Plagues and Peoples* (1976); D. W. Meinig, *Atlantic America, 1492–1800* (1986); Herman Viola and Carolyn Margolis, eds., *Seeds of Change: Five Hundred Years Since Columbus* (1991); Eric Wolf, *Europe and the People Without History* (1982).

Mesoamerican Civilizations

Inga Clendinnen, *Aztecs: An Interpretation* (1991); Michael Coe, *Mexico*, 3d. ed. (1984); Brian Fagan, *Kingdoms of Gold, Kingdoms of Jade: The Americas Before Columbus* (1991); Eduardo Matos Moctezuma and David Carrasco, *Moctezuma's Mexico: Visions of the Aztec World* (1992); Linda Schele and David Friedel, *A Forest of Kings* [on the Mayas] (1990); Smithsonian Institution, *Handbook of Middle American Indians*, 16 vols. (1964–1976).

North American Indians

Brian Fagan, *Ancient North America: The Archaeology of a Continent* (1991); Brian Fagan, *The Great Journey: The Peopling of Ancient America* (1987); Francis Jennings, *The Founders of America: From the Earliest Migrations to the Present* (1993); Alvin Josephy, Jr., ed., *America in 1492* (1992); Alice B. Kehoe, *North American Indians* (1981); Mark Mehrer, *Cahokia's Countryside: Household Archaeology, Settlement Patterns, and Social Power* (1995); Lynda N. Shaffer, *Native Americans Before 1492: The Moundbuilding Centers of the Eastern Woodlands* (1992); Smithsonian Institution, *Handbook of North American Indians*, 8 vols. (1978–1990); Colin F. Taylor, ed., *The Native Americans: The Indigenous People of North America* (1992); Bruce Trigger and Wilcomb Washburn, eds., *The Cambridge History of the Native Peoples of the Americas*, Vol. 1: *North America* (1996).

Africa

Jacob Ade Ajayi and Michael Crowder, *History of West Africa* (1985); Paul Bohannon and Philip Curtin, *Africa and Africans* (1988); John Iliffe, *Africans: The History of a Continent* (1996); Robert July, *A History of the African People* (1992); Roland Oliver, ed., *The Cambridge History of Africa*, vol. 3: *c. 1050–c. 1600* (1977); Roland Oliver and J. D. Fage, *A Short History of Africa* (1988); John Thornton, *Africa and Africans in the Making of the Atlantic World, 1400–1680* (1992).

Exploration and Discovery

Emerson Baker et al., eds., *American Beginnings: Exploration, Culture, and Cartography in the Land of Norumbega* (1994); Fredi Chiappelli et al., eds., *First Images of America: The Impact of the New World on the Old*, 2 vols. (1976); Felipe Fernández-Armesto, *Before Columbus: Exploration and Colonization from the Mediterranean to the Atlantic, 1229–1492* (1987); Felipe Fernández-Armesto, *Columbus* (1991); Jerald T. Milanich, *Florida Indians and the Invasion from Europe* (1995); Jerald T. Milanich and Susan Milbrath, eds., *First Encounters: Spanish Explorations in the Caribbean and the United States, 1492–1570* (1989); Samuel Eliot Morison, *The European Discovery of America: The Northern Voyages, A.D. 1500–1600* (1971); Samuel Eliot Morison, *The European Discovery of America: The Southern Voyages, A.D. 1492–1616* (1974); J. H. Parry, *The Age of Reconnaissance* (1963); J. H. Parry, *The Discovery of the Sea* (1974); William and Carla Phillips, *The Worlds of Christopher Columbus* (1992); David B. Quinn, *North America from Earliest Discovery to First Settlements* (1977); Irving Rouse, *The Tainos: Rise and Decline of the People Who Greeted Columbus* (1992); Kirsten Seaver, *The Frozen Echo: Greenland and the Exploration of North America, ca. A.D. 1000–1500* (1995); Roger C. Smith, *Vanguard of Empire: Ships of Exploration in the Age of Columbus* (1993); Paolo Emilio Taviani, *Columbus: The Great Adventure* (1991).

The Conquest of Mexico

Sandra Cypess, *La Malinche in Mexican Literature* (1991); Ross Hassig, *Mexico and the Spanish Conquest* (1994); Miguel León-Portilla, ed., *The Broken Spears: The Aztec Account of the Conquest of Mexico* (1992); James Lockhart, ed. and trans., *We People Here: Nahuatl Accounts of the Conquest of Mexico* (1993); Lord Thomas, *Conquest: Montezuma, Cortés, and the Fall of Old Mexico* (1993).

Early European Settlements

Kenneth Andrews, *Trade, Plunder and Settlement: Maritime Enterprise and the Genesis of the British Empire, 1480–1630* (1984); Nancy Farriss, *Maya Society Under Colonial Rule* (1984); Charles Gibson, *Spain in America* (1966); Karen O. Kupperman, *Roanoke, the Abandoned Colony* (1984); James Lockhart, *The Nahuas After the Conquest: A Social and Cultural History of the Indians of Central Mexico, Sixteenth Through Eighteenth Centuries* (1992); A. J. R. Russell-Wood, *A World on the Move: The Portuguese in Africa, Asia, and America, 1415–1808* (1993); David J. Weber, *The Spanish Frontier in North America* (1992).

2

Europeans Colonize North America

1600 – 1640

I n August 1630, Fray Alonso de Benavides brought thrilling news to Madrid. Franciscan friars in the remote territory called New Mexico had successfully converted to Roman Catholicism at least eighty thousand heathens. In village after village and even among the nomadic Apaches and Navajos, Indians had eagerly embraced baptism in the new faith, had built beautiful churches and schools with their own hands, and had demonstrated their willing adherence to the true religion of Jesus Christ. Moreover, the friars' missionary activities had repeatedly benefited from God's "wonders and miracles." For example, when an old woman from the Taos pueblo tried to convince four others to renounce their Christian marriages, "a bolt of lightning flashed from a clear untroubled sky, killing that infernal agent of the demon."

Fray Alonso, who was born in the Azores in the 1570s, supervised the New Mexico missions from 1626 to 1629. His account of the Franciscans' miraculous successes, like Theodor de Bry's depiction of America as in the illustration opposite, created a sensation in Europe. Alonso's *Memorial* not only was immediately published in Spanish but also was quickly translated into Latin, French, Dutch, and German. Fray Alonso undertook the arduous journey to Spain to convince the king to increase his financial and administrative support of the Franciscan missions. He achieved that goal: King Phillip IV agreed to send additional friars to New Mexico at his own personal expense, and he ordered the colonial governor to assist the missionaries' efforts actively.

Yet even Fray Alonso de Benavides's enthusiastic and optimistic report contained a troubling undercurrent. The colonial capital at Santa Fe, he noted, was inhabited by only about 250 Spaniards (along with another 750 Pueblos and mestizos). The soldiers were "few and poorly equipped," and the church had been "a miserable hut" before Fray Alonso ordered the construction of a new one. Furthermore, not all the local Indians had been receptive to the friars' message. The residents of Picurís pueblo, for one, were "treacherous" and "on various occasions" had tried to murder the priests stationed there. Many of the miracles Fray Alonso described (such as the one recounted above) had been necessitated by the Indians' resistance to Christianity. For example, the skepticism of some Hopis about Christian teachings had led one friar to cause a boy blind from birth to see for the first time, and a Franciscan attempting to convert a group of Apaches had been saved from death only because at the last minute his attackers miraculously "did not dare shoot" the arrows they were aiming at him.

So, while praising the Spaniards' stunning successes in New Mexico, Fray Alonso revealed their equally striking weaknesses: more than a few Native Americans staunchly combated their missionizing; both priests and soldiers lacked adequate financial resources; and the one tiny, impoverished European settlement was surrounded by tens of thousands of potentially troublesome Pueblos, Apaches, and Navajos. Fray Alonso furthermore failed to identify an additional problem: royal governors often clashed with the Franciscans in a struggle for primacy in the region. A half-century later, such weaknesses helped to lead to a successful Pueblo revolt.

By the time Fray Alonso arrived in Madrid in 1630, England, France, and the Netherlands had also founded permanent colonies in North America. No longer were the Spaniards the only Europeans on that vast continent. Just as Franciscans played a major role in the Spanish settlements, so too Jesuit priests were active in New France. The French and Dutch colonies, like the Spanish outposts, were peopled largely by European men. Like the conquistadors, French and Dutch merchants (on the mainland) and planters (in the Caribbean islands) hoped to make a quick profit and then perhaps return to their homelands. The English, as Thomas Harriot made clear in the 1580s, were just as interested in profiting from North America. But they pursued those profits in a different way.

In contrast to other Europeans, most of the English settlers came to America intending to stay. Especially along the northeast Atlantic coast of the continent, in the area that came to be known as New England, they arrived in family groups, sometimes along with friends and relatives from neighboring villages back home. They recreated European society and family life to an extent not possible in the other colonies, where migrant men had to find their sexual partners within the Native American or African populations. Among the English colonies, those in the Chesapeake region and on the Caribbean islands most closely resembled colonies founded by other nations. Their economies, like those of Hispaniola or Brazil, soon came to be based on large-scale production for the international market by a labor force composed of bonded servants and slaves.

Wherever they settled, the English, like other Europeans, did not prosper until they learned to adapt to the alien environment. The first permanent English colonies survived only because nearby Indians assisted the newcomers. The settlers had to learn to grow unfamiliar American crops such as maize (corn) and tobacco. They also had to develop extensive trading relationships with Native Americans and with colonies established by other European countries. In need of laborers for their fields, they first used English indentured servants, then later began to import African slaves, copying the example of the Spanish in the Atlantic and Caribbean islands, and the Portuguese in São Tomé and Brazil. Thus the early history of the region that became the United States and the English Caribbean can best be understood as a series of complex interactions among a variety of European, African, and American peoples and environments rather than as a simple story of English colonization.

New Spain, New France, New Netherland, and the Caribbean

Spaniards were the first Europeans to establish a permanent settlement within the boundaries of the modern United States, but they were not the first to attempt that feat. Twice in the 1560s groups of French Protestants (Huguenots) sought to escape from persecution in their homeland by planting colonies on the south Atlantic coast. The first colony, in present-day South Carolina, collapsed when its starving inhabitants had to

Florida

• *Important Events* •

1533	Henry VIII divorces Catherine of Aragon; English Reformation begins
1558	Elizabeth I becomes queen
1565	Founding of St. Augustine (Florida), oldest permanent European settlement in present-day United States
1598	Juan de Oñate conquers Pueblos in New Mexico for Spain
1603	James I becomes king
1607	Jamestown founded, first permanent English settlement in North America
1608	Quebec founded by the French
1609	Henry Hudson explores Hudson River for the Dutch
1610	Founding of Santa Fe, New Mexico
1611	First Virginia tobacco crop
1614	Fort Orange (Albany) founded by the Dutch
1619	First Africans arrive in Virginia Virginia House of Burgesses established, first representative assembly in the English colonies
1620	Plymouth colony founded, first permanent English settlement in New England
1622	Powhatan Confederacy attacks Virginia colony
1624	Dutch settle on Manhattan Island (New Amsterdam) English colonize St. Christopher, first island in Lesser Antilles to be settled by Europeans James I revokes Virginia Company's charter
1625	Charles I becomes king
1630	Massachusetts Bay colony founded
1634	Maryland founded
1635	Roger Williams expelled from Massachusetts Bay; founds Providence, Rhode Island
1636	Connecticut founded
1637	Pequot War in New England
1638	Anne Hutchinson expelled from Massachusetts Bay colony, goes to Rhode Island
c. 1640	Sugar cultivation begins on Barbados
1642	Montréal founded by the French
1646	Treaty ends hostilities between Virginia and Powhatan Confederacy

be rescued by a passing ship. The second, near modern Jacksonville, Florida, was destroyed in 1565 by a Spanish expedition under the command of Pedro Menéndez de Avilés. To ensure Spanish domination of the strategically important region (located near sea lanes used by Spanish treasure ships bound for Europe), Menéndez set up a small fortified outpost, which he named St. Augustine—now the oldest continuously inhabited European settlement in the United States. Franciscan missionaries soon followed, but nearby Indians fiercely resisted the friars' efforts to Christianize them. Only after the native peoples were forcibly moved to mission towns did many assent to baptism. Even so, by the end of the sixteenth century a chain of Franciscan missions stretched across northern Florida.

More than thirty years passed after the founding of St. Augustine before conquistadors ventured anew into the present-day United States. In 1598,

New Mexico

drawn northward by rumors of rich cities, Juan de Oñate, a Mexican-born adventurer, led a group of about five hundred soldiers and settlers to New Mexico. At first, the Pueblos greeted the interlopers cordially. When the Spaniards began to use torture, murder, and rape to extort food and clothing from the villagers, however, the residents of Acoma pueblo killed several soldiers. The invaders responded ferociously, killing more than eight hundred people and capturing the remainder. All the captives above the age of twelve were ordered enslaved for twenty years, and men older than twenty-five had one foot amputated. Not surprisingly, the other Pueblo villages surrendered.

Yet Oñate's bloody victory proved illusory, for New Mexico held little wealth. It also was too far

The women of Acoma pueblo have long been accomplished potters. Before the arrival of Europeans with iron utensils, residents of the pueblo stored food and water in pots like this. The unusual shape derived from its function: the low center of gravity allowed a woman to balance the pot easily on her head as she carried water from a cistern to the top of the mesa.   The Field Museum #A109998c.

from the Pacific coast to assist in protecting Spanish sea lanes, which had been one of Oñate's aims (he, like others, initially believed the continent to be much narrower than it actually is). Many of the Spaniards returned to Mexico, and officials considered abandoning the isolated colony, which lay 800 miles north of the nearest Spanish settlement. Instead, in 1609, the authorities decided to maintain a small military outpost and a few Christian missions in the area, with the capital at Santa Fe (founded in 1610). This was the constricted world in which Fray Alonso de Benavides arrived in 1626 and on which he made his mark.

After Spain's destruction of France's Florida settlement in 1565, the French turned their attention northward, to the area that Jacques Cartier had explored in the 1530s. Several

New France

times in the late sixteenth century they tried futilely to establish permanent bases along the coast of what is now Canada. Finally, in 1608 Samuel de Champlain founded a trading post at an interior site the local Iroquois had called Stadacona when Cartier spent the winter there seventy-five years earlier. Champlain renamed it Quebec. He had chosen well: Quebec was the most easily defended spot in

the entire St. Lawrence River valley, a stronghold that controlled access to the heartland of the continent. In 1642, the French established a second post, Montréal, at the falls of the St. Lawrence (and thus at the end of navigation by oceangoing vessels), a place the Indians called Hochelaga.

Before the founding of Quebec and Montréal, French fishermen served as the major conduits through which North American beaver pelts reached France, but the two new posts quickly took over control of the lucrative trade in furs. The settlements had only a few European residents, most of them men, some of whom married Native American women. The colony's leaders offered land grants along the river to prospective settlers, including wealthy seigneurs (nobles) who were expected to import tenants to work their farms. A small number of Frenchmen brought their wives and took up agriculture; even so, more than twenty-five years after Quebec's founding, it had just sixty-four resident families, along with traders and soldiers. With respect to territory occupied and farmed, northern New France never grew much beyond the confines of the river valley between Quebec and Montréal.

One other important group was part of the population of New France: missionaries of the Society of Jesus (Jesuits), a Roman Catholic order dedicated to converting nonbelievers to Christianity. First arriving in

Jesuit Missions in New France

the colony in 1625, the Jesuits, whom the Native Americans called Black Robes, initially tried to persuade indigenous peoples to live near French settlements and to adopt European agricultural methods as well as the Europeans' religion. When that effort failed, the Jesuits concluded that they could introduce Roman Catholicism to their new charges without insisting that they fundamentally alter their traditional ways of life. Accordingly, the Black Robes learned Native American languages and traveled to remote regions of the interior, where they lived in twos and threes among hundreds of potential converts.

Using a variety of strategies, Jesuits sought to undermine the authority of village shamans (the traditional religious leaders) and to gain the confidence of leaders who could influence others. Trained in rhetoric, they won admirers by their eloquence. Immune to smallpox (for all had survived the disease already), they explained epidemics among the Indians as God's punishment for sin, their arguments aided by the ineffectiveness of the shamans' traditional

The Founding of Permanent European Colonies in North America, 1565–1640

Colony	Founder(s)	Date	Basis of Economy
Florida	Pedro Menéndez de Avilés	1565	Farming
New Mexico	Juan de Oñate	1598	Livestock
Virginia	Virginia Company	1607	Tobacco
New France	France	1608	Fur trading
New Netherland	Dutch West India Company	1614	Fur trading
Plymouth	Pilgrims	1620	Farming, fishing
Maine	Sir Ferdinando Gorges	1622	Fishing
St. Kitts, Barbados, et al.	European migrants	1624	Sugar
Massachusetts Bay	Massachusetts Bay Company	1630	Farming, fishing, fur trading
Maryland	Cecilius Calvert	1634	Tobacco
Rhode Island	Roger Williams	1635	Farming
Connecticut	Thomas Hooker	1636	Farming, fur trading
New Haven	Massachusetts migrants	1638	Farming
New Hampshire	Massachusetts migrants	1638	Farming, fishing

remedies against the new pestilence. Drawing on European science, Jesuits predicted solar and lunar eclipses. Perhaps most important, they amazed the villagers by communicating with each other over long distances and periods of time by employing marks on paper. The Native Americans' desire to learn how to harness the extraordinary power of literacy was one of the most critical factors in making them receptive to the missionaries' message.

Although the process took many years, the Jesuits slowly gained thousands of converts, some of whom moved to reserves set aside for Christian Indians. In those communities they followed Catholic teachings with fervor and piety. The converts replaced their own culture's traditional equal treatment of men and women with notions more congenial to the Europeans' insistence on male dominance and female subordination. Further, they altered their practice of allowing premarital sexual relationships and easy divorce because Catholic doctrine prohibited both customs.

Jesuit missionaries faced little competition from other Europeans for Native Americans' souls, but French fur traders had to confront a direct challenge. In 1614, only five years after Henry Hudson sailed up the river that now bears his name, his sponsor, the Dutch West India Company, established an outpost (Fort Orange) on that river at the site of present-day Albany, New York. Like the French, the Dutch sought beaver pelts, and their presence so close to Quebec posed a threat to French domination of the region. The Netherlands, at the time the world's dominant commercial power, was interested primarily in trade rather than colonization. Thus New Netherland, like New France, remained small, also focused on a river valley that offered easy access to its settlements. The colony's southern anchor was New Amsterdam, a town founded in 1624 on Manhattan Island, at the mouth of the Hudson River.

As the Dutch West India Company's colony in North America, New Netherland was a relatively unimportant part of a vast commercial empire that included posts in Africa, Brazil, the West Indies, and modern-day Indonesia. Autocratic directors-general ruled the colony for the company; with no elected assembly, settlers felt little loyalty to their nominal leaders. Migration was sparse. Even a company policy of 1629 that offered a large land grant, or patroonship, to anyone who would bring fifty settlers to the province failed to attract takers. (Only

New Netherland

one such tract—Rensselaerswyck, near Albany—was ever fully developed.) As late as the mid-1660s, New Netherland had only about five thousand inhabitants. Some of those were Swedes, who resided in the former colony of New Sweden (founded in 1638 on the Delaware River; see map, page 40) which was taken over by the Dutch in 1655.

Despite their geographical proximity and their trading rivalry, New France and New Netherland did not come into armed conflict with each other. Yet their Native American allies did. In the 1640s, the Iroquois, who traded chiefly with the Dutch and lived in modern upstate New York, went to war against their northern neighbors the Hurons, who traded primarily with the French and lived in present-day Ontario. The Iroquois wanted to become the major supplier of pelts to Europeans and to ensure the security of their hunting territories. They achieved both goals by using guns supplied by the Dutch to largely exterminate the Hurons, whose population had already been decimated by an epidemic. The Iroquois thus established themselves as a major force in the region, one that Europeans could ignore only at their peril.

It was in the Caribbean, though, that France, the Netherlands, and England—the third entrant into the contest for North America—clashed most openly in the first half of the seventeenth century. The Spanish concentrated their colonization efforts on the Greater Antilles— Cuba, Hispaniola, Jamaica, and Puerto Rico. They left many smaller islands alone, partly because of resistance by their Carib inhabitants, partly because the mainland offered greater wealth for less effort. But to other European powers, the tiny islands were attractive targets: they could provide bases from which to attack Spanish vessels loaded with American gold and silver, and they could serve as sources of valuable tropical products such as spices, dyes, and fruits.

The Caribbean

England was the first northern European nation to establish a permanent foothold in the smaller West Indian islands (the Lesser Antilles). English people settled on St. Christopher (St. Kitts) in 1624, then later on other islands such as Barbados (1627). France was able to colonize Guadeloupe and Martinique only after overcoming fierce resistance by native Caribs, whereas the Dutch more easily gained control of St. Eustatius (strategically located near St. Kitts). In addition to native inhabitants, the European interlopers had to worry about conflicts with Spaniards and with each other. Most of the islands

were attacked at least once during the course of the century, and some changed hands. For example, the English drove the Spanish out of Jamaica in 1655, and the French soon thereafter took over half of Hispaniola, creating the colony of St. Domingue (modern Haiti).

Why did other Europeans devote so much energy to gaining control of these tiny bits of land neglected by Spain? The primary answer to that question was sugar. Early in the 1640s, English residents of Barbados discovered that the island's soil and climate were ideally suited for cultivating sugar cane, then the major source of sweetness in the human diet. Europeans at the time grew that expensive, desirable luxury food in only a few widely scattered locations: Madeira, the Canaries, São Tomé, and Brazil.

Satisfying Europe's Sweet Tooth

Sugar was one of the most important components of the post-Columbian exchange of plants and animals. First domesticated in the East Indies, it was being grown in North Africa and southern Spain by 1000 C.E. But neither those regions nor the Atlantic islands settled in the fifteenth century could supply the demands of Europe's insatiable sweet tooth. Canary Island sugar canes were among the plants Columbus carried to Hispaniola on his 1493 voyage; by the 1520s, plantations (probably worked by African slaves) in the Greater Antilles were regularly shipping cargoes of sugar to Spain. Because of its focus on the mainland, though, the Spanish government did not encourage Caribbean sugar cultivation. At the end of the sixteenth century, most American sugar was being produced in Brazil.

The Dutch provided the key to the introduction of sugar cane to the newly colonized Lesser Antilles. In 1630 they seized control of northeastern Brazil from the Portuguese, holding the region until 1654. There the Dutch learned how to grow the canes and to process them into molasses and refined brown and white sugars. When they taught those skills to Barbadians, they were not being altruistic. The Dutch expected to sell African slaves to West Indian planters and to carry to Europe barrels of molasses and rum, which was distilled from sugar. The results must have exceeded their wildest dreams. The Barbados sugar boom in the 1640s was both explosive and lucrative. Planters, slave traders, and Dutch shipping interests alike earned immense profits.

Of course, as other Caribbean planters adopted sugar-cane cultivation, Barbadians' profits fell. Even so, sugar remained the most valuable American

In the 1660s, a French book illustrated the various phases of sugar processing for curious European readers. Teams of oxen (A) turned the mill, the rollers of which crushed the canes (C), producing the sap (D), which was collected in a vat (E), then boiled down into molasses (K). African slaves, with minimal supervision by a few Europeans (foreground), managed all phases of the process.   Library Company of Philadelphia.

commodity for more than one hundred years. In the eighteenth century, sugar grown by slaves in British Jamaica and French St. Domingue dominated the world market. Yet, in the long run, the future economic importance of the Europeans' American colonies lay on the mainland rather than in the Caribbean.

England Colonizes Mainland North America

The failure of Raleigh's attempt to colonize Virginia ended English efforts to settle in North America for nearly two decades. When the English decided in 1606 to try once more, they again planned colonies that imitated the Spanish model. Success came only when they abandoned that model and founded settlements very different from those of other European powers. Unlike Spain, France, or the Netherlands, England eventually sent large numbers of men and women to set up agriculturally based colonies on the mainland. Two major developments prompted approximately 200,000 ordinary English men and women to move to North America in the seventeenth century and led their government to encourage that migration.

The first major development that led English folk to move to North America was the onset of dramatic social and economic change caused by the doubling of the English population in the 150-year period after 1530, largely as a result of the introduction of nutritious American crops into Europe. All those additional people needed food, clothing, and other goods. The competition for goods led to high inflation, coupled with a fall in real wages as the number of workers increased. In these new economic and demographic circumstances, some English people— especially those with sizable landholdings that could produce food and clothing fibers for the growing population—substantially improved their lot. Others, particularly landless laborers and those with very

Social Change in England

European Settlements and Indian Tribes in Eastern North America, 1650 *The few European settlements established in the east before 1650 were widely scattered, hugging the shores of the Atlantic Ocean and the banks of its major rivers. By contrast, America's native inhabitants controlled the vast interior expanse of the continent and Spaniards had begun to move into the West.*

small amounts of land, fell into unremitting poverty. When landowners raised rents or decided to enclose and combine small holdings into large units, they forced tenant farmers off the land. As a result, geographical as well as social mobility increased, and the population of the cities swelled. London, for example, more than tripled in size between 1550 and 1650. By the latter year 375,000 residents were living on its crowded streets.

Well-to-do English people reacted with alarm to what they saw as the disappearance of traditional ways of life. Steady streams of the landless and homeless filled the streets and highways. Obsessed with the problem of maintaining order, officials came to believe that England was overcrowded. They concluded that colonies established in North America could siphon off England's "surplus population," thus easing social strains at home. For similar reasons, many English people decided that they could improve their circumstances by migrating from a small, land-scarce, apparently overpopulated island to a large, land-rich continent. Such economic considerations were rendered even more significant in light of the second development, a major change in English religious practice.

The sixteenth century witnessed a religious transformation that eventually led large numbers of English dissenters to leave their homeland. In 1533,

English Reformation

Henry VIII, wanting a male heir and infatuated with Anne Boleyn, sought to annul his marriage to his Spanish-born queen, Catherine of Aragon, despite nearly twenty years of marriage and the birth of a daughter. When the pope refused to approve the annulment, Henry left the Roman Catholic Church. He founded the Church of England and—with Parliament's concurrence—proclaimed himself its head. The English people welcomed the schism. Many had little respect for the English Catholic Church, which at the time was filled with corrupt bishops and ignorant priests. At first the reformed Church of England differed little from Catholicism in its practices, but under Henry's daughter Elizabeth I (child of his marriage to Anne Boleyn), new currents of religious belief that had originated on the European continent early in the sixteenth century dramatically affected the English church.

The leaders of the continental Protestant Reformation were Martin Luther, a German monk, and John Calvin, a French cleric and lawyer. Combating the Catholic doctrine that priests must serve as in-

Tudor and Stuart Monarchs of England, 1509–1649

Monarch	Reign	Relation to Predecessor
Henry VIII	1509–1547	Son
Edward VI	1547–1553	Son
Mary I	1553–1558	Half-sister
Elizabeth I	1558–1603	Half-sister
James I	1603–1625	Cousin
Charles I	1625–1649	Son

termediaries between laypeople and God, Luther and Calvin insisted that each person could interpret the Bible for himself or herself. One result of that notion was the spread of literacy: to understand and interpret the Bible, people had to learn how to read. Both Luther and Calvin rejected Catholic rituals and denied the need for an elaborate church hierarchy. They also asserted that salvation came through faith alone, rather than—as Catholic teaching had it—through a combination of faith and good works. Calvin, though, went further than Luther in stressing God's absolute omnipotence and emphasizing the need for people to submit totally to God's will.

Elizabeth I tolerated religious diversity among her subjects as long as they generally acknowledged her authority as head of the Church of England.

Puritans

Accordingly, during her long reign (1558–1603) Calvin's ideas gained influence within the English church. By the late sixteenth century, many English Calvinists—those who came to be called Puritans because they wanted to purify the Church of England—believed that the English Reformation had not gone far enough. Henry had simplified the church hierarchy; they wanted to abolish it altogether. Henry had subordinated the church to the interests of the state; they wanted a church free from political interference. And the Church of England, like the Roman Catholic church, continued to include all English people in its membership. The Puritans preferred a more restricted definition; they wanted to confine church membership to persons they believed to be "saved."

Elizabeth I's Stuart successors, her cousin James I (1603–1625) and his son Charles I (1625–1649), were

London in 1616, with London Bridge at center right. Overcrowding in the city led many observers to conclude that American colonization could remove "excess" population and provide new employment for poverty-stricken persons. The rapidly growing community of London merchants also sought to develop new sources of overseas profits.   Trustees of the British Library.

less tolerant of Puritans than she. As Scots, they also had little respect for the traditions of representative government that had developed in England under the Tudors and their predecessors. The wealthy landowners who sat in Parliament had grown accustomed to having considerable influence on government policies, especially taxation. But James I, taking a position later endorsed by his son, publicly declared his adherence to the theory of the *divine right of kings*. The Stuarts insisted that a monarch's power came directly from God and that his subjects had a duty to obey him. A king's authority was absolute, they argued, just like the authority of a father over his children.

The First Stuart Monarchs

Both James I and Charles I believed that their authority included the power to enforce religious conformity among their subjects. Because Puritans were challenging many of the most important precepts of the English church, the monarchs authorized the removal of Puritan clergymen from their pulpits. In the 1620s and 1630s a number of English Puritans accordingly decided to move to America, where they hoped to put their religious beliefs into practice unmolested by the Stuarts or the church hierarchy.

However, the initial impetus for the establishment of what was to become England's first permanent colony in the Western Hemisphere came not from the Puritans but from a group of merchants and wealthy gentry. In 1606, envisioning the possibility of earning great profits by finding precious metals and opening new trade routes, the men established a joint-stock venture, the Virginia Company, to plant colonies in America.

Joint-stock companies had been developed in England during the sixteenth century as a mechanism for pooling the resources of many small investors. These forerunners of modern corporations were funded through the sale of stock. Until the founding of the Virginia Company, they had been used primarily to finance trading voyages. For that purpose they worked well: no one risked too much money, and investors usually received quick returns. Joint-stock companies turned out to be a poor way to finance colonies, because the early settlements required enormous amounts of capital and, with rare exceptions, failed to return much immediate profit. Colonies founded by joint-stock companies consequently suffered from a chronic lack of capital and from constant tension between stockholders and colonists, who claimed they were not being adequately supported by the investors.

Joint-Stock Companies

The Virginia Company was no exception to this rule. Chartered by James I in 1606, the company tried but failed to start a colony in Maine and barely succeeded in planting one in Virginia. In 1607 it dispatched to North America an expedition consisting exclusively of men and boys. In May, 104 Englishmen landed in a region called Tsenacomoco by the native inhabitants. There they established the settlement called Jamestown on a swampy peninsula in a river they also named for their monarch. The colonists were ill equipped for survival in the unfamiliar environment, and the settlement was afflicted by dissension and disease.

Founding of Virginia

By January 1608, only thirty-eight of the original colonists were still alive. Many of the first migrants were gentlemen unaccustomed to working with their hands and artisans with irrelevant skills like glassmaking. Having come to Virginia expecting to make easy fortunes, most could not adjust to the conditions they encountered. They resisted living "like savages," retaining English dress and casual work habits despite their desperate circumstances. Such attitudes, combined with the effects of chronic malnutrition and epidemic disease, took a terrible toll. Only when Captain John Smith, one of the colony's founders, imposed military discipline on the colonists in 1608 was Jamestown saved from collapse. But after Smith's departure the settlement experienced a severe "starving time" (the winter of 1609–1610), during which at least one colonist re-

Theodor de Bry's America *depicted crucial events in the continents' history. This illustration is de Bry's version of the kidnapping of Pocahontas, Powhatan's daughter, in 1612. In the foreground, two other Native Americans are enticing Pocahontas to join the English; at right center, she is being led onto a ship; in the background, English raiders are burning the villages of Powhatan's people.* Library of Congress.

sorted to cannibalism. Although more settlers (including a few women and children) arrived in 1608 and 1609 and living conditions slowly improved, as late as 1624 only 1,300 of approximately 8,000 English migrants to Virginia remained alive.

That Jamestown survived was a tribute not to the English but rather to the Native Americans within whose territories they settled, a group of six Algonkian tribes known as the Powhatan Confederacy (see map, page 40). A shrewd and powerful leader, Powhatan was aggressively consolidating his authority over some twenty-five other small bands when the Europeans arrived. Fortunately for the colonists, Powhatan at first viewed them as potential allies. He found the English colony a reliable source of items such as steel knives and guns, which gave him a technological advantage over his Indian neighbors. In return, Powhatan's people traded their excess corn and other foodstuffs to the starving settlers. The initially cordial relationship soon deteriorated, however. The English colonists kidnapped Powhatan's daughter, Pocahontas, holding her as a hostage in retaliation for Powhatan's seizure of several settlers. In captivity, she agreed in 1614 to

Powhatan Confederacy

marry a colonist, John Rolfe; she sailed with him to England, where she died in 1616.

The relationship between the Jamestown colony and the coastal Indians was uneasy. English and Algonkian peoples had much in common: deep religious beliefs, a lifestyle oriented around agriculture, clear political and social hierarchies, and sharply defined gender roles. Yet the English and the Powhatans themselves usually focused on their cultural differences, not their similarities. English men thought that Indian men were lazy because they did not work in the fields and spent much of their time hunting (which was a sport to the English). Indian men thought English men effeminate because they did "women's work" of cultivation. In the same vein, the English believed that Algonkian women were oppressed because they did heavy field labor.

Algonkian and English Cultural Differences

Other differences between the two cultures caused serious misunderstandings. Although both societies were hierarchical, the nature of the hierarchies differed considerably. Among the East Coast Algonkians, people were not born to positions of leadership, nor were political power and social status necessarily inherited through the male line. Members of the English gentry inherited their position from their fathers, and English political and military leaders tended to rule autocratically. By contrast, the authority of Algonkian leaders rested on consensus. Accustomed to the European concept of powerful kings, the English sought such figures in native villages. Often (for example, when negotiating treaties) they willfully overestimated the ability of chiefs to make independent decisions for their people.

Furthermore, the Algonkians and the English had very different notions of property ownership. In most Algonkian villages, land was held communally by the entire group. It could not be bought or sold absolutely, although certain rights to use the land (for example, for hunting or fishing) could be transferred. English people, in contrast, were accustomed to individual farms and to buying and selling land. In addition, the English refused to accept the validity of Indians' claims to traditional hunting territories, insisting that only land intensively cultivated could be regarded as owned or occupied. As one colonist put it, the English believed that "salvadge peoples" who "rambled" over a region without farming it could claim no "title or propertye" in the land.

Above all, the English settlers believed unwaveringly in the superiority of their civilization. Although in the early years of colonization they often anticipated living peacefully alongside Native Americans, they always assumed that they would dictate the terms of such coexistence. Like Thomas Harriot at Roanoke, they expected Native Americans to adopt English customs and to convert to Christianity. They showed little respect for traditional Indian ways of life, especially when they believed their own interests were at stake. That attitude was clearly revealed in the Virginia colony's treatment of the Powhatan Confederacy in subsequent years.

Tobacco: The Basis of Virginia's Success

The spread of tobacco cultivation upset the balance of power in early Virginia. In tobacco—the American crop previously introduced to Europe by the Spanish—the settlers and the Virginia Company found the salable commodity for which they had been searching. John Rolfe planted the first crop in 1611. In 1620 Virginians exported 40,000 pounds of cured leaves, and by the end of that decade shipments had jumped dramatically to 1.5 million pounds. The great tobacco boom had begun, fueled by high prices and substantial profits for planters. The price later fell almost as sharply as it had risen, and it fluctuated wildly from year to year in response to increasing supply and international competition. Nevertheless, tobacco became the foundation of Virginia's economic prosperity, and the colony developed from a small outpost peopled exclusively by males into an agricultural settlement inhabited by both men and women.

Successful tobacco cultivation required abundant land, since the crop quickly drained soil of nutrients. Planters soon learned that a field could produce only about three satisfactory crops before it had to lie fallow for several years to regain its fertility. Thus the once-small English settlements began to expand rapidly: eager planters applied to the Virginia Company for large land grants on both sides of the James River and its tributary streams. Lulled into a false sense of security by years of peace, the planters established farms at some distance from one another along the river banks—a settlement pattern convenient for tobacco cultivation but poorly designed for defense.

Opechancanough, Powhatan's brother and successor, watched the English colonists steadily encroaching on the confederacy's lands and attempting to convert its members to Christianity. Recognizing the

Indian Uprising

danger his brother had overlooked, the war leader launched coordinated attacks all along the river on March 22, 1622. By the end of the day, 347 colonists (about one-quarter of the total) lay dead, and only a timely warning from two Christian converts saved Jamestown itself from destruction.

Virginia reeled from the blow but did not collapse. Reinforced by new shipments of men and arms from England, the settlers attacked Opechancanough's villages. For some years an uneasy peace prevailed, but then in April 1644 Opechancanough tried one last time to repel the invaders. He failed, losing his life in the war that ensued. In 1646, survivors of the Powhatan Confederacy accepted a treaty formally subordinating them to English authority. Although they continued to live in the region, their alliance crumbled and their efforts to resist the spread of European settlement ended.

Life in the Chesapeake: Virginia and Maryland

The 1622 Powhatan uprising that failed to destroy the colony did succeed in killing its parent. The Virginia Company never made any profits from the enterprise, for all its earnings were offset by the heavy

Headrights

cost of supporting the settlers and by internal corruption. In 1624 James I revoked the charter, transforming Virginia into a *royal colony*—a colony ruled by the king through appointed officials. Yet he nevertheless continued the company policy (adopted in 1617) of attracting settlers through a "headright" system. Every new arrival paying his or her own way was promised a land grant of 50 acres; those who financed the passage of others received similar headrights for each person. To ordinary English farmers, many of whom owned little or no land, the headright system offered a powerful incentive to migrate to Virginia. To wealthy gentry, it promised even more: the possibility of establishing vast agricultural enterprises worked by large numbers of laborers.

In 1619, the company had introduced a second policy that James was more reluctant to retain: it had authorized the landowning men of the major Virginia settlements to elect representatives to an assembly called the House of Burgesses.

The House of Burgesses

Although England was a monarchy, English landholders had long been accustomed to electing members of Parliament and controlling their own local governments. In accordance with his belief in the absolute power of the monarchy and his distrust of legislative bodies, James at first abolished the assembly. But Virginians protested so vigorously that by 1629 the House of Burgesses was functioning once again. Only two decades after the first permanent English settlement was planted in North America, the colonists successfully insisted on governing themselves at the local level. Thus the political structure of England's American possessions came to differ from that of New Spain, New France, and New Netherland, all of which were ruled autocratically.

By the 1630s, tobacco was firmly established in Virginia as the staple crop and chief source of revenue. It quickly became just as important in the second English colony planted on Chesapeake Bay: Maryland,

Founding of Maryland

settled in 1634 and given by Charles I to the Calvert family as a personal possession, a *proprietorship*. (Because Virginia and Maryland both border Chesapeake Bay—see map, page 40—they are often referred to collectively as "the Chesapeake.") The Calverts intended the colony to serve as a haven for their fellow Roman Catholics, who were being persecuted in England. Cecilius Calvert, second Lord Baltimore, became the first colonizer to offer freedom of religion to all Christian settlers; he understood that protecting the Protestant majority was the only way to ensure Catholics' rights.

In everything but religion the two Chesapeake colonies resembled each other. In Maryland as in Virginia, tobacco planters spread out along the river banks, establishing isolated farms instead of towns. The region's deep, wide rivers offered dependable water transportation in an age of few and inadequate roads. Each farm or group of farms had its own wharf, where oceangoing vessels could take on or discharge cargo. As a result, Virginia and Maryland had few towns, for their residents did not need commercial centers in order to buy and sell goods.

The planting, cultivation, and harvesting of tobacco had to be done by hand; these tasks did not

How do historians know what seventeenth-century settlements looked like? Recent excavations at St. Mary's City, Maryland, founded as the capital and sole town of Calvert's colony in 1634, demonstrate the importance of cooperation between historians and archaeologists. St. Mary's City is one of only two major seventeenth-century English settlements in America not now buried under modern cities. (The other, Jamestown, was located in 1996, although for many years historians believed that it had been eroded into the James River.) The site of St. Mary's City was abandoned in 1696 when the colonial capital was moved to Annapolis; later the area was incorporated into a tobacco plantation. Working from written documents like deeds and wills, historians created

hypotheses about the layout of the town. But when archaeologists began digging into the soil, they discovered what the documents had not revealed: the town plan was based on triangles intersecting at the town's central square. A modern artist's reconstruction of the town as it might have looked in 1685 shows portions of those triangles. At far right, top, is the Jesuit chapel, the first Catholic church in Anglo-America. At center is the square, with the large Country's House, the building once used as the capitol, on the left. (The new state house constructed in 1676 is off this map to the far left, at the point of a triangle at the same distance from the square as the chapel.) The artist needed both archival and archaeological data to produce this drawing. Historic St. Mary's City Commission.

---

take much skill, but they were repetitive, time-consuming, and labor-intensive. Clearing land for new fields, a necessary process every few years, was also a slow, labor-intensive task. Above all else, then, successful Chesapeake tobacco plantations required laborers. But where and how could they be obtained? Nearby Indians, their numbers reduced by war and disease, could not supply the needed workers. Dutch traders carried a few Africans to the Chesapeake beginning in 1619, but such merchants could more easily and profitably sell slaves in the West Indies, their first American landfall. In the first half of the seventeenth century, therefore, only a few

Need for Laborers

Africans, some of them free, arrived in the Chesapeake. By 1650, about three hundred blacks lived in Virginia—a tiny fraction of the population.

Chesapeake tobacco planters thus looked primarily to England to supply their labor needs. Because of the headright system (which Maryland also adopted in 1640), a prospective tobacco planter anywhere in the Chesapeake could simultaneously obtain both land and labor by importing workers from England. Good management could make the process self-perpetuating: a planter could use his profits to pay for the passage of more workers and thereby gain title to more land.

Since men did the agricultural work in European societies, planters and workers alike assumed that field laborers should be men. Such male laborers, along with a few women, mi-

English Migrants

grated to America as *indentured servants*—that is, in return for their passage they contracted to work for planters for periods ranging from four to seven years. Indentured servants accounted for 75 to 85 percent of the approximately 130,000 English migrants to Virginia and Maryland during the seventeenth century; the rest were mostly young couples with one or two children.

Roughly three-quarters of the servant migrants were males between the ages of fifteen and twenty-four; only one in five or six was female. Most of the men had been farmers and laborers, and many came from parts of England experiencing severe social

disruption. Some had already moved several times within England before migrating to America; they came from the middling ranks of society—what their contemporaries called the "common sort." Their youth indicated that most of them probably had not yet established themselves in their homeland.

For such people the Chesapeake appeared to offer good prospects. After fulfilling the terms of their indentures, servants were promised "freedom dues"

Conditions of Servitude

consisting of clothes, tools, livestock, casks of corn and tobacco, and sometimes even land. From a distance at least, America seemed to hold out chances for advancement unavailable in England. Yet the migrants' lives were difficult. Servants typically worked six days a

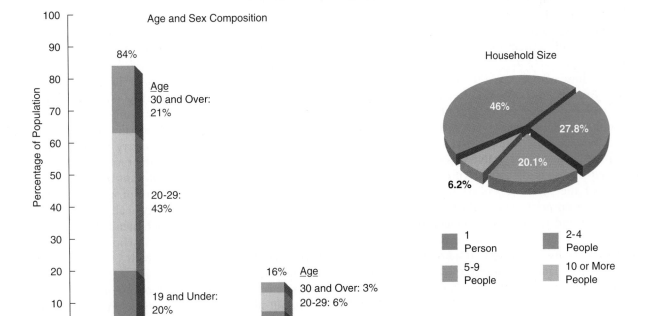

Population of Virginia, 1625   *The only detailed census taken in the English mainland North American colonies during the seventeenth century was prepared in Virginia in 1625. It listed a total of 1,218 people, comprising 309 "households" and living in 278 dwellings—so some houses contained more than one family. The chart shows, on the left, the proportionate age and gender distribution of the 765 individuals for whom full information was recorded, and, on the right, the percentage variation in the sizes of the 309 households. The approximately 42 percent of the residents of the colony who were servants were concentrated in 30 percent of the households. Nearly 70 percent of the households had no servants at all.*   Source of data: Robert V. Wells, *The Population of the British Colonies in America Before 1776: A Survey of Census Data* (Princeton: Princeton University Press, 1975), tables V-5 and V-6 and pp. 165–166.

week, ten to fourteen hours a day, in a climate much warmer than they were accustomed to. Their masters could discipline or sell them, and they faced severe penalties for running away. Even so, the laws did offer them some protection. For example, their masters were supposed to supply them with sufficient food, clothing, and shelter, and they were not to be beaten excessively. Servants who were especially cruelly treated turned to the courts for assistance, sometimes winning verdicts directing that they be sold to more humane masters or freed from their indentures.

Servants and planters alike had to contend with epidemic disease but not with the same illnesses that continued to kill Native Americans in large numbers. Migrants first had to survive the process the colonists called "seasoning"—a bout with disease (probably malaria) that usually occurred during their first Chesapeake summer. They then had to endure recurrences of malaria, along with dysentery, typhoid fever, and other diseases. As a result, approximately 40 percent of male servants did not survive long enough to become freedmen. Even young men of twenty-two who had successfully weathered their seasoning could expect to live only another twenty years at best.

For those who survived the term of their indentures, however, the opportunities for advancement were real. Until the last decades of the seventeenth century, former servants were usually able to become independent planters ("freeholders") and to live a modest but comfortable existence. Some even assumed positions of political prominence such as justice of the peace or militia officer. But in the 1670s tobacco prices entered a fifty-year period of stagnation and decline. Simultaneously, good land grew increasingly scarce and expensive. In 1681 Maryland dropped its legal requirement that servants receive land as part of their freedom dues, forcing large numbers of freed servants to live for years as wage laborers or tenant farmers. By 1700 the Chesapeake was no longer the land of opportunity it once had been.

Life in the early Chesapeake was hard for everyone, regardless of sex or status. Farmers (and sometimes their wives) toiled in the fields alongside servants, laboriously clearing land, then planting and harvesting tobacco and corn. Because hogs could forage for themselves in the forests and needed little tending, Chesapeake households subsisted mainly on pork and corn, which were filling but did not supply sufficient nutrients. Planter families supplemented this monotonous fare by eating fish, shellfish, and wildfowl, in addition to vegetables such as lettuce and peas, which they grew in small gardens. The health problems caused by epidemic disease were magnified by the near impossibility of preserving food for safe winter consumption. Salting, drying, and smoking, the only methods the colonists knew, did not always prevent spoilage.

Standard of Living

Few households had many material possessions other than farm implements, bedding, and basic cooking and eating utensils. Chairs, tables, candles, and knives and forks were luxury items. Most people rose and went to bed with the sun, sat on crude benches or storage chests, and held plates or bowls in their hands while eating meat and vegetable stews with spoons. The tiny houses were ramshackle dwellings with just one or two rooms. Planters devoted their income to improving their farms, buying livestock, and purchasing more laborers rather than to improving their standard of living. Instead of making items such as clothing and tools, planter families concentrated their energies chiefly on growing tobacco, importing necessary manufactured goods from England.

The predominance of males, the incidence of servitude, and the high mortality rates combined to produce unusual patterns of family life. Female servants normally were not allowed to marry during their terms of indenture because masters did not want pregnancies to deprive them of workers. Many male ex-servants could not marry at all because there were relatively few women; such men lived alone, in pairs, or as third members of households containing married couples. In contrast, nearly every adult free woman in the Chesapeake married, and widows usually remarried within a few months of a husband's death. Yet because their marriages were delayed by servitude or broken by death, Chesapeake women bore only one to three children, in contrast to English women, who normally had at least five.

Chesapeake Families

Thus Chesapeake families were few, small, and short-lived. The migrants could not reproduce the English system of family governance, for they came to America as individuals free of paternal control and tended to die while their own children were still quite young. In one Virginia county, for example, more than three-quarters of the children had lost at least one parent by the time they either married or reached age twenty-one.

As a result of the demographic patterns that led to a low rate of natural increase, migrants made up a majority of the Chesapeake population throughout the seventeenth century. That

Chesapeake Politics

fact had important implications for politics in Maryland and Virginia. Since migrants dominated the population, they also composed the vast majority of the membership of Virginia's House of Burgesses and Maryland's House of Delegates (established in 1635). So, too, in each colony they dominated the governor's council, which was simultaneously the colony's highest court, part of the legislature, and executive adviser to the governor.

English-born colonists naturally tended to look to England for solutions to their problems, and migrants frequently relied on English allies to advance their cause. Because of the low birth rates and high mortality, no cohesive native-born ruling elite emerged until the early eighteenth century. Before that, the Chesapeake colonies' immigrant leaders engaged in bitter and prolonged struggles for power and personal economic advantage. The incessant quarreling and convoluted political tangles thwarted the ability of the Virginia and Maryland governments to function effectively.

Representative institutions based on the consent of the governed are usually seen as a major source of political stability. In the seventeenth-century Chesapeake, most property-owning white males could vote, and such freeholders chose as their legislators the local elites who seemed to be the natural leaders of their respective areas. But because most such men were migrants without strong ties to each other or to the colonies, the assemblies' existence did not lead to political stability. Unusual demographic patterns thus produced the region's especially contentious politics.

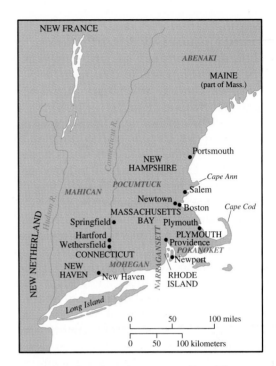

The Founding of New England

The economic motives that prompted English people to move to the Chesapeake colonies also drew men and women to New England (see map). But because Puritans organized the New England colonies, and also because of environmental differences between the two regions, the northern settlements turned out very differently from those in the South. The northern climate was too cold and the soil too infertile to raise tobacco on a large scale or to raise

New England Colonies, 1650 *The most densely settled region of the mainland was New England, where English settlements and Indian villages existed side by side.*

sugar cane at all. Accordingly, diversified small farms dominated the landscape. Except for the Catholics who moved to Maryland, migrants to the Chesapeake seem to have been little affected by religious motives. Yet religion was a primary motivating factor in the minds of many, though certainly not all, of the people who colonized New England. The Puritan church quickly became one of the most important institutions in colonial New England; neither the Church of England nor Roman Catholicism had much impact on the settlers or the development of the Chesapeake colonies.

Religion was a constant presence in the lives of pious Puritans. As followers of John Calvin, they believed that an omnipotent God predestined souls to

Puritan Beliefs

heaven or hell before birth and that Christians could do nothing to change their ultimate fate. One of their primary duties as Christians, though, was to assess the state of their own souls. They devoted themselves to self-examination and Bible study, and families prayed together each day under the guidance of the husband and father. Yet even the most pious could never be absolutely certain that they were numbered among the saved (or elect). Consequently, devout Puritans were filled with anxiety about their spiritual state. That anxiety lent a special intensity to their religious beliefs and to their concern with proper behavior— their own and others'.

Some Puritans (called Congregationalists) wanted to reform the Church of England rather than abandon it. Another group, known as Separatists, believed the Church of England to be so corrupt that it could not be salvaged. The only way to purify it, they believed, was to start anew, establishing their own religious bodies, with membership restricted to the saved, as nearly as they could be identified.

Separatists were the first to move to New England. In 1609 a group of them migrated to the Netherlands, where they found the freedom of worship denied them in Stuart England. But they were troubled by the Netherlands' tolerant atmosphere: the nation that tolerated them also tolerated religions and behaviors that they abhorred. Hoping to isolate themselves and their children from the corrupting influence of worldly temptations, these people, who were to become known as Pilgrims, received permission from the Virginia Company to colonize the northern part of its territory.

In September 1620, more than one hundred people, only thirty of them Separatists, set sail from England on the old and crowded *Mayflower*. Two months later they landed in America, but farther north than they had intended. Still, given the lateness of the season, they decided to stay where they were. They established their colony on a fine harbor previously visited by the French explorer Champlain, whose drawing of it appears on page 51. The English named their settlement Plymouth, locating it on the site of an Indian village whose inhabitants had died in the chickenpox epidemic of 1616–1618.

Founding of Plymouth

Even before they landed, the Pilgrims had to surmount their first challenge—from the "strangers," or non-Puritans, who had sailed with them to America. Because they landed outside the jurisdiction of the Virginia Company, some of the strangers questioned the authority of the colony's leaders. In response, the Mayflower Compact, signed in November 1620 while everyone was still on board the *Mayflower*, established a "Civil Body Politic" and a rudimentary legal authority for the colony. The settlers elected a governor and

at first made all decisions for the colony at town meetings. Later, after more towns had been founded and the population had increased, Plymouth, like Virginia and Maryland, created an assembly to which the landowning male settlers elected representatives.

A second challenge facing the Pilgrims was simple survival. Like the Jamestown settlers before them, they were poorly prepared to subsist in the new environment. Their difficulties were compounded by the season of their arrival, for winter quickly descended on them. Only half of the *Mayflower*'s passengers were still alive by spring. But, again like the Virginians, the Pilgrims benefited from the political circumstances of their Native American neighbors.

Pokanokets

The Pokanokets (a branch of the Wampanoags) controlled the area in which the Pilgrims had settled. Their villages had suffered terrible losses in the recent chickenpox epidemic, so to protect themselves from the powerful Narragansetts of the southern New England coast (who had been spared the ravages of the disease), the Pokanokets decided to ally themselves with the newcomers. In the spring of 1621, their leader, Massasoit, signed a treaty with the Pilgrims, and during the colony's first difficult years the Pokanokets supplied the English with essential foodstuffs. The settlers were also assisted by Squanto, a Pokanaket, who, like Malinche (see Chapter 1), served as a conduit between the Native Americans and the Europeans. Captured by fishermen in the early 1610s and taken to England, Squanto learned to speak English. When he returned to North America, he discovered that his village had been wiped out by the epidemic. Squanto became the Pilgrims' interpreter and a major source of information about the unfamiliar environment.

Massachusetts Bay Company

Before the 1620s ended, another group of Puritans—this time Congregationalists—launched the colonial enterprise that would come to dominate New England and would absorb Plymouth in 1691. The event that stimulated their interest in North America was Charles I's accession to the throne in 1625. Charles was more hostile to Puritan beliefs than his father had been, and for eleven years after 1629 he refused to call Parliament into session because it was dominated by Puritans. In 1633 he named William Laud, a prominent persecutor of Puritans, as archbishop of Canterbury, the most important post in the Church of England. Some non-Separatists

When Samuel de Champlain mapped the New England coast while on the exploratory voyage for France that led him to the St. Lawrence River, he drew the harbor on which the Pilgrims settled about a decade and a half later. Most of the people of the village he depicted, probably the home of Squanto before he was kidnapped and carried to England around 1611, died in the chicken pox epidemic of 1616–1618. John Carter Brown Library at Brown University.

therefore began to think about settling in America. A group of Congregationalist merchants sent out a body of colonists to Cape Ann, north of Cape Cod, in 1628. The following year the merchants obtained a royal charter, constituting themselves as the Massachusetts Bay Company.

The new joint-stock company quickly attracted the attention of Puritans of the "middling sort" who were becoming increasingly convinced that they no longer would be able to practice their religion freely in England. They remained committed to the goal of reforming the Church of England but concluded that they should pursue that aim in America rather than at home. In a dramatic move, the Congregationalist merchants boldly decided to transfer the Massachusetts Bay Company's headquarters to New England. The settlers would then be answerable to no one in the mother country and would be able to handle their affairs, secular and religious, as they pleased.

The most important recruit to the new venture was John Winthrop, a member of the lesser English gentry. In October 1629, the Massachusetts Bay Company elected Winthrop as its governor. (Until his death twenty years later, he served the colony continuously in one leadership post or another.) It fell to Winthrop to organize the initial segment of the great Puritan migration to America. In 1630 more than one thousand English men and women moved to Massachusetts—most of them to Boston,

Governor John Winthrop

which soon became the largest town in English North America. By 1643 nearly twenty thousand compatriots had followed them.

On board the *Arbella*, en route to New England in 1630, John Winthrop preached a sermon, "A Modell of Christian Charity," laying out his expectations for the new colony. Above all, he stressed the communal nature of the endeavor on which he and his fellow settlers had embarked. God, he explained, "hath so disposed of the condition of mankind as in all times some must be rich, some poor, some high and eminent in power and dignity, others mean and in subjection." But differences in status did not imply differences in worth. On the contrary: God had planned the world so that "every man might have need of other, and from hence they might be all knit more nearly together in the bond of brotherly affection." In America, Winthrop asserted, "we shall be as a city upon a hill, the eyes of all people are upon us." If the Puritans failed to carry out their "special commission" from God, "the Lord will surely break out in wrath against us."

Winthrop's was a transcendent vision. The society he foresaw in Puritan America was a true *commonwealth*, a community in which each person put the good of the whole ahead of his or her private concerns. Although, like seventeenth-century England, that society was to be characterized by social inequality and clear hierarchies of status and power, it was also to be a society whose members all lived according to the precepts of Christian love. Of course, such an ideal was beyond human reach. Early New England had its share of bitter quarrels and unchristian behavior. What is remarkable is how long the ideal prevailed as a goal to be sought, though seldom attained.

The Puritans expressed their communal ideal chiefly in the doctrine of the covenant. They believed God had made a covenant—that is, an agreement or contract—with them when they were chosen for the special mission to America. In turn they covenanted with each other, promising to work together toward their goals. The founders of churches and towns in the new land often drafted formal documents setting forth the principles on which such institutions would be based. The same was true of the colonial governments of New England. The Pilgrims' Mayflower Compact was a covenant; so too was the Fundamental Orders of Connecticut (1639), which laid down the basic law for the settlements established

Ideal of the Covenant

along the Connecticut River valley in 1636 and thereafter.

The leaders of Massachusetts Bay likewise transformed their original joint-stock company charter into the basis for a covenanted community based on mutual consent. Under pressure from landowning male settlers, they gradually changed the General Court—officially the company's small governing body—into a colonial legislature. They also granted the status of freeman, or voting member of the company, to all property-owning adult male church members residing in Massachusetts. Less than two decades after the first large group of Puritans had arrived in Massachusetts Bay, the colony had a functioning system of self-government composed of a governor and a two-house legislature. The General Court also established a judicial system modeled on England's.

The colony's method of distributing land helped to further the communal ideal. Unlike Virginia and Maryland, where individual applicants sought headrights for themselves and their servants, in Massachusetts groups of families—often from the same region of England—applied together to the General Court for grants of land on which to establish towns. The men who received the original town grant had the sole authority to determine how the land would be distributed.

New England Towns

Understandably, they copied the villages from which they had come. First they laid out town lots for houses and a church. Then they gave each family parcels of land scattered around the town center: pasture here, a woodlot there, an arable field elsewhere. They reserved the best and largest plots for the most distinguished among them (including the minister). People who had been low on the social scale in England were given much smaller and less desirable allotments. Still, every man received land, thus sharply differentiating these villages from their English counterparts.

When migrants began to move beyond the territorial limits of the Massachusetts Bay colony into Connecticut (1636), New Haven (1638), and New Hampshire (1638), the same pattern of town land grants was maintained. Only Maine, with coastal regions thinly populated by fishermen and their families, deviated from the standard practice.

Thus New England settlements initially tended to be more compact than those of the Chesapeake.

Town centers grew up quickly, developing in three distinctly different ways. Some, chiefly isolated agricultural settlements in the interior, tried to sustain Winthrop's vision of harmonious community life based on diversified family farms. A second group, the coastal towns like Boston and Salem, became bustling seaports, serving as places of entry for thousands of new migrants and as focal points for trade. The third category, commercialized agricultural towns, grew up in the Connecticut River valley, where easy water transportation made it possible for farmers to sell surplus goods readily. In Springfield, Massachusetts, for example, the merchant-entrepreneur William Pynchon and his son John began as fur traders and ended as large landowners with thousands of acres on which tenant farmers produced grain for export. Even in Puritan New England the acquisitive, individualistic spirit characteristic of the Chesapeake found some room for expression.

The migration to the Connecticut valley ended the Puritans' relative freedom from clashes with their Native American neighbors. The first English settlers in the valley moved there from Newtown (Cambridge, Massachusetts), under the direction of their minister, Thomas Hooker. Connecticut was fertile, though remote from the other English towns, and the wide river promised ready access to the ocean. The site had just one problem: it fell within the territory controlled by the powerful Pequots.

The Pequots' dominance was based on their role as primary middlemen in the trade between New England Indians and the Dutch in New Netherland.

Pequot War

The arrival of English settlers signaled the end of the Pequots' power over the regional trading networks, for their tributary bands could now trade directly with Europeans. Clashes between Pequots and English colonists began even before the Connecticut valley settlements were established, but their founding tipped the balance toward war. The Pequots tried without success to enlist other Indians in resisting English expansion. After two English traders were killed (probably not by Pequots), the English raided a Pequot village. In return, the Pequots attacked the new town of Wethersfield in April 1637, killing nine and capturing two of the colonists. To retaliate, a Massachusetts Bay expedition the following month attacked and burned the main Pequot town on the Mystic River. The Englishmen and their Narragansett allies

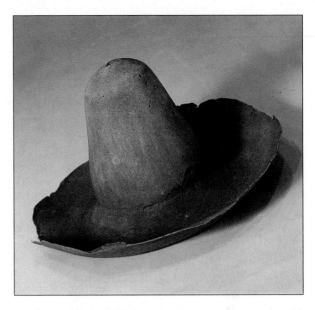

An English beaver felt hat, made by combining American beaver fur with wool and other fibers. Men and women in England and on the European continent wore such fashionable items, thus creating the insatiable demand for pelts that fueled the fur trade for many years. The Pilgrim Society, Plymouth, Massachusetts.

slaughtered at least four hundred Pequots, mostly women and children, and captured the few survivors.

For the next thirty years, the New England Indians tried to accommodate themselves to the spread of European settlement. They traded with the newcomers and sometimes worked for them, but for the most part they resisted acculturation or incorporation into English society. The Native Americans clung to their traditional farming methods, which did not employ plows or fences, and women rather than men continued to be the chief cultivators. When men whose hunting territories had become English farms did learn "European" trades in order to survive, they chose those that—like broom making, basket weaving, and shingle splitting—most nearly accorded with their customary occupations and simultaneously ensured both independence and income. The one European practice they adopted was keeping livestock, for in the absence of game, domesticated animals provided excellent alternative sources of meat.

Although the official seal of the Massachusetts Bay colony showed an Indian crying "Come over and

Among John Eliot's principal converts to Christianity was a young Native American named Daniel Takawampbartis. Ordained as a minister, he served at the head of the Indian congregation at Natick, Massachusetts, a "Praying Town," until his death in 1716. Members of his congregation made this desk for him in about 1677, incorporating elements of English design (brass pulls), Native American motifs (incised lines), and uniquely American hooved feet. The top, a hinged box, is intended to hold a Bible.   The Morse Institute, Natick, Massachusetts. Photo by Mark Sexton of the Peabody and Essex Museum, Salem.

he established, and just 10 percent of those town residents had been formally baptized.

The Jesuits' successful missions in New France contrasted sharply with the Puritans' failure to win many converts and the Franciscans' mixed results in New Mexico. Initially, Catholicism had several advantages over Puritanism (advantages more fully exploited by Jesuits than by Franciscans). The Catholic Church employed attractive rituals, instructed converts that through good works they could help to earn their own salvation, and offered Indian women an inspiring role model— the Virgin Mary. In Montréal and Quebec but not in New Mexico, communities of nuns taught Indian women and children and ministered to their needs. Furthermore, the few French colonists on the St. Lawrence did not alienate potential converts by encroaching steadily on their lands (as did New Englanders) or by demanding labor tribute (as did New Mexicans). Perhaps most important, the Jesuits understood that Christian beliefs were to some extent compatible with Native American culture. Unlike Puritans and Franciscans, Jesuits were willing to accept converts who did not wholly adopt European styles of life.

Puritan, Franciscan, and Jesuit Missions Compared

What attracted Native Americans to these religious ideas? Conversion often alienated the new Christians (both Catholic and Puritan) from their relatives and traditions—a likely outcome that must have caused many potential converts to think twice about making such a commitment. But surely one primary motive was a desire to use the Europeans' religion as a means of coping with the dramatic changes the intruders had wrought. The combination of disease, alcohol, new trading patterns, and loss of territory disrupted customary ways of life to an unprecedented extent. Shamans had little success in restoring traditional ways. Many Native Americans must have concluded that the Europeans' own ideas could provide the key to survival in the new circumstances.

John Winthrop's description of a smallpox epidemic that swept through southern New England in the early 1630s reveals the relationship among smallpox, conversion to Christianity, and English land claims. "A great mortality among the Indians," he noted in his diary in 1633. "Divers of them, in their sickness, confessed that the Englishmen's God was a good God; and that if they recovered, they

help us," most colonists showed little interest in converting the New England Algonkians to Christianity. Only a few Massachusetts clerics, most notably John Eliot, seriously undertook missionary activities. Eliot insisted that converts reside in towns, farm the land in English fashion, assume English names, wear European-style clothing and shoes, cut their hair, and stop observing a wide range of their own customs. Since Eliot was demanding a total cultural transformation from his adherents—on the theory that Indians could not be properly Christianized unless they were also "civilized"—he understandably met with little success. At the peak of Eliot's efforts, only eleven hundred Native Americans lived in the fourteen "Praying Towns"

John Eliot and the Praying Towns

Father Claude Chauchetière, a Jesuit in New France, sketched scenes of life in the colony's missions. His drawing of Indian women worshiping at a shrine of the Virgin Mary includes (at the rear) a view of one woman cutting her hair to conform more closely to European fashion. The other female converts show no evidence of having adopted European dress or hairstyles. Archives Departmentales de la Gironde, France.

would serve him." But most did not recover: in January 1634 an English scout reported that smallpox had spread "as far as any Indian plantation was known to the west." By July, Winthrop observed that most of the Indians within a 300-mile radius of Boston had died of the disease. Therefore, he declared with satisfaction, "the Lord hathe cleared our title to what we possess."

 ## Life in New England

New England's colonizers adopted lifestyles that differed considerably from those of both their Indian neighbors and their European counterparts in the Chesapeake. Algonkian bands usually moved four or five times each year to take full advantage of their environment. In spring, women planted the fields, but once crops were established they did not need regular attention for several months. Villages then divided into small groups, women gathering wild foods and men hunting and fishing. The villagers returned to their fields for harvest, then separated again for fall hunting. Finally, the people wintered together in a sheltered spot before returning to the fields to start the cycle anew the following spring.

Unlike the mobile Algonkians, English people lived year-round in the same location. And unlike residents of the Chesapeake, New Englanders constructed sturdy dwellings intended to last. (Indeed, some survive to this day.) They used the same fields again and again, believing it was less arduous to employ manure as fertilizer than to clear new fields every few years. Furthermore, they had to fence their croplands to prevent them from being overrun by the cattle, sheep, and hogs that were their chief sources of meat. When New Englanders began to spread out over the countryside, the reason was not so much human crowding as it was animal crowding. All that livestock constantly needed more pasturage.

Because Puritans commonly moved to America in family groups, the age range in early New England was wide; and because many more women went to New England than to the tobacco colonies, the population could immediately begin to reproduce itself. Moreover, New England was much healthier than the Chesapeake. Once Puritan settlements had survived the difficult first two or three years and established self-sufficiency in foodstuffs, New England proved to be even healthier than the mother country. Adult male migrants to the Chesapeake lost about ten years from their English life expectancy of fifty to fifty-five years; their Massachusetts counterparts gained five or more years.

New England Families

Consequently, while Chesapeake population patterns gave rise to families that were few in number, small in size, and transitory, the demographic characteristics of New England made families there numerous, large, and long-lived. In New England most men were able to marry; migrant women married young (at age twenty, on the average); and marriages lasted longer and produced more children, who were more likely to live to maturity. If seventeenth-century Chesapeake women could expect to rear one to three healthy children, New England women could anticipate raising five to seven.

Both children and older people flourished in the healthy climate of colonial New England. More infants survived their first year of life than in other contemporary societies, and more people lived longer. Thus settlers with numerous children needed highchairs, like this one made in seventeenth-century Massachusetts for the use of the Mather family. American Antiquarian Society. Gift of Hannah Mather Crocker, 1819.

The nature of the population had other major implications for family life. New England in effect created grandparents, since in England people rarely lived long enough to know their children's children. And whereas early southern parents commonly died before their children married, northern parents exercised a good deal of control over their adult children. Young men could not marry without acreage to cultivate, and because of the communal landgrant system they were dependent on their fathers to supply them with that land. Daughters, too, needed the dowry of household goods that their parents would give them when they married. Yet parents needed their children's labor and often were reluctant to see them marry and start their own households. These needs at times led to considerable conflict between the generations. On the whole, though, children seem to have obeyed their parents' wishes, for they had few alternatives.

Another important difference lay in the influence of religion on New Englanders' lives. Puritans controlled the governments of Massachusetts Bay, Plymouth, Connecticut, and all the other early northern colonies. Congregationalism was the only officially recognized religion; except in Rhode Island, which was founded by dissenters from Massachusetts, members of other sects had no freedom of worship. Some non-Puritans voted in town meetings, but in Massachusetts Bay and New Haven, church membership was a prerequisite for voting in colony elections. All households were taxed to build meetinghouses and pay ministers' salaries. Massachusetts's first legal codes (1641 and 1648) incorporated regulations drawn from Old Testament scriptures into the laws of the colony; those codes were later copied by New Haven, Plymouth, New Hampshire, and Connecticut. All colonists were required to attend religious services, whether or not they were church members, and anyone who expressed contempt for ministers or their preaching was punished with fines or whippings.

Impact of Religion

In addition, the Puritan colonies attempted to enforce strict codes of moral conduct. Colonists there were frequently tried for drunkenness, cardplaying, even idleness. Couples who had sex during their engagement—as revealed by the birth of a baby less than nine months after their wedding—were fined and publicly humiliated. (Maryland, by contrast, did not penalize premarital pregnancy, only bastardy.) More harshly treated in both regions were men—and a handful of women—who engaged in behaviors that today would be called homosexual. (The term did not then exist, nor were some people thought to be more likely than others to perform such acts.) Several men who had consenting same-sex relationships were hanged, as were other men suspected of bestiality (sex with animals). One unfortunate resident of New Haven was executed because the colonists believed he had fathered a piglet, now known to be a biological impossibility.

In New England, church and state were thus intertwined, for Puritans believed they were following Old Testament rules in assigning such penalties to moral miscreants. Puritans objected to secular interference in religious affairs but at the same time expected the church to influence the conduct of politics and the affairs of society. They also believed that the state had an obligation to support and protect the one true church—theirs. As a result, though they came to America seeking freedom to worship as they wished, they saw no contradiction in their refusal to grant that freedom to others. Indeed, the two most significant divisions in early Massachusetts were caused by religious disputes and by Massachusetts Bay's unwillingness to tolerate dissent.

Roger Williams

Roger Williams, a Separatist, migrated to Massachusetts Bay in 1631. He soon began to express some eccentric ideas: that the king of England had no right to give away land already occupied by Native Americans, that church and state should be kept entirely separate, and that Puritans should not impose their religious beliefs on others. Banished from Massachusetts in late 1635, Williams founded the town of Providence on Narragansett Bay a few months later. Because of Williams's beliefs, Providence and other towns in what became the colony of Rhode Island adopted a policy of tolerating all religions, including Judaism.

Anne Hutchinson

The other dissenter, and an even greater challenge to Massachusetts Bay orthodoxy, was Mistress Anne Marbury Hutchinson. A skilled medical practitioner popular with the women of Boston, she was a follower of John Cotton, a minister who stressed the *covenant of grace*, or God's free gift of salvation to unworthy human beings. By contrast, most Massachusetts clerics emphasized the need for Puritans to engage in good works, study, and reflection in preparation for receiving God's grace. (In its most extreme form, such a doctrine could verge on the *covenant of works*, or the idea that people could earn their own salvation.) After spreading her ideas for months in the context of childbed discussions (when no men were present), Mistress Hutchinson began holding women's meetings in her home to discuss Cotton's sermons. She emphasized the covenant of grace more than did Cotton himself, and she even adopted the belief that the elect could be assured of salvation and communicate directly with God. Such ideas had an immense appeal for Puritans. Anne Hutchinson offered them certainty of salvation instead of a state of constant anxiety. Her approach also lessened the importance of the institutional church and its ministers.

Mistress Hutchinson's ideas were a dangerous threat to Puritan orthodoxy. So in November 1637, the leaders of the General Court charged her with

Many New England men and women lived to become grandparents. Few, however, equaled the life span of Mary Mirick Davie, who died at the age of 117 in 1752. Massachusetts Historical Society.

having maligned the colony's ministers by accusing them of preaching the covenant of works. For two days she defended herself cleverly against her accusers, matching scriptural references and wits with John Winthrop himself. But then Mistress Hutchinson triumphantly and boldly declared that God had spoken to her "by an immediate revelation," telling her that he would curse the Puritans' descendants for generations if they harmed her. That assertion assured her banishment. After she had also been excommunicated from the church, she and her family, along with some faithful followers, were exiled to Rhode Island. Several years later, after she moved to New Netherland, she and most of her children were killed by Indians.

The authorities in Massachusetts Bay perceived Anne Hutchinson as doubly dangerous to the existing order: she threatened not only religious orthodoxy but also traditional gender roles. Puritans believed in the equality before God of all souls, including those of women, but they considered actual women (as distinct from their spiritual selves) inferior to men. Christians had long followed Saint Paul's dictum that women should keep silent in church and be submissive to their husbands. Mistress Hutchinson did neither. The magistrates' comments during her trial reveal that they were almost as outraged by her "masculine" behavior as by her religious beliefs. Winthrop charged her with having set wife against husband, since so many of her followers were women. A minister at her church trial told her bluntly: "You have stept out of your place, you have rather bine a Husband than a Wife and a preacher than a Hearer; and a Magistrate than a Subject."

The New England authorities' reaction to Anne Hutchinson reveals the depth of their adherence to European gender-role concepts. To them, an orderly society required the submission of wives to husbands as well as the obedience of subjects to rulers. English people intended to change many aspects of their lives by colonizing North America, but not the sexual division of labor or the assumption of male superiority.

 ## Conclusion

By the middle of the seventeenth century, Europeans had unquestionably come to North America to stay, a fact that signaled major changes for the peoples of both hemispheres. Europeans had indelibly altered not only their own lives but also those of the Native Americans. Europeans killed Indians with their weapons and diseases and had but limited success in converting them to European religions. Contacts with the Native Americans taught Europeans to eat new foods, speak new languages, and recognize—however reluctantly—the persistence of other cultural patterns. The prosperity and even survival of many of the European colonies depended heavily on the cultivation of American crops (maize and tobacco) and an Asian crop (sugar), thus attesting to the importance of post-Columbian ecological change.

European political rivalries, once confined to Europe, now spread around the globe, as England, Spain, Portugal, France, and the Netherlands vied for control of the peoples and resources of Asia, Africa, and the Americas. In America, Spaniards reaped the benefits of their South and Central American gold and silver mines, while French people earned their primary profits from Indian trade (in Canada) and cultivating sugar cane (in the Caribbean). Sugar also enriched the Portuguese.

The Dutch, by contrast, concentrated on commerce—trading in furs and sugar as well as carrying human cargoes of enslaved Africans to South America and the Caribbean.

Of these nations, only France and Spain went beyond the economic relationships they established with native peoples to attempt to Christianize them. In missions scattered in remote locations such as northern Florida, the St. Lawrence valley, and New Mexico, Catholic priests like Fray Alonso de Benavides worked with dedication to convert the Indians and to persuade them of the truth of Europeans' religious beliefs.

Although the English colonies, too, at first sought to rely on trade, they quickly took another form altogether when so many English people of the "middling sort" decided to migrate to North America. To a greater extent than their European counterparts, the English transferred the society and politics of their homeland to a new environment. Their sheer numbers, coupled with their need for vast quantities of land on which to grow their crops and raise their livestock, inevitably brought them into conflict with their Native American neighbors. New England and the Chesapeake differed in the sex ratio and age range of their migrant populations, in the nature of their developing economies, in their settlement patterns, and in the impact of religious beliefs on their settlers' lives. Yet both were English in origin, and in the years to come both regions would be drawn into the increasingly fierce rivalries besetting the European powers. Those rivalries would continue to affect Americans of all races until after France and England fought the greatest war yet known in the mid-eighteenth century and the Anglo-American colonies had won their independence.

Suggestions for Further Reading

General

Charles M. Andrews, *The Colonial Period of American History: The Settlements*, 3 vols. (1934–1937); David Hackett Fischer, *Albion's Seed: Four British Folkways in America* (1989); Karen O. Kupperman, ed., *America in European Consciousness, 1493–1750* (1995); D. W. Meinig, *Atlantic America, 1492–1800* (1986); Gary B. Nash, *Red, White, and Black: The Peoples of Early America*, 2d ed. (1982); Mary Beth Norton, *Founding Mothers & Fathers: Gendered Power and the Forming of American Society* (1996); John E. Pomfret, *Founding the American Colonies, 1583–1660* (1970); Paula Treckel, *To Comfort the Heart: Women in Seventeenth-Century America* (1996); Alden T. Vaughan, *Roots of American Racism* (1994).

New Spain, New Netherland, New France, and the Caribbean

Karen Anderson, *Chain Her by One Foot: The Subjugation of Native Women in Seventeenth-Century New France* (1991); Charles R. Boxer, *The Dutch Seaborne Empire, 1600–1800* (1965); Denys Delâge, *Bitter Feast: Amerindians and Europeans in Northeastern North America, 1600–64* (1993); Richard S. Dunn, *Sugar and Slaves: The Rise of the Planter Class in the English West Indies, 1624–1713* (1972); William J. Eccles, *France in America*, rev. ed. (1990); Carol Hoffecker et al., eds., *New Sweden in America* (1995); Jonathan Israel, *Dutch Primacy in World Trade, 1585–1740* (1989); Donna Merwick, *Possessing Albany, 1630–1710* (1990); Sidney Mintz, *Sweetness and Power: The Place of Sugar in Modern History* (1985); Marc Simmons, *The Last Conquistador: Juan de Oñate and the Settling of the Far Southwest* (1991); David J. Weber, *The Spanish Frontier in North America* (1992).

England

Susan Dwyer Amussen, *An Ordered Society: Gender and Class in Early Modern England* (1988); Carl Bridenbaugh, *Vexed and Troubled Englishmen, 1590–1642*, rev. ed. (1976); Peter Laslett, *The World We Have Lost*, 3d ed. (1984); Wallace Notestein, *The English People on the Eve of Colonization, 1603–1630* (1954); Michael Walzer, *The Revolution of the Saints* (1965); Keith Wrightson, *English Society, 1580–1680* (1982).

Early Contact Between Europeans and Indians

James Axtell, *The Invasion Within: The Contest of Cultures in Colonial North America* (1985); Philip Barbour, *Pocahontas and Her World* (1970); William Cronon, *Changes in the Land: Indians, Colonists, and the Ecology of New England* (1983); Francis Jennings, *The Invasion of America: Indians, Colonialism, and the Cant of Conquest* (1975); Karen O. Kupperman, *Settling with the Indians: The Meeting of English and Indian Cultures in America, 1580–1640* (1980); Patrick Malone, *The Skulking Way of War: Technology and Tactics Among the Indians of New England (1991)*; Kenneth Morrison, *The Embattled Northeast: The Elusive Ideal of Alliance in Abnaki-Euroamerican Relations* (1984); Helen C. Rountree, *Pocahontas's People: The Powhatan Indians of Virginia Through Four Centuries* (1990); Neal Salisbury, *Manitou and Providence: Indians, Europeans, and the Making of New England, 1500–1643* (1982); Bernard Sheehan, *Savagism and Civility: Indians and Englishmen in Colonial Virginia* (1980); Timothy Silver, *A New Face on the Countryside: Indians, Colonists, and Slaves in South Atlantic Forests, 1500–1800* (1990); Alden T. Vaughan, *The New England Frontier: Puritans and Indians, 1620–1675*, rev. ed. (1979); Peter Wood et al., eds., *Powhatan's Mantle: Indians in the Colonial Southeast* (1989).

Chesapeake Society and Politics

Lois Green Carr et al., *Robert Cole's World: Agriculture and Society in Early Maryland* (1991); David Galenson, *White Servitude in Colonial America: An Economic Analysis* (1981); James Horn, *Adapting to a New World: English Society in the Seventeenth-Century Chesapeake* (1994); Ivor Noël Hume, *The Virginia Adventure: Roanoke to James Towne* (1994); A. J. Leo Lemay, *The American Dream of Captain John Smith* (1991); Gloria L. Main, *Tobacco Colony: Life in Early Maryland, 1650–1720* (1983); Edmund S. Morgan, *American Slavery, American Freedom: The Ordeal of Colonial Virginia* (1975); James Perry, *The Formation of a Society on Virginia's Eastern Shore, 1615–1655* (1990); Darrett Rutman and Anita Rutman, *A Place in Time: Middlesex County, Virginia, 1650–1750* (1984); Alden T. Vaughan, *American Genesis: Captain John Smith and the Founding of Virginia* (1975).

New England Communities, Politics, and Religion

David Grayson Allen, *In English Ways: The Movement of Societies and the Transferral of English Law and Custom to Massachusetts Bay in the 17th Century* (1981); Virginia DeJohn Anderson, *New England's Generation: The Great Migration and the Formation of Society and Culture in the 17th Century* (1991); Charles Cohen, *God's Caress: The Psychology of Puritan Religious Experience* (1986); David D. Hall, *Worlds of Wonder, Days of Judgment: Popular Religious Belief in Early New England* (1989); Stephen Innes, *Creating the Commonwealth: The Economic Culture of Puritan New England* (1995); Stephen Innes, *Labor in a New Land: Economy and Society in 17th-Century Springfield* (1983); Sydney V. James, *Colonial Rhode Island* (1975); George Langdon, *Pilgrim Colony: A History of New Plymouth, 1620–1691* (1966); Kenneth A. Lockridge, *A New England Town: The First Hundred Years (Dedham, Massachusetts, 1636–1736)* (1970); John Frederick Martin, *Profits in the Wilderness: Entrepreneurship and the Founding of New England Towns in the 17th Century* (1991); Edmund S. Morgan, *The Puritan Dilemma: The Story of John Winthrop* (1958); Darrett Rutman, *Winthrop's Boston* (1965).

New England Women and Family Life

David Cressy, *Coming Over: Migration and Communication Between England and New England in the Seventeenth Century* (1987); John Demos, *A Little Commonwealth: Family Life in Plymouth Colony* (1970); Philip J. Greven, Jr., *Four Generations: Population, Land, and Family in Colonial Andover, Massachusetts* (1970); Lyle Koehler, *A Search for Power: The "Weaker Sex" in Seventeenth-Century New England* (1980); Edmund S. Morgan, *The Puritan Family*, rev. ed. (1966); Roger Thompson, *Sex in Middlesex: Popular Mores in a Massachusetts County, 1649–1699* (1986).

Why why should of this one be minding?
Therin a World of Euils Finding My Iarres
Then Farwell World, Farwell My Wiles thy Warrs
My Ioies thy Toyes thy Wiles thy Warrs
Truft Soules Retreat I am not forrye.
The Eternall Drawes to him my heart
By Faith (which cap my Force Subvert)
me me (after grace) with Glory.

CHAPTER

3

American Society
Takes Shape
1640 – 1720

Standing on a ladder with the condemned man, the hangman tightened the noose around his neck and shoved him off the ladder. The rope broke, and the notorious pirate Captain William Kidd lay on the ground, dazed. The hangman repeated the procedure with a new rope. This time it held, and Kidd died violently, as he had lived. It was May 23, 1701; the site was Wapping, near the London docks. As a warning to others, Kidd's body was left dangling from a gibbet on the bank of the Thames.

William Kidd, born in Scotland, had made his home in New York, the port once known as New Amsterdam. Merchants there were none too choosy about how they earned their profits, and at the end of the seventeenth century the vast expansion of worldwide trading networks opened practically unlimited opportunities for buccaneers who preyed on ships carrying valuable commodities long distances by sea. The merchants of Manhattan eagerly provisioned pirates' ships and purchased their loot. In the 1690s, the economy of the town depended on this illegal trade. For years Kidd and other pirates could count on the complicity of New York's governors, who ignored their activities in exchange for shares of the bounty.

Why was Captain Kidd condemned to die? His fatal buccaneering voyage began in London in early 1696, when he gained financial backing from several powerful and prominent English investors. After recruiting a crew in New York, Kidd sailed for Madagascar, the main pirate haven in the Indian Ocean. He captured all the likely vessels he encountered—a ship from Bombay flying the English flag, a Dutch merchantman, a Portuguese vessel. His most valuable prize, the *Quedah Merchant*, carried a large cargo of cloth, sugar, opium, and iron.

Captain Thomas Smith, a Boston mariner, painted this remarkable self-portrait in the late seventeenth century. It links his sailing career—illustrated in the background battle scene, which is thought to represent a combined Anglo-Dutch assault on a North African fort in 1670—with his pious Puritan faith. The skull under his hand serves to remind viewers of the brevity of life, which the poem underscores. "Why, why should I the World be minding?" the poet asks, looking forward to a future in which "The Eternall" would "Crowne me (after Grace) with Glory." *Worcester Art Museum.*

After more than a year of buccaneering, Kidd returned to New York by way of the Caribbean, hoping to avoid prosecution for piracy by paying off his investors in full and by bribing colonial officials. Unfortunately for Kidd, one of his financial backers, the earl of Bellomont, had become governor of New York. Bellomont was waging a vigorous campaign against piracy and could not afford to protect Kidd. In addition, as governor he could claim for his personal use one-third of any confiscated illegal cargo, whereas as a backer he was entitled to less than one-fifth of the partnership's proceeds. Kidd's fate was sealed when Bellomont ordered his arrest and shipped him back to England for trial.

The saga of William Kidd illustrates above all the involvement of the English mainland colonies in a growing network of trade and international contacts, not all of them legal. North America, like England itself, was becoming increasingly embedded in a worldwide matrix of exchange and warfare. The web woven by oceangoing vessels—once composed of only a few strands spun by Christopher Columbus, John Cabot, and their successors—now crisscrossed the globe, carrying West Indian sugar to Europe, Africans to America, cloth and spices from the East Indies to Africa, and New England fish and wood products to the Caribbean. Formerly tiny outposts, the North American colonies expanded their territorial claims and embarked on a deliberate course of economic development. In response, the English government for the first time began to adopt policies to systematize colonial administration, passing laws that regulated trade and reshaped the American governments.

Three developments shaped life in the mainland English colonies between 1640 and 1720: the introduction of a system of chattel slavery, especially in the south Atlantic coastal regions; changes in the colonies' relationship with their mother country; and increasing conflicts with their North American neighbors, both European and Native American. All these developments were intimately connected with the historical processes that produced Captain Kidd and others like him.

The explosive growth of the slave trade was of critical significance in the Anglo-American economy. Carrying human cargoes paid off handsomely, as many slave traders learned; planters who could afford to buy slaves also reaped huge profits. The arrival of large numbers of West African peoples dramatically reshaped colonial society and fueled the international trading system. The burgeoning North American economy, invigorated by the arrival of so many laborers, attracted new attention from colonial administrators. Especially after the Stuarts had been restored to the throne (having lost it for a time as a result of the English Civil War in the 1640s), rulers and bureaucrats in London attempted to supervise the American settlements more effectively and to ensure that the mother country benefited from their economic growth.

Neither English colonists nor London administrators could ignore other peoples living on the North American continent. As the English settlements expanded, they came into violent conflict not only with the powerful Indians of the interior but also with the Dutch, the Spanish, and especially the French. By 1720, war—between Europeans and Indians, among Europeans, and among Indians allied with different colonial powers—had become an all-too-frequent feature of American life. No longer isolated from each other or from Europe, the people and products of the North American colonies were now integral to the world trading system and inextricably enmeshed in its conflicts.

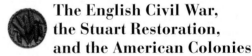

The English Civil War, the Stuart Restoration, and the American Colonies

In 1642, England erupted into civil war. Disputes over taxation, religion, and other issues led to armed conflict between supporters of the Puritan-dominated Parliament and King Charles I. After four

Stuart Monarchs of England, 1660–1714

Monarch	Reign	Relation to Predecessor
Charles II	1660–1685	Son
James II	1685–1688	Brother
Mary	1688–1694	Daughter
William	1688–1702	Son-in-law
Anne	1702–1714	Sister, sister-in-law

• *Important Events* •

1642–46	English Civil War; end of first New England economic system based on furs and migrants	**1681**	Pennsylvania chartered
1649	Charles I executed	**1685**	James II becomes king
1651	First Navigation Act passed to regulate colonial trade	**1686–89**	Dominion of New England established, superseding all charters of colonies from Maine to New Jersey
1660	Stuarts restored to throne; Charles II becomes king	**1688–89**	James II deposed in Glorious Revolution; William and Mary ascend throne
1662	Halfway Covenant drafted in New England, creating category of partial membership in Congregational churches	**1689–97**	King William's War fought on northern New England frontier
1663	Carolina chartered	**1692**	Witchcraft outbreak in Salem Village; nineteen executions result
1664	English conquer New Netherland; New York founded New Jersey established	**1696**	Board of Trade and Plantations established to coordinate English colonial administration
1670s	Jacques Marquette, Louis Jolliet, and Robert Cavelier de La Salle explore the Great Lakes and Mississippi valley for France	**1701**	Iroquois adopt neutrality policy toward France and England
1675–76	King Philip's (Metacom's) War devastates New England	**1702–13**	Queen Anne's War fought by French and English
1676	Bacon's Rebellion disrupts Virginia government; Jamestown destroyed	**1711–13**	Tuscarora War (North Carolina) leads to capture or migration of most Tuscaroras
1680–92	Pueblo revolt temporarily drives Spaniards from New Mexico	**1715**	Yamasee War nearly destroys South Carolina
		1718	New Orleans founded in French Louisiana
		1732	Georgia chartered

years of warfare, Parliament triumphed. Charles I was executed in 1649, and the parliamentary army's leader, Oliver Cromwell, assumed control of the government. Yet after Cromwell's death in 1658 Parliament decided to restore the monarchy if Charles I's son and heir would agree to restrictions on his authority. In 1660, Charles II ascended the throne, having promised to support the Church of England and to seek Parliament's consent for any new taxes. Thus ended the tumultuous chapter in English history known as the Interregnum (Latin for "between reigns") or Commonwealth period.

The Civil War, the Interregnum, and the reign of Charles II (1660–1685) had far-reaching significance for the Anglo-American colonies. During the Civil War and the Commonwealth period, Puritans controlled the English government. Thus the migration to New England largely ceased, and some colonists packed up to return home. During the subsequent reign of Charles II, six of the thirteen colonies that eventually would form the American nation were either founded or came under English rule: New York, New Jersey, Pennsylvania (including Delaware), and North and South Carolina (see map, page 64). All were proprietorships; like Maryland they were granted in their entirety to one man or to a group of men who held title to the soil and controlled the government. Charles II gave these vast American holdings as rewards to men who had supported him during the Civil War. Several of his favorites even shared in more than one grant. Collectively, these became known as the Restoration colonies, because they were created by the restored Stuart monarchy.

One of the first to benefit was Charles's younger brother James, the duke of York. In 1664, acting as

The Anglo-American Colonies in the Early Eighteenth Century   *By the early eighteenth century, the English colonies nominally dominated the Atlantic coastline of North America. But the colonies' formal boundary lines are deceiving, because the western reaches of each colony were still largely unfamiliar to Europeans and because much of the land was still inhabited by Native Americans.*

The Founding of English Colonies in North America, 1664–1732

Colony	Founder(s)	Date	Basis of Economy
New York (formerly New Netherland)	James, duke of York	1664	Farming, fur trading
New Jersey	Sir George Carteret, John Lord Berkeley	1664	Farming
North Carolina	Carolina proprietors	1665	Tobacco, forest products
South Carolina	Carolina proprietors	1670	Rice, indigo
Pennsylvania	William Penn	1681	Farming
Georgia	James Oglethorpe	1732	Rice, forest products

New Netherland Becomes New York

though the Dutch colony of New Netherland did not exist, Charles II gave James the region between the Connecticut and Delaware Rivers, including the Hudson valley and Long Island. James immediately organized an invasion fleet. In late August the vessels anchored off Manhattan Island and demanded New Netherland's surrender. The colony complied without resistance. Although the Netherlands briefly regained control of the colony in 1672, the Dutch permanently ceded the province in 1674.

Thus England acquired a tiny but heterogeneous possession. In 1664, an appreciable minority of English people (mostly Puritan New Englanders who had moved to Long Island) already lived in the colony. New York, as it was now called, also included sizable numbers of Native Americans, Germans, French-speaking Walloons (from the southern part of modern Belgium), Scandinavians, and Africans, as well as a smattering of other European peoples. The Dutch West India Company, the world's greatest slave-trading power at midcentury (see page 70), had actively imported slaves into the colony, intending some of them for resale in the Chesapeake. Many, though, remained in New Netherland as laborers; at the time of the English conquest, almost one-fifth of Manhattan's approximately fifteen hundred inhabitants were of African descent. In fact, slaves constituted a higher proportion of New York's urban population than of the Chesapeake's at the same time.

Recognizing the population's diversity, the duke of York's representatives moved cautiously in their efforts to establish English authority. The Duke's Laws, a legal code proclaimed in 1665, at first applied solely to the English settlements on Long Island, only later being extended to the rest of the colony. Dutch forms of local government were maintained, Dutch land titles confirmed, and Dutch residents allowed to maintain customary legal practices. Religious toleration was guaranteed through a multiple establishment: each town was permitted to decide which church to support with its tax revenues. Much to the dismay of English residents of the colony, the Duke's Laws made no provision for a representative assembly. Like other Stuarts, James was suspicious of legislative bodies, and not until 1683 did he agree to the colonists' requests for an elected legislature. Before then, New York was ruled by an autocratic governor as it had been under the Dutch.

The English takeover thus had little immediate effect on the colony. Its population grew slowly, barely reaching eighteen thousand by the time of the first English census in 1698. Until the second decade of the eighteenth century, New York City remained a commercial backwater within the orbit of Boston.

One of the chief reasons why the English conquest brought so little change to New York was that the duke of York in 1664 regranted the land between the Hudson and Delaware Rivers—East and West Jersey—to his friends Sir George Carteret and John Lord Berkeley. That grant left his own colony confined between Connecticut to the east and the Jerseys to the west and south, depriving it of much fertile land and hindering its economic growth. He also failed to

Founding of New Jersey

In 1679 a traveler drew this picture of the Stadt Huys (State House) on Manhattan Island, in the colony of New York. The government building and its adjoining houses, built under Dutch rule while the settlement was still called New Amsterdam, make the scene look more like the Netherlands than like England.   Brooklyn Historical Society.

promote migration. Meanwhile, the Jersey proprietors acted rapidly to attract settlers, promising generous land grants, limited freedom of religion, and—without authorization from the Crown—a representative assembly. In response, large numbers of Puritan New Englanders migrated southward to the Jerseys, along with some Dutch New Yorkers and a contingent of families from Barbados. New Jersey grew quickly; in 1726, at the time of its first census as a united colony, it had 32,500 inhabitants, only 8,000 fewer than New York.

Within twenty years, Berkeley and Carteret sold their interests in the Jerseys to separate groups of investors. The purchasers of all of Carteret's share (West Jersey) and portions of Berkeley's (East Jersey)

were members of the Society of Friends, seeking a refuge from persecution in England. The Society of Friends, also called Quakers, denied the need for intermediaries between individuals and God. They believed that anyone could receive the "inner light" and be saved and that all were equal in God's sight. They had no formally trained clergy; any Quaker, male or female, could become a "public Friend" and travel from meeting to meeting to discuss God's word. Moreover, any member could speak in meetings if he or she desired. The Quaker message of radical egalitarianism was not welcome in the hierarchical society of seventeenth-century England or, for that matter, in Puritan New England. For example, Mary Dyer—who had followed Anne Hutchinson into exile—became a Quaker, returned to Boston as a missionary, and was hanged (along with several men) for preaching Quaker doctrines.

The Quakers obtained their own colony in 1681, when Charles II granted the region between Maryland and New York to his close, personal friend William Penn, a prominent member of the sect. Penn was then thirty-seven years old; he held the colony as a personal proprietorship, one that earned profits for his descendants until the American Revolution. Even so, Penn, like the Roman Catholic Calverts of Maryland before him, saw his province not merely as a source of revenue but also as a haven for his persecuted coreligionists. Penn offered land to all comers on liberal terms, promised toleration of all religions (though only Christians were given the vote), guaranteed English liberties such as the right to bail and trial by jury, and pledged to establish a representative assembly.

Pennsylvania: A Quaker Haven

He also publicized the ready availability of land in Pennsylvania through promotional tracts printed in German, French, and Dutch and distributed widely throughout Europe.

Penn's activities and the attraction of his lands for Quakers gave rise to a migration whose magnitude was equaled only by the Puritan exodus to New England in the 1630s. By mid-1683, over three thousand people—among them Welsh, Irish, Dutch, and Germans—had already moved to Pennsylvania, and within five years the population reached twelve thousand. (By contrast, it took Virginia more than thirty years to achieve a comparable population.) Philadelphia, carefully planned to be the major city in the province, drew merchants and artisans from throughout the English-speaking world. From mainland and West Indian colonies alike came Quakers seeking religious freedom; they brought with them years of experience on American soil and well-established trading connections. Pennsylvania's lands were both plentiful and fertile, and the colony

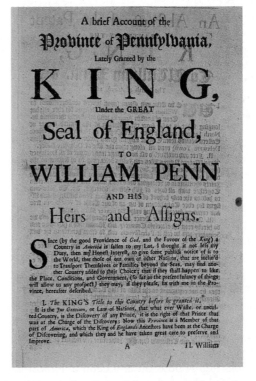

William Penn, later the proprietor of Pennsylvania, as he looked during his youth in Ireland. In such pamphlets as the one shown here, Penn spread the word about his new colony to thousands of readers in England and its other colonial possessions.   Portrait and Pamphlet: Historical Society of Pennsylvania.

soon began exporting flour and other foodstuffs to the West Indies. Practically overnight Philadelphia acquired more than two thousand citizens and began to challenge Boston's commercial dominance.

A pacifist with egalitarian principles, Penn attempted to treat Native Americans fairly. He learned to speak the language of the Delawares (or Lenapes),

William Penn's Indian Policy

from whom he purchased tracts of land to sell to European settlers. Penn also established strict regulations for trade and forbade the sale of alcohol to Indians.

His policies attracted Indians who moved to Pennsylvania near the end of the seventeenth century to escape repeated clashes with English colonists in Maryland, Virginia, and North Carolina. Most important were the Tuscaroras, whose experiences are described later in this chapter. Likewise, Shawnees and Miamis chose to move eastward from the Ohio valley. By a supreme irony, however, the same toleration that attracted Native Americans also brought non-Quaker Europeans who showed little respect for Indian claims to the soil. In effect, Penn's policy was so successful that it caused its own downfall. The Scots-Irish, Palatine Germans, and Swiss who settled in Pennsylvania in the first half of the eighteenth century clashed repeatedly over land with groups of Indians who had also recently migrated to the colony.

The other proprietary colony, granted by Charles II in 1663, encompassed a huge tract of land stretching from the southern boundary of Virginia to Spanish Florida. The area

Founding of Carolina

had great strategic importance; a successful English settlement there would prevent Spaniards from pushing farther north. The semitropical land was also extremely fertile, holding forth the promise of producing exotic and valuable commodities such as figs, olives, wines, and silk. The proprietors named their new province Carolina in honor of Charles, whose Latin name was *Carolus*. The "Fundamental Constitutions of Carolina," which they asked the political philosopher John Locke to draft for them, set forth an elaborate plan for a colony governed by a hierarchy of landholding aristocrats and characterized by a carefully structured distribution of political and economic power. But Carolina failed to follow the course the proprietors laid out. Instead, it quickly developed two distinct population centers, which in 1729 permanently split into two separate colonies.

The Albemarle region that became North Carolina was settled by Virginia planters. They established a society much like their own, with an economy based on tobacco cultivation and the export of such forest products as pitch, tar, and timber. Because North Carolina lacked a satisfactory harbor, its planters continued to rely on Virginia's ports and merchants to conduct their trade, and the two colonies remained tightly linked. Although North Carolina planters held some slaves, they never became as dependent on slave labor as did the other population center in Carolina.

Charleston, South Carolina, was founded in 1670 by a group of settlers from the island of Barbados, which was already overcrowded less than fifty years after English people first moved there. The English migrants from Barbados brought with them the slaves who had worked on their sugar plantations and the legal codes that had governed those laborers, thereby shaping the future of South Carolina and the subsequent history of the United States.

 ## The North American Slave Trade and the Enslavement of Africans

Since England had no tradition of slavery, why did English settlers in North America and the Caribbean islands begin to enslave Africans around the middle of the seventeenth century? The answer to that question lies in a combination of the settlers' need for labor and the experience of other Europeans.

Although the English had not previously practiced slavery, other Europeans had. As noted in Chapter 1, the Spanish and Portuguese imported enslaved Africans as laborers into the islands of the Mediterranean Atlantic during the fifteenth century. They then extended that practice to their American possessions, New Spain and Brazil. No free people of any description were willing to toil for wages in the difficult and dangerous conditions of South American mines or Caribbean sugar plantations. To produce the profitable goods they had come to America to seek, Europeans needed bound laborers—people who, by law or contract, could be forced to work at jobs that no person would do voluntarily. Dutch, French, and English Caribbean planters eagerly purchased slaves from the 1640s on. Then, twenty years later, the supply of English indentured servants in the Chesapeake started to dry up. Because population pressures had eased in England,

and because the founding of the new Restoration colonies meant that prospective migrants could choose other American destinations, Chesapeake planters were deprived of an ample number of English laborers. Consequently, they too turned to Africans.

In the early mainland English settlements, the few residents of African descent varied in status: some were free, some indentured, some enslaved. All came from a population that the historian Ira Berlin recently

Atlantic Creoles termed "Atlantic creoles"—people who participated in the new international system of trade and piracy that encompassed Captain Kidd. Often of mixed race, they were already familiar with Europeans and fitted easily into established niches in the many-faceted hierarchical social structures of the early colonies. Slave status was not clearly defined in law, and individuals moved back and forth across boundaries of freedom, indenture, and enslavement.

Before the 1660s, none of the English mainland colonies systematically categorized Africans as slaves.

But after Chesapeake planters began to import already enslaved Africans from Caribbean sugar islands and then to

Systematic Enslavement of Africans purchase slaves directly from Africa, that situation changed decisively. As increasing numbers of slaves arrived each year beginning in the 1670s, the enslaved population changed from acculturated creole to newly imported African, and the laws governing enslaved people were more comprehensively and tightly drawn. Most of the English colonies, even those without many bondspeople, adopted codes to govern slaves' behavior. By the end of the century, African slavery was firmly established as the basis of the economy in the Chesapeake as well as in the Caribbean.

One of the most remarkable aspects of the adoption of the slave system was English enslavers' evident lack of moral qualms. No one at the time seems to have questioned—or even felt the need to justify with racist rationalizations—the decision to hold Africans and their descendants in perpetual bondage. That fact suggests the importance both of

At forts along the African coast, Europeans purchased slaves from local rulers. This contemporary illustration of such a transaction is taken from a book published in 1729. Library of Congress.

prior Spanish and Portuguese practice and of economic motives in leading to this momentous development. Certainly economics, not racism, was the theme of one New Englander's argument for acquiring slaves in 1645. The problem with indentured servants, he pointed out, was that they would become free "and not stay but for verie great wages." Further, "wee shall maynteyne 20 Moores [Africans] cheaper then one Englishe servant." He concluded, "I doe not see how wee can thrive untill we gett into a stock of slaves suffitient to doe all our buisnes." Nowhere did he consider the morality of the course he advocated, nor did he contend that Africans were inferior to other peoples. Accepting their already enslaved status, he simply wanted to employ them to his advantage.

Between 1492 and 1770 more Africans than Europeans came to the Americas. The vast majority of them went to Brazil or the Caribbean: of at least 10 million enslaved people brought to the Americas during the existence of slavery, only about 120,000 by 1740, or 260,000 by 1775, were imported into the region that later became the United States. The magnitude of the slave trade raises three related questions. What was its impact on West Africa and Europe? How was the trade organized and conducted? What was its effect on the people it carried and on the region to which they were taken?

West Africa was one of the most fertile and densely inhabited regions of the continent, so the trade in human beings did not seriously depopulate the area. That was true even

West Africa and the Slave Trade

after the demand for slaves grew so great that the sale of previously enslaved prisoners could not meet it and African raiding parties began regularly setting out to capture the unwary. Even so, because American planters preferred to purchase male slaves, the trade significantly affected the sex ratio of the remaining population. The relative lack of men increased the work demands on women and simultaneously encouraged polygyny.

In Guinea, the primary consequences of the trade were political and economic. Coastal rulers—like the one pictured on page 69—served as middlemen, allowing the establishment of permanent slave-trading posts in their territories and supplying resident Europeans with slaves to fill ships that stopped regularly at the coastal forts. Such rulers controlled European traders' access to slaves and at the same time controlled inland peoples' access

to desirable European goods like cloth, alcohol, tobacco, firearms, and iron bars that could be made into useful tools. The centralizing tendencies of the slave trade helped to create such powerful eighteenth-century kingdoms as Dahomey and Asante (formed from the Akan States; see page 12). Smaller polities were destroyed and traditional economic patterns disrupted, as trade once sent north toward the Mediterranean was redirected to the coast, and as local manufactures declined in the face of European competition.

Europeans were the chief beneficiaries of this traffic in slaves, despite its importance to some African kings. The expanding network of trade between

Europe and the Slave Trade

Europe and its colonies in the seventeenth and eighteenth centuries was fueled by the sale and transportation of slaves, the exchange of commodities produced by slave labor, and the need to feed and clothe so many bound laborers. The sugar planters of the Caribbean and Brazil, along with the tobacco and rice planters of North America, eagerly purchased slaves from Africa, dispatched shiploads of valuable staple crops to Europe, and bought large quantities of cheap food, much of it from elsewhere in the Americas. By the 1720s, more than 80 percent of English cotton textile exports was traded to Africa or slaveholding American colonies.

The European economy, previously oriented toward the Mediterranean and Asia, shifted its emphasis to the Atlantic Ocean. Whereas European merchants' profits had once come primarily from trade with North Africa, the eastern Mediterranean, and China, by the late seventeenth century commerce in slaves and the products of slave labor constituted the basis of the European economic system. The irony of Columbus's discoveries was thus complete: seeking the wealth of Asia, Columbus found instead the lands that ultimately replaced Asia as the source of European prosperity.

European nations fought bitterly to control the slave trade. The Portuguese, who at first dominated the trade, were supplanted by the Dutch in the 1630s. The Dutch in turn lost out to the English, who controlled the trade through the Royal African Company, a joint-stock company chartered by Charles II in 1672. Holding a monopoly on all English trade with sub-Saharan Africa, the company built and maintained eight forts, dispatched to West Africa hundreds of ships carrying English manufactured goods, and transported more than 120,000

Slave traders tightly packed their human cargoes, attempting to carry as many people as possible on each voyage. This cutaway view of a typical vessel gives the ship's dimensions and shows the way slaves were transported in cramped quarters, with only small openings providing light and air. British Library.

slaves to England's colonies in the Caribbean and on the mainland. Yet even before the company's monopoly expired in 1712, many individual English traders had illegally entered the market for slaves. By the early eighteenth century, such independent traders were carrying most of the Africans imported into the colonies, earning huge profits from successful voyages.

The experience of the Middle Passage (thus named because it was the middle section of the so-called triangular trade among England, Africa, and the Americas; see pages 81–82) was always traumatic and sometimes fatal for the Africans who made up a ship's cargo. An average of 10 to 20 percent of slaves died en route. On voyages that were unusually long or plagued by epidemic diseases, mortality rates were much higher. In addition, some slaves died either before the ships left Africa or shortly after their arrival in the Americas. Their European captors also died at high rates, chiefly through exposure to dis-

The Middle Passage

eases endemic to Africa. Just 10 percent of the men sent to run the Royal African Company's forts in Lower Guinea lived to return home to England, and one in every four or five European sailors died on the Middle Passage. Once again, the exchange of diseases caused unanticipated death and destruction.

One of the most vivid accounts of the Middle Passage was written by Olaudah Equiano, who was eleven years old in 1756 when African raiders kidnapped him from his Ibo village in what is now Nigeria. Terrified by the light complexions, long hair, and strange language of the sailors, he was afraid that "I had gotten into a world of bad spirits and that they were going to kill me." Equiano was placed below decks, where "with the loathsomeness of the stench and crying together, I became so sick and low that I was not able to eat, nor had I the least desire to taste anything." The slavers flogged him to make him eat. Equiano thought about killing himself by jumping overboard but was too closely watched. At last some other Ibos told him that they were being taken to their captors' country to work.

"I then was a little revived," Equiano remembered, "and thought if it were no worse than working, my situation was not so desperate."

After a long voyage during which many of the Africans died of disease brought on by the cramped, unsanitary conditions and poor food, the ship arrived at Barbados. Equiano and his shipmates feared that "these ugly men" were cannibals, but experienced slaves came on board to assure them that they would not be eaten and that many Africans like themselves lived on the island. "This report eased us much," Equiano recalled, "and sure enough soon after we landed there came to us Africans of all languages." Equiano was not purchased in the West Indies, instead being carried to Virginia, where he was soon sold and put to work on a tobacco plantation before being resold to a visiting ship captain.

The voyage Equiano described was typical, for most slave ships followed the Northeast Trades to the Caribbean before heading north to Virginia. So

Slavery in the Chesapeake

many Africans were imported so rapidly that as early as 1690 the Chesapeake colonies had more African slaves than English indentured servants, and by 1710 one-fifth of the region's population was of African descent. Slaves usually cost about two-and-a-half times as much as servants, but they repaid the greater investment with a lifetime of service.

Yet many planters could not afford to purchase such expensive workers. Accordingly, the transition from indentured to enslaved labor increased the social and economic distance between richer and poorer planters. Those with enough money could acquire slaves and accumulate greater wealth, whereas the less affluent could not even buy indentured servants, whose price was driven up by scarcity. As time passed, Anglo-American society in the Chesapeake became more and more stratified—that is, the gap between rich and poor steadily widened. The introduction of large numbers of Africans into the Chesapeake thus had a significant impact on Anglo-American society, in addition to reshaping the population as a whole.

That impact involved cultural values as well as demographic and economic change. Without realizing it, Anglo-Americans in the Chesapeake adopted African modes of thought about the use of time and the nature of work. Africans were more accustomed than European migrants to life in a hot climate. Anglo-Americans soon learned the benefits of

African patterns of time usage—working early and late, taking a long rest in the midday heat. They also assimilated African attitudes toward work, which were far more casual than those of New England. There, Puritans emphasized the necessity of "improving" every moment and scorned all leisure-time activities. In the Chesapeake, Anglo- and African-Americans alike came to recognize the importance of recreation and to understand that work could be performed at a leisurely pace on most occasions.

Since Africans were included among the first colonists to come to South Carolina from Barbados in 1670, they composed one-quarter to one-third

African-Americans in South Carolina

of the early population. The Barbadian slaveowners quickly discovered that Africans had a variety of skills well suited to the semitropical environment of South Carolina. African-style dugout canoes became the chief means of transportation in the colony, which was crisscrossed by rivers. Fishing nets copied from African models proved more efficient than those of English origin. Baskets that enslaved laborers wove and gourds that they hollowed out came into general use as containers for food and drink. Africans' skill at killing crocodiles equipped them to handle alligators. And, finally, Africans adapted their traditional techniques of cattle herding for use in America. Since meat and hides—not the exotic products originally envisioned—were the colony's chief exports in its earliest years, Africans contributed significantly to South Carolina's prosperity.

The similarity of South Carolina's environment to West Africa's, coupled with the large proportion of Africans in the population, ensured that more aspects of West African culture survived in that colony than elsewhere on the North American mainland. Only in South Carolina did enslaved parents continue to give their children African names; only there did a dialect develop that combined English words with African terms. (Known as Gullah, it has survived to the present day in isolated areas.) African skills remained useful, so techniques that in other regions were lost when the migrant generation died were instead passed down to the migrants' children. And in South Carolina, as in Guinea, African women were the primary traders, dominating the markets of Charleston as they did those of Guinea.

Significantly, the importation of large numbers of Africans near the end of the seventeenth century

How do historians know that enslaved Africans were able to preserve at least some aspects of their cultural heritage in colonial North America? Although most enslaved people were illiterate and thus did not leave written records describing their cultural beliefs or practices, African-Americans did create objects that showed their connections to their homeland even more vividly than words on a page could have done. Many such objects have been found in the United States. The drum on the left was constructed on the Gold Coast of Africa in the nineteenth century, the one on the right in Virginia sometime before the middle of the eighteenth century. The similarities of style and decoration suggest strong cultural affinities between the two drum builders even though they were separated by 3,000 miles of ocean and at least one hundred years. Photo: Trustees of The British Museum; Smithsonian Institution, Washington, D.C.

 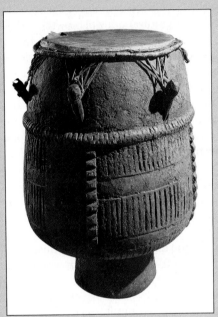

coincided with the successful introduction of rice as a staple crop in South Carolina. English people knew little about the techniques of growing and processing rice, and their first attempts to raise the crop were not successful. But people from Africa's Rice Coast (see Chapter 1, page 12) had spent their lives working with the crop. Although the evidence is circumstantial, it seems likely that the Africans' expertise enabled their English masters to cultivate the crop profitably. After rice had become South Carolina's major export, 43 percent of the Africans imported into the colony came from rice-producing regions, and enslaved Africans' central position in the economy was unchallenged.

Rice and Indigo

South Carolina later developed a second staple crop, and it too made use of slaves' special skills. The crop was indigo, much prized in Europe as a source of blue dye for clothing. In the early 1740s, Eliza Lucas, a young woman who was managing her father's plantations, began to experiment with indigo cultivation. Drawing on the knowledge of slaves and overseers from the West Indies, she developed the planting and processing techniques later adopted throughout the colony. Indigo was grown on high ground, and rice was planted in low-lying swampy areas; rice and indigo also had different growing seasons. Thus the two crops complemented each other perfectly. Although South Carolina indigo never matched the quality of that raised in the West Indies, the indigo industry flourished because Parliament offered Carolinians a bounty on every pound they exported to Great Britain.

After 1700, therefore, southern planters, large and small alike, were irrevocably committed to slavery as their chief source of labor. The same was not true of northerners. Only a

Slavery in the North

small proportion of the Africans brought to the English colonies in America went to the northern mainland provinces, and most of those worked as enslaved domestic servants. Lacking large-scale agricultural enterprises, the rural North did not demand many bound laborers. In northern urban areas, though, European domestic servants were hard to find and harder to keep because other jobs in the labor-scarce economy earned higher wages. Thus enslaved Africans there filled an identifiable need. In some northern colonial cities (notably Newport, Rhode Island, and New York City), slaves accounted for more than 10 percent of the population.

The introduction of large-scale slavery in the South, coupled with its near absence in the rural North, accentuated regional differences that already had begun to develop in England's American colonies. To the distinction between diversified agriculture and staple-crop production was now added a difference in the status of most laborers. That difference was one of degree, for slavery was legal everywhere in the colonies, but it was nonetheless crucial. For the next 150 years the continent's society and politics were to be indelibly shaped by decisions made in the late seventeenth century.

Relations Between Europeans and Indians

Everywhere in North America, European colonizers depended heavily on the labor of native peoples, but their reliance took varying forms in different parts of the continent. In the Northeast, France, England, and the Netherlands competed for the pelts supplied by Indian trappers. In the Southeast, England, Spain, and later France each tried to control a thriving trade with the Native Americans in deerskins and Indian slaves. In the Southwest, meanwhile, Spain attempted to exploit the agricultural and artisan skills of the Pueblo peoples (see map).

After Fray Alonzo de Benavides departed for Madrid in 1629 (see Chapter 2), Franciscan friars con-

tinued their conversion efforts, with mixed success.

Popé and the Pueblo Revolt

The Pueblo peoples were willing to add Christianity to their own religious beliefs but not to give up their indigenous rituals. Friars and secular colonists who held *encomiendas* also placed heavy demands on the Indians. As the decades passed, Franciscans adopted brutal and violent tactics in an attempt to wipe out all traces of the native religion. Finally, in 1680 the Pueblos revolted under the leadership of Popé, a respected shaman, and successfully drove the Spaniards out of New Mexico. Although Spanish authority was restored in 1692, Spain had learned its lesson. From that time on, Spanish governors stressed cooperation with the Pueblos, rather than confrontation, and no longer attempted to reduce them to bondage or to violate their cultural integrity. The Pueblo revolt was the most successful and longest-sustained Indian resistance movement in colonial North America.

When the Spanish expanded their territorial claims to the east and north, they followed the same strategy they had used in New Mexico, establishing

Spain's North American Possessions

their presence through military outposts and Franciscan missions. The army's role was to maintain order among the subject Indians—to protect them from attack and ensure the availability of their labor—and to guard the boundaries of the Spanish Empire from possible incursions, especially by the French. The friars concentrated on conversions. By the late eighteenth century, Spain claimed a vast territory that stretched from California (first colonized in 1769 to prevent Russian sea-otter trappers from taking over the region) through Texas (settled after 1700) to the Gulf Coast. Throughout that region, the Spanish presence consisted of a mixture of missions and forts dotting the countryside, sometimes at considerable distances from each other.

Europeans along the eastern seaboard valued Indians as hunters rather than as agricultural workers, but they were no less dependent on Indian labor than were Spaniards in the Southwest. To obtain pelts and deerskins from indigenous peoples, Europeans—French, Spanish, and English alike—had to supply trade goods the Indians wanted. Such commodities included ammunition, clothing, and alcohol (usually rum distilled from West Indian molasses). Although in the seventeenth century Indians

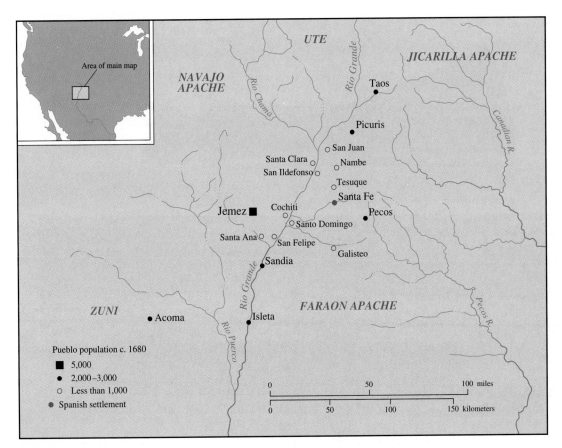

New Mexico, c. 1680 *In 1680, the lone Spanish settlement at Santa Fe was surrounded and vastly outnumbered by the many Pueblo villages nearby.* Source: Adapted from *Apache, Navaho, and Spaniard*, by Jack D. Forbes. Copyright © 1960 by the University of Oklahoma Press. Used by permission.

primarily obtained rum at settlers' taverns or in gift exchanges accompanying trade or treaty negotiations, by 1720 European and Indian traders were carrying casks of rum far into the American interior. Indians' demand for alcohol (a commodity to which they were introduced by the traders) made rum a key component of colonial commerce, and alcohol abuse hastened the deterioration of villages already devastated by disease and dislocation.

Also destructive of tribal communities was traffic in Indian slaves. Carolina Indians, especially the Creeks, profited from selling their captive enemies to the English, who either kept them as slaves or exported them to other mainland settlements or to the West Indies. There are no reliable statistics on the extent of the trade in Indian slaves, but in 1708 they composed 14 percent of the South

Indian Slave Trade in the Southeast

Carolina population. Many were Catholics converted by the Spanish missions in northern Florida, then captured by Englishmen or their Native American allies.

Bitter conflicts between the Carolina settlers and indigenous peoples produced not only slaves but also mass migrations. In 1711 the Tuscaroras, an Iroquoian people, attacked a Swiss-German settlement at New Bern, which had expropriated their lands without payment. The Tuscaroras had been avid slavers and had sold to the Europeans many captives seized from their Algonkian neighbors. Those Indians took the opportunity to settle old scores, joining with the English colonists to defeat their enemy in a bloody two-year war. In the end, more than a thousand Tuscaroras were themselves sold into slavery, and the remnants of the group

Tuscarora and Yamasee Wars

Trade between Europeans and Indians provided both societies with essential items. The Europeans manufactured tomahawks specifically for the Native American market. Likewise, the Indians of Long Island increased their production of wampum (made from clam shells) when English and Dutch colonists adopted the purple and white beads as a medium of exchange. Wampum served as a substitute for European coins, which were scarce in the remote colonial outposts. Tomahawk: Peabody and Essex Museum. Belt: Peabody and Essex Museum

drifted northward, where they joined the Five Nations Iroquois in New York.

The slave trade's abuses led to yet another Indian war in Carolina. Colonial traders regularly engaged in corrupt, brutal, and fraudulent practices. They were notorious for cheating Native Americans, physically abusing them (including raping women), and selling friendly peoples into slavery when no enemy captives came readily to hand. In the spring and summer of 1715, the Yamasees, aided by Creeks and others, retaliated by attacking English settlements. Refugees by the hundreds streamed into Charleston; the Creek-Yamasee offensive came close to driving the intruders from the mainland altogether. But colonial reinforcements arrived from

the north, and Cherokees joined English settlers to fight the Creeks, their ancient enemies.

The war pointed up both the difficulty of achieving unity among the Indians and their critical dependence on European weapons. When the Creeks and Yamasees depleted their stores of ammunition and could not repair their broken guns, their cause was lost. The Yamasees moved south to Florida, and the Creeks retreated to villages in the west. South Carolina did not fully recover from the effects of the Yamasee War for many years, but the existence of the colony was never again seriously threatened.

That the Yamasees could escape by migrating southward exposed the one remaining gap in the line of English coastal settlements, the area between South Carolina's southern border and Spanish Florida (see map, page 64). The gap was

Founding of Georgia

plugged in 1732 with the chartering of Georgia, the last of the colonies that would become part of the United States. Intended as a haven for English debtors by its founder James Oglethorpe, Georgia was specifically designed as a garrison province. Since all its landholders were expected to serve as militiamen to defend English settlements, the charter prohibited women from inheriting or purchasing land in the colony. The charter also prohibited slavery and the use of alcoholic beverages. Such provisions reveal the founders' intention that Georgia should be peopled by sturdy, sober yeoman farmers who could take up their weapons at a moment's notice against Native Americans or Spaniards. None of the original conditions of the charter were enforced, however, and all of them had been abandoned by 1752, when Georgia became a royal colony.

In the Northeast, relationships were complicated by the number of European and Indian nations involved in the fur trade. The key players were the Iroquois, not one tribe but five—the Mohawks, Oneidas,

Iroquois Confederacy

Onondagas, Cayugas, and Senecas. (In 1722, the Tuscaroras became the sixth.) Under the terms of a defensive alliance forged early in the sixteenth century, decisions of war and peace for the entire Iroquois Confederacy were made by a council composed of tribal representatives. Each nation retained some autonomy and could not be forced to comply with a council directive against its will.

The Iroquois were unique among Native Americans, not only because of the strength and persistence of their alliance but also because of the role played by their clan matrons. The older women of each village chose its chief and could either start wars (by calling for the capture of prisoners to replace dead relatives) or stop them (by refusing to supply warriors with necessary foodstuffs).

Philip Georg Friedrich von Reck, an artist who visited Georgia in the early years of English settlement there, recorded a festival celebrated by the local Yuchi Indians in 1736. European guns hang from the rafters of the open shelter, showing that extensive trade connections already existed between the two peoples. Royal Library, Copenhagen.

Louisiana, c. 1720 *By 1720, French forts and settlements dotted the Mississippi River and its tributaries in the interior of North America. Two isolated Spanish outposts were situated near the Gulf of Mexico.*   Source: Adapted from *France in America*, by William J. Eccles. Copyright © 1972 by William J. Eccles. Reprinted by permission of Harper & Row, Publishers, Inc.

Before the arrival of Europeans, the Iroquois waged wars primarily to acquire captives to replenish their population. Contact with foreign traders brought ravaging disease as early as 1633 and thus intensified the need for captives. Simultaneously, the Europeans' coming created an economic motive for warfare: the desire to control the fur trade and gain unimpeded access to European goods. The war with the Hurons in the 1640s (see page 38) was but the first of a series of conflicts with other tribes known as the Beaver Wars, in which the Iroquois fought desperately to maintain a dominant position in the trade.

In the mid-1670s, just when they were achieving their goal, the French stepped in; an Iroquois triumph would have destroyed France's plans to trade directly with the Indians of the Great Lakes and Mississippi valley. Over the next twenty years the French launched repeated attacks on Iroquois villages. The English offered little assistance other than weapons to their trading partners and nominal allies. Their people and resources depleted by constant warfare, the Iroquois in 1701 negotiated neutrality treaties with France, England, and their Indian neighbors. For the next half-century they maintained their power through trade and skillful diplomacy rather than warfare.

The wars against the Iroquois Confederacy were crucial components of French Canada's plan to penetrate the heartland of North America. In the 1670s, Louis de Buade de Frontenac, the governor-general of Canada, encouraged the explorations of Father Jacques Marquette, Louis Jolliet, and Robert Cavelier de La Salle in the Great Lakes and Mississippi valley regions. Officials in France approved the expeditions because they wanted to find a trade route to Mexico. La Salle and Frontenac, by contrast, hoped to profit personally, monopolizing the fur trade by establishing trading posts along the Mississippi River.

French Expansion

Unlike Spaniards, French adventurers did not attempt to subjugate the Native Americans they encountered. Nor, at first, did they even claim the territory formally for France. Still, when France decided to strengthen its presence near the Gulf of Mexico by founding New Orleans in 1718—to counter both the westward thrust of the English colonies and the eastward moves of the Spanish—the Mississippi posts became the glue of empire. *Coureurs de bois* (literally, "forest runners") used the rivers and lakes of the American interior to travel regularly between Quebec and Louisiana, carrying French goods to outposts such as Michilimackinac (at the junction of Lakes Michigan and Huron), Cahokia and Kaskaskia (in present-day Illinois), and Fort Rosalie (Natchez), on the lower Mississippi River (see map).

Most of the posts consisted of a small military garrison and a priest, surrounded by powerful nations such as the Choctaws, Chickasaws, Osages, and

Illinois. The Indians permitted French soldiers and traders to remain among them because they wanted easy access to valuable European goods. The French, for their part, sought political as well as economic ends, attempting to prevent the English from encroaching too far into the interior. Their goals were limited; they did not engage in systematic efforts to convert nearby Native American peoples to Christianity.

Along the Mississippi just south of modern St. Louis and north of Fort Chartres (see map, page 78), migrants from Quebec and Montréal established six small villages (known collectively as *le pays de Illinois*, the Illinois country) that produced wheat for export to New Orleans. But a shortage of manpower—the population never rose much above three thousand—meant that the French could not significantly expand the amount of land under cultivation. And the lack of French women led to interracial unions between French men and Native American women and to the creation of mixed-race people known as *metís*.

Matters were very different in the English colonies, where white colonists had an avid interest in acquiring more land. In Virginia, the conflict was especially acute because of the colonists' insatiable hunger for tobacco acreage.

By the early 1670s, some Virginians were eagerly eyeing rich lands north of the York River that early treaties had reserved for Native Americans.

Bacon's Rebellion

Using as a pretext the July 1675 killing of an English servant by some Doeg Indians, they attacked not only the Doegs but also the Susquehannocks, a powerful tribe that had recently occupied the area. In retaliation, Susquehannock bands raided frontier plantations in the winter of 1676. The land-hungry Anglo-Americans rallied behind the leadership of Nathaniel Bacon, a recently arrived planter, who, like many of his followers, had immigrated too late to acquire fertile lands in the already settled tidewater region. Bacon and his followers wanted, in his words, "to ruine and extirpate all Indians in general." Governor William Berkeley, however, hoped to avoid setting off a major war, which might devastate the colony.

Berkeley and Bacon soon clashed. After Bacon forced the House of Burgesses to authorize him to attack the Indians, Berkeley declared Bacon and his men to be in rebellion. As the chaotic summer of 1676 wore on, Bacon alternately pursued Indians and battled with the governor's supporters. In September Bacon marched on Jamestown itself and burned the capital to the ground. But when Bacon died of dysentery the following month, the rebellion collapsed. Even so, a new treaty signed in 1677 opened much of the disputed territory to English settlement.

More than coincidentally, New England—also colonized more than fifty years earlier—was wracked by conflict with Native Americans at precisely the same time. In both areas, the colonists' original accommodation with the Indians, reached after the defeat of the Pequots in the North and the Powhatan Confederacy in the South, no longer satisfied both parties. In New England, though, it was the indigenous peoples, rather than the colonists, who felt aggrieved.

In the half-century since the founding of New England, colonial settlement had spread far into the interior of Massachusetts and Connecticut. In

King Philip's War

the process, the colonists had completely surrounded the ancestral lands of the Pokanokets (Wampanoags) on Narragansett Bay. Their chief, Metacom (known to the English as King Philip), was the son of Massasoit, who had signed the treaty with the Pilgrims in 1621. Troubled by encroachments on Pokanoket lands and equally concerned about the impact European culture and Christianity were having on his people, Metacom led his warriors in attacks on nearby communities in June 1675.

The Nipmucks and the Narragansetts soon joined Metacom's forces. In the fall, the three Indian nations jointly attacked settlements in the northern Connecticut River valley. In early 1676, they devastated well-established villages and even attacked Plymouth and Providence. Altogether, the alliance totally destroyed twelve of the ninety Puritan towns and attacked forty others. One-tenth of the able-bodied adult male colonists in Massachusetts were captured or killed. Proportional to population, it was the most costly war in American history. New England's very survival seemed at stake.

But the tide turned in the summer of 1676. The Indian coalition ran short of food and ammunition, and colonists began to use Christian Indians as guides and scouts. After Metacom was killed in an ambush in August, the alliance crumbled. Many surviving Pokanokets, Nipmucks, and Narragansetts, including Metacom's wife and son, were captured and sold into slavery in the West Indies. The power of New England's coastal tribes was broken. Thereafter they lived in small clusters, subordinated to the colonists and often working as servants or sailors. Only on the isolated island of Martha's Vineyard were some surviving Wampanoags able to preserve their cultural identity intact.

New England and the Web of Imperial Trade

From the early years of colonization to the close of the seventeenth century, New England changed in three major ways. The population grew dramatically; the residents' relationship to Puritanism altered; and the economy developed in unanticipated ways.

Population expansion resulted not from continued migration from England (for that largely ceased after the outbreak of the English Civil War in 1642) but rather from natural increase. The original settlers' many children also produced many children, and subsequent generations followed suit. By 1700, New England's population had quadrupled to reach approximately 100,000. Such an increase placed great pressure on available land, and many members of the third and fourth generations of New Englanders had to migrate—north to New Hampshire or Maine, south to New York, west beyond the Connecticut River—to find sufficient farmland for themselves and their children. Others abandoned agriculture and learned skills like blacksmithing or carpentry so they could support themselves in the growing number of towns dotting the countryside.

Population Pressures

The passage of time also brought changes in Puritanism, for two of the Puritans' fundamental beliefs came inevitably into conflict. Puritans practiced infant baptism, yet at the same time they insisted that only the saved could be members of their churches. No one foresaw the problem that confronted congregations in the 1660s: young people baptized as children married and had babies before undergoing the searching examination of their faith required to join a church. Could the offspring of such couples be baptized? The need to answer that question led to the convening of a synod of clergymen in 1662 and to the adoption of the so-called Halfway Covenant, which established a category of "halfway" membership in Puritan congregations. If previously baptized adults acknowledged the

church's authority over them, the ministers declared, they could have their children baptized.

By the 1660s, women were far more likely than men to become either full or halfway members of Puritan congregations. Searching for the cause of this phenomenon, Cotton Mather, the most prominent member of a family of distinguished ministers, speculated that the fear of dying in childbirth made women especially sensitive to their spiritual state. By contrast, modern historians have argued that women were attracted to religion because the church offered them spiritual equality to offset their secular inferiority.

Women, Men, and Puritan Churches

Whatever the explanation, the increasingly female composition of his audiences prompted Mather to deliver sermons outlining women's proper role in church and society—the first formal examination of that theme in American history. Mather was the first of many men to publish sermons urging American women to be submissive to their husbands, watchful of their children, and attentive to religious duty.

If Mather thought to ask the parallel question—why had New England's men become more reluctant to acknowledge the church's authority over them?—he did not propose an answer, though scholars have done so. One historian hypothesizes that the connection between church membership and political obligation was critical. Believing with good reason that unchurched men were unlikely to be elected to office, male New Englanders may well have failed to join congregations because they wanted to avoid having to serve as constables or militia officers. Such time-consuming and onerous jobs not only took them away from their farms and families but also could cause dissension in their neighborhoods.

Another hypothesis focuses on the male residents of seaport towns such as Boston and Salem. Men in these urban areas, some historians argue, became more worldly and less interested in religion as the economy of the New England colonies changed after the outbreak of the English Civil War.

Initially, New England's economy rested on two foundations: the fur trade and the constant flow of migrants. Together, those had allowed New Englanders to acquire the manufactured goods they needed. The fur trade gave them valuable pelts to sell in England, and the migrants were always willing to exchange clothing and other items for the earlier settlers' surplus

New England's First Economy

The harbor of Christiansted, St. Croix, in the Danish West Indies. Although this view was painted over one hundred years after the events discussed in this chapter, the town had not changed much in the interim. Scenes like this would have been very familiar to Captain William Kidd and his contemporaries, for such tiny ports existed all over the Caribbean. Anchored merchant vessels await the hogsheads of molasses being prepared for shipment at the wharf.   MAPes MONDe Ltd.

seed, grains, and livestock. But New England's supply of furs was quickly exhausted by excessive trapping, and the migrants stopped coming after the English Civil War began. Thus in the early 1640s that first economic system collapsed.

The Puritans then began a search for new markets and salable crops. They found such crops in the waters off the coast—fish—and on their own land—grain and wood products. By 1643 they had also found the necessary markets: first the Wine Islands and then the English colonies in the Caribbean. All these islands lacked precisely the goods that New England could produce in abundance: cheap food (corn and salted fish) to feed to slaves and wood for barrels to hold wine and molasses (the form in which sugar was shipped).

Thus developed the series of transactions that has become known, inaccurately, as the triangular trade. The northern colonists sold their goods in the West Indies and elsewhere to earn the money with which to purchase English imports.

Atlantic Trading System

There soon grew up in New England's ports a cadre of merchants who acquired—usually through barter—cargoes of timber and foodstuffs, which they then dispatched to the West Indies for sale. In the Caribbean, the ships sailed from island to island, exchanging fish, barrel staves, and grains for molasses, fruit, spices, and slaves. Once they had a full load, the ships returned to Boston, Newport, or New Haven to dispose of their cargoes. New Englanders traded the items they did not use to other colonies or to England.

Most important, northerners distilled West Indian molasses into rum, a key component of the only

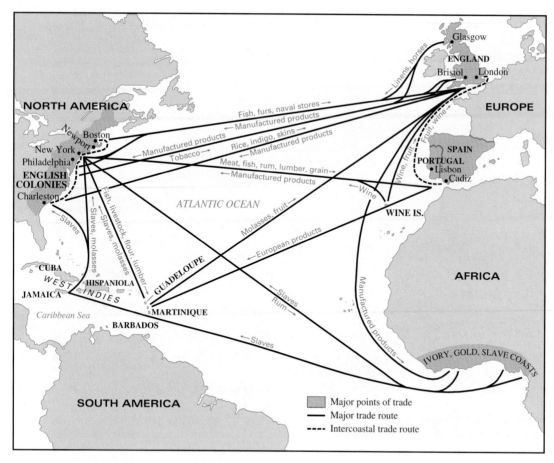

Atlantic Trade Routes   *By the late seventeenth century, an elaborate trade network linked the countries and colonies bordering the Atlantic Ocean. The most valuable commodities exchanged were enslaved people and the products of slave labor.*

part of the trade that could be termed triangular. Rhode Islanders took rum to Africa and traded it for slaves, whom they carried to the West Indies to exchange for more molasses to produce still more rum. With that exception, the trading pattern was not a triangle but a shifting set of two-way voyages (see map). Its sole constant was uncertainty, due to the weather, rapid shifts in supply and demand in the small island markets, and the delicate system of credit on which the entire structure depended.

The New Englanders who ventured into commerce were soon differentiated from their rural counterparts by their ties to a wider transatlantic world and their preoccupation with material endeavors. As time passed, increasing numbers of Puritans became involved in trade. Small investors who

owned shares of voyages soon dominated the field numerically if not monetarily.

The gulf between commercial and farming interests widened after 1660, when, with Stuart Restoration, merchants who were members of the Church of England (Anglicans) began to migrate to New England to participate directly in the booming trade in slaves and staple crops produced by enslaved laborers. Such men had little stake in the survival of Massachusetts Bay and Connecticut in their original forms, and some were openly antagonistic to Puritan traditions. As non-Congregationalists they were denied the vote, but they were still taxed to support the church. Further, Anglicans were forbidden to practice their own religion freely. They resented their exclusion from the governing elite, believing that their wealth and social status entitled them to political power. Congregationalist clergymen returned their hostility, preaching sermons lamenting New England's new commercial orientation. The Reverend Increase Mather (Cotton Mather's father) reminded his congregation in 1676 that "Religion and not the World was that which our Fathers came hither for."

But Mather spoke for the past, not for the future or even for many of his own contemporaries. By the 1670s, New England and the other American colonies were deeply enmeshed in an intricate international trading network. The early colonies may have been even more dependent on overseas markets and on imported goods than eighteenth-century America would be. During the 1600s the colonies lacked sufficient population to support manufacturing. For example, all attempts to establish ironworks or glass factories in the first decades of settlement failed because there simply were not enough colonial consumers. Furthermore, the colonies' economic fortunes depended on the sale of their exports in foreign markets: furs, deerskins, sugar, tobacco, rice, fish, and timber products together formed the basis for Anglo-America's prosperity.

English officials seeking a new source of revenue after the disruptions of the Civil War realized that the colonies could make important contributions to England's economic well-being. Chesapeake tobacco and West Indian sugar had obvious value, but other colonial products also had profitable potential. Additional tax revenues could put England back on a sound financial footing, and English merchants wanted to ensure that they—not their Dutch rivals—reaped the benefits of trading with the English colonies. Parliament and the restored Stuart monarchs accordingly began to draft laws designed to confine the profits of colonial trade primarily to the mother country.

Mercantilism

Like other European nations, England based its commercial policy on a series of assumptions about the operations of the world's economic system. Collectively, these assumptions are usually called *mercantilism*, though neither the term itself nor a unified mercantilist theory was formulated until a century later. The economic world was seen as a collection of national states, whose governments actively competed for shares of a finite amount of wealth. What one nation gained was automatically another nation's loss. Each nation's goal was to become as economically self-sufficient as possible while maintaining a favorable balance of trade with other countries by exporting more than it imported. Colonies had an important role to play in such a scheme. They could supply the mother country with valuable raw materials to be consumed at home or sent abroad, and they could serve as a market for the mother country's manufactured goods.

Parliament applied mercantilist thinking to the American colonies in laws known as the Navigation Acts. The major acts—passed between 1651 and 1673—established three main principles. First, only English or colonial merchants and ships could engage in trade in the colonies. Second, certain valuable American products could be sold only in the mother country or in other English colonies. At first, these "enumerated" goods were wool, sugar, tobacco, indigo, ginger, and dyes; later acts added rice, naval stores (masts, spars, pitch, tar, and turpentine), copper, and furs to the list. Third, all foreign goods destined for sale in the colonies had to be shipped by way of England and were subject to English import duties. Some years later, a new series of laws established a fourth principle: the colonies could not export items (such as wool clothing, hats, or iron) that competed with English products.

Navigation Acts

The intention of the Navigation Acts was clear: American trade was to center on England. The mother country was to benefit from colonial imports and exports both. England had first claim on the most valuable colonial exports, and all foreign imports into the colonies had to pass through England first, enriching its customs revenues in the process. Some colonies, like those in the West Indies and the Chesapeake, were adversely affected by the laws because they could not seek new markets for their staple crops. In others, the impact was less severe. Builders and owners of ships benefited from the monopoly on American trade given to English and colonial merchants. And the northern and middle colonies in particular produced many goods that were not enumerated—for example, fish, flour, and barrel staves. These products could be traded directly to foreign purchasers as long as they were carried in English or American ships.

The English authorities soon learned that it was easier to write mercantilist legislation than to enforce it. The many harbors of the American coast provided ready havens for smugglers, and colonial officials often looked the other way when illegally imported goods were offered for sale. In ports such as St. Eustatius in the Dutch West Indies, American merchants could easily dispose of enumerated goods and purchase foreign items on which duty had not been paid. Consequently, Parliament in 1696 enacted another Navigation Act. This law established in America a number of vice-admiralty courts, which operated without juries. In England such courts dealt only with cases involving piracy, vessels taken as wartime prizes, and the like. But since American juries had already demonstrated a tendency to favor local smugglers over customs officers (a colonial customs service was instituted in 1671), Parliament decided to remove Navigation Act cases from the regular colonial courts.

England took another major step in colonial administration in 1696 by creating the fifteen-member Board of Trade and Plantations, which thereafter served as the chief organ of government concerned with the American colonies. (Previously, no single body had that responsibility.) It gathered information, reviewed Crown appointments in America, scrutinized legislation passed by colonial assemblies, supervised trade policies, and advised successive ministries on colonial issues. Still, the Board of Trade did not have any direct powers of enforcement. It also shared jurisdiction over American affairs not only with the customs service and the navy but also with the secretary of state for the southern department, the member of the ministry responsible for the colonies. In short, although the Stuart monarchs' reforms considerably improved the quality of colonial administration, supervision of the American provinces remained decentralized and haphazard.

Board of Trade and Plantations

Colonial Political Development and Imperial Reorganization

English officials in the 1670s and 1680s confronted not only resistance to the Navigation Acts but also a bewildering array of colonial governments. Massachusetts Bay and Plymouth functioned under their original charters. Neighboring Connecticut (including the formerly independent New Haven) and Rhode Island had been granted charters by Charles II in 1662 and 1663, respectively. Virginia was a royal colony, and New York also became one when

its proprietor ascended the throne in 1685 as James II. All the other mainland settlements were proprietorships, whose royal charters gave the proprietors a great deal of leeway in how they governed their possessions.

Still, in political structure the colonies shared certain characteristics. Most were ruled by a governor and a two-house legislature. In New England, the governors were elected by property-holding men or by the legislature; in the Chesapeake and the middle colonies, they were appointed by the king or the proprietor. A council, either elected or appointed, advised the governor on matters of policy and sometimes served as the colony's highest court. The councils also served as upper houses of colonial legislatures. At first, councilors and elected representatives met jointly to debate and adopt laws affecting the colony. But as time passed, the fundamental differences between the two legislative groups' purposes and constituencies led them to separate (the first such division occurred in Massachusetts in 1644). Thus developed the two-house legislature still used in almost all of the states.

Colonial Political Structures

Meanwhile, local political institutions were taking shape. In New England, elected selectmen initially governed the towns, but by the end of the century town meetings—held at least annually and attended by most free adult male residents—handled matters of local concern. In the Chesapeake colonies and both of the Carolinas, appointed justices of the peace ran local governments. At first the same was true in Pennsylvania, but by the early eighteenth century elected county officials began to take over some government functions. And in New York, local elections were the rule even before the establishment of the colonial assembly in 1683.

By late in the seventeenth century, therefore, Anglo-American colonists were everywhere accustomed to exercising a considerable degree of local political autonomy. The tradition of consent was especially firmly established in New England. Massachusetts, Plymouth, Connecticut, and Rhode Island were, in effect, independent entities, subject neither to the direct authority of the king nor to a proprietor. Everywhere in the English colonies, free adult men who owned more than a stated minimum amount of property (which varied from province to province) expected to have an influential voice in how they were governed—and especially in how they were taxed.

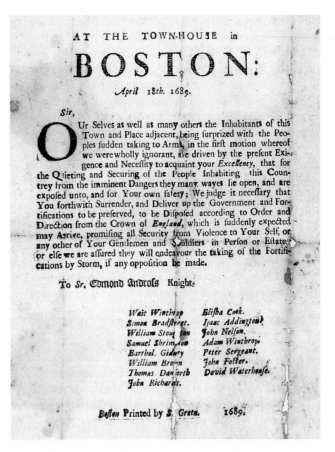

AT THE TOWN-HOUSE in

BOSTON:

April 18th. 1689.

Sir,

OUr Selves as well as many others the Inhabitants of this Town and Place adjacent, being surprized with the Peoples sudden taking to Arms, in the first motion whereof we were wholly ignorant, are driven by the present Exigence and Necessity to acquaint your *Excellency*, that for the Quieting and Securing of the People Inhabiting this Countrey from the imminent Dangers they many wayes lie open, and are exposed unto, and for Your own safety; We judge it necessary that You forthwith Surrender, and Deliver up the Government and Fortifications to be preserved, to be Disposed according to Order and Direction from the Crown of *England*, which is suddenly expected may Arrive, promising all Security from Violence to Your Self, or any other of Your Gentlemen and Souldiers in Person or Estate; or else we are assured they will endeavour the taking of the Fortifications by Storm, if any opposition be made.

To *Sr.* Edmond Andros *Knight.*

Wait Winthrop	*Elisha Cook.*
Simon Bradstreet.	*Isaac Addington.*
William Stoughton	*John Nelson.*
Samuel Shrimton	*Adam Winthrop.*
Barthol. Gidney	*Peter Sergeant.*
William Brown	*John Foster.*
Thomas Danforth	*David Waterhouse.*
John Richards.	

Boston Printed by *S. Green.* 1689.

Sir Edmund Andros (1637–1714), the much-detested autocratic governor of the Dominion of New England, and a broadside issued at the height of the crisis caused by the Glorious Revolution, calling on Andros to surrender control of the government. The signers were the foremost leaders of the Massachusetts Bay colony, among them a son and grandson of John Winthrop. Portrait: Massachusetts State Archives. Broadside: Massachusetts Historical Society.

After James II became king, these expectations clashed with those of the monarch. The new king and his successors sought to bring order to the apparently chaotic state of colonial administration by tightening the reins of government and reducing the colonies' political autonomy. (Simultaneously, they used the Navigation Acts to reduce the colonies' economic autonomy.) They began to chip away at the privileges granted in colonial charters and to reclaim proprietorships for the Crown. New Hampshire (1679), its parent colony Massachusetts (1691), New Jersey (1702), and the Carolinas (1729) all became royal colonies. The charters of Rhode Island, Connecticut, Maryland, and Pennsylvania were temporarily suspended but ultimately were restored to their original status.

The most drastic reordering of colonial administration targeted Puritan New England. Reports from America convinced English officials that New

Dominion of New England

England was a hotbed of smuggling. Moreover, Puritans refused to allow freedom of religion to non-Congregationalists and insisted on maintaining laws that ran counter to English practice. New England thus seemed an appropriate place to exert English authority with greater vigor. The charters of all the colonies from New Jersey to Maine (then part of Massachusetts) were revoked, and a Dominion of New England was established in 1686. (For the boundaries of the Dominion, see the map on page 64.) Sir Edmund Andros, the governor, was given immense power: all the assemblies were dissolved, and he needed only the consent of an appointed council to make laws and levy taxes.

New Englanders endured Andros's autocratic rule for more than two years. Then came the dramatic news that James II had been overthrown in a bloodless coup known as the Glorious Revolution and had been replaced on the throne by his daughter Mary and her husband, the Dutch prince William of Orange. James II, like his father Charles I, had levied taxes without parliamentary approval. He also had announced his conversion to Roman Catholicism. When Parliament offered the throne to the Protestants William and Mary, the Glorious Revolution affirmed the supremacy of both Parliament and Protestantism.

Seizing the opportunity to rid themselves of the hated Dominion, New Englanders jailed Andros and his associates, proclaimed their loyalty to William and Mary, and wrote to England for instructions about the form of government they should adopt. Most of Massachusetts Bay's political leaders hoped that the new monarchs would renew their original charter, revoked in 1684 prior to establishment of the Dominion.

Glorious Revolution in America

In other American colonies, too, the Glorious Revolution was a signal for revolt. In Maryland the Protestant Association overturned the government of the Catholic proprietor, and in New York a militia officer of German origin, Jacob Leisler, assumed control of the government. Like the New Englanders, the Maryland and New York rebels allied themselves with the supporters of William and Mary. They saw themselves as carrying out the colonial phase of the English revolt against Stuart absolutism.

William and Mary, however, like James II, believed that England should exercise tighter control over its unruly American possessions. Consequently, the only American rebellion that received royal sanction was that in Maryland, primarily because of its anti-Catholic thrust. In New York, Jacob Leisler was hanged for treason, and Massachusetts (including the formerly independent jurisdiction of Plymouth) became a royal colony with an appointed governor. The province was allowed to retain its town meeting system of local government and to elect its council, but the new charter issued in 1691 eliminated the traditional religious test for voting and officeholding. An Anglican parish was set up in the heart of Boston. The "city upon a hill" as John Winthrop had envisioned it was no more.

Compounding New England's difficulties in a time of political upheaval and economic uncertainty was a war with the French and their Native American allies. King Louis XIV of France allied himself with the deposed James II, and England declared war on France in 1689. The conflict, which lasted until 1697, was known in Europe as the War of the League of Augsburg, but the colonists called it King William's War. The American war was fought chiefly on the northern frontiers of New England and New York; among the English settlements devastated by enemy attacks in 1690 were Schenectady, New York, and Casco (now Falmouth), Maine. Expeditions organized by the colonies against Montréal and Quebec that same year both failed miserably, and throughout the rest of the war New England found itself on the defensive.

In this period of extreme stress occurred an outbreak of witchcraft accusations in Salem Village (now Danvers), Massachusetts. Like their contemporaries elsewhere, seventeenth-century New Englanders believed in the existence of witches, whose evil powers came from the Devil. If people could not find other explanations for their troubles, they tended to suspect they were bewitched. Before 1689, 103 New Englanders, most of them middle-aged women, had been charged with practicing witchcraft, chiefly by neighbors who attributed their misfortunes to the suspected witch. Only a few of the accused were convicted, and fewer still were executed. Most such incidents were isolated; nothing else in New England's history came close to matching the Salem Village cataclysm.

Witchcraft in Salem Village

The crisis began in early 1692 when a group of girls and young women accused some older female neighbors of having bewitched them. Before the hysteria spent itself ten months later, nineteen people (including several men, most of them related to convicted female witches) were hanged, one was pressed to death with heavy stones, and more than one hundred persons were jailed. Historians have proposed various explanations for this puzzling episode, but to be understood it must be seen in the context of political and legal disorder, Indian war, and religious and economic crises. Puritan New Englanders must have felt as though their entire world was collapsing. At the very least they could have had no sense of security about their future.

Nowhere was that more true than in Salem Village, a farming town torn between old and new styles of life because of its position on the edge of the bustling port of Salem. And no residents of the village had more reason to feel insecure than those who issued the first accusations. Many of them had been orphaned in the recent Indian attacks on Maine; they were living in Salem Village as domestic servants. Their involvement with witchcraft began as an experiment with fortunetelling as a means of foreseeing their futures, in particular the identities of their eventual husbands. As the most powerless people in a town apparently powerless to direct its fate, they offered their fellow New Englanders a compelling explanation for the seemingly endless chain of troubles afflicting them: their province was under direct attack from the Devil and his legion of witches. Accordingly, it is not so much the number of witchcraft prosecutions that seems surprising but rather their abrupt cessation in the fall of 1692.

There were three reasons for the rapid end to the crisis. First, the accusers grew too bold. When they began to charge some of the colony's most distinguished and respected residents with being in league with the Devil, members of the ruling elite began to doubt their veracity. Second, the colony's ministers, led by Increase Mather, formally expressed strong reservations about the validity of the spectral evidence used against most of the accused. Third, the implementation of the new royal charter ended the worst period of political uncertainty, eliminating a major source of stress. King William's War continued, but, although the Puritans were not entirely pleased with the new charter, at least order had formally been restored.

Over the course of the next three decades, Massachusetts and the rest of the English colonies in America accommodated themselves to the new imperial order. Most colonists resented alien officials who arrived in America determined to implement the policies of king and Parliament, but they adjusted to their demands and to the trade restrictions imposed by the Navigation Acts. They fought another imperial war—the War of the Spanish Succession, or Queen Anne's War—from 1702 to 1713, without enduring the stresses of the first, despite the heavy economic burdens the conflict imposed. Colonists who allied themselves with royal government received patronage in the form of offices and land grants and composed "court parties" that supported English officials. Others, who were either less fortunate in their friends or more principled in defense of colonial autonomy, made up the opposition, or "country" interest. By the end of the first quarter of the eighteenth century, most men in both

No seventeenth-century New Englander ever drew a picture of a witchcraft trial or execution, but an artist did record the hanging of several witches in England around 1650. The multiple executions of Salem witches in the summer of 1692 probably resembled this gallows scene. Folger Shakespeare Library.

groups had been born in America and were members of elite families whose wealth derived from staple-crop production in the South and commerce in the North.

 Conclusion

The eighty years from 1640 to 1720 established the basic economic and political patterns that were to structure all subsequent changes in mainland colonial society. In 1640 there were just two isolated centers of English population, New England and the Chesapeake. In 1720, nearly the entire east coast of North America was in English hands, and Indian power east of the Appalachian Mountains had been broken. What had been a migrant population was now mostly American-born; economies originally based on the fur trade had become far more complex and more closely linked with the mother country; and a wide variety of political structures had been reshaped into a more uniform pattern. Yet at the same time the introduction of large-scale slavery into the Chesapeake and the Carolinas irrevocably differentiated their societies from those of the colonies to the north. Staple-crop production for the market was not the key distinguishing feature of the southern regional economies; rather, their uniqueness lay in their reliance on a system of perpetual servitude.

Meanwhile, from a small outpost in Santa Fe, New Mexico, and missions in Florida, the Spanish had expanded their influence throughout the Gulf Coast region and, by just after midcentury, as far north as California. The French had moved from a few settlements along the St. Lawrence to dominate the length of the Mississippi River and the entire Great Lakes region. Both groups of colonists lived near Indian nations and were dependent on the indigenous people's labor and goodwill. The French and Spanish could not fully control their Native American allies—and the French did not even try. The extensive Spanish and French presence to the south and west of the English settlements meant that future conflicts among the European powers in North America were nearly inevitable.

By 1720, the essential elements of the imperial administrative structure that would govern the English colonies until 1775 were firmly in place. The regional economic systems originating in the late seventeenth and early eighteenth centuries also continued to dominate North American life for another century—until after independence had been won. And Anglo-Americans had developed the commitment to autonomous local government that later would lead them into conflict with Parliament and the king.

Suggestions for Further Reading

General

Wesley Frank Craven, *The Colonies in Transition, 1660–1713* (1968); W. J. Eccles, *France in America*, rev. ed. (1990); Jack P. Greene and J. R. Pole, eds., *Colonial British America* (1984); John J. McCusker and Russell R. Menard, *The Economy of British America, 1607–1789* (1985).

New Netherland and the Restoration Colonies

Edwin Bronner, *William Penn's "Holy Experiment": The Founding of Pennsylvania, 1681–1701* (1962); Wesley Frank Craven, *New Jersey and the English Colonization of North America* (1964); Joyce Goodfriend, *Before the Melting Pot: Society and Culture in Colonial New York City, 1664–1730* (1992); Oliver Rink, *Holland on the Hudson: An Economic and Social History of Dutch New York* (1986); Robert C. Ritchie, *The Duke's Province: A Study of Politics and Society in Colonial New York, 1660–1691* (1977); Robert M. Weir, *Colonial South Carolina: A History* (1983).

Africa and the Slave Trade

Jay Coughtry, *The Notorious Triangle: Rhode Island and the African Slave Trade, 1700–1807* (1981); Philip D. Curtin, *The Atlantic Slave Trade: A Census* (1969); David Brion Davis, *The Problem of Slavery in Western Culture* (1966); Joseph Inikori and Stanley Engerman, eds., *The Atlantic Slave Trade* (1992); Herbert Klein, *The Middle Passage* (1978); Robin Law, *The Slave Coast of West*

Africa, 1550–1750: The Impact of the Atlantic Slave Trade on an African Society (1991); Daniel C. Littlefield, *Rice and Slaves: Ethnicity and the Slave Trade in Colonial South Carolina* (1981); James Rawley, *The Transatlantic Slave Trade: A History* (1981); Barbara Solow, ed., *Slavery and the Rise of the Atlantic System* (1991).

Africans in Anglo-America

T. H. Breen and Stephen Innes, *"Myne Owne Ground": Race and Freedom on Virginia's Eastern Shore, 1640–1676* (1980); Douglas Deal, *Race and Class in Colonial Virginia: Indians, Englishmen, and Africans on the Eastern Shore During the Seventeenth Century* (1993); Allan Kulikoff, *Tobacco and Slaves: The Development of Southern Cultures in the Chesapeake, 1680–1800* (1986); Edgar J. McManus, *Black Bondage in the North* (1973); Edmund S. Morgan, *American Slavery, American Freedom: The Ordeal of Colonial Virginia* (1975); Peter H. Wood, *Black Majority: Negroes in Colonial South Carolina from 1670 Through the Stono Rebellion* (1974).

European–Native American Relations in the North

Russell Bourne, *The Red King's Rebellion: Racial Politics in New England, 1675–1678* (1991); John Demos, *The Unredeemed Captive: A Family Story from Early America* (1994); Matthew Dennis, *Cultivating a Landscape of Peace: Iroquois-European Encounter in Seventeenth-Century America* (1993); Francis Jennings, *The Ambiguous Iroquois Empire* (1984); Peter Mancall, *Deadly Medicine: Indians and Alcohol in Early America* (1995); Michael Puglisi, *Puritans Beseiged: The Legacies of King Philip's War in the Massachusetts Bay Colony* (1991); Daniel Richter, *The Ordeal of the Longhouse: The Peoples of the Iroquois League in the Era of European Colonization* (1992); Daniel Richter and James Merrell, eds., *Beyond the Covenant Chain: The Iroquois and Their Neighbors in Indian America, 1600–1800* (1987); Dean Snow, *The Iroquois* (1992); Richard White, *The Middle Ground: Indians, Empires, and Republics in the Great Lakes Region, 1650–1815* (1991).

European–Native American Relations in the South and West

David H. Corkran, *The Creek Frontier, 1540–1783* (1967); Verner W. Crane, *The Southern Frontier, 1660–1732* (1929); Ramón Gutiérrez, *When Jesus Came, the Corn Mothers Went Away: Marriage, Sexuality, and Power in New Mexico, 1500–1846* (1991); Elizabeth A. H. John, *Storms Brewed in Other Men's Worlds: The Confrontation of Indians, Spanish, and French in the Southwest, 1540–1795* (1975); Andrew Knaut, *The Pueblo Revolt of 1680* (1995); James Merrell, *The Indians' New World: Catawbas and Their Neighbors from European Contact through the Era of Removal* (1989); Daniel H. Usner, Jr., *Indians, Settlers, and Slaves in a Frontier Exchange Economy: The Lower Mississippi Valley before 1783* (1992).

New England

Bernard Bailyn, *The New England Merchants in the Seventeenth Century* (1955); Richard Bushman, *From Puritan to Yankee: Character and the Social Order in Connecticut, 1690–1765* (1967); Christine Heyrman, *Commerce and Culture: The Maritime Communities of Colonial Massachusetts, 1690–1750* (1984); Richard Melvoin, *New England Outpost: War and Society in Colonial Deerfield* (1990); Robert Pope, *The Half-Way Covenant* (1969); Amanda Porterfield, *Female Piety in Puritan New England* (1991);

Laurel Thatcher Ulrich, *Good Wives: Image and Reality in the Lives of Women in Northern New England, 1650–1750* (1982).

New England Witchcraft

Paul Boyer and Stephen Nissenbaum, *Salem Possessed: The Social Origins of Witchcraft* (1974); Elaine Breslaw, *Tituba, Reluctant Witch of Salem: Devilish Indians and Puritan Fantasies* (1996); John Demos, *Entertaining Satan: Witchcraft and the Culture of Early New England* (1982); Richard Godbeer, *The Devil's Dominion: Magic and Religion in Early New England* (1992); Peter Hoffer, *The Devil's Disciples: Makers of the Salem Witchcraft Trials* (1996); Carol Karlsen, *The Devil in the Shape of a Woman: Witchcraft in Early New England* (1987); Bernard Rosenthal, *Salem Story: Reading the Witch Trials of 1692* (1993); Richard Weisman, *Witchcraft, Magic, and Religion in 17th-Century Massachusetts* (1984).

Colonial Politics

Lois Green Carr and David W. Jordan, *Maryland's Revolution of Government, 1689–1692* (1974); Richard P. Johnson, *Adjustment to Empire: The New England Colonies, 1675–1715* (1981); David S. Lovejoy, *The Glorious Revolution in America* (1972); Jack M. Sosin, *English America and Imperial Inconstancy: The Rise of Provincial Autonomy, 1696–1715* (1985); Jack M. Sosin, *English America and the Restoration Monarchy of Charles II* (1980); Jack M. Sosin, *English America and the Revolution of 1688* (1982).

Imperial Trade and Administration

Robert M. Bliss, *Revolution and Empire: English Politics and the American Colonies in the Seventeenth Century* (1991); Lawrence W. Harper, *The English Navigation Laws: A Seventeenth-Century Experiment in Social Engineering* (1939); Marcus Rediker, *Between the Devil and the Deep Blue Sea: Merchant Seamen, Pirates, and the Anglo-American Maritime World, 1700–1750* (1987); Robert C. Ritchie, *Captain Kidd and the War Against the Pirates* (1986); I. K. Steele, *Politics of Colonial Policy: The Board of Trade in Colonial Administration* (1968); Stephen Saunders Webb, *Lord Churchill's Coup: The Anglo-American Empire and the Glorious Revolution Reconsidered* (1995); Stephen Saunders Webb, *1676: The End of American Independence* (1984); Stephen Saunders Webb, *The Governors-General: The English Army and the Definition of the Empire, 1569–1681* (1979).

CHAPTER

4

Growth and Diversity
1720–1770

Maturina, a free black resident of New Orleans, awoke with a start at 3 A.M. on June 2 to the shouts of her neighbor, a slave woman named Louisa. "Maturina, someone has stolen your hens!" Louisa yelled. Leaping from her bed, Maturina ran to investigate, accompanied by her son and her brother Nicolas. They quickly located three of the hens, which had escaped from the robber's grasp, but could search no more until daylight.

Maturina knew where to look for missing chickens. At dawn, she and her relatives went to the city market on the levee (river bank), where they soon encountered a man carrying three fowls they recognized as hers. By threatening him with prosecution, they extracted the information that he had purchased the hens from a French grocer named La Rochelle. So the three confronted La Rochelle at his hut, where they found yet another of the birds. Under their questioning, the grocer reluctantly admitted that "it was a negro who had brought them to him to sell," informing Maturina and Nicolas "that he must be on the levee, or in some of the huts."

Suspicious, Maturina searched La Rochelle's own hut, rousting out the thief, who was hiding within. He tried to escape, but Nicolas pursued and captured him. Brought before the authorities, the thief proved to be Juan, a runaway slave from the countryside. The official investigation revealed that several times in the previous month Juan had successfully sold other stolen poultry at the levee market.

That much of the action in the story of Maturina, Nicolas, and Juan took place on the Mississippi River levee is not surprising. In the mid-eighteenth century, the crude market centered there was as much a focal point of New Orleans as were its formal government buildings. (The theft occurred in 1782, when New Orleans was ruled by Spain [see page 125], but the same events could have happened at any time in

More than fifty years after Maturina found her missing chickens at the New Orleans market (see vignette), Benjamin Henry Latrobe sketched these "Market Folks" buying and selling goods on the levee. Maturina would have recognized this scene, even though it occurred in 1819. African-Americans, European-Americans, and Native Americans all actively participated in market exchanges in both eras. *Maryland Historical Society, Baltimore.*

the preceding three decades.) To the levee came Indian traders, French and German farmers, free and enslaved Africans—all intent on buying and selling. One contemporary observed in 1761 that the Germans' Saturday morning market on the levee supplied the city with "cabbages, salads, fruits, greens . . . as well as vast quantities of wildfowl, salt pork, and many excellent sorts of fish." About 2,000 people, or one-fourth of the population of Louisiana, lived in New Orleans in 1763, and they regularly mingled at the levee market.

The lively markets in New Orleans and Anglo-American cities such as Boston and Philadelphia illuminate several key themes of colonial development in the mid-eighteenth century: population growth, ethnic diversity, the increasing importance of colonial urban centers, the creation of an urban elite that purchased food and clothing from other colonists, rising levels of consumption for all social ranks, and the new significance of internal markets. In the French and English mainland colonies, exports continued to dominate the economy. Settlers along the Atlantic and Gulf of Mexico coasts were tied to an international commercial system that fluctuated wildly for reasons having little to do with the colonies but inescapable in their effects. Yet expanding local populations demanded greater quantities and types of goods, and Europe could not supply all those needs. Therefore, in English and French America, as well as in the northern portions of New Spain known as the Borderlands (where exports were never an important element of the economy), colonists came increasingly to depend on exploiting and consuming their own resources.

Ethnic diversity was especially pronounced in the small colonial cities, but even the countryside attracted settlers from a wide range of nations. For example, an Englishman traveling in the vicinity of New Orleans in 1770 encountered not merely the French, Indian, and African residents one might expect, but also Germans, Acadians (see page 124), Irish, Scots, a native of the Spanish island of Minorca, a Slav, and several Anglo-Americans. The Spanish Borderlands and rural New England were the only exceptions; they attracted few new migrants of any description, their population growth stemming entirely from natural increase. The middle and southern Anglo-American colonies attracted by far the largest number of newcomers, both free and enslaved. Their arrival not only swelled the total population but also altered political balances and affected the religious climate by introducing new sects.

The ruling elites in the colonies paid little heed to the newcomers. In New France and New Spain, ordinary settlers were already denied any voice in their government, but even in English America elected and appointed leaders often refused to allow recent migrants from Europe adequate representation and government services. A series of violent clashes ensued after midcentury. By that time, native-born elites dominated the English colonies and contended with governors and other officials born in the mother country for control of the government machinery.

Intermarried webs of wealthy families developed in each of Europe's American possessions by the 1760s. Such well-off, educated colonists participated in transatlantic intellectual communities, whereas many colonists of the "lesser sort" could neither read nor write. The elites lived in comfortable houses and enjoyed leisure-time activities. Most colonists, whether free or enslaved, struggled just to survive, working daily from dawn to dark. Such divisions were most pronounced in British America, the largest and most prosperous settlements on the continent. By the last half of the century, the social and economic distance among different ranks of Anglo-Americans had widened noticeably.

Wealthy Anglo-Americans in particular were heavily influenced by the Enlightenment, the prevailing European intellectual movement of the day. The Enlightenment stressed reason and empirical knowledge, deliberately discarding superstition and instinct as guides to human behavior. Enlightened thinkers saw God as a distant presence who had ordered the world, setting forth natural laws that humans could discover through careful investigation and logical thought. From this perspective grew a distaste for emotion of any sort. Thus the religious revival known as the Great Awakening, which erupted in the English colonies in the 1740s, aroused much opposition from elites, because that revival drew primarily on the Calvinistic concept of a God that people could never fully comprehend. To a believer in the primacy of reason, the passions of the newly "awakened" were incomprehensible.

In 1720, much of the North American continent still fell under Indian control. By 1770, in sharp contrast, settlements of Europeans and Africans ruled by Great Britain filled almost all of the region between the Appalachian Mountains and the Atlantic Ocean; and the British, thanks to their victory over France in the Seven Years War (see pages 124–125), dominated the extensive system of rivers and lakes

• *Important Events* •

1690	Locke's *Essay Concerning Human Understanding* published, a key example of Enlightenment thought
1720–40	Black population of Chesapeake begins to grow by natural increase, contributing to rise of large plantations
1739	Stono Rebellion (South Carolina) leads to increased white fears of slave revolts
George Whitefield arrives in America; Great Awakening broadens
1739–48	King George's War disrupts American economy
1741	New York City "conspiracy" reflects whites' continuing fears of slave revolts
1760s	Baptist congregations take root in Virginia
1760–75	Peak of eighteenth-century European and African migration to English colonies
1765–66	Hudson River land riots pit tenants and squatters against large landlords
1767–69	Regulator movement (South Carolina) tries to establish order in back country
1771	North Carolina Regulators defeated by eastern militia at Battle of Alamance

running through the heart of the continent. Spanish missions extended in a great arc from present-day northern California to the Gulf Coast. Such geographic, economic, and social changes transformed the character of Europe's North American possessions.

 ## Population Growth and Ethnic Diversity

One of the most striking characteristics of the English mainland colonies in the eighteenth century was their rapid population growth. Only about 250,000 European- and African-Americans resided in the colonies in 1700. Thirty years later, that number had more than doubled, and by 1775 it had become 2.5 million. Such rapid expansion appears even more remarkable when compared to the modest changes that occurred in Louisiana, New Mexico, California, and Texas. By the last quarter of the eighteenth century, Texas had only about 2,500 Spanish residents and California even fewer; the largest Spanish colony, New Mexico, included just 20,000 or so. The total European population of New France expanded from approximately 15,000 in 1700 to about 70,000 in the 1760s, but only along the St. Lawrence River between Quebec and Montréal and in New Orleans were there significant concentrations of French settlers.

Although migration accounted for a considerable share of the growth in English America, most of the growth resulted from natural increase. Once the difficult early decades of settlement had passed, the American population doubled approximately every twenty-five years. Such a rate of growth was unparalleled in human history until very recent times. It had a variety of causes, chief among them women's youthful age at the onset of childbearing (early twenties for Europeans, late teens for Africans). Since married women became pregnant every two or three years, women normally bore five to ten children. Because the colonies were healthful places to live (especially north of Virginia), a large proportion of children who survived infancy reached maturity and began families of their own. As a result, about half of the American population was under sixteen years old in 1775. (By contrast, only about one-third of the American population was under sixteen in 1990.)

Africans (about 278,000) constituted the largest racial or ethnic group that came to the mainland English colonies during the eighteenth century.

Newcomers from Africa and Europe

In the slaveholding societies of South America and the Caribbean, a surplus of males over females and appallingly high mortality rates meant that only a large, continuing flow of enslaved Africans could maintain the captive work force at constant levels. South Carolina, where rice cultivation was difficult and unhealthy (chiefly because malaria-carrying mosquitoes bred in the rice swamps), and where planters preferred to purchase men, bore some resemblance to such colonies because it too required an inflow of Africans to sustain as well as expand its labor force. But in the Chesapeake the number of black residents grew especially

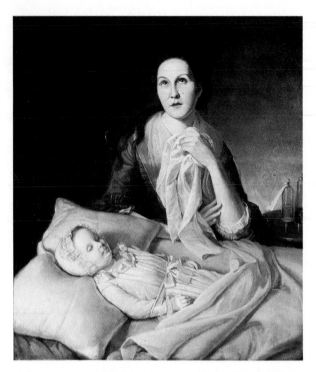

"Rachel Weeping" by Charles Willson Peale conveys as few other colonial portraits can the affection of eighteenth-century parents for their children and the grief they felt when those children died (as was so often the case) at an early age. Peale movingly revealed his wife's sorrow at the death of their daughter; thus his painting helps to refute the interpretation—advanced by some historians—that high levels of infant mortality led colonists to avoid becoming too attached to their young children. Philadelphia Museum of Art, the Barra Foundation.

rapidly, because the new African workers were added to a population that began to sustain itself through natural increase after 1740.

The offspring of slaves were also slaves, whereas the children of servants were free. The consequences of this important difference between enslaved and indentured labor were not clear until after 1720. It then became evident that a planter who owned adult female slaves could watch the size of his labor force increase steadily—through the births of their children—without making additional major investments in workers. Not coincidentally, the first truly large Chesapeake plantations appeared in the 1740s. Some years later, the slaveholder Thomas Jefferson indicated that he fully understood the connections when he declared, "I consider a woman who brings a child every two years more profitable than the best man of the farm. What she produces is an addition to the capital, while his labors disappear in mere consumption."

In addition to the new group of Africans, about 585,000 Europeans moved to North America during the eighteenth century, most of them after 1730 (see maps, page 95). Because some of these migrants (for example, convicts sentenced to exile by English courts) and all the slaves did not freely choose to come to the colonies, approximately one-third of the newcomers moved to America against their will. That contrasts sharply with later voluntary migrations from Europe, Asia, and the Americas in the nineteenth and twentieth centuries.

One of the largest groups of immigrants— nearly 150,000—came from Ireland or Scotland. About 66,000 were Scots-Irish, descended from

Scots-Irish, Germans, and Scots

Presbyterian Scots who had settled in the north of Ireland during the seventeenth century. Some 35,000 people came directly to America from Scotland. Another 43,000, both Protestants and Catholics, migrated from southern Ireland. Fleeing economic distress and (in Ireland) religious discrimination, they were also lured by hopes of obtaining land. Scots, Irish, and Scots-Irish immigrants usually landed in Philadelphia. They moved west and south, settling chiefly in Pennsylvania, Maryland, Virginia, and the Carolinas. Frequently unable to afford any acreage, they squatted on land belonging to Indians, land speculators, or colonial governments.

Migrants from Germany numbered about 85,000. Most emigrated from the Rhineland between 1730 and 1755, also usually arriving in Philadelphia. They became known locally as Pennsylvania Dutch (a corruption of *Deutsch*, as the Germans called themselves); late in the century they and their descendants accounted for one-third of Pennsylvania's residents. But many other Germans moved west and then south along the eastern slope of the Appalachian Mountains, eventually finding homes in western Maryland and Virginia. Others sailed first to Charleston or Savannah and settled in the interior of South Carolina or Georgia, often initially living under very difficult conditions, as is evident in the drawing on page 96. The Germans belonged to a wide variety of Protestant sects—primarily Lutheran, German Reformed, and Moravian—and therefore added to the already substantial religious diversity of the middle colonies.

The most concentrated period of immigration to the colonies fell between 1760 and 1775. Tough times in Germany and the British Isles led many to

Non-English Ethnic Groups in the British Colonies, c. 1775 *Non-African immigrants arriving in the years after 1720 were pushed to the peripheries of settlement, as is shown by these maps. Scottish, Scots-Irish, French, and German newcomers had to move to the frontiers. The Dutch remained where they had originally settled in the seventeenth century. Africans were concentrated in coastal plantation regions.*

decide to seek a better life in America; simultaneously, the slave trade burgeoned. In those fifteen years alone arrived more than 220,000 persons—or nearly 10 percent of the entire population of British North America in 1775. Late-arriving free immigrants had little choice but to remain in the cities or move to the edges of settlement; land elsewhere was fully occupied. In the peripheries they became the tenants of, or bought property from, land speculators who had purchased giant tracts in the (usually vain) hope of making a fortune.

Because of these migration patterns and the concentration of slaveholding in the South, half of the colonial population south of New England was of non-English origin by 1775. Whether the migrants assimilated readily into Anglo-American culture depended on patterns of settlement, the size of the group, and the strength of the migrants' ties to their common culture. For example, the Huguenots—French Protestants who fled religious persecution in their homeland after

Effects of Ethnic Diversity

1685—settled in tiny enclaves in American cities like Charleston and New York. They were unable to sustain either their language or their religious practices, and within two generations they were almost wholly absorbed into Anglo-American culture. By contrast, the equally small group of colonial Jews maintained a distinct identity. Most Jews in early America were Sephardic—that is, they were descended from the group of Jews who had escaped persecution in Spain and Portugal by migrating to the Netherlands and later to Dutch colonies in the New World. In a few cities—notably New York and Newport, Rhode Island—they established synagogues and worked actively to preserve their culture (for example, by opposing intermarriage with Christians).

Members of the larger groups of migrants (Germans, Irish, and Scots) found it easier to sustain Old World ways. Countless localities were settled almost exclusively by one group or another. Near Frederick, Maryland, a visitor would have heard more German than English; in Anson and Cumberland Counties, North Carolina, the same visitor might have

The first German immigrants in Georgia lived in crude shelters they erected in the wilderness at the settlement they named New Ebenezer. Notice the similarity to the structures inhabited by the Indians of the region, illustrated in a painting by the same artist, Philip Georg Friedrich von Reck, on page 77.   The Royal Library, Copenhagen.

thought she was in Scotland. Where migrants from different countries settled in the same region, ethnic antagonisms often surfaced. One German clergyman, for example, explained his efforts to prevent German youths from marrying people of different ethnic origins by asserting that the Scots-Irish were "lazy, dissipated and poor" and that "it is very seldom that German and English blood is happily united in wedlock."

Recognizing the benefits of keeping other racial and ethnic groups divided, the English elites on occasion deliberately fostered such antagonisms. When the targets of their policies were European migrants, the goal was the maintenance of political and economic power. When the targets were Indians and Africans, as they were in South Carolina, the stakes were considerably higher. In 1758 one official reported, "It has been allways the policy of this government to create an aversion in them [Indians] to Negroes." South Carolinians of English origin, a minority of the population, wanted to prevent Indians and Africans from making common cause against them. To keep slaves from running away to join the Indians, Anglo-Americans hired Indians as slave catchers. To keep Indians from trusting Africans, slaves were employed as soldiers in Indian wars.

The elites probably would have preferred to ignore the English colonies' growing racial and ethnic diversity, but they could not do so for long and still maintain their power. When such men decided to lead a revolution in the 1770s, they recognized that they needed the support of non-English Americans. Quite deliberately, they then began to speak of "the rights of man," rather than "English liberties," when they sought recruits for their cause.

 ## Economic Growth and Development

The dramatic increase in the population of Anglo-America served as a source of stability for the colonial economy and provided a firm basis for further growth. Again, a comparison to French and Spanish America reveals significant differences. The population and economy of New Spain's Borderlands stagnated. The isolated settlements produced few items for export (notably, hides and skins, most obtained through trade with Indians); residents were more likely to exchange goods illegally with their French and English neighbors than with the distant centers of Spanish Mexico or the Caribbean. French Canada exported large quantities of furs and fish, but monopolistic trade practices ensured that most of the profits ended up in the home country. The Louisiana colony required substantial government subsidies to survive, despite its active internal trade and some agricultural exports such as tobacco and rice. Of France's American possessions, only the Caribbean islands flourished economically.

British, French, and Spanish Colonies Compared

In British North America, by contrast, each year the rising population generated ever-greater demands for goods and services, which led to the development of small-scale colonial manufacturing and a complex network of internal trade. As the area of settlement expanded, roads, bridges, mills, and stores were built to serve the new communities. A lively coastal trade developed; by the late 1760s, 54 percent of the vessels leaving Boston harbor were sailing to other mainland colonies rather than to foreign ports. Such ships not only collected goods for export and distributed imports but also sold items made in America. The colonies thus began to move away from their earlier pattern of near total dependence on Europe for manufactured goods. For the

Who Moved to America from England and Scotland in the Early 1770s, and Why?

	English Emigrants	Scottish Emigrants	Free American Population
Destination			
13 British colonies	81.1%	92.7%	—
Canada	12.1%	4.2%	—
West Indies	6.8%	3.1%	—
Age Distribution			
Under 21	26.8%	45.3%	56.8%
21–25	37.1%	19.9%	9.7%
26–44	33.3%	29.5%	20.4%
45 and over	2.7%	5.3%	13.1%
Sex Distribution			
Male	83.8%	59.9%	—
Female	16.2%	40.1%	—
Unknown	4.2%	13.5%	—
Traveling Alone or with Families			
In families	20.0%	48.0%	—
Alone	80.0%	52.0%	—
Known Occupation or Status			
Gentry	2.5%	1.2%	—
Merchandising	5.2%	5.2%	—
Agriculture	17.8%	24.0%	—
Artisanry	54.2%	37.7%	—
Laborer	20.3%	31.9%	—
Why They Left			
Positive reasons (e.g., desire to better one's position)	90.0%	36.0%	—
Negative reasons (e.g., poverty, unemployment)	10.0%	64.0%	—

Source of data: Bernard Bailyn, *Voyagers to the West* (New York: Knopf, 1986), Tables 4.1, 5.2, 5.4, 5.7, 5.23, and 6.1.

Note: Between December 1773 and March 1776, the British government questioned individuals and families leaving ports in Scotland and England for the American colonies to learn who they were, where they were going, and why they were leaving. This table summarizes just a few of the findings of the official inquiries, which revealed a number of significant differences between the Scottish and English emigrants.

How do historians know that the residents of colonial North America began to purchase luxury items in the eighteenth century and that those goods came from wide-ranging trade networks? Probate inventories—written records of what people possessed at the time of their deaths—are a useful documentary source. But perhaps even more revealing are the results of archaeological excavations at the sites of colonial settlements. The shards shown below were found at one of the first French outposts in Louisiana—Old Mobile, established in 1702 on Mobile Bay, in what is now Alabama. The pots, of which only these small pieces remain (see the complete example), represent the final stage in a long trade route originating in China. The Chinese sold ceramics to traders in the Philippines, which Spain controlled, in exchange for Mexican silver. Spanish ships then carried the porcelain across the Pacific to Mexico, where it was purchased at annual fairs in Acapulco, carried by mule train across Mexico to Vera Cruz, then shipped to Caribbean ports and to Spain itself. The three hundred or so residents of Old Mobile bought such items from the Spanish settlement at Pensacola in nearby Florida. A brief description in an inventory could not convey so much information nearly as vividly as do these small bits of pottery.   Fragments: The Magazine Antiques. Pot: The Metropolitan Museum of Art.

first time, the American population was generating sufficient demand to encourage manufacturing enterprises. The largest indigenous industry was iron making; by 1775, 82 American furnaces and 175 forges were producing more iron than was England itself. Almost all of that iron was for domestic consumption.

The major energizing, yet destabilizing, influence on the colonial economy nevertheless remained foreign trade. Colonial prosperity still depended heavily on overseas demand for American products like tobacco, rice, indigo, fish, and barrel staves; the sale of such items earned the colonists the credit they needed to purchase English and European imports. If demand for American exports slowed, the colonists' income dropped and so did their ability to buy imported goods. Merchants were particularly vulnerable to economic downswings, and bankruptcies were common.

Despite fluctuations, the economy grew slowly during the eighteenth century. That growth, which resulted in part from Americans' higher earnings

Growth of Consumption

from their exports, in turn produced better standards of living for all property-owning Americans. In the first two decades of the century, as the price of British manufactures fell in relation to Americans' incomes, households began to acquire amenities such as chairs and earthenware dishes. Diet also improved as trading networks brought access to more varied foodstuffs. After 1750, luxury items like silver plate could be found in the homes of the wealthy, and the "middling sort" started to purchase imported English ceramics and teapots. Even the poorest property owners had more and better household possessions. Thus the colonists became *consumers*, in the sense that for the first time they could make choices among a wide variety of products and also could afford to buy items not absolutely essential for survival and subsistence.

Yet the benefits of economic growth were not evenly distributed: wealthy Americans improved their position relative to other colonists. The native-born elite families who dominated American political, economic, and social life by 1750 were those who had begun the century with sufficient capital to take advantage of the changes caused by population growth. They were the urban merchants who exported raw materials and imported luxury goods, the large landowners who rented small farms to immigrant tenants, the slave traders who supplied equally wealthy planters with their bondspeople, and the owners of rum distilleries. The rise of this group of moneyed families helped to make the social and economic structure of mid-eighteenth-century America more stratified than before.

New arrivals did not have the opportunities for advancement that had greeted their predecessors. Even so, there seems to have been relatively little severe poverty among free settlers in rural areas, where 90 percent of the colonists lived. But in the cities, the story was different. Families of urban laborers lived on the edge of desti-

Urban Poverty

tution. In Philadelphia, for instance, a male laborer's average annual earnings fell short of the amount needed to supply his family with the bare necessities. Even in a good year, his wife or children had to do wage work; in a bad year, the family could be reduced to beggary. By the 1760s public urban poor-relief systems were overwhelmed with applicants for assistance, and some cities began to build workhouses or almshouses to shelter the growing number of poor people. Among them were recent immigrants, the elderly and infirm, and widows, especially those with small children.

Within this overall picture, it is important to distinguish among the various regions: New England, the middle colonies, the Chesapeake, and the Lower South (the Carolinas and Georgia). Each region of the colonies had its own economic rhythm derived from the nature of its export trade.

In New England, three elements combined to influence economic development: the nature of the landscape, New England's leadership in colonial

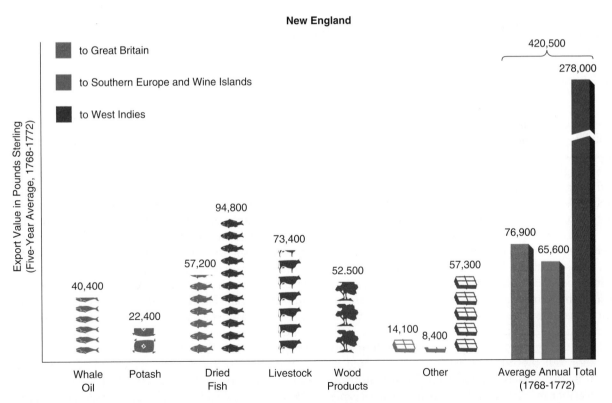

Regional Trading Patterns: New England *New England's major exports—dried fish, livestock, and wood products—were sold primarily in the West Indies.* Source: James F. Shepherd and Gary M. Walton, *Shipping, Maritime Trade, and the Economic Development of Colonial North America* (Cambridge: Cambridge University Press, 1972). Copyright 1972. Used by permission of Cambridge University Press.

Middle Colonies

Regional Trading Patterns: Middle Colonies *The middle colonies' major trading partners were the West Indies, the Wine Islands, and southern Europe. Bread, flour, and grains were the region's most valuable exports.* Source: James F. Shepherd and Gary M. Walton, *Shipping, Maritime Trade, and the Economic Development of Colonial North America* (Cambridge: Cambridge University Press, 1972). Copyright 1972. Used by permission of Cambridge University Press.

New England and King George's War

shipping, and the impact of imperial wars. New England's poor soil did not produce salable surpluses other than livestock, so wood products constituted a major cash crop. Farms were worked primarily by family members; the region had relatively few hired laborers. It also had the lowest average wealth per freeholder in the colonies. But New England had many wealthy men: merchants and professionals whose income was drawn from trade with the West Indies in items such as dried fish, livestock, and molasses.

Boston, by the 1730s a major shipbuilding center, soon felt the effects when warfare resumed in 1739. British vessels clashed with Spanish ships in the Caribbean, setting off a conflict that became known in America as King George's War. Nominally the war was fought to determine who would sit on the Austrian throne (in Europe it was called the War of the Austrian Succession), but one of its causes was

European commercial rivalries in the Americas, as nations jockeyed for position in the lucrative West Indian trade. The war's first impact on Boston's economy was positive. Ships—and sailors—were in great demand to serve as privateers (privately owned vessels authorized by the British to capture the enemy's commercial shipping). Wealthy merchants became even wealthier by profiting from contracts to supply military expeditions.

But Boston suffered heavy losses of manpower in Caribbean battles and in forays against the French in Canada. The most successful expedition was also the most costly. In 1745 a Massachusetts force captured the French fortress of Louisbourg (in modern Nova Scotia), which guarded the sea lanes leading to New France. Afterward, though, Massachusetts had to levy heavy taxes on its residents to pay for the expensive effort. For decades Boston's economy felt the continuing effects of King George's War. The city was left with unprecedented numbers of widows and children on its relief rolls. The boom in shipbuilding ended when the war did, and taxes remained high. As a final blow to the colony, Britain gave Louisbourg back to France in the Treaty of Aix-la-Chapelle (1748).

The middle colonies were more positively affected by King George's War and its aftermath because of the greater fertility of the soil in New York and Pennsylvania, where commercial farming was the norm.

Prosperity of the Middle Colonies

An average Pennsylvania farm family consumed only 40 percent of what it produced, selling the rest. New York and New Jersey both had many tenant farmers, who rented acreage from large landowners and often paid their rental fees by sharing crops with their landlords. Prosperous landlords and farmers were thus in an ideal position to profit from the wartime demand for grain and meat, especially in the West Indies. After the war a series of poor grain harvests in Europe caused flour prices to rise rapidly. Philadelphia and New York, which could draw on large fertile grain- and livestock-producing areas, took the lead in the foodstuffs trade. Meanwhile, Boston, which had no such fertile hinterland, found its economy stagnating.

Increased European demand for grain had a significant impact on the Chesapeake as well. After 1745, when the price of grain began rising faster than that of tobacco, some Chesapeake planters began to convert tobacco fields to wheat and corn. By diversifying their crops, they could avoid dependency on one product for their income. Tobacco still ruled the region and remained the largest single export from the mainland colonies. (The value of tobacco exports was nearly double that of grain products, the next contender.) Yet the conversion to grain cultivation brought about the first significant

Change in the Chesapeake

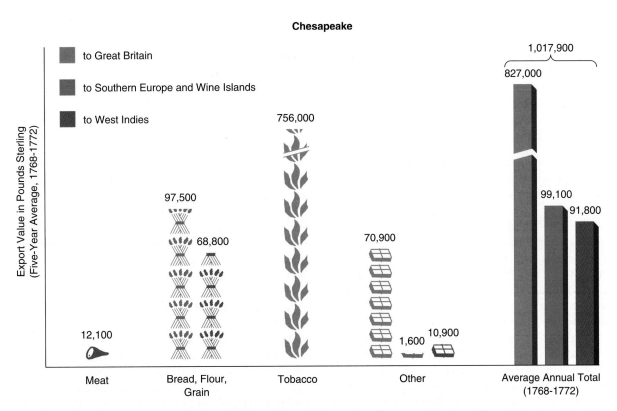

Chesapeake

to Great Britain
to Southern Europe and Wine Islands
to West Indies

Export Value in Pounds Sterling (Five-Year Average, 1768-1772)

Meat — 12,100
Bread, Flour, Grain — 97,500, 68,800
Tobacco — 756,000
Other — 70,900, 1,600, 10,900
Average Annual Total (1768-1772) — 1,017,900, 827,000, 99,100, 91,800

Regional Trading Patterns: The Chesapeake *Tobacco—legally exported only to Great Britain under the terms of the Navigation Acts—was the Chesapeake's dominant product. Grain made up an increasing proportion of the crops this region sold to other destinations.*   Source: James F. Shepherd and Gary M. Walton, *Shipping, Maritime Trade, and the Economic Development of Colonial North America* (Cambridge: Cambridge University Press, 1972). Copyright 1972. Used by permission of Cambridge University Press.

Regional Trading Patterns: The Lower South   *Rice and indigo, sold primarily in the mother country,*
dominated the exports of the Lower South.   Source: James F. Shepherd and Gary M. Walton, *Shipping, Maritime Trade, and*
the Economic Development of Colonial North America (Cambridge: Cambridge University Press, 1972). Copyright 1972. Used by permission of Cambridge University Press.

change in Chesapeake settlement patterns by encouraging the development of port towns (like Baltimore) to house the merchants who marketed the
new products.

Like the Chesapeake, the Lower South depended on staple crops and an enslaved labor force,
but its pattern of economic growth was distinctive.

**Trade and the
Lower South**

In contrast to tobacco prices,
which rose slowly through the
middle decades of the century,
rice prices climbed steeply,
doubling by the late 1730s. The
sharp rise was caused primarily by heavy demand for
rice in southern Europe. Because Parliament removed rice from the list of enumerated products (see
page 83) in 1730, South Carolinians were able to do
what colonial tobacco planters never could: trade directly with continental Europe. But dependence on
European sales had its drawbacks, as rice growers
discovered at the outbreak of King George's War in
1739. Trade with the European continent was dis-

rupted, rice prices plummeted, and South Carolina
entered a depression from which it did not emerge
for a decade. Still, prosperity returned by the 1760s
because of rapidly rising European demand for
South Carolina's exports; indeed, the Lower South
experienced more rapid economic growth in that period than did the other regions of the colonies.
Partly as a result, it had the highest average wealth
per freeholder in Anglo-America by the time of the
American Revolution.

Although King George's War at first helped
New England and hurt the Lower South, in the long
run those effects were reversed. In the Chesapeake
and the middle colonies, the war ushered in a long
period of prosperity. These variations in economic
experience point up a crucial fact about the English
mainland colonies: they did not compose a unified
whole. They were linked economically into regions,
but they had few political or social ties beyond or
even within those regions. Despite the growing
coastal trade, the individual colonies' economic for-

tunes depended not on their neighbors in America but rather on the shifting markets of Europe and the West Indies. Had it not been for an unprecedented crisis in the British imperial system (discussed in Chapter 5), it is hard to see how they could have been persuaded to join in a common endeavor. Even with that impetus, they found unity difficult to maintain.

Colonial Cultures

A seventeenth-century resident of England's American possessions miraculously transported to 1750 would have been surprised not only by the denser and more diverse population but also by what the historian Richard Bushman has termed "the refinement of America." Those colonists who acquired wealth through trade, agriculture, or manufacturing spent their money ostentatiously, dressing at the height of fashion, traveling in horse-drawn carriages driven by uniformed servants, and entertaining each other at lavish parties. Most notably, they built large houses containing rooms specifically designed for such forms of socializing as dancing, cardplaying, or drinking tea. Sufficiently well-off to enjoy "leisure" time (a first for North America), they attended concerts and the theater, gambled at horse races, and

Genteel Culture

played billiards and other games. They also cultivated polite manners, adopting stylized forms of address and paying attention to "proper" ways of behaving. Although the effects of accumulated wealth were most pronounced in Anglo-America, elite families in New Mexico, Louisiana, and Quebec as well, set themselves off from the "lesser sort." Together these wealthy families deliberately constructed a genteel culture quite different from that of the seventeenth-century colonies or of ordinary colonists in their own day.

Men from such families prided themselves not only on their possessions and on their positions in the colonial political, social, and economic hierarchy, but also on their level of education and their intellectual connections to Europe. Many had been tutored by private teachers hired by their families; some even attended college in Europe or America. (Harvard, the first colonial college, founded in 1636, was joined by William and Mary in 1693, Yale in 1701, and later by several others—for example, Princeton, established in 1747.) In the seventeenth century, only aspiring clergymen attended college, and their studies focused heavily on ancient languages and theology. But by the mid-eighteenth century, colleges broadened their curricula to include courses on mathematics, the natural sciences, law, and medicine. Accordingly, young men from elite

Education and the Enlightenment

The profits earned by tobacco planters with large holdings of land and slaves enabled them to buy luxurious items unimaginable to earlier colonists. This handpainted ivory fan and elaborate gold and enamel watch belonged to female members of the Byrd family of Virginia in the mid-eighteenth century.   Watch: Virginia Historical Society. Fan: Virginia Historical Society.

Nabby Martin, an eighteenth-century girl living in Providence, depicted in her needlework sampler buildings representing higher education (University Hall at Brown University) and politics (the Rhode Island State House). Ironically, she was excluded from participating in both on account of her sex. Museum of Art, Rhode Island School of Design, Providence, R.I.

or upwardly mobile families enrolled in college to study for careers other than the ministry. American women, though, were uniformly excluded from advanced education. The only exceptions were some of the young women who joined convents in Canada or Louisiana; a few were able to engage in sustained study within the convent walls.

The learned clergymen who headed colonial colleges in the eighteenth century were deeply affected by the intellectual current known as the Enlightenment. About the middle of the previous century, some European thinkers began to analyze nature in an effort to determine the laws that govern the universe. They employed experimentation and abstract reasoning to discover general principles behind phenomena such as the motions of planets and

stars, the behavior of falling objects, and the characteristics of light and sound. Above all, Enlightenment philosophers emphasized acquiring knowledge through reason, taking particular delight in challenging previously unquestioned assumptions. John Locke's *Essay Concerning Human Understanding* (1690), for example, disputed the notion that human beings are born already imprinted with innate ideas. All knowledge, Locke asserted, derives from one's observations of the external world.

The Enlightenment had an enormous impact on educated, well-to-do people in Europe and America. It supplied them with a common vocabulary and a unified view of the world, one that insisted that the enlightened eighteenth century was better than all previous ages. It joined them in a common endeavor, the effort to make sense of God's orderly creation. Thus American naturalists like John and William Bartram supplied European scientists with information about New World plants and animals so that they could be included in newly formulated universal classification systems. So, too, Americans interested in astronomy took part in an international effort to learn about the solar system by studying a rare occurrence, the transit of Venus across the face of the sun in 1769.

Enlightenment rationalism affected politics as well as science. Locke's *Two Treatises of Government* (1691) and other works by French and Scottish philosophers challenged previous concepts of a divinely sanctioned political order. Governments, declared Locke, were created by men and so could be altered by them. If a ruler broke his contract with the people and did not protect their rights, he could legitimately be ousted from power by peaceful—or even violent—means. The aim of government was the good of the people, Enlightenment theorists proclaimed. A proper political order could prevent the rise of tyrants; even the power of monarchs was subject to God's natural laws.

Yet the world in which such ideas were discussed was that of the few, not the many. Most residents of North America did not know how to read or write. Even those with basic literacy skills—a small proportion in French or Spanish America, about half of the people in British America—were familiar only with the rudiments. Books were scarce and expensive (the one book households tended to own was the Bible), and ordinary folk rarely had occasion to write a letter. Public schools supported by tax levies were few and

Oral Cultures

far between, even in such colonies as Massachusetts, which nominally required towns to provide schooling for local children. European youngsters who learned to read usually did so in their own homes, taught by their parents or older siblings. A few months at a private "dame school" run by a literate local widow might complete their education by teaching them the basics of writing and simple arithmetic. Enslaved African-American children were denied even that level of learning; teaching slaves to read and write was forbidden as too subversive of the social order. And only the most zealous Indian converts were taught Europeans' literacy skills.

Thus the cultures of colonial North America were primarily oral, communal, and—at least through the first half of the eighteenth century—intensely local. In the absence of literacy, the major means of communication was face-to-face conversation. Information tended to travel slowly and within relatively confined regions. Different locales developed divergent cultural traditions, and racial and ethnic variations heightened those differences. Public rituals served as the chief means through which the colonists forged their cultural identities.

Attendance at church was perhaps the most important such ritual. In Congregational (Puritan) churches, seating was assigned by church leaders to reflect standing in the community. In early New England, men and women sat on opposite sides of a central aisle, arranged in ranks according to age, wealth, and church membership. By the mid-eighteenth century, wealthy men and their wives sat in privately owned pews; their children, servants, and the less fortunate were still seated in sex-segregated fashion at the rear or sides of the church. In eighteenth-century Virginia, seating in Anglican parishes also conformed to the local status hierarchy. Planter families purchased their own pews, and in some parishes landed gentlemen customarily strode into church as a group just before the service, deliberately drawing attention to their exalted position. In the city of Quebec, Catholic feast days were celebrated by formal processions of men into the parish church; each participant's rank determined his placement in the procession. By contrast, Quaker meetinghouses in Pennsylvania and elsewhere used an egalitarian but sex-segregated seating system. The rituals surrounding people's entrance into and seating in colonial churches, in other words, symbolized their place in society and the values of the local community.

Religious Rituals

Communal culture centered on the civic sphere as well. In New England, colonial governments proclaimed official days of thanksgiving (for good harvests, victories in war, and so forth) and days of fasting and prayer (when the colony was experiencing difficulties such as droughts or epidemics). Everyone was expected to participate in the public rituals held in churches on such occasions. Monthly militia musters (known as training days) also brought the community together, since all able-bodied men between the ages of sixteen and sixty were members of the militia.

Civic Rituals

In the Chesapeake, important cultural rituals occurred on court and election days. When the county court was in session, men would come from miles around to file suits, appear as witnesses, serve as jurors, or simply observe the goings-on. Attendance at court functioned as a method of civic education; from watching the proceedings men learned what behavior their neighbors expected of them. Elections served the same purpose, for freeholders voted in public. An election official, often flanked by the candidates for the office in question, would call each man forward to declare his preference. The voter would then be thanked politely by the gentleman for whom he had cast his oral ballot. Traditionally, the candidates treated their supporters to rum at nearby taverns.

Everywhere in colonial North America, the public punishment of criminals served not just to humiliate the offender but also to remind the community of proper standards of behavior. Public hangings and whippings expressed the community's outrage about crimes and restored harmony to its ranks. Judges often assigned penalties that shamed miscreants in especially appropriate ways. In San Antonio, Texas, for example, one cattle thief was sentenced to be led through the town's streets "with the entrails hanging from his neck"; and when a New Mexico man assaulted his father-in-law, he was directed not merely to pay medical expenses but also to kneel before him and to beg his forgiveness publicly, in front of the entire community. New Englanders who were convicted of capital offenses but not hanged did not thereby escape public humiliation: frequently they were ordered to wear nooses around their necks for years as a constant reminder to themselves, their families, and their neighbors of their heinous violation of community norms.

The wide availability of consumer goods after the early years of the eighteenth century fostered

Convicted criminals were publicly punished and shamed in front of their friends, relatives, and neighbors. A man might be put in the stocks for offenses such as contempt of authority, drunken and disorderly conduct, or theft. The intent was not simply to deter him from future misbehavior but to let his fate serve as a warning to all who saw his humiliating posture.   Library of Congress.

Rituals of Consumption

new rituals centered on consumption, establishing novel links among the various residents of North America and creating what historians have termed "an empire of goods." The rituals began with the acquisition of desirable items. In the seventeenth century, settlers acquired necessities by bartering with neighbors or by ordering products from a home-country merchant. By the middle of the eighteenth century, specialized shops selling nonessentials had proliferated in cities such as New York, Philadelphia, and New Orleans. In 1770, Boston alone had more than five hundred stores, which offered consumers a vast selection of millinery, sewing supplies, tobacco, gloves, tableware, and the like. Even small and medium-size towns had one or two retail establishments by then. A colonist with money to spend would set aside time to "go shopping," a novel and pleasurable activity. A shopkeeper would display his (or occasionally her) wares to the customer, who was treated with respect and offered choices undreamed of by previous generations of colonists. The subsequent purchase of a desired object—for example, a ceramic bowl, a mirror, or a length of beautiful fabric—marked only the beginning of consumption rituals.

Consumers would then deploy their purchases in an appropriate manner: hanging the mirror prominently on a wall of the house, displaying the bowl on a table or sideboard, turning the fabric into a piece of clothing that could be worn on special occasions. Individual colonists clearly took personal pleasure in owning lovely objects, but they also could take pride in displaying their acquisitions (and thus their wealth and good taste) publicly to kin and neighbors. A particularly rich man might even hire a portraitist to paint his family using the objects and wearing the clothing, thereby creating a pictorial record that also would be displayed to others.

Tea drinking played an especially important role in Anglo-American consumption rituals. From early in the eighteenth century, households with aspirations to genteel status sought to acquire the items necessary for the proper consumption of tea: not just pots and cups but also strainers, sugar tongs, bowls, and even special tables. Tea provided a focal point for socializing and, because of its cost, served as a crucial marker of status. A hot drink that was mildly stimulating, it was seen as healthful as well. Thus poor households also consumed tea, although they could not afford the fancy equipment used by their better-off neighbors. Even some Mohawk Indians adopted the custom, much to the surprise of a traveler from Sweden, who observed them drinking tea in the late 1740s.

Just as civic, religious, and consumption rituals helped to bring certain communities together, so too they allowed the disparate cultures of colonial North America to interact with one another. Particularly important were the rituals that developed on what the historian Richard White has termed "the middle ground"—that is, the psychological and geographical space in which Indians and Europeans encountered each other. Most of those cultural encounters occurred in the context of trade or warfare.

Intercultural Rituals

When Europeans sought to trade with Indians, they came into contact with an indigenous system of exchange that stressed gift giving rather than formalized buying and selling. Although French and English traders complained constantly about the need to present Indians with gifts prior to negotiating with them for furs and skins, such a step was essential to successful bargaining. Over time, an appropriate ritual developed. A European trader arriving at a village would give gifts (cloth, rum, gunpowder, and other items) to Indian hunters. Eventually, those gifts would be reciprocated, and further exchanges would then take place. To the detriment of Indian societies, rum became a crucial component of these intercultural trading rituals. With some reason, traders came to believe that drunken Indians would sell their furs more cheaply; and some Indians refused to hunt or trade unless they were first supplied with alcohol.

Rituals surrounding murders were also critical points of cultural interaction. Indians and Europeans both believed that murders required a compensatory act, but the two groups had different notions of what that act should be. Europeans sought primarily to identify the murderer and to punish, perhaps to kill, that person. Such "eye for an eye" re-

This trade card (advertisement) issued by a Philadelphia tobacco dealer in 1770 shows a convivial group of wealthy men at a tavern. Both the leisurely activity depicted here and the advertisement itself were signs of the new rituals of consumption. Merchants began to advertise only when their customers could choose among different ways of spending money.   Library Company of Philadelphia.

venge was for Indians only one of a number of possible responses to murder. Compensation could also be accomplished by capturing someone who could take the dead person's place or—most important for maintaining peace on the frontiers—by "covering the dead," or providing the family of the deceased with goods that could compensate for the loss. Eventually, the French and the Algonkians in particular evolved an elaborate ritual for handling frontier murders—a ritual that encompassed elements of both societies' traditions: murders were investigated and murderers identified, but by mutual agreement deaths were usually "covered" by trade goods rather than by blood revenge.

Throughout colonial North America, therefore, a variety of rituals both cemented ties and established rank within communities and allowed those communities to interact peacefully with one another. Such rituals were economic, political, and religious in nature, and all residents of the continent participated in them to some extent.

 ## Colonial Families

As Europeans consolidated their hold on the North American continent during the first three quarters of the eighteenth century, Native Americans were forced to adapt to novel circumstances. As noted in Chapter 1, Spanish horses dramatically changed the lives of Plains Indians, and diseases ravaged even those groups that had little direct contact with Europeans. Bands reduced in numbers by disease and warfare recombined into new units; for example, the group later known as the Catawbas emerged in the 1730s in the western Carolinas from the fragmentary remains of several earlier Indian nations, including the Yamasees. Likewise, Indian family forms were reshaped under pressure from European secular and religious authorities. Whereas many Indian societies had permitted easy divorce, English, French, and Spanish missionaries frowned on such practices; and those societies that had allowed polygynous marriages (including New England Algonkians) redefined such relationships, designating one wife as "legitimate" and others as "concubines."

Indian and Mixed-Race Families

Continued high mortality rates created Indian societies in which extended kin took on new importance, for when parents died, aunts, uncles, and other relatives—even occasionally nonkin—assumed child-rearing responsibilities. Furthermore, once European dominance was established in any region, Indians there were commonly unable to pursue traditional modes of subsistence. That led to unusual family forms as well as to a variety of economic strategies. In New England, for instance, Algonkian husbands and wives often could not live together, for adults sought to support themselves by working separately for Anglo-Americans (perhaps wives as domestic servants, husbands as sailors). And in New Mexico, detribalized Navajos, Pueblos, and Apaches employed as servants by Spanish settlers clustered in the small towns of the Borderlands. Known collectively as *genizaros*, they lost contact with Indian cultures and instead lived on the fringes of Hispanic society.

Wherever there were relatively few European women in the population, sexual liaisons (both inside and outside marriage) occurred among European men and Indian women. The resulting mixed-race population of mestizos and métis worked as a familial "middle ground" to ease other cultural interactions. In New France and the Anglo-American backcountry, such families frequently resided in Indian villages and were enmeshed in trading networks; often, children of these unions became prominent leaders of Native American societies. (For example, Peter Chartier, the son of a Shawnee mother and a French father, led a pro-French Shawnee band in western Pennsylvania in the 1740s.) By contrast, in the Spanish Borderlands the offspring of Europeans and genizaros were treated as degraded individuals. Largely denied the privilege of legal marriage, they bore generations of "illegitimate" children of various racial mixtures, giving rise in Hispanic society to a wide range of labels describing degrees of skin color with a precision unknown in English or French America.

Family life among the many European migrants to North America was far more stable than that among Indian and mestizo peoples. Families (rather than individuals) constituted the basic units of colonial society. Headed by European men or their widows, households were the chief mechanisms of production and consumption. Their members—bound by ties of blood or servitude—worked together to produce goods for consumption or sale. The head of the household represented it to the outside world, managing the finances and hold-

European-American Families

Farmer Abraham's Almanac, *published in Philadelphia in 1759, contained this crude woodcut showing women engaged in chores associated with dairying: at right, milking a cow; at left, churning butter.* American Antiquarian Society.

ing legal authority over the rest of the family—his wife, his children, and his servants or slaves. (Eighteenth-century Americans used the word *family* for people who occupied one house, whether or not they were blood kin.) Such households were considerably larger than American families today; in 1790, the average home in the United States housed 5.7 whites. Most of those large families were nuclear—that is, unlike Indian families they did not include extended kin like aunts, uncles, or grandparents.

In English, French, and Spanish America alike, the vast majority of European families supported themselves through agriculture by cultivating crops and raising livestock. The scale and nature of the work varied: the production of indigo in Louisiana or tobacco in the Chesapeake required different sorts of labor from subsistence farming in New England or cattle ranching in New Mexico and Texas. Still, just as in the European, African, and Native American societies discussed in Chapter 1, household tasks were allocated by sex. The master, his sons, and his male servants or slaves performed one set of chores; the mistress, her daughters, and her female servants or slaves, an entirely different set.

The mistress was responsible for what Anglo-Americans called "indoor affairs." She and her female helpers prepared food, cleaned the house, did laundry, and often made clothing. These basic chores were complex and time-consuming. Preparing food, for instance, involved planting and cultivating a garden, harvesting and preserving vegetables, salting and smoking meat, drying apples and pressing cider, milking cows and making butter and cheese, not to mention cooking and baking. The head of the household and his male helpers, responsible for "outdoor affairs," also had heavy workloads. They had to plant and cultivate the fields, build fences, chop wood for the fireplace, harvest and market crops, care for livestock, and butcher cattle and hogs to provide the household with meat. So extensive was the work involved in maintaining a farm household that a married couple could not do it alone. They had to have help. If they had no children, they then turned to servants or slaves.

The larger population in colonial towns and cities offered women opportunities for employment unknown in the countryside. One such Bostonian was Ann Arnold, a wet nurse known as Jersey Nanny (probably a native of the English Isle of Jersey), who was portrayed in 1748 by John Greenwood. Museum of Fine Arts, Boston. Gift of Henry Lee Shattuck.

A European-American man's household could include African-American families as well as his own kin. More than 95 percent of colonial African-Americans were held in perpetual bondage. Although many African-Americans lived on farms with only one or two other slaves, the majority had the experience of living and working in a largely black setting. In South Carolina and Louisiana, a majority of the population was of African origin; in Georgia, about half; and in the Chesapeake, 40 percent. Indeed, portions of the Carolina low country were nearly 90 percent African-American by 1790.

Large plantations allowed for the specialization of labor. Each had its own enslaved male blacksmiths, carpenters, and shoemakers, along with slave women who worked as seamstresses, cooks, dairymaids, and midwives. These skilled slaves—between 10 and 20 percent of the African-American population—were essential to the smooth functioning of the plantation. But most

African-American Families

slaves, male or female, worked in the fields. Since West African women were accustomed to agricultural labor, that task must have coincided with their own cultural expectations. To European-Americans, however, black women's work in the fields connoted inferior status.

Because all the colonies legally permitted slavery, African-Americans had few potential refuges from bondage. Some recently arrived Africans stole boats to try to return home or ran off in groups to frontier regions to join the Indians. Some slaves from South Carolina and Georgia managed to reach Spanish Florida, where they were allowed to establish a free community, Gracia Real de Santa Teresa de Mose, on the outskirts of St. Augustine. Violent resistance had even less to recommend it than running away. European-American colonists may have been in the minority in some areas, but they controlled the guns and ammunition. Even if a revolt succeeded for a time, masters could easily muster the armed force necessary to put it down. Only in unusual circumstances, then, did colonial slaves rebel collectively.

Yet the lack of rebellion did not imply an absence of resistance to enslavement. Family ties often provided a key means for such resistance. Even though slaves were not allowed to marry legally, they established strong family structures in which youngsters usually carried their parents' and grandparents' names. Extended-kin groups protested excessive punishment of relatives and asked to live in the same quarters. The links that developed among African-American families who had lived on the same plantation for several generations served as insurance against the uncertainties of existence under slavery. If a nuclear family was broken up by sale, other relatives could help with child rearing and similar tasks. Among African-Americans, just as among Indians, the extended family served a more important function than it did among European-Americans.

Most slave families managed to carve out a small measure of autonomy, especially in their working and spiritual lives. Enslaved Muslims often clung to their Islamic faith, a pattern especially evident in Louisiana. Many other Africans, though, converted to Christianity, finding comfort in the assurances of their new religion that all people would be free and equal in heaven. On many plantations, slaves were allowed or required to plant their own gardens, hunt, or fish in order to supplement the minimal diet their masters supplied. In some regions, most notably South Carolina and Louisiana, enslaved people were allowed to accumulate personal property by working for themselves once they had finished their assigned tasks. Late in the century, some Chesapeake planters with a surplus of laborers began to hire out slaves to others, often allowing the workers to keep a small part of their earnings. Such accumulated property could buy desired goods or serve as a legacy for children.

Just as African- and European-Americans lived together on plantations, so too both groups were found in cities. Yet the few colonial cities were nothing but large towns by today's standards. In 1750 the largest, Boston and Philadelphia, had just seventeen thousand and thirteen thousand inhabitants respectively. Life in the cities differed considerably from that on northern farms, southern plantations, or southwestern ranches. City dwellers everywhere, not just those in New Orleans who went to the levee, purchased foodstuffs and wood at markets and cloth in shops, instead of laboriously producing such items themselves. City people also had much more contact with the world beyond their own homes than did their rural counterparts.

Life in the Cities

By the 1750s, most major cities had at least one weekly newspaper, and some had two or three. Anglo-American newspapers printed the latest "advices from London" (usually two to three months old) and news from other English colonies, as well as local reports. Newspapers were available at taverns and inns, so people who could not afford to buy them could catch up on the news. Even illiterates could do so, since literate customers often read the papers aloud. Contact with the outside world, however, had drawbacks. Sailors sometimes brought exotic and deadly diseases into port. Boston, New York, Philadelphia, and New Orleans endured terrible epidemics of smallpox and yellow fever, which Europeans and Africans in the countryside largely escaped.

Politics and Religion: Stability and Crisis in British America

In the first decades of the eighteenth century, Anglo-American political life exhibited a new stability. Despite substantial migration from overseas, most residents of the mainland had been born in America. Men from genteel families dominated the political structures in each province, for voters (free male property holders) tended to defer to their well-educated "betters" on election days.

Throughout the Anglo-American colonies, political leaders sought to increase the powers of elected assemblies relative to the powers of the governors and other appointed officials. Assemblies began to claim privileges associated with the British House of Commons, such as the rights to initiate all tax legislation and to control the militia. The assemblies also developed effective ways of influencing British appointees, especially by threatening to withhold their salaries. In some colonies (Virginia and South Carolina, for example), elite members of the assemblies usually presented a united front to royal officials, but in others (like New York), they fought with each other long and bitterly. New York took the first steps on the road to modern American democracy. In an attempt to win hotly contested elections, the province's genteel leaders began to appeal to "the people," competing openly for the votes of ordinary freeholders. Yet in 1733 that same New York government imprisoned a newspaper editor, John Peter Zenger, who had too vigorously criticized its actions. Defending Zenger against the charge of "seditious libel," his lawyer argued that the truth could not be defamatory, thus helping to establish a free-press principle now found in American law.

Rise of the Assemblies

Eighteenth-century assemblies bore little resemblance to twentieth-century state legislatures. Much of their business would today be termed administrative; only on rare occasions did they formulate new policies or pass laws of real importance. Members of the assemblies also saw their roles differently than do modern legislators. Instead of believing that they should act positively to improve the lives of their constituents, eighteenth-century assemblymen saw themselves as acting defensively to prevent encroachments on the people's rights. In their minds, their primary function was, for example, to stop the governors or councils from enacting oppressive taxes, rather than to pass laws that would actively benefit their constituents.

By midcentury, politically aware colonists commonly drew analogies between their own governments and Great Britain's balance of king, lords, and

In 1713, the colony of Massachusetts constructed its impressive State House in Boston. Here met the assembly and the council. The solidity and imposing nature of the building must have symbolized for its users the increasing consolidation of power in the hands of the Massachusetts legislature.   The Bostonian Society.

commons—a combination that had been thought to produce a stable polity since the days of ancient Greece and Rome. Although the analogy was not exact, political leaders equated their governors with the monarch, their councils with the aristocracy, and their assemblies with the House of Commons. All three were thought essential to good government, but Americans did not regard them with the same degree of approval. They viewed governors and appointed councils as posing potential threats to colonial freedoms and customary ways of life. As representatives of England rather than America, the governors and councils were to be feared rather than trusted. Colonists saw the assemblies, however, as the people's protectors. And in turn the assemblies regarded themselves as representatives of the people.

Again, though, such beliefs should not be equated with modern practice. The assemblies, firmly controlled by dominant families whose members were reelected year after year, rarely responded to the concerns of their poorer constituents. Although settlement continually spread westward, assemblies failed to reapportion themselves to provide adequate representation for newer communities—a lack of action that led to serious grievances among frontier dwellers, especially those from non-English ethnic groups. Thus it is important to distinguish between the colonial ideal, which placed the assembly at the forefront in the protection of people's liberties, and the reality, which was that most of those who were protected tended to be the wealthy and the assembly members themselves.

At midcentury, the political structures that had stabilized in a period of relative calm were confronted with a series of crises. None affected all the mainland provinces, but no colony escaped wholly untouched by at least one. The crises were of various sorts—ethnic, racial, economic, religious. They exposed the internal tensions building in the pluralistic American society, foreshadowing the greater disorder of the revolutionary era. Most important, they demonstrated that the political accommodations arrived at in the aftermath of the Glorious Revolution were no longer adequate to govern Britain's American empire. Once again, changes appeared necessary.

One of the first and greatest crises occurred in South Carolina. Early one morning in September 1739, about twenty South Carolina slaves gathered near the Stono River south of Charleston. Seizing guns and ammunition from a store, they killed the storekeepers and some nearby planter families. Then, joined by other local slaves, they headed south toward Florida in hopes of finding refuge at Gracia Real de Santa Teresa de Mose. By midday, however, the alarm had been sounded among slaveowners in the district. That afternoon a troop of militia attacked the fugitives, who then numbered about a hundred, killing some and dispersing the rest. More than a week later, most of the remaining conspirators were captured. Those not killed on the spot were later executed, but for over two years renegades were rumored to be at large.

Stono Rebellion

The Stono Rebellion shocked slaveholding South Carolinians and residents of other colonies as well. Throughout British America, laws governing the behavior of African-Americans were stiffened. But the most immediate response came in New York City, which had suffered a slave revolt in 1712. There the news from the South, coupled with fears of Spain generated by the outbreak of King George's War, set off a reign of terror in the summer of 1741. Hysterical whites interpreted a biracial gang of thieves and arsonists as malevolent conspirators who wanted to foment a slave uprising under the guidance of a supposed priest in the pay of Spain. By summer's end, thirty-one blacks and four whites had been executed for participating in the supposed plot. The Stono Rebellion and the New York conspiracy not only exposed and confirmed Anglo-Americans' deepest fears about the dangers of slaveholding but also revealed the assemblies' inability to prevent serious internal disorder. Events of the next two decades confirmed that pattern.

By midcentury, most of the fertile land east of the Appalachians had been purchased or occupied. As a result, conflicts over land titles and conditions of landholding grew in number and frequency as colonists competed for control of land good for farming. In 1746, for example, some New Jersey farmers clashed violently with agents of the East Jersey proprietors. The proprietors claimed the farmers' land as theirs and demanded annual payments, called quitrents, for the use of the property. Similar violence occurred in the 1760s in the region that later became Vermont. There, farmers holding land grants issued by New Hampshire battled with speculators claiming title to the area through grants from New York authorities.

Land Riots in New Jersey and New York

The most serious land riots of the period took place along the Hudson River in 1765 and 1766. Late in the seventeenth century, Governor Benjamin Fletcher of New York had granted several huge tracts in the lower Hudson valley to prominent colonial families. The proprietors in turn divided these estates into small farms, which they rented chiefly to poor Dutch and German migrants who regarded tenancy as a step on the road to independent freeholder status. By the 1750s some proprietors were earning large sums annually from quitrents and other fees.

After 1740, though, increasing migration from New England brought conflict to the great New York estates. The New Englanders did not want to become tenants. Many squatted on vacant portions of the manors and resisted all attempts at eviction. In the mid-1760s the Philipse family brought suit against the New Englanders, some of whom had lived on Philipse land for twenty or thirty years. New York courts upheld the Philipse claim and ordered squatters to make way for tenants with valid leases. Instead of complying, the farmers organized a rebellion against the proprietors. For nearly a year insurgent farmers controlled much of the Hudson valley. They terrorized proprietors and loyal tenants, freed their friends from jail, and on one occasion battled a county sheriff and his posse. The rebellion was put down only after British troops dispatched from New York City captured the rebellion's leaders.

Built in the late eighteenth century and still standing in Fairfax County, Virginia, the Frying Pan Meetinghouse was one of the Baptist churches with a racially integrated congregation from its earliest years. The existence of such egalitarian religious bodies directly challenged the colony's hierarchical society. Virginia Department of Historic Resources, VA.

Violent conflicts of a different sort erupted just a few years later in the Carolinas. The Regulator movements of the late 1760s (South Carolina) and early 1770s (North Carolina) pitted backcountry farmers against wealthy eastern planters who controlled the provincial governments. Frontier dwellers, most of whom were Scots-Irish, protested their lack of an adequate voice in colonial political affairs. South Carolinians for months policed the countryside in vigilante bands, contending that law enforcement in the region was too lax and biased against them. North Carolinians, whose primary grievance was heavy taxation, fought and lost a battle with eastern militiamen at Alamance in 1771. Regional, ethnic, and economic tensions thus com-

Regulators in the Carolinas

bined to create these disturbances, which ultimately arose from frontier people's dissatisfaction with the Carolina governments.

The most widespread crisis, however, was religious. From the late 1730s through the 1760s, waves of religious revivalism—today known collectively as the Great Awakening—swept over various parts of the colonies, primarily New England (1735–1745) and Virginia (1750s and 1760s). Orthodox Calvinists were eager to combat Enlightenment rationalism, which denied innate human depravity. Simultaneously, the economic and political uncertainty accompanying King George's War made colonists receptive to the spiritual certainty offered by evangelical religion. In addition, many recent immigrants and residents of the backcountry had no prior religious affiliation, thus presenting evangelists with a potential source of converts.

First Great Awakening

The first signs of what was to become the Great Awakening appeared in western Massachusetts, in the Northampton Congregational Church led by the Reverend Jonathan Edwards, a noted preacher and theologian. During 1734 and 1735, Edwards noticed a remarkable response among the youthful members of his flock to a message based squarely on Calvinist principles. Individuals could attain salvation, Edwards contended, only through recognition of their own depraved natures and the need to surrender completely to God's will. Such surrender brought to members of his congregation an intensely emotional release from sin and came to be seen as a single identifiable moment of conversion.

The effects of such conversions remained isolated until 1739, when George Whitefield, an English Anglican cleric, arrived in America. For fifteen months he toured the British colonies, preaching to large audiences from Georgia to New England and concentrating his efforts in the major cities: Boston, New York, Philadelphia, Charleston, and Savannah. A gripping orator, Whitefield was the chief generating force behind the Great Awakening. The historian Harry Stout has termed him "the first modern celebrity," because he was skilled at self-promotion and cleverly manipulated both his listeners and the newspapers. Everywhere he traveled, his fame preceded him. Thousands turned out to listen—and to experience conversion. Whitefield's journey, the first such ever undertaken, created

George Whitefield

new interconnections among the previously distinct colonies.

Regular clerics initially welcomed Whitefield and the American-born itinerant evangelist preachers who sprang up to imitate him. Soon, however, many clergymen began to realize that although "revived" religion filled their churches, it ran counter to their own approach to doctrine and matters of faith. They disliked the emotional style of the revivalists, whose itinerancy also disrupted normal patterns of church attendance because it took churchgoers away from the services they usually attended.

Opposition to the Awakening heightened rapidly, causing large numbers of congregations to splinter. "Old Lights"—traditional clerics and their followers—engaged in bitter disputes with the "New Light" evangelicals. Already characterized by numerous sects, American Protestantism became further divided as the major denominations split into Old Light and New Light factions and as new evangelical sects—Methodists and Baptists—gained adherents. Paradoxically, the angry fights and the rapid rise in the number of distinct denominations eventually led to an American willingness to tolerate religious diversity. No single sect could make an unequivocal claim to orthodoxy, so they had to coexist if they were to exist at all.

The most important effect of the Awakening was its impact on American modes of thought. The revivalists' message directly challenged the colonial tradition of deference. Itiner-

Impact of the Awakening

ant preachers, only a few of whom were ordained clergymen, claimed they understood the will of God better than did orthodox clerics. The Awakening's emphasis on emotion rather than learning undermined the validity of received wisdom, and New Lights questioned not only religious but also social and political orthodoxy. For example, New Lights began to defend the rights of groups and individuals to dissent from a community consensus, thereby challenging one of the most fundamental tenets of colonial political life.

Nowhere was this trend more evident than in Virginia, where the plantation gentry and their ostentatious lifestyle dominated society. By the 1760s

Virginia Baptists

Baptists had gained a secure foothold in Virginia; their beliefs and behavior were openly at odds with the way most genteel families lived. They rejected as sinful the horseracing, gambling, and dancing that occupied much of the gentry's leisure time. Like Quakers before them, they dressed plainly, in contrast to the gentry's fashionable opulence. They addressed each other as "brother" and "sister" regardless of social status, and they elected the leaders of their congregations—more than ninety of them by 1776. Their monthly "great meetings," which attracted hundreds of people, introduced new public rituals that rivaled the weekly Anglican services.

Strikingly, almost all the Virginia Baptist congregations included both black and white members. When the Dan River Baptist Church was founded in 1760, for example, eleven of its original seventy-four members were African-Americans, and other congregations had African-American majorities. Church rules applied equally to all members; interracial sexual relationships, divorce, and adultery were forbidden to everyone. In addition, masters were directed not to break up slave marriages through sale. Biracial committees investigated complaints about church members' misbehavior. Churches excommunicated slaves for stealing from their masters, but they also excommunicated masters for physically abusing their slaves. One such slaveowner excommunicated in 1772 experienced a true conversion. Penalized for "burning" one of his slaves, Charles Cook apologized to the congregation and became a preacher in a largely African-American church. Other Baptists decided that owning slaves was "unrighteous" and freed their bondspeople; Robert Carter manumitted more than nine hundred slaves.

 Conclusion

The Great Awakening thus injected an egalitarian strain into Anglo-American life at midcentury and further disrupted traditional structures of existence. Although primarily a religious movement, the Awakening also had important social and political consequences, calling into question habitual modes of behavior in the secular as well as the religious realm. In short, the Great Awakening helped to break Anglo-Americans' ties to their limited seventeenth-century origins. So, too, did the newcomers from Germany, Scotland, Ireland, and Africa, who brought their languages, customs, and religions to British North America. The European immigrants settled throughout the English colonies but were concentrated in the growing cities and in the backcountry. By contrast, enslaved migrants from Africa lived and worked primarily within 100 miles of the Atlantic coast. In many areas of the colonial South, 50 to 90 percent of the population was of African origin.

The economic life of all Europe's North American colonies proceeded simultaneously on two levels. On the farms, plantations, and ranches on which most colonists resided, the daily, weekly, monthly, and yearly rounds of chores for men, women, and children alike dominated people's lives while providing the goods consumed by households and sold in the marketplace. At the same time, the British, French, and Spanish colonies were enmeshed in an international network of trade that affected their local economic circumstances. The bitter wars fought by European nations during the eighteenth century inevitably involved the colonists by creating new opportunities for overseas sales or by disrupting their traditional markets. Above all, the colonial economy was volatile, fluctuating for reasons beyond Americans' control. Those fortunate few who—through skill, control of essential resources, or luck—reaped the profits of international trade made up the wealthy class of merchants and landowners who dominated colonial political and social life.

A century and a half after European peoples first settled in North America, the colonies mixed diverse European, American, and African traditions into a novel cultural blend that owed much to Europe but just as much, if not more, to North America itself. Europeans who interacted regularly with peoples of African and American origin—and with Europeans who came from nations other than their own—had to develop new methods of accommodating intercultural differences in addition to creating ties within their own potentially fragmenting communities. Yet at the same time the dominant colonists continued to identify themselves as French, Spanish, or British rather than as Americans. That did not change in Canada, Louisiana, or the Spanish Borderlands, but in the 1760s some Anglo-Americans began to realize that their interests were not necessarily identical to those of Great Britain or its monarch. For the first time, they offered a direct challenge to British authority.

Suggestions for Further Reading

General

Jack P. Greene, *Pursuits of Happiness: The Social Development of the Early Modern British Colonies and the Formation of American Culture*

(1988); Richard Hofstadter, *America at 1750: A Social Portrait* (1971); Peter C. Mancall, *Deadly Medicine: Indians and Alcohol in Early America* (1995); D. W. Meinig, *Atlantic America, 1492–1800* (1986); Stephanie G. Wolf, *As Various as Their Land: The Everyday Lives of 18th Century Americans* (1992).

New France and New Spain

Ramón Gutiérrez, *When Jesus Came, the Corn Mothers Went Away: Marriage, Sexuality, and Power in New Mexico, 1500–1846* (1991); Gwendolyn Midlo Hall, *Africans in Colonial Louisiana: The Development of Afro-Creole Culture in the Eighteenth Century* (1992); Dale Miquelon, *New France, 1701–1744* (1987); G. F. G. Stanley, *New France, 1744–1760* (1968); Daniel H. Usner, Jr., *Indians, Settlers, and Slaves in a Frontier Exchange Economy: The Lower Mississippi Valley Before 1783* (1992); David J. Weber, *The Spanish Frontier in North America* (1992); Richard White, *The Middle Ground: Indians, Empires, and Republics in the Great Lakes Region, 1650–1815* (1991).

Anglo-American Society

T. H. Breen, *Tobacco Culture* (1985); Carl Bridenbaugh, *Cities in Revolt: Urban Life in America, 1743–1776* (1955); Lois Green Carr et al., eds., *Colonial Chesapeake Society* (1988); David Conroy, *In Public Houses: Drink and the Revolution of Authority in Colonial Massachusetts* (1995); Rhys Isaac, *The Transformation of Virginia, 1740–1790* (1982); Christopher Jedrey, *The World of John Cleaveland: Family and Community in Eighteenth-Century New England* (1979); Sung Bok Kim, *Landlord and Tenant in Colonial New York: Manorial Society, 1664–1775* (1978); Peter C. Mancall, *Valley of Opportunity: Economic Culture Along the Upper Susquehanna, 1700–1800* (1991); Gary B. Nash, *The Urban Crucible: Social Change, Political Consciousness, and the Origins of the American Revolution* (1979); Michael Zuckerman, *Peaceable Kingdoms: New England Towns in the Eighteenth Century* (1970).

Anglo-American Economic Development

Richard Bushman, *The Refinement of America: Persons, Houses, Cities* (1992); Cary Carson et al., eds., *Of Consuming Interests: The Style of Life in the Eighteenth Century* (1994); Stephen Innes, ed., *Work and Labor in Early America* (1988); Alice Hanson Jones, *Wealth of a Nation to Be: The American Colonies on the Eve of the Revolution* (1980); John J. McCusker and Russell R. Menard, *The Economy of British America, 1607–1789* (1985); Edwin J. Perkins, *The Economy of Colonial America* (1980); Gary M. Walton and James F. Shepherd, *The Economic Rise of Early America* (1979).

Anglo-American Politics

Bernard Bailyn, *The Origins of American Politics* (1968); Patricia U. Bonomi, *A Factious People: Politics and Society in Colonial New York* (1971); Richard Bushman, *King and People in Provincial Massachusetts* (1985); Edward M. Cook, Jr., *The Fathers of the Towns: Leadership and Community Structure in Eighteenth-Century New England* (1976); Jack P. Greene, *The Quest for Power: The Lower Houses of Assembly in the Southern Royal Colonies, 1689–1776* (1963).

Immigration to British America

Bernard Bailyn, *The Peopling of British North America* (1986); Bernard Bailyn, *Voyagers to the West* (1986); Bernard Bailyn and

Philip Morgan, eds., *Strangers Within the Realm* (1991); Jon Butler, *The Huguenots in America* (1983); R. J. Dickson, *Ulster Immigration to Colonial America, 1718–1775* (1966); David Dobson, *Scottish Immigration to Colonial America, 1607–1785* (1994); A. Roger Ekirch, *Bound for America: The Transportation of British Convicts to the Colonies, 1718–1775* (1987); Ned Landsman, *Scotland and Its First American Colony* (1985); A. G. Roeber, *Palatines, Liberty, and Property: German Lutherans in Colonial British America* (1993).

African-Americans

Ira Berlin and Philip Morgan, eds., *Cultivation and Culture: Labor and the Shaping of Slave Life in the Americas* (1993); Thomas J. Davis, *A Rumor of Revolt: The "Great Negro Plot" in Colonial New York* (1985); Marvin L. Michael Kay and Lorin Lee Cary, *Slavery in North Carolina, 1748–1775* (1995); Allan Kulikoff, *Tobacco and Slaves: The Development of Southern Cultures in the Chesapeake, 1680–1800* (1986); Gerald [Michael] Mullin, *Flight and Rebellion: Slave Resistance in Eighteenth-Century Virginia* (1972); Michael Mullin, *Africa in America: Slave Acculturation and Resistance in the American South and the British Caribbean, 1736–1834* (1992); William Pierson, *Black Yankees: The Development of an Afro-American Subculture in Eighteenth-Century New England* (1988); Mechal Sobel, *The World They Made Together: Black and White Values in Eighteenth-Century Virginia* (1987); Betty Wood, *Women's Work, Men's Work: The Informal Slave Economies of Low Country Georgia* (1995); Anne Yentsch, *A Chesapeake Family and Their Slaves* (1994).

Anglo-American Women and Families

Kathleen M. Brown, *Good Wives, Nasty Wenches, and Anxious Patriarchs: Gender, Race, and Power in Colonial Virginia* (1996); Cornelia Hughes Dayton, *Women Before the Bar: Gender, Law, and Society in Connecticut, 1639–1789* (1995); Philip J. Greven, *The Protestant Temperament: Patterns of Child-Rearing, Religious Experience, and the Self in Early America* (1977); Joan Gundersen,

To Be Useful to the World: Women in Eighteenth-Century America (1996); Barry J. Levy, *Quakers and the American Family* (1988); June Namias, *White Captives: Gender and Ethnicity on the American Frontier* (1993); Marylynn Salmon, *Women and the Law of Property in Early America* (1986); Daniel Blake Smith, *Inside the Great House: Planter Family Life in Eighteenth-Century Chesapeake Society* (1980); Merril D. Smith, *Breaking the Bonds: Marital Discord in Pennsylvania, 1730–1830* (1992).

Anglo-American Education, Science, and the Enlightenment

Patricia Cline Cohen, *A Calculating People: The Spread of Numeracy in Early America* (1982); Lawrence A. Cremin, *American Education: The Colonial Experience, 1607–1783* (1970); Richard Beale Davis, *Intellectual Life in the Colonial South, 1585–1763* (1978); Brooke Hindle, *The Pursuit of Science in Revolutionary America* (1956); Kenneth Lockridge, *Literacy in Colonial New England* (1974); Henry F. May, *The Enlightenment in America* (1976); Thomas P. Slaughter, *The Natures of John and William Bartram* (1996); William Sloan and Julie Williams, *The Early American Press, 1690–1783* (1994); Raymond P. Stearns, *Science in the British Colonies of America* (1970).

Religion and the Great Awakening

Patricia U. Bonomi, *Under the Cope of Heaven: Religion, Society, and Politics in Colonial America* (1986); J. M. Bumstead and John E. Van de Wetering, *What Must I Do to Be Saved? The Great Awakening in Colonial America* (1976); Jon Butler, *Awash in a Sea of Faith: Christianizing the American People* (1990); Michael Crawford, *Seasons of Grace: Colonial New England's Revival Tradition in Its British Context* (1991); Alan E. Heimert, *Religion and the American Mind: From the Great Awakening to the Revolution* (1966); David S. Lovejoy, *Religious Enthusiasm in the New World* (1985); Harry S. Stout, *The Divine Dramatist: George Whitefield and the Rise of Modern Evangelicalism* (1991); Patricia Tracy, *Jonathan Edwards, Pastor* (1980).

CHAPTER

5

Severing the Bonds
of Empire
1754–1774

T he two men must have found the occasion remarkable. The artist customarily painted portraits of the wealthy and high born, not of artisans, even well-connected, affluent ones. The subject himself was an artist—a maker of beautiful silver and gold objects, an engraver of cartoons and townscapes. The political sympathies of the painter, John Singleton Copley, lay primarily with Boston's conservatives, whereas the sitter, Paul Revere, was a noted leader of resistance to British policies. Yet some time in 1768 Revere commissioned Copley to paint his portrait, and the result (opposite page) is one the greatest works of American art.

Copley was thirty, Revere thirty-four. Each man had learned his trade from a parent. Revere's father Apollos, who arrived in Boston as a teenage Huguenot refugee early in the century, was an accomplished gold- and silversmith; Paul served as his father's apprentice and took over the family business when Apollos died in 1754. Copley, whose Irish parents had immigrated to Boston in the 1730s, was taught to paint by his stepfather, Peter Pelham, an English artist. The two young tradesmen had undoubtedly known each other for years. In 1763 and thereafter Copley hired Revere to make silver and gold frames for the miniature portraits that were among his earliest works.

But their finest collaboration was the painting reproduced here. Copley portrayed Revere surrounded by the tools of his trade and contemplating a teapot he was crafting. The silversmith wears a loose-fitting linen shirt and an open vest rather than the formal dress usually worn by colonial artists' subjects. Even so, Revere is not actually at work: his clothes are too clean, the table too polished to be a work surface. The

John Singleton Copley's portrait of Paul Revere is generally regarded as one of his masterpieces. Copley captured Revere's character as a hard-working, respectable artisan—a man unafraid of displaying his humble origins to the world.

Museum of Fine Arts, Boston. Gift of Joseph W., William B., and Edward H. R. Revere.

119

silversmith's pose and apparel convey an impression of thoughtfulness, virtuous labor, and solidity. The teapot too carries a message, especially in the year 1768. Simultaneously a reflection of a craftsman's skills and a prominent emblem of the new "empire of goods" in British America, it resonated with symbolism because, as shall be seen later in this chapter, tea boycotts were an important component of colonial resistance to Great Britain. Both artist and subject, indeed, were to be active participants (though in very different ways) in the 1773 event known to history as the Boston Tea Party.

In retrospect, John Adams identified the years between 1760 and 1775 as the era of the true American Revolution. The Revolution, Adams declared, was completed before the fighting started, for it was "in the Minds of the people," involving not the actual winning of independence but a fundamental shift of allegiance from Britain to America. Today, not all historians would agree with Adams's assertion that that shift constituted the Revolution. But none would deny the importance of the events of those crucial years, which divided the American population along political lines and set the colonies on the road to independence.

The story of the 1760s and early 1770s describes an ever-widening split between Great Britain and Anglo-America and among their respective supporters in the colonies. In the long history of British settlement in the Western Hemisphere, considerable tension at times had marred the relationship between individual provinces and the mother country. Still, that tension rarely had been sustained for long, nor had it been widespread, except during the crisis following the Glorious Revolution in 1689. The primary divisions affecting the colonies had been internal rather than external. In the 1750s, however, a series of events began to draw the colonists' attention from domestic matters to their relations with Great Britain. It all started with the Seven Years War.

Britain's overwhelming victory in that war, confirmed by treaty in 1763, forever altered the balance of power in North America. France was ousted from the continent and Spain from Florida, events with major consequences for both the indigenous peoples of the interior and the residents of the British colonies. Indians could no longer play off European powers against one another and so lost one of their major diplomatic tools. Anglo-Americans, for their part, no longer had to fear the French threat on their northern and western borders or the Spanish in the Southeast. The British colonies along the coast would never have dared to break with their mother country, some historians contend, if France and its Indian allies had continued to control the interior of the continent.

The British victory in 1763, then, constituted a major turning point in American history because of

The Colonial Wars, 1689–1763

American Name	European Name	Dates	Participants	American Sites	Dispute
King William's War	War of the League of Augsburg	1689–97	England, Holland versus France, Spain	New England, New York, Canada	French power
Queen Anne's War	War of Spanish Succession	1702–13	England, Holland, Austria versus France, Spain	Florida, New England	Throne of Spain
King George's War	War of Austrian Succession	1739–48	England, Holland, Austria versus France, Spain, Prussia	West Indies, New England, Canada	Throne of Austria
French and Indian War	Seven Years War	1756–63	England versus France, Spain	Ohio country, Canada	Possession of Ohio country

• *Important Events* •

1754	Albany Congress meets to try to forge colonial unity Fighting breaks out with Washington's defeat at Fort Necessity		**1766**	Stamp Act repealed Declaratory Act insists that Parliament can tax the colonies
1756	Britain declares war on France; Seven Years War officially begins		**1767**	Townshend Acts lay duties on trade within the empire, send new officials and judges to America
1759	British forces take Quebec		**1768–70**	Resistance to Townshend duties takes form of boycotts and public demonstrations but divides merchants and urban artisans
1760	American phase of war ends with fall of Montréal to British troops George III becomes king		**1770**	Lord North becomes prime minister Townshend duties repealed, except for tea tax Boston Massacre kills five colonial rioters
1763	Treaty of Paris ends Seven Years War Pontiac's allies attack British forts in West Proclamation of 1763 attempts to close land west of Appalachians to English settlement		**1772**	Boston Committee of Correspondence formed
1764	Sugar Act lays new duties on molasses, tightens customs regulations Currency Act outlaws paper money issued by the colonies		**1773**	Tea Act aids East India Company Boston Tea Party protests the Tea Act
1765	Stamp Act requires stamps on all printed materials in colonies Sons of Liberty formed		**1774**	Coercive Acts punish Boston and Massachusetts as a whole Quebec Act reforms government of Quebec

its direct effect on all the residents of North America. It also had a significant impact on Great Britain, one that soon affected the colonies as well. To win the war, Britain went heavily into debt. To reduce the debt, Parliament for the first time imposed revenue-raising taxes on the colonies in addition to the customs duties that had long regulated trade. That decision exposed differences in the political thinking of Americans and Britons—differences that until then had been obscured by a shared political vocabulary.

During the 1760s and early 1770s a broad coalition of the residents of Anglo-America, men and women alike, resisted new tax levies and attempts by British officials to tighten controls over provincial governments. The colonies' elected leaders became ever more suspicious of Britain's motives as the years passed. They laid aside old antagonisms to coordinate their response to the new measures, and they slowly began to reorient their political thinking. As late as the summer of 1774, though, most were still seeking a solution within the framework of the empire; few harbored thoughts of independence.

 ### Renewed Warfare Among Europeans and Indians

The English colonies along the Atlantic seaboard were surrounded by hostile, or potentially hostile, neighbors: Indians everywhere, the Spanish in Florida and along the coast of the Gulf of Mexico, the French along the great inland system of rivers and lakes that stretched from the St. Lawrence to the Mississippi. The Spanish outposts posed little direct threat, for Spain's days as a major power had passed. The French were another matter. Their long chain of forts and settlements dominated the North American interior, facilitating trading partnerships and alliances with the Indians. In none of the three wars fought between 1689 and 1748 was England able to shake France's hold on the American frontier. Under the Peace of Utrecht, which ended Queen Anne's War in 1713, the English won control of such peripheral northern areas as Newfoundland, Hudson's Bay, and Nova Scotia (Acadia). But Britain made no territorial gains in King George's War (see map, page 126).

An eighteenth-century Iroquois warrior as depicted by a European artist. Such men of the Six Nations confederacy dominated the North American interior before the Seven Years War. Lines drawn on maps by colonizing powers and the incursions of traders made little impact on their power.   Library of Congress, Rare Book and Special Collections Division.

During both Queen Anne's War and King George's War, the Iroquois Confederacy maintained the policy of neutrality it first developed in 1701.

Iroquois Neutrality

While British and French forces fought for nominal control of the North American continent, the confederacy—which actually dominated a large portion of that continent—skillfully played the Europeans off against each other, refusing to commit its warriors fully to either side despite being showered with gifts by both. Instead, the Iroquois fought only their traditional southern enemies, the Catawbas. Since France repeatedly urged them to attack the Catawbas, who were allied with Britain, the Iroquois achieved desirable goals. They kept the French

happy and simultaneously consolidated their control over the entire interior region north of Virginia. The campaign against a common enemy also enabled the confederacy to cement its alliance with its weaker tributaries, the Shawnees and Delawares, and to ensure the continued subordination of those groups.

But even careful Iroquois diplomats could not prevent the region inhabited by the Shawnees and Delawares (now western Pennsylvania and eastern Ohio) from providing the spark that set off a major war. That conflict spread from America to Europe (a significant reversal of previous patterns), proving decisive in the contest for North America. Trouble began in 1752 when Anglo-American fur traders ventured into the area known as the Ohio country (see map, page 123). The French could not permit their rivals to gain a foothold in the region, for it contained the source of the Ohio River, which offered direct access by water to French posts on the Mississippi. A permanent British presence in the Ohio country could challenge France's control of the western fur trade and even threaten its prominence in the Mississippi valley. Accordingly, in 1753 the French pushed southward from Lake Erie, building fortified outposts at strategic points.

In response to the French threat to their western frontiers, delegates from seven northern and middle colonies gathered in Albany, New York, in

Albany Congress

June 1754. With the backing of administrators in London, they sought two goals: to persuade the Iroquois to abandon their traditional neutrality and to coordinate the defenses of the colonies. They succeeded in neither. The Iroquois listened politely to the colonists' arguments but saw no reason to change a policy that had served them well for half a century. And although the Albany Congress delegates adopted a Plan of Union (which would have established an elected intercolonial legislature with the power to tax), their provincial governments uniformly rejected the plan—primarily because those governments feared a loss of autonomy.

While the Albany Congress delegates deliberated, the war they sought to prepare for was already beginning. Governor Robert Dinwiddie of Virginia had sent a small militia force westward to counter the French moves. Virginia claimed ownership of the Ohio country, and Dinwiddie was eager to prevent the French from establishing a permanent post there. But the Virginia militiamen arrived too late.

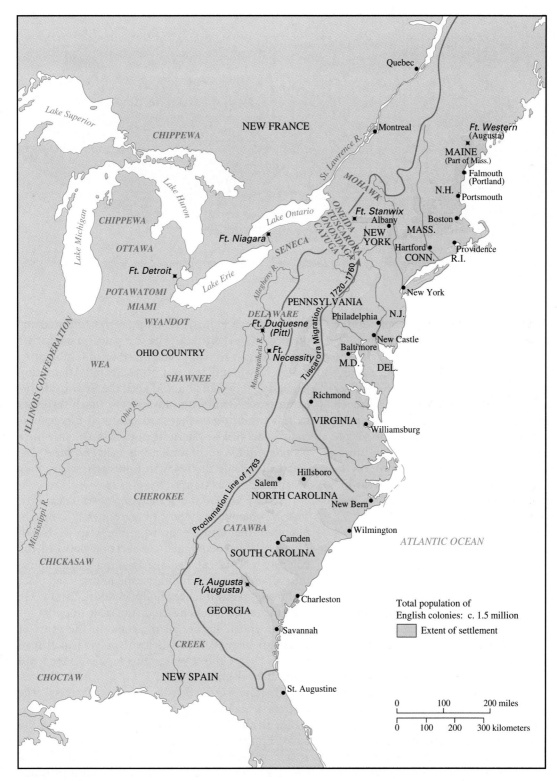

European Settlements and Native American Tribes, 1750 *By 1750, Europeans had expanded the limits of the English colonies to the eastern slopes of the Appalachian Mountains. Few independent Indian nations still existed in the East, but beyond the mountains they controlled the countryside. Only a few widely scattered English and French forts maintained the Europeans' presence there.*

A colonial soldier in 1758 etched onto his powder horn images of Indians and English troops fighting in the Seven Years War.   New York Historical Society.

The French had already taken possession of the strategic point—now Pittsburgh—where the Allegheny and Monongahela Rivers meet to form the Ohio, and they were busily engaged in constructing Fort Duquesne. The inexperienced young officer who commanded the Virginians attacked a French detachment and then allowed himself to be trapped in his crudely built Fort Necessity at Great Meadows, Pennsylvania. After a day-long battle (on July 3, 1754), during which more than one-third of his men were killed or wounded, twenty-two-year-old George Washington surrendered. He and his men were allowed to return to Virginia.

Washington had blundered grievously, setting off a war that eventually would encompass nearly the entire world. He also en-

Seven Years War

sured that the Ohio valley Indians, many of whom had moved west to escape Iroquois domination and to trade with the French, would for the most part support France in the conflict. The Indians took Washington's mistakes as an indication of Britain's inability to win the war, and nothing that occurred in the next four years made them change their minds. In July 1755, a few miles south of Fort Duquesne, a combined force of French and Indians ambushed British and colonial troops readying for a renewed assault on the fort. General Edward Braddock was killed, and his men were demoralized by a devastating defeat. After news of the debacle reached London, Britain declared war on France in 1756, thus formally beginning the conflict known as the Seven Years War.

For three more years one disaster followed another for Great Britain. The war went so badly that Britain began to fear that France would attempt to retake Newfoundland and Nova Scotia. Attempting to solidify their hold on that area, the British administrators of Nova Scotia forced its French residents to leave the homes they had occupied for generations—the first modern deportation of an entire people. After years of wandering, many of these Acadian exiles made their way to Louisiana, where they became known as Cajuns.

At last, under the leadership of William Pitt, who was named secretary of state in 1757, Britain mounted the effort that won the war in North America. Pitt encouraged cooperation between the colonists and Great Britain, agreeing to reimburse the colonies for their military expenditures and placing troop recruitment wholly in local hands. He thereby gained wholehearted American support for the war effort. Earlier in the war—in the years of England's many defeats—British officers had instead tried to coerce the colonies into supplying men and materiel to the army.

In July 1758, British forces recaptured the fortress at Louisbourg, winning control of the entrance to the St. Lawrence River and breaking the major French supply route. Then, in a surprise night attack in September 1759, General James Wolfe's soldiers defeated the French on the Plains of Abraham and took Quebec. Sensing a British victory, the Iroquois abandoned their policy of neutrality and allied themselves with Britain, hoping to gain some diplomatic leverage. A year later the British captured

Montréal, the last French stronghold on the continent, and the American phase of the war ended.

In the Treaty of Paris (1763), France ceded its major North American holdings to Britain. Spain, an ally of France toward the end of the war, gave Florida to the victors. Britain, fearing the presence of France on its western borders, forced the French to cede Louisiana to Spain. The British thus gained control of the fur trade of the entire continent. And no longer would the English seacoast colonies have to worry about the threat to their existence posed by France's extensive North American territories (see maps, page 126).

American Soldiers

Because most of the fighting had occurred in the Northeast, the war had especially pronounced effects on New Englanders. As many as one-third of all Massachusetts men between the ages of sixteen and twenty-nine served for a time in the provincial army. Wartime service left a lasting impression on these soldiers. For the first time, ordinary Americans came into extended contact with Britons—and they did not like what they saw. The provincials regarded the British troops (called "redcoats" because of the color of their uniforms) as haughty, profane Sabbath-breakers who arbitrarily imposed overly harsh punishments on anyone who broke the rules. Nearly sixty years later a veteran still vividly recalled an incident in 1762 when a British soldier inflicted hundreds of lashes on three men for "some trifling offense. . . . I felt at the time as though I could have taken summary vengeance on those who were the authors of it," he wrote in his memoirs.

The New England soldiers also learned that British troops did not share their adherence to principles of contract and consensus—the values that had governed their lives at home. Colonial regiments mutinied or rebelled en masse if they believed they were being treated unfairly, as happened, for example, when they were not allowed to leave at the end of their formal enlistments. One private in these

On the night of September 13, 1759, British forces under General James Wolfe scaled the heights of Quebec and defeated the French army led by General Louis Joseph Montcalm. Both generals died on the battlefield. Library of Congress.

European Claims in North America *The dramatic results of the British victory in the Seven Years (French and Indian) War are vividly demonstrated in these maps, which depict the abandonment of French claims to the mainland after the Treaty of Paris in 1763.*

circumstances grumbled in his journal in 1759, "Although we be Englishmen born, we are debarred Englishmen's liberty. . . . [The British soldiers] are but little better than slaves to their officers. And when I get out of their [power] I shall take care how I get in again." Such men would later recall their personal experience of British "tyranny" when they decided to support the Revolution.

The overwhelming British triumph stimulated some Americans to think expansively about the colonies' future. People like the Philadelphia printer Benjamin Franklin, who had long touted the colonies' wealth and potential, predicted a glorious new future for British North America—a future that included not just geographical expansion but also economic development and population growth. Such men were to lead the resistance to British measures in the years after 1763. They uniformly opposed any laws that would retard America's growth and persistently supported steps to increase Americans' control over their own destiny.

 1763: A Turning Point

The great victory over France had an irreversible impact on North America, felt first by the indigenous peoples of the interior. With France excluded from the continent altogether and Spanish territory now confined to the area west of the Mississippi, the diplomatic strategy that had served the Indians well for so long could no longer be employed. The consequences were immediate and devastating.

Even before the Treaty of Paris, southern Indians had to adjust to the new circumstances. After Britain gained the upper hand in the American war in 1758, Creeks and Cherokees lost their ability to force concessions by threatening to turn instead to France or Spain. In desperation, and in retaliation for British atrocities, Cherokees attacked the Carolina and Virginia frontiers in 1760. Though initially victorious, the Indians were defeated the following year by a force of British regulars and colonial militia. Late in 1761 the two sides concluded a treaty under which the Cherokees allowed the construction of British forts in their territories and opened a large tract of land to European settlement.

The fate of the Cherokees in the South was a portent of things to come in the Ohio country. There, the Ottawas, Chippewas, and Potawatomis reacted angrily when Great Britain, no longer facing French competition, raised the price of trade goods and ended traditional gift-giving practices. Britain also allowed settlers to move into the Monongahela and Susquehanna valleys, onto Delaware and Iroquois lands. A shaman named Neolin (also known as the Delaware Prophet) warned his people of impending doom and urged them to resist British encroachments.

Pontiac, the war chief of an Ottawa village near Detroit, understood the implications of British policies. Only unity among the western tribes, he realized, could prevent total de-

Pontiac's Uprising

pendence on and subordination to the victorious British. Using his considerable powers of persuasion, in the spring of 1763 he forged an unprecedented alliance among Hurons, Chippewas, Potawatomis, Delawares, Shawnees, and even some Mingoes (Pennsylvania Iroquois). Pontiac then laid siege to Fort Detroit while war parties attacked other British outposts in the Great Lakes region. Detroit withstood the siege, but by late June all the other forts west of Niagara and north of Fort Pitt (old Fort Duquesne) had fallen to the Indian alliance.

That was the high point of the uprising. Indians raided the Virginia and Pennsylvania frontiers at will throughout the summer, killing at least two thousand settlers. But they could not take the strongholds of Niagara, Fort Pitt, or Detroit. In early August, colonial militiamen soundly defeated a combined force of Delawares, Shawnees, Hurons, and Mingoes at Bushy Run, Pennsylvania. Conflict ceased when Pontiac broke off the siege of Detroit in late October. A treaty ending the war was finally negotiated three years later.

Pontiac's uprising showed Great Britain that the huge territory it had just acquired from France would not be easy to govern. The central administration in London had no prior experi-

Proclamation of 1763

ence managing such a vast tract of land, particularly one inhabited by such restive peoples—the remaining French settlers along the St. Lawrence and the many different Indian

Benjamin West, the first well-known American artist, engraved this picture of a prisoner exchange at the end of Pontiac's Uprising, with Colonel Henry Bouquet supervising the return of settlers abducted during the war. In the foreground, a child resists leaving the Indian parents he had grown to love. Many colonists were fascinated by the phenomenon West depicted—the reluctance of captives to abandon their adoptive Indian families.   Ohio Historical Society.

groups. In October, in a futile attempt to assert control over the interior, the British ministry issued the Proclamation of 1763, which declared the headwaters of rivers flowing into the Atlantic from the Appalachian Mountains to be the temporary western boundary for colonial settlement (see map, page 123). The proclamation was intended to prevent clashes between Indians and colonists by forbidding whites to move onto Indian lands until tribes had given up their land by treaty. But many whites had already established farms or purchased property west of the proclamation line, and from the outset the unenforceable policy was doomed to failure.

Other decisions made in London in 1763 and thereafter had a wider impact in British North

America. The hard-won victory created both problems and opportunities for the British government. The most pressing problem, Britain's immense war debt, had to be solved by King George III and his new prime minister, George Grenville.

George III succeeded his grandfather, George II, on the British throne in 1760. The twenty-two-year-old king, a man of mediocre intellect and even more mediocre education,

George III

was unfortunately also an erratic judge of character. During the crucial years between 1763 and 1770, when the rift with the colonies was growing ever wider, he replaced ministries with bewildering rapidity. Though determined to assert the power of the monarchy, the king was immature and unsure of himself. He often substituted stubbornness for intelligence, and he regarded adherence to the status quo as the hallmark of patriotism.

The man he selected as prime minister in 1763, George Grenville, believed that the American colonies should be more tightly administered than in the past. Grenville confronted a financial crisis: England's burden of indebtedness had nearly doubled since 1754, from £73 million to £137 million. Annual expenditures before the war had amounted to no more than £8 million; now the yearly interest on the debt alone came to £5 million. Grenville's ministry had to find new sources of funds, and the British people themselves were already heavily taxed. Since the colonists had benefited greatly from the wartime expenditures, Grenville concluded that Anglo-Americans should be asked to pay a greater share of the cost of running the empire.

Grenville did not question Great Britain's right to levy taxes on the colonies. Like all his countrymen, he believed that the government's legitimacy derived ultimately from the consent of the people, but he defined consent far more loosely than did the colonists. Americans had come to believe that they could be represented only by men for whom they or their property-holding neighbors actually voted; otherwise, they could not count on legislators to represent their interests properly. Grenville and his English contemporaries, however, believed that Parliament—king, lords, and commons acting together—by definition represented all British subjects, wherever they resided (even overseas) and whether or not they could vote.

Theories of Representation

Parliament saw itself as collectively representing the entire nation; the particular constituency that chose a member of the House of Commons had no special claim on that member's vote. According to this theory of government, called *virtual representation*, the colonists were seen as virtually, if not actually, represented in Parliament. Thus their consent to acts of Parliament could be presumed. By contrast, in the colonies members of the lower houses of the assemblies were viewed as specifically representing the regions that had elected them. Before Grenville proposed to tax the colonists, the two notions coexisted without apparent contradiction. But the events of the 1760s pointed up the difference between the two definitions of representation.

The same events threw into sharp relief Americans' attitudes toward political power. The colonists had become accustomed to a central government

Real Whigs

that wielded only limited authority over them and affected their daily lives very little. In consequence, they believed that a good government was one that largely left them alone, a view in keeping with the theories of a group of British writers known as the Real Whigs. Drawing on a tradition of dissenting thought that reached back to John Locke and even to the Civil War, the Real Whigs stressed the dangers inherent in a powerful government, particularly one headed by a monarch. Some of them even favored republicanism, which proposed to eliminate monarchs altogether and rest political power more directly on the will of the people. Real Whigs warned the people to guard constantly against government's attempts to encroach on their liberty and seize their property. Political power was always to be feared, wrote John Trenchard and Thomas Gordon in their essay series *Cato's Letters* (originally published in London in 1720–1723 and reprinted many times thereafter in the colonies). Rulers would try to corrupt and oppress the people. Only the perpetual vigilance of people and their elected representatives could preserve their fragile yet precious liberty, which was closely linked to their right to hold private property.

Britain's attempts to tighten the reins of government and raise revenues from the colonies in the 1760s and early 1770s convinced many Americans that the Real Whigs' reasoning applied to their circumstances, especially because of the link between liberty and property rights. Excessive and unjust taxation, they believed, could destroy their freedoms.

They began to interpret British measures in light of the Real Whigs' warnings and to see oppressive designs behind the actions of Grenville and his successors. Historians disagree over the extent to which those perceptions were correct, but by 1775 a large number of colonists believed they were. In the mid-1760s, however, colonial leaders did not immediately accuse Grenville of an intent to oppress them. They at first simply questioned the wisdom of the laws he proposed.

Parliament passed the first such measures, the Sugar and Currency Acts, in 1764. The Sugar Act (also known as the Revenue Act) revised existing customs regulations and laid new duties on some foreign imports into the colonies. It also established a vice-admiralty court at Halifax, Nova Scotia, and included provisions aimed at stopping the widespread smuggling of molasses, one of the chief commodities in American trade. Although the Sugar Act appeared to resemble the Navigation Acts, which the colonies had long accepted as legitimate, it broke with tradition because it was explicitly designed to raise revenue, not to channel American trade through Britain. The Currency Act effectively outlawed colonial issues of paper money. (British merchants had complained that Americans were paying their debts in inflated local currencies.) Americans could accumulate little sterling, since they imported more than they exported; thus the act seemed to the colonists to deprive them of a useful medium of exchange.

Sugar and Currency Acts

The Sugar and Currency Acts were imposed on an economy already in the midst of depression. A business boom accompanied the Seven Years War, but the brief spell of prosperity ended abruptly in 1760 when the war shifted overseas. Urban merchants could not sell all their imported goods to colonial customers alone, and without the military's demand for foodstuffs, American farmers found fewer buyers for their products. The bottom dropped out of the European tobacco market, threatening the livelihood of Chesapeake planters. Sailors were thrown out of work, and artisans found few customers. In such circumstances, the prospect of increased import duties and inadequate supplies of currency aroused merchants' hostility.

Individual American essayists and colonial governments protested the new policies. But, lacking any precedent for a united campaign against acts of Parliament, Americans in 1764 took only hesitant and uncoordinated steps. Eight colonial legislatures sent separate petitions to Parliament requesting the Sugar Act's repeal. They argued that its commercial restrictions would hurt Britain as well as the colonies and that they had not consented to its passage. The protests had no effect. The law remained in force, and Grenville proceeded with another revenue plan.

 ## The Stamp Act Crisis

The Stamp Act (1765), Grenville's most important proposal, was modeled on a law that had been in effect in Great Britain for almost a century. It touched nearly every colonist by requiring tax stamps on most printed materials, but it placed the heaviest burden on merchants and other members of the colonial elite, who used printed matter more frequently than did ordinary folk. Anyone who purchased a newspaper or pamphlet, made a will, transferred land, bought dice or playing cards, needed a liquor license, accepted a government appointment, or borrowed money would have to pay the tax. Never before had a revenue measure of such scope been proposed for the colonies. The act also required that tax stamps be paid for with sterling, which was scarce, and that violators be tried in vice-admiralty courts, which operated without juries. (Previously, such courts had heard only cases involving violations of maritime law.) Americans feared the loss of their right to trial by a jury of their peers. Finally, such a law would break decisively with the colonial tradition of self-imposed taxation.

The most important colonial pamphlet protesting the Sugar Act and the proposed Stamp Act was *The Rights of the British Colonies Asserted and Proved*, by James Otis, Jr., a brilliant young Massachusetts attorney. Otis starkly exposed the ideological dilemma that was to confound the colonists for the next decade. How could they justify their opposition to certain acts of Parliament without questioning Parliament's authority over them? On the one hand, Otis asserted, Americans were "entitled to all the natural, essential, inherent, and inseparable rights" of Britons, including the right not to be taxed without their consent. "No man or body of men, not excepting the parliament . . . can

James Otis's *Rights of the British Colonies*

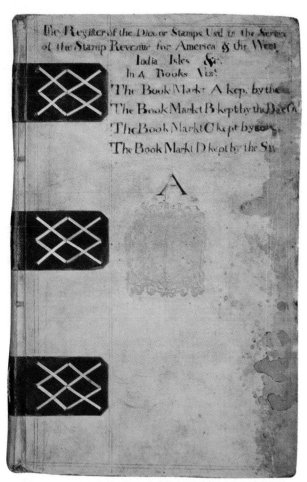

In 1765 a clerk in the offices of British tax officials prepared this register to contain examples of the tax stamps intended for use in the American colonies. But because the law was never enforced and soon repealed, the register is largely empty, and the other volumes the clerk anticipated were never readied at all.   The British Library Philatelic Section, Inland Revenue Archives.

ment: that Parliament was the sole, supreme authority in the empire. Even unconstitutional laws enacted by Parliament had to be obeyed until Parliament decided to repeal them.

According to orthodox British political theory, there could be no middle ground between absolute submission to Parliament and a frontal challenge to its authority. Otis tried to find such a middle ground by proposing colonial representation in Parliament, but his idea was never taken seriously on either side of the Atlantic. The British believed that colonists were already virtually represented in Parliament, and Anglo-Americans quickly realized that a handful of colonial delegates to London would simply be outvoted.

Otis published his pamphlet before the Stamp Act was passed. When Americans first learned of the act's adoption in the spring of 1765, they were uncertain how to react. Few colonists—even appointed government officials—publicly favored the law. But colonial petitions had already failed to prevent its adoption, and further lobbying appeared futile. Perhaps Otis was right that the only course open to Americans was to pay the stamp tax, reluctantly but loyally. Acting on that assumption, colonial agents in London sought the appointment of their American friends as stamp distributors so that the law would at least be enforced equitably.

Not all the colonists were resigned to paying the new tax. Among them was a twenty-nine-year-old lawyer serving his first term in the Virginia House of

Patrick Henry and the Virginia Stamp Act Resolves

Burgesses. Patrick Henry later recalled that he was "young, inexperienced, unacquainted with the forms of the house and the members that composed it"— and appalled by his fellow legislators' unwillingness to oppose the Stamp Act. Henry decided to act. "Alone, unadvised, and unassisted, on a blank leaf of an old law book," he wrote the Virginia Stamp Act Resolves.

Little in Henry's earlier life foreshadowed his success in the political arena he entered so dramatically. The son of a prosperous Scottish immigrant to western Virginia, Henry had little formal education. After marrying at eighteen, he failed at both farming and storekeeping before turning to the law as a means of supporting his wife and their six children. Henry lacked legal training, but his oratorical skills made him an effective advocate, first for his clients and later for his political beliefs. A prominent Virginia lawyer

take [those rights] away," he declared. On the other hand, Otis was forced to admit, under the British system established after the Glorious Revolution, "the power of parliament is uncontrollable but by themselves, and we must obey. . . . Let the parliament lay what burthens they please on us, we must, it is our duty to submit and patiently bear them, till they will be pleased to relieve us."

Otis's first contention, drawing on colonial notions of representation, implied that Parliament could not constitutionally tax the colonies because Americans were not represented in its ranks. Yet his second point both acknowledged political reality and accepted the prevailing theory of British govern-observed, "He is by far the most powerful speaker I ever heard. Every word he says not only engages, but commands the attention; and your passions are no longer your own when he addresses them."

Patrick Henry introduced his seven proposals near the end of the legislative session, when many burgesses had already departed for home. Henry's fiery speech led the Speaker of the House to accuse him of treason. (Henry denied the charge, contrary to the nineteenth-century myth that he exclaimed, "If this be treason, make the most of it!") The few burgesses remaining in Williamsburg adopted five of Henry's resolutions by a bare majority. Although they repealed the most radical of the five the next day, their action had far-reaching effects. Some colonial newspapers printed Henry's seven original resolutions as if they had been uniformly passed by the House, even though one had been rescinded and two others were never debated or voted on at all.

The four propositions adopted by the burgesses repeated Otis's arguments, asserting that the colonists had never forfeited the rights of British subjects, among which was consent to taxation. The other three resolutions went much further. The one that was repealed claimed for the burgesses "the only exclusive right" to tax Virginians, and the final two (those never considered) asserted that residents of Virginia need not obey tax laws passed by other legislative bodies (namely Parliament), terming any opponent of that opinion "an Enemy to this his Majesty's Colony."

The burgesses' decision to accept only the first four of Henry's resolutions anticipated the position most Americans would adopt throughout the following decade. Though willing to contend for their rights, the colonists did not seek independence. They rather wanted some measure of self-government. Accordingly, they backed away from the assertions that they owed Parliament no obedience and that only their own assemblies could tax them. Indeed, declared the Maryland lawyer Daniel Dulany, whose *Considerations on the Propriety of Imposing Taxes on the British Colonies* was the most widely read pamphlet of 1765, "The colonies are dependent upon Great Britain, and the supreme authority vested in the king, lords, and commons, may justly be exercised to secure, or preserve their dependence." But, warned Dulany, a superior did not have the right "to seize the property of his inferior when he pleases"; there was a

Continuing Loyalty to Britain

crucial distinction between a condition of "dependence and *inferiority*" and one of "absolute *vassalage* and slavery."

Over the next ten years, America's political leaders searched for a formula that would enable them to control their internal affairs, especially taxation, but remain under British rule. The chief difficulty lay in British officials' inability to compromise on the issue of parliamentary power. The notion that Parliament could exercise absolute authority over all colonial possessions was basic to the British theory of government. Even the harshest British critics of the ministries of the 1760s and 1770s questioned only the wisdom of specific policies, not the principles on which they were based. In effect, the Americans wanted British leaders to revise their fundamental understanding of the workings of their government. But that was simply too much to expect.

The ultimate effectiveness of Americans' opposition to the Stamp Act rested on more than ideological arguments over parliamentary power. What

In 1795 the artist Lawrence Sully painted the only known life portrait of Patrick Henry. The old man's fierce gaze reflects the same intensity that marked his actions thirty years earlier, when he introduced the Virginia Stamp Act Resolves in the House of Burgesses. Mead Art Museum, Amherst College. Bequest of Herbert L. Pratt, Class of 1985.

gave the resistance its primary force were the decisive and inventive actions of some colonists during the late summer and fall of 1765.

In August the Loyal Nine, a Boston social club of printers, distillers, and other artisans, organized a demonstration against the Stamp Act. Hoping to

Loyal Nine

show that people of all ranks opposed the act, they approached the leaders of the city's rival laborers' associations, based in Boston's North End and South End neighborhoods. The two gangs, composed of unskilled workers and poor tradesmen, often battled each other, but the Loyal Nine convinced them to lay aside their differences to participate in the demonstration. All colonists, not just affluent ones, would have to pay the stamp taxes.

Early on August 14, the demonstrators hung an effigy of Andrew Oliver, the province's stamp distributor, from a tree on Boston Common. That night a large crowd led by a group of about fifty well-dressed tradesmen paraded the effigy around the city. The crowd tore down a small building they thought was intended as the stamp office and built a bonfire near Oliver's house with wood from the destroyed building. They then beheaded the effigy and added it to the flames. Demonstrators broke most of Oliver's windows and threw stones at officials who tried to disperse them. In the midst of the melée, the North End and South End leaders drank a toast to their successful union. The Loyal Nine achieved success when Oliver publicly promised not to fulfill the duties of his office. One Bostonian jubilantly wrote to a relative, "I believe people never was more Universally pleased not so much one could I hear say he was sorry, but a smile sat on almost every ones countinance."

But another crowd action twelve days later, aimed this time at Oliver's brother-in-law, Lieutenant Governor Thomas Hutchinson, drew no praise from Boston's respectable citizens. On the night of August 26, a mob reportedly led by the South End leader Ebenezer MacIntosh attacked the homes of several customs officers. The crowd then completely destroyed Hutchinson's elaborately furnished townhouse in one of Boston's most fashionable districts. The lieutenant governor reported that by the next morning "one of the best finished houses in the Province had nothing remaining but the bare walls and floors." His trees and garden were ruined, his valuable library was lost, and the mob "emptied

the house of every thing whatsoever except a part of the kitchen furniture." But Hutchinson took some comfort in the fact that "the encouragers of the first mob never intended matters should go this length and the people in general express the utmost detestation of this unparalleled outrage." (A portrait of Hutchinson is on page 141.)

The differences between the two Boston mobs of August 1765 exposed divisions that would continue to characterize subsequent colonial protests.

**Americans'
Divergent
Interests**

Few residents of the colonies sided with Great Britain during the 1760s, but various colonial groups had divergent goals. The skilled craftsmen who composed the Loyal Nine, and merchants, lawyers, and other members of the educated elite preferred orderly demonstrations confined to political issues. For the city's laborers, by contrast, economic grievances may have been paramount. Certainly, their "hellish Fury" as they wrecked Hutchinson's house suggests a resentment against his ostentatious display of wealth.

Colonists, like Britons, had a long tradition of crowd action in which disfranchised people took to the streets to redress deeply felt local grievances. But the Stamp Act controversy drew ordinary urban folk into the vortex of transatlantic politics for the first time. Matters that previously had been of concern only to the gentry or to members of colonial legislatures were now discussed on every street corner. Benjamin Franklin's daughter observed as much when she informed her father, then serving as a colonial agent in London, that "nothing else is talked of, the Dutch [Germans] talk of the stompt act the Negroes of the tamp, in short every body has something to say."

The entry of unskilled workers, slaves, and women into the realm of imperial politics both threatened and afforded an opportunity to the elite men who wanted to mount effective opposition to British measures. On the one hand, crowd action could have a stunning impact. Anti–Stamp Act demonstrations occurred in cities and towns stretching from Halifax, Nova Scotia, in the north, to the Caribbean island of Antigua in the south (see maps, page 133). They were so successful that by November 1, when the law was scheduled to take effect, not one stamp distributor was willing to carry out his official duties. Thus the act could not be enforced. But on the other hand, wealthy men recognized that mobs composed of the formerly

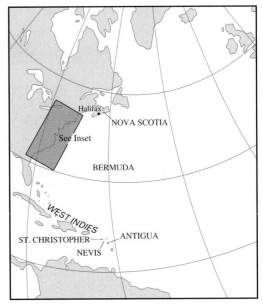

Sites of Major Demonstrations Against the Stamp Act   *Every place named on these maps was the site of a demonstration against the Stamp Act of 1765; British colonies outside the eventual United States joined in the nearly universal opposition to the hated measure.*   Source: From Lester J. Cappon et al., eds., *Atlas of Early American History: The Revolutionary Era, 1760–1790.* Copyright © 1976 by Princeton University Press. Reprinted by permission of Princeton University Press.

powerless—whose goals were not always identical to theirs (as the Boston experience showed)—could endanger their own dominance of the society. What would happen, they wondered, if the "hellish Fury" of the crowd were turned against them?

They therefore attempted to channel resistance into acceptable forms by creating an intercolonial association, the Sons of Liberty. The first such group was created in New York in early November, and branches spread rapidly through the coastal cities. Composed of merchants, lawyers, prosperous tradesmen like Paul Revere, and others, the Sons of Liberty by early 1766 linked protest leaders from Charleston, South Carolina, to Portsmouth, New Hampshire.

Sons of Liberty

The Sons of Liberty could influence events but not control them. In Charleston in October 1765, an informally organized crowd shouting "Liberty Liberty and stamp'd paper" forced the resignation of the South Carolina stamp distributor. The victory celebration a few days later—the largest demonstration the city had ever known—featured a British flag with the word "Liberty" emblazoned on it. But the new Charleston chapter of the Sons of Liberty was horrified when in January 1766 local slaves paraded through the streets similarly crying "Liberty." That was not the sort of liberty elite slaveowners had in mind.

In Philadelphia, resistance leaders were dismayed when an angry mob threatened to attack Benjamin Franklin's house. The city's laborers believed Franklin to be partly responsible for the Stamp Act, since he had obtained the post of stamp distributor for a close friend. But Philadelphia's artisans—the backbone of the opposition movement there and elsewhere—were fiercely loyal to Franklin, one of their own who had made good. They gathered to protect his home and family from the crowd. The house was saved, but the resulting split between the

British Ministries and Their American Policies

Head of Ministry	Major Acts
George Grenville	Sugar Act (1764) Currency Act (1764) Stamp Act (1765)
Lord Rockingham	Stamp Act repealed (1766) Declaratory Act (1766)
William Pitt/Charles Townshend	Townshend Acts (1767)
Lord North	Townshend duties (except for the tea tax) repealed (1770) Coercive Acts (1774) Quebec Act (1774)

better-off tradesmen and the common laborers prevented the establishment of a successful workingmen's alliance like that of Boston.

During the fall and winter of 1765–1766, opposition to the Stamp Act proceeded on three separate fronts. Colonial legislatures petitioned Parliament to repeal the hated law and in October sent delegates to an intercolonial congress, the first since 1754. The Stamp Act Congress met in New York to draft a unified but conservative statement of protest. At the same time, the Sons of Liberty held mass meetings, attempting to rally public support for the resistance movement. Finally, American merchants organized nonimportation associations to pressure British exporters. By the 1760s, one-quarter of all British exports were being sent to the colonies, and American merchants reasoned that London merchants whose sales suffered severely would lobby for repeal. Since times were bad and American merchants were finding few customers for imported goods anyway, a general moratorium on future purchases would also help to reduce their bloated inventories.

Repeal of the Stamp Act

In March 1766, Parliament repealed the Stamp Act. The nonimportation agreements had had the anticipated effect, creating allies for the colonies among wealthy London merchants. But boycotts, formal protests, and crowd actions were less important in winning repeal than was the appointment of a new prime minister, chosen by George III for reasons unrelated to colonial politics. Lord Rockingham, who replaced Grenville in the summer of 1765, had opposed the Stamp Act, not because he believed

Parliament lacked power to tax the colonies but because he thought the law unwise and divisive. Thus although Rockingham proposed repeal, he linked it to passage of the Declaratory Act, which asserted Parliament's ability to tax and legislate for Britain's American possessions "in all cases whatsoever."

News of the repeal arrived in Newport, Rhode Island, in May, and the Sons of Liberty quickly dispatched messengers to carry the welcome tidings throughout the colonies. They organized celebrations commemorating the glorious event, which all stressed the Americans' unwavering loyalty to Great Britain. Their goal achieved, the Sons of Liberty dissolved. Few colonists saw the ominous implications of the Declaratory Act.

 Resistance to the Townshend Acts

The colonists had accomplished their immediate aim, but the long-term prospects were unclear. In the summer of 1766, another change in the ministry in London revealed how fragile their victory had been. The new prime minister was William Pitt, who as Britain's secretary of state had fostered cooperation between the colonies and Great Britain during the Seven Years War (see page 124). Now, however, Pitt was ill much of the time, and another minister, Charles Townshend, became the dominant force in the ministry. An ally of Grenville and a supporter of colonial taxation, Townshend decided to renew the attempt to obtain additional funds from Britain's American possessions.

The taxes Townshend proposed in 1767 were to be levied on trade goods like paper, glass, and tea, and thus seemed to be nothing more than extensions of the existing Navigation Acts. But the Townshend duties differed from previous customs duties in two ways. First, they were levied on items imported into the colonies from Britain, not from foreign countries. Thus they were at odds with mercantilist theory (see page 83). Second, they were designed to raise money to pay the salaries of some royal officials in the colonies. That posed a direct challenge to the colonial assemblies, which derived considerable power from threatening to withhold officials' salaries. In addition, Townshend's scheme provided for the creation of an American Board of Customs Commissioners and of vice-admiralty courts at Boston, Philadelphia, and Charleston. Both moves angered merchants, whose profits would be threatened by more vigorous enforcement of the Navigation Acts.

In 1765, months had passed before the colonists began to protest the Stamp Act. The passage of the Townshend Acts, however, drew a quick response.

John Dickinson's Farmer's Letters

One series of essays in particular, *Letters from a Farmer in Pennsylvania* by the prominent lawyer John Dickinson, expressed a broad consensus. Eventually all but four colonial newspapers printed Dickinson's essays; in pamphlet form they went through seven American editions. Dickinson contended that Parliament could regulate colonial trade but could not exercise that power to raise revenue. By drawing a distinction between trade regulation and unacceptable commercial taxation, Dickinson avoided the sticky issue of consent and how it affected colonial subordination to Parliament. But his argument created a different, and equally knotty, problem. In effect it obligated the colonies to assess Parliament's motives in passing any law pertaining to trade before deciding whether to obey it. That was in the long run an unworkable position.

Massachusetts Assembly Dissolved

The Massachusetts assembly responded to the Townshend Acts by drafting a letter to be circulated among the other colonial legislatures, calling for unity and suggesting a joint petition of protest. Not the letter itself but the ministry's reaction to it united the colonies. When Lord Hillsborough, recently named to the new post of secretary of state for America, learned of the circular letter, he ordered Governor Francis Bernard of Massachusetts to insist that the assembly recall it. He also directed other governors to prevent their assemblies from discussing the letter. Hillsborough's order gave colonial assemblies the incentive they needed to join forces to oppose this new threat to their prerogatives. In late 1768 the Massachusetts legislature met, debated, and resoundingly rejected recall by a vote of 92 to 17. Bernard immediately dissolved the assembly, and other governors followed suit when their legislatures debated the circular letter.

The number of votes cast against recalling the circular letter—92—assumed ritual significance for the supporters of resistance. The figure 45 already had symbolic meaning because John Wilkes, a radical Londoner sympathetic to the American cause, had been jailed for libel in Britain for publishing an essay entitled *The North Briton No. 45*. In Boston, Paul Revere made a punchbowl weighing 45 ounces that held 45 gills (half-cups) and was engraved with the names of the 92 legislators; James Otis, John Adams, and others publicly drank 45 toasts from it. In Charleston, the city's tradesmen decorated a tree with 45 lights and set off 45 rockets. Carrying 45 candles, they adjourned to a tavern, where 45 tables were set with 45 bowls of wine, 45 bowls of punch, and 92 glasses.

Rituals of Resistance

Such public rituals served important educational functions. Just as the pamphlets by Otis, Dulany, Dickinson, and others acquainted literate colonists with the issues raised by British actions, so public rituals taught illiterate Americans about the reasons for resistance and familiarized them with the terms of the argument. When Boston's revived Sons of Liberty invited hundreds of city residents to dine with them each August 14 to commemorate the first Stamp Act uprising, and the Charleston Sons of Liberty held their meetings in public, crowds gathered to watch and listen. Likewise, the public singing of songs supporting the American cause helped to spread the word. The participants in such events were openly expressing their commitment to the cause of resistance and encouraging others to join them.

During the campaign against the Townshend duties, the Sons of Liberty and other American leaders made a deliberate effort to involve ordinary folk in the resistance movement. Most important, they urged colonists of all ranks and both sexes to sign agreements not to purchase or consume British

A Society of Patriotic Ladies *(1775), attributed to Philip Dawes, an English printmaker. This grotesque caricature of female patriots shows the women emptying their tea into a chamber pot (at left) and flirting with their male counterparts (at center), while a neglected child sits below the table. The cartoon bears no resemblance to the actual event, the signing of an anti-British petition by female residents of Edenton, North Carolina.* Library of Congress.

walking through town in a solemn procession. Women throughout the colonies exchanged recipes for tea substitutes or drank coffee instead. The best known of the protests (because it was satirized in a British cartoon reproduced here), the so-called Edenton Ladies Tea Party, actually had little to do with tea. It was a meeting of prominent North Carolina women who pledged formally to work for the public good and to support resistance to British measures.

Women also encouraged home manufacturing. In many towns, young women calling themselves Daughters of Liberty met to spin in public in an effort to persuade other women to make homespun and thus end the colonies' dependence on British cloth. These symbolic displays of patriotism— publicized by newspapers and broadsides—served the same purpose as the male rituals involving the numbers 45 and 92. When young ladies from well-to-do families sat publicly at spinning wheels all day, eating only American food and drinking local herbal tea, and later listening to patriotic sermons, they were serving as political instructors. Many women took great satisfaction in their new-found role. When a New England satirist hinted that women discussed only "such triffling subjects as Dress, Scandal and Detraction" during their spinning bees, three Boston women replied angrily: "Inferior in abusive sarcasm, in personal invective, in low wit, we glory to be, but inferior in veracity, sincerity, love of virtue, of liberty and of our country, we would not willingly be to any."

But the colonists were by no means united in support of nonimportation and nonconsumption. If the Stamp Act protests had occasionally (as in Boston and Philadelphia) revealed a division between artisans and merchants on the one side and common laborers on the other, resistance to the Townshend Acts exposed new splits in American ranks. The most significant divided urban artisans and merchants, allies in 1765 and 1766, and it arose from a change in economic circumstances.

Divided Opinion over Boycotts

The Stamp Act boycotts had helped to revive a depressed economy by creating a demand for local products and reducing merchants' inventories. But in 1768 and 1769, merchants were enjoying boom times and had no financial incentive to support a boycott. As a result, merchants signed the agreements only reluctantly, sometimes violating them se-

products. The new consumerism that previously had linked colonists economically now linked them politically as well, supplying them with a ready method of displaying their allegiance. As "A Tradesman" wrote in a Philadelphia paper in 1770, it was essential "for the Good of the Whole, to strengthen the Hands of the Patriotic Majority, by agreeing not to purchase British Goods."

As the primary purchasers of textiles and household goods, women played a central role in the nonconsumption movement. In Boston more than three hundred matrons publicly promised not to buy or drink tea, "Sickness excepted." The women of Wilmington, North Carolina, burned their tea after

Daughters of Liberty

A

VERSE,

Occasioned by seeing the North-Spinning, in *BOSTON*.

BOSTON, behold the pretty Spinners here,
    And see how gay the pretty Sparks appear :
See Rich and Poor all turn the Spinning Wheel,
All who Compassion for their Country feel,
All who do love to see Industry live,
And see Frugality in *Boston* thrive.

   Britain, behold thy Trade stole from thy Hand,
And carried on in *Boston's* distant Land :
See now thy Trade and Tradesmen, all expire,
And see them all cut short of their Desire,
Th' Desire they had that *Boston's* Trade should spoil,
That they might reap the Fruit of all our Toil ;
     they might take what we'he been slaving for,
And rule us by the Parlimental Law :
But thanks to God, their ill Designs are cropt,
And their Tirannical Designs are stopt.

   Now they have run their Chain's extended Length,
And exhausted all their once encourag'd Strength :
Now have their ill Designs all found an end,
Now they have made a Foe of ev'ry Friend :
Now let them starve and die the Death of those,
Who do the Interest of their King oppose.

BOSTON: Printed and Sold 1769.

A 1769 Boston broadside commended the spinners, "Rich and Poor," who had "Compassion for their Country" and promoted "Frugality" during the Townshend Act crisis. The poet put into verse precisely the message the spinners intended to convey. Massachusetts Historical Society.

cretly. In contrast, artisans supported nonimportation enthusiastically, recognizing that the absence of British goods would create a ready market for their own manufactures. Thus tradesmen formed the core of the crowds that coerced both importers and their customers by picketing stores, publicizing offenders' names, and sometimes destroying property.

Such tactics were effective: colonial imports from England dropped dramatically in 1769, especially in New York, New England, and Pennsylvania.

But they also aroused heated opposition, creating a second major division among the colonists. Some Americans who supported resistance to British measures began to question the use of violence to force others to join the boycott. In addition, wealthier and more conservative colonists were frightened by the threat to private property inherent in the campaign. Political activism by ordinary colonists challenged the ruling elite's domination, just as its members had feared in 1765.

Disclosures that leading merchants were violating the nonimportation agreement caused dissension in the ranks of the boycotters, so Americans

Repeal of the Townshend Duties

were relieved when news arrived in April 1770 that the Townshend duties had been repealed, with the exception of the tea tax. A new prime minister, Lord North, had persuaded Parliament that duties on trade within the empire were bad policy. Although some colonial leaders argued that nonimportation should continue until the tea tax was repealed, merchants quickly resumed importing. The rest of the Townshend Acts remained in force, but repeal of the taxes made the other laws appear less objectionable.

 ## Growing Rifts

At first the new ministry in London did nothing to antagonize the colonists. Yet on the very day Lord North proposed repeal of the Townshend duties, a clash between civilians and soldiers in Boston led to the death of five Americans. The origins of the event that patriots called the Boston Massacre lay in repeated clashes between customs officers and the people of Massachusetts. The decision to base the American Board of Customs Commissioners in Boston was the source of the problem.

From the day of their arrival in November 1767, the customs commissioners were frequent targets of mob action. In June 1768 their seizure of patriot leader John Hancock's sloop *Liberty* on suspicion of smuggling caused a riot in which prominent customs officers' property was destroyed. The riot in turn helped to convince the ministry in London that troops were needed to maintain order in the unruly port. The assignment of two regiments of regulars to their city confirmed Bostonians' worst fears; the redcoats were a constant reminder of the oppressive potential of British power.

Bostonians found themselves hemmed in at every turn. Guards on Boston Neck, the entrance to the city, checked all travelers and their goods. Redcoat patrols roamed the city day and night, questioning and sometimes harassing passersby. Military parades were held on Boston Common, accompanied by martial music and often the public whipping of deserters and other violators of army rules. Parents began to fear for the safety of their daughters, who were subjected to soldiers' coarse sexual insults. But the greatest potential for violence lay in the uneasy relationship between the soldiers and Boston laborers. Many redcoats sought employment in their off-duty hours, competing for unskilled jobs with the city's ordinary workingmen. Members of the two groups brawled repeatedly in taverns and on the streets.

Early on the evening of March 5, 1770, a crowd of laborers began throwing hard-packed snowballs at soldiers guarding the Customs House. Goaded beyond endurance, the sentries acted against express orders to

Boston Massacre

the contrary and fired on the crowd, killing four and wounding eight, one of whom died a few days later. Resistance leaders idealized the dead rioters as martyrs for the cause of liberty, holding a solemn funeral and later commemorating March 5 annually with patriotic orations. Paul Revere's engraving of the massacre (based on a drawing by John Singleton Copley's half brother Henry Pelham and reproduced on page 139) was part of the propaganda campaign.

Leading patriots wanted to ensure that the soldiers did not become martyrs as well. Despite the political benefits the patriots derived from the massacre, it is unlikely that they approved of the crowd action that provoked it. Ever since the destruction of Hutchinson's house in August 1765, men allied with the Sons of Liberty had supported orderly demonstrations and expressed distaste for uncontrolled riots, of which the Boston Massacre was a prime example. Thus when the soldiers were tried for the killings in November, they were defended by John Adams and Josiah Quincy, Jr., both unwavering patriots. All but two of the accused men were acquitted, and those convicted were released after being branded on the thumb. Undoubtedly the favorable outcome of the trials prevented London officials from taking further steps against the city.

For more than two years after the Boston Massacre and the repeal of the Townshend duties, a superficial calm descended on the colonies. The most outspoken colonial newspapers, such as the *Boston Gazette*, the

A British Plot?

Pennsylvania Journal, and the *South Carolina Gazette*, published essays drawing on Real Whig ideology and accusing Great Britain of a deliberate plan to oppress the colonies. After the Stamp Act's repeal, the patriots had praised Parliament; following repeal of the Townshend duties, they warned of impending tyranny. What had seemed to be an isolated mistake, a single ill-chosen stamp tax, now appeared to be part of a plot against American liberties. Essayists pointed to Parliament's persecution of the British radical John Wilkes, the stationing of troops in Boston, and the growing number of vice-admiralty courts as evidence of plans to enslave the colonists. Indeed, patriot writers played repeatedly on the word *enslavement*. Most white colonists had direct knowledge of slavery (either as slaveholders themselves or as neighbors of slaveowners), and the threat of enslavement by Britain must have hit them with peculiar force.

Still, no one yet advocated complete independence from the mother country. Though the patriots were becoming increasingly convinced that they should seek freedom from parliamentary authority, they continued to acknowledge their British identity and their allegiance to George III. They began, therefore, to envision a system that would enable them to be ruled by their own elected legislatures while remaining loyal to the king. But any such scheme was alien to Britons' conception of the nature of their government, which was that Parliament held sole undivided sovereignty over the empire. Furthermore, in the British mind, Parliament encompassed the king as well as lords and commons, so separating the monarch from the legislature was impossible.

Then, in the fall of 1772, the North ministry began to implement the Townshend Act that provided for governors and judges to be paid from customs revenues. In early November, voters at a Boston town meeting established a Committee of Correspondence to publicize the decision by exchanging letters with other Massachusetts towns. Heading the committee was the man who had proposed its formation, Samuel Adams.

Samuel Adams was fifty-one in 1772, thirteen years older than his distant cousin John and by a

How do historians know whether ordinary people were familiar with the ideas propounded by the leaders of the American Revolution? This is a difficult question to answer, because most of the evidence about the patriots' ideology comes from pamphlets and newspapers aimed at the well educated. People who could read at only a basic level might not have been able to understand the sophisticated criticisms of British policies advanced in such writings. But because an engraver made his point visually rather than verbally, anyone, even illiterate folk, could interpret an image like Paul Revere's masterful portrayal of the Boston Massacre. The label "Butcher's Hall" on the Customs House merely reinforces the patriot view of the incident on March 5, 1770. The British soldiers are shown firing on an unresisting crowd (not the aggressive, angry mob described at the soldiers' trial), and a gun with smoke drifting up from its barrel emerges from a window above the redcoats, suggesting the complicity of civilian officials in what the patriots interpreted as an outrageous act.   Photo: Library of Congress.

decade the senior of most other leaders of American resistance. He had been a Boston tax collector, a member and clerk of the Massachusetts assembly, an ally of the Loyal Nine, and a member of the Sons of Liberty. His primary forum

Samuel Adams

was the Boston town meeting. Unswerving in his devotion to the American cause, Adams drew a sharp contrast between a corrupt, vice-ridden Britain and the colonies, peopled by simple, liberty-loving folk. An experienced political organizer, Adams continually stressed the necessity of prudent collective action. His Committee of Correspondence thus undertook the task of creating an informed consensus among all the residents of Massachusetts.

Such committees, which were eventually established throughout the colonies, represented the next logical step in the organization of American resistance. Until 1772, the pro-

Boston Committee of Correspondence

test movement was largely confined to the seacoast and primarily to major cities and towns (see maps, page 133). Adams realized that the time had come to widen the movement's geographic scope, to attempt to involve the residents of the interior in the struggle. Accordingly, the Boston town meeting directed the Committee of Correspondence "to state the Rights of the Colonists and of this Province in particular," to list "the Infringements and Violations thereof that have been, or from time to time may be made," and to send copies to the other towns in the province. In return, Boston requested "a free communication of their Sentiments on this Subject."

The statement of colonial rights prepared by the Bostonians declared that Americans had absolute rights to life, liberty, and property. The idea that "a British house of commons, should have a right, at pleasure, to give and grant the property of the colonists" was "irreconcileable" with "the first principles of natural law and Justice . . . and of the British Constitution in particular." The list of grievances complained of taxation without representation, the presence of unnecessary troops and customs officers on American soil, the use of imperial revenues to pay colonial officials, the expanded jurisdiction of vice-admiralty courts, and even the nature of the instructions given to American governors by their superiors in London.

The entire document, which was printed as a pamphlet for distribution to the towns, exhibited none of the hesitation that had characterized colonial claims against Parliament in the 1760s. No longer were patriots—at least in Boston—preoccupied with defining the precise limits of parliamentary authority. No longer did they mention the necessity of obedience to Parliament. They were committed to a course that placed American rights first, loyalty to Great Britain a distant second.

The response of the Massachusetts towns to the committee's pamphlet must have caused Samuel Adams to rejoice. Some towns disagreed with Boston's assessment of the state of affairs, but most

aligned themselves with the city. From Braintree came the assertion that "all civil officers are or ought to be Servants to the people and dependent upon them for their official Support, and every instance to the Contrary from the Governor downwards tends to crush and destroy civil liberty." The town of Holden declared that "the People of New England have never given the People of Britain any Right of Jurisdiction over us." The citizens of Petersham commented that resistance to tyranny was "the first and highest social Duty of this people." And Pownallborough warned, "Allegiance is a relative Term and like Kingdoms and commonwealths is local and has its bounds." Beliefs like these made the next crisis in Anglo-American affairs the final one.

 ## The Boston Tea Party

The only one of the Townshend duties still in effect by 1773 was the tax on tea. In the years after 1770 some Americans continued to boycott English tea, while others resumed drinking it either openly or in secret. As explained in Chapter 4, tea was important in the colonists' diet and in their social lives, so observing the boycott required them not only to forgo a favorite beverage but also to alter habitual forms of socializing. Tea thus retained an explosively symbolic character even though the boycott was less than fully effective after 1770.

In May 1773, Parliament passed an act designed to save the East India Company from bankruptcy. The company, which held a legal monopoly on

Tea Act

British trade with the East Indies, was of critical importance to the British economy (and to the financial well-being of many prominent British politicians who had invested in its stock). According to the Tea Act, certain duties paid on tea were to be returned to the company, and tea was to be sold only by designated agents, a method of distribution that would enable the East India Company to avoid colonial middlemen and undersell any competitors, even smugglers.

The net result of bypassing the middlemen would be cheaper tea for American consumers. Resistance leaders, however, interpreted the new measure as a pernicious device to make them admit Parliament's right to tax them, for the less-expensive tea would still be taxed under the Townshend law. Others saw the Tea Act as the first step in the establishment of an East India Company monopoly of all colonial trade. Residents of the four cities designated to receive the first shipments of tea accordingly prepared to respond to what they perceived as a new threat to their freedom.

In New York City, the tea ships failed to arrive on schedule. In Philadelphia, the governor of Pennsylvania persuaded the captain to turn around and sail back to Britain. In Charleston, the tea was unloaded, stored under the direction of local tradesmen, and later destroyed. The only confrontation occurred in Boston, where both sides—the town meeting, joined by participants from nearby towns, and Governor Thomas Hutchinson, two of whose sons were tea agents—rejected compromise.

The first of three tea ships, the *Dartmouth*, entered Boston harbor on November 28. The customs laws required cargo to be landed and the appropriate duty paid by its owners within twenty days of a ship's arrival; otherwise, the cargo had to be seized by customs officers and sold at auction. After a series of mass meetings, Bostonians voted to post guards on the wharf to prevent the tea from being unloaded. Hutchinson, for his part, refused to permit the vessels to leave the harbor. John Singleton Copley, whose father-in-law was a tea agent, tried to mediate the dispute.

On December 16, one day before the cargo would have been confiscated, more than five thousand people (nearly a third of the city's population) crowded into Old South Church. The meeting, chaired by Samuel Adams, made a final attempt to persuade Hutchinson to send the tea back to England. But the governor remained adamant. In the early evening Adams reportedly announced "that he could think of nothing further to be done—that they had now done all they could for the Salvation of their Country." Cries then rang out from the back of the crowd: "Boston harbor a tea-pot tonight! The Mohawks are come!" Small groups pushed their way out of the meeting. Within a few minutes, about sixty men crudely disguised as Indians assembled at the wharf, boarded the three ships, and dumped the cargo into the harbor. By 9 P.M. their work was done: 342 chests of tea worth approximately £10,000 floated in splinters on the water.

Among the "Indians" were many representatives of Boston's artisans, including Paul Revere. Five masons, eleven carpenters and builders, three leatherworkers, a blacksmith, two barbers, a coachmaker, and twelve apprentices have been identified as par-

Thomas Hutchinson, the governor of Massachusetts, helped to incite the Boston Tea Party by refusing to allow the tea ships to leave the harbor. This portrait conveys the governor's haughty demeanor. Massachusetts Historical Society.

ticipants. That their ranks also included four farmers from outside Boston, ten merchants, two doctors, a teacher, and a bookseller illustrated the widespread support for the resistance movement. The next day John Adams exulted in his diary that the Tea Party was "so bold, so daring, so firm, intrepid and inflexible" that "I can't but consider it as an epocha in history."

The North administration reacted with considerably less enthusiasm when it learned of the Tea Party. In March 1774, Parliament adopted the first of four laws that became known as the Coercive, or Intolerable, Acts. It ordered the port of Boston closed until the tea was paid for, prohibiting all but coastal trade in food and firewood. Later in the spring, Parliament passed three other punitive measures. The Massachusetts Government Act altered

Coercive and Quebec Acts

the province's charter, substituting an appointed council for the elected one, increasing the governor's powers, and forbidding most town meetings. The Justice Act provided that a person accused of committing murder in the course of suppressing a riot or enforcing the laws could be tried outside the colony where the incident had occurred. Finally, the Quartering Act gave broad authority to military commanders seeking to house their troops in private dwellings. Thus the Coercive Acts punished not only Boston but also Massachusetts as a whole, alerting other colonies to the possibility that their residents, too, could be subject to retaliation if they opposed British authority.

After passing the last of the Coercive Acts, Parliament turned its attention to much-needed reforms in the government of Quebec. The Quebec Act thereby became linked with the Coercive Acts in the minds of the patriots. Intended to ease strains that had arisen since the British conquest of the formerly French colony, the Quebec Act granted greater religious freedom to Catholics—alarming Protestant colonists, who equated Roman Catholicism with religious and political despotism. It also reinstated French civil law, which had been replaced by British procedures in 1763, and it established an appointed council (rather than an elected legislature) as the governing body of the colony. Finally, in an attempt to provide northern Indians with some protection against Anglo-American settlement, the act annexed to Quebec the area east of the Mississippi River and north of the Ohio River. That region, parts of which were claimed by individual seacoast colonies, was thus removed from their jurisdiction.

Members of Parliament who voted for the punitive legislation believed that the acts would be obeyed and that at long last they had solved the problem posed by the troublesome Americans. But the patriots showed little inclination to bow to the wishes of Parliament. In their eyes, the Coercive Acts and the Quebec Act proved what they had feared since 1768: that Great Britain had embarked on a deliberate plan to oppress them. If the port of Boston could be closed, why not the ports of Philadelphia or New York? If the royal charter of Massachusetts could be changed, why not the charter of South Carolina? If certain people could be removed from their home colonies for trial, why not

Implications of the Coercive Acts

all violators of all laws? If troops could be forcibly quartered in private houses, did not that action pave the way for the occupation of all of America? If the Roman Catholic Church could receive favored status in Quebec, why not everywhere? It seemed as though the full dimensions of the plot against American rights and liberties had at last been revealed.

The Boston Committee of Correspondence urged all the colonies to join in an immediate renewed boycott of British goods. But the other provinces were not yet ready to take such a drastic step. They suggested that another intercolonial congress be convened to consider an appropriate response. Few people wanted to take hasty action; even the most ardent patriots remained loyal to Britain and hoped for reconciliation with its leaders. Despite their objections to British policy, they continued to see themselves as part of the empire. Americans were approaching the brink of confrontation, but they had not committed themselves to an irrevocable break. So the colonies agreed to send delegates to Philadelphia in September to attend a Continental Congress.

 Conclusion

During the preceding decade, momentous changes had occurred in the ways colonists thought about themselves and their allegiance. The number of colonists who defined themselves as political actors had increased substantially. Once linked unquestioningly to Great Britain, they had begun to develop a sense of their own identity as Americans, including a recognition of the cultural and social gulf that separated them from Britons. They had started to realize that their concept of the political process differed from that held by people in the mother country. They also had come to understand that their economic interests did not necessarily coincide with those of Great Britain. Colonial political leaders reached such conclusions only after a long train of events, some of them violent, had altered their understanding of their relationship with the mother country. Parliamentary acts such as the Stamp Act and the Townshend Acts had elicited colonial responses—both ideological and practical—that produced further responses from Britain. Tensions escalated until they climaxed in the Tea Party. From that point on, there was to be no turning back.

In the late summer of 1774, the Americans were committed to resistance but not to independence.

Even so, they had started to sever the bonds of empire. During the next decade, they would forge the bonds of a new American nationality to replace those rejected Anglo-American ties.

Suggestions for Further Reading

General

Ian R. Christie and Benjamin W. Labaree, *Empire or Independence, 1760–1776: A British-American Dialogue on the Coming of the American Revolution* (1976); Edward Countryman, *The American Revolution* (1985); Marc Egnal, *A Mighty Empire: The Origins of the American Revolution* (1988); Ronald Hoffman and Peter Albert, eds., *The Transforming Hand of Revolution: Reconsidering the American Revolution as a Social Movement* (1995); Merrill Jensen, *The Founding of a Nation: A History of the American Revolution, 1763–1776* (1968); John Phillip Reid, *The Constitutional History of the American Revolution* (1995); Robert W. Tucker and David C. Hendrickson, *The Fall of the First British Empire: Origins of the War of American Independence* (1982).

Colonial Warfare and the British Empire

Fred Anderson, *A People's Army: Massachusetts Soldiers and Society in the Seven Years' War* (1984); Lawrence Henry Gipson, *The British Empire Before the American Revolution* (1936–1970); Douglas Leach, *Roots of Conflict: British Armed Forces and Colonial Americans, 1677–1763* (1986); Robert C. Newbold, *The Albany Congress and Plan of Union of 1754* (1955); William Pencak, *War, Politics, and Revolution in Provincial Massachusetts* (1981); Alan Rogers, *Empire and Liberty: American Resistance to British Authority, 1755–1763* (1974); John Shy, *Toward Lexington: The Role of the British Army in the Coming of the American Revolution* (1965); James Titus, *The Old Dominion at War: Society, Politics, and Warfare in Late Colonial Virginia* (1991).

British Politics and Policy

Colin Bonwick, *English Radicals and the American Revolution* (1977); James E. Bradley, *Popular Politics and the American Revolution in England* (1986); John Brewer, *Party Ideology and Popular Politics at the Accession of George III* (1976); John Brooke, *King George III* (1972); John L. Bullion, *A Great and Necessary Measure: George Grenville and the Genesis of the Stamp Act, 1763–1765* (1981); Michael Kammen, *A Rope of Sand: The Colonial Agents, British Politics, and the American Revolution* (1968); Nancy F. Koehn, *The Power of Commerce: Economy and Governance in the First British Empire* (1994); P. D. G. Thomas, *Tea Party to Independence* (1991); P. D. G. Thomas, *The Townshend Duties Crisis* (1987); P. D. G. Thomas, *British Politics and the Stamp Act Crisis* (1975).

Native Americans and the West

Richard Aquila, *The Iroquois Restoration: Iroquois Diplomacy on the Colonial Frontier, 1701–1754* (1983); David H. Corkran, *The Cherokee Frontier: Conflict and Survival, 1740–1762* (1962); Gregory Dowd, *A Spirited Resistance: The North American Indian Struggle for Unity, 1745–1815* (1992); Francis Jennings, *Empire of Fortune: Crowns, Colonies and Tribes in the Seven Years' War in America* (1988); Howard H. Peckham, *Pontiac and the Indian Uprising* (1947); Jack M. Sosin, *Whitehall and the Wilderness: The Middle West in British Colonial Policy, 1760–1775* (1961); Richard White, *The Middle Ground: Indians, Empires and Republics in the Great Lakes Region, 1650–1815* (1991).

Political and Economic Thought

Bernard Bailyn, *The Ideological Origins of the American Revolution* (1967); J. C. D. Clark, *The Language of Liberty, 1660–1832: Political Discourse and Social Dynamics in the Anglo-American World* (1994); J. E. Crowley, *This Sheba, Self: The Conceptualization of Economic Life in Eighteenth-Century America* (1974); Jay Fliegelman, *Prodigals and Pilgrims: The American Revolution Against Patriarchal Authority, 1750–1800* (1982).

American Resistance

David Ammerman, *In the Common Cause: American Response to the Coercive Acts of 1774* (1974); T. H. Breen, *Tobacco Culture: The Mentality of the Great Tidewater Planters on the Eve of the Revolution* (1985); Richard D. Brown, *Revolutionary Politics in Massachusetts: The Boston Committee of Correspondence and the Towns, 1772–1774* (1970); Joseph Albert Ernst, *Money and Politics in America, 1755–1775: A Study in the Currency Act of 1764 and the Political Economy of Revolution* (1973); Paul Gilje, *The Road to Mobocracy: Popular Disorder in New York City, 1763–1834* (1987); Dirk Hoerder, *Crowd Action in Revolutionary Massachusetts, 1765–1780* (1977); Benjamin W. Labaree, *The Boston Tea Party* (1964); Pauline R. Maier, *The Old Revolutionaries: Political Lives in the Age of Samuel Adams* (1980); Pauline R. Maier, *From Resistance to Revolution: Colonial Radicals and the Development of American Opposition to Britain, 1765–1776* (1972); Edmund S. Morgan and Helen M. Morgan, *The Stamp Act Crisis: Prologue to Revolution* (1953); Gary B. Nash, *The Urban Crucible: Social Change, Political Consciousness, and the Origins of the American Revolution* (1979); Bruce A. Ragsdale, *A Planters' Republic: The Search for Economic Independence in Revolutionary Virginia* (1996); Richard Ryerson, *The Revolution Has Now Begun: The Radical Committees of Philadelphia, 1765–1776* (1978); Peter Shaw, *American Patriots and the Rituals of Revolution* (1981); John W. Tyler, *Smugglers and Patriots: Boston Merchants and the Advent of the American Revolution* (1986); Richard Walsh, *Charleston's Sons of Liberty: A Study of the Artisans, 1763–1789* (1959); Hiller B. Zobel, *The Boston Massacre* (1970).

CHAPTER

6

A Revolution, Indeed
1774–1783

W hen John Provey and Richard Weaver appeared before the loyalist claims commissioners in London at the end of the Revolution, the commissioners were not impressed with their descriptions of losses and loyal service to the king. Such men had "no right to ask or expect any thing from Government," the commissioners declared. Their applications "hardly deserve[d] a serious Investigation or a serious Answer." So Provey and Weaver, along with most of the forty-five other men in the same circumstances, were denied any assistance from the funds allocated by Parliament to compensate loyalists for the damages they had incurred by opposing the Revolution. Why were Weaver and Provey treated thus? They were African-Americans.

John Provey, a North Carolinian, had been the slave of a lawyer; Richard Weaver, a Philadelphian, was freeborn. Provey served in a black corps of the British army during the war; Weaver left Philadelphia with the British troops when they evacuated that city in 1778 and made his way to London the following year. Both had wives and children at the time they requested government assistance. Because they were denied the help they sought, they and their families, along with hundreds of other African-Americans, became dependent on charity disbursed by a group of civic-minded London merchants, the Committee to Aid the Black Poor, which was formed in 1786.

Seeing no future for themselves in London, they both agreed to emigrate to West Africa, to the new colony of Sierra Leone, which was sponsored by the Black Poor Committee. John Provey died on shipboard before the vessels even left London. But Richard Weaver went to Sierra Leone and was elected the first governor of the tiny colony, composed largely of exiled African-American loyalists. Conflicts with a nearby ruler and with slavers who established a post near the settlement almost

In 1787, John Trumbull painted Washington and his officers participating in "The Surrender of Lord Cornwallis at Yorktown" six years earlier. Trumbull devoted his career to painting large, patriotic canvases that illustrated important moments in the nation's history. Although he was not present at the events he portrayed, he sketched his subjects from life and relied on their descriptions when he composed his works, which always depicted the nation's leaders in heroic fashion.
Yale University Art Gallery (a detail) Trumbull Collection

"The Wise Men of Gotham and Their Goose," published in 1776, was a British satirist's look at his nation's American policy. The cartoonist showed British politicians in the process of killing the colonial goose that laid the golden eggs (displayed in a basket in the background) while the British lion slumbers overhead and the king watches unemotionally. As in the cartoon of the "Patriotic Ladies" on page 136, a urinating dog symbolizes the artist's disgust with the proceedings. John Carter Brown Library at Brown University.

destroyed it. But in 1792 the future of the colony was assured when an additional twelve hundred African-American refugees arrived from Nova Scotia, where they had fled immediately after the war.

The little-known tale of the black loyalists who returned to the homeland of their ancestors is but one dramatic example of the disruptive effects of the American Revolution. The Revolution was more than just a series of clashes between British and patriot armies with the victors emerging nobly, as the illustration on page 144 might imply. The Revolution uprooted thousands of families, disrupted the economy, reshaped society by forcing many colonists into permanent exile, led Americans to develop new conceptions of politics, and created a na-

tion from thirteen separate colonies. Thus it marked a significant turning point in Americans' collective history.

The struggle for independence required revolutionary leaders to accomplish three separate but closely related tasks. The first was political and ideological: transforming a consensus favoring loyal resistance into a coalition supporting independence. They accordingly adopted a variety of measures (ranging from persuasion to coercion) to enlist all European-Americans in the patriot cause. Fearing with some reason that Indians and blacks would side with Britain, the colonies' elected leaders hoped at least to ensure those groups' neutrality in the impending conflict.

The second task involved foreign relations. To win independence, patriot leaders knew they needed international recognition and aid, particularly from France. Thus they dispatched to Paris the most experienced American diplomat, Benjamin Franklin, who had served for years as a colonial agent in London. Franklin skillfully negotiated the Franco-American alliance of 1778, which was to prove crucial to winning independence.

Only the third task directly involved the British. George Washington, commander-in-chief of the American army, soon recognized that his primary goal should be not to win battles but to avoid losing them decisively. The outcome of any one battle was less important than ensuring that his army survived to fight another day. Consequently, the story of the Revolutionary War reveals British action and American reaction, British attacks and American defenses. The American war effort was aided by the failure of British military planners to analyze accurately the problem confronting them. Until it was too late, they treated the war against the colonists as they treated wars against other Europeans: they concentrated on winning battles and did not consider the difficulties of achieving their main goal, retaining the colonies' allegiance. In the end, the Americans' triumph owed more to their own endurance and to Britain's mistakes than to their military prowess.

 Government by Congress and Committee

When the fifty-five delegates to the First Continental Congress convened in Philadelphia in September 1774, they knew that any measures they adopted were likely to enjoy support among many of their

• *Important Events* •

1774	First Continental Congress meets in Philadelphia, adopts Declaration of Rights and Grievances Continental Association implements economic boycott of Britain; committees of observation established to oversee boycott		British evacuate Boston Declaration of Independence adopted New York City falls to British
1774–75	Provincial conventions replace collapsing colonial governments	**1777**	British take Philadelphia Burgoyne surrenders at Saratoga
1775	Battles of Lexington and Concord; first shots of war fired Second Continental Congress begins Lord Dunmore's proclamation offers freedom to patriots' slaves if they join British forces	**1778**	French alliance brings vital assistance to the United States British evacuate Philadelphia
		1779	Sullivan expedition destroys Iroquois villages
		1780	British take Charleston
		1781	Cornwallis surrenders at Yorktown
		1782	Peace negotiations begin
1776	Thomas Paine publishes *Common Sense*, advocating independence	**1783**	Treaty of Paris signed, granting independence to the United States

fellow countrymen and countrywomen. That summer, open meetings held throughout the colonies had endorsed the idea of another nonimportation pact. Participants in such meetings promised (in the words of the freeholders of Johnston County, North Carolina) to "strictly adhere to, and abide by, such Regulations and Restrictions as the Members of the said General Congress shall agree to and judge most convenient." Committees of correspondence publicized these meetings so effectively that Americans everywhere knew about them. Most of the congressional delegates were selected by extralegal provincial conventions whose members were chosen at such local gatherings, since governors had forbidden regular assemblies to conduct formal elections. Thus the very act of designating delegates to attend the Congress involved Americans in open defiance of British authority.

The colonies' leading political figures—most of them lawyers, merchants, and planters—attended the Philadelphia Congress. The Massachusetts delegation included both Samuel Adams, the experienced organizer of Boston resistance, and his younger cousin John, an ambitious lawyer. Among others, New York sent John Jay, a talented young attorney. From Pennsylvania came the

First Continental Congress

conservative Joseph Galloway and his long-time rival, John Dickinson. Virginia elected Richard Henry Lee and Patrick Henry, both noted for their patriotic zeal, as well as George Washington. Most of these men had never met, but in the weeks, months, and years that followed they became the chief architects of the new nation.

The congressmen faced three tasks when they convened at Carpenters Hall on September 5, 1774. The first two were explicit: defining American grievances and developing a plan for resistance. The third—outlining a theory of their constitutional relationship with Great Britain—was less clear-cut and proved troublesome. The most radical congressmen, like Lee of Virginia, argued that colonists owed allegiance only to George III and that Parliament was nothing more than a local legislature for Great Britain with no authority over the colonies. The conservatives—Joseph Galloway and his allies—proposed a formal plan of union that would have required Parliament and a new American legislature to consent jointly to all laws pertaining to the colonies. After heated debate, delegates narrowly rejected Galloway's proposal, but they were not prepared to accept the radicals' position either.

Finally, they accepted a compromise position worked out by John Adams. The crucial clause that Adams drafted in the Congress's Declaration of

Declaration of Rights and Grievances

Rights and Grievances read in part: "From the necessity of the case, and a regard to the mutual interest of both countries, we cheerfully consent to the operation of such acts of the British parliament, as are bona fide, restrained to the regulation of our external commerce." Notice the key phrases. "From the necessity of the case" declared that Americans would obey Parliament only because they thought that doing so was in the best interest of both countries. "Bona fide, restrained to the regulation of our external commerce" made it clear to Lord North that they would continue to resist taxes in disguise, like the Townshend duties. Most striking of all was that such language—which only a few years before would have been regarded as irredeemably radical—could be presented and accepted as a compromise in the fall of 1774. The Americans had come a long way since their first hesitant protests against the Sugar Act ten years earlier.

With the constitutional issue resolved, the delegates readily agreed on the laws they wanted repealed (notably the Coercive Acts) and decided to implement an economic boycott while petitioning the king for relief. They adopted the Continental Association, which called for nonimportation of British goods (effective December 1, 1774), nonconsumption of British products (effective March 1, 1775), and nonexportation of American goods to Britain and the British West Indies (effective September 10, 1775, so that southern planters could market their 1774 tobacco crop, which had to be dried and cured before sale).

To enforce the Continental Association, Congress recommended the election of committees of observation and inspection in every American locality. By specifying that committee members be chosen by all persons qualified to vote for members of the lower house of the colonial legislatures, Congress guaranteed the committees a broad popular base. In some places the committeemen were former local officeholders; in other towns they were men who had never before held office. Everywhere, these committeemen—perhaps seven to eight thousand of them in the colonies as a whole—became the local leaders of American resistance.

Such committees were officially charged only with overseeing implementation of the boycott, but over the next six months they became de facto governments. They examined merchants' records and published the names of those who continued to import British goods. They also promoted home manufactures, encouraging Americans to adopt simple modes of dress and behavior to symbolize their commitment to liberty and virtuous behavior. Since expensive leisure-time activities were believed to reflect vice and corruption, Congress urged Americans to forgo dancing, gambling, horseracing, cockfighting, and other forms of "extravagance and dissipation." Some committees accordingly forbade dancing, extracted apologies from people caught gambling or racing, prohibited the slaughter of lambs (because of the need for wool), and offered prizes for the best locally made cloth.

Thus the committees gradually extended their authority over many aspects of American life. They attempted to identify opponents of American resistance, developing elaborate spy networks, circulating copies of the Continental Association for signatures, and investigating reports of dissident remarks and activities. Suspected dissenters were first urged to support the colonial cause; if they failed to do so, the committees had them watched, restricted their movements, or tried to force them to leave the area. People engaging in casual political exchanges with friends one day could find themselves charged with "treasonable conversation" the next. One Massachusetts man, for example, was called before his local committee for maligning the Congress as "a Pack or Parcell of Fools" that was "as tyrannical as Lord North and ought to be opposed & resisted." When he refused to recant, the committee ordered him watched.

Those who dissented more openly received harsher treatment, as the experiences of the Reverend John Agnew of Virginia demonstrate. Agnew, an Anglican, insisted on warning his congregation of "the danger and sin of rebellion." He rejected the committee's summons and was thereafter ostracized by its order. Millers would not grind his corn, and doctors would not treat his sick wife and children. The committee tried to intimidate him by sending armed men to his church to beat drums and drill during services. When that failed, patriots nailed shut the church's doors and windows. Finally Agnew and his oldest son fled, but the persecution of his wife and younger children continued. She was, she later recalled, "daily insulted and robbed . . . [and] searched under various pretense."

Committees of Observation

While the committees of observation were expanding their power during the winter and early spring of 1775, the regular colonial governments were collapsing. Only in Con-

Provincial Conventions

necticut, Rhode Island, Delaware, and Pennsylvania did legislatures continue to meet without encountering patriot challenges to their authority. In every other colony, popularly elected provincial conventions took over the task of running the government, sometimes entirely replacing the legislatures and at other times holding concurrent sessions. In late 1774 and early 1775, these conventions approved the Continental Association, elected delegates to the Second Continental Congress (scheduled for May), organized militia units, and gathered arms and ammunition. Unable to stem the tide of resistance, the British-appointed governors and councils watched helplessly as their authority crumbled.

The frustrating experience of Governor Josiah Martin of North Carolina is a case in point. After a provincial convention was called to meet at New Bern on April 4, 1775—the same day the legislature was to convene—Martin asked all citizens to "renounce disclaim and discourage all such meetings cabals and illegal proceedings . . . which can only tend to introduce disorder and anarchy." When the convention met at New Bern, its membership proved to be virtually identical to that of the colonial legislature. The delegates proceeded to act alternately in both capacities and even passed some joint resolves. Continuing the farce, the exasperated Martin delivered a speech to the assembly denouncing the convention. Three days later, Martin wrote to officials in London, admitting that his government was "absolutely prostrate, impotent, and that nothing but the shadow of it is left."

Royal officials in other colonies suffered similar humiliations. Courts were prevented from holding sessions; taxes were paid to the conventions' agents rather than to provincial tax collectors; sheriffs' powers were challenged; and militiamen would muster only when committees ordered. In short, during the six months preceding the battles at Lexington and Concord, independence was being won at the local level, but without formal acknowledgment and for the most part without bloodshed. Not many Americans fully realized what was happening. The vast majority still proclaimed their loyalty to Great Britain and denied that they sought to leave the empire. Among the few who most clearly recognized the trend toward independence were those who opposed it.

Choosing Sides: Loyalists, African-Americans, and Indians

The first protests against British measures, in the mid-1760s, had won the support of most colonists. Only in the late 1760s and early 1770s did a significant number of Americans begin to question both aims and tactics of the resistance movement. By 1774 and 1775 such people found themselves in a difficult position. Like their more radical counterparts, most of them objected to parliamentary policies, favoring some kind of constitutional reform. Joseph Galloway, for instance, was a conservative by American standards, but his plan for restructuring the empire was too novel for Britain to accept. Nevertheless, if forced to a choice, these colonists sympathized with Great Britain rather than with an independent America. The events of the crucial year between the passage of the Coercive Acts and the outbreak of fighting in Massachusetts crystallized their thinking. Their objections to violent protest, their desire to uphold the legally constituted colonial governments, and their fears of anarchy combined to make them especially sensitive to the dangers of resistance.

Some conservatives began in 1774 and 1775 to publish essays and pamphlets critical of the Congress and its allied committees. In New York City, a group of Anglican clergymen jointly wrote pamphlets and essays arguing the importance of maintaining a cordial connection between Britain and America. In Pennsylvania, Joseph Galloway published *A Candid Examination of the Mutual Claims of Great Britain and the Colonies,* attacking the Continental Congress for rejecting his plan of union. In Massachusetts, the young attorney Daniel Leonard, writing under the pseudonym Massachusettensis, engaged in a prolonged newspaper debate with Novanglus (John Adams). Leonard and others realized that what had begun as a dispute over the nature of American subordination to Parliament was now raising the question of whether the colonies would remain linked to Great Britain at all. "Rouse up at last from your slumber!" the Reverend Thomas Bradbury Chandler of New Jersey cried out to Americans. "There is a set of people

John Singleton Copley married into a loyalist family. His father-in-law, Richard Clarke, was one of the Boston tea agents in 1773. Copley was in Italy studying art when the war began but joined his exiled wife and father-in-law in London in 1776. His sentimental portrait of the family (with himself in the background) commemorated their reunion. The only person in the painting who ever returned to America was his daughter Elizabeth (center), who grew up to marry a Bostonian.   Andrew W. Mellon Fund © National Gallery of Art, Washington, D.C.

among us . . . who have formed a scheme for establishing an independent government or empire in America."

Some colonists heeded the conservative pamphleteers' warnings. About one-fifth of the Anglo-American population remained loyal to Great Britain, actively opposing independence and remaining true to a self-conception that patriots proved willing to abandon. That there were so few active loyalists is surprising, since joining the patriot cause required a far more significant change of allegiance than did loyalism.

Loyalists, Patriots, and Neutrals

With notable exceptions, most people of the following descriptions remained loyal to the Crown: British-appointed government officials; merchants whose trade depended on imperial connections; Anglican clergy everywhere and lay Anglicans in the North, where their denomination was in the minority (the king was the head of their church as well as head of state); former officers and enlisted men from the British army, many of whom had settled in America after 1763; non-English ethnic minorities, especially Scots; tenant farmers, particularly those whose landlords sided with the patriots; members of persecuted religious sects; and many of the back-country southerners who had rebelled against eastern rule in the 1760s and early 1770s. All these people had one thing in common: patriot leaders were their long-standing opponents, though for varying reasons. Ethnic minorities in particular had long felt excluded from the colonial political process. Local and provincial disputes thus helped to determine which side people chose in the imperial conflict.

Active patriots, who accounted for about two-fifths of the population, came chiefly from the groups that had dominated colonial society, either numerically or politically. Among them were yeoman farmers, members of dominant Protestant sects (both Old and New Lights), Chesapeake gentry, merchants dealing mainly in American commodities, city artisans, elected officeholders, and people of English descent. Wives usually but not always adopted their husbands' political beliefs. Although all these patriots supported the Revolution, they pursued divergent goals within the broader coalition, as they had in the 1760s. Some sought limited political reform, others extensive political change, and still others social and economic reforms. (The ways in which their concerns interacted are discussed in Chapter 7.)

There remained in the middle perhaps two-fifths of the white population. Some of those who tried to avoid taking sides were sincere pacifists, such as Quakers. Others opportunistically shifted their allegiance to whatever side happened to be winning at the time. Still others simply wanted to be left alone; they cared little about politics and usually obeyed whoever was in power. But such colonists also resisted British and Americans alike when the demands on them seemed too heavy—when taxes became too high, for example, or when calls for militia service came too often. Their attitude might best be summed up in the phrase "a plague on both your houses." Such persons made up an especially large proportion of the population in the southern back-country, where Scots-Irish settlers had little love for either the patriot gentry or the English authorities.

To American patriots, apathy or neutrality was a crime as heinous as loyalism. In their minds, those who were not for them were against them. By the winter of 1775–1776, the Second Continental Congress was recommending that all "disaffected" persons be disarmed and arrested. State legislatures passed laws prescribing severe penalties for suspected loyalists. Many began to require all voters (or, in some cases, all free adult men) to take oaths of allegiance; the penalty for refusal was usually banishment or extra taxes. After 1777, many states confiscated the property of banished loyalists and used the proceeds for the war effort.

During the war, loyalists congregated in cities held by the British army. When those posts were evacuated at war's end, loyalists scattered to different parts of the British Empire—Britain, the West Indies, and especially Canada. In the provinces of Nova Scotia, New Brunswick, and Ontario they re-created their lives as colonists, laying the foundations of British Canada. All told, perhaps as many as 100,000 Americans preferred to leave their homeland rather than live in a nation independent of British rule. That preference attests to the depth of their loyalty to the monarchy and their Anglo-American identity.

The patriots' policies helped to ensure that the scattered and persecuted loyalists could not band together to threaten the revolutionary cause. But loyalists were not the patriots' only worry. They feared that Indians and slaves might join the forces arrayed against them. Early in the war, free blacks from New England enlisted in local patriot militias, but the revolutionaries could not assume that enslaved African-Americans would also support the struggle for independence.

African-Americans' Dilemma

Bondspeople faced a dilemma at the beginning of the Revolution: how could they best pursue their goal of escaping slavery? Should they fight with or against their masters? With no correct choice immediately apparent, African-Americans made different decisions. Some indeed joined the revolutionaries, but to most an alliance with Great Britain appeared more promising. Thus news of slave conspiracies surfaced in different parts of the colonies in late 1774 and early 1775. All shared a common element: a plan to assist the British in return for freedom. One group of slaves futilely petitioned General Thomas Gage, the commander-in-chief of the British army in Boston, promising to fight for the redcoats if he would liberate them. The most serious incident occurred in 1775 in Charleston, where Thomas Jeremiah, a free black harbor pilot, was brutally executed after being convicted of attempting to foment a slave revolt.

Fear of such acts made sugar planters in the British West Indian colonies more cautious in their opposition to parliamentary policies than were their counterparts on the mainland. On most of the Caribbean islands, slaves outnumbered their masters by six or seven to one. With the ever-present threat of slave revolt or foreign attack hanging over their heads, planters could not afford to risk opposing Britain, their chief protector. The Jamaica assembly agreed with the mainland colonial legislatures that citizens should not be bound by laws to which they had not consented. Nevertheless, its members assured the king in 1774 that "it cannot be supposed, that we now intend, or ever could have intended Resistance to Great Britain." They cited as reasons Jamaica's "weak and feeble" condition, "its very small number of white inhabitants, and . . . the incumbrance of more than Two hundred thousand Slaves."

Slavery and Patriotic Fervor

Slavery affected politics in the continental colonies as well. In the North, with few resident slaves, revolutionary fervor was at its height. In Virginia and Maryland, where free people also constituted a safe majority, there was occasional alarm over potential slave revolts but no disabling fear. But South Carolina and Georgia, where slaves composed more than half of the population, were noticeably less enthusiastic about resistance. Georgia sent no delegates to the First Continental Congress and reminded its representatives at the second one to consider its circumstances, "with our blacks and tories [loyalists] within us," when voting on the question of independence.

The slaveowners' worst fears were realized in November 1775, when Lord Dunmore, the governor of Virginia, offered to free any slaves and indentured servants who would leave their patriot masters to join the British forces. Dunmore hoped to use African-Americans in his fight against the revolutionaries and to disrupt the economy by depriving planters of their labor force. But at most only two thousand African-Americans rallied to the British standard, and many of them perished in a smallpox epidemic. Even so, Dunmore's proclamation led Congress in January 1776 to modify an earlier policy that had prohibited the enlistment of African-Americans in the regular American army.

Although slaves did not pose a serious threat to the revolutionary cause in its early years, the patriots turned rumors of slave uprisings to their own advantage. In South Carolina, resistance leaders argued that unity under the Continental Association would protect masters from their slaves at a time when royal government was unable to muster adequate defense forces. Undoubtedly many wavering Carolinians were drawn into the revolutionary camp by fear

that an overt division among the colony's free people would encourage a slave revolt.

Similarly, the threat of Indian attacks helped persuade some reluctant westerners to support the struggle against Great Britain. In the years since the Proclamation of 1763, British officials had won the trust of the interior tribes by attempting to protect them from land-hungry European-Americans. British-appointed superintendents of Indian affairs, John Stuart in the South and Sir William Johnson in the North, lived among and understood the Indians. In 1768, Stuart and Johnson negotiated separate agreements modifying the proclamation line and attempting to draw realistic, defensible boundaries between tribal holdings and European-American settlements. The treaties supposedly established permanent western borders for the colonies. But just a few years later, in 1770 and 1773, the British pushed the southern boundary even farther west to accommodate the demands of settlers in western Georgia and Kentucky.

By 1775, many Indian groups were impatient with European-Americans' aggressive pressure on their lands. Relationships on the frontier were filled with bitterness, misunderstanding, and occasional bloody encounters. In combination with the tribes' confidence in Stuart and Johnson, such grievances predisposed most Indians toward an alliance with Great Britain. Even so, the latter hesitated to make full and immediate use of these potential allies. The superintendents were aware that neither the Indians' style of fighting nor tribal war aims were necessarily compatible with those of the British. Accordingly, Stuart and Guy Johnson (who became northern superintendent following his uncle's death) sought from the tribes only a promise of neutrality. The superintendents even helped to avert a general Indian uprising in the summer of 1774 by preventing the Shawnees from recruiting allies for attacks on frontier villages in Kentucky. Lord Dunmore's War, between the Shawnees and the Virginia militia, thus ended with Kentucky being opened to European-American settlement but with hunting and fishing rights still reserved to the Shawnees.

Indians' Grievances

Recognizing that their standing with native peoples was poor, the patriots also sought the Indians' neutrality. In 1775 the Second Continental Congress sent a general message to Indian nations describing the war as "a family quarrel between us and Old England" and requesting that they "not join on either side" since "you Indians are not concerned in it." A group of Cherokees led by Chief Dragging Canoe nevertheless decided that the "family quarrel" would allow them to settle some old scores. They attacked settlements along the western borders of the Carolinas and Virginia in the summer of 1776. But a militia campaign destroyed many of their towns, along with crops and large quantities of supplies. Dragging Canoe and his diehard followers fled to the west, establishing new outposts; the rest of the Cherokees agreed to a treaty that ceded still more of their land.

The fate of the Shawnees and Cherokees foreshadowed the history of Indian involvement in the Revolution. The British victory over France in

Native Americans' Diverse Interests

1763 had removed the Indians' strongest weapon: their ability to play the European powers off against one another. Successful strategies were difficult to envision under these new circumstances, and even if the interests of several neighboring tribes coincided, old enmities kept them from forming alliances. Consequently, during the Revolution many Indian nations pursued a course that aligned them with neither side and (as the American leaders wanted) avoided active involvement in the war.

Thus although patriots could never completely ignore the threats posed by loyalists, neutrals, slaves, and Indians, only rarely did fear of these groups seriously hamper the revolutionary movement. Occasionally frontier militiamen refused to turn out for duty on the seacoast because they feared Indians would attack in their absence. Sometimes southern troops refused to serve in the North because they (and their political leaders) were unwilling to leave their regions unprotected against a slave insurrection. But the practical impossibility of a large-scale slave revolt, coupled with tribal feuds and the patriots' successful campaign to disarm and neutralize loyalists, ensured that the revolutionaries would remain firmly in control as they fought for independence.

 War Begins

On January 27, 1775, Lord Dartmouth, secretary of state for America, addressed a fateful letter to General Thomas Gage in Boston. Expressing his belief

In 1776 Benjamin West painted this portrait of Colonel Guy Johnson, the superintendent for Indian affairs in the northern district of America, while Johnson was in London for consultations with British officials. In the background is a man thought to be the Mohawk chief Joseph Brant (see page 163). Andrew Mellon Fund © National Gallery of Art, Washington, D.C.

that American resistance was nothing more than the response of a "rude rabble without plan," Dartmouth urged Gage to take a decisive step. Opposition could not be "very formidable," Dartmouth wrote, and even if it were, "it will surely be better that the Conflict should be brought on, upon such ground, than in a riper state of Rebellion."

Dartmouth's letter did not reach Gage until April 14. He responded by sending an expedition to confiscate provincial military supplies stockpiled at

Battles of Lexington and Concord

Concord. Bostonians dispatched two messengers, William Dawes and Paul Revere (later joined by Dr. Samuel Prescott), to rouse the countryside. So when the British vanguard of several hundred

In 1775, an unknown artist painted the redcoats entering Concord. The fighting at North Bridge, which occurred just a few hours after this triumphal entry, signaled the start of open warfare between Britain and the colonies.   Photography Courtesy of Concord Museum, Concord, MA.

men approached Lexington at dawn on April 19, they found a ragtag group of seventy militiamen—about half of the adult male population of the town—drawn up before them on the common. The Americans' commander ordered his men to withdraw, realizing they could not halt the redcoats' advance. But as they began to disperse, a shot rang out; the British soldiers then fired several volleys. When they stopped, eight Americans lay dead and another ten had been wounded. The British moved on to Concord, 5 miles away.

There the contingents of militia were larger, Concord residents having been joined by groups of men from nearby towns. An exchange of gunfire at the North Bridge spilled the first British blood of the Revolution: three men were killed and nine wounded. Thousands of militiamen then fired from houses and from behind trees and bushes at the British forces as they retreated to Boston. By the end of the day, the redcoats had suffered 272 casualties, including 70 deaths. Only the arrival of reinforcements and the American militia's lack of coordination prevented much heavier British losses. The patriots suffered just 93 casualties.

By the evening of April 20, perhaps as many as twenty thousand American militiamen had gathered around Boston, summoned by local committees that spread the alarm across the countryside. Many did not stay long, since they were needed at home for spring planting, but those who remained dug in along siege lines encircling the city. For nearly a year the two armies sat and stared at each other across those lines. The redcoats attacked their besiegers only once, on June 17, when they drove the Americans from

First Year of War

trenches atop Breed's Hill in Charlestown. In that misnamed Battle of Bunker Hill, the British incurred their greatest losses of the entire war: over 800 wounded and 228 killed. The Americans, though forced to abandon their position, lost less than half that number.

During the same eleven-month period, patriots captured Fort Ticonderoga, a British fort on Lake Champlain, acquiring much-needed cannon. Trying to bring Canada into the war on the American side, they also mounted an uncoordinated northern campaign that ended in disaster at Quebec in early 1776. But the chief significance of the war's first year lay in the long lull in fighting between the main armies at Boston. The delay gave both sides a chance to regroup, organize, and plan their strategies.

Lord North and his new American secretary, Lord George Germain, made three central assumptions about the war they faced. First, they concluded

British Strategy

that patriot forces could not withstand the assaults of trained British regulars. They and their generals were convinced that the 1776 campaign would be the first and last of the war. Accordingly, they dispatched to America the largest force Great Britain had ever assembled anywhere: 370 transport ships carrying 32,000 troops and tons of supplies, accompanied by 73 naval vessels and 13,000 sailors. Such an extraordinary effort, they thought, would ensure a quick victory. Among the troops were thousands of Hessian mercenaries (from the German state of Hesse); eighteenth-century armies were often composed of such professional soldiers who hired out to the highest bidder.

Second, British officials and army officers treated this war as comparable to wars they had fought successfully in Europe. They adopted a conventional strategy of capturing major American cities and defeating the rebel army decisively without suffering serious casualties themselves. Third, they assumed that a clear-cut military victory would automatically bring about their goal of retaining the colonies' allegiance.

All these assumptions proved false. North and Germain, like Lord Dartmouth before them, vastly underestimated Americans' commitment to armed resistance. Battlefield defeats did not lead patriots to abandon their political aims and sue for peace. The ministers in London also failed to recognize the significance of the American population's dispersal over an area 1,500 miles long and more than 100 miles

wide. Although Great Britain would control each of the most important American ports at one time or another during the war, less than 5 percent of the population lived in those cities. Furthermore, the coast offered so many excellent harbors that essential commerce was easily rerouted. In other words, the loss of cities did little to damage the American cause, whereas the aim of capturing such ports repeatedly led redcoat generals astray.

Most of all, British officials did not at first understand that military triumph would not necessarily lead to political victory. Securing the colonies permanently would require hundreds of thousands of Americans to return to their original allegiance. The conquest of America was thus a far more complicated task than the defeat of France twelve years earlier. Great Britain needed not only to overpower the patriots but also to convert them. After 1778, the ministry adopted a strategy designed to achieve that goal through the expanded use of loyalist forces and the restoration of civilian authority in occupied areas. But the new policy came too late. Britain's leaders never fully realized that they were fighting not a conventional European war but rather an entirely new kind of conflict: the first modern war of national liberation.

Great Britain at least had a bureaucracy ready to supervise the war effort. The Americans had only the Second Continental Congress, originally planned as a brief gathering to consider the ministry's response

Second Continental Congress

to the Continental Association. Instead, the delegates who convened in Philadelphia on May 10, 1775, found that they had to assume the mantle of intercolonial government. "Such a vast Multitude of objects, civil, political, commercial and military, press and crowd upon us so fast, that we know not what to do first," John Adams wrote a close friend early in the session. Yet as the summer passed, Congress slowly organized the colonies for war. It authorized the printing of money with which to purchase necessary goods, established a committee to supervise relations with foreign countries, and took steps to strengthen the militia. Most important, it created the Continental Army and appointed its generals.

Until Congress met, the Massachusetts provincial congress had taken responsibility for organizing the militiamen encamped at Boston. But that army, composed of men from all the New England states,

The plight of the redcoat soldiers besieged in Boston during the fall and winter of 1775–1776 attracted the sympathies of a British cartoonist. For "Six-Pence a Day," he noted, soldiers were exposed to "Yankees, Fire and Water, Sword and Famine," while their wives and children begged for assistance at home. The artist hoped to persuade men not to enlist in the British army. The British Museum, Department of Prints and Drawings, Satires.

constituted a heavy drain on limited local resources. Consequently, Massachusetts asked the Continental Congress to assume the task of directing the army. As a first step, Congress had to choose a commander-in-chief. Since the war had thus far been a wholly northern affair, many delegates recognized the importance of naming someone who was not a New Englander. There seemed only one obvious candidate: they unanimously selected their fellow delegate, the Virginian George Washington.

Washington was no fiery radical, nor was he a reflective political thinker. He had not played a prominent role in the prerevolutionary agitation, but his devotion to the American cause was unquestioned. He was dignified, conservative, and respectable—a man of unimpeachable integrity. The younger son of a Virginia planter, Washington did not expect to inherit sub-

George Washington: A Portrait of Leadership

stantial property and planned to make his living as a surveyor. But the early death of his older brother and his marriage to the wealthy widow Martha Custis made George Washington a rich man. Though unmistakably an aristocrat, he was unswervingly committed to representative government. He had other desirable traits as well. His stamina was remarkable: in more than eight years of war, Washington never had a serious illness and took only one brief leave of absence. Moreover, he both looked and acted like a leader. More than six feet tall in an era when most men were five inches shorter, he displayed a stately and commanding presence. Other patriots praised his judgment, steadiness, and discretion, and even a loyalist admitted that Washington could "atone for many demerits by the extraordinary coolness and caution which distinguish his character."

Washington needed all the coolness and caution he could muster when he took command of the army

outside Boston in July 1775. It took him months to
impose hierarchy and discipline on the unruly troops and to bring order to the supply system. But by March 1776, when the arrival of cannon from Ticonderoga finally enabled him to put direct pressure on the redcoats in the city, the army was prepared to act. As it happened, an assault on Boston proved unnecessary. Sir William Howe, who had replaced Gage, had for some time been considering an evacuation; he wanted to transfer his troops to New York City. The patriots' new cannon decided the matter. On March 17, the British and more than a thousand of their loyalist allies abandoned Boston forever.

British Evacuate Boston

That spring of 1776, as the British fleet left Boston for the temporary haven of Halifax, Nova Scotia, the colonies were moving inexorably toward the act the Massachusetts loyalists on board the British ships feared most: a declaration of independence. Even months after fighting began, American leaders still denied seeking a break with Great Britain. But in January 1776 there appeared a pamphlet by a man who both thought and advocated the unthinkable.

Thomas Paine's *Common Sense* exploded on the American scene like a bombshell. Within three months of publication, it sold 120,000 copies. The author, a radical English printer who had lived in America only since 1774, called stridently and stirringly for independence. More than that: Paine challenged many common American assumptions about government and the colonies' relationship to Britain. Rejecting the notion that a balance of monarchy, aristocracy, and democracy was necessary to preserve freedom, he advocated the establishment of a *republic*, a government by the people with no king or nobility. Instead of acknowledging the benefits of links to the mother country, Paine insisted that Britain had exploited the colonies unmercifully. In place of the frequently heard assertion that an independent America would be weak and divided, he substituted an unlimited confidence in America's strength when freed from European control.

Thomas Paine's *Common Sense*

These striking statements were expressed in equally striking prose. Scorning the rational style of most other pamphleteers, Paine adopted a furious, enraged tone. The king, he declared, was a "royal brute," a "wretch" who only pretended concern for the colonists' welfare. The pamphlet indeed reflected the oral culture of ordinary folk. Couched in everyday language, it relied heavily on the Bible—the only book familiar to most Americans—as a primary source of authority. No wonder the pamphlet had a wider distribution than any other political publication of its day.

There is no way of knowing how many people were converted to the cause of independence by reading *Common Sense*. But by late spring in 1776 independence had become inevitable. On May 10, the Second Continental Congress formally recommended that individual colonies "adopt such governments as shall, in the opinion of the representatives of the people, best conduce to the happiness and safety of their constituents in particular, and America in general." From that source stemmed the first state constitutions. Perceiving the trend of events, the few loyalists still connected with Congress severed their ties to that body.

Thomas Paine, the English radical who wrote Common Sense. *James Watson prepared this 1783 engraving from a portrait by Charles Willson Peale, who depicted his subject accompanied by the tools of the writer's trade—several sheets of paper and a quill pen.* National Portrait Gallery, Smithsonian Institution, Washington, D.C.

Then on June 7 came confirmation of the movement toward independence. Richard Henry Lee of Virginia, seconded by John Adams of Massachusetts, introduced the crucial resolution: "that these United Colonies are, and of right ought to be, free and independent States, that they are absolved of all allegiance to the British Crown, and that all political connection between them and the State of Great Britain is, and ought to be, totally dissolved." Congress debated but did not immediately adopt Lee's resolution. Instead, it postponed a vote until early July, to allow time for consultation and public reaction. In the meantime, a five-man committee—including Thomas Jefferson, John Adams, and Benjamin Franklin—was directed to draft a declaration of independence.

The committee assigned primary responsibility for writing the declaration to Jefferson, who was well known for his apt and eloquent style. Years later John Adams recalled that Jefferson had modestly protested his selection, suggesting that Adams prepare the initial draft. The Massachusetts revolutionary recorded his frank response: "You can write ten times better than I can."

Thomas Jefferson was at the time thirty-four years old, a Virginia lawyer educated at the College of William and Mary and in the law offices of a

Thomas Jefferson and the Declaration of Independence

prominent attorney. A member of the House of Burgesses, he had read widely in history and political theory. His broad knowledge was evident not only in the declaration but also in his draft of the Virginia state constitution, completed just a few days before his appointment to the committee. Jefferson, an intensely private man, loved his home and family deeply. This early stage of his political career was marked by his beloved wife Martha's repeated difficulties in childbearing. While he wrote and debated in Philadelphia, she suffered a miscarriage at their home, Monticello. Not until after her death in 1782, from complications following the birth of their sixth (but only third surviving) child in ten years of marriage, did Jefferson fully commit himself to public service.

The draft of the declaration was laid before Congress on June 28, 1776. The delegates officially voted for independence four days later, then debated the wording of the declaration for two more days, adopting it with some changes on July 4. Since

Americans had long ago ceased to see themselves as legitimate subjects of Parliament, the Declaration of Independence concentrated on George III (see the Appendix). That focus also provided an identifiable villain. The document accused the king of attempting to destroy representative government in the colonies and of oppressing Americans through the unjustified use of excessive force.

The declaration's chief long-term importance, however, did not lie in its lengthy catalogue of grievances against George III (including, in a section omitted by Congress, Jefferson's charge that the British monarchy had introduced slavery into America). It lay instead in the ringing statements of principle that have served ever since as the ideal to which Americans aspire: "We hold these truths to be self-evident: That all men are created equal; that they are endowed by their Creator with certain unalienable rights; that among these are life, liberty and the pursuit of happiness; that, to secure these rights, governments are instituted among men, deriving their just powers from the consent of the governed; that whenever any form of government becomes destructive of these ends, it is the right of the people to alter or to abolish it, and to institute new government." These phrases have echoed down through American history like no others.

The delegates in Philadelphia who voted to accept the Declaration of Independence did not have the advantage of our two centuries of hindsight. When they adopted the declaration, they risked their necks: they were committing treason. Thus when they concluded the declaration with the assertion that they "mutually pledge[d] to each other our lives, our fortunes, and our sacred honor," they spoke no less than the truth. The real struggle still lay before them, and few had Thomas Paine's boundless confidence in success.

 The Long Struggle in the North

In late June 1776, the first ships carrying Sir William Howe's troops from Halifax appeared off the coast of New York (see map, page 159). On July 2, the day

Loss of New York City

Congress voted for independence, redcoats landed on Staten Island. Howe, though, waited until mid-August, after the arrival of more troops from England, to begin his attack on the city. The delay gave Washington sufficient time to march his army of seventeen thousand south from Boston to meet the threat. But both he and his men, still inexperienced in fighting and maneuvering, made major mistakes, losing battles at Brooklyn Heights and on Manhattan Island. The city fell to the British, who captured nearly three thousand American soldiers. Those men spent most of the rest of the war imprisoned on British vessels anchored in New York harbor, where many died of disease.

During the autumn months, Washington retreated across New Jersey, with Howe in leisurely pursuit. The British took control of most of the state, and hundreds of New Jerseyites and Pennsylvanians (among them Joseph Galloway) accepted pardons for their "treasonous" activities. Occupying troops met little opposition, and the revolutionary cause appeared to be in disarray. "These are the times that try men's souls," wrote Thomas Paine in his pamphlet *The Crisis.* "The summer soldier and the sunshine patriot will, in this crisis, shrink from the service of his country; . . . yet we have this consolation with us, that the harder the conflict, the more glorious the triumph."

Campaign in New Jersey

The British let their advantage slip away as redcoats stationed in New Jersey went on a rampage of rape and plunder. Because loyalists and patriots were indistinguishable to British and Hessian troops, families on both sides suffered nearly equally. Livestock, crops, and firewood were seized for use by the British army. Houses were looted and burned, churches and public buildings desecrated. Yet nothing was better calculated to rally doubtful Americans to the cause than the murder of innocent civilians and the rape of women.

The soldiers' marauding alienated potentially loyal New Jerseyites and Pennsylvanians whose allegiance the British could ill afford to lose. It also spurred Washington's determination to strike back. Moving quickly, he attacked a Hessian encampment at Trenton early in the morning of December 26, while the redcoats were still reeling from their Christmas celebration. The patriots captured more than nine hundred Hessians and killed another thirty; only three Americans were wounded. A few days later, Washington attacked again at Princeton. Having gained command of the field and buoyed American spirits with the two swift victories, Wash-

The War in the North, 1775–1777 *The early phase of the Revolutionary War was dominated by British troop movements in the Boston area, the redcoats' evacuation to Nova Scotia in the spring of 1776, and the subsequent British invasion of New York and New Jersey.*

ington set up winter quarters at Morristown, New Jersey.

The 1776 campaign established patterns that persisted throughout much of the war, despite changes in British leadership and strategy. The British forces were usually more numerous and often better led than the Americans. But their ponderous style of maneuvering, lack of familiarity with the terrain, and inability to live off the land without antagonizing the populace partially offset those advantages. Furthermore, although Washington always seemed to lack regular troops—the Continental Army never numbered more than 18,500 men—he could usually count on the militia to join him at crucial times. American militiamen did not like to sign up for long terms of service or to fight far from home; but when their homes were threatened, they rallied to the cause. Washington and his officers complained about the militiamen's habit of disappearing during planting or harvesting. But time and again their presence, however brief, enabled the Americans to launch an attack or counter an important British thrust.

As the war dragged on, the Continental Army and the militia took on decidedly different characters. State governments, responsible for filling

At the Battle of Princeton in early 1777, American forces under George Washington cemented the victory they had won a few days earlier at Trenton. This view was painted in 1787 by James Peale, who fought in the battle.   Princeton University Library.

The American Army

military quotas, discovered that most men willing to enlist for long periods in the regular army were young, single, and footloose. Farmers with families tended to prefer short-term militia duty. As the supply of men willing to sign up with the Continentals dwindled, recruiters in northern states turned increasingly to African-Americans, both slave and free. Perhaps as many as five thousand blacks eventually served in the army, and most of them won their freedom as a result. They commonly served in racially integrated units but were assigned tasks that others shunned, such as cooking, foraging for food, and driving wagons. Also attached to the American forces were a number of women, the wives and widows of poor soldiers. Such camp followers worked as cooks, nurses, and launderers in return for rations and low wages. The presence of women, as well as militiamen who floated in and out of the American camp at irregular intervals, made for an unwieldy army that officers found difficult to manage. Yet the army's shapelessness also reflected its greatest strength: an almost unlimited reservoir of manpower and womanpower.

The officers of the Continental Army—those who enlisted for long periods or for the war's duration—developed an intense sense of pride and commitment to the revolutionary cause. The hardships they endured, the battles they fought, the difficulties they overcame all helped to forge an esprit de corps that outlasted the war. The realities of warfare were often dirty, messy, and corrupt, but the officers drew strength from a developing image of themselves as professionals who sacrificed personal gain for the good of the entire nation. When Benedict Arnold—an officer who fought heroically for the patriot cause early in the war—violated that virtuous self-image by defecting to the British, they made his name a metaphor for villainy. "How black, how despised, loved by none, and hated by all," wrote one patriot.

In 1777, the chief British effort was planned by the flashy "Gentleman Johnny" Burgoyne, a playboy general as much at home at the gaming tables of London as on the battlefield. A subordinate of Howe, Burgoyne spent the winter of 1776–1777 in London, where he gained the ear of Lord George Germain. Burgoyne convinced Germain that he could lead an invading force of redcoats and Indians down the Hudson River from Canada, cutting off New England from the rest of the states. He proposed to rendezvous near Albany with a similar force that would move east along the Mohawk River valley. The combined forces would then presumably link up with Sir William Howe's troops in New York City.

Planning the 1777 Campaign

That Burgoyne's scheme would give "Gentleman Johnny" all the glory and relegate Howe to a supporting role did not escape Sir William's notice. While Burgoyne was plotting in London, Howe was laying his own plans in New York. Joseph Galloway and other Pennsylvania loyalists persuaded Howe that Philadelphia could be taken easily and that many loyal residents would welcome his troops. Just as Burgoyne left Howe out of his plans, Howe left Burgoyne out of his. Thus the two major British armies in America would operate independently in 1777, and the result would be a disaster (see map).

Howe captured Philadelphia, but he did so in inexplicable fashion, delaying for months before beginning the campaign, then taking six weeks to transport his troops by sea instead of marching them overland. That maneuver cost him at least a month, debilitated his men, and depleted his supplies. Incredibly, at the end of the lengthy voyage, he was only 40 miles closer to Philadelphia than when he started. By the time Howe was ready to move on Philadelphia, Washington had had time to prepare its defenses. Twice, at Brandywine Creek and again at Germantown, the two armies clashed near the patriot capital. Although the British won both engagements, the Americans handled themselves well. The redcoats took Philadelphia in late September, but to little effect. The campaign season was nearly over; the revolutionary army had gained confidence in itself and its leaders; few welcoming loyalists had ma-

Howe Takes Philadelphia

Campaign of 1777 *The crucial campaign of 1777 was fought on two fronts: along the upper Hudson and Mohawk river valleys, and in the vicinity of Philadelphia. The rebels won in the north; the British triumphed—at least nominally—in the south. The capture of Philadelphia, however, did the redcoats little good, and they abandoned the city the following year.*

terialized; and, far to the north, Burgoyne was going down to defeat.

Burgoyne and his men set out from Montréal in mid-June 1777, floating down Lake Champlain into New York in canoes and flat-bottom boats. They easily took Fort Ticonderoga from its outnumbered and outgunned patriot defenders. Trouble began, however, when Burgoyne began an overland march. His clumsy artillery carriages and baggage wagons foundered in the heavy forests and ravines. Patriot militia felled giant trees across

Burgoyne's Campaign in New York

This kettledrum belonged to the band of the Royal Norfolk Regiment, a British infantry unit that surrendered to the Americans at Saratoga. The drum was sent to West Point, where it has remained ever since, a symbol of the new nation's first great victory of the Revolution. The West Point Museum Collection, U.S. Military Academy, West Point, NY. Photo by Paul Warchal.

his path to slow his progress. Consequently, Burgoyne's troops took twenty-four days to travel 23 miles. In August, the campaign suffered two sharp blows—first, when the redcoats and Indians marching east along the Mohawk River turned back after a battle at Oriskany, New York; second, when in a clash near Bennington, Vermont, American militiamen nearly wiped out eight hundred of Burgoyne's German mercenaries. Yet the general continued to dawdle, giving the Americans more than enough time to prepare for his coming. After several skirmishes with an American army commanded by General Horatio Gates, Burgoyne was surrounded near Saratoga, New York. On October 17, 1777, he surrendered his entire force of more than six thousand men.

The August 1777 battle at Oriskany was also important because it revealed a division in the Iroquois Confederacy (see pages 77–78). In 1776 the Six

Split of the Iroquois Confederacy

Nations had formally pledged to remain neutral in the Anglo-American struggle. But two influential Mohawk leaders, Joseph and Mary Brant, worked tirelessly to persuade their fellow Iroquois to join the British. Mary Brant, a powerful tribal matron, was also the widow of the Indian superintendent Sir William Johnson. Her younger brother Joseph, a renowned warrior, was convinced that the Six Nations should ally themselves with the British in order to prevent American encroachment on their lands. The Brants won over to the British the Senecas, Cayugas, and Mohawks, all of whom contributed warriors to the 1777 expedition. But the Oneidas—who had been converted to Christianity by Protestant missionaries—preferred the American side and brought the Tuscaroras with them. The Onondagas split into three factions, one on each side and one supporting neutrality. At Oriskany, some Oneidas and Tuscaroras joined patriot militiamen in fighting their Iroquois brethren; thus a league of friendship that had survived over three hundred years was torn apart.

The collapse of Iroquois unity and the confederacy's abandonment of neutrality had significant consequences. In 1778, Iroquois warriors allied with the British raided frontier villages in Pennsylvania and New York. To retaliate, the Americans dispatched an expedition under General John Sullivan the following summer to burn Iroquois crops, orchards, and settlements. The destruction was so thorough that many bands had to leave their ancestral homeland to seek food and shelter north of the Great Lakes during the winter of 1779–1780. A large number of Iroquois people never returned to New York but settled permanently in British Canada.

Burgoyne's surrender at Saratoga brought joy to patriots, discouragement to loyalists and Britons. In exile in London, Thomas Hutchinson wrote of "universal dejection" among loyalists there. "Everybody in a gloom," he commented; "most of us expect to lay our bones here." The disaster prompted Lord North to authorize a peace commission to offer the Americans what they had requested in 1774—in effect, a return to the imperial system of 1763. It was, of course, far too late for that: the patriots rejected the overture, and the peace commission sailed back to England empty-handed in mid-1778.

Most important of all, the American victory at Saratoga drew France formally into the conflict. Ever since 1763, the French had sought to avenge their defeat in the Seven Years War, and the American Revolution gave them that opportunity. Even before Benjamin Franklin arrived in Paris in late 1776, France was covertly supplying the revolutionaries with military necessities. Indeed, 90 percent of the gunpowder used by the Americans during the war's first two years came from France.

Benjamin Franklin worked tirelessly to strengthen ties between the two nations. He deliberately assumed a plain style of dress that made him stand out amid the luxury of the court of King Louis XVI. Presenting himself as a representative of American simplicity, he played on the French image of Americans as virtuous yeomen. Franklin's efforts culminated in 1778 when the countries signed two treaties. In the Treaty of Amity and Commerce, France recognized

Franco-American Alliance of 1778

Joseph Brant, the Iroquois leader who helped to persuade the Mohawks, Senecas, and Cayugas to support the British in the latter stages of the Revolution, as painted by Charles Willson Peale in 1797. Independence National Historic Park Collection.

American independence and established trade ties with the new nation. In the Treaty of Alliance, France and the United States promised—assuming that France would go to war with Britain, which it soon did—that neither would negotiate peace with the enemy without consulting the other. France also abandoned all its claims to Canada and to North American territory east of the Mississippi River. The most visible symbol of Franco-American cooperation in the years that followed was the Marquis de Lafayette, a young nobleman who volunteered for service with George Washington in 1777 and fought with American forces until the conflict ended.

The French alliance had two major benefits for the patriot cause. First, France began to aid the Americans openly, sending troops and naval vessels in addition to arms, ammunition, clothing, and blankets. Second, Great Britain could no longer focus solely on the American mainland, for it had to fight France in the Caribbean and elsewhere. Spain's entry into the war in 1779 as an ally of France (but not of the United States) further magnified Britain's problems, for the Revolution then became a global

James Armistead Lafayette, a Virginia slave, was first a spy and later a courier for General Lafayette during the Revolution. After the war, he adopted Lafayette's surname as his own and was freed by a special act of the state legislature. Valentine Museum, Gift of Mr. Louis E. Franck, Jr.

war. French assistance was important to Americans throughout the conflict, but in its last years the aid was particularly vital.

 ## The Long Struggle in the South

In the aftermath of the Saratoga disaster, Lord George Germain and British military officials reassessed their strategy. Maneuvering in the North had done them little good; perhaps shifting the field of battle southward would bring success. Many loyalist exiles in London encouraged this line of thinking. They argued that loyal southerners would welcome the redcoat army as liberators and that the region could serve as a base for attacking the North, once it had been pacified and returned to civilian control.

In early 1778 Sir William Howe was replaced by Sir Henry Clinton, who oversaw the regrouping of British forces in America. He ordered the evacuation of Philadelphia in June 1778 and dispatched a small expedition to Georgia at the end of the year. When Savannah and then Augusta fell easily into British hands, Clinton became convinced that a southern strategy would succeed. In late 1779 he sailed down the coast from New York to attack Charleston, the most important city in the South (see map, page 166).

The Americans worked hard to bolster Charleston's defenses, but the city fell to the British on May 12, 1780. General Benjamin Lincoln surrendered the entire southern army—5,500 men—to the invaders. In the weeks that followed, the redcoats spread through South Carolina, establishing garrisons at key points in the interior. Hundreds of South Carolinians renounced allegiance to the United States and proclaimed their loyalty to the Crown. Clinton organized loyalist regiments, and the process of pacification began.

Fall of Charleston

Yet the British triumph was less complete than it appeared. The success of the southern campaign depended on British control of the seas, for the British armies were so widely dispersed and travel by land so difficult that only through British naval vessels could the armies coordinate their efforts. For the moment, the Royal Navy safely dominated the American coastline, but French naval power posed a threat to the entire southern enterprise. Moreover, the redcoats never managed to establish full control of the areas they seized. Patriot bands operated freely throughout the state, and loyalists could not be guaranteed protection against their enemies. Last but not least, the fall of Charleston did not dishearten the patriots; instead, it spurred them to greater exertions. As one Marylander declared confidently, "The Fate of America is not to be decided by the Loss of a Town or Two." Patriot women in four states formed the Ladies Association, which collected money to purchase shirts for needy soldiers. Recruiting efforts were stepped up.

Nevertheless, the war in South Carolina went badly for the patriots throughout most of 1780. In August, a reorganized southern army under Horatio Gates was crushingly defeated at Camden by the forces of Lord Cornwallis, the new British commander in the South. The redcoats were joined wherever they went by hundreds, even thousands, of enslaved African-Americans seeking freedom on the basis of Lord Dunmore's proclamation. They ran away from their patriot masters individually and as families in such numbers that they seriously disrupted planting and harvesting in 1780 and 1781. More than fifty-five thousand slaves were lost to their owners as a result of the war. Not all of them joined the British or won their freedom if they did, but their flight had exactly the effect Dunmore wanted. Many served the British well as scouts, guides, and laborers.

A British cartoon published in 1780. Even after Spain and the Netherlands had joined France in supporting the Americans' quest for independence, this artist had confidence in Britain's ability to outweigh the alliance in "The Ballance of Power."   Miriam and Ira D. Wallach Division of Art, Prints and Photographs, The New York Public Library.

After the defeat at Camden, Washington (who had to remain in the North to oppose the British army occupying New York) appointed General Nathanael Greene of Rhode Island to command the southern campaign. Greene was appalled by what he found in South Carolina. "The word difficulty when applied to the state of things here . . . is almost without meaning, it falls so far short" of reality, he wrote to a friend. His troops needed clothing, blankets, and food, but "a great part of this country is already laid waste and in the utmost danger of becoming a desert." Incessant guerrilla warfare had, he commented, "so corrupted the principles of the people that they think of nothing but plundering one another."

In such circumstances, Greene had to move cautiously. He adopted a conciliatory policy toward loy-

Greene Rallies South Carolina

alists and neutrals, persuading the governor of South Carolina to offer pardons to those who had fought for the British if they would join the patriot militia. He also ordered his troops to treat captives fairly and not to loot loyalist property. Greene recognized that the patriots could win only by convincing the populace that they could bring stability to the region. He thus helped the shattered provincial congresses of Georgia and South Carolina to begin reestablishing civilian authority in the interior—a goal the British were never able to accomplish, even along the coast.

Greene also took a conciliatory approach to the southern Indians. With his desperate need for soldiers, he could not afford to have frontier militia companies occupied in defending their homes against Indian attacks. Since he had so few regulars (only sixteen hundred when he took command), Greene had to rely on western volunteers. Although

The War in the South *The southern war— after the British invasion of Georgia in late 1778—was characterized by a series of British thrusts into the interior, leading to battles with American defenders in both North and South Carolina. Finally, after promising beginnings, Cornwallis's foray into Virginia ended with disaster at Yorktown in October 1781.*

royal officials cooperating with the redcoat invaders initially won some Indian allies, Greene's careful diplomacy eventually proved successful. By war's end, only the Creeks remained allied with Great Britain.

Even before Greene took command of the southern army in December 1780, the tide had begun to turn. In October, at King's Mountain, a force from the settlements west of the Appalachians defeated a large party of redcoats and loyalists. Then in January 1781 Greene's trusted aide Brigadier General Daniel Morgan brilliantly defeated the crack British regiment Tarleton's Legion at Cowpens. Greene himself confronted the main body of British troops under Lord Cornwallis at Guilford Court House, North Carolina, in March. Although Cornwallis controlled the field at the end of the day, most of his army had been destroyed. He had to retreat to

Wilmington, on the coast, to receive supplies and fresh troops from New York by sea. Meanwhile, Greene returned to South Carolina, where, in a series of swift strikes, he forced the redcoats to abandon their interior posts and retire to Charleston.

Cornwallis had already ignored explicit orders not to leave South Carolina unless the state was safely in British hands. He headed north into Virginia, where he joined forces with a detachment of redcoats commanded by the American traitor Benedict Arnold. Instead of acting decisively with his new army of 7,200 men, Cornwallis withdrew to the peninsula between the York and James Rivers, where he fortified Yorktown and waited for supplies and reinforcements. Seizing the opportunity, Washington quickly moved more than 7,000 troops south from New York City. When a French fleet under the Comte de Grasse arrived from the Caribbean in time to defeat the Royal Navy vessels sent to relieve Cornwallis, the British general was trapped (see map). On October 19, 1781, Cornwallis surrendered to the combined American and French forces.

Surrender at Yorktown

When news of the surrender reached London, Lord North's ministry fell. Parliament voted to cease offensive operations in America and authorized peace negotiations. But guerrilla warfare between patriots and loyalists continued to ravage the Carolinas and Georgia for more than a year, and in the North vicious raids by both sides kept the frontier aflame. The persistence of conflict among guerrillas, frontiersmen, and Indians after the Battle of Yorktown, too often overlooked in accounts of the Revolution, serves to underscore the significance of the internal conflict that accompanied the more famous battles between the British and American armies.

Often overlooked also are the heavy costs of winning independence. More than twenty-five thousand American men died in the war, only about one-quarter of them from wounds suffered in battle. The rest were declared missing in action or died of disease or as prisoners of war. In the South, years of guerrilla warfare and the loss of thousands of runaway slaves shattered the economy. Indebtedness soared, and local governments were crippled for lack of funds, since few people could afford to pay their taxes. In the 1780s in Charles County, Maryland, for example, men commonly refused to serve in elective or appointive office because their personal estates would become liable for any taxes or fines they were unable to collect. Many of the county's formerly

How do historians know that Americans had only incomplete knowledge of the boundaries of their new nation? They know from consulting written documents and from looking at early maps like this one, "A New and Correct Map of the United States of North America," produced in 1784. New it certainly was, but correct it was not. A comparison with a standard map of the United States and Canada today shows many errors of scale, proportion, and placement of natural features. To point out just a few: the Ohio River is shown much too far south; the northern part of the Mississippi River is misplaced to the west; Lake Superior is too small, and its islands are too large; and the Nova Scotia peninsula is misshapen. What links all these features is that they were on the periphery of the new nation and thus on the margins of Americans' knowledge. But even so well known a waterway as Chesapeake Bay is inaccurately drawn, suggesting that residents of the United States still had much to learn about the geography of their country.   Photo: New Jersey Historical Society.

Measles, typhus, diphtheria, dysentery, and other diseases ravaged military encampments, so medicine chests like the one shown here were essential equipment for the army. Doctors used crude remedies that often did more harm than good, for little was known about the causes of such afflictions. Smallpox was one of the few epidemics that eighteenth-century doctors could combat: inoculation was known to be an effective preventive measure as early as the 1720s. The West Point Museum Collection, U.S. Military Academy, West Point, NY. Photo by Josh Nefsky.

wealthy planters descended into insolvency as a result of the war, and in the 1790s a traveler observed that "the country . . . wears a most dreary aspect," remarking on the "old dilapidated mansions" that had once housed well-to-do slaveowners.

Yet Charles County residents and Americans in general "all rejoiced" when they learned of the signing of a preliminary peace treaty at Paris in November 1782. The American diplomats—Benjamin Franklin, John Jay, and

Treaty of Paris

John Adams—ignored their instructions from Congress to be guided by France and instead negotiated directly with Great Britain. Their instincts were sound: the French government was more an enemy to Britain than a friend to the United States. In fact, French ministers worked secretly behind the scenes to try to prevent the establishment of a strong and unified government in America. Spain's desire to lay claim to the region between the Appalachian Mountains and the Mississippi River further complicated the negotiations. But the American delegates proved adept at power politics and achieved their main goal: independence as a united nation. The new British ministry, headed by Lord Shelburne (formerly an outspoken critic of Lord North's American poli-

cies), was weary of war and made numerous concessions—so many, in fact, that Parliament ousted the ministry shortly after peace terms were approved.

The treaty, signed formally on September 3, 1783, granted the Americans unconditional independence. The boundaries of the new nation were generous: to the north, approximately the present-day boundary with Canada; to the south, the 31st parallel (about the modern northern border of Florida); to the west, the Mississippi River. Florida, which Britain had acquired in 1763, was returned to Spain. The Americans also gained unlimited fishing rights off Newfoundland. In ceding so much land to the United States, Great Britain ignored the territorial rights of its Indian allies, sacrificing their interests to the demands of European politics. Loyalists and British merchants were also poorly served by British diplomats. The treaty's ambiguously worded clauses pertaining to the payment of prewar debts and the postwar treatment of loyalists caused trouble for years to come and proved impossible to enforce.

 Conclusion

The long war was finally over, and the victorious Americans could look back on their achievement with satisfaction and awe. In 1775, with an inexperienced ragtag army, they had taken on the greatest military power in the world—and eight years later they had won. They accomplished their goal more through persistence and commitment than through brilliance on the battlefield. Actual victories were few, but their army always survived defeats and standoffs to fight again. Ultimately, the Americans simply wore their enemy down.

In winning the war, the Americans reshaped the physical and mental landscapes in which they lived. They abandoned the British identity that once was so important to them, excluding from their new nation all those unwilling to make a break with the mother country. In the Continental Army in particular they began the process of creating loyalty to an entity that had no prior existence—a nation they named "the United States of America." They also established a claim to most of the territory east of the Mississippi River and south of the Great Lakes, thereby greatly expanding the land potentially open to their settlements.

In achieving independence, Americans surmounted formidable challenges. But in the future they faced perhaps even greater ones: establishing stable republican governments at the state and national levels to replace the monarchy they had rejected, and ensuring their government's continued existence in a world of bitter rivalries among the major powers—Britain, France, and Spain. Those European rivalries worked to the Americans' advantage during the war, but in the decades to come they would pose significant threats to the survival of the new nation.

Suggestions for Further Reading

General

Colin Bonwick, *The American Revolution* (1991); Edward Countryman, *The American Revolution* (1985); Theodore Draper, *A Struggle for Power: The American Revolution* (1996); Stephen G. Kurtz and James H. Hutson, eds., *Essays on the American Revolution* (1973); Robert Middlekauff, *The Glorious Cause: The American Revolution, 1763–1783* (1982); Harry M. Ward, *The American Revolution: Nationhood Achieved, 1763–1788* (1995); Alfred F. Young, ed., *Beyond the American Revolution* (1993); Alfred F. Young, ed., *The American Revolution: Explorations in the History of American Radicalism* (1976).

Military Affairs

Jeremy Black, *War for America: The Fight for Independence, 1775–1783* (1991); E. Wayne Carp, *To Starve the Army at Pleasure: Continental Army Administration and American Political Culture, 1775–1783* (1984); Stephen Conway, *The War of American Independence, 1775–1783* (1995); John C. Dann, ed., *The Revolution Remembered: Eyewitness Accounts of the War for Independence* (1980); Don Higginbotham, *The War of American Independence: Military Attitudes, Policies, and Practice, 1763–1789* (1971); Ronald Hoffman and Peter Albert, eds., *Arms and Independence: The Military Character of the American Revolution* (1984); Piers Mackesy, *The War for America, 1775–1783* (1964); James K. Martin, *Benedict Arnold, Revolutionary Hero* (1997); Charles P. Niemeyer, *America Goes to War: A Social History of the Continental Army* (1997); Charles Royster, *A Revolutionary People at War: The Continental Army and American Character, 1775–1783* (1980); John Shy, *A People Numerous and Armed: Reflections on the Military Struggle for American Independence*, rev. ed. (1990).

Local and Regional Studies

Richard Buel, *Dear Liberty: Connecticut's Mobilization for the Revolutionary War* (1980); Edward Countryman, *A People in Revolution: The American Revolution and Political Society in New York, 1760–1790* (1981); Jeffrey Crow and Larry Tise, eds., *The Southern Experience in the American Revolution* (1978); Thomas Doerflinger, *A Vigorous Spirit of Enterprise: Merchants and Economic Development in Revolutionary Philadelphia* (1986); David Hackett Fischer, *Paul Revere's Ride* (1994); Robert A. Gross, *The Minutemen and Their World* (1976); Ronald Hoffman, *A Spirit of Dissension: Economics, Politics, and the Revolution in Maryland* (1973); Ronald Hoffman, Thad W. Tate, and Peter Albert, eds., *An Uncivil War: The Southern Backcountry During the American Revolution* (1985); Jean B. Lee, *The Price of Nationhood: The American Revolution in Charles County* (1994); Bruce A. Ragsdale,

A Planters' Republic: The Search for Economic Independence in Revolutionary Virginia (1996); Stephen Rosswurm, *Arms, Country, and Class: The Philadelphia Militia and the "Lower Sort" During the American Revolution* (1988); John Selby, *The Revolution in Virginia, 1775–1783* (1988).

Indians and African-Americans

Colin Calloway, *The American Revolution in Indian Country: Crisis and Diversity in Native American Communities* (1995); Sylvia Frey, *Water from the Rock: Black Resistance in a Revolutionary Age* (1991); Barbara Graymont, *The Iroquois in the American Revolution* (1972); Isabel T. Kelsey, *Joseph Brant, 1743–1807: Man of Two Worlds* (1984); James H. O'Donnell III, *Southern Indians in the American Revolution* (1973); Anthony F. C. Wallace, *The Death and Rebirth of the Seneca* (1969).

Loyalists

Bernard Bailyn, *The Ordeal of Thomas Hutchinson* (1974); Robert McCluer Calhoon, *The Loyalists in Revolutionary America, 1760–1781* (1973); Mary Beth Norton, *The British-Americans: The Loyalist Exiles in England, 1774–1789* (1972); Janice Potter, *The Liberty We Seek: Loyalist Ideology in Colonial New York and Massachusetts* (1983); Paul H. Smith, *Loyalists and Redcoats: A Study in British Revolutionary Policy* (1964); James W. St. G. Walker, *The Black Loyalists: The Search for a Promised Land in Nova Scotia and Sierra Leone, 1783–1870* (1976).

Women

Richard Buel and Joy Buel, *The Way of Duty: A Woman and Her Family in Revolutionary America* (1984); Ronald Hoffman and Peter Albert, eds., *Women in the Age of the American Revolution* (1989); Linda K. Kerber, *Women of the Republic: Intellect and Ideology in Revolutionary America* (1980); Mary Beth Norton, *Liberty's Daughters: The Revolutionary Experience of American Women, 1750–1800* (1980).

Foreign Policy

Jonathan Dull, *A Diplomatic History of the American Revolution* (1985); Ronald Hoffman and Peter Albert, eds., *Peace and the Peacemakers: The Treaty of 1783* (1986); Ronald Hoffman and Peter Albert, eds., *Diplomacy and Revolution: The Franco-American Alliance of 1778* (1981); Lawrence Kaplan, ed., *The American Revolution and a "Candid World"* (1977); Jan Willem Schulte Nordholt, *The Dutch Republic and American Independence* (1982); Richard W. Van Alstyne, *Empire and Independence: The International History of the American Revolution* (1965).

Patriot Leaders

Fawn M. Brodie, *Thomas Jefferson: An Intimate History* (1974); Richard Brookhiser, *Founding Father: Rediscovering George Washington* (1996); Joseph Ellis, *American Sphinx: The Character of Thomas Jefferson* (1997); John E. Ferling, *The First of Men: A Life of George Washington* (1988); Eric Foner, *Tom Paine and Revolutionary America* (1976); Norman Risjord, *Thomas Jefferson* (1994); Charles Royster, *Light-Horse Harry Lee and the Legacy of the American Revolution* (1981); Peter Shaw, *The Character of John Adams* (1976); Sheila Skemp, *Benjamin and William Franklin: Father and Son, Patriot and Loyalist* (1994); Esmond Wright, *Franklin of Philadelphia* (1986).

CHAPTER

7

Forging a National Republic
1776–1789

On January 25, 1787, an army of fifteen hundred farmers from the hills and valleys of western Massachusetts advanced on the Springfield federal armory, which housed 450 tons of military supplies, including seven thousand muskets and thirteen hundred barrels of gunpowder. Inside the arsenal, General William Shepard prepared his group of one thousand militiamen to resist the assault. First, though, he dispatched two aides to warn the farmers that they would soon "inevitably" draw the fire of men who had been their officers during the Revolutionary War. "That is all we want, by God!" replied one of the rebels. The farmers moved toward the armory, urged on by the commands of Daniel Shays, one of their leaders. "March, God Damn you, March!" he shouted. Shepard fired two cannon over the heads of the farmers, and then—when that did not frighten them—ordered his men to shoot directly at the straggling ranks. Four men died, twenty were wounded, and the rebels withdrew.

What caused this violent clash between former comrades in arms, so soon after the war? Massachusetts farmers were angered by high taxes and the scarcity of money. Since the preceding summer, they had organized committees and crowd actions—the tactics used so successfully in the 1760s and early 1770s—to halt state efforts to seize property for nonpayment of taxes. Many of the insurgents were respected war veterans, described as "gentlemen" in contemporary accounts of the riots. Daniel Shays, their nominal leader (he disclaimed the title), had been a captain in the Continental Army. Clearly the episode could not be dismissed as the work of an unruly rabble. What did the uprising mean for the republic's future? Was it a sign of impending anarchy?

The protesters explained their position in an address to the Massachusetts government. They proclaimed their loyalty to the nation but

A woodcut of Daniel Shays and one of his chief officers, Job Shattuck, in 1787.   National Portrait Gallery, Smithsonian Institution, Washington, D.C.

objected to the state's fiscal policies, which, they said, prevented them from providing adequately for their families. Referring to their experience as revolutionary soldiers, they asserted that they "esteem[ed] one moment of Liberty to be worth an eternity of Bondage." One rebel sympathizer explained, "Whenever any encroachments are made either upon the liberties or properties of the people, if redress cannot be had without, it is virtue in them to disturb government." The Massachusetts government was "tyrannical," Shays asserted, and, like that of Great Britain, deserved to be overthrown.

To the state's elected leaders, the most ominous aspect of the uprising was the farmers' attempt to link their rebellion with the earlier struggle for independence. The state legislature insisted that "in a republican government the majority must govern. If the minor part governs it becomes aristocracy; if every one opposed at his pleasure, it is no government, it is anarchy and confusion." In short, the crowd actions that once had been a justifiable response to British tyranny were no longer legitimate.

In a republic, reform had to come through the ballot box rather than by force. If the nation's citizens refused to submit to legitimate authority, the result would be chaos and political collapse.

The confrontation at the Springfield armory symbolized for many Americans the trials facing the new nation. That the rebels were dispersed easily, that their leaders (including Shays) had to flee to neighboring states for asylum, that two of the insurgents were hanged, and that a newly elected legislature adopted conciliatory measures—none of these outcomes altered American political leaders' interpretation of the events in western Massachusetts. In Shays's Rebellion they thought they discerned the first signs of disintegration of the republic they had worked so hard to establish.

Republicanism—the idea that governments should be based wholly on the consent of the people—originated with political theorists in ancient Greece and Rome. Republics, such writers declared, were desirable yet fragile forms of government. Unless their citizens were especially virtuous—that is,

• *Important Events* •

1776	Second Continental Congress directs states to draft constitutions	**1788**	Hamilton, Jay, and Madison write *The Federalist* to urge ratification of the Constitution by New York Constitution ratified
1777	Articles of Confederation sent to states for ratification	**1794**	Defeat of Miami Confederacy at Fallen Timbers
1781	Articles of Confederation ratified	**1795**	Treaty of Greenville opens Ohio to white settlement
1786	Annapolis Convention meets, discusses reforming government	**1800**	Mason Locke Weems publishes his *Life of Washington*
1786–87	Shays's Rebellion in western Massachusetts raises questions about future of the republic		
1787	Northwest Ordinance organizes territory north of Ohio River and east of Mississippi River Constitutional Convention drafts new form of government		

sober, moral, and industrious—and largely in agreement on key issues, republics were doomed to failure. When Americans left the British Empire, they abandoned the idea that the best system of government balanced monarchy, aristocracy, and democracy—or, to put it another way, that a stable polity required participation by a king, the nobility, and the people. They substituted a belief in the superiority of republicanism, in which the people, not Parliament, were sovereign. Now Americans had to deal with the potentially unwelcome consequences of that decision. How could they best ensure political stability? How could they foster consensus among the populace? How could they create and sustain a virtuous republic?

America's political and intellectual leaders worked hard to inculcate virtue in their fellow countrymen and countrywomen. After 1776, American literature, theater, art, architecture, and education all pursued explicitly moral goals. The education of women was considered particularly important, for as the mothers of the republic's children, they were primarily responsible for ensuring the nation's future. On such matters Americans could agree, but they disagreed on many other critical issues. Almost all white men concurred that women, Indians, and African-Americans should be excluded from formal participation in politics, but they found it difficult to reach a

consensus on how many of their own number should be included, how often elections should be held, or how their new governments should be structured.

Republican citizens had to make many other decisions as well. Should a republic conduct its dealings with Indian nations and foreign countries any differently than other types of governments did? Were republics, in other words, obliged to negotiate fairly and honestly at all times? And then there were Thomas Jefferson's words in the Declaration of Independence: "all men are created equal." Given that bold statement of principle, how could white republicans justify holding African-Americans in perpetual bondage? Some answered that question by freeing their slaves or by voting for state laws that abolished slavery. Others responded by denying that blacks were "men" in the same sense as whites.

The most important task facing Americans in these years was the construction of a genuinely national government. Before 1765, the British mainland colonies had rarely cooperated on common endeavors. Many circumstances separated them: their diverse economies, varying religious traditions and ethnic compositions, competing land claims (especially in the West), and different political systems. But fighting the Revolutionary War brought them together and created a new nationalistic spirit, especially among those who served in the Continental

Army or the diplomatic corps. Wartime experiences broke down at least some of the boundaries that previously had divided Americans, replacing loyalties to state and region with loyalties to the nation.

Still, forging a national republic (as opposed to a set of loosely connected state republics) was neither easy nor simple. America's first such government, under the Articles of Confederation, proved to be inadequate. But some of the nation's political leaders learned from their experiences and tried another approach when they drafted the Constitution in 1787. Some historians have argued that the Articles of Confederation and the Constitution reflect opposing political philosophies, the Constitution representing an "aristocratic" counterrevolution against the "democratic" Articles. The two documents are more accurately viewed as successive attempts to solve the same problems. Both applied theories of republicanism to practical problems of governance; neither was entirely successful in resolving those difficulties.

 ## Creating a Virtuous Republic

When the colonies declared their independence from Great Britain, John Dickinson recalled many years later, "there was no question concerning forms of Government, no enquiry whether a Republic or a limited Monarchy was best. . . . We knew that the people of this country must unite themselves under some form of Government and that this could be no other than the republican form." But how should that goal be implemented?

Three different definitions of *republicanism* emerged in the new United States. The first, held chiefly by members of the educated elite (such as the Adamses of Massachusetts), was based directly on ancient history and political theory. The histories of popular governments in Greece and Rome seemed to prove that republics could succeed only if they were small in size and homogeneous in population. Unless a republic's citizens were willing to sacrifice their own private interests for the good of the whole, the government would collapse. A truly virtuous man, classical republican theory insisted, had to forgo personal profit and work solely for the best interests of the nation. In return for sacrifices, though, a republic offered its citizens equality of opportunity. Under such a government, rank would be based

Varieties of Republicanism

on merit rather than on inherited wealth and status. Society would be governed by members of a "natural aristocracy," men whose talent had elevated them from what might have been humble beginnings to positions of power and privilege. Rank would not be abolished but instead would be founded on merit.

A second definition, advanced by other members of the elite but also by some skilled craftsmen, drew more on economic theory than on political thought. Instead of perceiving the nation as an organic whole composed of people nobly sacrificing for the common good, this version of republicanism followed the Scottish theorist Adam Smith in emphasizing individuals' pursuit of rational self-interest. The applicability of this approach was underscored by the huge profits some men reaped from patriotism by selling supplies to the army. The nation could only benefit from aggressive economic expansion, argued men such as Alexander Hamilton. When republican men sought to improve their own economic and social circumstances, the entire nation would benefit. Republican virtue would be achieved through the pursuit of private interests, rather than through subordination to some communal ideal.

The third notion of republicanism was more egalitarian than the other two, which both contained considerable potential for inequality. This view was less influential because many of its proponents were illiterate or barely literate and thus wrote little to promote their beliefs. Men who advanced the third version of republicanism, the most prominent of whom was Thomas Paine, called for widening men's participation in the political process. They also wanted government to respond directly to the needs of ordinary folk, rejecting any notion that the "lesser sort" should automatically defer to their "betters." They were, indeed, democrats in more or less the modern sense. For them, republican virtue was embodied in the untutored wisdom of the people as a whole, rather than in the special insights of a natural aristocracy or the pronouncements of wealthy individuals.

Despite the differences, the three strands of republicanism shared many of the same assumptions. For example, all three contrasted a virtuous, industrious America to the corruption of Britain and Europe. In the first version, that virtue manifested itself in frugality and self-sacrifice; in the second, it would prevent self-interest from becoming vice; in the third, it was the justification for including even propertyless free men in the ranks of voters. "Virtue,

Virtue alone . . . is the basis of a republic," asserted Dr. Benjamin Rush of Philadelphia, an ardent patriot, in 1778. His fellow Americans concurred, even if they defined virtue in divergent ways. Most agreed that a virtuous country would be composed of hardworking citizens who would dress simply and live plainly, elect wise leaders to public office, and forgo the conspicuous consumption of luxury goods.

As citizens of the United States set out to construct their republic, they believed they were embarking on an unprecedented enterprise. With great pride in their new nation, they

Virtue and the Arts

expected to replace the vices of monarchical Europe—immorality, selfishness, and lack of public-spiritedness—with the sober virtues of republican America. They wanted to embody republican principles not only in their governments but also in their society and culture. They looked to painting, literature, drama, and architecture to convey messages of nationalism and virtue to the public.

Americans faced a crucial contradiction at the very outset of their efforts. To some republicans, the fine arts themselves were manifestations of vice. Their existence in a virtuous society, many contended, signaled the arrival of luxury and corruption. What need did a frugal yeoman have for a painting—or, worse yet, a novel? Why should anyone spend hard-earned wages to see a play in a lavishly decorated theater? The first American artists, playwrights, and authors thus confronted an impossible dilemma. They wanted to produce works embodying virtue, but those very works, regardless of their content, were viewed by many as corrupting.

Still, they tried. William Hill Brown's *The Power of Sympathy* (1789), the first novel written in the United States, was a lurid tale of seduction intended as a warning to young women, who made up a large proportion of America's fiction readers. In Royall Tyler's *The Contrast* (1787), the first successful American play, the virtuous conduct of Colonel Manly was contrasted (hence the title) with the reprehensible behavior of the fop Billy Dimple. The most popular book of the era, Mason Locke Weems's *Life of Washington*, published in 1800 shortly after George Washington's death, was intended by its author to "hold up his great Virtues . . . to the imitation of Our Youth." Weems could hardly be accused of subtlety. The famous tale he invented—six-year-old George bravely admitting cutting down his father's favorite cherry tree—ended

with George's father exclaiming, "Run to my arms, you dearest boy. . . . Such an act of heroism in my son, is worth more than a thousand trees, though blossomed with silver, and their fruit of purest gold."

Painting and architecture, too, were expected to embody high moral standards. Two of the most prominent artists of the period, Gilbert Stuart and Charles Willson Peale, painted innumerable portraits of upstanding republican citizens. John Trumbull's vast canvases depicted milestones of American history such as the Battle of Bunker Hill, Burgoyne's surrender at Saratoga, and Cornwallis's capitulation at Yorktown. Such portraits and historical scenes were intended to instill patriotic sentiments in their viewers. Architects likewise hoped to convey in their buildings a sense of the young republic's ideals. When the Virginia government asked Thomas Jefferson, then minister to France, for advice on the design of the state capitol in Richmond, Jefferson unhesitatingly recommended copying a Roman building, the Maison Carrée at Nîmes. "It is very simple," he explained, "but it is noble beyond expression." Jefferson set forth ideals that would guide American architecture for a generation to come: simplicity of line, harmonious proportions, a feeling of grandeur. Nowhere were these rational goals of republican art manifested more clearly than in Benjamin H. Latrobe's plans for the majestic domed United States Capitol in Washington, D.C., built shortly after the turn of the century.

Despite the artists' efforts (or, some would have said, because of them), some Americans were beginning to detect signs of luxury and corruption by the mid-1780s. The resumption of European trade after the war brought a return to fashionable clothing for both men and women and abandonment of the simpler homespun garments patriots had once worn with pride. Elite families again attended balls and concerts. Parties no longer seemed complete without gambling and cardplaying. Social clubs for young people multiplied; Samuel Adams worried in print about the opportunities for corruption lurking behind plans for tea drinking and genteel conversation among Boston youths. Especially alarming to fervent republicans was the establishment in 1783 of the Society of the Cincinnati, a hereditary organization of Revolutionary War officers and their descendants. Many feared that the group would become the nucleus of a native-born aristocracy. All these developments directly challenged the United States's self-image as a virtuous republic.

Thomas Jefferson's design for the front of the Virginia state capitol (c. 1785) epitomized the architectural ideals of the republic. Massachusetts Historical Society.

Americans' deep-seated concern for the future of the infant republic focused their attention on their children, the "rising generation." Throughout the history of the colonies, education had been seen chiefly as a private means to personal advancement, of concern only to individual families. Now, though, education would serve a public purpose. If young people were to resist the temptations of vice, they would have to learn the lessons of virtue at home and at school. In fact, the very survival of the nation depended on it. The early republican period was thus a time of major educational reform.

Educational Reform

The 1780s and 1790s brought two significant changes in American educational practice. First, in contrast to the colonies, where nearly all education had been privately financed, some northern states began to use tax money to support public elementary schools. In 1789, Massachusetts became one of the first states to require towns to offer their citizens free public elementary education.

Second, schooling for girls was improved. Americans' recognition of the importance of the rising generation led to the realization that mothers would have to be properly educated if they were to instruct their children adequately. Therefore Massachusetts insisted in its 1789 law that town elementary schools be open to girls as well as boys. Throughout the United States, private academies were founded to give teenage girls from well-to-do families an opportunity for advanced schooling. No one yet proposed opening colleges to women, but a few fortunate girls could study history, geography, rhetoric, and mathematics. The academies also trained female students in fancy needlework—the only artistic endeavor considered appropriate for genteel women.

The chief theorist of women's education in the early republic was Judith Sargent Murray of Gloucester, Massachusetts. In a series of essays

Judith Sargent Murray and Women's Education

published in the 1780s and 1790s, Murray argued that women and men had equal intellectual capacities, though women's inadequate education might make them seem less intelligent. "We can only reason from what we know," she declared, "and if an opportunity of acquiring knowledge hath been denied us, the inferiority of our sex cannot fairly be deduced from thence." Therefore, concluded Murray, boys and girls should be offered equivalent scholastic training. She further contended that girls should be taught to support themselves by their own efforts: "Independence should be placed within their grasp."

Murray's direct challenge to the traditional colonial belief that, as one man put it, girls "knew quite enough if they could make a shirt and a pudding" was part of a general rethinking of women's position that occurred as a result of the Revolution. Male patriots who enlisted in the army or served in Congress were away from home for long periods of time. In their absence their wives, who previously had handled only the "indoor affairs" of the household, shouldered the responsibility for "outdoor affairs" as well. As the wife of a Connecticut militiaman later recalled, her husband "was out more or less during the remainder of the war [after 1777], so much so as to be unable to do anything on our farm. What was done, was done by myself." Similarly, John and Abigail Adams took great pride in Abigail's developing skills as a "farmeress." Like her female contemporaries, Abigail Adams stopped calling the farm "yours" in letters to her husband and began referring to it as "ours"—a revealing change of pronoun. Both men and women realized that female patriots had made vital and important contributions to winning the war through their work at home and that their notions of proper gender roles had to be rethought. Americans began to develop new ideas about the role women should play in a republican society.

The best-known example of those new ideas is a letter Abigail Adams addressed to her husband

Judith Sargent (1751–1820), later Mrs. John Murray, painted by John Singleton Copley when she was in her late teens. Although her steady gaze suggests clear-headed intelligence, there is little in the stylized portrait—typical of Copley's work at the time—to suggest her later emergence as the first notable American feminist theorist. Frick Art Reference Library.

in March 1776. "In the new Code of Laws which I suppose it will be necessary for you to make I desire you

Abigail Adams: "Remember the Ladies"

would Remember the Ladies," she wrote. "Remember all Men would be tyrants if they could. . . . If perticuliar care and attention is not paid to the Laidies we are determined to foment a Rebelion, and will not hold ourselves bound by any Laws in which we have no voice, or Representation." With these words, Abigail Adams took a step that was soon to be duplicated by other disfranchised Americans. She deliberately applied the ideology developed to combat parliamentary supremacy to purposes revolutionary leaders had never intended. Since men were

"Naturally Tyrannical," she argued, the United States should reform colonial marriage laws, which made wives subordinate to their husbands.

Abigail Adams did not ask that women be allowed to vote, but others claimed that right. The men who drafted the New Jersey state constitution in 1776 defined voters carelessly as "all free inhabitants" who met certain property qualifications. They thereby unintentionally gave the vote to property-holding white spinsters and widows, as well as to free blacks. Qualified women and African-Americans regularly voted in New Jersey's local and congressional elections until 1807, when they were disfranchised by the state legislature, which falsely alleged that they had engaged in widespread vote fraud. Yet the fact that women voted at all was evidence of their altered perception of their place in the political life of the country.

Such dramatic episodes were unusual. After the war, European-Americans still viewed women in traditional terms, continuing to believe that women's primary function was to be good wives, mothers, and mistresses of households. They perceived significant differences between male and female characters.

Women's Role in the Republic

That distinction eventually enabled Americans to resolve the conflict between the two most influential strands of republican thought and led to new roles for some women. Because wives could not own property or participate directly in economic life, women in general came to be seen as the embodiment of self-sacrificing, disinterested republicanism. Through new female-run charitable associations founded after the war, better-off women assumed public responsibilities, in particular through caring for poor widows and orphaned children. Thus men were freed from the naggings of conscience as they pursued their economic self-interest (that other republican virtue), secure in the knowledge that their wives and daughters were fulfilling the family's obligation to the common good. The ideal republican man, therefore, was an individualist, seeking advancement for himself and his family. The ideal republican woman, by contrast, always put the well-being of others ahead of her own.

Together white men and women established the context for the creation of a virtuous republic. But nearly 20 percent of the American population was black. How did approximately 700,000 African-Americans fit into the developing national plan?

Emancipation and the Growth of Racism

Revolutionary ideology exposed one of the primary contradictions in American society. Both blacks and whites saw the irony in slaveholding Americans' claims that one of their aims in taking up arms was to prevent Britain from "enslaving" them. Many revolutionary leaders voiced the theme. In 1773 Dr. Benjamin Rush called slavery "a vice which degrades human nature," warning ominously that "the plant of liberty is of so tender a nature that it cannot thrive long in the neighborhood of slavery." Common folk also saw the contradiction. When Josiah Atkins, a Connecticut soldier marching south, saw Washington's plantation, he observed in his journal: "Alas! That persons who pretend to stand for the rights of mankind for the liberties of society, can delight in oppression, & that even of the worst kind!"

African-Americans did not need revolutionary ideology to tell them that slavery was wrong, but they quickly took advantage of that ideology. In 1779 a group of slaves from Portsmouth, New Hampshire, asked the state legislature "from what authority [our masters] assume to dispose of our lives, freedom and property," pleading "that the name of slave may not more be heard in a land gloriously contending for the sweets of freedom." The same year several bondspeople in Fairfield, Connecticut, petitioned the legislature for their freedom, characterizing slavery as a "dreadful Evil" and "flagrant Injustice." How could men who were "nobly contending in the Cause of Liberty," they asked, continue "this detestable Practice"?

Both legislatures responded negatively, but the postwar years did witness the gradual abolition of slavery in the North. Vermont abolished slavery in its 1777 constitution. Massachusetts courts decided in the 1780s that a clause in the state constitution prohibited slavery. Pennsylvania passed an abolition law in 1780; four years later Rhode Island and Connecticut provided for gradual emancipation, followed by New York (1799) and New Jersey (1804). Although New Hampshire did not formally abolish slavery, only eight slaves were reported on the 1800 census, and none remained a decade later.

Gradual Emancipation

No southern state adopted similar general emancipation laws, but the legislatures of Virginia (1782), Delaware (1787), and Maryland (1790 and

1796) altered laws that previously had restricted slaveowners' ability to free their bondspeople. South Carolina and Georgia never considered adopting such acts, and North Carolina insisted that all manumissions (emancipations of individual slaves) be approved by county courts.

Revolutionary ideology thus had limited impact on the well-entrenched economic interests of large slaveholders. Only in the North, where slaves were relatively rare and where little money was invested in human capital, could state legislatures easily vote to abolish slavery. Even there, legislators' concern for property rights—the Revolution, after all, was fought for property as well as life and liberty—led them to favor gradual emancipation over immediate abolition. Most states provided only for the freeing of children born after passage of the law, not for the emancipation of adults. And even those children were to remain slaves until reaching adulthood. Still, by 1840 in only one northern state—New Jersey—were African-Americans legally held in bondage.

Despite the slow progress of abolition, the number of free people of African descent in the United States grew dramatically in the first years after the Revolution. Before the war there had been few free blacks in America. According to a 1755 Maryland census, for example, only 4 percent of the African-Americans in the colony were free. Most blacks emancipated before the war were *mulattos*, born of unions between enslaved women and their masters, who then manumitted the children. But wartime disruptions radically changed the size and composition of the freed population. Slaves who had escaped from plantations during the war, others who had served in the American army, and still others who had been emancipated by their owners or by state laws were now free. By 1790 there were nearly 60,000 free people of color in the United States; ten years later they numbered more than 108,000, nearly 11 percent of the total African-American population.

The effects of postwar manumissions were felt most sharply in the Chesapeake, where they were fostered by economic changes such as declining soil fertility and the shift from tobacco to grain production. Since grain cultivation was less labor-intensive than tobacco growing, planters began to complain about "excess" slaves. They occasionally solved that problem by freeing some of their less productive or

Growth of Free Black Population

Robert Carter was one of the largest slaveholders in Virginia. After the state altered its manumission laws and he had become a Baptist, he decided to free all his bondspeople. He worked out a plan of gradual emancipation, freeing some slaves each year for several years. Hannah, one of his weavers, wrote to him in April 1792, requesting that she be allowed to buy her loom when she was emancipated the following January. This is one of only a handful of documents known to be written by literate slave women during the eighteenth century. Chicago Historical Society, Robert Carter Papers.

more favored bondspeople. The free black population of Virginia more than doubled between 1790 and 1810, and by the latter year nearly one-quarter of Maryland's African-American population was no longer in legal bondage.

In the 1780s and thereafter, freed people often made their way to northern port cities. Boston and Philadelphia, where slavery was abolished sooner than in New York City, were popular destinations. Women outnumbered men among the migrants by a margin of three to two. Black women found more opportunities for employment, particularly as domestic servants, in the cities than in the countryside. Some freedmen also worked in domestic service, but larger numbers were employed as unskilled laborers and seamen. A few of the women

Migration to Northern Cities

How do historians know that the 1780s and 1790s marked a key turning point in the history of slavery and racism in the United States? The emancipation and manumission laws adopted by state legislatures, coupled with debates in pamphlets and newspapers, are important indications of a shift in Americans' thinking. But a painting such as the one reproduced here, Liberty Displaying the Arts and Sciences, *offers a unique visual perspective on the same developments. In 1792, the Library Company of Philadelphia, a private lending library founded in the mid-eighteenth century, commissioned the artist Samuel Jennings to produce a depiction of slavery and abolitionism showing the "figure of Liberty (with her Cap and proper Insignia) displaying the arts." The library's directors reportedly were well pleased with the results. The painting, probably the first to celebrate emancipation, shows the blonde goddess presenting books (symbolizing knowledge and freedom) to several suppliant and grateful blacks, while in the background a group of former slaves dances joyfully around a liberty pole. Although the theme is abolition and the African-Americans in the foreground have realistic features, the portrayal of blacks in passive roles and diminutive sizes portends future stereotypical images. Thus the picture simultaneously linked emancipation and the growth of racism.* The Library Company of Philadelphia.

and a sizable proportion of men (nearly one-third of those in Philadelphia in 1795) were skilled workers or retailers. These people chose new names for themselves, exchanging the surnames of former masters for names like Newman or Brown, and as soon as possible they established independent two-parent nuclear families instead of continuing to live in their employers' households. They also began to occupy distinct neighborhoods, probably as the combined result of discrimination and a desire for racial solidarity.

Emancipation did not bring equality. Even whites who recognized African-Americans' right to freedom were unwilling to accept them as equals. Laws discriminated against emancipated blacks as they had against slaves. South Carolina, for example, did not permit free blacks to testify against whites in court. Public schools often refused to educate their children. Freedmen found it difficult to purchase property and find good jobs. And though in many areas African-Americans were accepted as members—even ministers—of evangelical churches, whites rarely allowed them an equal voice in church affairs.

Gradually, freed people developed their own institutions, often based in their own neighborhoods. In Charleston, mulattos formed the Brown Fellowship Society, which provided insurance coverage for its members, financed a school, and helped to support orphans. In 1794, blacks in Philadelphia and Baltimore founded societies that eventually became the African Methodist Episcopal (AME) denomination. AME churches later sponsored schools in a number of cities and, along with African Baptist, African Episcopal, and African Presbyterian churches, became cultural centers of the free black community. Freed people quickly learned that, to survive and prosper, they had to rely on their own collective efforts rather than on the benevolence or goodwill of their white compatriots.

Freed People's Churches and Associations

Their endeavors were all the more necessary because the postrevolutionary years witnessed the development of a coherent racist theory in the United States. Whites had long regarded their slaves as inferior, but the most influential writers on race attributed that inferiority to environmental factors. They argued that blacks' seemingly debased character derived from their enslavement,

Development of Racist Theory

rather than enslavement being the consequence of inherited inferiority. In the Revolution's aftermath, though, white southerners needed to defend their enslavement of other human beings against the notion that "all men are created equal." Consequently, they began to argue that blacks were less than fully human and that the principles of republican equality applied only to whites. In other words, to avoid having to confront the contradiction between their practice and the egalitarian implications of revolutionary theory, they redefined the theory so that it would not apply to African-Americans.

This racism had several intertwined elements. First was the assertion that, as Thomas Jefferson suggested in 1781, blacks were "inferior to the whites in the endowments both of body and mind." Then came the belief that blacks were congenitally lazy, dishonest, and uncivilized (or uncivilizable). Third, and of crucial importance, was the notion that all blacks were sexually promiscuous and that black men lusted after white women. The specter of interracial sexual intercourse involving black men and white women haunted early American racist thought. Significantly, the more common reverse circumstance—the sexual exploitation of enslaved women by their white masters—aroused little comment.

African-Americans did not allow these developing racist notions to go unchallenged. Benjamin Banneker, a free black surveyor, astronomer, and mathematical genius, directly disputed Thomas Jefferson's belief in blacks' intellectual inferiority. In 1791 Banneker sent Jefferson a copy of his latest almanac (which included his astronomical calculations) as an example of blacks' mental powers. Jefferson's response admitted Banneker's capability but indicated that he regarded Banneker as exceptional; Jefferson insisted that he needed more evidence before he would change his mind.

At its birth, then, the republic was defined by its leaders as an exclusively white enterprise. Indeed, some historians have argued that the subjugation of blacks was a necessary precondition for equality among whites. They have pointed out that identifying a common racial antagonist helped to create white solidarity and to lessen the threat to gentry power posed by the enfranchisement of poorer whites. Some have asserted that it was less dangerous to allow whites with little property to participate formally in politics than to open the possibility that

A Republic for Whites Only

they might join with former slaves to question the rule of the "better sort." That was perhaps one reason why after the Revolution the division of American society between slave and free was transformed into a division between blacks—some of whom were free—and whites. The wielders of power ensured their continued dominance in part by substituting race for enslavement as the primary determinant of African-Americans' status.

Designing Republican Governments

In May 1776, even before adoption of the Declaration of Independence, the Second Continental Congress directed states to devise new republican governments to replace the provincial congresses and committees that had met since 1774. Thus Americans initially concentrated on drafting state constitutions and devoted little attention to their national government—an oversight they later were forced to remedy.

At the state level, they immediately faced the problem of defining just what a constitution was. The British Constitution could not serve as a model because it was a mixture of law and custom; Americans wanted tangible documents specifying the fundamental structures of government. Several years passed before states concluded that their constitutions, unlike ordinary laws, could not be drafted by regular legislative bodies. Following the lead established by Vermont in 1777 and Massachusetts in 1780, they began to call conventions for the sole purpose of drafting constitutions. Thus states sought direct authorization from the people—the theoretical sovereigns in a republic—before establishing new governments. After preparing new constitutions, delegates submitted them to voters for ratification.

Drafting of State Constitutions

The framers of state constitutions concerned themselves primarily with outlining the distribution of and limitations on government power. Both issues were crucial to the survival of republics. If authority was improperly distributed among the branches of government, or not confined within reasonable limits, the states might become tyrannical, as Britain had. Americans' experience with British rule permeated every provision of their new constitutions. States experimented with different solutions to the problems the framers perceived, and the early constitutions varied considerably in specifics while remaining broadly comparable in outline.

Under their colonial charters, Americans had learned to fear the power of the governor—usually, the appointed agent of king or proprietor—and to see the legislature as their defender. Accordingly, the first state constitutions typically provided for the governor to be elected annually (commonly by the legislature), limited the number of terms he could serve, and gave him little independent authority. Simultaneously, the constitutions expanded the legislature's powers. Every state except Pennsylvania and Vermont retained a two-house structure, with members of the upper house having longer terms and being required to meet higher property-holding standards than members of the lower house. But they also redrew electoral districts to reflect population patterns more accurately, and they increased the number of members in both houses. Finally, most states lowered property qualifications for voting. As a result the legislatures came to include some members who before the war would not have been eligible to vote. Thus the revolutionary era witnessed the first deliberate attempt to broaden the base of American government, a process that has continued into our own day.

But the state constitutions' authors knew that governments designed to be responsive to the people would not necessarily provide sufficient protection if tyrants were elected to office. They consequently included explicit limitations on government authority in the documents they composed. Seven of the constitutions contained formal bills of rights, and the others had similar clauses. Most guaranteed citizens freedom of the press and of religion, the right to a fair trial, the right of consent to taxation, and protection against general search warrants. An independent judiciary was charged with upholding such rights.

Limits on State Governments

In sum, the constitution makers put far greater emphasis on preventing state governments from becoming tyrannical than on making them effective wielders of political authority. Their approach to shaping governments was understandable, given the American experience with Great Britain. But establishing such weak political units, especially in wartime, practically ensured that the constitutions soon would need revision. As early as the 1780s some states began to rewrite constitutions they had drafted in 1776 and 1777.

Invariably, the revised versions increased the powers of the governor and reduced the scope of the legislature's authority. Only then, a decade after the Declaration of Independence, did Americans start to develop a formal theory of checks and balances as the primary means of controlling government power. Once they realized that legislative supremacy did not in itself guarantee good government, Americans attempted to achieve that goal by balancing the powers of the legislative, executive, and judicial branches against one another. The national constitution they drafted in 1787 embodied that principle.

The constitutional theories that Americans applied at the state level did not at first influence their conception of national government. Since American political leaders had little time to devote to legitimizing their de facto government while organizing the military struggle against Britain, the powers and structure of the Continental Congress evolved by default early in the war. Not until late 1777 did Congress send the Articles of Confederation to the states for ratification.

Articles of Confederation

The Articles largely wrote into law the unplanned arrangements of the Continental Congress. The chief organ of national government was a unicameral (one-house) legislature in which each state had one vote. Its powers included conducting foreign relations, settling disputes between states, controlling maritime affairs, regulating Indian trade, and valuing state and national coinage. The Articles did not give the national government the ability to raise revenue effectively or to enforce a uniform commercial policy. The United States of America was described as "a firm league of friendship" in which each state "retains its sovereignty, freedom and independence, and every Power, Jurisdiction and right, which is not by this confederation expressly delegated to the United States, in Congress assembled." (See the Appendix for the text of the Articles.)

The Articles required the unanimous consent of the state legislatures for ratification or amendment, and a clause concerning western lands proved troublesome. The draft accepted by Congress allowed states to retain all land claims derived from their original colonial charters. But states with definite western boundaries spelled out in their charters (like Maryland and New Jersey) wanted other states to cede to the national government their landholdings west of the Appalachian Mountains. Otherwise, they feared, states with large claims could expand and overpower their smaller neighbors. Maryland refused to accept the Articles until 1781, when Virginia finally promised to surrender its western holdings to national jurisdiction (see map, page 184). Other states followed suit, establishing the principle that unorganized lands would be held by the nation as a whole.

The capacity of a single state to delay ratification for three years was a portent of the fate of American government under the Articles of Confederation. The unicameral legislature, whether it was called the Second Continental Congress (until 1781) or the Confederation Congress (thereafter), was too inefficient and unwieldy to govern effectively. The Articles' authors had not given adequate thought to the distribution of power within the national government or to the relationship between the Confederation and the states. The Congress they created was simultaneously a legislative body and a collective executive, but it had no independent income and no authority to compel the states to accept its rulings. What is surprising is not how poorly the Confederation functioned but rather how much the government was able to accomplish.

Trials of the Confederation

The most persistent problem faced by the American governments, state and national, was finance. Because legislators at all levels were reluctant to levy taxes, both Congress and the states tried to finance the war by printing currency. Even though the money was backed by nothing but good faith, it circulated freely and without excessive depreciation during 1775 and most of 1776. Demand for military supplies and civilian goods was high, stimulating trade (especially with France) and local production. Indeed, the amount of money issued in those years was probably no more than what a healthy economy required as a medium of exchange.

Financial Problems

But in late 1776, as the American army suffered reverses in New York and New Jersey, prices began to rise and inflation set in. The currency's value rested on Americans' faith in their government, a faith that was sorely tested in the years that followed, especially during the dark days of early British triumphs in the South (1779 and 1780). State governments fought inflation by controlling wages and

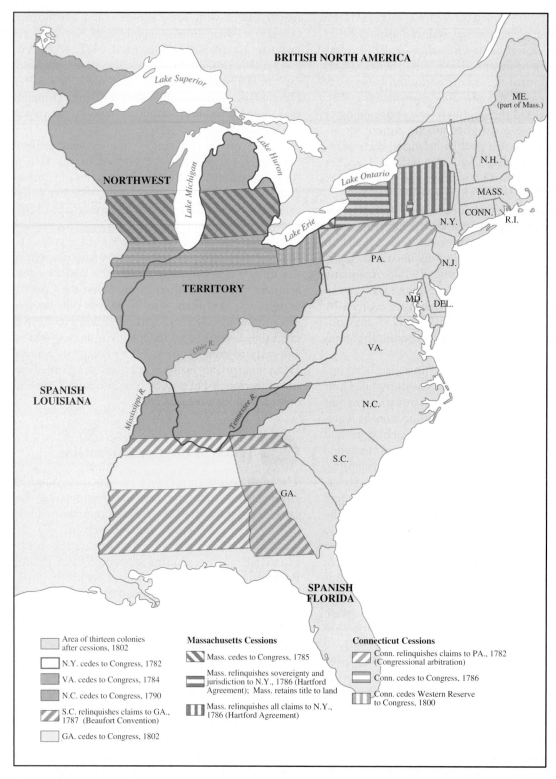

Western Land Claims and Cessions, 1782–1802   *After the United States achieved independence, states competed with each other for control of valuable lands to which they had possible claims under
their original charters. That competition led to a series of compromises among the states or between individual states and the new nation, which are indicated on this map.*

prices and requiring acceptance of paper currency on an equal footing with hard money. States also borrowed funds, established lotteries, and even levied taxes. Their efforts were futile. So too was Congress's attempt to stop printing currency altogether and to rely solely on money contributed by the states. By early 1780 it took forty paper dollars to purchase one silver dollar. Soon, Continental currency was worthless.

In 1781, faced with total collapse of the monetary system, the congressmen undertook ambitious reforms. After establishing a department of finance under the wealthy Philadelphia merchant Robert Morris, they asked the states to amend the Articles of Confederation to allow Congress to levy a duty of 5 percent on imported goods. Morris put national finances on a solid footing, but the customs duty was never adopted. First Rhode Island and then New York refused to agree to the tax. The states' resistance reflected fear of a too-powerful central government. As one worried citizen wrote in 1783, "If permanent Funds are given to Congress, the aristocratical Influence, which predominates in more than a major part of the United States, will fully establish an arbitrary Government." But states too needed revenue; when they enacted new, heavy taxes after the war, farmers resisted *their* authority. Shays's Rebellion was the most dramatic result of that resistance.

Congress also faced major diplomatic problems at the close of the war. Chief among them were issues involving the peace treaty itself. Article 4, which promised the repayment of prewar debts (most of them owed by Americans to British merchants), and Article 5, which recommended that states allow loyalists to recover their confiscated property, aroused considerable opposition. States passed laws denying British subjects the right to sue for recovery of debts or property in American courts, and town meetings decried the loyalists' return. As residents of Norwalk, Connecticut, put it, few Americans wanted to permit the "Tory Villains" to return "while filial Tears are fresh upon our Cheeks and our Murdered Brethren scarcely cold in their Graves." State governments also had reason to oppose enforcement of the treaty. Sales of loyalists' land, houses, and other possessions had helped to finance the war. Since most of the purchasers were prominent patriots, states had no desire to raise questions about the legitimacy of their property titles.

Weakness in Foreign Affairs and Commerce

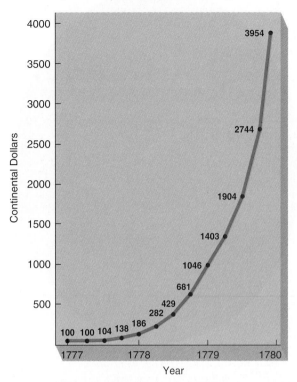

Depreciation of Continental Currency, 1777–1780

* Currency abandoned in April 1780

Depreciation of Continental Currency, 1777–1780 *The depreciation of Continental currency accelerated in 1778, as is shown in this graph measuring its value against one hundred silver dollars. Thereafter, its value dropped almost daily.* Source: Data from John J. McCusker, "How Much Is That in Real Money? A Historical Price Index for Use as a Deflator of Money Values in the Economy of the United States," *Proceedings of the American Antiquarian Society*, Vol. 101, Pt. 2 (1991), Table C-1.

The refusal of state and local governments to comply with Articles 4 and 5 gave Britain an excuse to maintain military posts on the Great Lakes long after its troops were supposed to have withdrawn. Furthermore, Congress's inability to convince states to implement the treaty pointed up its lack of power, even in an area—foreign affairs—in which it had authority under the Articles of Confederation. Concerned nationalists argued publicly that enforcement of the treaty, however unpopular, was a crucial test for the republic. "Will foreign nations be willing to undertake anything with us or for us," asked Alexander Hamilton, "when they find that the nature of our

Because of their citizens' resistance to taxation, the early state governments found it hard to raise sufficient revenues. Some, like Massachusetts, turned to state-run lotteries to make up the shortfall. Here a New Englander proudly poses with a lottery ticket, demonstrating his support for the state.   Milwaukee Art Museum Purchase, Layton Art Collection.

governments will allow no dependence to be placed on our engagements?"

Congress's weakness was especially evident in the realm of trade because the Articles of Confederation denied it the power to establish a national commercial policy. Immediately after the war, Britain, France, and Spain all restricted American trade with their colonies. Americans, who had hoped independence would bring about trade with all nations, were outraged but could do little to change matters. Members of Congress watched helplessly as British manufactured goods flooded the United States while American produce could no longer be sold in the British West Indies, once its prime market. Although Americans reopened commerce with other European countries and started a profitable trade with China in 1784, neither substituted for access to closer and larger markets.

Congress also had difficulty dealing with the threat posed by Spain's presence on the nation's southern and western borders. Determined to prevent the

Failed Negotiations with Spain

republic's expansion, Spain in 1784 closed the Mississippi River to American navigation. It thus deprived the growing settlements west of the Appalachians of their major access route to the rest of the nation and the world. Congress opened negotiations with Spain in 1785, but even John Jay, one of the nation's most experienced diplomats, could not win the necessary concessions on navigation. The talks collapsed the following year after Congress divided sharply on the question of whether agreement should be sought on other issues. Southerners, voting as a bloc, insisted on navigation rights on the Mississippi; northerners were willing to abandon that claim in order to win commercial concessions. The impasse raised doubts about the possibility of a national consensus on foreign affairs.

Diplomatic problems of another sort confronted congressmen when they considered the status of land beyond the Appalachians. Although tribal claims were not discussed by British and American diplomats, the United States assumed that the Treaty of Paris (1783) cleared its title to all land east of the Mississippi except the area still held by Spain. But recognizing that some sort of land cession should be obtained from the most powerful tribes, Congress initiated negotiations with both northern and southern Indians (see map, page 187). At Fort Stanwix, New York, in 1784, and at Hopewell, South Carolina, in late 1785 and early 1786, American diplomats signed separate treaties with chiefs purporting to represent the Iroquois and with emissaries from the Choctaw, Chickasaw, and Cherokee nations. Later, both groups of Indians denied that the men who agreed to the treaties had been authorized to speak for them. But the United States still took the treaties as confirmation of its sovereignty over the territories in question and authorized settlers to move onto the land. European-Americans soon poured over the southern Appalachians, provoking the Creeks—who had not agreed to the Hopewell treaties—to defend their territory by declaring war. Only in 1790 did they come to terms with the United States.

Encroachment on Indian Lands

In the North, meanwhile, the Iroquois Confederacy was in disarray. Members of the Six Nations who had not fled to Canada in 1779 found that they had little bargaining power left. In 1786 they repudiated the Fort Stanwix treaty and threatened new attacks on frontier settlements, but everyone knew the threat was empty. The flawed treaty stood by default. At intervals until the end of the decade New York State purchased large tracts of land from individual Iroquois nations. By 1790 the once-dominant confederacy was confined to a few scattered reservations.

Led by a remarkable prophet, Handsome Lake, the Iroquois sought to adapt to their new circumstances by embracing the traditional values of their culture and renouncing drinking alcohol, gambling, and other destructive European customs. Yet simultaneously, with Handsome Lake's approval, Quaker missionaries taught the Iroquois Anglo-American styles of agricultural subsistence. Men were now to be cultivators rather than hunters—since their hunting territories were lost—and women to be housekeepers rather than cultivators. Paradoxically, only by adopting a sexual division of labor that had originated in Europe could the Iroquois maintain a semblance of their culture.

Handsome Lake's Reforms

Western nations such as the Shawnees, Chippewas, Ottawas, and Potawatomis previously had allowed the Iroquois to speak for them. After the collapse of Iroquois power, they formed their own confederacy and demanded direct negotiations with the United States. Their aim was to present a united front so as to avoid the piecemeal surrender of land by individual bands and villages.

At first the national government ignored the western confederacy. Shortly after state land cessions were completed, Congress began to organize the Northwest Territory, bounded by the Mississippi River, the Great Lakes, and the Ohio River (see map). Ordinances passed in 1784, 1785, and 1787 outlined the process through which the land could be sold to settlers and formal governments could be organized.

Northwest Ordinances

To ensure orderly development, Congress in 1785 directed that the land be surveyed into townships 6 miles square, each divided into thirty-six sections of 640 acres (1 square mile). Revenue from the sale of the sixteenth section of each township was to be reserved for the support of public schools—the first instance of federal aid to education in American history. The minimum price per acre was set at one dollar, and the minimum sale was one section. Congress was not especially concerned about helping the

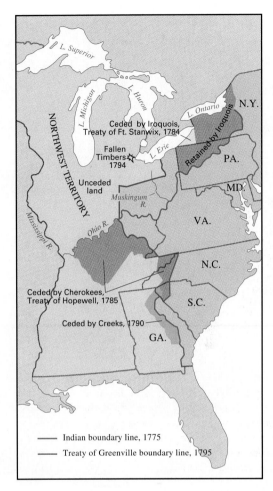

Cession of Tribal Lands to the United States, 1775–1790 *The land claims of the United States meant little as long as Indian nations still controlled vast territories within the new country's formal boundaries. A series of treaties in the 1780s and 1790s opened some lands to white settlement.* Source: From Lester J. Cappon et al., eds., *Atlas of Early American History: The Revolutionary Era, 1760–1790.* Copyright © 1976 by Princeton University Press. Reprinted by permission of Princeton University Press.

small farmer: the resulting minimum outlay of $640 was beyond the reach of ordinary Americans (except those veterans who received part of their army pay in land warrants). Proceeds from land sales were the first independent revenues available to the national government.

The most important ordinance was the third, passed in 1787. The Northwest Ordinance contained a bill of rights guaranteeing settlers freedom

In 1784, Thomas Jefferson proposed a scheme for organizing the new nation's western lands. His plan would have divided the region on a grid pattern, yielding fourteen new states (with names such as "Metropotamia" and "Pelisipia") composed of 10-mile-square "hundreds." After a year of debate, Jefferson's plan was replaced by the one adopted in the Land Ordinance of 1785, which is described in the text. Notice that Jefferson's outline map contains some of the same errors evident in "A New and Correct Map" on page 167. Clements Library, University of Michigan.

of religion and the right to a jury trial, forbidding cruel and unusual punishments, and nominally prohibiting slavery. Eventually, that prohibition was to become an important symbol for antislavery northerners, but at the time it had little effect. Some residents of the territory already held slaves, and Congress did not intend to deprive them of their property. Moreover, the ordinance also contained a provision allowing slaveowners to "lawfully reclaim" runaway bondspeople who took refuge in the territory—the first national fugitive slave law. The ordinance prevented slavery from taking deep root by discouraging slaveholders from moving into the territory with their human chattel, but not until 1848

was enslavement abolished throughout the region, now known as the Old Northwest.

The ordinance also specified the process by which residents of the territory could organize state governments and seek admission to the Union "on an equal footing with the original States." Early in the nation's history, therefore, Congress laid down a policy of admitting new states on the same basis as the old and assuring residents of the territories the same rights held by citizens of the original states. Having suffered under the rule of a colonial power, congressmen understood the importance of preparing the new nation's first "colony" for eventual self-government. Nineteenth- and twentieth-century

Americans were to be less generous in their attitudes toward residents of later territories, many of whom were non-European or non-Protestant. But the nation never fully lost sight of the egalitarian principles of the Northwest Ordinance.

In a sense, though, the ordinance was purely theoretical at the time it was passed. The Miamis, Shawnees, and Delawares refused to acknowledge American sovereignty. They opposed settlement violently, attacking unwary pioneers who ventured too far north of the Ohio River. In 1788 the Ohio Company, to which Congress had sold a large tract of land at reduced rates, established the town of Marietta at the juncture of the Ohio and Muskingum Rivers. But Indians prevented the company from extending settlement very far into the interior. After General Arthur St. Clair, the Northwest Territory's first governor, failed to negotiate a meaningful treaty with the Indians in early 1789, it was apparent that the United States could not avoid a clash with a western confederacy composed of eight nations and led by the Miamis.

Little Turtle, the able war chief of the Miami Confederacy, defeated first General Josiah Harmar (1790) and then St. Clair himself (1791) in major battles near the present border between Indiana and Ohio. More than six hundred of St. Clair's men were killed and scores more wounded; it was the whites'

War in the Old Northwest

worst defeat in the entire history of the American frontier. In 1793 the Miami Confederacy declared that peace could be achieved only if the United States recognized the Ohio River as its northwestern boundary. But the national government refused to relinquish its claim in the region. A new army under the command of General Anthony Wayne, a Revolutionary War hero, attacked and defeated the confederacy in August 1794 at the Battle of Fallen Timbers (near present-day Toledo, Ohio; see map, page 187). Peace negotiations began after the victory.

In the summer of 1795, the United States and the Miami Confederacy signed the Treaty of Greenville, bringing an end to open conflict after several years of warfare. All the participants smoked the calumet (peace pipe) pictured here, symbolizing their acceptance of the treaty. Because there were so many signatories, the ceremony took a long time. Pipe: Ohio Historical Society, Treaty: National Archives.

By the summer of 1795, Wayne reached agreement with the Miami Confederacy. The Treaty of Greenville gave each side a portion of what it wanted. The United States gained the right to settle much of what was to become Ohio, the indigenous peoples retaining only the northwest corner of the region. Indians, though, received the acknowledgment they had long sought: American recognition of their rights to the soil. At Greenville, the United

States formally accepted the principle of Indian sovereignty, by virtue of residence, over all lands the native peoples had not ceded. Never again would the United States government claim that it had acquired Indian territory solely through negotiation with a European or North American country.

The problems the United States encountered in ensuring safe settlement of the Northwest Territory pointed up the basic weakness of the Confederation government. Not until after the Articles of Confederation were replaced with a new constitution could the United States muster sufficient force to implement the Northwest Ordinance. Thus, although the ordinance is often viewed as one of the few lasting accomplishments of the Confederation Congress, it must be seen within a context of political impotence.

 ## From Crisis to the Constitution

The Americans most deeply concerned about the inadequacies of the Articles of Confederation were those involved in finance, overseas trade, and foreign affairs. In those areas the Articles were obviously deficient: Congress could not levy taxes, nor could it impose its will on the states to establish a uniform commercial policy or to ensure the enforcement of treaties.

The problems involving trade were particularly serious. Less than a year after the war's end, the American economy slid into a depression. Exporters of staple crops (especially tobacco and rice) and importers of manufactured goods were harmed by the postwar restrictions European powers imposed on American commerce. Although some of the restrictions were eased and recovery began by 1786, the war's effects proved impossible to erase entirely, particularly in the Lower South. Some estimates suggest that between 1775 and 1790 America's per capita gross national product declined by nearly 50 percent.

The war, indeed, had wrought permanent change in the American economy. The near total cessation of foreign commerce in nonmilitary items during the war years stimulated domestic manufacturing. Con-

Economic Change

sequently, despite the influx of European goods after 1783, the postwar period witnessed the stirrings of American industrial development. For ex-

ample, the first American textile mill began production in Pawtucket, Rhode Island, in 1793. Because of continuing population growth, the domestic market assumed greater relative importance in the overall economy. Moreover, foreign trade patterns shifted from Europe and toward the West Indies, continuing a trend that had begun before the war. Foodstuffs shipped to the French and Dutch Caribbean islands became America's largest single export, replacing tobacco (and thus accelerating the Chesapeake's conversion from tobacco to grain production).

Recognizing the Confederation Congress's inability to deal with commercial matters, Virginia invited the other states to a convention at Annapolis, Maryland, to discuss trade pol-

Annapolis Convention

icy. Although eight states named representatives to the meeting in September 1786, only five delegations attended. Those present realized that they were too few in number to have any real impact on the political system. They issued a call for another convention, to be held in Philadelphia nine months later, "to devise such further provisions as shall . . . appear necessary to render the constitution of the federal government adequate to the exigencies of the Union."

The other states did not respond immediately. But then Shays's Rebellion convinced many political leaders that the nation's problems extended far beyond trade policy. The reaction to the rebellion hastened the movement toward comprehensive revision of the Articles. After most of the states had already appointed delegates, the Confederation Congress belatedly endorsed the convention. In mid-May 1787, fifty-five men, representing all the states but Rhode Island, assembled in Philadelphia to begin their deliberations.

The vast majority of delegates to the Constitutional Convention were men of property and substance. They all favored reform; otherwise, they would not have come to Philadelphia. Most wanted to invigorate

Constitutional Convention in Philadelphia

the national government and to give it new authority over taxation and foreign commerce. Many had been members of state legislatures, and some had helped to draft state constitutions. All were influenced in their Philadelphia deliberations by their understanding of the success or failure of those constitutions' provisions. Among their number were merchants, planters, physicians,

The Constitutional Convention met in the state capitol of Pennsylvania, now known as Independence Hall. This view dates from 1778.   Independence National Historic Park.

generals, governors, and especially lawyers—twenty-three had studied the law. Most had been born in America, and many came from families that had arrived in the seventeenth century. In an era when only a tiny proportion of the population had any advanced education, more than half of the delegates had attended college. A few had been educated in Britain, but most were graduates of American institutions: Princeton, with ten, had the most alumni participants. The youngest delegate was twenty-six, the oldest—Benjamin Franklin—eighty-one. Like George Washington, whom they elected their presiding officer, most were in their vigorous middle years. A dozen men did the bulk of the convention's work. Of these, James Madison of Virginia was by far the most important; he truly deserves the title "Father of the Constitution."

The frail, shy James Madison was thirty-six years old in 1787. Raised in western Virginia, he attended

James Madison: Father of the Constitution

Princeton, served on the local Committee of Safety, and was elected successively to the provincial convention, the state's lower and upper houses, and the Continental Congress (1780–1783). Although Madison returned to Virginia to serve in the state legislature in 1784, he remained in touch with national politics, partly through his continuing correspondence with his close friend Thomas Jefferson. A promoter of the Annapolis Convention, he strongly supported its call for further reform.

Madison was unique among the delegates in his systematic preparation for the Philadelphia meeting. Through Jefferson in Paris he bought more than two hundred books on history and government, carefully analyzing their accounts of past confederacies and republics. A month before the Constitutional Convention began, he summed up the results

James Madison (1751–1836), the youthful scholar and skilled politician who earned the title "Father of the Constitution." Library of Congress.

of his research in a lengthy paper entitled "Vices of the Political System of the United States." After listing the flaws he perceived in the current structure of the government (among them "encroachments by the states on the federal authority" and lack of unity "in matters where common interest requires it"), Madison revealed the conclusion that would guide his actions over the next few months. What the government most needed, he declared, was "such a modification of the sovereignty as will render it sufficiently neutral between the different interests and factions, to controul one part of the society from invading the rights of another, and at the same time sufficiently controuled itself, from setting up an interest adverse to that of the whole Society."

Thus Madison set forth the principle of checks and balances. The government, he believed, had to be constructed in such a way that it could not become tyrannical or fall wholly under the influence of a particular interest group. He regarded the large size of a potential national republic as an advantage in that respect. Rejecting the common assertion that republics had to be small to survive, Madison argued that a large, diverse republic should be preferred. Because the nation would include many different interest groups, no one of them would be able to control the government. Political stability would result from compromises among the contending parties.

Madison's conception of national government was embodied in the so-called Virginia Plan, introduced on May 29 by his fellow Virginian Edmund Randolph. The plan provided for a two-house legislature, the lower house elected directly by the people and the upper house selected by the lower; proportional representation in both houses; an executive elected by Congress; a national judiciary; and congressional veto over state laws. The Virginia Plan gave Congress the broad power to legislate "in all cases to which the separate states are incompetent." Had it been adopted intact, it would have created a government in which national authority reigned unchallenged and state power was greatly diminished. Proportional representation in both houses would also have given large states a dominant voice in the national government.

Virginia and New Jersey Plans

The convention included many delegates who recognized the need for change but believed the Virginians had gone too far in the direction of national consolidation. After two weeks of debate on Randolph's proposal, the disaffected delegates united under the leadership of William Paterson of New Jersey. On June 15 Paterson presented an alternative scheme, the New Jersey Plan, calling for modifying the Articles rather than completely overhauling the government. Paterson proposed retaining a unicameral congress but giving it new powers of taxation and trade regulation. Paterson earlier had made his position clear in debate. Asserting that the Articles were "the proper basis of all the proceedings of the convention," he contended that the delegates' proper task was "to mark the orbits of the states with due precision and provide for the use of coercion" by the national government. Although the convention initially rejected Paterson's position, he and his allies won a number of victories in the months that followed.

The delegates began their work by discussing the structure and functions of Congress. They readily agreed that the new national government should

The Debates: Houses of Congress

have a two-house (bicameral) legislature. But they then discovered that they differed widely in their answers to three key questions: Should representation in both houses of Congress be proportional to population? How was representation in either or both houses to be apportioned among the states? And, finally, how were the members of the two houses to be elected?

The last issue was the easiest to resolve. To quote John Dickinson, the delegates thought it "essential" that members of the lower branch of Congress be elected directly by the people and "expedient" that members of the upper house be chosen by state legislatures. Since legislatures had selected delegates to the Confederation Congress, they would expect a similar privilege in the new government. If the convention had not agreed to allow state legislatures to elect senators, the Constitution would have aroused significant opposition among state political leaders.

Considerably more difficult was the matter of proportional representation in the Senate. The delegates accepted without much debate the principle of proportional representation in the lower house. But small states, through their spokesman Luther Martin of Maryland, argued for equal representation in the Senate, while large states supported a proportional plan for the upper house. For weeks the convention deadlocked on the issue, neither side able to obtain a majority. A committee appointed to work out a compromise recommended equal representation in the Senate, coupled with a proviso that all appropriation bills originate in the lower house. But not until the convention accepted a suggestion that a state's two senators vote as individuals rather than as a unit was a breakdown averted.

The Debates: Slavery and Representation

The remaining critical question divided the nation along sectional lines rather than by size of state: how was representation in the lower house to be apportioned among states? Delegates from states with large numbers of slaves wanted African and European inhabitants to be counted equally; delegates from states with few slaves wanted only free people to be counted. So slavery became inextricably linked to the foundation of the new government. Delegates resolved the dispute by using a formula developed by the Confederation Congress in 1783 to allocate financial assessments among states: three-fifths of slaves would be included in population totals. (The formula reflected delegates' judgment that slaves were less efficient producers of wealth than free people, not that they were 60 percent human and 40 percent property.) The three-fifths compromise on representation won unanimous approval. Only two delegates, Gouverneur Morris of New York and George Mason of Virginia, later spoke out against the institution of slavery.

Constitutional Protections for Slavery

Although the words *slave* and *slavery* do not appear in the Constitution (the framers used euphemisms such as *other persons*), direct and indirect protections for slavery were deeply embedded in the document. The three-fifths clause, for example, assured white southern voters not only congressional representation out of proportion to their numbers but also a disproportionate influence on the selection of the president, since the number of each state's electoral votes was determined by the size of its congressional delegation. Congress was prevented from outlawing the slave trade for at least twenty years, and the fugitive slave clause required all states to return runaways to their masters. By guaranteeing that the national government would aid any states threatened with "domestic violence," the Constitution promised aid in putting down future slave revolts, as well as incidents like Shays's Rebellion.

Once agreement was reached on the knotty, conjoined problems of slavery and representation, the delegates readily achieved consensus on the other issues confronting them. All agreed that the national government needed the authority to tax and to regulate commerce. But instead of giving Congress the nearly unlimited scope proposed in the Virginia Plan, delegates enumerated congressional powers and then provided for flexibility by granting all authority "necessary and proper" to carry out those powers. Discarding the legislative veto contained in the Virginia Plan, the convention implied a judicial veto instead. The Constitution plus national laws and treaties would constitute "the supreme law of the land; and the judges in every state shall be bound thereby." As another means of circumscribing state powers, delegates drafted a long list of actions forbidden to states.

The convention placed primary responsibility for conducting foreign affairs in the hands of the president, who was also designated commander-in-chief of the armed forces. That

The Presidency decision raised the question, left unspecified in the Constitution's text, of whether the president (or Congress, for that matter) acquired special powers in times of war. With the consent of the Senate, the president could appoint judges and other federal officers. To select the president, delegates established an elaborate mechanism, the electoral college, whose members would be chosen in each state by legislatures or qualified voters. This system, they hoped, would ensure that the executive would be independent of the national legislature—and of the people. They also agreed that the chief executive should serve a four-year term but be eligible for reelection.

The final document still showed signs of its origins in the Virginia Plan, but compromises created a system of government less powerful at the national level than Madison and Randolph had envisioned. The key

Separation of Powers to the Constitution was the distribution of political authority—separation of powers among executive, legislative, and judicial branches of the national government, and division of powers between states and nation. Concurrence of two-thirds of Congress and three-fourths of the states, for example, was required for amendments. The branches were balanced against one another, their powers deliberately entwined to prevent them from acting independently. The president was given a veto over congressional legislation, but his treaties and major appointments required the Senate's consent. Congress could impeach the president and federal judges, but courts appeared to have the final say on interpreting the Constitution. These checks and balances would make it difficult for the government to become tyrannical. At the same time, though, the elaborate system would sometimes prevent the government from acting quickly and decisively. Furthermore, the line between state and national powers was so ambiguously and vaguely drawn that the United States had to fight a civil war in the next century before the issue was fully resolved.

The convention held its last session on September 17, 1787. Of the forty-two delegates present, only three refused to sign the Constitution. (Two of the three declined in part because of the lack of a bill of rights.) Benjamin Franklin had written a speech calling for unity; because his voice was too weak to

be heard, another delegate read it for him. "I confess that there are several parts of this constitution which I do not at present approve," Franklin admitted. Yet he urged its acceptance "because I expect no better, and because I am not sure, that it is not the best." Only then was the Constitution made public. The convention's proceedings had been entirely secret—and remained so until the delegates' private notes were published in the nineteenth century. (See the Appendix for the full text of the Constitution.)

 ## Opposition and Ratification

Later the same month, the Confederation Congress submitted the Constitution to the states but did not formally recommend approval. The ratification clause provided for the new system to take effect once it was approved by special conventions in at least nine states, with delegates being elected by qualified voters. Thus the national Constitution, unlike the Articles of Confederation, would rest directly on popular authority (and the presumably hostile state legislatures would be circumvented).

As states began to elect delegates to the special conventions, discussion of the proposed government grew more heated. Federalists (supporters of the Constitution) and Antifederalists (its opponents) published newspaper essays and pamphlets vigorously defending or attacking the convention's decisions. The extent of the debate was unprecedented. Every newspaper in the country printed the full text of the Constitution, and most newspapers supported its adoption. Even so, it quickly became apparent that the disputes within the Constitutional Convention had been mild compared with divisions of opinion within the populace as a whole. Although most politically aware citizens concurred that the national government should have more power over taxation and foreign commerce, some believed that the proposed government held the potential for tyranny.

Federalists built on the notions of classical republicanism, holding forth a vision of a virtuous, self-sacrificing republic vigorously led by an aristocracy of talent. They claimed that the

Federalists nation did not need to fear centralized authority when good men were in charge and that the carefully structured government would preclude the possibility of tyranny. A republic could be large, they declared, if the government was designed to prevent any one group from controlling it. The separation of powers among legislative, executive, and judicial branches, and the division of powers between states and nation, would accomplish that goal. Thus people did not need to be protected from the powers of the new government in a formal way.

Antifederalists feared a too-powerful central government, although they recognized the need for a national source of revenue. They saw the states as the chief protectors of individual rights; consequently, their weakening could bring the onset of arbitrary power. Antifederalist arguments against the Constitution often consisted of lists of potential abuses of government authority.

Antifederalists

Heirs of the Real Whig ideology of the late 1760s and early 1770s, Antifederalists stressed the need for constant popular vigilance to avert oppression. Indeed, some of the Antifederalists were the very men who originally promulgated those ideas—Samuel Adams, Patrick Henry, and Richard Henry Lee were leaders of the opposition to the Constitution. The Antifederalist ranks were heavily peopled by such older Americans, whose political opinions had been shaped prior to the centralizing, nationalistic Revolution. Joining them were small farmers, who were preoccupied with guarding their property against excessive taxation, and ambitious, upwardly mobile men who would gain more from an economic and political system less tightly controlled than the one the Constitution promised to establish.

As public debate continued, Antifederalists focused on the Constitution's lack of a bill of rights. Even if states were weakened by the new system, they believed, people could still be protected from tyranny if their rights were specifically guaranteed. The Constitution did contain some prohibitions on congressional power. For example, the writ of habeas corpus, which prevented arbitrary imprisonment, could not be suspended except in dire emergencies. But Antifederalists found such constitutional provisions inadequate. Nor were they reassured by Federalist assertions that, since the new government was one of limited powers, it could not violate people's rights.

Importance of a Bill of Rights

Letters of a Federal Farmer, perhaps the most widely read Antifederalist pamphlet, listed the rights that should be protected: freedom of the press and of religion, the right to trial by jury, and guarantees against unreasonable search warrants. From Paris, Thomas Jefferson added his voice to the chorus. Re-

The Federal Almanack *for 1789 trumpeted the virtues of the new Constitution. Not all Americans were so certain that the national government, here symbolized as an edifice supported by thirteen pillars, was as "solid, strong as time" as the printer proclaimed.* American Antiquarian Society.

plying to Madison's letter conveying a copy of the Constitution, Jefferson declared, "I like much the general idea" but not "the omission of a bill of rights. . . . A bill of rights is what the people are entitled to against every government on earth, general or particular, and what no just government should refuse, or rest on inference."

As state conventions met to consider ratification, the lack of a bill of rights loomed ever larger as

Ratification of the Constitution

a flaw in the proposed government. Four of the first five states to ratify did so unanimously, but serious disagreements then surfaced. Massachusetts, in which Antifederalist forces had been bolstered by a backlash against the state government's heavy-handed treatment of the Shays rebels, ratified by a majority of only 19 votes out of 355 cast. In June 1788, when New Hampshire ratified, the requirement of nine states was satisfied. But New York and Virginia had not yet voted, and everyone realized the new Constitution could not succeed unless those key states accepted it.

Despite a valiant effort by the Antifederalist Patrick Henry, pro-Constitution forces won by 10 votes in the Virginia convention. In New York, James Madison, John Jay, and Alexander Hamilton campaigned for ratification by publishing *The Federalist*, a political tract that explained the theory behind the Constitution and masterfully answered its critics. Their reasoned arguments, coupled with Federalists' promise to add a bill of rights to the Constitution, helped win the battle. On July 26, 1788, New York ratified the Constitution by the slim margin of 3 votes. Although the last state (Rhode Island) did not formally join the Union until 1790, the new government was a reality.

the political context of American life in the 1780s. At the outset of the war, most politically aware Americans believed that "that government which governs best governs least," but by the late 1780s many had changed their minds. These were the drafters and supporters of the Constitution, who concluded from the republic's vicissitudes under the Articles of Confederation that the United States needed a more powerful central government. They contended during ratification debates that their proposed solution to the nation's problems was just as "republican" in conception (if not more so) as the Articles.

Both sides concurred in a general adherence to republican principles, but they emphasized different views of republicanism. Federalists advanced a position based on the principles of classical republicanism. Antifederalists, fearing that elected leaders would not subordinate personal gain to the good of the whole, wanted a weak central government, formal protection of individual rights, and a loosely regulated economy.

The Federalists won their point when the Constitution was adopted, however narrowly. The process of consolidating the states into a national whole was thereby formalized. The 1790s, the first decade of government under the Constitution, would witness hesitant steps toward the creation of a true nation, the *United* States of America.

 Conclusion

During the 1770s and 1780s the nation took shape as a political union. It began to develop an economy independent of the British Empire, and it designed a foreign policy that attempted to chart its own course in the world in order to protect the national interest, defend the country's borders, and promote beneficial trade. Some Americans prescribed rules for the cultural and intellectual life they thought appropriate for a republic, outlining artistic and educational goals for a properly virtuous people. An integral part of the formation of the Union was the systematic formulation of American racist thought. Emphasizing race (rather than status as slave or free) as a determinant of African-Americans' standing in the nation allowed white men to define republicanism to exclude all people but themselves and to ensure that they would dominate the country for the foreseeable future.

The experience of fighting a war and of struggling for survival as an independent nation altered

Suggestions for Further Reading

General

Richard Beeman et al., eds., *Beyond Confederation: Origins of the Constitution and American National Identity* (1987); John E. Crowley, *The Privileges of Independence: Neomercantilism and the American Revolution* (1993); Ronald Hoffman et al., eds., *The Economy of Early America: The Revolutionary Period, 1763–1790* (1988); Cathy Matson and Peter S. Onuf, *A Union of Interests: Political and Economic Thought in Revolutionary America* (1990); Forrest McDonald, *Novus Ordo Seclorum: The Intellectual Origins of the Constitution* (1985); Edmund S. Morgan, *Inventing the People: The Rise of Popular Sovereignty in England and America* (1988); Gordon S. Wood, *The Radicalism of the American Revolution* (1992); Gordon S. Wood, *The Creation of the American Republic, 1776–1787* (1969); Alfred F. Young et al, eds., *We the People: Voices and Images of the New Nation* (1993); Rosemarie Zagarri, *The Politics of Size: Representation in the United States, 1776–1850* (1988).

Continental Congress and Articles of Confederation

E. James Ferguson, *The Power of the Purse: A History of American Public Finance, 1776–1790* (1961); H. James Henderson, *Party Politics in the Continental Congress* (1974); Merrill Jensen, *The New Nation: A History of the United States During the Confederation,*

1781–1789 (1950); Jerrilyn G. Marston, *King and Congress: The Transfer of Political Legitimacy, 1774–1776* (1987); Richard B. Morris, *The Forging of the Union, 1781–1789* (1987); Peter S. Onuf, *Statehood and Union: A History of the Northwest Ordinance* (1987); Jack N. Rakove, *The Beginnings of National Politics: An Interpretive History of the Continental Congress* (1979); Ann Withington, *Toward a More Perfect Union: Virtue and the Formation of American Republics* (1992).

State Politics

Willi Paul Adams, *The First American Constitutions: Republican Ideology and the Making of the State Constitutions in the Revolutionary Era* (1980); Robert Gross, ed., *In Debt to Shays* (1992); Ronald Hoffman and Peter Albert, eds., *Sovereign States in an Age of Uncertainty* (1981); Donald Lutz, *Popular Consent and Popular Control: Whig Political Theory in the Early State Constitutions* (1980); Jackson Turner Main, *Political Parties Before the Constitution* (1973); Jackson Turner Main, *The Sovereign States, 1775–1783* (1973); David P. Szatmary, *Shays' Rebellion: The Making of an Agrarian Insurrection* (1980).

The Constitution

Thornton Anderson, *Creating the Constitution: The Convention of 1787 and the First Congress* (1993); Lance Banning, *The Sacred Fire of Liberty: James Madison and the Founding of the Federal Republic* (1995); Roger H. Brown, *Redeeming the Republic: Federalists, Taxation, and the Origins of the Constitution* (1993); Christopher Duncan, *The Anti-Federalists and Early American Political Thought* (1995); Jackson Turner Main, *The Anti-Federalists: Critics of the Constitution, 1781–1788* (1961); Frederick W. Marks III, *Independence on Trial: Foreign Affairs and the Making of the Constitution* (1973); Jack N. Rakove, *Original Meanings: Politics and Ideas in the Making of the Constitution* (1996); Robert A. Rutland, *The Ordeal of the Constitution: The Antifederalists and the Ratification Struggle of 1787–88* (1966); Abraham Sofaer, *War, Foreign Affairs, and Constitutional Power*, vol. 1, *The Origins* (1976).

Education and Culture

Cathy N. Davidson, *Revolution and the Word: The Rise of the Novel in America* (1987); Joseph M. Ellis, *After the Revolution: Profiles of Early American Culture* (1979); Carl F. Kaestle, *Pillars of the Republic: Common Schools and American Society, 1780–1860* (1983); Russel B. Nye, *The Cultural Life of the New Nation, 1776–1803*

(1960); Kenneth Silverman, *A Cultural History of the American Revolution* (1976).

Women

Edith Gelles, *Portia: The World of Abigail Adams* (1992); Ronald Hoffman and Peter Albert, eds., *Women in the Age of the American Revolution* (1989); Susan Juster, *Disorderly Women: Sexual Politics and Evangelicalism in Revolutionary New England* (1994); Linda K. Kerber, *Women of the Republic: Intellect and Ideology in Revolutionary America* (1980); Mary Beth Norton, *Liberty's Daughters: The Revolutionary Experience of American Women, 1750–1800* (1980); Rosemarie Zagarri, *A Woman's Dilemma: Mercy Otis Warren and the American Revolution* (1995).

African-Americans and Slavery

Ira Berlin and Ronald Hoffman, eds., *Slavery and Freedom in the Age of the American Revolution* (1983); David Brion Davis, *The Problem of Slavery in the Age of Revolution, 1770–1823* (1975); Paul Finkelman, *Slavery and the Founders: Race and Liberty in the Age of Jefferson* (1996); Carol V. R. George, *Segregated Sabbaths: Richard Allen and the Emergence of Independent Black Churches, 1760–1840* (1973); Winthrop Jordan, *White over Black: American Attitudes Toward the Negro, 1550–1812* (1968); Duncan J. Macleod, *Slavery, Race, and the American Revolution* (1974); Gary Nash, *Forging Freedom: The Formation of Philadelphia's Black Community, 1720–1840* (1988); Donald L. Robinson, *Slavery in the Structure of American Politics, 1765–1820* (1971); Shane White, *Somewhat More Independent: The End of Slavery in New York City, 1770–1810* (1991); Arthur Zilversmit, *The First Emancipation: The Abolition of Slavery in the North* (1967).

Indians

Harvey L. Carter, *The Life and Times of Little Turtle* (1987); Gregory E. Dowd, *A Spirited Resistance: The North American Indian Struggle for Unity, 1745–1815* (1992); Dorothy Jones, *License for Empire: Colonialism by Treaty in Early America* (1982); Francis Paul Prucha, *American Indian Policy in the Formative Years: The Indian Trade and Intercourse Acts, 1790–1834* (1962); Wiley Sword, *President Washington's Indian War: The Struggle for the Old Northwest, 1790–1795* (1985); Anthony F. C. Wallace, *The Death and Rebirth of the Seneca* (1969); Richard White, *The Middle Ground: Indians, Empires, and Republics in the Great Lakes Region, 1650–1815* (1991).

8

Politics and Society in the Early Republic

1789–1800

"Shall I commence my journal, my dear Elizabeth, with a description of the pain I felt at taking leave of all my friends, or shall I leave you to imagine?" wrote Margaret Dwight as she began a chronicle of her arduous journey from New Haven, Connecticut, to Warren, Ohio. An orphan at age twenty, Margaret was traveling west to live with relatives who had already migrated to the region known as New Connecticut. Her diary, kept at a cousin's request, described not only the difficult trip but also the reactions of a genteely bred young woman to the rough life of the early American frontier.

Margaret filled her pages with comments on poor roads, dangerous river crossings, dirty taverns, profane wagoneers, troublesome fellow travelers, and brawling "dutchmen" (Germans), whose failure to observe the Sabbath disgusted her. "We have concluded the reason so few are willing to return from the Western country," she remarked, "is not that the country is so good, but because the journey is so bad." Disconcerted by her inability to understand the Germans' "Jabbering," Margaret also noticed differences in English usage: "The people here talk curiously, they all reckon instead of expect—Youns is a word I have heard used several times, but what it means I don't know."

Many people she encountered assumed that Margaret was moving west to find a husband. One innkeeper's wife predicted that she "would certainly be married in a little while"; a man "at once concluded" that she and a traveling companion "were going to the Hio . . . to get husbands." But Margaret resisted, writing that she was "determin'd not to oblige myself to spend my days there, by marrying should I even have an opport[unit]y." She was "encouraged" by meeting a young *"unmarried"* woman traveling from Ohio back to the East, "a thing I never before heard of, & had begun to think impossible." Yet at the end of her trip Margaret found Warren "pleasanter than I expected." About a year later, she married William Bell, a local merchant who soon relocated to Pittsburgh, the western Pennsylvania town that had grown up around Fort Pitt. Eventually, she gave birth to eight children in the West she had disdained.

Margaret Dwight was just one of the many thousand people who moved west in the decades following the Revolution. Their mobility signaled the beginnings of a new age, as large numbers of European-Americans and African-Americans poured through the Appalachian Mountains for the first time. North of the Ohio River (Margaret's destination), the strength of the Miami Confederacy blocked westward expansion until after the Treaty of Greenville in 1795. South of the river, western settlements appeared as early as the 1770s, but they were isolated from the Atlantic coast by the long chain of mountains. Not until the first years of the nineteenth century did those settlements become more fully integrated into American life through the vehicle of the Second Great Awakening, a religious revival that swept both the East and the West.

The dispersal of the population was accompanied by political fragmentation and economic difficulties. The United States economy still depended on the export trade. When warfare between England and France resumed in 1793, Americans found their commerce disrupted yet again, with consequent fluctuations in their income and profits. And the fight over the Constitution presaged an even wider division over the major political, economic, and diplomatic questions confronting the young republic. To make matters worse, Americans did not anticipate the political disagreements that characterized the 1790s. Believing that the Constitution would resolve the problems that had arisen during the Confederation period, they expected the new government to rule largely by consensus.

Accordingly, many Americans found it difficult to understand the partisan tensions that accompanied disputes over fundamental issues such as the extent to which authority (especially fiscal authority) should be centralized in the national government, the formulation of foreign policy in an era of continual warfare in Europe, and the limits of dissent. They could not understand or fully accept the division of America's political leaders into two fac-

tions—not yet political parties—known as Federalists and Republicans, because factions were believed to be legitimate only in monarchies. In republics, it was thought, the rise of factions was a sign of decay and corruption. As the decade closed with the first fully partisan presidential election, Americans still had not come to terms with the implications of partisan politics.

 ## Building a Workable Government

Americans in many cities celebrated the ratification of the Constitution with a series of parades on July 4, 1788. The processions were carefully planned to

Celebrating Ratification

symbolize the unity of the new nation and to recall its history to the minds of the watching throngs. Like prerevolutionary protest meetings, the parades served as political lessons for literate and illiterate Americans alike. Men and women who could not read were thereby educated about the significance of the new Constitution for the nation. They also were instructed about political leaders' hopes for industry and frugality on the part of a virtuous American public.

The Philadelphia parade, planned by the artist Charles Willson Peale, was filled with symbols that expressed those goals. About five thousand people took part in the procession, which stretched for a mile and a half and lasted three hours. The parade featured floats portraying themes such as "The Grand Federal Edifice." Marchers representing the first pioneers and revolutionary war troops were joined by groups of farmers and artisans dramatizing their work. More than forty groups of tradesmen, including barbers, hatters, printers, cloth manufacturers, and clockmakers, sponsored floats. The artisans were followed by lawyers, doctors, clergymen of all denominations, and congressmen. Bringing up the rear was a symbol of the nation's future, students from the University of Pennsylvania and other city schools, bearing a flag labeled "The Rising Generation." After the parade, the marchers imbibed beer and cider, the "Federal liquors" celebrated in a broadside circulated at the time.

The nationalistic spirit expressed in the ratification processions carried over to the first session of Congress. Only a few Antifederalists ran for office in

• *Important Events* •

1789	George Washington inaugurated as first president
	Judiciary Act of 1789 organizes federal court system
	French Revolution begins
1790	Alexander Hamilton's *Report on Public Credit* proposes assumption of state debts
1791	First ten amendments (Bill of Rights) ratified
1793	France declares war on Britain, Spain, and Holland
	Washington's neutrality proclamation keeps the United States out of the war
	Democratic-Republican societies founded, the first grassroots political organizations
1794	Whiskey Rebellion in western Pennsylvania protests taxation
1795	Jay Treaty with England
1796	First contested presidential election: John Adams elected president, Thomas Jefferson vice president
1798	XYZ affair arouses American opinion against France
	Alien and Sedition Acts punish political dissenters
	Virginia and Kentucky resolutions protest suppression of dissent
1798–99	Quasi-War with France
1800	Franco-American Convention ends the Quasi-War
	Jefferson elected president, Aaron Burr vice president
	Gabriel's Rebellion threatens Virginia whites
1801	Second Great Awakening sweeps through Kentucky

Nationalism in the First Congress

the congressional elections held late in 1788, and even fewer were elected. Thus the First Congress consisted chiefly of men who supported a strong national government. The drafters of the Constitution had deliberately left many key issues undecided, so the nationalists' domination of Congress meant that their views on those points quickly prevailed.

Congress faced four immediate tasks when it convened in April 1789: raising revenue to support the new government, responding to state ratification conventions' call for a bill of rights, setting up executive departments, and organizing the federal judiciary. The last task was especially important. The Constitution established a Supreme Court but left it to Congress to decide whether to have other federal courts as well.

James Madison, who had been elected to the House of Representatives, soon became as influential in Congress as he had been at the Constitutional Convention. A few months into the first session, he persuaded Congress to adopt the Revenue Act of 1789, imposing a 5 percent tariff on certain imports. Thus the First Congress quickly achieved what the

IN HONOUR of AMERICAN

BEER and CYDER,

It is hereby recorded, for the information of strangers and posterity, that 17 000 people assembled on this green, on the 4th of July, 1788, to celebrate the establishment of the constitution of the United States, and that they separated at an early hour, without intoxication, or a single quarrel.----They drank nothing but Beer and Cyder. Learn, reader, to prize those invaluable FEDERAL liquors, and to consider them as the companions of those virtues that can alone render our country free and respectable.

Learn likewise to despise

SPIRITOUS LIQUORS, as

Anti-federal, and to consider them as the companions of all those vices, that are calculated to dishonour and enslave our country.

Drinking beer and cider (instead of imported spirits like brandy) took on patriotic meaning in the celebrations of the Constitution's ratification. Other forms of alcohol, this broadside proclaimed, were "Anti-federal" and thus inappropriate for the nation's citizens. Rare Book and Manuscript Division, New York Public Library, Astor, Lenox, and Tilden Foundations.

The first census in 1790, demonstrating that the United States had nearly 4 million residents, was a source of pride to the young republic. A jug of Liverpool ware commemorated the count by reproducing the figures surrounded by symbols of the nation's prosperity—agricultural produce, buildings, a ship, and other items. Division of Political History, Smithsonian Institution, Washington, D.C.

Confederation Congress never had: an effective national tax law. The new government would have problems in its first years, but lack of revenue was not one of them.

Madison also took the lead on the issue of constitutional amendments. At the convention and thereafter, he had consistently opposed additional

Bill of Rights

limitations on the national government. He believed it unnecessary to guarantee people's rights explicitly when the government was one of delegated powers. But Madison recognized that public opinion, as expressed in state ratifying conventions, was against him. Accordingly, he placed nineteen proposed amendments before the House. Eventually, the states ratified ten, which officially became part of the Constitution on December 15, 1791 (see the Appendix for the Constitution and all amendments). Their adoption defused Antifederalist opposition and rallied support for the new government.

The First Amendment specifically prohibited Congress from passing any law restricting the right to freedom of religion, speech, press, peaceable assembly, or petition. The next two amendments arose directly from the former colonists' fear of standing armies as a threat to freedom. The Second Amendment guaranteed people's right "to keep and bear arms" because of the need for a "well-regulated Militia." Thus the constitutional right to bear arms was based on the expectation that most able-bodied men would serve the nation as citizen soldiers and there would be little need for a standing army. The Third Amendment defined the circumstances in which troops could be quartered in private homes. The next five pertained to judicial procedures. The Fourth Amendment prohibited "unreasonable searches and seizures"; the Fifth and Sixth established the rights of accused persons; the Seventh specified the conditions for jury trials in civil (as opposed to criminal) cases; and the Eighth forbade "cruel and unusual punishments." The Ninth and Tenth Amendments reserved to the people and the states other unspecified rights and powers. In short, the amendments' authors made clear that, in listing some rights, they did not mean to preclude the exercise of others.

While debating proposed amendments, Congress also considered the organization of the executive branch. It readily agreed to continue the three

Executive Branch

administrative departments established under the Articles of Confederation: War, Foreign Affairs (renamed State), and Treasury. Congress instituted two lesser posts: the attorney general—the nation's official lawyer—and the postmaster general. Controversy arose over whether the president alone could dismiss officials whom he originally had appointed with the Senate's consent. After some debate, the House and Senate agreed that he had such authority. Thus was established the important principle that the heads of executive departments are responsible to the president.

Aside from constitutional amendments, the most far-reaching piece of legislation enacted by the First Congress was the Judiciary Act of 1789,

Judiciary Act of 1789

which defined the jurisdiction of the federal judiciary and established a six-member Supreme Court, thirteen district courts, and three circuit courts of appeal. Its most important provision, Section 25, allowed appeals from state courts to federal courts when cases raised certain types of constitutional issues. Section 25 thus implemented Article VI of the Constitution, which stated that federal laws and treaties were to be considered "the supreme Law of the Land." For Article VI to be enforced uniformly, the national judiciary had to be able to overturn state court decisions in cases involving the Constitution, federal laws, or treaties. Yet nowhere did the Constitution explicitly permit such action by federal courts. The Judiciary Act of 1789 presumed that the wording of Article VI implied the right of appeal from state to federal courts. In the nineteenth century, however, judges and legislators committed to states' rights challenged that interpretation.

During its first decade, the Supreme Court handled few cases of any importance, and there was considerable turnover in its membership. (John Jay, the first chief justice, served only six years.) But in a significant 1796 decision, *Ware* v. *Hylton*, the Court for the first time declared a state law unconstitutional. That same year it also reviewed the constitutionality of an act of Congress, upholding its validity in the case of *Hylton* v. *U.S.* The most important case of the decade, *Chisholm* v. *Georgia* (1793), established that states could be sued in federal courts by citizens of other states. This decision, unpopular with state governments, was overruled five years later by the Eleventh Amendment to the Constitution.

The Early Supreme Court

Domestic Policy Under Washington and Hamilton

George Washington did not seek the presidency. In 1783 he returned to Mount Vernon, his plantation on the Potomac River, eager for the peaceful life of a Virginia planter. But his fellow countrymen never regarded Washington as just another private citizen. He was unanimously elected the presiding officer of the Constitutional Convention. As such, he did not participate in debates, but he consistently voted for a strong national government and served as a steadying influence. Once the proposed structure of the government was presented to the public, Americans concurred that only George Washington had sufficient stature to serve as the re-

Election of the First President

public's first president. The unanimous vote of the electoral college was just a formality.

Washington was reluctant to return to public life but knew he could not ignore his country's call. Awaiting the summons to New York City, the nation's capital, he wrote to an old friend, "My movements to the chair of Government will be accompanied by feelings not unlike those of a culprit who is going to the place of his execution. . . . I am sensible, that I am embarking the voice of my Countrymen and a good name of my own, on this voyage, but what returns will be made for them, Heaven alone can foretell."

Washington acted cautiously during his first months in office, knowing that whatever he did would set precedents for the future. When the title by which he should be addressed aroused controversy (Vice President John Adams favored "His Highness, the President of the United States of America, and Protector of their Liberties"), Washington said nothing. The accepted title soon became a plain "Mr. President." By using the heads of the executive departments collectively as his chief advisers, he created the cabinet. As the Constitution required, he sent Congress an annual State of the Union message. Washington also concluded that he should exercise his veto power over congressional legislation very sparingly—only, indeed, if he was convinced a bill was unconstitutional.

Washington's First Steps

Washington's first major task as president was to choose the heads of the executive departments. For the War Department he selected an old comrade-in-arms, Henry Knox, who had been his reliable general of artillery during much of the Revolution. His choice for the State Department was his fellow Virginian Thomas Jefferson, who had just returned to the United States from his post as minister to France. And for the crucial position of secretary of the treasury, the president chose the brilliant, intensely ambitious Alexander Hamilton.

The illegitimate son of a Scottish aristocrat and a woman whose husband had divorced her for adultery and desertion, Hamilton was born in the British West Indies in 1757. His early years were spent in poverty; after his mother's death when he was eleven, he worked as a clerk for a mercantile firm. In 1773 Hamilton enrolled in King's College (later Columbia University) in New York City; only eighteen months

Alexander Hamilton

John Trumbull, known primarily for his larger-than-life portraits of patriot leaders, painted this miniature of George Washington, who posed for it during his presidency (c. 1792–1794). Division of Political History, Smithsonian Institution, Washington, D.C.

later, the precocious seventeen-year-old contributed a pamphlet to the prerevolutionary publication wars of late 1774. Devoted to the patriot cause, Hamilton volunteered for service in the American army, where he came to the attention of George Washington. In 1777 Washington appointed the young man as one of his aides, and the two developed great affection for one another. Indeed, in some respects Hamilton became the son Washington never had.

The general's patronage helped the poor youth of dubious background to marry well. At twenty-three he took as his wife Elizabeth Schuyler, daughter of a wealthy New York family. After the war, Hamilton practiced law in New York City and served as a delegate first to the Annapolis Convention and then to the Constitutional Convention. Though he exerted little influence at either gather-

ing, his contributions to *The Federalist* in 1788 revealed him to be one of the chief political thinkers in the republic.

In his dual role as secretary of the treasury and one of Washington's major advisers, two traits distinguished Hamilton from most of his contemporaries. First, he displayed an undivided loyalty to the nation as a whole. As a West Indian who had lived on the mainland only briefly before the war, Hamilton had no ties to a particular state. He showed little sympathy for, or understanding of, demands for local autonomy. Thus the aim of his fiscal policies was always to consolidate power at the national level. Further, he never feared the exercise of centralized executive authority, as did older counterparts who had clashed repeatedly with colonial governors, nor was he afraid of maintaining close political and economic ties with Britain.

Second, he regarded his fellow human beings with unvarnished cynicism. Perhaps because of his difficult early life and his own overriding ambition, Hamilton believed people to be motivated primarily, if not entirely, by self-interest—particularly economic self-interest. He placed no reliance on people's capacity for virtuous and self-sacrificing behavior. This outlook set him apart from those Americans who foresaw a rosy future in which public-spirited citizens would pursue the common good rather than their own private advantage. Although other Americans (like Madison) also stressed the role of private interests in a republic, Hamilton went beyond them in his emphasis on self-interest as the major motivator of human behavior. And his beliefs significantly influenced the way in which he tackled the monumental task before him: straightening out the new nation's tangled finances.

In 1789, Congress ordered the new secretary of the treasury to assess the public debt and to submit recommendations for supporting the government's credit. Hamilton found that the country's remaining war debts fell into three categories: those owed by the nation to foreign governments and investors, mostly to France (about $11 million); those owed by the national government to merchants, former soldiers, holders of revolutionary bonds, and the like (about $27 million); and, finally, similar debts owed by state governments (roughly $25 million). With respect to the national debt, there was little disagreement: politically aware Americans recognized that if their new

National and State Debts

government was to succeed it would have to repay at full face value those financial obligations incurred by the nation while winning independence.

The state debts were another matter. Some states—notably Virginia, Maryland, North Carolina, and Georgia—already had paid off most of their war debts. They would oppose the national government's assumption of responsibility for other states' debts, because their citizens would be taxed to pay such obligations. Massachusetts, Connecticut, and South Carolina, by contrast, still had sizable unpaid debts and would welcome a system of national assumption. The possible assumption of state debts also had political implications. Consolidating the debt in the hands of the national government would help to concentrate economic and political power at the national level. A contrary policy would reserve greater independence of action for the states.

Hamilton's first *Report on Public Credit*, sent to Congress in January 1790, reflected both his national loyalty and his cynicism. He proposed that Congress assume outstanding state debts, combine them with national obligations, and issue new securities covering both the principal and the accumulated unpaid interest. Current holders of state or national debt certificates would have the option of taking a portion of their payment in western lands. Hamilton's aims were clear: he wanted to expand the financial reach of the United States government, simultaneously reducing the states' economic power. He also wanted to ensure that holders of public securities—many of them wealthy merchants and speculators—would have a significant financial stake in the survival of the national government.

Hamilton's Financial Plan

Hamilton's plan stimulated lively debate in Congress. The opposition coalesced around his former ally James Madison, who opposed the assumption of state debts because his own state of Virginia had already paid off most of its obligations. As a congressman tied to agrarian rather than moneyed interests, Madison also criticized the proposal to compensate only the current holders of public securities. Well aware that speculators had purchased large quantities of debt certificates at a small fraction of their face value, Madison proposed that the original holders of the debt also be compensated by the government. Madison's plan, though fairer than Hamilton's, would have been difficult, if not impossible, to administer. The House of Representatives rejected it.

Alexander Hamilton (1757–1804) sat for this miniature by Charles Willson Peale in 1780. The determination and purposefulness of the future secretary of the treasury are reflected even in this early portrait. Columbiana Collection, Columbia University.

At first, the House also rejected the assumption of state debts. The Senate, however, adopted Hamilton's plan largely intact, and a series of compromises followed. Hamilton agreed to changes in the assumption plan that would benefit Virginia in particular. The assumption bill also became linked in a complex way to the other controversial issue of that congressional session: the location of the permanent national capital. Both northerners and southerners wanted the capital in their region. The legend that Hamilton and Madison agreed over Jefferson's dinner table to exchange assumption of state debts for a southern site is not supported by the surviving evidence, but a political deal was undoubtedly struck. The Potomac River was designated as the site for the capital, and the first part of Hamilton's financial program became law in August 1790.

Four months later Hamilton submitted to Congress a second report on public credit, recommending the chartering of a national bank. This proposal too aroused considerable opposition, though primarily after Congress had already passed the bill to establish the bank.

First Bank of the United States

Hamilton modeled his bank on the Bank of England. The Bank of the United States was to be capitalized at $10 million, of which only $2 million would come from public funds. Private investors would supply the rest. The bank's charter would run for twenty years, and the government would name one-fifth of the directors. The bank's notes would circulate as the nation's currency. The bank would also act as collecting and disbursing agent for the Treasury and would lend money to the government. Most political leaders recognized that such an institution would be beneficial, especially because it would solve the problem of America's perpetual shortage of an acceptable medium of exchange. But another issue loomed large: did the Constitution give Congress the power to establish such a bank?

James Madison answered that question with a resounding no. He pointed out that Constitutional Convention delegates had specifically rejected a clause authorizing Congress to issue corporate charters. Consequently, he argued, that power could not be inferred from other parts of the Constitution.

Madison's contention disturbed President Washington, who decided to request other opinions before signing the bill into law. Edmund Randolph, the attorney general, and Thomas Jefferson, the secretary of state, agreed with Madison that the bank was unconstitutional. Jefferson referred to Article I, Section 8, of the Constitution, which gave Congress the power "to make all Laws which shall be necessary and proper for carrying into Execution the foregoing Powers." The key word, Jefferson argued, was *necessary:* Congress could do what was needed but could not do (without specific constitutional authorization) what was merely desirable. Thus Jefferson formulated the strict-constructionist interpretation of the Constitution.

Strict and Broad Constructions of the Constitution

Washington asked Hamilton to reply to the negative assessments of his proposal. Hamilton's *Defense of the Constitutionality of the Bank,* presented to the president in February 1791, was a brilliant exposition of what has become known as the broad-

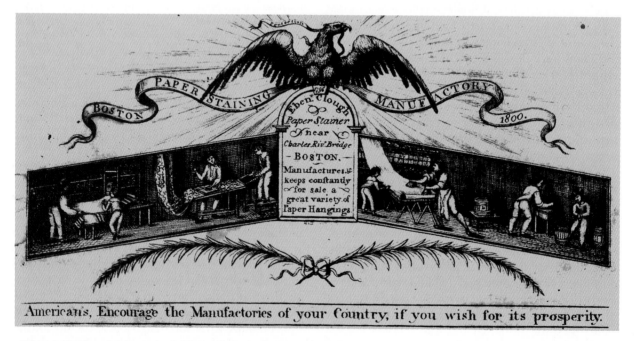

Although Congress did not react positively to the arguments in Hamilton's Report on Manufactures, *the owners of America's burgeoning industries recognized the importance of the policy Hamilton advocated. Ebenezer Clough, a Boston maker of wallpaper, incorporated into his letterhead the exhortation "Americans, Encourage the Manufactories of your Country, if you wish for its prosperity."* American Antiquarian Society.

constructionist view of the Constitution. Hamilton argued forcefully that Congress could choose any means not specifically prohibited by the Constitution to achieve a constitutional end. If the end was constitutional and the means was not unconstitutional, then the means also was constitutional.

Washington was convinced. The bill became law; the bank proved successful. So did the scheme for funding the national debt and assuming the states' debts. The new nation's securities became desirable investments for its own citizens and for wealthy foreigners, especially those in the Netherlands, who rushed to purchase American debt certificates. The influx of new capital, coupled with the high prices American produce now commanded in European markets, eased farmers' debt burdens and contributed to a new prosperity. But two other aspects of Alexander Hamilton's wide-ranging financial scheme did not fare so well.

In December 1791, Hamilton presented to Congress his *Report on Manufactures*, the third and last of his prescriptions for the American economy. In it he outlined an ambitious plan for encouraging and protecting the United States's infant industries, like shoemaking and textile manufacturing. Hamilton argued that the nation could never be truly independent as long as it relied heavily on Europe for manufactured goods. He thus urged Congress to promote the immigration of technicians and laborers and to support industrial development through a limited use of protective tariffs. Many of Hamilton's ideas were implemented in later decades, but few congressmen in 1791 could see much merit in his proposals. They firmly believed that America's future lay in agriculture and the carrying trade and that the mainstay of the republic was the virtuous yeoman farmer. Therefore, Congress rejected the report.

That same year Congress accepted another feature of Hamilton's financial program, an excise tax on whiskey. Although proceeds from the Revenue Act of 1789 were sufficient to pay interest on the national debt alone, the decision to fund state debts meant that the national government required additional income. An excise tax on whiskey was attractive because it affected relatively few farmers—those in the West who sold their grain in the form of distilled spirits as a means of avoiding the high cost of transportation—and because it might reduce consump-

Whiskey Rebellion

tion of whiskey. (Eighteenth-century Americans were notorious for their heavy drinking; annual per capita consumption of alcohol was about double today's rate.) Moreover, Hamilton knew that those western farmers were Jefferson's supporters, and he saw the benefits of taxing them rather than the merchants who supported his own policies.

News of the excise law set off protests in frontier areas of Pennsylvania, where residents were already dissatisfied with the army's as yet unsuccessful attempts to defeat the Miami Confederacy (see pages 188–189). To their minds, the same government that was protecting them inadequately was now proposing to tax them disproportionately. Unrest continued for two years on the frontiers of Pennsylvania, Maryland, and Virginia. Crowds of men drafted petitions protesting the excise, raised liberty poles (deliberately imitating actions taken in the 1760s), and occasionally harassed tax collectors.

President Washington responded with restraint until violence erupted in July 1794, when western Pennsylvania farmers resisted a federal marshal and a tax collector trying to enforce the law. Three rioters were killed and several militiamen wounded. About seven thousand rebels convened on August 1 to plot the destruction of Pittsburgh but decided not to face the heavy guns of the fort guarding the town. Washington then took decisive action to prevent a crisis reminiscent of Shays's Rebellion. On August 7, he called on the insurgents to disperse and summoned nearly thirteen thousand militia from Pennsylvania and neighboring states. By the time federal forces marched westward in October and November (led at times by Washington himself), the disturbances had ended. The troops met little resistance and arrested only twenty suspects. Two, neither of them prominent leaders of the rioters, were convicted of treason, but—continuing his policy of restraint—Washington pardoned both. The leaderless and unorganized rebellion ended almost without bloodshed.

The chief importance of the Whiskey Rebellion was not military victory over the rebels—for there was none—but the forceful message it conveyed to the American public. The national government, Washington had demonstrated, would not tyrannize its citizens, but it also would not allow violent resistance to its laws. In the republic, change would be effected peacefully, by legal means. People dissatisfied with the law should try to amend or repeal it, not take extralegal action.

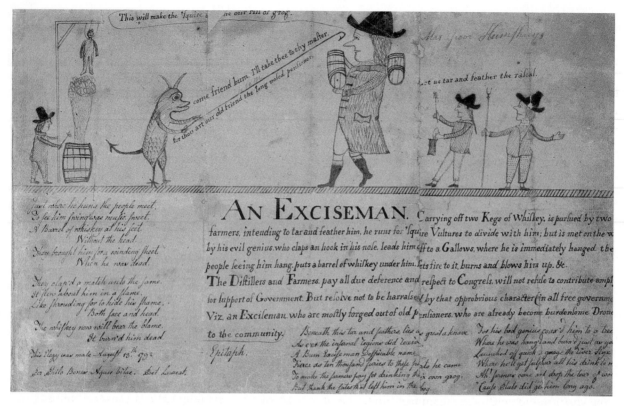

A cartoon from the mid-1790s showed the fate of an exciseman who confiscated two kegs of whiskey: pursued by two farmers, he allies himself with a devil and is hanged from a gallows.   Atwater Kent Museum.

Republicans and Federalists

By 1794, a group of Americans were already beginning to seek change systematically through electoral politics, even though traditional political theory regarded organized opposition—especially in a republic—as illegitimate. In a monarchy, opposition groups were to be expected, even encouraged. In a government of the people, by contrast, serious and sustained disagreement was taken as a sign of corruption and subversion. Yet the opposition leaders Thomas Jefferson and James Madison became convinced as early as 1792 that Hamilton's policies of favoring wealthy commercial interests at the expense of agriculture aimed at imposing a corrupt, aristocratic government on the United States. They contended that they were the true heirs of the Revolution and that Hamilton was plotting to subvert republican principles. To dramatize their point, Jefferson, Madison, and their followers in Congress began calling themselves *Republicans.*

Hamilton in turn accused Jefferson and Madison of the same crime: attempting to destroy the republic. Hamilton and his supporters began calling themselves *Federalists,* to legitimize their claims and link themselves with the Constitution. In short, each group accused the other of being an illicit faction working to destroy the republican principles of the Revolution. (In the traditional sense of the term, a *faction* was by definition dangerous and opposed to the public good.)

At first, President Washington tried to remain aloof from the political dispute that divided Hamilton and Jefferson, his chief advisers. Even so, the controversy helped persuade him to seek a second term of office in 1792 in hopes of promoting political unity. But in 1793 and thereafter, developments in foreign affairs magnified the disagreements.

Partisan Politics and Foreign Policy

The initial years under the Constitution were blessed by international peace. Soon, however, the French Revolution, which began in 1789, brought about the resumption of hostilities between France, America's wartime ally, and Great Britain, America's most important trading partner.

At first Americans welcomed the news that France was turning toward republicanism. The French people's success in limiting, then overthrowing, an oppressive monarchy seemed to vindicate America's own revolution. Americans saw themselves as the vanguard of an inevitable historical trend that would reshape the world for the better. But by the early 1790s the reports from France were disquieting. Outbreaks of violence continued; ministries succeeded each other with bewildering rapidity; executions were commonplace. The king himself was beheaded in early 1793. Although many Americans, including Jefferson and Madison, retained their sympathy for the revolutionaries, others began to view France as a prime example of the perversion of republicanism. As might be expected, Alexander Hamilton fell into the latter group.

The French Revolution

When France declared war on Britain, Spain, and Holland in 1793, the Americans faced a dilemma. The 1778 Treaty of Alliance with France bound them to that nation "forever," and a mutual commitment to republicanism created ideological bonds. Yet the United States was connected to Great Britain as well. Aside from their shared history and language, America and Britain were economic partners. Americans still purchased most of their manufactured goods from Great Britain. Indeed, since the financial system of the United States depended heavily on import tariffs as a source of revenue, the nation's economic health in effect required uninterrupted trade with the former mother country.

The political and diplomatic climate was further complicated in April 1793, when Citizen Edmond Genêt, a representative of the French government, landed in Charleston. As Genêt made his way northward to New York City, he recruited Americans for expeditions against British and Spanish colonies in the Western Hemisphere, and he distributed privateering commissions with a

Citizen Genêt

generous hand. Genêt's arrival raised a series of troubling questions for President Washington. Should he receive Genêt, thus officially recognizing the French revolutionary government? Should he acknowledge an obligation to aid France under the terms of the 1778 Treaty of Alliance? Or should he proclaim American neutrality?

For once, Hamilton and Jefferson saw eye to eye. Both told Washington that the United States could not afford to ally itself with either side. Washington agreed. He received Genêt but also issued a proclamation informing the world that the United States would adopt "a conduct friendly and impartial toward the belligerent powers." In deference to Jefferson's continued support for France, the word *neutrality* did not appear in the declaration, but its meaning was clear.

Genêt himself was removed from politics when his faction fell from power in Paris; he subsequently sought political asylum in the United States. But his disappearance from the diplomatic scene did not lessen the impact of the French Revolution in America. The domestic divisions Genêt helped to widen were perpetuated by clubs called Democratic-Republican societies, formed by Americans sympathetic to the French Revolution and worried about the policies of the Washington administration. Such societies expressed a growing grassroots concern about the same developments that troubled Jefferson and Madison.

More than forty Democratic-Republican societies were organized between 1793 and 1800. Their members saw themselves as heirs of the Sons of Liberty, seeking the same goal as their predecessors: protection of people's liberties against encroachments by corrupt and self-serving rulers. To that end, they publicly protested government fiscal and foreign policy and repeatedly proclaimed their belief in "the equal rights of man," particularly the rights to free speech, free press, and assembly. Like the Sons of Liberty, the Democratic-Republican societies were composed chiefly of artisans and craftsmen, although professionals, farmers, and merchants also joined.

Democratic-Republican Societies

The rapid growth of such groups, outspoken in their criticism of the Washington administration for its failure to come to the aid of France and for its domestic economic policies, deeply disturbed Hamilton and eventually Washington himself. Some news-

Citizen Edmond Genêt's visit caused the first major diplomatic crisis in the new nation. His attempts to enlist Americans in support of the French Revolution raised troubling questions about the international role of the United States. Collection of the Albany Institute of History and Art. Bequest of George Genêt.

papers charged that the societies were subversive agents of a foreign power. Their "real design," one asserted, was "to involve the country in war, to assume the reins of government and tyrannize over the people." The climax of the counterattack came in the fall of 1794, when Washington accused the societies of having fomented the Whiskey Rebellion.

In retrospect, Washington and Hamilton's reaction to the Democratic-Republican societies seems disproportionately hostile. But it must be recalled that factional disputes were believed to endanger the survival of republics. As the first organized political dissenters in the United States, the Democratic-Republican societies alarmed elected officials, who had not yet accepted the idea that one component of a free government was an organized loyal opposition.

Also in 1794 George Washington dispatched Chief Justice John Jay to London to negotiate four unresolved questions affecting Anglo-American af-

fairs. The first point at issue was recent British seizures of American merchant ships trading in the French West Indies. The United States wanted to establish the principle of freedom of the seas and to assert its right, as a neutral nation, to trade freely with both combatants. Second, in violation of the 1783 peace treaty, Great Britain had not yet evacuated its posts in the American Northwest. Settlers there believed that the British were responsible for the renewed warfare in the region (see pages 183–189), and they wanted that threat removed. The Americans also hoped for a commercial treaty and sought compensation for the slaves who had left with the British army at the end of the war.

Jay Treaty

The negotiations in London proved difficult, since Jay had little to offer in exchange for the concessions he sought. Britain did agree to evacuate the western forts and ease restrictions on American trade to England and the West Indies. (Some limitations were retained, however, violating the Americans' stated commitment to open commerce.) No compensation for slaves was agreed to, but the treaty established two arbitration commissions—one to deal with prewar debts Americans owed to British creditors and the other to hear claims for captured American merchant ships. Under the circumstances, Jay did remarkably well: the treaty averted war with England at a time when the United States, which lacked an effective navy, could not have hoped to win such a conflict. Nevertheless, most Americans, including the president, were dissatisfied with at least some parts of the treaty.

At first, potential opposition was blunted because the Senate debated and ratified the treaty in secret. Not until after it was approved by a vote of 20 to 10 in June 1795 was the public informed of its provisions. The Democratic-Republican societies led protests against the treaty, which were especially intense in the South. Planters criticized the commission on prewar debts and the failure to obtain compensation for runaway slaves. Once President Washington had signed the treaty, though, there seemed to be little the Republicans could do to prevent it from taking effect. Just one opportunity remained: Congress had to appropriate funds to carry out the treaty provisions and, according to the Constitution, appropriation bills had to originate in the House of Representatives.

When the House debated the issue in March 1796, members opposing the treaty tried to prevent approval of the appropriations. To that end, they asked Washington to submit to the House all documents pertinent to the negotiations. In successfully resisting the House's request, Washington established the doctrine of *executive privilege*—the power of the president to withhold information from Congress if he believes circumstances warrant doing so.

The treaty's opponents initially appeared to be in the majority, but pressure for approval built as time passed. Frontier residents were eager to have the British posts evacuated, fearing a new outbreak of Indian war despite the signing of the Treaty of Greenville. Merchants wanted to reap benefits from expanded trade. Furthermore, Thomas Pinckney of South Carolina had negotiated a treaty with Spain giving the United States navigation privileges on the Mississippi, which would be an economic boost to the West and South. The popularity of Pinckney's Treaty (the Senate ratified it unanimously) helped to overcome opposition to the Jay Treaty. For all these reasons, the House voted the necessary funds by the narrow margin of 51 to 48.

Analysis of the vote reveals both the regional nature of the division and the growing cohesion of the Republican and Federalist factions in Congress.

Partisan Divisions in Congress

Voting for the appropriations were 44 Federalists and 7 Republicans; voting against were 45 Republicans and 3 Federalists. The final tally was also split by region. The vast majority of votes against the bill were cast by southerners (including three Virginia Federalists). The bill's supporters were from New England and the middle states, with the exception of two South Carolina Federalists. The seven Republicans who voted for the appropriations were from commercial areas in New York, Pennsylvania, and Maryland.

The small number of defectors on both sides reveals a new force at work in American politics: partisanship. Voting statistics from the first four Congresses show the ever-increasing tendency of members of the House of Representatives to vote as cohesive groups, rather than as individuals. If factional loyalty is defined as voting together at least two-thirds of the time on national issues, the percentage of nonaligned congressmen dropped from 42 percent in 1790 to just 7 percent in 1796. Significantly, this trend toward party cohesion occurred even though Congress experienced heavy turnover. Most congressmen served only one or two terms in office, and fewer than 10 per-

cent were reelected more than three times. During the 1790s the majority slowly shifted from Federalist to Republican. Federalists controlled the first three Congresses, through the spring of 1795. Republicans gained ascendancy in the Fourth Congress. Federalists returned to power with slight majorities in the Fifth and Sixth Congresses, but the Republicans took over—more or less for good—in the Seventh Congress in 1801.

To describe these shifts is easier than to explain them. The growing division cannot be accurately explained in the terms used by Jefferson and Madison (aristocrats versus the people) or by Hamilton and Washington (true patriots versus subversive rabble). Simple economic differences between agrarian and commercial interests do not provide the answer either, since more than 90 percent of Americans in the 1790s lived in rural areas. Moreover, Jefferson's vision of a prosperous agrarian America was based on commercial farming, not rural self-sufficiency. Nor did the Federalist-Republican division simply repeat the Federalist-Antifederalist debate of 1787–1788. Even though most Antifederalists became Republicans, the party's leaders, Madison and Jefferson, had supported the Constitution.

Bases of Partisanship

Yet certain distinctions can be made. Republicans, who were especially prominent in the southern and middle states, tended to be self-assured, confident, and optimistic about both politics and the economy. Southern planters, firmly in control of their region and of a class of enslaved laborers, did not fear instability, at least among the European-American population. They foresaw a prosperous future based partly on continued westward expansion, which they expected to dominate. Republicans employed democratic rhetoric to win the allegiance of small farmers south of New England. Members of non-English ethnic groups—especially Irish, Scots, and Germans—found Republicans' words attractive. Also included in the Republican coalition were artisans, who saw themselves as the urban equivalent of yeoman farmers and valued their independence from domineering bosses. Republicans of all descriptions emphasized developing America's own resources and were less concerned than the Federalists about the nation's position in the world. Republicans also remained sympathetic to France in international affairs.

By contrast, Federalists, concentrated in New England, came mostly from English stock. They

How do historians know that Americans were intensely patriotic in the early years of the republic? One piece of evidence is supplied by the many items incorporating patriotic motifs that decorated the homes of American citizens. The artisans of the new nation (and of England as well) quickly recognized that "patriotism sold," so they created a wide variety of objects to satisfy Americans' demand for furniture, wallpaper, curtains, and pottery goods displaying such themes. (See, for example, the jug made in England and reproduced on page 202.) Only middling and well-to-do Americans could afford to buy such items, but a less-well-off American woman could produce some of these goods for herself. We do not know who made this eagle hooked rug, but a poor woman with just a few moments to spare each day could well have labored for months to display her allegiance to the new nation in this fashion.   New York State Historical Association, Cooperstown.

drew considerable support from commercial interests and were insecure, uncertain of the future. They stressed the need for order, authority, and regularity in the political world. Federalists had no grassroots political organization and put little emphasis on involving ordinary people in government. Not all Federalists were wealthy merchants; many were farmers who, prevented from expanding agricultural production because of New England's poor soil, gravitated toward the more conservative party. Federalists, like Republicans, assumed that southern interests would dominate the land west of the mountains, so they had little incentive to work actively to develop that potentially rich territory. In Federalist eyes, the nation was perpetually threatened by potential enemies, both internal and external, and was best protected by a continuing alliance with Great Britain. Their vision of international affairs may have been more accurate than that of the Republicans, given the warfare in Europe, but it was also narrow and unattractive. Since the Federalist view held out little hope of a better future to the voters of any region, it is not surprising that Republicans eventually prevailed.

The presence of the two organized groups—not yet parties in the modern sense but active contenders for office nonetheless—made the presidential election of 1796 the first that was seriously contested. Tired of the criticism to which he had been subjected, George Washington decided to retire from office. (Presidents had not yet been limited to two terms by constitutional amendment.) In September Washington published his Farewell Address, most of which had been written by Hamilton. In it Washington out-

Washington's Farewell Address

lined two principles that guided American foreign policy at least until the late 1940s: to maintain commercial but not political ties to other nations and to enter no permanent alliances. He also drew sharp distinctions between the United States and Europe, stressing America's uniqueness and the need for unilateralism (independent action in foreign affairs).

Domestically, Washington lamented the existence of factional divisions among his countrymen. Historians have often interpreted his call for an end to partisan strife as the statement of a man who could see beyond political affiliations to the good of the whole. But it is more accurately read in the context of its day as an attack on the legitimacy of the Republican opposition. What Washington wanted was unity behind the Federalist banner, which he saw as the only proper political stance. The Federalists (like the Republicans) continued to see themselves as the sole guardians of the truth and the only true heirs of the Revolution; they perceived their opponents as misguided, unpatriotic troublemakers who were undermining the revolutionary ideals.

To succeed Washington, the Federalists in Congress put forward Vice President John Adams, with the diplomat Thomas Pinckney as his running mate.

Election of 1796

Congressional Republicans caucused and chose Thomas Jefferson as their presidential candidate; the lawyer, Revolutionary War veteran, and active Republican politician Aaron Burr of New York agreed to run for vice president.

That the election was contested did not mean that its outcome was decided by the people. Voters could cast their ballots only for electors, not for the candidates themselves, and not all electors publicly declared their preferences. More than 40 percent of the members of the electoral college were chosen by state legislatures rather than by popular vote, and some were picked even before the presidential candidates had been named by congressional caucuses. Moreover, the method of voting in the electoral college did not take into account the possibility of party slates. The Constitution's drafters had not foreseen the development of competing national political organizations, so the Constitution provided no way to express support for one person for president and another for vice president. The electors simply voted for two people. The man with the highest total became president; the second highest, vice president.

This procedure proved to be the Federalists' undoing. Adams won the presidency with 71 votes, but a number of Federalist electors (especially those from New England) did not cast ballots for Pinckney. Thomas Jefferson won 68 votes, 9 more than Pinckney, and became vice president. The incoming administration was thus politically divided. The next four years were to see the new president and vice president, once allies and close friends, become bitter enemies.

 ## John Adams and Political Dissent

John Adams took over the presidency peculiarly blind to the partisan developments of the previous four years. As president he never abandoned an outdated notion discarded by George Washington as early as 1794: that the president should be above politics, an independent and dignified figure who did not seek petty factional advantage. Thus Adams kept Washington's cabinet intact, despite its key members' allegiance to his chief rival, Alexander Hamilton. Adams often adopted a passive posture, letting others (usually Hamilton) take the lead when he should have acted decisively. As a result, his administration gained a reputation for inconsistency. When Adams's term ended, the Federalists were severely divided, and the Republicans had won the presidency. But Adams's detachment from Hamilton's maneuverings did enable him to weather the greatest international crisis the republic had yet faced: the so-called Quasi-War with France.

The Jay Treaty improved America's relationship with Great Britain, but it provoked retaliation by France. Angry that the United States had reached agreement with its enemy, the French government ordered its vessels to seize American ships carrying British goods. In response, Adams appointed three commissioners to try to reach a settlement with France. Simultaneously, Congress increased military spending, authorizing the building of ships and the stockpiling of weapons and ammunition.

For months, the American commissioners sought negotiations with Talleyrand, the French foreign minister, but Talleyrand's agents demanded a

XYZ Affair

bribe of $250,000 before talks could begin. The Americans retorted, "No, no; not a sixpence," and reported the incident in dispatches that President Adams received in early March 1798. Adams informed Congress of the impasse and recommended increased appropriations for defense.

This cartoon drawn during the XYZ affair depicts the United States as a maiden being victimized by the five leaders of the French government's directorate. In the background, John Bull (England) watches from on high, while other European nations discuss the situation. The Lilly Library, Indiana University, Bloomington, Indiana.

Convinced that Adams had deliberately sabotaged the negotiations, congressional Republicans insisted that the dispatches be turned over to Congress. Adams complied, aware that releasing the reports would work to his advantage. He withheld only the names of the French agents, referring to them as *X*, *Y*, and *Z*. The revelation that the Americans had been treated with contempt stimulated a wave of anti-French sentiment in the United States. A journalist's version of the commissioners' reply, "Millions for defense, but not a cent for tribute," became the national slogan. Cries for war filled the air. Congress formally abrogated the Treaty of Alliance and authorized American ships to seize French vessels.

Thus began an undeclared war with France. The so-called Quasi-War was fought in the West Indies, between warships of the United States Navy and French privateers seeking to capture American merchant vessels. Although initial American losses of merchant shipping were heavy, by early 1799 the United

Quasi-War with France

States Navy had established its superiority in Caribbean waters. Its ships captured eight French privateers and naval vessels, easing the threat to America's vital West Indian trade.

The Republicans, who opposed war and continued to sympathize with France, could do little to stem the tide of anti-French feelings. Since Agent Y had boasted of the existence of a "French party in America," Federalists flatly accused Republicans of traitorous designs. A New York newspaper declared that anyone who remained "lukewarm" after reading the XYZ dispatches was a "criminal—and the man who does not warmly reprobate the conduct of the French must have a soul black enough to be *fit* for *treason Strategems* and *spoils*." John Adams wavered between calling the Republicans traitors and acknowledging their right to oppose administration measures. His wife was less tolerant. "Those whom the French boast of as their Partizans," Abigail Adams declared, should be "adjudged traitors to their country." If Jefferson had been president, she added, "we should all have been sold to the French."

Federalists saw this climate of opinion as an opportunity to deal a death blow to their Republican opponents. Now that the country seemed to see the truth of what they had been saying ever since the Whiskey Rebellion in 1794—that Republicans were subversive foreign agents—Federalists sought to codify that belief into law. In 1798, the Federalist-controlled Congress adopted a set of four laws known as the Alien and Sedition Acts, intended to suppress dissent and to prevent further growth of the Republican party.

Alien and Sedition Acts

Three of the acts were aimed at immigrants, whom Federalists accurately suspected of being Republican in their sympathies. The Naturalization Act lengthened the residency period required for citizenship and ordered all resident aliens to register with the federal government. The two Alien Acts provided for the detention of enemy aliens in time of war and gave the president authority to deport any alien he deemed dangerous to the nation's security. Neither act was implemented during the Adams administration, however.

The fourth act, the Sedition Act, sought to control both citizens and aliens. It outlawed conspiracies to prevent the enforcement of federal laws and set the maximum punishment for such offenses at five years in prison and a $5,000 fine. The act also tried to control speech. Writing, printing, or uttering "false, scandalous and malicious" statements against the government or the president "with intent to defame . . . or to bring them or either of them, into contempt or disrepute" became a crime punishable by as much as two years' imprisonment and a fine of $2,000. Today any such law punishing speech alone would be considered unconstitutional. But in the eighteenth century, when organized political opposition was regarded with suspicion, the restrictions that the Sedition Act placed on speech were acceptable to many.

The Sedition Act led to fifteen indictments and ten convictions. Most of the accused were outspoken Republican newspaper editors who failed to mute their criticism of the administration in response to the law. But the first victim—whose story may serve as an example of the rest—was a hot-tempered Republican congressman from Vermont, Matthew Lyon. The Irish-born Lyon, a former indentured servant who had purchased his freedom and fought in the Revolution, was indicted for declaring in print

that John Adams had displayed "a continual grasp for power" and "an unbounded thirst for ridiculous pomp, foolish adulation, and selfish avarice." Though convicted, fined $1,000, and sent to prison for four months, Lyon was not silenced. He conducted his reelection campaign from jail, winning an overwhelming majority. The fine was ceremoniously paid for him by contributions from leading Republicans around the country.

Faced with prosecutions of their supporters, Jefferson and Madison sought an effective means of combating the acts. Petitioning the Federalist-controlled Congress to repeal the laws would clearly do no good. Furthermore, Federalist judges refused to allow accused individuals to question the Sedition Act's constitutionality. Accordingly, the Republican leaders turned to the only other forum available for protest: state legislatures. Carefully concealing their own role—it would not have been desirable for the vice president to be indicted for sedition—Jefferson and Madison each drafted a set of resolutions. Introduced into the Kentucky and Virginia legislatures, respectively, in the fall of 1798, the resolutions differed somewhat but had the same import. Since the Constitution was created by a compact among the states, they contended, people speaking through their states had a legitimate right to judge the constitutionality of actions taken by the federal government. Both sets of resolutions pronounced the Alien and Sedition Acts null and void and asked other states to join in the protest.

Virginia and Kentucky Resolutions

Although no other state endorsed them, the Virginia and Kentucky resolutions were nevertheless influential. First, they were superb political propaganda, rallying Republican opinion throughout the country. They placed the opposition party squarely in the revolutionary tradition of resistance to tyrannical authority. Second, the theory of union that they proposed inspired southern states' rights advocates in the 1830s and thereafter. Jefferson and Madison had identified a key constitutional issue: how far could states go in opposing the national government? How could a conflict between the two be resolved? These questions were not to be definitively answered until the Civil War.

Ironically, just as the Sedition Act was being implemented and northern state legislatures were rejecting the Virginia and Kentucky resolutions,

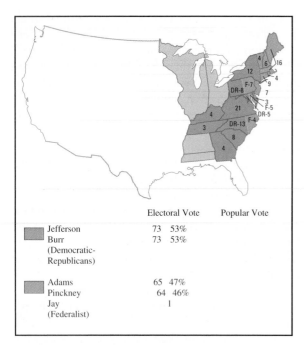

	Electoral Vote	Popular Vote
Jefferson	73	53%
Burr	73	53%
(Democratic-Republicans)		
Adams	65	47%
Pinckney	64	46%
Jay	1	
(Federalist)		

Presidential Election, 1800 The Democratic-Republicans, with their candidates Thomas Jefferson and Aaron Burr, won the electoral votes of the southern states, while the Federalists, the party of John Adams and Charles Cotesworth Pinckney, received votes primarily in New England. The parties split the votes of the middle states, but the Democratic-Republicans dominated the electoral-vote count there and won the election.

Convention of 1800

Federalists split over the course of action the United States should take toward France. Hamilton and his supporters still called for a declaration legitimizing the undeclared naval war. But Adams received a number of private signals that the French government regretted its treatment of the American commissioners. Acting on these assurances, he dispatched the envoy William Vans Murray to Paris. The United States asked for two things: compensation for ships the French had seized since 1793 and abrogation of the treaty of 1778. The Convention of 1800, which ended the Quasi-War, provided for the latter but not the former. Still, it freed the United States from its only permanent alliance, thus allowing it to follow the independent diplomatic course George Washington outlined in his Farewell Address.

The results of the negotiations were not known in the United States until after the presidential election of 1800. Even so, since Hamilton and many of his followers wanted to widen the Quasi-War, Adams's decision to seek a peaceful settlement probably cost him reelection because of the divisions it caused in Federalist ranks.

The Republicans entered the 1800 presidential race firmly united behind Jefferson and Burr. Although they won the election, their lack of foresight almost cost them dearly. The problem was the system of voting in the electoral college, which Federalists understood better than Republicans.

Election of 1800

The Federalists arranged in advance for one of their electors to fail to vote for Charles Cotesworth Pinckney, their vice-presidential candidate. John Adams thus received the higher number of Federalist votes (65 to Pinckney's 64). The Republicans failed to make the same distinction between their candidates, and all 73 of their electors cast ballots for both Jefferson and Burr (see map). Because neither Republican had a plurality, the Constitution required that the contest be decided in the House of Representatives, with each state's congressmen voting as a unit. Since the new House, dominated by Republicans, would not take office for some months, Federalist congressmen decided the election. It took them thirty-five ballots to decide that Jefferson would be a lesser evil than Burr. In response to the tangle, the Twelfth Amendment to the Constitution (1804) changed the method of voting in the electoral college to allow for a party ticket.

Westward Expansion, Social Change, and Religious Ferment

The United States experienced a dramatic increase in internal migration in the postrevolutionary years. As much as 5 to 10 percent of the population moved each year, approximately half relocating to another state. Young European-American men were the most mobile segment of the populace, but all groups moved with similar frequency. The major population shifts were from east to west (see map, page 218): from New England to upstate New York and Ohio, from New Jersey to western Pennsylvania, from the Chesapeake to the new states of Kentucky

In 1805, an unidentified artist painted Benjamin Hawkins, a trader and United States agent to the Indians of the Southeast, at the Creek agency near Macon, Georgia. Hawkins introduced European-style agriculture to the Creeks, who are shown here with vegetables from their fields. Throughout the eastern United States, Indian nations had to make similar adaptations of their traditional lifestyles in order to maintain their group identity.   Collection of the Greenville County Art Museum, South Carolina.

and Tennessee, which entered the Union in 1792 and 1796 respectively. Very few people moved north or south, but some southerners (perhaps yeoman farmers escaping the expansion of slavery) did seek new homes farther north.

Some of these migrants moved west of the Appalachian Mountains. The first permanent white settlements beyond the mountains were established in western North Carolina in 1771. But not until after the defeat of the Shawnees in 1774 and the Cherokees in 1776 (see pages 152–153) was the way cleared for a more general migration. Small groups of families filtered through the Cumberland Gap into Kentucky, following the Wilderness Road carved out in 1775. At war's end, Americans streamed over the

Settlement in the West

mountains in considerably larger numbers. In 1783, only about 12,000 whites and blacks lived west of the mountains and south of the Ohio River; less than a decade later, the 1790 census counted more than 100,000 residents of the future states of Kentucky and Tennessee.

Settlements grew more slowly north of the Ohio River because of the strength of the Miami Confederacy. But once the Treaty of Greenville was signed in 1795, the Ohio country also grew rapidly. Many easterners traveled by land to Pittsburgh, then floated down the Ohio River on flatboats and rafts to Marietta. Others, like Margaret Dwight, moved to land that Connecticut had claimed under its colonial charter—the so-called Western Reserve (see map, page 184). All these settlers repeated the process of transforming the environment that their fore-

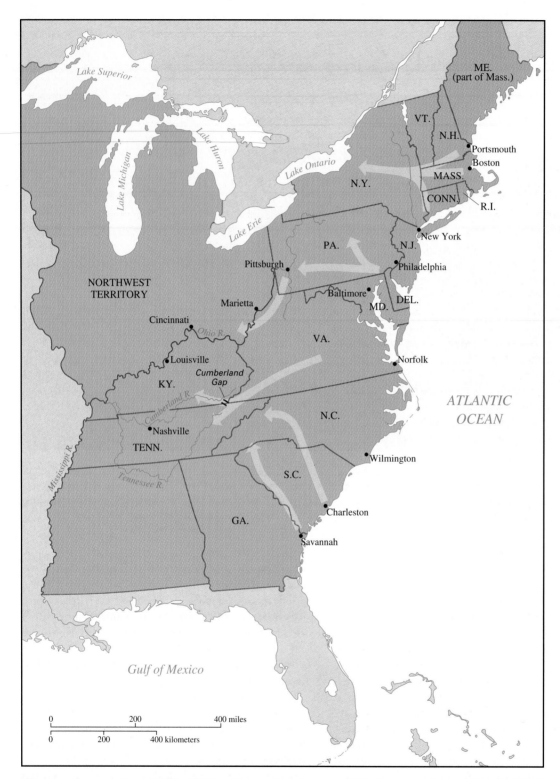

Western Expansion, 1785–1805   *After the Revolutionary War, large numbers of white and black Americans ventured west of the Appalachian Mountains for the first time. Following certain distinct routes, they moved along rivers like the Mohawk (in New York) and the Ohio or through passes like the Cumberland Gap.*

bears had undertaken: cutting down forests, clearing fields, building fences, and, in general, imposing patterns of land usage derived from European practice on a landscape previously managed quite differently by Indians.

The transplanted New Englanders in particular did their best to re-create the societies they had left behind, laying out farms and towns in neat checkerboard patterns and founding libraries and Congregational churches. Early arrivals' enthusiastic letters describing Ohio's rich soil and potential for growth recruited others to join them, setting off a phenomenon known in New England as "Ohio Fever." The New Englanders, proud of their literate, orderly culture, viewed their neighbors with disdain. Ohioans, said one, were "intelligent, industrious, and thriving," whereas the Virginians who had settled across the river in Kentucky were "ignorant, lazy, and poor." He continued the contrast: "Here the buildings are neat, . . . there the habitations are miserable cabins. Here the grounds are laid out in a regular manner . . . ; there the fields are surrounded by a rough zigzag log fence."

The westward migration of slaveholders, first to Kentucky and Tennessee and then later into the rich lands of western Georgia and eventually the Gulf Coast, had an adverse impact on African-Americans. The web of family connections built up over several generations of residence in the Chesapeake was torn apart by the population movement. Even those few large planters who moved their entire slave force west rarely owned all the members of every family on their plantations. Most commonly the migrants were either younger sons of eastern slaveholders, whose inheritance included only a portion of the family's slaves, or small farmers with just one or two bondspeople. In the early years of American settlement in the West, the population was widely dispersed; accordingly, African-Americans raised among large numbers of kin in the Chesapeake had to adapt to lonely lives on isolated farms, far from their parents, siblings, or even spouses and children. The approximately 100,000 African-Americans forcibly moved west by 1810 had to begin to build new families there to replace those unwillingly left behind in the East. They succeeded well, as Chapter 11 shows.

The mobility of the population created a volatile mix in southern frontier areas. Everyone was new to the region, and few had relatives nearby. Since most

African-Americans in the West

Second Great Awakening

of the migrants were young, single men just starting to lead independent lives, western society was at first unstable. Like the seventeenth-century Chesapeake, the late-eighteenth-century American West was a society in which single women like Margaret Dwight married quickly. The other side of the same coin was that the few women among the migrants lamented their lack of congenial female friends. Isolated, far from familiar surroundings, women and men strove to create new communities to replace those left behind. Perhaps the most meaningful of the new communities was the affiliation supplied by evangelical religion.

Among the migrants to Kentucky and Tennessee were clergymen and committed lay members of the evangelical sects that had arisen in America after the Great Awakening of the 1730s through the 1760s—Baptists, Presbyterians, and Methodists. That First Awakening had flourished in the southern backcountry well into the 1760s, and the Second Great Awakening, which began around 1800 in the West and continued into the 1840s (see pages 348–349), was an extension of the earlier revival. Laymen and clerics alike spread the doctrine of evangelical Christianity through the countryside, carrying the message of salvation to the rootless and mostly uneducated frontier folk.

At camp meetings, sometimes attended by thousands of people and usually lasting from three days to a week, clergymen exhorted their audiences to repent their sins and become genuine Christians. Many declared that salvation was open to all, rejecting the Calvinistic doctrine of predestination. Stressing the emotional nature of the conversion experience and downplaying the need for Bible study, such preachers brought the message of religion to the people in more ways than one. They were in effect democratizing American religion, making it available to all rather than to a preselected and educated elite.

The most famous camp meeting took place in August 1801 at Cane Ridge, in central Kentucky. At a time when the largest settlement in the state had no more than two thousand inhabitants, about ten thousand people came to Cane Ridge, attracted to a scheduled Presbyterian communion service after a summer filled with smaller revivals. Twenty Presbyterian and Methodist clergymen preached to the throngs; they were joined by an estimated three hundred lay exhorters, who began speaking to the crowd

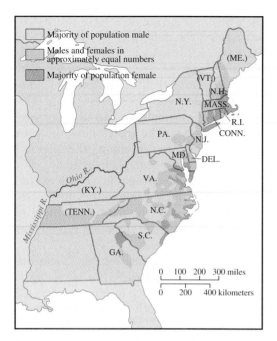

Sex Ratio of White Population, 1790
The first census revealed that the sex ratio varied dramatically in different parts of the country. In many older, coastal areas, women predominated; on the frontier, men were in the majority. The variations had important implications for life in those regions, as the text points out.   Source: From Lester J. Cappon et al., eds., *Atlas of Early American History: The Revolutionary Era, 1760–1790.* Copyright © 1976 by Princeton University Press. Reprinted by permission of Princeton University Press.

spontaneously. One witness saw "sinners dropping down on every hand, shrieking, groaning, crying for mercy, . . . some singing, some shouting, clapping their hands, hugging and even kissing, laughing." Such scenes were to be repeated many times in the decades that followed. Revivals swept across different regions of the country until nearly the middle of the century, leaving an indelible legacy of evangelism to many American Protestant churches.

The established churches of the colonial era—supported, like the Congregationalists in Massachusetts or the Anglicans in Virginia, by tax revenues—

Attacks on Established Churches

came under vigorous attack from dissenters who used revolutionary ideology to great advantage. Isaac Backus, a New England Baptist, pointed out forcefully that "many, who are filling the

nation with the cry of liberty and against *oppressors* are at the same time themselves violating that dearest of all rights, liberty of conscience." Legislators found it impossible to resist the logic of such arguments. Many states dissolved their ties to churches during or immediately after the war, and others vastly reduced state support for established denominations.

These changes meant that congregations could no longer rely on public funds and that all churches were placed on the same footing with respect to government. Church membership became voluntary, as did monetary contributions from members. If congregations were to survive, they had to generate new sources of support. Revivals, which were genuine outpourings of religious sentiment, also proved a convenient means of increasing church membership.

An analysis of secular society can help to explain the conversion patterns of the Second Awakening. Unlike the First Great Awakening, when converts were evenly divided by sex, more women than men—particularly

Women and the Second Awakening

young women—answered the call of Christianity during the Second Awakening. The increase in female converts seems to have been directly related to fundamental changes in women's circumstances in the late eighteenth century. In some areas of the country, especially New England (where the revival movement flourished), women outnumbered men after 1790, for many young men had migrated westward (see map). Thus eastern girls could no longer count on finding marital partners. The uncertainty of their social and familial position seems to have led them to seek spiritual certainty in the church.

Young women's domestic roles changed dramatically at the same time, for cloth production was beginning to move from the household to the factory (see page 349). Deprived of their chief household role as spinners and weavers, New England daughters found in the church a realm where they could continue to make useful contributions to society. Church missionary societies and charitable associations provided an acceptable outlet for their talents. One of the most striking developments of the early nineteenth century was the creation of hundreds of female associations to aid widows and orphans, collect money for foreign missions, and improve the quality of maternal care. Thus American women collectively assumed the role of keepers of the nation's conscience, taking the lead in charitable enterprises and freeing their husbands from concern for such moral issues.

The religious ferment in frontier regions of the Upper South contributed to racial ferment as well, for people of both races attended the camp meetings

Unrest Among African-Americans

to hear black and white preachers. When revivals spread eastward into more heavily slaveholding areas, planters became fearful of the egalitarianism implied in the evangelical message of universal salvation and harmony. Their fear was heightened by events in the West Indies. In 1793, in the French colony of Saint Domingue (Haiti), mulattos and blacks under the leadership of Toussaint L'Ouverture overthrew European rule in a bloody revolt characterized by numerous atrocities on both sides. News of the successful rebellion traveled rapidly among slaves and slaveowners in the South, which at that time was experiencing rapid demographic change.

The expansion of cotton production after the invention of the cotton gin in 1793 and the beginnings of large-scale westward migration increased the demand for slaves. Planters rushed to purchase new enslaved laborers, both to take advantage of the new technology and to replace the bondspeople lost during the Revolution. The postwar decades therefore witnessed the single most massive inflow of Africans into North America since the beginnings of the slave trade. Before the legal trade was halted in 1808, more than ninety thousand new Africans had been imported into the United States (see map). Their mere presence increased slaveholders' anxieties about the possibilities for revolt, while simultaneously the postwar increase in the number of free blacks severely challenged the slave system. Like their white compatriots, African-Americans (both slave and free) had become familiar with notions of liberty and equality. They also had witnessed the benefits of fighting collectively for freedom, rather than resisting individually or running away. The circumstances were ripe for an explosion.

At this juncture in Virginia, Gabriel, an enslaved Richmond blacksmith who argued that African-Americans should fight for their freedom, planned a large-scale revolt. Identifying his targets not as all whites but

Gabriel's Rebellion

rather as those "merchants" who oppressed artisans of both races, Gabriel first recruited to his cause other skilled African-Americans who like him-

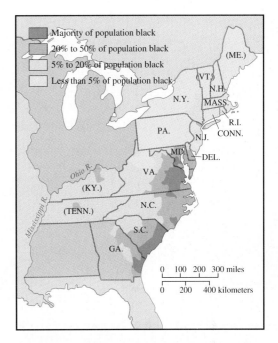

African-American Population, 1790: Proportion of Total Population *The first census clearly indicated that the African-American population was heavily concentrated in just a few areas of the United States, most notably in coastal regions of South Carolina, Georgia, and Virginia. Although there were growing numbers of blacks in the backcountry—presumably taken there by migrating slaveowners—most parts of the North and East, with the exception of the immediate vicinity of New York City, had few African-American residents.*   Source: From Lester J. Cappon et al., eds., *Atlas of Early American History: The Revolutionary Era, 1760–1790.* Copyright © 1976 by Princeton University Press. Reprinted by permission of Princeton University Press.

self lived in semifreedom under minimal supervision. Next he enlisted rural slaves. The conspirators planned to attack Richmond on the night of August 30, 1800, setting fire to the city, seizing the state capitol, and capturing the governor. At that point, Gabriel believed, other slaves and sympathetic poor whites would join in.

The plan showed considerable political sophistication, but heavy rain forced a postponement. Several planters then learned of the plan from their slaves and spread the alarm. Gabriel avoided capture for some weeks, but most of the other leaders of the rebellion were quickly arrested and interrogated.

Richmond, Virginia, at the time of Gabriel's Rebellion. This was the city as Gabriel knew it. The state capitol, the rebels' intended target, dominates the city's skyline as it dominated Gabriel's thinking.   Virginia Historical Society.

Twenty-six conspirators, including Gabriel himself, were hanged, but that outcome did not put an end to unrest among Virginia's slaves.

In 1802, a waterman named Sancho—a peripheral participant in Gabriel's plot—revived the plans for a revolt. This time word spread along Virginia and North Carolina rivers, carried by slaves who, like Sancho, worked on the boats that plied the two states' interconnected waterways. The plans were still incomplete when the plots were revealed. Again, trials and executions followed, and twenty-five more African-Americans lost their lives on the gallows.

At his trial two years earlier, one of Gabriel's followers had made explicit the links that so frightened Chesapeake slaveholders. He told his judges that, like George Washington, "I have adventured my life in endeavouring to obtain the liberty of my country-men, and am a willing sacrifice in their cause." Southern state legislatures responded to such claims by increasing the severity of the laws regulating slav-ery. Before long, all talk of emancipation (gradual or otherwise) ceased, and slavery became even more firmly entrenched as an economic institution and way of life.

 Conclusion

As the nineteenth century began, inhabitants of the United States were moving toward an accommodation to their changed lives in the new republic. Native American peoples east of the Mississippi found that they had to give up some parts of their traditional culture to preserve others. African-Americans and European-Americans tried to create new lives for themselves in the West and to adjust to changed economic circumstances in the East. Building on successful negotiations with both Britain (the Jay Treaty) and France (the Convention of 1800), the United States developed its diplomatic independence, striving to avoid entanglement with the European powers. The 1790s spawned vigorous debates over foreign and domestic policy and saw the beginnings of a system of political parties. Dissent was discouraged but not successfully suppressed. Religious revivals swept portions of the countryside and contributed to social unrest, as they had done in the eighteenth century.

At the end of the 1790s, after years of struggle, the Jeffersonian interpretation of republicanism finally prevailed over Hamilton's approach. As a result, in the years to come the country would be characterized by a decentralized economy, minimal government (especially at the national level), and maximum freedom of action and mobility for individual white men. Jeffersonian Republicans, like other white men before them, failed to extend to white women, Indian peoples, and African-Americans the freedom and individuality they recognized as essential for themselves.

Suggestions for Further Reading

National Government and Administration

Kenneth Bowling, *The Creation of Washington, D.C.* (1991); Ralph Adams Brown, *The Presidency of John Adams* (1975); William R. Casto, *The Supreme Court in the Early Republic: The Chief Justiceships of John Jay and Oliver Ellsworth* (1995); Stanley Elkins and Eric McKitrick, *The Age of Federalism, 1788–1800* (1993); Morton Frisch, *Alexander Hamilton and the Political Order* (1991); Richard H. Kohn, *Eagle and Sword: The Federalists and the Creation of the Military Establishment in America, 1783–1802* (1975); Tadahisa Kuroda, *The Origins of the Twelfth Amendment: The Electoral College in the Early Republic, 1787–1804* (1994); Forrest McDonald, *Alexander Hamilton* (1979); Forrest McDonald, *The Presidency of George Washington* (1974); John R. Nelson, Jr., *Liberty and Property: Political Economy and Policymaking in the New Nation, 1789–1812* (1987); James R. Sharp, *American Politics in the Early Republic: The New Nation in Crisis* (1993); Garry Wills, *Cincinnatus: George Washington and the Enlightenment* (1984).

Partisan Politics

Joyce Appleby, *Capitalism and a New Social Order: The Republican Vision of the 1790s* (1984); Lance Banning, *The Jeffersonian Persuasion: Evolution of a Party Ideology* (1978); Richard Buel, *Securing the Revolution: Ideology in American Politics, 1789–1815* (1972); Joseph Charles, *The Origins of the American Party System* (1956); Noble E. Cunningham, *The Jeffersonian Republicans: The Formation of Party Organization, 1789–1801* (1957); Manning J. Dauer, *The Adams Federalists* (1953); Richard Hofstadter, *The Idea of a Party System: The Rise of Legitimate Opposition in the United States, 1780–1840* (1970); John Zvesper, *Political Philosophy and Rhetoric: A Study of the Origins of American Party Politics* (1977).

Foreign Policy

Harry Ammon, *The Genêt Mission* (1973); Samuel F. Bemis, *Jay's Treaty*, 2d ed. (1962); Samuel F. Bemis, *Pinckney's Treaty*, 2d ed. (1960); Jerald A. Combs, *The Jay Treaty* (1970); Alexander DeConde, *The Quasi-War: Politics and Diplomacy of the Undeclared War with France, 1797–1801* (1966); Alexander DeConde, *Entangling Alliance: Politics and Diplomacy Under George Washington* (1958); Felix Gilbert, *To the Farewell Address: Ideas of Early American Foreign Policy* (1961); Reginald Horsman, *The Diplomacy of the New Republic, 1776–1815* (1985); Lawrence Kaplan, *"Entangling Alliances with None": American Foreign Policy in the Age of Jefferson* (1987); Bradford Perkins, *The First Rapprochement: England and the United States, 1795–1805* (1967); William Stinchcombe, *The XYZ Affair* (1981).

Civil Liberties

Leonard W. Levy, *Emergence of a Free Press* (1985); Leonard W. Levy, *Origins of the Fifth Amendment* (1968); Robert A. Rutland, *The Birth of the Bill of Rights, 1776–1791*, rev. ed. (1983); James Morton Smith, *Freedom's Fetters: The Alien and Sedition Laws and American Civil Liberties* (1956).

Social Change and Westward Expansion

Andrew Cayton, *The Frontier Republic: Ideology and Politics in the Ohio Country, 1789–1812* (1986); Nancy F. Cott, *The Bonds of Womanhood: "Woman's Sphere" in New England, 1780–1835* (1977); Douglas Egerton, *Gabriel's Rebellion: The Virginia Slave Conspiracies of 1800 and 1802* (1993); John Mack Faragher, *Daniel Boone: The Life and Legend of an American Pioneer* (1992); Reginald Horsman, *The Frontier in the Formative Years, 1783–1815* (1970); Allen Kulikoff, *The Agrarian Origins of American Capitalism* (1992); Malcolm Rohrbough, *The Trans-Appalachian Frontier: Peoples, Societies, and Institutions, 1775–1850* (1979); Thomas Slaughter, *The Whiskey Rebellion* (1986).

Religion

Catharine Albanese, *Sons of the Fathers: The Civil Religion of the American Revolution* (1976); Ruth Bloch, *Visionary Republic: Millennial Themes in American Thought* (1985); Jon Butler, *Awash in a Sea of Faith: Christianizing the American People* (1990); Paul Conkin, *Cane Ridge: America's Pentecost* (1990); Nathan O. Hatch, *The Democratization of American Christianity* (1990); Ronald Hoffman and Peter J. Albert, eds., *Religion in a Revolutionary Age* (1994); Fred J. Hood, *Reformed America, 1783–1837* (1980); William McLoughlin, *Revivals, Awakenings, and Reform* (1978).

9

The Empire of Liberty
1801–1824

Nez Perce villagers on the western slope of the Rockies were stunned on September 20, 1805, when a ragtag group of white men descended on them. Some boys playing in a field first spotted the intruders, a scouting group headed by William Clark. Terrified, the boys fled. Clark, leaving his gun and horse behind him, chased the boys and found them hiding. The boys returned to their village with gifts of ribbon.

An old man soon came to greet the bearded strangers. Using signs to communicate, he invited them to his village. As elderly men and women of all ages looked on with fear, the Indian leader told Clark that the village head, Broken Arm, and the men were away on a raid. They fed Clark and his group with pieces of buffalo, dried salmon, and camas bread.

In the next village, the Nez Perce greeted the Clark party in much the same way. They welcomed the strangers and watched them gather food. A Nez Perce chief mapped out the terrain for them, indicating that in another camp was an important leader, Twisted Hair. Clark then sent a message to his partner Meriwether Lewis and the majority of the exploring group, saying he and his companions would meet them at Twisted Hair's settlement. The villagers watched on September 22 as the two separate groups joined.

According to the Nez Perce's oral tradition, their cautious but friendly welcome of Lewis and Clark was due in part to the efforts of an elderly woman whose experience with white people had been positive. Watkuweis, whose name meant "returned from a far country," had once been a slave of a white trader. When Clark arrived at her village, she said: "These are the people who helped me. Do them no hurt." The Nez Perce also welcomed Lewis and Clark because they wanted guns and ammunition, which the expedition was carrying. In the spring of 1805 men

Shoshone guide Sacagawea showing Black Eagle Falls in what is now Montana to Meriwether Lewis, William Clark, and Clark's servant York. Artist Olaf Seltzer depicted the Lewis and Clark expedition's role in extending the American "empire of liberty." *Detail of "Capt. Lewis at the Black Eagle Falls of the Missouri River—June 13, 1805," by Olaf C. Seltzer, oil on canvas, 0137.753, From the Collection of Gilcrease Museum, Tulsa.*

from Broken Arm's band had traded with other Indians for six guns and had heard about the Lewis and Clark expedition. Lewis and Clark gave the chiefs the usual gifts—tobacco, clothing, flags, and medals—but Nez Perce self-interest, not trading goods, was responsible for the good relations.

The Nez Perce crossed the rugged mountains regularly and safely, but the Lewis and Clark expedition found the terrain perilous. Early in September 1805 as the explorers had moved through the Rockies in present-day Montana and Idaho, they crossed what expedition member Sergeant Patrick Gass in his diary described as "the most terrible mountains I ever beheld." Shoshone Indians had warned them that the trail was treacherous, and that little game was to be had. But they also told Lewis and Clark that the Nez Perce traversed it frequently, and the American explorers believed that if the Indians could make the climb, so could they.

The trip had proved as difficult as predicted. The Americans lost their way a number of times and tumbled down steep mountain trails. They slept in the snow, bone cold. Short of food, they killed a horse for meat. Finally, the thirty survivors of the fifty-man group reached level land and the Nez Perce villages. From there they went on to the Pacific Ocean and then spent another year on the return journey.

President Thomas Jefferson had commissioned Lewis and Clark in 1803 to explore the newly purchased Lousiana Territory. The twenty-nine-year-old Lewis had been a regular army officer in the 1790s and was Jefferson's private secretary. The thirty-three-year-old Clark was an explorer and former soldier who had fought and negotiated with Native Americans. Aware of the risks as well as the scientific and political importance of their mission, both itched to explore the West. They gathered information on the natural history of the areas they passed through, but they had political goals as well: to counter British advances to the Indians and to map the territory so that it could be opened to settlement and exploitation.

The Lewis and Clark expedition (1804–1806) proved successful. The explorers reached the Pacific, and their good relations with the Indians and the fame of their travels led to the opening of the territory to settlement and prevented British advances. Their collection of information about natural specimens and artifacts from the area was thorough. Along the way they had been aided by trappers and

Native Americans, including Sacagawea, a young Shoshone woman companion to a French-Canadian trader, who joined the expedition. Sacagawea helped negotiate safe passage in the Far West, and she interpreted the terrain and the languages of the West for the explorers.

The Lewis and Clark expedition was part of American expansion. Like the purchase of the Louisiana Territory from France in 1803 it extended, in Jefferson's phrase, the American "empire of liberty." Through buckskin diplomacy, Lewis and Clark made friends beyond the limits of United States settlement. They were harbingers of the future, of the expansion and settlement of the United States.

Americans passed a political test at home when President Jefferson succeeded President Adams peacefully in 1800, despite the bitterness of the election and political intrigue. Presidential succession by ballot rather than arms helped secure constitutional government.

The transfer of power to the Republicans from the Federalists intensified political conflict. In the tradition of the Revolution, Republican presidents would seek to restrain the national government, believing that limited government would foster republican virtue. The Federalists would advocate a strong national government with centralized authority to promote economic development. As both factions competed for popular support, they laid the basis for the evolution of democratic politics. But factionalism, personal animosities, and partisanship within each group prevented the development of cohesive political parties, and the Federalists, unable to build a strong base of popular support, slowly faded away.

Events abroad and in the West encouraged and threatened Americans. Seizing one opportunity, the United States purchased the Louisiana Territory, pushing its border to the Pacific Ocean. But then from the high seas came war. Caught between the warring British and French, the United States found its ships seized and its sailors impressed, in violation of its rights as a neutral and independent nation. When the humiliation and threat to United States interests became too great, Americans took up arms in the War of 1812 both to defend their rights as a nation and to expand farther to the west and north. Though unprepared for combat, the United States fought Great Britain to a standstill. The Americans also routed Indian resistance and shattered Native American unity. A peace treaty restored the prewar

• *Important Events* •

1801	John Marshall becomes Chief Justice of the United States Thomas Jefferson inaugurated as first Republican president	**1814**	Andrew Jackson's defeat of Creeks at Battle of Horseshoe Bend begins Indian removal from the South Treaty of Ghent ends the War of 1812
1801–05	United States defeats Barbary pirates in Tripoli War	**1814–15**	Hartford Convention undermines Federalists
1803	*Marbury* v. *Madison* establishes judicial review United States purchases Louisiana Territory from France	**1815**	Battle of New Orleans makes Jackson a national hero
1804	Burr kills Hamilton in a duel Jefferson reelected	**1816**	Second Bank of the United States chartered James Monroe elected president
1804–06	Lewis and Clark explore Louisiana Territory	**1817**	Rush-Bagot Treaty limits British and American naval forces on Lake Champlain and the Great Lakes
1805	Prophet emerges as Shawnee leader	**1819**	*McCulloch* v. *Maryland* establishes supremacy of federal over state law Adams-Onís Treaty with Spain gives Florida to United States and defines Louisiana territorial border
1807	*Chesapeake* affair almost leads to war with Great Britain Embargo Act halts foreign trade		
1808	Congress bans importation of slaves to the United States James Madison elected president	**1819–23**	Financial panic and depression: hard times for Americans
1808–13	Prophet and Tecumseh organize Native American tribal resistance	**1820**	Missouri Compromise creates a formula for admitting slave and free states Monroe reelected
1812–15	United States and Great Britain fight the War of 1812	**1823**	Monroe Doctrine closes Western Hemisphere to European intervention
1813	Death of Tecumseh ends effective pan-Indian resistance		

status quo, but the war and the treaty reaffirmed American independence and strengthened American determination to steer clear of European conflicts.

The War of 1812 unleashed a wave of nationalism and self-confidence. War needs promoted domestic manufacturing and internal improvements. With peace, the federal government championed business and the construction of roads and canals. The new spirit encouraged economic growth and western expansion at home, trade abroad, and assertiveness throughout the Western Hemisphere. By the 1820s, the United States was no longer an experiment; a new nation had emerged. Free of its colonial past, the country began energetically shaping its own identity.

Economic growth and territorial expansion, however, generated new problems. In 1819 a finan-

cial panic brought hardship and conflict that sowed the seeds for the Jacksonian movement in the 1820s and 1830s. More ominously, sectional differences and the presence of slavery created divisions that would widen in the wake of further westward expansion during the 1840s and 1850s.

 Jefferson in Power

Thomas Jefferson viewed the election of 1800 as a revolution that restored government to its limited role. He stressed republican virtues of independence, self-reliance, and equality. He believed in a limited and frugal government. In contrast to the formality of the Federalist presidents Washington and Adams, Jefferson and his fellow Republicans

This portrait of President Thomas Jefferson was painted by Rembrandt Peale in 1805. Charles Willson Peale (Rembrandt's father) and his five sons helped establish the reputation of American art in the new nation. Rembrandt Peale was most famous for his presidential portraits; here he captured Jefferson in a noble pose without the usual symbols of office or power, befitting the Republican age. New-York Historical Society.

preferred simplicity, wearing ordinary clothes instead of the aristocratic wigs and breeches (knee-length trousers) the first two presidents had favored.

Jefferson considered the United States "the world's best hope" and set the United States on a course to live up to that assessment. Although as president he cut federal operations, he and his Republican successors (James Madison and James Monroe) invigorated the federal government over the next two decades. He did not hesitate to use federal power, even when questionable, as in the purchase of Louisiana. Although he stressed the importance of domestic issues, during his term of office foreign crises, in particular, strengthened federal institutions.

The election campaign of 1800 had been so bitter that Jefferson in his inaugural address sought unity by declaring, "We are all Republicans, we are all Federalists." Still, the Federalists and Republicans continued to distrust each other. John Adams, the outgoing president, and Jefferson had once been close friends but now disliked each other intensely. Both were thin-skinned and not only quick to take offense but also quick to give it. On inaugural day Adams had left Washington before dawn to avoid the Republican takeover. Republicans considered Federalists antidemocratic. Federalists accused Republicans of favoring egalitarianism, which they believed had recently led to anarchy in France. By doing away with Federalist social pomp and excessive government, Jefferson intended to restore the simplicity and civic virtue that had fueled the American Revolution.

Jefferson aggressively extended the Republicans' grasp on the national government. Virtually all of the six hundred or so officials appointed during the administrations of Washington and Adams were loyal Federalists; only six were known Republicans. To bring into his administration men who shared his vision of an agrarian republic and individual liberty, Jefferson refused to recognize appointments that Adams had made in the last days of his presidency, and he dismissed Federalist customs collectors from New England ports and awarded vacant treasury and judicial offices to Republicans. By July 1803 Federalists still held only 130 of 316 presidentially controlled offices. Jefferson adroitly used patronage to build a party organization, compete with the Federalists, and restore political balance in government.

Republican Appointments

The Republican Congress proceeded to affirm its belief in limited government. Albert Gallatin, secretary of the treasury, and John Randolph of Virginia, Jefferson's ally in the House of Representatives, translated ideology into policy, putting the federal government on a diet. Congress repealed all internal taxes, including the whiskey tax. Gallatin cut the army budget in half and reduced the 1802 navy budget by two-thirds. Gallatin moved to reduce the national debt—which Alexander Hamilton viewed as the engine of economic growth—from $83 million to $57 million, as part of a plan to retire it altogether by 1817. Jefferson even closed two of the nation's five diplomatic missions abroad—at The Hague and Berlin—to save money.

More than frugality, however, distinguished Republicans from Federalists. Before Jefferson's election, opposition to the Alien and Sedition Acts of 1798 had helped unite Republicans (see page

215). Jefferson now declined to use the acts against his opponents (as President Adams had done in suppressing Republican editors) and pardoned those who had been convicted under the acts. Congress let expire the Sedition Act in 1801 and the Alien Act in 1802. Congress also repealed the Naturalization Act of 1798, which had required fourteen years of residency for citizenship. The 1802 act that replaced it required only five years of residency, loyalty to the Constitution, and the forsaking of foreign allegiance and titles. It also, however, continued provisions for the registration of aliens. The new act, which made it easier to become a citizen, would remain the basis of naturalized American citizenship into the twentieth century.

The Republicans turned next to the judiciary, the last stronghold of Federalist power. During the 1790s not a single Republican had occupied the federal bench. The Judiciary Act of 1801, passed in the final days of the Adams administration, created fifteen new judgeships, which Adams filled by signing midnight appointments until his term was just hours away from expiring. The act also reduced by attrition the number of justices on the Supreme Court from six to five. Since that reduction would have denied Jefferson a Supreme Court appointment until two vacancies had occurred, the new Republican-dominated Congress repealed the 1801 act.

The Republicans also targeted opposition judges for removal. Federalist judges had refused to review the Sedition Act under which Federalists had prosecuted critics of the Adams administration. At Jefferson's prompting, the House impeached (indicted) Federal District Judge John Pickering of New Hampshire, an emotionally disturbed alcoholic, and in 1804 the Senate removed him from office. The Republicans were moving against the partisan Federalist judiciary.

Attacks on the Judiciary

The day Pickering was convicted, the House impeached Supreme Court Justice Samuel Chase for judicial misconduct. A staunch Federalist, Chase had led in pressing for convictions under the Sedition Act and repeatedly had denounced Jefferson's administration from the bench. The Republicans, however, failed to muster the two-thirds majority of senators necessary to convict him. Their failure to remove Chase preserved the Court's independence and established the precedent that criminal actions, not political disagreements, were the only proper grounds for impeachment. Time soon cured the Re-

publicans' grievances; in his tenure as president, Jefferson appointed three new Supreme Court justices. Nonetheless, the Court remained a Federalist stronghold under Chief Justice of the United States John Marshall.

Marshall, a Virginia Federalist, was an astute lawyer with keen political sense. He had served as minister to France and then secretary of state under Adams before being named to the Supreme Court. Though an autocrat by nature, Marshall possessed a grace and openness of manner that complemented the new Republican political style. Charles de Saint-Memin's portrait of Marshall in 1801 captured both his autocratic bearing and his direct manner. Under Marshall's domination, however, the Supreme Court retained a Federalist outlook even after Republican justices achieved a majority in 1811. Throughout his tenure (from

John Marshall

John Marshall (1755–1835) was Chief Justice of the United States from 1801 to 1835. He posed for this portrait by the French artist Charles Balthazar Julien Fevret de Saint-Memin in 1801, the year he joined the Court. The artist captured the power and strength with which Marshall would dominate the Court.   Duke University Archives.

1801 until 1835), the Court consistently upheld federal supremacy over the states and protected the interests of commerce and capital.

Marshall made the Court an equal branch of government in practice as well as theory. Service on the Court became a coveted honor for ambitious and talented men. Marshall unified the Court, influencing the justices to issue joint majority opinions rather than a host of individual concurring judgments. Marshall himself became the voice of the majority: from 1801 through 1805 he wrote twenty-four of the Court's twenty-six decisions; through 1810 he wrote 85 percent of the Court's opinions, including every important decision.

Marshall also increased the Court's power, notably in the landmark case *Marbury* v. *Madison* (1803). William Marbury, one of Adams's midnight

**Marbury
v. *Madison***

appointees, had been named a justice of the peace in the District of Columbia. James Madison, Jefferson's new secretary of state, declined to certify Marbury's appointment so that the president could appoint a Republican. Marbury sued, requesting a writ of mandamus (a court order forcing the president to appoint him). The case presented a political dilemma. If the Supreme Court ruled in favor of Marbury and issued a writ of mandamus, the president probably would not comply with it, and the Supreme Court had no way to force him to do so. But if the Federalist-dominated Court refused to issue the writ, it would be handing the Republicans a victory.

Marshall avoided both pitfalls. Speaking for the Court, he ruled that Marbury had a right to his appointment but that the Court could not compel Madison to honor the appointment because the Constitution did not grant the Court power to issue a writ of mandamus. In the absence of any specific mention in the Constitution, Marshall ruled, the section of the Judiciary Act of 1789 that authorized the Court to issue such writs was unconstitutional. In *Marbury* v. *Madison*, the Supreme Court denied itself the power to issue writs of mandamus but established its great power to judge the constitutionality of laws passed by Congress.

In succeeding years Marshall fashioned the theory of *judicial review*, the power of the Court to decide the constitutionality of legislation. Since the Constitution was the supreme law, he reasoned, any federal or state act contrary to the Constitution

must be null and void. The Supreme Court, whose duty it was to uphold the law, would decide whether or not a legislative act contradicted the Constitution. The power of judicial review established with *Marbury* v. *Madison* permanently enhanced the independence of the judiciary.

While Marshall was enlarging the power of the Court, President Jefferson had his eye on enlarging the borders of the nation. Jefferson shared with other Americans the belief that the United States was destined to expand its "empire of liberty." But there were four obstacles: the French in New Orleans and in the Louisiana Territory; the Spanish in Florida and Mexico; the British in Canada; and Native Americans throughout the continent. The obstacle posed by the French in New Orleans and Louisiana was the first to be overcome.

Since American independence, Louisiana had held a special place in the young nation's expansionist dreams. Louisiana defined the western border

**Louisiana
Purchase**

of the United States along the Mississippi from the Gulf of Mexico to present-day Minnesota. Spain had acquired the Louisiana Territory from France in 1763, at the end of the Seven Years War (see page 125). By 1800 hundreds of thousands of Americans in search of land had settled in the rich Mississippi and Ohio valleys, intruding on tribal lands. These settlers floated their farm goods down the Mississippi and Ohio Rivers to New Orleans for export. Whoever controlled the port of New Orleans thus had a hand on the throat of the American economy. Americans preferred Spanish control of Louisiana to control by France, a much stronger power.

Rumors of the transfer of Louisiana back to France proved true in 1802. France had acquired the territory in secret pacts with Spain in 1800 and 1801, but the United States learned of the transfer only in 1802, when Napoleon threatened to rebuild a French empire in the New World. "Every eye in the United States is now focused on the affairs of Louisiana," Jefferson wrote to Robert R. Livingston, the American minister in Paris. American concerns intensified in October 1802 when Spanish officials, on the eve of ceding control to the French, violated Pinckney's Treaty (see page 211) by denying Americans the privilege of storing their products at New Orleans prior to transshipment to foreign markets. "The Mississippi," Secretary of State James Madison wrote, "is to them everything. It is the Hudson, the

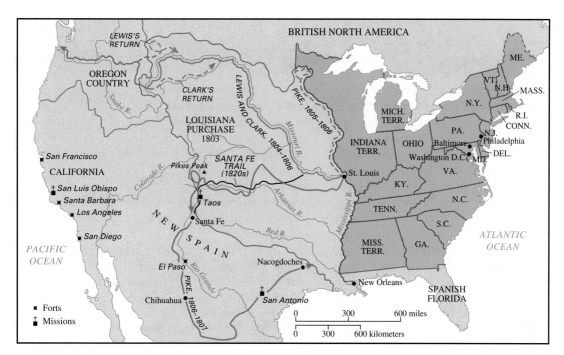

Louisiana Purchase *The Louisiana Purchase (1803) doubled the area of the United States and opened the trans-Mississippi West for American settlement.*

Delaware, the Potomac and all navigable rivers of the Atlantic States formed into one stream." Western farmers and eastern merchants thought a devious Napoleon had closed the port; they grumbled and talked war.

To relieve the pressure for war and to win western farm support, Jefferson prepared for war while sending James Monroe to join Robert Livingston in France to try to buy the port of New Orleans. Meanwhile, Congress authorized the call-up of eighty thousand militiamen in case war became necessary. Arriving in Paris in April, Monroe was astonished to learn that France already had offered to sell all 827,000 square miles of Louisiana to the United States for a mere $15 million. On April 30 Monroe and Livingston signed the Louisiana treaty to purchase the vast territory, whose borders were undefined and whose land was uncharted (see map).

At one stroke of a pen, the Louisiana Purchase doubled the size of the nation and opened the way for continental expansion. It was also the most popular achievement of Jefferson's presidency. But for Jefferson, the purchase presented a dilemma. It promised fulfillment of his dream of a continental nation

reaching to the Pacific, "with room enough for our descendants to the hundredth and thousandth generation." It provided a means to resolve Indian-settler conflict in the West by making available land to which eastern tribes could be forcibly removed. But was it legal?

The Constitution did not authorize the president to acquire new territory and incorporate it into the nation. Jefferson considered proposing a constitutional amendment to allow the purchase but decided not to. His justification for authorizing the purchase was that he was exercising the president's implied powers to protect the nation. The people signaled their approval of Jefferson's decision on election day in 1804.

Americans eager to expand the nation sought information and routes westward. Lieutenant Zebulon Pike followed Lewis and Clark in 1805 and 1806 in

Exploration of the West

search of the source of the Mississippi and a navigable water route to the Far West. The vast lands were not uninhabited, as Lewis and Clark had demonstrated. When Pike and his men wandered into

Spanish territory to the south, the Spanish held them captive for several months in Mexico. After his release, Pike wrote an account of his experiences that set commercial minds spinning. He described a potential commercial market in southwestern Spanish cities as well as bountiful furs and precious minerals. Over the next few decades, as Americans avidly read accounts of western exploration, expansion seized their imagination. The vision of a road to the Southwest became a reality with the opening of the Santa Fe Trail in the 1820s, and settlement followed the trail.

Tejas—Texas—was a buffer province between Spain's Mexican colonies and the Louisiana Territory. Texas officials welcomed Americans interested in the land south of Louisiana. American immigrants began to drift in, and some fought as volunteers with Indians and Mexican rebels in a twelve-year war with Spain that ended in 1821 with Mexican independence. The establishment of an independent Mexico stirred dreams of an independent Texas nation. Many Americans, however, were suspicious of all Mexicans. They did not want to include Mexicans—a mix of European, Indian, and African peoples—in the "empire of liberty."

 ## Republicans Versus Federalists

Prior to the Republican victory in 1800, most Federalists had disdained popular campaigning. They believed in government by the "best" people—those whose education, wealth, and experience qualified them to be leaders. For candidates to debate their own merits in front of their inferiors—the voters—was believed to be demeaning. The direct appeals of the Republicans struck the Federalists as a subversion of the natural political order.

After the resounding Federalist defeat in 1800, however, a younger generation of Federalists began to imitate the Republicans. Led by men like Josiah Quincy, a Massachusetts congressman, the Younger Federalists campaigned for popular support. Quincy cleverly presented the Federalists as the people's party, attacking Republicans as autocratic planters. "Jeffersonian Democracy," Quincy gibed in 1804, was "an Indian word, signifying '*a great tobacco planter who had herds of black slaves.*'" In attacking frugal government, the Younger Federalists played on fears of a weakened army and navy. Eastern

Political Campaigning

merchants depended on a strong navy to protect ocean trade; westerners looked to the army for support as they encroached on the territory of Native Americans.

In states where both factions organized and ran candidates, people became more involved in politics. In some states about 90 percent of the eligible voters—nearly all of whom were white males—cast ballots between 1804 and 1816. As popular interest and participation in elections increased, states expanded suffrage. But the popular base remained restricted: property qualifications for voting and holding office persisted, and in six states the legislatures still selected presidential electors in 1804. Fearing the divisiveness of partisanship, even Republicans restrained their organizational efforts, and most leaders shied away from cohesive political movements.

Yet political competition and a vigorous, partisan press prompted grassroots campaigning. Political barbecues symbolized the new style of campaign. In New York the factions roasted oxen; on the New England coast they baked clams; in Maryland they served oysters. Guests washed down their meals with beer and punch and sometimes competed in corn shuckings or horse pulls. Voters displayed their allegiance by attending these events and displaying images of their party leaders, such as the portrait of Jefferson on a snuff box. Oratory was a popular form of entertainment, and candidates delivered lengthy and uninhibited speeches at barbecues. They often made wild accusations, which—given the slow speed of communications—might go unanswered until after the election.

Both factions held political barbecues, but the Federalists never fully mastered the art of wooing voters. Older Federalists still opposed blatant campaigning. And though strong in Connecticut, Delaware, and a few other states, the Federalists never offered the Republicans sustained competition. Divisions among Federalists often undermined their success, and the extremism of some Older Federalists discredited them all. A case in point was Timothy Pickering, a Massachusetts congressman and former secretary of state. Pickering opposed the Louisiana Purchase, feared Jefferson's reelection, and urged the secession of New England in 1803 and 1804. He won some support, but most Federalists opposed his plan for secession. Ever the opportunist, Vice President Aaron Burr flirted with Pickering, fantasizing about leading New York into secession, with other states following. But when Burr lost his bid to become governor of New York in 1804, his

How do historians know that popular interest in elections was increasing early in the nineteenth century? Election data are not available, but paintings like John Lewis Krimmel's Election Day in Philadelphia *(1815) convey that interest. Only white males could vote at the time, and the crowd is composed mostly of white men, although at least one African-American and some women and children are present. The artist depicts a festive occasion. Citizens riding on a float in the background carry their own flag; they have created a parade. A holiday spirit seems to prevail as men cluster in groups talking, arguing, sharing jokes, and generally appearing to have a good time. Perhaps there is a hint of overindulgence as well. The man sitting in front of an overturned chair (left foreground), with his hat on the ground behind him,* seems to have fallen, perhaps from too much drink—a common affliction in the party atmosphere of election day. Among the spectators are two women (center foreground), one of whom is holding the hand of a little girl. They suggest a restraining force on the raucous scene. The woman dressed in white and her friend offer a common female image of the time: the woman as an emblem of republican virtue. The space between the female and male figures suggests that the women stand apart not only as nonvoters but also as symbols of virtue and seriousness absent in the male world. Overall, the painting depicts a popular event, mixing a party atmosphere with civic duty. From a sober exercise of democratic responsibility, voting had become a popular, festive occasion.   Photo: Winterthur Museum.

and Pickering's dream of a northern confederacy evaporated.

The controversies surrounding Burr highlight some of the shortcomings of the emerging political system. Personal animosities were as strong a force as ideology, and temporary factions flourished. Moreover, although politicians courted voters and participation in politics broadened, the electoral base remained narrow. The election of 1804 showed the Federalists could offer only weak competition at

Voters expressed their party loyalty by displaying portraits of party leaders, as in this Thomas Jefferson commemorative pitcher. It also shows the extent of grass-roots involvement in presidential politics. Collection of David J. and Janet L. Frent.

the national level. And where Federalists were too weak to pose a threat, Republicans fought among themselves.

Both Republicans and Federalists suffered from divisiveness and personal animosities. The charismatic and ambitious Aaron Burr and Alexander Hamilton, for instance, had long

Hamilton-Burr Duel

despised each other. Hamilton always seemed to block Burr's path. He thwarted Burr's attempt to steal the election of 1800 from Jefferson, and in the 1804 New York gubernatorial race Burr lost to a rival Republican faction backed by the Federalist Hamilton. Burr turned his resentment on Hamilton, who had charged that he was too dangerous and unfit to hold office, and challenged Hamilton to a duel. His honor at stake, Hamilton accepted Burr's challenge, though he found dueling repugnant. Because New York had outlawed dueling, the two men met across the Hudson River at Weehawken, New Jersey. Hamilton did not fire and paid for that decision with his life. But in killing Hamilton, Burr only added to his dishonor in the public's

eyes. He was indicted for murder in New York and New Jersey and faced immediate arrest if he returned to either state.

His political career in ruins, Burr plotted to create in the Southwest a new empire carved out of the Louisiana Territory. With the collusion of General James Wilkinson, the United States commander in the Mississippi valley, Burr planned to raise a private army to grab land from the United States or from Spain (his exact plans remain uncertain). Wilkinson switched sides and informed President Jefferson of Burr's intention. Jefferson personally assisted the prosecution in Burr's 1807 trial for treason, over which Chief Justice Marshall presided. The jury acquitted Burr, who fled to Europe to avoid further prosecution.

Campaigning for reelection in 1804, Jefferson claimed credit for western expansion and the restoration of republican values. He considered the ac-

Jefferson's Reelection

quisition of Louisiana among his greatest presidential accomplishments. Jefferson and the Republicans bragged of ending the Federalist threat to liberty by repealing the Alien and Sedition and Judiciary Acts. They also had reduced the size of government by cutting spending. Despite his opponents' charges, Jefferson had demonstrated that Republicans supported commerce and promoted free trade. American trade with Europe was flourishing. Unwisely, Federalists who earlier had criticized Jefferson for not seizing Louisiana now attacked the president for paying too much for it and for exceeding his powers in buying it.

Jefferson's opponent was Charles Cotesworth Pinckney, a wealthy South Carolina lawyer and former Revolutionary War aide to George Washington. As Adams's vice-presidential running mate in 1800, Pinckney had inherited the Federalist leadership. Jefferson dumped the disloyal and unreliable Aaron Burr from the 1804 ticket, and he and his running mate, George Clinton of New York, swamped Pinckney and New Yorker Rufus King in the electoral college by 162 votes to 14, carrying fifteen of the seventeen states.

Jefferson's reelection was both a personal and an organizational triumph. The political dissenters of the 1790s had fashioned the Democratic-Republican societies into successful political organizations. More than anything else, opposition to the Federalists had given them cohesion. Indeed, in areas where the Federalists were strongest—in commercial New York and Pennsylvania in the 1790s and in New England in the 1800s—the Republicans had organized most effectively.

Although this period is commonly called the era of the first party system, parties as such were not fully developed. Competition at the polls encouraged rudimentary party organization, but personal ambition, personality clashes, and local, state, and regional loyalties undermined it. Increasingly, too, external events overpowered party ties.

Preserving American Neutrality in a World at War

"Peace, commerce, and honest friendship with all nations, entangling alliance with none," President Jefferson had proclaimed in his first inaugural address. Jefferson's efforts to stand aloof from European conflict were successful until 1805. Thereafter, the pursuit of peace and undisturbed commerce occupied nearly his entire second administration, but they proved elusive goals.

After the Senate ratified Jay's Treaty in 1795 (see page 210), the United States and Great Britain appeared to reconcile their differences. Britain withdrew from its western forts and interfered less in American trade with France. Increased trade helped: the United States became Britain's best customer, and the British Empire in turn bought the bulk of American exports.

But in May 1803, two weeks after Napoleon sold Louisiana to the United States, renewal of the Napoleonic wars between France and Britain (and Britain's continental allies, Prussia, Austria, and Russia) again trapped the United States between Britain and France on the high seas. For two years American commerce benefited from the conflict. As the world's largest neutral carrier, the United States became the chief supplier of food to Europe. American merchants also gained control of most of the West Indian trade.

Meanwhile, United States victory in the Tripoli War on the north coast of Africa (against the Barbary states) provided Jefferson with his one clear success in protecting American trading rights. In 1801 the sultan of Tripoli had demanded payment not to prey on American vessels and sailors in the Mediterranean. Jefferson refused to pay and instead sent a naval squadron to protect American merchant ships from the Barbary pirates. In 1803–1804, under Lieutenant Stephen Decatur, the navy blockaded Tripoli

harbor while marines marched overland from Egypt to seize the port of Derna. The United States ransomed its hostages and signed a peace treaty with Tripoli in 1805 but continued to pay tribute to other Barbary states until 1815. That year the navy, again under Decatur, forced Algiers and Tunis to renounce attacks against Americans. The Tripoli War and its aftermath made clear that the United States would protect its commerce anywhere, and it helped make the Mediterranean safe for commerce again.

American merchants grew increasingly concerned about Anglo-French interference with trade. In October 1805 Britain tightened its control of the high seas by defeating the French and Spanish fleets at the Battle of Trafalgar. Two months later Napoleon defeated the Russian and Austrian armies at Austerlitz. Stalemated, France and Britain launched a commercial war, blockading each other's trade. As a trading partner of both countries, the United States paid a high price.

Britain, whose navy was the world's largest, was suffering a severe shortage of sailors. Few men were enlisting, and those in service frequently deserted, demoralized by poor shipboard conditions. Some British subjects found work on United States merchant ships, where conditions were better. The Royal Navy resorted to stopping American ships and seizing British deserters, British-born naturalized American seamen, and other unlucky sailors suspected of being British. Perhaps six to eight thousand Americans were impressed (forcibly drafted) in this way between 1803 and 1812. Americans saw impressment as a direct assault on the independence of their new republic. The principle of "once a British subject, always a British subject" ignored United States citizenship and sovereignty. The alleged deserters—many of them American citizens—faced British court-martial.

Impressment of American Sailors

In February 1806 the Senate denounced British impressment as aggression and a violation of America's neutral rights. In protest, Congress passed the Non-Importation Act, prohibiting importation from Great Britain of cloth and metal articles. In November Jefferson suspended the act temporarily while William Pinckney, a Baltimore lawyer, joined James Monroe in London to negotiate a settlement. But the treaty Monroe and Pinckney carried home violated their instructions—it did not mention impressment—and Jefferson never submitted it to the Senate for ratification.

The United States merchant marine facilitated economic growth in the early republic. But protection of neutral shipping rights and impressment of American seamen by the British navy stirred conflict between the United States and Britain and helped bring about the War of 1812. Here George Ropes, Jr., depicts the launching of the merchant ship Fame *in 1802 at Salem, Massachusetts.* Peabody Essex Museum.

Less than a year later, the *Chesapeake* affair exposed American military weakness and intensified the emotional impact of impressment on the public.

Chesapeake Affair

In June 1807 the forty-gun frigate U.S.S. *Chesapeake* left Norfolk, Virginia, on a mission to protect American ships in the Mediterranean. About 10 miles out, still inside American territorial waters, it met the fifty-gun British frigate *Leopard*. When the *Chesapeake* refused to be searched for deserters, the *Leopard* repeatedly fired its guns broadside into the American ship. Three Americans were killed and eighteen wounded, including the ship's captain. The British seized four deserters from the Royal Navy—three of them American citizens; one of them, Jenkin Ratford, was hanged. Damaged and humiliated, the *Chesapeake* returned to port.

Had the United States been better prepared militarily, the ensuing howl of public indignation might have brought about a declaration of war. But the United States was ill equipped to defend its neutral rights with force; it was no match for the British navy. With Congress in recess, Jefferson was able to avoid hostilities. In July, the president closed American waters to British warships to prevent similar incidents, and soon thereafter he increased military and naval expenditures. In December Jefferson again put economic pressure on Great Britain by invoking the Non-Importation Act, followed eight days later by a new restriction, the Embargo Act.

The Embargo Act was intended to avoid war. Jefferson thought of it as a short-term measure to prevent confrontation between American merchant vessels and British and French warships and to put pressure on France and England by denying them American products. The embargo forbade virtually all exports from the United States to any country. Foreign ships deliver-

Embargo Act

ing goods left American ports with empty holds. Smuggling blossomed overnight.

Few American policies were as well intentioned or as unpopular and unsuccessful as Jefferson's embargo. Although "peaceable coercion" was an enlightened concept in international affairs, some Republicans felt uneasy about interfering with trade. Federalists opposed the embargo vociferously. Some feared its impact abroad. "If England [were to] sink," Federalist vice-presidential candidate Rufus King said in 1808, "her fall will prove the grave of our liberties." Mercantile New England, the heart of Federalist opposition to Jefferson, felt the brunt of the resulting economic depression. Shipping collapsed as exports fell by 80 percent between 1807 and 1808. In the winter of 1808–1809, talk of secession spread through New England port cities.

Although general unemployment soared, some individuals benefited from the embargo. Merchants with ships abroad (thus not idled by the embargo) and merchants willing to risk the lax enforcement to trade illegally could garner enormous profits. United States manufacturers—the early textile mills, for instance—received a boost, since the domestic market became theirs exclusively.

Great Britain, meanwhile, was only mildly affected by the embargo. The British most severely hurt—West Indians and factory workers—had no voice in policy. English merchants actually gained because they took over the Atlantic carrying trade from the stalled American ships. And because of a successful British blockade of Europe, the embargo had little practical effect on the French. Indeed, it gave France an excuse to set privateers against American ships that had escaped the embargo. The French cynically claimed that such ships were British ships in disguise, because the embargo prevented American vessels from sailing.

In the election of 1808, the Republicans faced not only the Federalists but also dissatisfaction with the embargo and factional dissent. Although nine state legislatures passed resolutions urging Jefferson to run again, the president followed Washington's lead in renouncing a third term. He supported James Madison, his secretary of state, as the Republican standard-bearer. For the first time, however, the Republican nomination was contested. Madison won the endorsement of the Republican congressional caucus, but Virginia Republicans put forth James Monroe (who later withdrew), and some east-

Election of 1808

ern Republicans supported Vice President George Clinton.

Charles Cotesworth Pinckney and Rufus King again headed the Federalist ticket, but with new vigor. The Younger Federalists, led by Harrison Gray Otis and other Bostonians, made the most of the widespread disaffection with Republican policy, especially the embargo. Although Pinckney received only 47 electoral votes to Madison's 122, the Federalists offered genuine competition. Pinckney carried all of New England except Vermont, and he won Delaware and some electoral votes in two other states. Federalists also gained seats in Congress and captured the New York state legislature. The Federalist future looked promising.

Under the pressure of domestic opposition, the embargo eventually collapsed. Jefferson felt the weight of his failure: "never did a prisoner, released from his chains," he wrote on leaving office, "feel such relief as I in shaking off the shackles of power." In his last days in office Jefferson had tried to lighten the burden through the Non-Intercourse Act of 1809. This act reopened trade with all nations except Britain and France, and it authorized the president to resume trade with Britain or France if either of them ceased to violate neutral rights.

Non-Intercourse Act

The new act solved only the problems created by the embargo; it did not prevent further British and French interference with American commerce. For one brief moment it appeared to work. In June 1809 President Madison reopened trade with England after the British minister to the United States assured him that Britain would repeal restrictions on American commerce. His Majesty's government in London, however, repudiated the minister's assurances, and Madison reverted to nonintercourse.

When the Non-Intercourse Act expired in 1810, Congress substituted a variant, Macon's Bill Number 2, that exchanged the proverbial stick for a carrot. The bill reopened trade with both Great Britain and France but provided that when either nation stopped violating American commercial rights, the president could suspend American commerce with the other. Madison, eager to avoid war, was tricked at his own game. When Napoleon accepted the offer, Madison declared nonintercourse with Great Britain in 1811. Napoleon, however, did not keep his word. The French continued to seize American ships, and nonintercourse failed a second time. But because the Royal Navy dominated the seas, Britain,

The Shawnee chiefs Prophet (left) and Tecumseh (right). The two brothers led a revival of traditional Shawnee culture and preached Native American federation against white encroachment. In the War of 1812 they allied themselves with the British, but Tecumseh's death at the Battle of the Thames (1813) and British indifference thereafter caused Native Americans' resistance and unity to collapse. Prophet: National Museum of American Art, Smithsonian Institution; Tecumseh: Field Museum of Natural History, FMNH Neg. #A93851.

not France, became the main target of American hostility.

Angry American leaders tended to blame even Indian resistance in the West on British agitation, ignoring the Native Americans' legitimate protests against treaty violations. In the early 1800s two Shawnee brothers, Prophet and Tecumseh, attempted to build a pan-Indian federation, taking advantage of Anglo-American friction. Prophet's early experiences typified the experiences of the Indians of the Old Northwest. Born in 1775, a few months after his father's death in battle, Prophet, called Lalawethika ("Noisemaker") as a young man, was expelled to Ohio along with other Shawnees under the 1795 Treaty of Greenville (see page 189), and he later moved to Indiana. Within the shrunken territory granted the Shawnees, game soon became scarce. Encroachment by whites and the periodic ravages of disease brought further misery, and, like many other

Shawnee Resistance

Native Americans, Lalawethika turned to whiskey. He also turned to traditional folk knowledge and remedies and in 1804 became a tribal medicine man. His medicine, however, could not stop the white man's diseases from ravaging his village.

Lalawethika emerged from his own battle with illness in 1805 as a new man, called Tenskwatawa ("the Open Door"), or "the Prophet." Claiming to have died and been resurrected, he traveled widely in the Ohio River valley as a religious leader, attacking the decline of moral values among Native Americans, warning of damnation for those who drank whiskey, condemning intertribal battles, and stressing harmony and respect for elders. He urged Indians to return to the old ways and abandon white customs: to hunt with bows and arrows, not guns; to stop wearing hats; and to refrain from eating bread and instead to cultivate corn and beans.

Prophet's message reassured the Shawnees, Potawatomis, and other western Indians who felt unsettled and threatened by non-Indians. Prophet won converts by performing miracles—he seemed to darken the sun by timing his invocations to coincide with a solar eclipse—and he used opposition to federal Indian policy to draw others into his camp. His message spread to southern tribes as well, and the federal government and white settlers became alarmed.

By 1808, Prophet and his older brother Tecumseh were talking less about spiritual renewal and more about resisting American aggression. Their

The Prophet and Tecumseh

refusal to leave lands claimed by the government was encouraged by the British, who looked to alliances with Native Americans after renewed Anglo-American hostilities followed the *Chesapeake* affair of 1807. In repudiating land cessions to the government under the Treaty of Fort Wayne (1809), Tecumseh told Indiana's governor William Henry Harrison at Vincennes in 1810 that "the only way to check and stop this evil is, for all the red men to unite in claiming a common and equal right in the land, as it was at first, and should be yet; for it . . . belongs to all, for the use of each. . . . No part has a right to sell, even to each other, much less to strangers."

Tecumseh, a towering six-foot warrior and charismatic orator, soon overshadowed his brother as Shawnee leader; his message found greater reception among younger Indians. Warriors found Tecumseh's political visions more relevant than Prophet's spirituality in protecting themselves against the United States. Convinced that only an Indian federation could stop the advance of white settlement, Tecumseh sought to unify northern and southern Indians. He traveled widely, preaching Indian resistance. And he warned Harrison that Indians would resist white occupation of the 2.5 million acres on the Wabash River that they had ceded in the Treaty of Fort Wayne.

 ## The War of 1812

Conflict over Native American loyalties in the West and over impressment on the seas strained relations between Britain and the United States. Having exhausted all efforts to alter British policy, the United States in 1811 and early 1812 drifted toward war with Great Britain until Republican "War Hawks" elected to Congress in 1810 led the charge to war. Meanwhile, in June 1812, Britain reopened the seas to American shipping. Hard times had hit the British Isles: the Anglo-French conflict had blocked much

of British commerce with the European continent, and exports to the United States had fallen 80 percent. But two days after the change in British policy, before word of it had crossed the Atlantic, Congress declared war.

The War of 1812, the nation's first general war, was the logical outcome of United States policy after the renewal of warfare in Europe in 1803.

The Vote for War

The grievances President Madison enumerated in his message to Congress on June 1, 1812, were old ones: impressment, interference with neutral commerce, and British alliances with the western tribes. What brought the United States to this point, however, were Republicans' resolve to defend American independence and honor and American expansionists' thirst for British Canada.

The war Congress was a partisan one. Much of the war fever came from the so-called War Hawks, land-hungry southerners and westerners, all Republicans, led by John C. Calhoun of South Carolina and first-term congressman and House Speaker Henry Clay of Kentucky. Westerners had increased their numbers in Congress following reapportionment after the 1810 census, and the enlarged delegation was concerned equally with national honor and expansion. Most representatives from the coastal states opposed war, because armed conflict with the great naval power would interrupt American shipping. On June 4, the House voted 79 to 49 for war; two weeks later the Senate voted 19 to 13 in favor. Republicans favored war by a vote of 98 to 23; Federalists opposed it 39 to 0. On June 19, President Madison signed the declaration of war.

Though unprepared for war in 1812, the United States could not avoid it. The United States had tried economic pressure but had failed to protect American ships and sailors. The United States Army and Navy and the state militias were not fully prepared to wage war against the British.

The war turned out to be mostly a series of scuffles and skirmishes. The military campaigns were poorly executed; full-scale battles were rare (see map, page 240). The Americans had the advantage of fighting close to home. The war's outcome affirmed the freedom won in the Revolutionary War and dealt a serious blow to Indian resistance to American expansion. It also stimulated American nationalism and self-confidence.

After six months of preparation, American forces were still not ready for war. The United

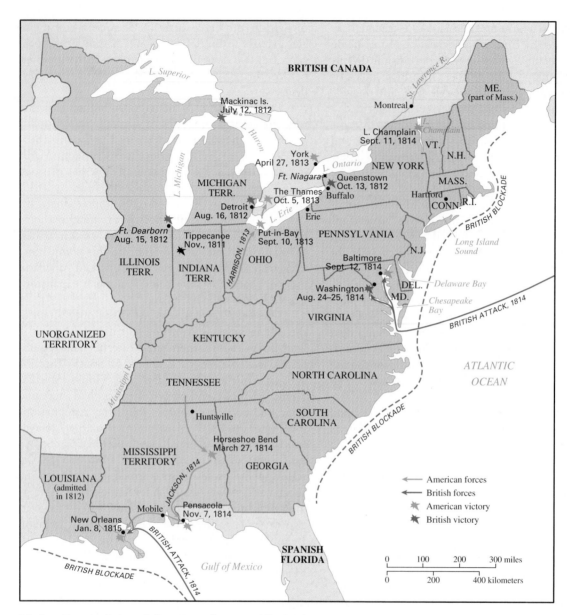

Major Campaigns of the War of 1812 *The land war centered on the American-Canadian border,*
the Chesapeake Bay, and the Louisiana and Mississippi Territories.

States Navy had a corps of experienced officers who
had proved their mettle in pro-

**Recruiting
an Army**

tecting American merchant ships
from the Barbary pirates. But
in comparison with the Royal
Navy, the ruler of the seas, the
American navy was minuscule. Jefferson's warning
that "our constitution is a peace establishment—it is
not calculated for war" proved true. The United
States Army had neither an able staff nor an adequate force of enlisted men. By 1812 the United

States Military Academy at West Point, founded in
1802, had produced only eighty-nine regular officers. The American army thus turned to political
leaders and the state militias to recruit volunteers,
and not all states cooperated. Much of the war
effort, including planning, was decentralized. The
government offered enlistees a sign-up bonus of
$16, monthly pay of $5, a full set of clothes, and a
promise of three months' pay and 160 acres of western land upon discharge. Forty-two percent of the
enlistees were illiterate.

At first, recruitment in the West went well. Civic spirit, desire for land, and strong anti-Indian sentiment stimulated thousands of enlistments from the Old Northwest, Kentucky, Tennessee, and the southern frontier. The army made itself more acceptable to new recruits by abolishing flogging in 1812. Within a year, however, frontier enlistments were declining. Word spread that the War Department was often slow in meeting its payroll and supplying clothing.

In New England, raising an army proved even more difficult. Many viewed the conflict as a Republican war—"Mr. Madison's War"—and Federalists discouraged enlistments. Even some New England Republicans declined to raise volunteer companies. Those who accepted promised their men that they would serve only a defensive role, as in Maine where they guarded the coastline. Indeed, the inability of the United States to mount a successful invasion of Canada was due in part to the army's failure to assemble an effective force. State militias in New England and New York often declined to fight outside the borders of their own state.

Canada offered the United States the only readily available battlefront on which to confront Great Britain and conquer land. The mighty Royal Navy

Invasion of Canada

could not reach the Great Lakes separating the United States and Canada, because there was no river access to them from the Atlantic (see map, page 240). Canada, thousands of miles from British supply sources, was vulnerable to American attack.

Begun with high hopes, the invasion of Canada ended in disaster. The American strategy concentrated on the West, aiming to split Canadian forces and isolate the Indians who were supporting the British. Tecumseh joined the British when the war began in return for the promise of an Indian nation in the Great Lakes region. United States General William Hull, governor of the Michigan Territory, marched his troops into Upper Canada, near Detroit. More experienced as a politician than as a soldier, Hull had surrounded himself with newly minted colonels who were as politically astute and militarily ignorant as he was. Although his forces in the area were twice as large as those of the British and their Indian allies, Hull waged a timid campaign, retreating more than he attacked. His abandonment of Mackinac Island and Fort Dearborn in Chicago and his surrender of Fort Detroit left the entire Midwest exposed to the enemy. The only

bright spot was the September 1812 defense of Fort Harrison in Indiana Territory by Captain Zachary Taylor, who provided the Americans with their first land victory. By the winter of 1812–1813, the British controlled about half of the Old Northwest.

The United States had no greater success on the Niagara front, where New York borders Canada. At the Battle of Queenstown, in Canada north of Niagara, the United States Army met defeat because the New York militia refused to leave New York. This scenario was repeated near Lake Champlain, where American plans to attack Montréal were foiled when the New York militia again declined to cross the border into Canada. The American offensives in the North were probably doomed to fail anyway; the United States lacked the means to hold any part of Canada permanently.

The navy provided the only bright ray in the first year of the war: the U.S.S. *Constitution*, the U.S.S. *Wasp*, and the U.S.S. *United States* all bested British warships on the Atlantic. The *Constitution's* rout of H.M.S. *Guerrière* in the Atlantic emboldened the United States Navy and earned the American ship the nickname "Old Ironsides." In victory, the Americans lost 20 percent of their ships. In defeat, however, the British lost just 1 percent of their naval strength. The British admiralty simply shifted its fleet away from the American ships, and by 1813 the Royal Navy again commanded the seas.

The Royal Navy blockaded the Chesapeake and Delaware Bays in December 1812, and by 1814 the blockade covered nearly all American ports along the Atlantic and Gulf coasts. Since 1811, American trade overseas had declined nearly 90 percent, and the decline in revenues from customs duties threatened to bankrupt the federal government.

The contest for control of the Great Lakes, the key to the war in the Northwest, was largely a shipbuilding race. Under Master Commandant Oliver

Great Lakes Campaign

Hazard Perry and shipbuilder Noah Brown, the United States outbuilt the British on Lake Erie and defeated them at the bloody Battle of Put-in-Bay on September 10, 1813. With this costly victory, the Americans gained control of Lake Erie.

General William Henry Harrison then began the march that proved to be among the United States's most successful moments in the war. The volunteers who constituted the majority of Harrison's command were a ragged group. Volunteers in the Kentucky militia, they had been drafted into the

In the first year of the War of 1812, only the United States Navy proved equal to British forces. In August 1812, the U.S.S. Constitution *defeated and sank* H.M.S. Guerrière *in the Atlantic 750 miles east of Boston. The Guerrière had long plagued American ships, and the victory was widely cheered in the states. Thomas Birch's painting* Constitution and the Guerrière *re-creates the fury of the encounter.*   United States Naval Academy Museum.

regular army and sent to fight in Upper Canada; they marched 20 to 30 miles a day to join Harrison's forces in Ohio, receiving no training and armed only with swords and knives.

Harrison's force of forty-five hundred men attacked and took Detroit and then entered Canada. They pursued the British, Shawnee, and Chippewa forces, defeating them on October 5 at the Battle of the Thames. This victory permitted the United States to retain control of the Old Northwest. Tecumseh died in the battle, and with his death expired Native American unity. After the Battle of the Thames, the Americans razed York (now Toronto), the Canadian capital. They looted and burned the Parliament building before withdrawing; they did not have enough troops to hold the city.

After defeating Napoleon in April 1814, the British stepped up the land campaign against the United States, concentrating on the Chesapeake Bay region. In retaliation for the burning of York—and

to divert American troops from Lake Champlain, where the British planned a new offensive—royal troops occupied Washington, D.C., in August and set it ablaze, leaving the presidential mansion scarred by fire. The attack on the capital, however, was only a diversion. The major battle occurred at Baltimore, where the Americans held firm. Francis Scott Key, witnessing the British fleet's bombardment of Fort McHenry in Baltimore harbor, was inspired to write the verses of "The Star-Spangled Banner" (which became the national anthem in 1931). Although the British inflicted heavy damage both materially and psychologically, they achieved little militarily. Equally unsuccessful was their offensive at Lake Champlain, where an American fleet turned back a British flotilla at Plattsburgh. The offensive was discontinued, and the war was essentially a stalemate.

The last campaigns of the war were waged in the South, along the Gulf of Mexico against the Creeks and against the British around New Orleans (see map, page 240). The Creeks—also known as the Red Sticks—

Campaign Against the Creeks

had responded to Tecumseh and Prophet's calls to resist United States expansion. Some had died in Indiana Territory, at Prophetstown on Tippecanoe Creek, when General Harrison's troops routed Shawnee forces there in 1811. In December 1812 General Andrew Jackson raised his Tennessee militia to fight the Creeks. By late 1813 his anti-Creek campaign was stalled by lack of supplies, and his men, who had signed up for a year, were talking about going home. Jackson refused to discharge them; they could not, he said, leave their posts on enemy ground. Officers repeatedly threatened to shoot any man who left. In March 1814 Jackson executed John Woods, a militiaman, for disobedience and mutiny. This act broke the opposition within the ranks, and Jackson's men defeated the Creek nation at the Battle of Horseshoe Bend in Mississippi Territory in March 1814.

Andrew Jackson's defeat of the Creek nation began his rise to political prominence. In the August 1814 Treaty of Fort Jackson, the Creeks ceded two-thirds of their land and withdrew to the southern and western part of Mississippi Territory, in what is now Alabama; the removal of Indians from the South had begun. Jackson became a major general in the regular army and continued south toward the Gulf of Mexico. To forestall a British invasion at Pensacola Bay, which guarded an overland route to New Orleans, Jackson seized Pensacola—in Spanish Florida—in November 1814. Then, after securing Mobile, he marched on to New Orleans to defend it against the British.

The Battle of New Orleans was the last campaign of the war. Early in December the British fleet landed fifteen hundred men east of the city, hoping

Battle of New Orleans

to control the Mississippi River and thus strangle the lifeline of the American West. They faced American regulars, Tennessee and Kentucky volunteers, and two

Andrew Jackson imposed the Treaty of Fort Jackson on the Creek nation, ending the campaign against the Red Sticks. The treaty required the Creeks to pay the costs of the war, which Jackson estimated at the equivalent of 20 million acres. In forcing the Creeks out of what is now central Alabama, Jackson initiated the Indians' forced removal from the South. Ironically, of the thirty-five chiefs who made their mark on the treaty, part of which is shown here, only one was a member of the Creek nation. National Archives.

companies of free African-American volunteers from New Orleans. For three weeks the British under Sir Edward Pakenham and the Americans led by Jackson played cat-and-mouse. Finally, on January 8, 1815, the two forces met head-on. In fortified positions, Jackson's poorly trained army held its ground against two frontal assaults from a British contingent of six thousand. At day's end, more than two thousand British soldiers lay dead or wounded; the Americans suffered only twenty-one casualties. Andrew Jackson emerged a national hero, and the battle was memorialized in song and paintings. The Battle of New Orleans actually was fought two weeks after the end of the war. Unknown to the participants, a treaty had been signed in Ghent, Belgium, on December 24, 1814.

The United States government had gone to war reluctantly and throughout the conflict probed for a diplomatic end to hostilities. In 1813, President Madison eagerly accepted a Russian offer to mediate, but Great Britain balked. Three months later, British foreign minister Lord Castlereagh suggested opening peace talks. It took over ten months to arrange meetings, but in August 1814 a team of American negotiators, including John Quincy Adams and Henry Clay, began talks with the British in Ghent.

Treaty of Ghent

The Ghent treaty made no mention of the issues that had led to war. The United States received no satisfaction on impressment, blockades, or other maritime rights for neutrals. British demands for an independent Indian nation in the Northwest and territorial cessions from Maine to Minnesota were not satisfied. Essentially, the Treaty of Ghent restored the prewar status quo. It provided for an end to hostilities with the British and with Native Americans, release of prisoners, restoration of conquered territory, and arbitration of boundary disputes.

Why did the negotiators settle for so little? Events in Europe had made peace and the status quo acceptable at the end of 1814, as they had not been in 1812. Napoleon's fall from power allowed the United States to abandon its demands, since peace in Europe made impressment and interference with American commerce moot questions. Similarly, war-weary Britain—its treasury nearly depleted—stopped pressing for a military victory.

The War of 1812 affirmed the independence of the American republic. Nearly three hundred thousand troops had taken up arms to maintain independence; almost two thousand died and four thousand were wounded. Although conflict with Great Britain continued, it never again led to war. The experience strengthened America's resolve to steer clear of European politics, for it had been the British-French conflict that had drawn the United States into war. For the rest of the century the United States would shun involvement in European political issues and wars.

Consequences of the War of 1812

The war had disastrous results for most Native Americans. Although they were not a party to the Treaty of Ghent, the ninth article of the treaty pledged the United States to end hostilities and to restore "all the possessions, rights, and privileges" that Indians had enjoyed before the war. More than a dozen treaties were signed with midwestern Indian leaders in 1815, but they had little meaning. With the death of Tecumseh, the Indians had lost their most powerful political and military leader; with the withdrawal of the British, they had lost their strongest ally. The Shawnees, Potawatomis, Chippewas, and others had lost the means to resist American expansion.

Domestically, the war exposed weaknesses in defense and transportation. American generals had found American roads inadequate to move troops and supplies. In the Northwest, General Harrison's troops had depended on homemade cartridges and gifts of clothing from Ohio residents; in Maine, troops had melted down spoons to make bullets. Improved transportation and a well-equipped army became national priorities; both were vital for westward expansion. In 1815, President Madison responded by centralizing control of the military and by building a line of forts for coastal defense, and Congress voted a standing army of ten thousand men—one-third of the army's wartime strength but three times the size of the army during Jefferson's administration. After the war, improved transportation would facilitate western settlement.

Perhaps most important of all, the war stimulated economic growth. The embargo, the Non-Importation and Non-Intercourse Acts, and the war itself spurred the production of manufactured goods: New England capitalists began to invest in home manufactures. The effects of these changes were to be far-reaching (see Chapter 10).

Finally, the war sealed the fate of the Federalists. Realizing that they could not win a presidential election in wartime, the Federalists joined renegade Republicans in supporting DeWitt Clinton of New York in 1812. This was the high point of Federalist organization at the state level, and the Younger Federalists campaigned hard. Clinton nevertheless lost to President Madison by 128 to 89 electoral votes; areas that favored the war (the South and West) remained solidly Republican. The Federalists gained some congressional seats and carried many local elections, but once again extremism undermined the Federalists.

During the war Federalists had revived talk of secession. With the war stalemated, delegates from New England states met in Hartford, Connecticut,

Hartford Convention

for three weeks in the winter of 1814–1815 to discuss revising the national compact or pulling out of the republic. Moderates prevented a resolution of secession, but convention members condemned the war and the embargo and endorsed radical changes in the Constitution. They wanted to restrict the presidency to one term and require a two-thirds congressional vote to admit new states to the Union. They proposed forbidding naturalized citizens from holding office. The proceedings were a fruitless attempt to preserve New England Federalist political power as electoral strength shifted to the South and West and immigrants became politically active.

The timing of the Hartford Convention proved lethal. The victory at New Orleans and news of the peace treaty made the convention, with its talk of secession and constitutional amendments, look ridiculous if not treasonous. Rather than harassing a beleaguered wartime administration, the Federalists found themselves in retreat before a rising tide of nationalism. Though Federalism survived in a handful of states until the 1820s, the Federalist faction began to dissolve. The War of 1812, at first a source of revival as opponents of war flocked to the Federalist banner, helped bring its demise.

 ## Postwar Nationalism and Diplomacy

With peace came a new surge of American nationalism. Self-confident, the nation asserted itself at home and abroad as Republicans borrowed a page from Federalists' agenda and encouraged commerce and economic development. In his message to Congress in December 1815, President Madison embraced Federalist doctrine by recommending military expansion and a program of economic growth. Wartime experiences, he said, had demonstrated the need for a national bank (the charter of the first Bank of the United States had expired in 1811) and for better transportation. To raise government revenues and perpetuate the wartime growth of manufacturing, Madison called for a protective tariff—a tax on imported goods designed to protect American manufactures. Though he strayed from Jeffersonian Republicanism, Madison did so within limits. Only a constitutional amendment, he argued, could give the federal government the authority to build roads and canals that were less than national in scope.

The congressional leadership pushed Madison's nationalist program energetically in the belief that it would unify the country. Republican Congressman John C. Calhoun of South Carolina and Speaker of the House

Nationalist Program

Henry Clay of Kentucky believed the tariff would stimulate industry. The agricultural South and West would sell cotton to the new mills and sell food to the millworkers. New roads would make possible the flow of produce and goods, and tariff revenues would provide the money to build them. A national bank would facilitate all these transactions.

The Republican Congress enacted much of the nationalist program. They chartered the Second Bank of the United States just five years after they had let the charter of the first Bank of the United States run out. The Republicans recognized that they needed a national bank to assist the government and to issue currency. The bank opened its doors in Philadelphia in 1817. The government provided $7 million of the initial $35 million in capital and appointed one-fifth of the directors.

Congress did not share Madison's scruples about the constitutionality of using federal funds to build local roads. "Let us, then, bind the republic together," Calhoun declared, "with a perfect system of roads and canals." Madison, however, vetoed Calhoun's internal-improvements bill, which would have funded mostly local roads, declaring it unconstitutional. Internal improvements, Madison insisted, were the province of the states and of private enterprise. He did, however, approve funds for the extension of the National Road, which began in western Maryland, to Ohio, on the grounds that the road was a military necessity.

To aid American industry, Congress passed the first substantial protective tariffs. The embargo and the war had stimulated domestic industry—especially the manufacture of cloth and iron—but resumption of overseas trade after the war revived competition from abroad. The Tariff of 1816 levied taxes on imported woolens and cottons and on iron, leather, hats, paper, and sugar, in effect raising their prices in the United States. Some New England congressmen viewed the tariff as interference in free trade, and southern congressmen (except Calhoun and a few others) opposed it because it would increase the prices that southern families paid for imported goods. But with support in the western and Middle Atlantic states, the tariff passed.

James Monroe, elected president in 1816, continued Madison's domestic program, supporting tariffs and vetoing internal improvements on constitutional grounds. Monroe was the third Virginian elected president between 1801 and 1825. A former senator, twice governor of Virginia, and an experienced diplomat, he had served under Madison as secretary of state and secretary of war. Monroe fulfilled his ambition to be president largely through perseverance and close association with Jefferson and Madison.

Even Madison's admirers admitted that, among the nation's founders, he was an ordinary and colorless man who rarely had an original idea. He rode into office on Republican coattails, easily defeating the last Federalist nominee, Rufus King, and sweeping all the states except the Federalist strongholds of Massachusetts, Connecticut, and Delaware. "Discord does not belong to our system," Monroe optimistically declared, calling the American people "one great family with a common interest." A Boston newspaper dubbed the one-party period the "Era of Good Feelings."

Led by Federalist chief justice John Marshall, the Supreme Court became the bulwark of a nationalist point of view. In *McCulloch* v. *Maryland* (1819),

McCulloch v. Maryland

the Court struck down a Maryland law taxing a branch of the federally chartered Second Bank of the United States. Maryland had imposed the tax in an effort to destroy the bank's Baltimore branch. The issue was thus one of state versus federal jurisdiction. Speaking for a unanimous Court, Marshall asserted the supremacy of the federal government over the states. "The Constitution and the laws thereof are supreme," he declared. "They control the constitution and laws of the respective states and cannot be controlled by them."

The Court went on to consider whether Congress could issue a bank charter. The Constitution did not spell out such power, but Marshall noted that Congress had the authority to pass "all laws which shall be necessary and proper for carrying into execution" the enumerated powers of the government. Echoing Alexander Hamilton's notion of implied powers, Marshall ruled that Congress could legally exercise "those great powers on which the welfare of the nation essentially depends." If the ends were legitimate and the means were not prohibited, Marshall ruled, a law was constitutional. The Constitution was, in Marshall's words, "intended to endure for ages to come, and consequently, to be adapted to the various causes of human affairs." The bank charter was declared legal.

McCulloch v. *Maryland* thus joined Federalist nationalism and Federalist economic views. By asserting federal supremacy, Marshall was protecting the commercial and industrial interests that favored a national bank; this was federalism in the tradition of Alexander Hamilton. The decision was only one in a series. In *Fletcher* v. *Peck* (1810), the Court had voided a Georgia law that violated individuals' rights to make contracts. In *Dartmouth College* v. *Woodward* (1819), the Court nullified a New Hampshire act altering the charter of Dartmouth College. Marshall ruled that the charter was a contract, and in protecting such contracts he thwarted state interference in commerce and business. *Gibbons* v. *Ogden* (1824) confirmed federal supremacy in interstate commerce.

Monroe's secretary of state, John Quincy Adams, matched the self-confident Marshall Court in assertiveness and nationalism. A small, austere

John Quincy Adams as Secretary of State

man once described by a British official as a "bulldog among spaniels," Adams, the son of John and Abigail Adams, was a superb diplomat who spoke six languages. From 1817 to 1825 he brilliantly managed the nation's foreign policy, stubbornly pushing for expansion, fishing rights for Americans in Atlantic waters, political distance from the Old World, and peace. An ardent expansionist, he nonetheless placed conditions on expansion, believing that it must come about through negotiations, not war, and that newly acquired territories must bar slavery. He urged restraint. The United States, Adams said in an 1821 Fourth of July speech, "goes not abroad, in search of monsters to destroy. She is the well-wisher to the freedom and independence of all."

An Anglophobe, Adams nonetheless worked to strengthen the peace with Great Britain. In 1817 the two nations agreed in the Rush-Bagot Treaty to limit their naval forces to one ship each on Lake Champlain and Lake Ontario and to two ships each on the four other Great lakes. This first disarmament treaty of modern times led to the demilitarization of the border between the United States and Canada.

Adams then pushed for the Convention of 1818, which fixed the United States–Canadian border from Lake of the Woods in Minnesota westward to the Rockies along the 49th parallel (see map, page 250). When agreement could not be reached on the territory west of the Rockies, Britain and the United States settled on joint occupation of Oregon for ten years (renewed indefinitely in 1827). Adams wanted to fix the border along the 49th parallel all the way to the Pacific Ocean, thereby gaining the important inland waterways of Juan de Fuca Strait and Puget Sound, and he hoped for a better negotiating position when the treaty lapsed.

Adams's next moved to settle long-term disputes with Spain. Although the 1803 Louisiana Purchase had omitted reference to Spanish-ruled West Florida, the United States claimed the territory as far east as the Perdido River (the present-day Florida-Alabama border) but occupied only a small finger of the area. During the War of 1812 the United States had seized Mobile and the remainder of West Florida. After the war Adams took advantage of Spain's preoccupation with domestic and colonial troubles to negotiate for the purchase of East Florida. During the talks, which took place in 1818, General Andrew Jackson took it on himself to occupy much of present-day Florida on the pretext of suppressing Seminole raids against American settlements across the border. Adams was furious with Jackson but defended his brazen act.

The following year, Don Luís de Onís, the Spanish minister to the United States, agreed to cede Florida to the United States without payment.

Adams-Onís Treaty

The Adams-Onís, or Transcontinental, Treaty also defined the southwestern boundary of the Louisiana Purchase, a jagged line across the West from Texas to the Pacific Ocean (see map, page 231). (Spain retained present-day Texas, New Mexico, and California.) In return, the United States government assumed $5 million worth of claims by American citizens against Spain and gave up its dubious claim

John Quincy Adams (1767–1848), architect of the Monroe Doctrine, was secretary of state from 1817 to 1825. Thomas Sully's portrait, painted in 1825, captured Adams's determination and stubbornness.   New York State, Office of Parks, Recreation, and Historic Preservation, Philipse Manor Hall State Historic Site.

to northern Mexico (Texas). Expansion was thus achieved at little cost and without war.

When the Spanish flag was last raised over St. Augustine on July 10, 1821, and at Pensacola on July 17, the residents of Florida differed in the welcome they gave to the United States and the American colonial governor, General Andrew Jackson. Some planter-slaveholders and traders were pleased to be living under the American flag, but Creeks and Seminoles, free blacks, runaway slaves who had escaped to Florida, smugglers who worked the coast, and Spanish-speaking town dwellers, were not pleased. General Jackson had led raids against the Seminoles in Florida in 1814 and 1818 and was feared by many. The last colonial Spanish governor, José María Coppinger, encouraged residents to resettle in Mexico, Cuba, or Texas. The Spanish urged the Seminoles to move to the Texas–United States border to discourage American penetration into

Texas. Most Florida residents stayed put but were wary of the United States.

Conflict between the United States and European nations was temporarily resolved by the Rush-Bagot Treaty, the Convention of 1818, and the Adams-Onís Treaty, but events to the south still threatened American interests. John Quincy Adams's desire to insulate the United States and the Western Hemisphere from European conflict brought about his greatest achievement: the Monroe Doctrine.

The immediate issue was the recognition of new governments in Latin America. Between 1808 and 1822, the United Provinces of the Río de la Plata (present-day northern Argentina, Paraguay, and Uruguay), Chile, Peru, Colombia, and Mexico all broke free from Spain. Mindful of the United States's own revolutionary tradition, many Americans favored recognizing their independence, but Monroe and Adams moved cautiously. They sought to avoid conflict with Spain and to be assured of the stability of the new regimes. Then in 1822, shortly after the Adams-Onís Treaty was signed and ratified, the United States became the first nation outside Latin America to recognize the new states, including Mexico.

Soon events in Europe again threatened the stability of the New World. Spain suffered a domestic revolt, and France, in an attempt to bolster the weak Spanish monarchy against the rebels, occupied Spain. The United States feared that France would return the new Latin American states to colonial rule. Great Britain, similarly distrustful of France, proposed a joint United States–British declaration against European intervention in the Western Hemisphere and a joint disavowal of territorial ambitions in the region. Adams rejected the British overture. In accordance with George Washington's admonition to avoid foreign entanglements, he insisted that the United States act independently.

Determined to avoid joint action with Great Britain, Adams would not budge. Those who favored joint action believed the United States needed British naval power to prevent French or Russian expansion in the New World. But Adams won. "It would be more candid, as well as more dignified," he argued, "to avow our principles explicitly to Russia and France, than to come in as a cockboat in the wake of the British man-of-war." Adams interpreted the British proposal to disavow territorial ambitions as a deliberate attempt by London to prevent further American expansion.

President Monroe presented the American position—the Monroe Doctrine—to Congress in December 1823. His message called for *noncolonization* of the Western Hemisphere by European nations, a principle that addressed American anxiety not only about Latin America but also about Russian expansion on the West Coast. (Russia held Alaska and had built settlements and forts as far south as California.) He also demanded *nonintervention* by Europe in the affairs of independent New World nations, and he pledged *noninterference* by the United States in European affairs, including those of Europe's existing New World colonies.

Monroe Doctrine

The Monroe Doctrine proved popular at home as an anti-British, anti-European assertion of American nationalism, and it eventually became the foundation of American policy in the Western Hemisphere. Monroe's words, however, carried no force. Indeed, the policy could not have succeeded without the support of the British, who already were committed to keeping other European nations out of the hemisphere to protect their dominance in the Atlantic trade. Europeans ignored the Monroe Doctrine; it was the Royal Navy they respected, not American policy.

The Panic of 1819 and Renewed Sectionalism

Monroe's domestic record did not match the diplomatic successes of his administration. In 1819, financial panic subverted postwar confidence and revived sectional loyalties. Neither panic nor the resurgence of sectionalism hurt Monroe politically; without a rival political party to rally opposition, he won a second term in 1820 unopposed.

But hard economic times spread. The postwar expansion has been built on easy credit; state banks had printed notes too freely, fueling speculative buying of western land. Speculators had bought acreage to sell at a profit rather than to farm. When manufacturing fell in 1818, prices spiraled downward. The Second Bank of the United States cut back on loans, thus further contracting the economy. Distressed urban workers became politically involved by demonstrating for easy credit and internal improvements. Farmers

Hard Times

clamored for lower tariffs on imported manufactured goods. Hurt by a sharp decline in the price of cotton, southern planters railed at the protective Tariff of 1816, which had raised prices on all imported goods. The Virginia Agricultural Society of Fredericksburg, for example, protested that the tariff violated the principles on which the nation had been founded. In a memorial to Congress in 1820, the society called the tariff an unequal tax that awarded exclusive privileges to manufacturers—"oppressive monopolies, which are ultimately to grind both us and our children after us 'into dust and ashes.'" Manufacturers, by contrast, demanded greater tariff protection and eventually got it in the Tariff of 1824.

Western farmers suffered, too. Those who had purchased public land on credit could not repay their loans. To avoid mass bankruptcy, Congress delayed the deadlines for repayment, and western state legislatures passed "stay laws" restricting mortgage foreclosures. Many westerners blamed the panic on the Second Bank of the United States for tightening the money supply. As state banks folded, westerners bitterly accused the Second Bank of saving itself while the nation went to ruin. Although the economy recovered in the mid-1820s, resentment of the bank contributed to the rise of the Jacksonian movement (see pages 358–361).

Far more divisive was the question of slavery. Ever since the drafting of the Constitution, political leaders had tried to avoid the issue. The one exception was an act ending the foreign slave trade after January 1, 1808, which passed without much opposition. The act followed the expiration of the constitutional ban (Article I, Section 9) on ending the slave trade before 1808. In 1819, however, slavery crept onto the political agenda when Missouri residents petitioned Congress for admission to the Union as a slave state. For the next two-and-a-half years the issue dominated all congressional action. "This momentous question," wrote Thomas Jefferson, fearful for the life of the Union, "like a fire bell in the night, awakened and filled me with terror."

The debate transcended slavery in Missouri. At stake were the compromises that had kept the issue under wraps since the Constitutional Convention. Five new states had joined the Union since 1812: Louisiana (1812), Indiana (1816), Mississippi (1817), Illinois (1818), and Alabama (1819). Of these, Louisiana, Mississippi, and Alabama permitted slav-

"Fire Bell in the Night"

ery. Because Missouri was on the same latitude as free Illinois, Indiana, and Ohio (a state since 1803), its admission as a slave state would thrust slavery farther northward. It would also tilt the uneasy political balance in the Senate toward the slave states. In 1819 the Union consisted of eleven slave and eleven free states. If Missouri joined, slave states would have a one-vote edge in the Senate.

The moral issues made slavery an explosive question. The settlers of Missouri were mostly Kentuckians and Tennesseans who had grown up with slavery. But in the North slavery was slowly dying out, and many northerners had concluded that it was evil. When Representative James Tallmadge, Jr., of New York proposed gradual emancipation in Missouri, a passionate and sometimes violent debate ensued. Southerners accused the North of threatening to destroy the Union. "If you persist, the Union will be dissolved," Thomas W. Cobb of Georgia shouted at Tallmadge. "Seas of blood can only extinguish" the fire Tallmadge was starting, Cobb warned. "Let it come," retorted Tallmadge. The House, which had a northern majority, passed the Tallmadge amendment, but the Senate rejected it. The two sides were deadlocked.

A compromise emerged in 1820 under pressure from House Speaker Henry Clay: the admission of free Maine, carved out of Massachusetts, was linked with the admission of slave Missouri. In the rest of the Louisiana Territory north of latitude 36°30' (Missouri's southern boundary), slavery was prohibited forever (see map, page 250). The compromise carried, but the agreement almost came apart in November when Missouri submitted a constitution that barred free blacks from entering the state. Opponents contended that the proposed state constitution violated the federal Constitution's provision that "the citizens of each State shall be entitled to all privileges and immunities of citizens in the several States." Advocates argued that restrictions on free blacks were common in both North and South. In 1821, Clay produced a second compromise: Missouri guaranteed that none of its laws would discriminate against citizens of other states. (Once admitted to the Union, however, Missouri twice adopted laws banning free blacks.)

Missouri Compromise

Although political leaders succeeded in removing slavery from the congressional agenda, sectional issues undermined Republican unity and ended the

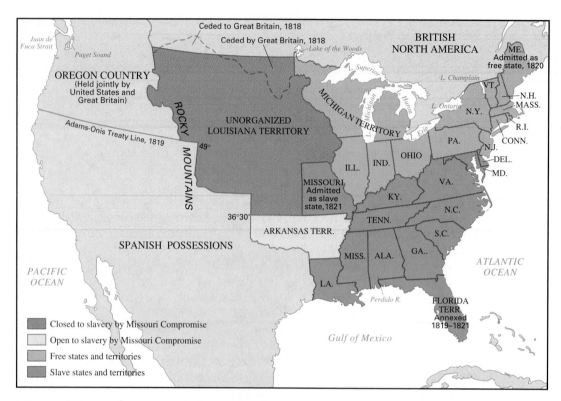

Missouri Compromise and the State of the Union, 1820 *The compromise worked out by House Speaker Henry Clay established a formula that avoided debate over whether new states would allow or prohibit slavery. In the process, it divided the United States into northern and southern regions.*

reign of the Virginia presidential dynasty. The Republican party came apart in 1824 as presidential candidates from different sections of the country scrambled for support. Sectionalism and the question of slavery ultimately would threaten the Union itself.

 Conclusion

The first decades of the nineteenth century were a time of self-definition and growth for the young republic. Political parties broadened white male involvement in politics and quieted factional divisions. A tradition of peaceful transition of power through presidential elections was established. And the United States expanded continuously, from the acquisition of Louisiana to the purchase of Florida.

The Revolution still cast a shadow over the new nation. Federalists harked back to British precedents. Republicans sought to maintain the ideals and virtues associated with the Revolution and the founding of a republic in which citizens would place civic virtue above individual gain. A second war with Britain—the War of 1812—reaffirmed American independence and thwarted Indian opposition to United States expansion; thereafter the nation was able to settle most foreign disputes at the bargaining table.

The War of 1812 and diplomatic assertiveness brought a sense of national identity and self-confidence. Americans claimed victory, and after the war, all branches of the government, responding to the popular mood, pursued a vigorous national policy. The Supreme Court promoted national unity by extending federal power over the states and encouraging commerce and economic growth. In spite of Jefferson's vision of an agrarian society, the country was gradually shifting to a market economy in which people produced goods to sell to others (see Chapter 10). Embargo and war had promoted the manufacturing of goods in the United States, lessening dependence on imports from Europe. Developments in transportation further stimulated the economy and expansion. Under the guidance of John Quincy Adams, the United States pursued its interests through diplomacy, not direct intervention. The Monroe Doctrine was among his finest achievements.

Sectionalism accompanied nationalism and geographic expansion. War, tariffs, economic hard times, and slavery brought out sectional discord. While manufacturers and merchants in the North and agricultural producers in the West became linked through transportation and trade, the South was developing its own economy and culture based on cotton, export markets, a plantation system, and slavery (see Chapter 11). Politicians kept the question of slavery off the national agenda as long as possible and worked out the Missouri Compromise as a stopgap measure. But territorial acquisitions and further westward expansion in the 1840s and 1850s would collide with a rising tide of reform to make the question of slavery unavoidable (see Chapters 13 and 14).

Over the next two decades, the way Americans lived and worked changed at a quickening pace. The colonial and revolutionary generations were fading away. The deaths of John Adams and Thomas Jefferson within a few hours of each other on July 4, 1826—the fiftieth anniversary of the signing of the Declaration of Independence—symbolized that passing. As citizens mourned those political giants, they recognized that their future would be very different from the world of the founders. Economic development, rising population, the spread of settlement, and the growth of cities were transforming people, their lives, and their communities.

Suggestions for Further Reading

General

Henry Adams, *History of the United States of America During the Administration of Thomas Jefferson and of James Madison*, 9 vols. (1889–1891); Noble E. Cunningham, Jr., *The United States in 1800: Henry Adams Revisited* (1988); George Dangerfield, *The Awakening of American Nationalism, 1815–1828* (1965); George Dangerfield, *The Era of Good Feelings* (1952); Jean V. Matthews, *Toward a New Society: American Thought and Culture, 1800–1830* (1991); John Mayfield, *The New Nation, 1800–1845* (1981); Marshall Smelser, *The Democratic Republic, 1801–1815* (1968).

Party Politics

James M. Banner, *To the Hartford Convention: The Federalists and the Origins of Party Politics in the Early Republic, 1789–1815* (1967); Noble E. Cunningham, Jr., *The Jeffersonian Republicans in Power: Party Operations, 1801–1809* (1963); David Hackett Fischer, *The Revolution of American Conservatism: The Federalist Party in the Era*

of Jeffersonian Democracy (1965); Linda K. Kerber, *Federalists in Dissent* (1970); Shaw Livermore, *Twilight of Federalism: The Disintegration of the Federalist Party, 1815–1830* (1962); Milton Lomask, *Aaron Burr*, 2 vols. (1979, 1983); Richard P. McCormick, *The Presidential Game: The Origins of American Presidential Politics* (1982); Drew McCoy, *The Elusive Republic* (1980); Robert V. Remini, *Henry Clay: Statesman for the Union* (1991); James Sterling Young, *The Washington Community, 1800–1828* (1966).

The Virginia Presidents

Harry Ammon, *James Monroe: The Quest for National Identity* (1971); Noble E. Cunningham, Jr., *In Pursuit of Reason: The Life of Thomas Jefferson* (1987); Noble E. Cunningham, Jr., *The Process of Government Under Jefferson* (1978); Ralph Ketcham, *Presidents Above Party: The First American Presidency, 1789–1829* (1984); Drew R. McCoy, *The Last of the Fathers: James Madison and the Republican Legacy* (1989); Merrill D. Peterson, *Thomas Jefferson and the New Nation* (1970); Norman K. Risjord, *Thomas Jefferson* (1994); Robert Allen Rutland, *The Presidency of James Madison* (1990); Robert W. Tucker and David C. Hendrickson, *Empire of Liberty: The Statecraft of Thomas Jefferson* (1990).

The Supreme Court and the Law

Leonard Baker, *John Marshall: A Life in Law* (1974); Robert Lowry Clinton, *Marbury v. Madison and Judicial Review* (1989); Richard E. Ellis, *The Jeffersonian Crisis: Courts and Politics in the Young Republic* (1971); Morton J. Horowitz, *The Transformation of American Law, 1780–1860* (1977); R. Kent Newmyer, *The Supreme Court Under Marshall and Taney* (1968); Thomas C. Shevory, *John Marshall's Law: Interpretation, Ideology, and Interest* (1994); Francis N. Stites, *John Marshall: Defender of the Constitution* (1981).

Expansionism, the War of 1812, and Diplomacy

Roger H. Brown, *The Republic in Peril* (1964); Alexander De Conde, *This Affair of Louisiana* (1976); R. David Edmunds, *Tecumseh and the Quest for Indian Leadership* (1984); R. David Edmunds, *The Shawnee Prophet* (1983); Clifford L. Egan, *Neither Peace nor War: Franco-American Relations, 1803–1812* (1983); Kenneth J. Hagan, *This People's Navy* (1991); Donald R. Hickey, *The War of 1812* (1989); Bradford Perkins, *The Creation of a Republican Empire, 1776–1865* (1993); Julius W. Pratt, *Expansionists of 1812* (1925); James P. Ronda, *Lewis and Clark Among the Indians* (1984); Greg Russell, *John Quincy Adams and the Public Virtues of Diplomacy* (1995); J. C. A. Stagg, *Mr. Madison's War: Politics, Diplomacy, and Warfare in the Early Republic, 1783–1830* (1983); Anders Stephanson, *Manifest Destiny: American Expansionism and the Empire of Right* (1995); Steve Watts, *The Republic Reborn: War and the Making of a Liberal America, 1790–1820* (1987); David J. Weber, *The Spanish Frontier in North America* (1992).

The Monroe Doctrine

Samuel F. Bemis, *John Quincy Adams and the Foundations of American Foreign Policy* (1949); Walter LaFeber, ed., *John Quincy Adams and American Continental Empire* (1965); Ernest R. May, *The Making of the Monroe Doctrine* (1976); Dexter Perkins, *Hands Off: A History of the Monroe Doctrine* (1941).

THE OLD GRANITE STATE,

Judson.   Abby.   John.   Asa.

LITH. OF ENDICOTT.   22 JOHN ST. NEW YORK.

A SONG,

Price 50 Cts N.

COMPOSED, ARRANGED AND SUNG, BY

THE HUTCHINSON FAMILY

CHAPTER

10

Rails, Markets, and Mills:
The North and West
1800–1860

T he Hutchinson family, also known as the Tribe of Jesse, was the most popular singing group in nineteenth-century America. Abby, Asa, Jesse, John, and Judson Hutchinson—five members of a family of sixteen children from rural New Hampshire—performed throughout the United States and across the Atlantic, singing the patriotic, religious, and sentimental songs that had dominated popular music since the Revolution. Twentieth-century commentators have compared them to Woody Guthrie, Chuck Berry, Bruce Springsteen, and even the Beatles for initiating new musical styles, for their popularity and energy as performers, and for writing their own socially aware lyrics.

The family members were accomplished entertainers. Unlike most groups that just sang, the Tribe of Jesse presented well-rehearsed and elaborately produced performances. They used traditional airs that the audiences knew and found comforting, but they wrote new lyrics exploring controversial social problems and reform, abolitionism, and temperance. For example, "'Get Off the Track!' represented the railroad with all its terrible enginery and speed and danger," according to a contemporary editor. When first performed in 1844, the song was too inflammatory for any publisher to print. The Hutchinsons sang it on stage, and the abolitionist press carried its lyrics until a publisher finally printed songsheets.

The Hutchinson Family celebrated their native rural New Hampshire in "The Old Granite State," their most popular song. They made a business of performing, and hawkers sold their sheet music at concerts. *Lynn Historical Society.*

Ho! the Car Emancipation
Rides majestic thro' our nation
Bearing on its Train, the story.
LIBERTY! a Nation's Glory.
    Roll it along, thro' the Nation
    Freedom's Car, Emancipation.

The song became one of the Hutchinsons' trademarks, rousing antislavery audiences.

The Hutchinson Family was part of a new phenomenon: singers, songwriters, musicians, publishers, and managers who made a business of music and entertainment. Drawing their largest audiences in the growing cities, they entered the commercial world and made a living from writing and performing music. The Hutchinson Family's fee for a single night in the 1840s reached $1,000. Each performance was planned and choreographed, and the group had an entourage of managers, agents, publishers, and concert-hall representatives. Hawkers sold sheet music, portraits, and songbooks at the Hutchinsons' concerts. A traditional rural pastime had become a big business.

The Hutchinsons' own lives, too, bridged the old and the new. Their roots were in the farm country of New Hampshire, the "Old Granite State" celebrated in their most popular song. But they left the farm to sing to millworkers, laborers, homemakers, and reformers in the industrial North.

Besides their musical talent, the Hutchinson Family seemed to offer their audiences reassurance in a time of rapid and thoroughgoing change. By setting their lyrics to traditional hymns, they connected change and reform with time-tested values. And by describing a bucolic future, they reassured their audiences that the present, with all its turmoil and change, would turn out well.

The Hutchinsons were able to tour the nation in concert because of advances in transportation and communications that linked the growing national economy between 1800 and 1860. The canal boat, steamboat, locomotive, and telegraph made possible a Hutchinson Family concert tour. But more enduringly, these technological advances opened up the frontier and helped expand farm production for markets at home and abroad. Ready-made men's garments manufactured in New York and Cincinnati could be purchased across the nation. Increasingly, farmers grew more crops for the internal market, and urban producers worked for wages. Improved transportation was the most tangible change, but equally significant was increased specialization in agriculture, manufacturing, and finance, which fostered a nationwide, capitalist, market-oriented economy.

This dramatic transformation began early in the century and spread nearly everywhere. In 1800 most of the 5.3 million Americans earned their living working the land or serving those who did. Settlements clustered on the East Coast, along the Ohio and Mississippi river valleys, along the Gulf Coast, across present-day Texas, and on the West Coast. By 1860, 31.4 million Americans had spread across the continent: some midwestern farms were 1,500 miles from the Atlantic, and settlement on the Pacific Slope was booming. A continental nation had been forged. Meanwhile, the economy, though still primarily agricultural, was being transformed by enormous commercial and manufacturing expansion.

Promotion of economic growth became the hallmark of the federal government, especially during the period of fervent nationalism after the War of 1812. The government encouraged individual enterprise by promoting an environment in which farming and industry could flourish. New financial institutions amassed the capital for large-scale enterprises like factories and railroads. Mechanization took hold; factories and precision-made machinery competed successfully with home workshops and handmade goods, and reapers and sowers revolutionized farming.

New tensions accompanied economic expansion, and not everyone profited in wealth and opportunity as the Hutchinson Family did. The experience of a journeyman tailor displaced by retailers and cheaper labor was far different than that of the new merchant princes. New England farm daughters who became wage workers found their world changing no less radically. Farmers everywhere experienced tensions between their traditional way of life and the opportunities and demands of market-oriented production. Moreover, boom-and-bust cycles became part of the fabric of ordinary life. And canals, railroads, and urban and industrial growth brought with them destruction of the environment. But whatever its benefits and drawbacks, economic development was irreversible.

 Transportation and Regionalization

The North, South, and West followed distinct economic paths between 1800 and 1860. Everywhere, agriculture remained the foundation of the American economy. Nevertheless, the North increasingly invested its resources in industry, commerce, and finance; the South in plantations and subsistence farms; and the West in commercialized family farms, agricultural processing, and implement manufactur-

• *Important Events* •

1790	First American textile mill, using water-powered spinning machines, opens in Pawtucket, Rhode Island	**1825**	Erie Canal completed
1807	Robert Fulton's steamboat, *Clermont*, makes its debut	**1830**	Baltimore and Ohio Railroad begins operation
1812–15	War of 1812 stimulates domestic manufactures War of 1812 fought	**1831**	McCormick invents the reaper
		1834	Women workers strike at Lowell textile mills
1813	New England capitalists found the Boston Manufacturing Company and build the first large-scale American factory	**1836**	Second Bank of the United States closes
		1837	*Charles River Bridge* v. *Warren Bridge* encourages new enterprises
1816	Tariff of 1816 introduces first substantial protective tariff Congress charters the Second Bank of the United States	**1839–43**	Hard times strike again
		1844	A government grant develops telegraph line between Baltimore and Washington
1818	National Road reaches Wheeling, Virginia, opening the West	**1848**	Regularly scheduled steamship passage begins between Liverpool and New York City
1819	*Dartmouth College* v. *Woodward* protects the sanctity of contracts	**1849**	California gold rush transforms the West Coast
1819–23	Hard times bring unemployment and business bankruptcies	**1853**	British study of American system of manufacturing
1820s	New England textile mills expand	**1854**	Railroad reaches the Mississippi River
1824	*Gibbons* v. *Ogden* affirms federal over state authority in interstate commerce	**1857**	Hard times mark end of third boom-or-bust cycle

ing. This tendency toward regional specialization made the various sections of the country at once less alike and more interdependent. All looked to transportation to link the various sections' economic activities.

The revolution in transportation and communications was probably the single overriding cause of these changes. Heavy investment in canals and railroads made the North the center of American commerce; its growing seaboard cities distributed western produce and New England textiles. New York financial and commercial houses linked the southern cotton-exporting economy to the North and Europe. The South, with most of its capital invested in slave labor, built fewer canals, railroads, and factories and remained mostly rural and undeveloped (see Chapter 11).

Before the 1820s and 1830s, it was by no means certain that New England and the Middle Atlantic states would dominate American finance and commerce. Indeed, the natural orientation of the 1800 frontier—Tennessee, Kentucky, and Ohio—was toward the South. The southward-flowing Ohio and Mississippi Rivers were the lifelines of early western settlement. Flatboats transported western grain and hogs southward for consumption or transfer to oceangoing vessels at New Orleans. Southern products—first tobacco, then lumber and cotton—flowed directly to Europe. Steamboats, successfully introduced in 1807 when Robert Fulton's *Clermont* paddled up the Hudson River from New York City, began in 1815 to carry cargo upstream on the Mississippi and Ohio Rivers, further reinforcing ties between the South and the West.

Change in Trade Routes

But this pattern changed in the 1820s when new arteries opened up east-west travel. The National

The town of Lockport, New York, owed its existence to the Erie Canal, and serving boats, freight, and passengers was its major industry. This view of the town was rendered in 1836, eleven years after the canal was opened.   Library of Congress, hand-colored by Sandi Rygiel, Picture Research Consultants, Inc.

Road—a stone-based, gravel-topped highway originating in Cumberland, Maryland—reached Wheeling, Virginia (now West Virginia), in 1818 and Columbus, Ohio, in 1833. (Today, highways U.S. 40 and I-70 follow the same route.) More important, the Erie Canal, completed in 1825, linked the Great Lakes with New York City and the Atlantic Ocean. The canal carried easterners and then immigrants to settle the Old Northwest and the frontier beyond; in the opposite direction, it transported western grain to the large and growing eastern markets. Railroads and later the telegraph would solidify these east-west links. By contrast, at only one place—Bowling Green, Kentucky—did northern and southern railroads connect with one another. Although trade still moved southward along the Ohio and Mississippi, the bulk of western trade flowed eastward by 1850. Thus by the eve of the Civil War, the northern and Middle Atlantic states were closely linked to the former frontier of the Old Northwest.

Construction of the 363-mile-long Erie Canal was a visionary enterprise. When the state of New

Canals

York authorized it in 1817, the longest American canal was only 28 miles long. Vigorously promoted by Governor DeWitt Clinton, the Erie cost $7 million, much of it in loans from British investors. The canal shortened the journey between Buffalo and New York City from twenty to six days and reduced freight charges from $100 to $5 a ton. By 1835, traffic was so heavy that the canal had to be widened from forty to seventy feet and deepened from four to seven feet. Skeptics who had called the canal "Clinton's big ditch" had long since fallen silent. The expanding midwestern population would lay the basis for Chicago to dominate the central region.

The success of the Erie Canal triggered an explosion of canal building. Sensing the advantage New York had gained, other states and cities rushed to follow suit. By 1840, canals crisscrossed the Northeast and Midwest, and total canal mileage reached 3,300—an increase of more than 2,000 miles in a single decade (see map, page 257). Unfortunately for investors, none of these canals enjoyed the financial success achieved by the Erie. As the high cost of construction combined with an economic contraction, investment in canals began to slump in the 1830s. By 1850 more miles were being abandoned than built, and the canal era had unmistakably ended.

Meanwhile, railroad construction boomed. The railroad era in the United States began in 1830 when Peter Cooper's locomotive Tom Thumb first steamed along 13 miles of track

Railroads

constructed by the Baltimore and Ohio Railroad. In 1833 the nation's second railroad ran 136 miles from Charleston to Hamburg in South Carolina. By 1850 the United States had nearly 9,000 miles of railroad; by 1860, roughly 31,000 (see map below and figure on page 258). Canal fever stimulated this early railroad construction. Promoters of the Baltimore and Ohio believed that railroads

would compete successfully with canals. Similarly, the line between Boston and Worcester in Massachusetts was intended as the first link in a rail line to Albany, at the eastern end of the Erie Canal. In Providence, Rhode Island, and other port cities, the railroads extended to the water's edge.

The earliest railroads connected nearby cities; not until the 1850s did railroads offer long-distance service at reasonable rates. The early lines had technical problems to overcome. Locomotives heavy enough to climb steep grades and pull long trains required strong rails and resilient trackbeds. Engineers met those needs by replacing wooden tracks with iron rails and by supporting the rails with ties embedded in gravel. A new wheel alignment—the swivel truck—permitted heavy engines to hold the track on sharp curves. Other problems persisted: the use of hand brakes severely restricted speed, and

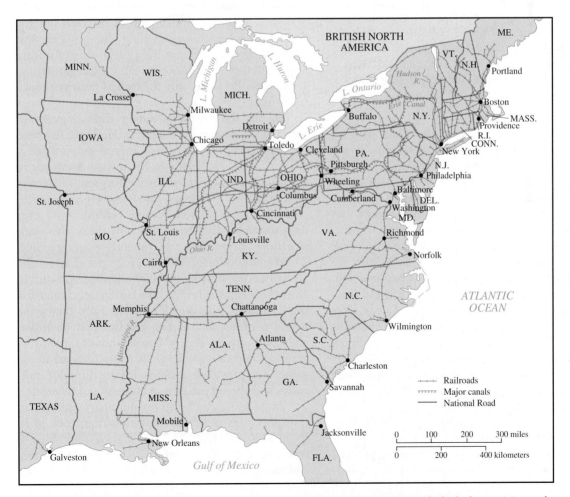

Major Railroads, Canals, and Roads in 1860 *Transportation networks linked port cities to the interior. These links were most dense in the populous Northeast and the Old Northwest.*

Railroad Mileage, 1830–1860

Railroad Mileage, 1830–1860 In the 1850s, railroads developed a national rail network east of the Mississippi River. Source: U.S. Bureau of the Census, *Historical Statistics of the United States, Colonial Times to 1970*, 2 parts (Washington, D.C., 1975), Part 2, p. 731.

the lack of a standard gauge for the width of track thwarted development of a national system. Pennsylvania and Ohio railroads, for instance, had no fewer than seven different track widths. A journey from Philadelphia to Charleston, South Carolina, involved eight different gauges, which meant that passengers had to change trains seven times.

In the 1850s technological improvements, competition, economic recovery, and a desire for national unity prompted development of regional and, eventually, national rail networks. By 1853 rail lines linked Chicago to eastern cities, and a year later track reached the Mississippi River. By 1860 rails stretched as far west as St. Joseph, Missouri. Short lines merged to create two unified systems, the New York Central and the Pennsylvania Railroad. Most lines, however, were still independently run. Differences in gauge, scheduling, car design, and a commitment to serve their hometowns first and foremost prevented cooperation and mergers.

Railroads were the most popular symbol of technological change. The Hutchinson Family capitalized on that image in "Get Off the Track!"; they dressed emancipation in railroad symbolism: all-out speed, unstoppable power, and energetic change.

Railroads did not completely replace water transportation. The federal government assisted water transportation by improving ports and clearing rivers for navigation. Shipping routes linked newer areas, like Texas and California, to the rest of the United States. At mid-century, steamships still carried bulk cargo more cheaply than railroads except during freezing weather. The sealike Great Lakes accommodated giant ships with propellers in place of paddlewheels; these leviathans carried heavy bulk cargoes like lumber, grain, and ore. On the high seas, steamships gradually replaced sailing vessels, which were dependent on prevailing winds and thus usually could not meet regular schedules. The biggest breakthrough occurred in 1848, when Samuel Cunard introduced regularly scheduled steamships between Liverpool and New York, reducing travel time across the Atlantic from twenty-five days eastbound and forty-nine days westbound to between ten and fourteen days each way. Sailing ships quickly lost first-class passengers and light cargo to steamships, although they continued to carry immigrants and bulk cargo. By 1860, only the freight trade remained to them.

Steamboats

By far the fastest-spreading technological advance of the era was the magnetic telegraph. Invented by artist Samuel F. B. Morse, the telegraph made it possible for distant messages to travel faster than any messenger could; instantaneous communication became possible even over long distances. By 1853, only nine years after construction of the first experimental telegraph line, 23,000 miles of telegraph wire had spread across the United States; by 1860, 50,000 miles were in use. In 1861 the telegraph bridged the continent, connecting the East, Gulf, and West Coasts, literally joining the nation together and ending the isolation of Texans and Californians. Rarely has an innovation had so great an impact so quickly: it revolutionized newsgathering, provided advance information for railroads, and altered patterns of business and finance.

Telegraph

Time was key to the revolutionary changes in transportation and communications that took place from 1800 to 1860. In 1800 it took four days to travel by coach from New York City to Baltimore and nearly four weeks to reach Detroit. By 1830 Baltimore was only a day-and-a-half away, and Detroit was only a two-week journey by way of the Erie Canal. By 1857 Detroit was an overnight train ride

In Providence, Rhode Island, locomotives replaced horses in transporting freight and people. In Atlantic ports and cities on navigable rivers, the rail lines extended to the water's edge to meet the steamers and sailing ships. Museum of Art, Rhode Island School of Design.

from New York City, and in a week a traveler could reach Texas or western Missouri by rail. Reduced travel time not only saved money and facilitated commerce but also brought frontier areas under the control of Chicago and eastern businesses. During the first two decades of the century, wagon transportation cost 30 to 70 cents per ton per mile. By 1860, railroads in New York State carried freight at an average charge of 2.2 cents per ton-mile, and wheat moved from Chicago to New York for 1.2 cents per ton-mile. In sum, the transportation revolution transformed the economy.

The Market Economy

Before the transportation revolution, most farmers had geared production to family needs and to local and foreign markets. They lived in interdependent communities and kept detailed accounts of labor and goods exchanged with their neighbors. Farm families produced much of what they needed—food, clothing, candles, soap, and the like—and traded for or purchased items they could not produce, such as cooking pots, horseshoes, coffee, tea, and sugar.

By the Civil War the United States was industrializing, and most Americans were involved in the market economy. More men and women worked for wages, and most people outside the South—farmers and workers alike—purchased increasing amounts of store-bought goods produced in workshops and factories.

In the market economy, men and women grew crops and produced goods for sale at home or abroad. The money that individuals received from market transactions—from the sale of goods or from the sale of a person's labor—purchased items produced by other people. Such a system encouraged specialization. Farmers began to grow only one or two crops or raise only cows, pigs, or sheep for market. Farm women gave up spinning and weaving and purchased fabric produced by wage-earning farm girls in Massachusetts textile mills.

Definition of a Market Economy

Improvements in transportation and technology, the division of labor, and new methods of financing all fueled the expansion of the economy. Goods and services multiplied. This growth, in turn, prompted new improvements and greater opportunities for wage labor. The effect was cumulative; by the 1840s the economy was growing at a faster rate than in the previous four decades. While per capita

E. Didier painted Auction in Chatham Street *in 1834. Auction houses in New York and other cities boomed during hard times.*   Museum of the City of New York.

income doubled between 1800 and 1860, the price of manufactured goods and food fell.

The pace of economic growth, however, was uneven. Prosperity reigned during two long periods, from 1823 to 1835 and from 1843 to 1857. But there were long stretches of economic contraction as well. The interruption in trade between Jefferson's 1807 embargo and the end of the War of 1812 had contributed to a negative growth rate—that is, fewer goods and services were produced. Contraction and deflation (decline in the general price level) occurred again during the hard times of 1819–1823, 1839–1843, and 1857. During these periods banks collapsed, businesses went under, wages and prices declined, and jobs were hard to find or to keep.

Boom-and-Bust Cycles

As a Baltimore physician noted in 1819, working people felt hard times "a thousand fold more than the merchants." Wage earners could not build up sufficient financial reserves in good times to get them through the next bout of hard times; often they could not even make it through the winter without drawing on charity for food, clothing, and firewood. In the 1820s and 1830s, free laborers in Baltimore typically found steady work from March through October, then unemployment and hunger from November through February.

If even good times were hard on workers and their families, hard times devastated them. In 1839 in Baltimore, when hundreds of small manufacturers for the local market closed their doors, tailors, shoemakers, milliners, and shipyard and construction workers lost their jobs. Ninety miles to the north, Philadelphia took on an eerie aura. "The streets seemed deserted," Sidney George Fisher observed in 1842. "The largest [merchant] houses are shut up and to rent, there is no business . . . no money, no confidence." Only auctions boomed, as sheriffs sold off seized property at a quarter of predepression prices, as the artist E. Didier portrayed in *Auction in Chatham Street* in nearby New York. In Philadelphia and other cities, soup societies fed the hungry. In New York, bread lines and beggars crowded the sidewalks. In smaller cities like Lynn, Massachusetts, the poor became scavengers, digging for clams and harvesting dandelions.

Hard times struck again in 1857. The Mercantile Agency—the forerunner of Dun and Bradstreet—recorded 5,123 bankruptcies in 1857, nearly double the number of the previous year. The bankrupt firms owed $300 million, only half of which would be paid off. Contemporary reports estimated twenty to thirty thousand unemployed people in Philadelphia, and thirty to forty thousand in New York City. Female benevolent societies expanded their soup kitchens and distributed free firewood to the needy. In Chicago, charities reorganized to meet the needs of the poor; in New York, the city hired the unemployed to repair streets and develop Central Park. And in Fall River, Massachusetts, a citizens' committee disbursed public funds on a weekly basis to nine hundred families. The soup kitchen, the bread line, and public aid had become fixtures in urban America.

What caused the boom-and-bust cycles that brought about such suffering? Generally speaking, they were a direct result of the market economy.

Cause of Boom-and-Bust Cycles

Prosperity stimulated demand for staples and for finished goods such as clothing and furniture. Increased demand in turn led not only to higher prices and still higher production but also, because of business confidence and expectation of higher prices, to speculation in land and to the flow of foreign currency into the country. Eventually production surpassed demand, causing prices and wages to fall; in response, inflated land and stock values collapsed. The inflow of foreign money led first to easy credit and then to collapse when unhappy investors withdrew their funds.

Some contemporary economists considered this process beneficial—a self-adjusting cycle in which unprofitable economic ventures were eliminated. In theory, people concentrated on the activities they did best, and the economy as a whole became more efficient. Advocates of the system also argued that it enhanced individual freedom, since theoretically each seller, whether of goods or labor, was free to determine the conditions of the sale. But in fact the system tied workers to a perpetual roller coaster; they became dependent on wages—and on the availability of jobs—for their very existence. The cycles that governed the market economy dominated every

corner of the country as even small localities became tied to regional and national markets.

People experienced the market economy in a variety of ways. In the course of the nineteenth century, traditional farm women who had contributed to the family as unpaid labor—producing cloth, clothing, and dairy products for family use—found their lives altered. They increasingly contributed cash, first from the sale of eggs, butter, cheese, and poultry, and then, in New England and the Middle Atlantic states, from industrial work at home, weaving cloth and sewing shoes for contractors who paid them by the piece. By midcentury many women's earnings sustained their families.

The market economy also ushered in another type of boom-and-bust cycle: harvest and destruction. Canals and railroads stimulated demand for distant resources, then accelerated the destruction of forests, natural waterways, and any landscape features that represented obstacles. Railroads made possible large-scale lumbering of pinewood forests in northern Michigan, Wisconsin, and Minnesota. During the 1850s, 40 million acres were cleared of lumber, leaving most of that land unfit even for agriculture. Similarly, the extension of railroads to Kansas and Nebraska brought hunters who slaughtered the great herds of bison for sport. The process of harvest and destruction eventually would change the ecology of the United States.

Government Promotes Economic Growth

The eighteenth-century political ideas that had captured the imagination of the Revolutionary War generation and found expression in the ideal of republican virtue had economic counterparts in the writings of Adam Smith, a Scottish political economist. Smith's *The Wealth of Nations* first appeared in 1776, the year of the Declaration of Independence. Both works emphasized individual liberty, and both were reactions against active government: Thomas Jefferson denounced monarchy and distant government; Smith rejected mercantilism, or government regulation of the economy to benefit the state (see page 83). Both declared that virtue resided in individual freedom and that the community would benefit most from individuals' pursuit of their own self-interest.

Jefferson, influenced by the economic and egalitarian ideas of republicanism (see pages 172–174), believed that freedom thrived where individuals had scope for independence, creativity, and choice—individuals fettered by government, monopoly, or economic dependence could not be free. Limited government was not an end, according to Jefferson, but a means to greater freedom. Committed to the idea that republican democracy would flourish best in a nation of independent farmers and artisans and in an atmosphere of widespread political participation, Jefferson recognized that government was needed to promote individual freedom. Beginning with the purchase of Louisiana in 1803, Republican policy, no less than that of the Federalists, endorsed using the federal government to promote economic growth. The result was faith in a market economy in which government played an active role.

After acquiring Louisiana, the federal government facilitated economic growth and geographic expansion by encouraging westward exploration and settlement, by promoting agriculture, and by developing transportation. The Lewis and Clark expedition (see page 231) began ongoing federal interest in geographic and geologic surveying and opened western lands to exploitation and settlement.

New steps followed quickly. In 1817–1818 Henry Rowe Schoolcraft explored the Missouri and Arkansas region, reporting on its geology and mineral resources. In 1819–1820 Major Stephen Long explored the Great Plains, mapping the area between the Platte and Canadian Rivers. Between 1827 and 1840 the government surveyed about fifty potential railroad routes. The final door to western settlement was opened in 1843–1844 by John C. Frémont's expedition, which followed the Oregon Trail to the Pacific, turned south to California, and then returned east by way of the Great Salt Lake. Frémont, later a California senator and in 1856 the first Republican presidential candidate, gained fame as a soldier-surveyor of the West. His report of his journey dispelled a long-standing myth that the middle of the continent was a desert.

To encourage settlement and cultivation of western lands, the federal government evicted Indians from their traditional lands and offered the land at reasonable prices (see pages 281–282). And because transportation was crucial to the development of the frontier, the government first financed roads and canals and later subsidized railroad construction by means of land grants. Even the State Department aided agriculture: its consular offices overseas collected horticultural information, seeds, and cuttings,

and it published technical reports in an effort to improve American farming.

The federal government also played an active role in technological and industrial growth. Federal arsenals pioneered new manufacturing techniques and helped to develop the machine-tool industry. The United States Post Office provided a communications link that stimulated interregional trade and briefly played a crucial role in the development of the telegraph. The federal government financed the first telegraph line, from Washington to Baltimore, in 1844; it was briefly managed by the Post Office. To create an atmosphere conducive to economic growth and individual creativity, the government protected inventions and domestic industries. Patent laws gave inventors a seventeen-year monopoly on their inventions, and tariffs protected American industry from foreign competition.

The federal judiciary validated government promotion of the economy and encouraged business enterprise. In *Gibbons* v. *Ogden* (1824), the Supreme Court overturned the New York State law that had given Robert Fulton and Robert Livingston a monopoly on the New York–New Jersey steamboat trade. Aaron Ogden, their successor, lost the monopoly when Chief Justice of the United States John Marshall ruled that the congressional prerogative of licensing new enterprises took precedence over New York's grant of monopoly rights to Fulton and Livingston. Marshall declared that Congress's power under the commerce clause of the Constitution extended to "every species of commercial intercourse," including transportation systems. Within a year, forty-three steamboats were plying Ogden's route.

Legal Foundations of Commerce

In defining interstate commerce broadly, the Marshall Court expanded federal powers over the economy while restricting the ability of states to control economic activity within their borders. Its action was consistent with the Court's earlier decision in *Dartmouth College* v. *Woodward* (1819), which protected the sanctity of contracts against interference by the states (see page 246). "If business is to prosper," Marshall wrote, "men must have assurance that contracts will be enforced."

Federal and state courts, in conjunction with state legislatures, also encouraged the proliferation of corporations—organizations entitled to hold property and transact business as if they were a per-

The Marshall Court encouraged business competition by ending state-licensed monopolies on inland waterways. Gibbons v. Ogden *(1824) opened up the New York–New Jersey trade to new lines, and within a short time dozens of steamboats were ferrying passengers and freight across the Hudson River.* New-York Historical Society.

son. Corporation owners, called shareholders, were granted *limited liability*, or freedom from responsibility for the company's debts. An attractive feature to potential investors, limited liability encouraged people to back new business ventures. In 1800 the United States had about three hundred incorporated firms; in 1817 there were about two thousand. By 1830 the New England states alone had issued nineteen hundred charters, one-third to manufacturing and mining firms. At first each firm needed a special legislative act to incorporate, but after the 1830s applications became so numerous that states established routine procedures allowing firms to incorporate.

Though legislative action created corporations, the courts played a crucial role in defining their status, extending their powers, and protecting them. A particular encouragement to corporate development and free enterprise was the Supreme Court's ruling in *Charles River Bridge* v. *Warren Bridge* (1837) that new enterprises could not be restrained by implied privileges under old charters. The case involved issues of great importance: should a new interest be allowed to compete against existing enterprises,

and should the state protect existing privilege or encourage innovation and the growth of commerce through competition?

The Massachusetts legislature had chartered the Charles River Bridge Company in 1785 and six years later extended its charter for seventy years. In return for assuming the risk of building a bridge between Charlestown and Boston, the owners were granted the privilege of collecting tolls. In 1828 the legislature chartered another company to build the Warren Bridge across the Charles nearby; the owner would have the right to collect tolls for six years, after which the bridge would be turned over to the state and be free of tolls. The Charles River Bridge Company sued in 1829, claiming that the new bridge breached the earlier charter and contradicted the principles in *Dartmouth College* v. *Woodward*.

Speaking for the Court majority, Marshall's successor Roger Taney declared that the original charter did not confer the privilege of monopoly and that exclusivity could not therefore be implied. Focusing on the question of corporate privilege rather than the law of contracts, Taney ruled that charter grants should be interpreted narrowly and that ambiguities would be decided in favor of the public interest. New enterprises should not be restricted by old charters, and economic growth would best be served by narrowing the application of the *Dartmouth College* decision. Thus the judiciary supported economic expansion and individual economic opportunity.

In promoting the economy, state governments far surpassed the federal government. From 1815 through 1860, for example, 73 percent of the $135 million invested in canals was government money, most of it from the states. In the 1830s the states started to invest in rail construction. Though the federal government played a larger role in constructing railroads than in building canals, state and local governments provided more than half of the capital for southern rail lines. State governments also invested in corporate and bank stocks, providing corporations and banks with much-needed capital. In fact, states actually equaled or surpassed private enterprise in their investments.

State Promotion of the Economy

Pennsylvania, probably the most active state in promoting its economy, invested a total of $100 million in canals, railroads, banks, and manufacturing firms; its appointees sat on more than 150 corporate boards of directors. Pennsylvania was the largest state in area, extending west from the Delaware River to beyond the mountains, and thus developed the most extensive program of internal improvements to stimulate settlement and economic growth. But Pennsylvania and other states did more than invest in industry. Through special acts and incorporation laws, they regulated the nature and activities of corporations and banks. They also used their licensing capacity to regulate industry. Georgia, for example, regulated the grading and marketing of tobacco.

Largely as a result of these government efforts, the United States experienced uneven but sustained economic growth from the end of the War of 1812 until 1860. Political controversy raged over questions of state versus federal activity—especially with regard to internal improvements and banking—but all parties agreed on the general goal of economic expansion. Indeed, during these years the major restraint on government action was not philosophical but financial: the public purse was small. As the private sector grew more vigorous, entrepreneurs looked less to government for financial support, and the states played less of a role in investment.

The Rise of Manufacturing and Commerce

The London *Times* ridiculed the McCormick reaper, invented by Virginia farmer Cyrus McCormick in 1831, as "a cross between a flying machine, a wheelbarrow, and an Astly chariot." In one continuous motion, a revolving drum on the horse-drawn reaper positioned grain stalks in front of a blade; the cut grain fell onto a platform. Put to a competitive test through rain-soaked wheat, only the Chicago-made reaper passed, to the cheers of the skeptical English spectators.

The reaper and hundreds of other American products made their international debut at the 1851 London Crystal Palace Exhibition, the first modern world's fair. There the design and quality of American machines and wares—from familiar farm tools to exotic devices such as the reaper and an ice-cream freezer—astonished observers. American manufacturers returned home with dozens of medals, including all three prizes for piano making. Most impressive to the Europeans were three simple machines: Alfred C. Hobb's unpickable padlocks, Samuel Colt's revolvers, and Robbins and Lawrence's rifles with completely interchangeable parts. All were machine-tooled rather than handmade, products of what the British called the American system of manufacturing.

So impressed were the British—whose nation was the leading industrial power of the time—that in 1853 they sent a parliamentary commission to study the American system. A year later a second committee returned to examine the firearms industry in detail. The committee's report described an astonishing experiment performed at the federal armory in Springfield, Massachusetts. To test the interchangeability of machine-made musket parts, the committee selected rifles made in each of the previous ten years. While the committee watched, the guns were dismantled "and the parts placed in a row of boxes, mixed up together." The Englishmen "then requested the workman, whose duty it is to 'assemble' the arms, to put them together, which he did—the Committee handing him the parts, taken at hazard—with the use of a turnscrew only, and as quickly as though they had been English muskets, whose parts had carefully been kept separate." Britain's Enfield arsenal subsequently converted to American equipment. Other nations quickly followed Great Britain's lead, sending delegations across the Atlantic to bring back American machines.

The American system of manufacturing used precision machinery to produce interchangeable parts that did not require individual adjustment to fit. Eli Whitney, a Yale graduate and inventor, had promoted the idea of interchangeable parts in 1798 when he contracted with the federal government to make ten thousand rifles in twenty-eight months. By the 1820s the United States Ordnance Department had contracted with private firms to introduce machine-made interchangeable parts for firearms. The American system quickly spread beyond the arsenals, giving birth to the machine-tool industry—the manufacture of machines for the purposes of mass production. One outcome was an explosion in consumer goods. Because the time and skill involved in manufacturing were greatly reduced, the new system permitted mass production at low cost: Waltham watches, Yale locks, and other goods became household items, inexpensive yet of uniformly high quality.

American System of Manufacturing

Interchangeable parts and the machine-tool industry were uniquely American contributions to the industrial revolution. Both paved the way for the swift industrialization that the nation experienced after the Civil War. In 1800, however, manufacturing was a relatively unimportant component of the American economy. Most took place in small workshops and homes, where master craftsmen supervised journeymen and taught apprentices and women worked alone spinning thread and weaving cloth. Tailors, shoemakers, and blacksmiths made articles by hand, to order for specific customers.

The rise of textile mills illustrates the changes in manufacturing wrought by the market economy. Some farm families continued to make their own cloth, but mill-produced cloth increasingly became the source of clothing. The nineteenth-century machine-tool industry made textile and clothing production a function of mills and factories rather than kitchens and home workshops. Cotton-textile mills in New England processed cotton grown in the slave South. Fed by the population boom, the expanding market economy created a demand for manufactured cotton goods. The first American textile mill—Almy and Brown's 1790 Pawtucket, Rhode Island, factory—used water-powered spinning machines constructed from British models by the

Production of Cloth

English immigrant Samuel Slater. Slater employed women and children as cheap labor and sold the thread they manufactured from Maine to Maryland. Soon other mills sprang up, stimulated by the embargo on British imports from 1807 through 1815. From 1809 through 1813 alone, 151 cotton and woolen companies incorporated.

These early mills, dependent on waterpower, were located in rural areas. By erecting dams and watercourses, mill owners diverted water from farmers and destroyed fishing, an important source of income and protein in rural and village America. To protect their customary rights, fishermen and farmers fought the manufacturers in New England state legislatures, but petitions from hopeful job seekers in the mill environs supported the manufacturers. The ensuing compromises promoted mill development.

Construction of the first American power loom and the chartering of the Boston Manufacturing Company in 1813 radically transformed textile manufacturing. The corporation was capitalized at $400,000—ten times the amount behind the Rhode Island mills—by Francis Cabot Lowell and other Boston merchants. Its goal was to eliminate the problems of coordination, quality control, and shipping inherent in the subcontracting of work in the putting-out system. The owners erected their factories in Waltham, Massachusetts, bringing all the manufacturing processes to a single location. They employed a resident manager to run the mill, thus separating ownership from management. Workers were paid by the piece or by the hour, and the cloth was sold throughout the United States.

Waltham (Lowell) System

The company's cloth was so inexpensive that many women began to purchase it rather than make their own. Nonetheless, spinning and especially weaving remained women's work in many rural homes. Women who traditonally had spun their own yarn and woven it into cloth now received yarn from the mills and returned finished cloth. The change was subtle but significant: although the work itself was familiar, women were operating their looms for piece-rate wages, not primarily to make cloth for their families.

When managers could not find enough hands in rural Waltham to staff the mill, they recruited New England farm daughters, accepting responsibility for their living conditions. As inducements, they offered

In the 1830s an unknown artist painted Middlesex Company Woolen Mills, *portraying the bulking mass of the mill buildings. The company organized all the manufacturing processes at a single location, in Lowell, Massachusetts, on the Merrimack River.* Museum of American Textile History.

cash wages, company-run boarding houses, and cultural events such as evening lectures—none of which was available on the farm. This paternalistic approach, called the Waltham (or Lowell) system, was adopted in other mills erected alongside New England rivers.

By 1860 a cotton mill resembled a modern factory. The work force consisted mainly of immigrant Irish women who lived at home, not in mill-subsidized housing. New England farm women continued to live in the few remaining boarding houses.

Textile Mills

Technological improvements in the looms and other machinery had made the work less skilled and more routine. The mills could thus pay lower wages, drawing from a reservoir of unskilled labor.

Textile manufacturing changed New England and had its greatest impact on Lowell, Massachusetts. Among the Lowell mills was the Middlesex Company. The population of Lowell, the "city of spindles" and the prototype of early American industrialization, grew from twenty-five hundred to thirty-three thousand between 1826 and 1850. It was the largest of the cotton-mill towns before the Civil War and had the biggest work force, the greatest output, and the most capital invested. It also led in technological change.

Textiles became the most important industry in the nation before the Civil War, employing 115,000 workers in 1860, more than half of them women and immigrants. The key to the success of the textile industry was that the machines, not the women, spun the yarn and wove the cloth. Workers watched the machines and intervened to maintain smooth operation. When a thread broke, the machine stopped automatically; a worker found the break, pieced the ends together, and restarted the machine. New England textile mills used increasingly specialized machines, relying heavily on advances in the machine-tool industry. Their application of the American system of manufacturing enabled American firms to compete successfully with British cotton mills (see figure, page 267).

Outside New England—for example, in Pennsylvania's Delaware valley—the textile industry grew more slowly, combining traditional ways with technology. A decade after the Waltham mills first appeared, entrepreneurs in Rockdale, Pennsylvania, converted paper mills to cotton manufacturing. Organized as partnerships rather than corporations, these businesses could not raise the large sums available to the Lowell mills. Unlike their counterparts in Waltham and Lowell, the owners lived and worked in the mill villages. Small factories employed entire families, and unmarried workers boarded in other workers' homes. Many Pennsylvania textile workers sought to save money to buy western land, and a number of them were successful. Growth and change occurred at a modest pace; not until the 1850s would a major manufacturing center arise in once-rural southeastern Pennsylvania.

The appearance of ready-made clothing was the other great change in the textile industry. Before the 1820s, most clothing was sewn at home by women, and some people purchased used clothing. Tailors and seamstresses made wealthy men's and women's clothing to order. By the 1820s and 1830s, ready-made clothing became common. Manufacturers used two methods, either separately or in combination, to produce it. One was production within a factory. The other was, again, the putting-out system: this time, typically, a journeyman tailor cut the fabric panels in the factory, and the sewing was put out at piece rates to unskilled or semiskilled labor, often women working in their own homes.

Ready-made Clothing

In 1832, Boston manufacturers employed three hundred journeyman tailors at $2 per day and thirteen hundred women and one hundred boys at 50 cents a day. Apprentices, if used at all, were no longer learning a trade; they were a permanent source of cheap labor. Women learned their sewing skills at home; they were passed down from mother to daughter. By the late 1850s, as many as seventeen different pairs of hands were involved in making a single pair of pants under the putting-out system.

Most of the first mass-produced clothes, crudely made and limited to a few loose-fitting sizes, were produced for men, and they were purchased by men who lived in city boarding houses and rooming houses, far from the female kin who previously would have made their clothes. Most women made their own clothes, but those who could afford to do so employed seamstresses. Improvements in fit and changes in men's fashion eventually made ready-to-wear apparel more acceptable to white-collar and

New England Cotton Industry Cloth Production, 1810–1860

New England Cotton-Industry Cloth Production, 1810–1860 *Textiles was the most important manufacturing industry in the United States in the 1830s, 1840s, and 1850s. The production of cloth increased six-fold during that time.* Source: James F. Willis and Martin L. Primack, *An Economic History of the United States,* 2d ed. (Englewood Cliffs, N.J.: Prentice-Hall, 1989), p. 171.

professional men. By the 1850s the short sack coat, which did not taper at the waist, had replaced the embroidered waistcoat. This forerunner of the modern suit jacket fit loosely and needed little custom tailoring. Now even upper-class men were willing to consider ready-made apparel. In 1818 Henry Sands Brooks (later Brooks Brothers), offered tailoring services and ready-made apparel to the carriage trade.

Retail clothing stores well stocked with ready-made clothes appeared in the 1820s. T. S. Whitmarsh of Boston advertised in 1827 that "he keeps constantly for Sale, from 5 to 10,000 Fashionable ready-made Garments." In 1830, J. T. Jacobs of New York boasted that "Gentlemen can rely upon being as well fitted from the shelves as if their measures were taken—their stock being very extensive and

F. B. Locke adapted to the new market for ready-made clothing by becoming a manufacturer, wholesaler, and retailer of men's shirts. Although he continued to make shirts to order, the staple of his Shirt Depot was mass-produced shirts, as this advertisement from the Boston Directory *for 1848–1849 indicates.* Warshaw Collection of Business Americana, Smithsonian Institution, Washington, D.C.

their sizes well assorted." F. B. Locke of Boston made and sold "shirts for the million."

Such merchants often bought goods wholesale, though many manufactured garments in their own factories. Lewis and Hanford of New York City boasted of cutting more than one hundred thousand garments in the winter of 1848–1849. The New York firm sold most of its clothing in the South and owned its own retail outlet in New Orleans. Paul Tulane, a New Orleans competitor, owned a New York factory that made goods for his Louisiana store. In the West, Cincinnati became the center of the new men's clothing industry. By midcentury, Cincinnati's ready-to-wear apparel industry employed fifteen hundred men and ten thousand women. As in Boston, most of the women did outwork.

Though cotton-textile mills and factories were in the vanguard, large-scale manufacturing also transformed woolen textiles, farm implements, machine tools, iron, steel, glass, and finished consumer goods. "White coal"—waterpower—was widely used to run the machines. By 1860, manufacturing accounted for one-third of the nation's total production, an increase of 200 percent in twenty years.

To a striking extent, large-scale manufacturing in this period was an outcome rather than an agent of change in American life. Ever since Alexander Hamilton's *Report on Manufactures* (see page 207), national pride had spurred the development of American industry. Contrary to Hamilton's hopes, however, more capital flowed into the merchant marine than into industry between 1789 and 1808. In the early republic, greater profits could be made by transporting British products to the United States than by producing the same items at home. But the embargo and the War of 1812 reversed this situation, and merchants began to shift their capital from shipping to manufacturing (see pages 239–245). It was in this new economic environment that the Waltham system took root.

Stimulants to Industry

Other factors also stimulated industry. Population growth, especially in urban areas and the Old Northwest, created a large domestic market for finished goods (see maps, page 269). As the rise of commercial agriculture drew farmers more into the market economy, they purchased more manufactured goods. Specialty merchants and new modes of transportation hastened the development of these new markets. To sell more, merchants had to find ways to produce more goods with less skilled labor. Government policy assisted manufacturing expansion. Beginning with the Tariff of 1816 and culminating in the Tariff of Abominations of 1828, Congress imposed tariffs more to protect the market for domestic manufactures than to increase government revenue.

Specialization of Commerce

Commerce expanded hand in hand with manufacturing. Cotton, for instance, had once been traded by plantation agents, who sold the raw cotton and bought manufactured goods that they then sold to plantation owners, extending them credit when necessary. As cotton became a great staple export after the invention of the cotton gin in 1793, cotton exports rose from half a million pounds in that year to 83 million pounds in 1815. Gradually, some agents came to specialize in finance alone: they were cotton brokers, who for a commission brought together buyers and sellers. Similarly, wheat and hog brokers sprang up in the West—in Cincinnati, Louisville, and St. Louis. The distribution of finished goods also became more specialized as wholesalers bought large quantities of particular items from manufacturers, and jobbers broke down the wholesale lots for retail stores and country merchants.

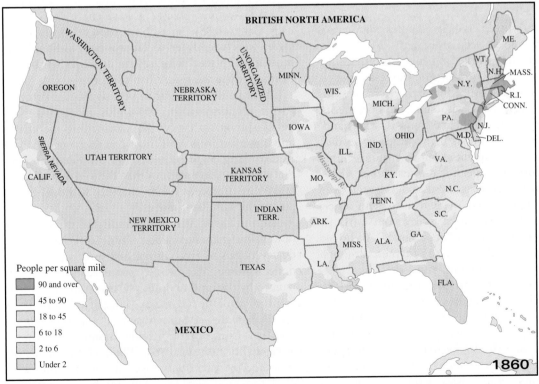

United States Population, 1820 and 1860 *Between 1820 and 1860, the population of the United States grew from 9.6 million to 31.4 million, and the density increased significantly in the North, the Old Northwest, and California. Settlement, too, spread farther away from the eastern seaboard.*

General merchants persisted longer in small towns than in cities. Such merchants continued to exchange some goods with local farm women—trading flour or pots and pans for eggs or other produce. They left the sale of finished goods, such as shoes and clothing, to local craftsmen. In some rural areas and on the frontier, peddlers acted as general merchants. But as transportation improved and towns grew, even small-town merchants began to specialize.

Commercial specialization transformed some traders in big cities, especially New York, into virtual merchant princes. New York had emerged as the dominant port in the late 1790s, outstripping Philadelphia and Boston. After the Erie Canal opened, New York City became a standard stop on every major trade route from Europe, the southern ports, and the West. New York traders were the middlemen for southern cotton and western grain trading. Merchants in other cities played a similar role within their own regions. Newly rich traders in turn invested their profits in processing enterprises and then in manufacturing, further stimulating the growth of northern cities. Some cities specialized: Rochester became a milling center, and Cincinnati—"Porkopolis"—became the first meatpacking center.

Merchants who engaged in complex commercial transactions required large office staffs. Most of the all-male office staff worked on high stools, laboriously copying business forms and correspondence. At the bottom of the office hierarchy were messenger boys, often preteens, who delivered documents. Above them were the ordinary copyists, who hand-copied documents in ink as many times as needed. Clerks handled assignments such as customs-house clearances, shipping papers, and translations. Above them were the bookkeeper and the confidential chief clerk. Those seeking employment in such an office, called a countinghouse, often took a course from a writing master to acquire a "good hand." All hoped to rise someday to the status of partner, although their chances of doing so were dim.

Banks and other financial institutions, which played a significant role in the expansion of commerce and manufacturing, also became a leading industry themselves. Financial institutions (banks, insurance companies, and corporations) linked savers—those who deposited money in banks—with producers and speculators who wished to borrow money. The expiration

Banking and Credit Systems

of the first Bank of the United States in 1811 acted as a stimulus to state-chartered banks, and over the next five years the number of such banks more than doubled. When state banks proved inadequate to spur national growth, Congress chartered the Second Bank of the United States in 1816 (see page 245). Many farmers, local bankers, and politicians, however, denounced the bank as a monster, claiming that it served national, not local, interests. Western landowners, like Andrew Jackson, suffered severe losses when the Second Bank reduced loans in the western states during the Panic of 1819. In 1836 critics finally succeeded in killing the bank (see pages 362–363).

The closing of the Second Bank in 1836 caused a nationwide credit shortage, which, in conjunction with the Panic of 1837, stimulated fundamental reforms in banking. Michigan and New York introduced charter laws promoting what was called *free banking*. Many other states soon followed suit. Previously, every new bank needed a special legislative charter before it could open for business; thus each bank incorporation was in effect a political decision. Under the new laws, any proposed bank that met certain minimum conditions—amount of capital invested, number of notes issued, and types of loans to be made—would receive a state charter automatically. Banks in Michigan, New York, and soon, other states were thus freer to incorporate, although the legislatures placed some restrictions on their operation to reduce the risk of bank failure.

Free banking proved to be a significant stimulus to the economy in the late 1840s and 1850s. New banks sprang up everywhere, providing merchants and manufacturers with the credit they needed. The free-banking laws also served as a precedent for general incorporation statutes that allowed manufacturing firms to receive state charters without special acts of the state legislature.

In the 1850s, with both credit and capital easily obtainable, manufacturing spread. In the North, industry began to rival agriculture and commerce in dollar volume. Meanwhile, commercial farming, financed by the credit boom, was integrating the early frontier into the northern economy. By 1860 six northern states—Massachusetts, New York, Pennsylvania, Connecticut, Rhode Island, and Ohio—were highly industrialized. Their clothing, textile, and shoe industries employed more than one hundred thousand workers each; lumber, seventy-five thousand; iron, sixty-five thousand; and woolens and leather, fifty thousand. Although agriculture still predominated even in these states, industrial employment would soon surpass it.

Workers and the Workplace

Oh, sing me the song of the Factory Girl!
So merry and glad and free!
The bloom in her cheeks, of health how it speaks,
Oh! a happy creature is she!
She tends the loom, she watches the spindle,
And cheerfully toileth away,
Amid the din of wheels, how her bright eyes kindle,
And her bosom is ever gay.

This idyllic portrait of factory work appeared in the Chicopee, Massachusetts, *Telegraph* in 1850. It was a fitting anthem for the teenage single women who first left the villages and farms of New England to work in the mills. New England mill owners, convinced that the degradation of English factory workers arose from their living conditions and not from the work itself, designed boarding-house communities offering airy courtyards and river views, prepared meals, and cultural activities. Housekeepers enforced strict curfews, banned alcohol, and reported to the corporations on workers' behavior and church attendance.

The promise of steady work, good pay, and kinship ties at first lured eager rural young women to the mills. Many pairs of sisters and cousins worked in the same mill and lived in the same boarding house. They helped each other adjust, and their letters home drew other kin to the mills. Young women then had few opportunities for work outside their own homes, and the commercial production of yarn and cloth had reduced their workload in New England farm households. Averaging sixteen and one-half years of age when they entered the mills, the girls usually stayed only about five years—few intended to stay longer. Their earnings brought them independence and the freedom of deciding whether to spend or save their earnings. That satisfaction was not sufficient, however, to change their ambitions to be wives and mothers. Most left the mills to marry and were replaced by other women interested in earning a wage.

Between 1837 and 1842, most mills ran only part-time because of a decline in demand for cloth. Subsequently managers applied still greater pressures on workers by means of the speed-up, the stretch-out, and the premium system. The speed-up

This young mill girl at Waltham or Lowell, probably in the late 1840s, posed for an early daguerreotype. Her swollen and rough hands contrast with her youth, neat dress, and carefully tied, beribboned hair. Her hands suggest that she worked, as did most twelve- and thirteen-year-olds, as a warper, straightening the strands of cotton or wool as they entered the looms. Courtesy of Jack Naylor.

increased the speed of the machines; the stretch-out increased the number of machines each worker had to operate; and premiums paid to the overseers whose departments produced the most cloth encouraged them to pressure workers for greater output. The result in Lowell was that the number of spindles and looms increased 150 and 140 percent respectively between 1836 and 1850, while the number of workers increased by only 50 percent. The corporation's goal of building an industrial empire and maximizing profits took precedence over its paternalistic concern for workers' living conditions. In the race for profits, owners lengthened hours, cut wages, and tightened discipline. Some millworkers began to think of themselves as slaves. The boarding houses became more crowded.

New England millworkers responded to their deteriorating working conditions by organizing and striking. In 1834, in reaction to a 25 percent wage cut, they unsuccessfully "turned out" (struck) against the Lowell mills. Two years later, when boarding-house rates increased, they turned out again.

Protests by Mill Women

As conditions continued to worsen, workers adopted new methods of resistance. In the 1840s, strikes gave way to a concerted effort to shorten the workday. Massachusetts mill women joined forces with other workers to press for state legislation mandating a ten-hour day. Eliza R. Hemingway, a three-year veteran of two different Lowell mills, told a Massachusetts House of Representatives committee in 1845 that workers' hours were too long, "her time for meals too limited. In the summer season, the work is commenced at 5 o'clock, A.M., and continued 'til 7 o'clock, P.M., with half an hour for breakfast and three quarters of an hour for dinner."

They aired their complaints in worker-run newspapers: in 1842, the *Factory Girl* appeared in New Hampshire, the *Wampanoag and Operatives' Journal* in Massachusetts. Two years later the *Factory Girl's Garland* and the *Voice of Industry*, nicknamed "the factory girl's voice," were founded. Even the *Lowell Offering*, the owner-sponsored paper that was the pride of millworkers and managers alike, became embroiled in controversy when workers charged that articles critical of working conditions had been suppressed.

The millworkers' rebellion against paternalism and exploitation took many forms. Their newspapers exposed worsening work conditions, their strikes provoked confrontations, and their songs expressed their resolve and unity, as in "The Factory Girl's Come-All-Ye" (about 1850):

No more I'll take my bobbins out,
No more I'll put them in,
No more the overseer will say
"You're weaving your cloth too thin!"

No more will I eat cold pudding,
No more will I eat hard bread,
No more will I eat those half-baked beans,
For I vow! They're killing me dead!

I'm going back to Boston town
And live on Tremont Street;
And I want all you fact'ry girls
To come to my house and eat!

The women's labor organizations were weakened by the short tenure of most workers. Few of the militant native-born millworkers stayed on to fight the managers and owners, and gradually there were fewer New England daughters to enter the mills. By the end of the 1850s the women who constituted the majority of millworkers were mostly Irish immigrants, driven to the mills by the need to support their families and unable to afford to complain about their working conditions.

A growing gender division in the workplace, especially in the textile, clothing, and shoemaking industries, was one important outcome of large-scale manufacturing. Although women and men in traditional agricultural and artisan households tended to perform different tasks, they worked as a family unit. As wage work spread, however, men's and women's work cultures became increasingly separate. The women and girls who left home to work in textile mills worked and lived in a mostly female world. In the clothing and shoemaking industries, whose male artisans had once worked at home assisted by unpaid family labor, men began working outside the home while women continued to work at home through the putting-out system. Tasks and wages, too, became rigidly differentiated: women sewed, whereas men shaped materials and finished products, receiving higher wages in shops employing men only. These new work patterns contributed to social and economic differences between men and women (see pages 327–328).

Gender Divisions in Work

The market system, wage labor, and the specialization of labor had an impact on unpaid household labor as well. As home and workplace became separate and labor came to be defined in terms of wages (what could be sold in the marketplace) rather than production, the unpaid labor of women was devalued. In a money-based economy in which families increasingly recorded their incomes and expenditures in account books, there was no category in which to enter women's unpaid labor and services. Yet those labors were extensive; indeed, the family depended on women's work within the household. And as the family became more dependent on wage labor, more family members sought outside employment and had less time to do their share of household labor. Thus gender defined household labor and placed a low value on it.

The new textile mills, shoe factories, iron mills, wholesale stores, and railroads were the antithesis of traditional workshop and household production.

Changes in the Workplace

Factories created a workplace in which authority was hierarchically organized. Factory workers lost their sense of autonomy as impersonal market forces seemed to dominate their lives. Competition among mills in the growing textile industry of the 1820s and 1830s led to layoffs and the replacement of operatives with cheaper, less-skilled workers or children. The formal rules of the factory contrasted sharply with the more relaxed pace and atmosphere of artisan shops and farm households. Supervisors represented owners whom workers never saw. The division of labor and the use of machines narrowed the skills required of workers. And the flow of work was governed by the bell, the steam whistle, or the clock. In 1844 the *Factory Girl's Garland* published a poem describing how the ringing of the factory bell controlled when the workers awoke, ate, began and ended work, and went to sleep. The central problem, of course, was the quickening pace of the work between the bells. Since owners and managers no longer shared the workers' tasks, they did not consider the plight of the worker when they imposed a speed-up.

Many workers welcomed the new manufacturing methods at first; new jobs and higher wages seemed adequate compensation. But wage reductions, speed-ups, and stretch-outs later changed their minds. Other conditions were trying, too. Millworkers had to tolerate the roar of the looms, and all workers on power machines risked accidents that could kill or maim. Perhaps most demoralizing, opportunities for advancement in the new system were virtually nil.

Changes in the workplace in turn transformed the workers. Initially, mill women drew on kinship, village, and gender ties to build supportive networks in factories. In the 1840s and after, as recently arrived Irish immigrant women came to predominate, more workers were strangers to each other before they entered the mills. Once employed, their only bases for friendship and mutual support were their work experiences. As a sense of distance from their employers took hold, so did deep-seated differences among workers.

Nationality, religion, education, and future prospects separated Irish and Yankee millworkers. Many New England women resented the immigrants, and management set one group against the other through selective hiring and promotions. Mill work was not a stage in the life of most Irish women; it was permanent employment. Unlike their Yankee sisters, they could not risk striking and losing their jobs; they and their families were dependent on their earnings. With legions of unskilled immigrants looking for work, Irish millworkers considered themselves fortunate to hold on to their jobs, even though the mills cut wages three times in the 1850s and continued the speed-ups and stretch-outs. The Irish workers assisted one another as much as possible but rarely engaged in formal protest.

As wage work became common and workers sensed a loss of independence, they experienced an erosion of the republican virtues that an earlier generation of artisans had shared with the Revolutionary War generation. Thomas Jefferson had hoped to preserve these values with the purchase of the Louisiana Territory and the encouragement of a market economy, but factory work and boom-and-bust cycles did not enhance individual freedom. Those who stayed in the master-journeyman-apprentice system or remained on farms after the 1830s saw themselves as distinct from the new wage workers. So, too, did many of the first generation of Yankee millworkers, for whom factory work was a stage in the life cycle before marriage.

While female textile workers and shoemakers organized and protested, male workers responded to changes in the nature of work by participating actively in reform politics. Labor parties arose in Pennsylvania, New York, and Massachusetts in the 1820s and eventually spread to a dozen states. These parties advocated free public education, abolition of imprisonment for debt, and opposition to banks and monopolies. The interests of workers' reform parties often coincided with those of middle-class benevolent movements. The two groups shared a concern not only for public education but also for public morals: temperance, observance of the Sabbath, and suppression of vice (see Chapter 13). Ironically, however, reform politics tended to divide workers. Many of the reforms—moral education, temperance, Sabbath closings—served the interests of merchants and industrialists seeking a more disciplined work force. Temperance and Sabbath closings also pitted the native-born against immigrant workers, many of whom were Catholic. Anti-immigrant and anti-Catholic movements further divided workers.

Journeymen recognized that the new system of manufacturing threatened them. When master

How do historians know what working conditions New England millworkers experienced? This 1853 timetable from the Lowell Mills is among the rich sources historians consult to reconstruct workers' experiences in the mills. Textile factories were the first corporations to impose rigid work rules. The size of the labor force, the management structure, and the organization of the work made it necessary to publish work rules. Exact times were established for beginning and ending work and for meals. Few workers carried their own timepieces, so a system of bells regulated the lives of the factory community. From March 20 to September 19, when work began at 6:30 A.M., bells alerted the workers at 4:30 and 5:50 A.M. and again at 6:20 A.M., ten minutes before they had to be at the factory. For their main meal at midday, they had forty-five minutes away from work; the 12:35 P.M. bell warned that they had ten minutes to return. For young mill women from the New England countryside, and later for Irish women, such regimentation must have seemed a world apart from the rhythms of rural life. Photo: Museum of American Textile History.

TIME TABLE OF THE LOWELL MILLS,

Arranged to make the working time throughout the year average 11 hours per day

TO TAKE EFFECT SEPTEMBER 21st, 1853.

The Standard time being that of the meridian of Lowell, as shown by the Regulator Clock of AMOS SANBORN, Post Office Corner, Central Street.

From March 20th to September 19th, inclusive.

COMMENCE WORK, at 6.30 A. M.   LEAVE OFF WORK, at 6.30 P. M., except on Saturday Evenings.
BREAKFAST at 6 A. M.   DINNER, at 12 M.   Commence Work, after dinner, 12.45 P. M.

From September 20th to March 19th, inclusive.

COMMENCE WORK, at 7.00 A. M.   LEAVE OFF WORK, at 7.00 P. M., except on Saturday Evenings.
BREAKFAST at 6.30 A. M.   DINNER, at 12.30 P.M.   Commence Work, after dinner, 1.15 P. M.

BELLS.

From March 20th to September 19th, inclusive.

Morning Bells.	Dinner Bells.	Evening Bells.
First bell,..........4.30 A. M.	Ring out,............12.00 M.	Ring out,..........6.30 P. M.
Second, 5.30 A. M. ; Third, 6.20.	Ring in,..........12.35 P.M.	Except on Saturday Evenings.

From September 20th to March 19th, inclusive.

Morning Bells.	Dinner Bells.	Evening Bells.
First bell,..........5.00 A. M.	Ring out,............12.30 P. M.	Ring out at..........7.00 P. M.
Second, 6.00 A. M. ; Third, 6.50.	Ring in,............1.05 P. M.	Except on Saturday Evenings.

SATURDAY EVENING BELLS.

During APRIL, MAY, JUNE, JULY, and AUGUST, Ring Out, at 6.00 P. M.
The remaining Saturday Evenings in the year, ring out as follows :

SEPTEMBER.		NOVEMBER.		JANUARY.	
First Saturday, ring out 6.00 P. M.		Third Saturday ring out 4.00 P. M.		Third Saturday, ring out 4.25 P. M.	
Second " " 5.45 "		Fourth " " 3.55 "		Fourth " " 4.35 "	
Third " " 5.30 "					
Fourth " " 5.20 "		DECEMBER.		FEBRUARY.	
		First Saturday, ring out 3.50 P. M.		First Saturday, ring out 4.45 P. M.	
OCTOBER.		Second " " 3.55 "		Second " " 4.55 "	
First Saturday, ring out 5.05 P. M.		Third " " 3.55 "		Third " " 5.00 "	
Second " " 4.55 "		Fourth " " 4.00 "		Fourth " " 5.10 "	
Third " " 4.45 "		Fifth " " 4.00 "			
Fourth " " 4.35 "				MARCH.	
Fifth " " 4.25 "				First Saturday, ring out 5.25 P. M.	
		JANUARY.		Second " " 5.30 "	
NOVEMBER.		First Saturday, ring out 4.10 P. M.		Third " " 5.35 "	
First Saturday, ring out 4.15 P. M.		Second " " 4.15 "		Fourth " " 5.45 "	
Second " " 4.05 "					

YARD GATES will be opened at the first stroke of the bells for entering or leaving the Mills.

. *SPEED GATES commence hoisting three minutes before commencing work.*

craftsmen in shoemaking, textiles, and apparel manufacturing attempted to keep up with change by turning their workshops into small factories with themselves as managers, the gap between master and journeymen threatened to become insurmountable. The market economy seemed to free masters and to make journeymen more dependent. Masters stressed individuals' freedom to contract for their labor; journeymen sought out the mutual protection of their fellow workers.

Organized labor's greatest achievement during this period was to gain relief from the threat of conspiracy laws. When journeyman shoemakers

Emergence of a Labor Movement

organized during the first decade of the century, their employers turned to the courts, charging criminal conspiracy. The cordwainers' (shoemakers') cases, which resulted in six trials between 1806 and 1815, left labor organizations in a tenuous position. Although the journeymen's right to organize was acknowledged, the courts ruled unlawful any coercive action by them that would harm other businesses or the public. In other words, strikes were ruled illegal. Eventually a Massachusetts case, *Commonwealth* v. *Hunt* (1842), effectively reversed this decision when Chief Justice Lemuel Shaw ruled that Boston journeyman bootmakers could strike "in such manner as best to subserve their own interests." Conspiracy laws no longer thwarted unionization.

Yet permanent labor organizations were difficult to maintain. Most workers outside the crafts were unskilled or semiskilled at best. Moreover, religion, race, ethnicity, and gender divided workers. The first unions arose among urban journeymen in printing, woodworking, shoemaking, and tailoring. These early labor unions tended to be local; the strongest resembled medieval guilds in that members sought to protect themselves against the competition of inferior workmen by regulating apprenticeship and establishing minimum wages. They also excluded women and African-Americans. (Massachusetts mill women organized their own unions.)

Umbrella organizations composed of individual craft unions, like the National Trades Union (1834), arose in several cities in the 1820s and 1830s. But the movement fell apart amid wage reductions and unemployment in the hard times of 1839–1843. In the 1850s the deterioration of working conditions strengthened the labor movement again, and affiliated craft unions began to organize into national unions. Workers won a reduction in hours, and the ten-hour day became standard. Though the Panic of 1857 wiped out the umbrella organizations, some of the new national unions in specific trades—notably printers, hat finishers, and stonecutters—survived. By 1860 national unions had also been organized by the painters, cordwainers, cotton spinners, iron molders, and machinists.

Economic and technological change inevitably affected individual workers more heavily than it affected their organizations. As a group, workers' share of the national wealth declined after the 1830s.

Individual producers—craftsmen, factory workers, and farmers—had less economic power than they had had a generation or two earlier. And workers were increasingly losing control over their own work.

 Commercial Farming

Although manufacturing increased steadily, agriculture remained the backbone of the economy. In 1800 New England and Middle Atlantic farmers worked as their fathers and mothers had. Life centered around a household economy in which the needs of the family and the labor at its disposal determined what was produced and in what amounts. Most implements—wooden plows, rakes, shovels, and yokes—were homemade, with iron parts obtained from the local blacksmith.

When canals and railroads began transporting grain, especially wheat, eastward from the fertile Old Northwest, northeastern agriculture could not compete. Eastern farmers had already cultivated all the land available to

Northeastern Agriculture

them; expansion was impossible. Moreover, small New England farms with their uneven terrain did not lend themselves to the new labor-saving farm implements introduced in the 1830s—mechanical sowers, reapers, threshers, and balers. In response to these problems and to competition from the West, many northern farmers either moved west or gave up farming for jobs in the merchant houses and factories.

Many eastern farm sons and daughters moved to western New York. After the Erie Canal was completed, these Yankees and New Yorkers settled on more fertile and cheaper land in Ohio and Indiana and then in Michigan, Illinois, and Wisconsin. Farm daughters who did not go west flocked to the early textile mills. Still other New Englanders—urban, better educated, and often experienced in trade—flocked to the countinghouses in New York, Boston, and Philadelphia. Between 1820 and 1860 the percentage of the population of the North living on farms declined from 71 to 40 percent.

But neither the countinghouse nor the factory depleted New England agriculture. The farmers who remained proved as adaptable on the farm as were their children working at copy desks and water-powered looms. By the 1850s many New England and Middle Atlantic farm families had abandoned the commercial production of wheat and corn and

Many women made butter for market in the early nineteenth century. Women's production and sale of butter, cheese, and other goods were an essential part of farm families' adaptation to the market economy. The Sinclair Hamilton Collection of American Illustrated Books, Princeton University Library.

stopped tilling poor land. Instead, they were improving their livestock, especially cattle, and specializing in vegetable and fruit production and dairy farming, financing these initiatives through land sales and borrowing. In fact, their greatest potential profit was from increasing land values, not from farming itself.

Farm families everywhere gradually adjusted to market conditions. In 1820 about one-third of all food produced was intended for market. By 1860 the amount had increased to about two-thirds. Middlemen specializing in the grain and food trades replaced the country storekeepers who had handled all transactions for local farmers, acting both as retailers and as marketing and purchasing agents.

Women's earning power from wages or market sales was an important factor in the market economy. With increasing commercialization and dependency on cash, women's earnings became essential to the survival of the family farm. The put-out work that women did in New England had its parallel in the

Women's Paid Labor

Middle Atlantic states and in Ohio—especially near towns and cities—in women's dairy production, which was crucial to family income. Butter and cheese making for local and regional markets replaced spinning and weaving as farm women's major activity, now that cloth could be purchased so cheaply. The work was physically demanding and did not replace regular home and farm chores but was added to them. Yet women took pride in their work; it gave many a sense of independence. Esther Lewis, a widow who sent from seventy-five to one hundred pounds of butter monthly to Philadelphia in the 1830s, even hired other women to increase production of milk products.

Women's success at butter and cheese making led some farms to specialize in dairy products and some entrepreneurs to seize the opportunity to profit by expanding production. Beginning in 1847 in Ohio, entrepreneurs built cheese factories in rural towns and contracted to buy curd from local dairy farmers. One such factory in Gustavus, Ohio, produced 5,000 pounds of cheese a day from the milk of 2,500 cows in 1852. The cheese was shipped by canal and railroad to cities and eastern ports, where merchants sold to consumers as far away as California, England, and China. By 1860 Ohio dairies were producing 21.6 million pounds of cheese a year for market.

Most farm families seemed to welcome the opportunities offered by the market economy. While continuing to take pride in self-sufficiency and to value rural culture, they shifted toward specialization and market-oriented production. The rewards for such flexibility were great. Produce sold at market financed land and equipment purchases and made credit arrangements possible. Many farm families flourished.

Meanwhile, the economic distance widened between farm owners on the one hand and tenants and hired hands on the other. The rising cost of land and of farming meant that opportunities for hired hands to acquire their own farms were shrinking. By the 1850s it took from ten to twenty years for a rural laborer to save enough money to farm for himself. Thus the number of tenant farmers increased. Previously farmers had relied on the labor of unpaid family members or enslaved workers; now paid farm labor became commonplace. In the North in 1860 there was one hired hand for every 2.3 farms.

Individually and collectively, Americans still valued agrarian life. State governments energetically promoted commercial agriculture to spur economic growth and sustain the values of an agrarian-based republic. Massachusetts in 1817 and New York in 1819 subsidized agricultural prizes and county fairs. New York required contestants to submit written descriptions of how they grew their prize crops; the state then published the best essays to encourage the use of new methods and promote specialization. Farm journals also helped familiarize farmers with developments in agriculture. By 1860 nearly sixty journals had a combined circulation of from 250,000 to 300,000.

Even so, the Old Northwest gradually and inevitably replaced the northeastern states as the center of American family agriculture. Farms in the Old Northwest were much

Mechanization of Agriculture

larger and better suited to the new mechanized farming implements than were their northeastern counterparts. The farmers of the region bought machines such as the McCormick reaper on credit and paid for them with the profits from their high yields. By 1847 Cyrus McCormick was selling a thousand reapers a year. By introducing interchangeable parts, he expanded production to five thousand a year, but demand still outstripped supply. Similarly, John Deere's steel plow, invented in 1837, replaced the inadequate iron plow; steel blades kept the soil from sticking and were tough enough to break the roots of prairie grass. By 1856, Deere's sixty-five employees were making 13,500 plows a year.

Mechanized farming was the basis of expanded production. In the 1850s alone wheat production surged 70 percent. By that time the area that had been the western wilderness in 1800 had become one of the world's leading agricultural regions. Midwestern farm families fed an entire nation, including a generation of immigrants—and still had enough food to export.

 ## Settling and Conquering the West

Integral to the development of the market economy was the steady expansion of the United States. In 1800 the edge of settlement within the United States extended in an arc from western New York State through the new states of Kentucky and Tennessee and south to Georgia. By 1820, with the acquisition of the Louisiana Territory and Florida, it had shifted westward to Ohio, Indiana, and Illinois in the North, and Louisiana, Alabama, and Mississippi in the South. By 1860, Texas and California were states, and settlement had reached its twentieth-century continental limits. Unsettled and sporadically settled land remained—mostly the plains and mountain territory between the Mississippi River and the Sierra Nevada—but elsewhere the land and its Native American inhabitants had given way to white settlement (see pages 334–339).

The legal boundaries of the country were also changing rapidly during this period. Between 1803 and 1853 the United States pushed its original boundaries to their present continental limits (except for Alaska). The Louisiana Purchase roughly doubled the nation's size, and the acquisition of Florida from Spain in 1819 secured the Southeast. In the 1840s the United States annexed the Republic of Texas, defined its northern border with Canada, and acquired California, Nevada, Utah, and most of Arizona through war with Mexico (see pages 376–378). Finally, in 1853 the Gadsden Purchase added southern Arizona and New Mexico.

Most Americans saw western settlers as civilizers; a minority, including Indians, viewed them

SIR JOS JEBB.

The fur trade was part of a market system that extended from the Far West through St. Louis, Montréal, and New York to the hat merchants of Europe. These Ottawa fur traders, painted at Fort Michilimackinac in Upper Michigan, most likely traded with fur merchants based in Montréal. National Archives of Canada.

as conquerors. In myth, literature, and song Americans glorified the explorers, fur trappers and scouts, and pioneers.

Conquerors and Civilizers

James Fenimore Cooper's Leatherstocking tales, a series of novels that began appearing in 1823, introduced Hawkeye (Natty Bumppo), America's first popular fictional hero. At heart a romantic, Hawkeye preferred the freedom of the virgin forest to domesticated society. Yet whatever noble Eden the wilderness offered, it inevitably gave way, as Cooper described in *The Last of the Mohicans* (1826), to civilization. Like the Hutchinson Family's emancipation railroad, progress was unstoppable. The public snapped up tales of pioneers civilizing the wilderness.

The Hutchinson Family expressed doubt about the price of American expansion. In "The Indian's Lament" (1846) they took an Indian voice and imagined Indian culture dying out:

And I, and I stand alone as the last of my race,
Upon this earth I feel I no more have a place,
Since my home, friends, and kindred are driven away,
For the steel of the white man, has swept them away.

What awaits the Indian is death, but it would bring release, in "the bright blissful shores, and the fair forest shade. / Where the steel of the white man, will never invade."

"The steel of the white man" referred to an iron will as well as to the military might that conquered the West. The frontier represented not only the peaceful settlement of the West and the extension of farming and republican virtue but also the conquering of the native inhabitants and the environment.

The history of the West was often violent and intolerant. The Mormons who sought a new Jerusalem near the Great Salt Lake were fleeing the gehenna (hell) imposed on them by frontier folk farther east (see page 317). Those who sought to farm the land, dig the gold, trap the furs, and cut the lumber destroyed the natural landscape and ecological balance in the name of progress and development.

The market economy provided a great impetus for expansion. Early on, the fur trapper system brought the Far West—way beyond settlement—into a market system that extended through St. Louis, Montréal, and New York to the hat merchants of Europe. Then, in the late 1840s, settlement jumped over the trapping areas to the West Coast of the American continent, when the promise of instant wealth in the form of gold sparked a gold rush.

Gold stimulated a mass migration to the West Coast. The United States had acquired Alta California in the Treaty of Guadalupe Hidalgo (see page 378) from Mexico, and the

California Gold Rush

province was inhabited mostly by native peoples, some Mexicans living on large estates, and a chain of small settlements around military forts (presidios) and missions. That changed almost overnight after James Marshall, a

carpenter, spotted gold particles in the millrace at Sutter's Mill (now Coloma, California, northwest of Sacramento) in January 1848. Word of the discovery spread, and other Californians rushed to scrabble for instant fortunes. When John C. Frémont reached San Francisco five months later, he found that "all, or nearly all, its male inhabitants had gone to the mines." The town, "which a few months before was so busy and thriving, was then almost deserted."

By 1849 the news had spread around the world, and hundreds of thousands of fortune seekers, mostly young men, streamed in from Mexico, England, Germany, France, Ireland, and all over the United States. The newcomers came for one reason: instant wealth. In search of gold and silver, they mined the lodes and washed away the surface soil with hydraulic mining, leaving the land unsuitable for anything after they abandoned it.

Success in the market economy required capital, hard labor, and time; by contrast, gold mining seemed to promise instant riches. Most "forty-niners," however, never found enough gold to pay their expenses. "The stories you hear frequently in the States," one gold seeker wrote home, "are the most extravagant lies imaginable—the mines are a humbug. . . . The almost universal feeling is to get

Frank Marryat, a young English artist and writer, painted this scene of San Francisco around 1849. Gateway to the gold fields, San Francisco grew from one thousand residents in 1848 to thirty-five thousand two years later. Ships bringing people and supplies are anchored in the harbor. Print collection of Miriam and Ira D. Wallach, Division of Arts, Prints, and Photographs. The New York Public Library. Astor, Lenox and Tilden Foundations.

Women who traveled west with their husbands found their domestic skills in great demand. In this watercolor entitled Laying Out of Karns' City, Minnesota *(1856), E. Whitefield shows a woman preparing a meal out of her lean-to kitchen for her husband and their guests.*   Chicago Historical Society.

home." But many stayed, either unable to afford the passage home or tempted by the growing labor shortage in California's cities and agricultural districts.

San Francisco, the former presido and mission of Yerba Buena, the gateway from the West Coast to the interior, became an instant city, ballooning to thirty-five thousand people in 1850. In 1848 it had been a small settlement of about a thousand Mexicans, Anglos, soldiers, friars, and Indians. Ships bringing people and supplies continuously jammed the harbor, a scene that artist Frank Marryat captured in an 1849 painting. A French visitor in that year wrote, "At San Francisco, where fifteen months ago one found only a half dozen large cabins, one finds today a stock exchange, a theater, churches of all Christian cults, and a large number of quite beautiful homes."

The forty-niners had their eyes on gold nuggets, but they had to be fed. Thus began the great Cali-

fornia agricultural boom. Wheat was the preferred staple; it required minimal investment, was easily planted, and offered a quick return at the end of a relatively short growing season. California farmers eagerly imported machinery, since labor was scarce (and thus expensive) and the flat, treeless valleys were well suited to horse-drawn machines. By the mid-1850s, California was exporting wheat. Meanwhile, enterprising merchants rushed to supply, feed, and clothe the new settlers. One such merchant was Levi Strauss, a German Jewish immigrant, whose tough mining pants found an enduring and eventually worldwide market as blue jeans.

In the Midwest, family farms were the basic unit of production. In California, by contrast, mining, grazing, and large-scale wheat farming were overwhelmingly male occupations. The experiences of women, who **Women Settlers** constituted about one-seventh of the travelers on the overland trails, differed from those of men moving westward. Most men came alone, drawn by a sense of adventure and personal opportunity. Women who accompanied their husbands found their lives uprooted. Moving was a traumatic experience for many; they left behind networks of friends and kin to journey, often with children, along an unknown path to a strange environment. Yet in the West their domestic skills were in great demand. They received high fees for cooking, laundering, and sewing, and they ran boarding houses and hotels (men shunned domestic work).

Not all women, however, were entrepreneurs. Some wives, at their spouses' behest, cooked for and served their husbands' friends, enabling their husbands to build reputations as hosts. Abigail Scott Duniway, a leading western crusader for women's suffrage and a veteran of the Overland Trail to Oregon, wrote in 1859 that she lived in a "neighborhood composed chiefly of bachelors, who found comfort in mobilizing at meal time at the homes of the few married men of the township, and seemed especially fond of congregating at the hospitable cabin home of my good husband, who was never quite so much in his glory as when entertaining men at this fireside, while I, if not washing, scrubbing, churning, or nursing the baby, was preparing their meals in our lean-to kitchen."

Gold altered the pattern of settlement along the entire Pacific coast. Before 1848 most overland traffic flowed north over the Oregon Trail; few pioneers turned south to California. By 1849 a pioneer observed that the Oregon Trail "bore no evidence of having been much traveled this year." Traffic was flowing south instead, and California was becoming the new population center of the Pacific Slope. One measure of this shift was the overland mail routes. In the 1840s the Oregon Trail had been the main communications link between the Midwest and the Pacific. But the post office officials who organized mail routes in the 1850s terminated them in California, not Oregon; there was no route north of Sacramento.

By 1860 farmers in California, as in the Great Plains and prairies farther east, had become firmly linked to the market economy. They cleared the land of trees or prairie grass, hoed corn and wheat, fenced in animals, and constructed cabins of logs or sod. Success often depended on their access to water, and they sought to divert the streams and rivers of

Western Farming

the West to irrigate their land. As settled areas expanded, farmers built roads to carry their stock and produce to market and bring back supplies they could not produce for themselves. Growth brought specialization; as western farmers shifted from self-sufficiency to commercial farming, they too tended to concentrate on one crop. As land prices rose, families seeking new land had to go farther west to find land they could afford.

Though often thought of as outposts of rugged individualism, many early agricultural settlements depended heavily on family and kinship networks and communal cooperation. Sugar Creek on the Sangamon River in central Illinois exemplified this cooperative spirit. The white settlers who arrived in 1817 named the settlement for its sugar maples, tapped first by the Kickapoos and then by the American settlers. Although the settlement was based on private land ownership, most newcomers over the next decade were members of kin networks who assisted each other in clearing land and turning temporary dwellings into permanent cabins. Whether raising hogs or children, Sugar Creek families depended on kin and friends for support. In crises, too, they rose to the occasion. When someone "would be sick with chills or jaundice, or something else," Sugar Creek farmer James Megredy recalled, "his neighbors would meet and take care of his harvest, get up wood, or repair his cabin, or plant his corn." Neighbors set up a "borrowing system" whereby scarce tools and labor constantly circulated through the neighborhood. Settlers who came without previous ties, if they stayed, did not long remain strangers.

What made possible settlements such as Sugar Creek was the availability of land and credit. Some public lands were granted as a reward for military service: veterans of the War of 1812 received 160 acres; veterans of the Mexican War (see Chapter 14) could purchase land at reduced prices. And until 1820, civilians could buy government land at $2 an acre (a relatively high price) on a liberal four-year payment plan. From 1800 to 1817 the government successively reduced the minimum purchase from 640 to 80 acres, bringing the land within the reach of more Americans. But when the availability of land prompted the flurry of land speculation that ended in the Panic of 1819 (see page 248), the government discontinued credit sales. Instead, it reduced the price further, to $1.25 an acre.

Land Grants and Sales

Some eager pioneers settled land before it had been surveyed and offered for sale. Such illegal settlers, or squatters, then had to buy the land at auction and faced the risk of being unable to purchase it. Often neighbors protected squatters; in Sugar Creek, Illinois, they even helped them buy land. In 1841, to facilitate settlement and end property disputes, Congress passed the Pre-emption Act, which legalized settlement prior to surveying.

Since most settlers needed to borrow money, private credit systems arose: banks, private investors, country storekeepers, and speculators all extended credit to farmers. Railroads also sold land on credit—land they had received from the government as construction subsidies. (The Illinois Central, for example, received 2.6 million acres in 1850.) Indeed, nearly all economic activity in the West involved credit, from land sales to the shipping of produce to railroad construction. In 1816, 1836, and 1855, easy credit helped boost land prices. When land prices increased beyond farmers' abilities to pay interest or repay their loans, or when farm prices or weather conditions reduced farmers' income, farmland values collapsed, ending the speculative bubble. Mortgage bankers and speculators then purchased much land cheaply. As a consequence, many farmers because renters instead of owners of land; tenancy became more common in the West than it had been in New England.

From the start, the agricultural West was dependent on its links with towns and cities. Cities along the Ohio River—Louisville and Cincinnati—and the

Frontier Cities

old French settlements—Detroit on the Great Lakes, St. Louis on the Mississippi River—predated and promoted the earliest settlement of much of the West. New population centers, however, bypassed such old French towns as Vincennes and Kaskaskia. Chicago spearheaded settlement farther west. Steamboats connected the river cities with eastern markets and ports, carrying grain east and returning with finished goods. As the center of a rail network, Chicago exercised sway over the settling and development of most of the middle United States. Like cities in the Northeast, these western cities eventually developed into manufacturing centers as merchants shifted their investments from commerce to industry. Chicago became a center for the manufacture of farm implements, Louisville, of textiles. Smaller cities specialized in flour mills, and all produced consumer goods for the hinterlands.

Urban growth in the West was so spectacular that by 1860 Cincinnati, St. Louis, and Chicago each had populations exceeding one hundred thousand, and Buffalo, Louisville, San Francisco, Pittsburgh, Detroit, and Milwaukee had surpassed forty thousand. Thus commerce, urban growth, and industrialization overtook the farmers' frontier, wedding the West to the Northeast.

 ## Conclusion

For the North and the West the period from 1800 through 1860 was one of explosive growth. Population increased sixfold. The United States now extended from sea to sea, incorporating new peoples—Indians, Mexicans, Californians—sending out settlers to plow the land and inhabit the cities, and recruiting immigrants from around the world. Agriculture, which had completely dominated the nation at the turn of the century, was by midcentury being challenged by a booming manufacturing sector. And agriculture itself was becoming market-oriented and mechanized.

Economic development changed the way people lived. Canals, railroads, steamboats, and telegraph lines linked economic activities hundreds and even thousands of miles apart. The market economy brought sustained growth; it also ushered in cycles of boom and bust. Hard times and unemployment became frequent occurrences. The growing economy also meant larger-scale destruction of the environment: mills exploited New England waterways as a source of power, Michigan was denuded of its pine forests, and the gold rush destroyed land in California.

Large-scale manufacturing also altered traditional patterns of production and consumption. Farmers began to purchase goods formerly made by their wives and daughters, and farm families geared production to faraway markets. Farm women increasingly contributed income from market sales to the family farm. In New England many young women left the family farm to become the first factory workers in the new textile industry. As workshops and factories replaced household production, and the master-journeyman-apprentice system faded away, workplace relations became more impersonal and working conditions harsher, and men's and women's work became increasingly dissimilar. Industrial jobs began to attract large numbers of immigrants, and some workers organized labor unions.

The American people, too, were changing. Immigration and western expansion were making the population more diverse. Urbanization, commerce, and industry were creating significant divisions among Americans, reaching deeply into the home as well as the workshop. The South was not totally insulated from these changes, but its dependence on slave rather than free labor set it apart. Above all else, slavery defined the South.

Suggestions for Further Reading

General

Stuart Bruchey, *The Roots of American Economic Growth, 1607–1861: An Essay in Social Causation* (1965); David Klingaman and Richard Vedder, eds., *Essays in Nineteenth-Century History* (1975); Jack Larkin, *The Reshaping of Everyday Life, 1790–1840* (1988); Otto Mayr and Robert C. Post, eds., *Yankee Enterprise: The Rise of the American System of Manufactures* (1981); D. W. Meinig, *The Shaping of America: A Geographical Perspective on 500 Years of History*, vol. 2, *Contininental America, 1800–1867* (1993); Douglass C. North, *Economic Growth of the United States, 1790–1860* (1966); Nathan Rosenberg, *Technology and American Economic Growth* (1972); Melvyn Stokes and Stephen Conway (eds.), *The Market Revolution in America: Social, Political, and Religious Expressions, 1800–1860* (1996).

Transportation

Robert G. Albion, *The Rise of New York Port, 1815–1860* (1939); Albert Fishlow, *American Railroads and the Transformation of the Ante-Bellum Economy* (1965); Carter Goodrich, *Government Promotion of American Canals and Railroads, 1800–1890* (1960); Louis C. Hunter, *Steamboats on the Western Rivers* (1949); Harry N. Scheiber, *Ohio Canal Era: A Case Study of Government and the Economy, 1820–1861* (1969); Ronald E. Shaw, *Canals for a Nation: The Canal Era in the United States, 1790–1860* (1990); George R. Taylor, *The Transportation Revolution, 1815–1860* (1951); James A. Ward, *Railroads and the Character of America, 1820–1887* (1986).

Commerce and Manufacturing

Alfred D. Chandler, Jr., *The Visible Hand: Managerial Revolution in American Business* (1977); Thomas C. Cochran, *Frontiers of Change: Early Industrialization in America* (1981); Robert F. Dalzell, Jr., *Enterprising Elite: The Boston Associates and the World They Made* (1987); Louis Hartz, *Economic Policy and Democratic Thought: Pennsylvania, 1776–1860* (1954); David A. Hounshell, *From the American System to Mass Production, 1800–1932: The Development of Manufacturing Technology in the United States* (1984); David J. Jeremy, *Transatlantic Industrial Revolution: The Diffusion of Textile Technologies Between Britain and America, 1790s–1830s* (1981); Stanley I. Kutler, *Privilege and Creative Destruction: The Charles River Bridge Case* (1971); Walter Licht, *Industrializing America: The Nineteenth Century* (1995); Merritt

Roe Smith, *Harpers Ferry Armory and the New Technology* (1977); Theodore Steinberg, *Nature Incorporated: Industrialization and the Waters of New England* (1991); Barbara M. Tucker, *Samuel Slater and the Origins of the American Textile Industry, 1790–1860* (1984); Anthony F. C. Wallace, *Rockdale: The Growth of an American Village in the Early Industrial Revolution* (1978).

Agriculture

"American Agriculture, 1790–1840, A Symposium," *Agricultural History* 46 (January 1972); Jeremy Atack and Fred Bateman, *To Their Own Soil: Agriculture in the Antebellum North* (1987); Allen G. Bogue, *From Prairie to Corn Belt: Farming on the Illinois and Iowa Prairies in the Nineteenth Century* (1963); Christopher Clark, *The Roots of Rural Capitalism: Western Massachusetts, 1780–1860* (1990); Clarence Danhof, *Change in Agriculture: The Northern United States, 1820–1870* (1969); John Mack Faragher, *Sugar Creek: Life on the Illinois Prairie* (1986); Paul W. Gates, *The Farmer's Age: Agriculture, 1815–1860* (1962); Benjamin H. Hibbard, *A History of Public Land Policies* (1939); Joan M. Jensen, *Loosening the Bonds: Mid-Atlantic Farm Women, 1750–1850* (1986); Robert Leslie Jones, *History of Agriculture in Ohio to 1880* (1983); Sally McMurry, *Transforming Rural Life: Dairying Families and Agricultural Change, 1820–1885* (1995).

Conquerors and Civilizers

William Cronon, *Nature's Metropolis: Chicago and the Great West* (1991); John Mack Faragher, *Women and Men on the Overland Trail* (1979); William H. Goetzmann, *Exploration and Empire: The Explorer and the Scientist in the Winning of the American West* (1966); Julie Roy Jeffrey, *Frontier Women: The Trans-Mississippi West, 1840–1880* (1979); Theodore J. Karamanski, *Fur Trade and Exploration: Opening the Far Northwest, 1821–1852* (1983); Lillian Schlissel, *Women's Diaries of the Westward Journey* (1982); Duane A. Smith, *Mining America: The Industry and the Environment, 1800–1980* (1987); John D. Unruh, Jr., *The Overland Emigrants and the Trans-Mississippi West, 1840–1860* (1979); David J. Weber, *The Spanish Frontier in North America* (1992).

Workers

Mary H. Blewett, *Men, Women, and Work: Class, Gender, and Protest in the New England Shoe Industry, 1780–1910* (1988); Jeanne Boydston, *Home and Work: Housework, Wages, and the Ideology of Labor in the Early Republic* (1990); Alan Dawley, *Class and Community: The Industrial Revolution in Lynn* (1977); Thomas Dublin, *Transforming Women's Work: New England Lives in the Industrial Revolution* (1994); Thomas Dublin, *Women at Work: The Transformation of Work and Community in Lowell, Massachusetts, 1826–1860* (1979); Bruce Laurie, *Artisans into Workers: Labor in Nineteenth-Century America* (1989); Jonathan Prude, *The Coming of Industrial Order: Town and Factory Life in Rural Massachusetts, 1810–1860* (1983); Howard B. Rock, Paul A. Gilje, and Robert Asher, eds., *American Artisans: Crafting Social Identity, 1750–1850* (1995); Norman Ware, *The Industrial Worker, 1840–1860* (1924); Sean Wilentz, *Chants Democratic: New York City and the Rise of the American Working Class, 1788–1850* (1984); David A. Zonderman, *Aspirations and Anxieties: New England Workers and the Mechanized Factory System, 1815–1850* (1992).

11
Slavery and the Growth of the South
1800–1860

She looked out of place in the dirty yard of the slave trader's establishment. Dressed in silk and adorned in jewelry, Eliza seemed bewildered as she clung to the hands of her children, a little boy and a girl. That morning in 1841 Eliza had been told that she was going into Washington, D.C., to receive her long-promised freedom. Now she found herself in "a slave pen within the very shadow of the Capitol."

Eliza had been the concubine of her owner, Elisha Berry, but a division of his property placed her under the control of his resentful daughter, who promptly decided to remove all evidence of her father's illicit relationship. As the reality of her situation sank in, Eliza began to fear most that she would be separated from her children.

Within a few days the slave trader moved her and the children to Richmond, Virginia, and then by ship to New Orleans, where planters in the booming Gulf region needed many more slaves. At the New Orleans slave market a man offered to purchase her son. Eliza pleaded with him to buy the family group and promised "to be the most faithful slave that ever lived." When he answered that he could not afford it, Eliza "burst into a paroxysm of grief, weeping plaintively." Later, when her daughter was sold away, Eliza had to be physically torn apart from the last person she loved.

Sent to work in the fields of a plantation on Bayou Boeuf, Eliza grew "feeble and emaciated" though she was still a young woman. Within two years she was dead. Eliza's fate was one of many human tragedies accompanying the vast expansion of plantation slavery that took place between 1800 and 1860. Tens of thousands of African-Americans suffered as slavery spread westward; across the Mississippi River and into Texas.

Louisiana sugar planters were among the richest of the southern slaveholders. Those who had enjoyed their wealth for a few decades often laid out spacious plantations and built large mansions, many of which survive today.
Louisiana State University Museum of Art, Baton Rouge.

Many northerners remained undisturbed in this period by the progress of human bondage, but a growing number came to see it as shocking and backward. In the years after the Revolution, northerners—possessing few slaves and influenced by the revolutionary concept of natural rights—had adopted gradual emancipation laws (see page 178). At the same time they developed a dynamic market economy and embarked on an industrial revolution. These changes rendered forced labor obsolete. An industrializing, free-labor society saw no use for slavery (see Chapter 10).

Meanwhile, the South witnessed a different kind of growth and prosperity. New lands were settled and new states peopled, but as the North grew and changed, economically the South merely grew. And growth there only reinforced existing economic patterns. Steadily the South emerged as the world's most extensive and vigorous slave economy. Slavery had a far-reaching influence on the whole society. Southerners were slaves, slaveholders, and nonslaveholders rather than farmers, merchants, mechanics, mill girls, and manufacturers. Southern wealth came from export crops rather than from commerce, manufacturing, and crops sold at home. The southern population was almost wholly rural rather than both rural and urban.

These facts meant that the economic and social lives of southerners were unavoidably distinct from those of northerners. Nonslaveholders operated their family farms in a society dominated by slaveholding planters. A handful of planters developed an aristocratic lifestyle, while slaves—one-third of the South's people—lived without freedom, struggling to develop a culture that sustained hope. The influence of slavery spread throughout the social system, affecting not just southern economics but southern values, customs, and laws.

Migration, Growth, and the Cotton Boom

Between 1800 and 1860, small farmers and slaveowning planters migrated westward and brought new territory under cultivation. As human labor, both voluntary and coerced, built a vastly larger slaveholding society, farms and plantations spread across the landscape. The attraction of rich new lands drew thousands of southerners across the Appalachian Mountains. Early settlers told people back east about "dark, heavy forests, . . . wide, thick canebrakes, [and] clear running river[s], full of fish." These accounts created in many men an irresistible urge to move. Small farmers and ambitious slaveowners poured across the mountains, pushing the Indians off their lands in the Gulf region (see pages 334–339). The floodtide of westward migration reached Alabama and Mississippi in the 1830s, then spilled into Texas in the 1850s.

The earliest settlers in the swelling stream of migration were often yeomen—small farmers, most of whom owned no slaves. Yeomen pioneered the southern wilderness, moving into undeveloped regions and building log cabins. After the War of 1812 they moved in successive waves down the southern Appalachians into new Gulf lands, first as herders of livestock and then as farmers.

Yeoman Farmers

Migration became almost a way of life for some yeoman families. Lured by stories of good land beyond the horizon, many men uprooted their wives and children repeatedly. Each new land seemed "like a paradise" to many eager settlers. The Alabama Territory, wrote one new arrival, had "the greatest prospect of corn and cotton I ever saw." Writing to friends in older parts of the South, he asked, "Why will you stay . . . and work them poor stony ridges when one half of the labor and one third of the ground heare will bring you more?" So many shared the excitement over new lands that one North Carolinian wrote in alarm, "The *Alabama Fever* rages here with great violence. . . . I am apprehensive if it continues to spread as it has done, it will almost depopulate the country."

On the southern frontier men worked hard to clear fields and establish a farm, while their wives labored in the household economy and patiently re-created the social ties—to relatives, neighbors, fellow churchgoers—that enriched everyone's experience. Women seldom shared the men's excitement about moving. They dreaded the isolation and loneliness of the frontier, but few had a voice in the decision. "We have been [moving] all our lives," lamented one woman. "As soon as ever we git comfortably settled, it is time to be off to something new." Maria Lides's father took the family from South Carolina to Alabama, but "his having such a good crop" there, Maria wrote to a relative, "seems to make him more anxious to move." She almost wished that another restless relative, her brother, would decide on California, because "he would be obliged to stop then for he could go no farther."

• *Important Events* •

1793	Eli Whitney invents the cotton gin Production of short-staple cotton begins to expand
1800	Gabriel's conspiracy is discovered in Virginia
1808	Congress bans further importation of slaves
1810–20	137,000 slaves are forced to move from North Carolina and the Chesapeake to Alabama, Mississippi, and other western regions
1812	Louisiana gains admission to the Union
1817	Mississippi gains admission to the Union
1819	Alabama gains admission to the Union
1822	Denmark Vesey's plot is discovered in South Carolina
1831	Nat Turner leads a violent rebellion in Virginia
1832	Virginia holds last serious debate in South about the future of slavery
1832 and after	Legislators in several states increase restrictions on slaves
1830s	Class tensions lead to electoral reforms in much of the South
1836	Arkansas gains admission to the Union
1839	Mississippi's Married Women's Property Act gives married women some property rights
1845	Florida and Texas gain admission to the Union
1857	North Carolina slaveholder Hinton R. Helper denounces the slave system in *The Impending Crisis*

Some yeomen acquired large tracts of level land, purchased slaves, and became wealthy. Others clung to the beautiful mountainous areas they loved or kept moving as independent subsistence farmers because, as one frontiersman put it, he disliked "seeing the nose of my neighbor sticking out between the trees." Those who moved tended to stick to the climate and soils they knew best. Yeomen could not afford the richest bottomlands, which were swampy and required expensive draining, but they acquired land almost everywhere else.

For slaveholding southerners another powerful motive impelled westward movement: the chance to profit from a spectacular cotton boom. Southern planters were not sentimentalists, holding onto slavery while northerners grew rich from commerce and the industrial revolution. Like other Americans, slaveholding southerners were profit oriented, and the cotton boom caused nonmechanized, slave-based agriculture to remain highly profitable in the South, sustaining the plantation economy.

Rise of the Cotton South

This outcome had not always seemed likely. At the time of the Revolution, slave-based agriculture was not very profitable in the Upper South, where most southerners then lived. Persistent debt plagued Virginia's extravagant and aristocratic tobacco growers. Farther south, along the coast of the Carolinas and Georgia, slaves grew rice and some indigo. Cotton was a profitable crop only for the Sea Island planters of South Carolina and Georgia, who grew the luxurious long-staple variety. Short-staple cotton, which grew readily in the interior, was unmarketable because its sticky seeds lay tangled in the fibers. Yet, in spite of the limited usefulness of slavery, much wealth was tied up in it. Ingrained social forces and fear of slave revolts prevented its abolition.

Then, late in the eighteenth century, England's burgeoning textile industry demanded more and more cotton. Sea Island cotton became so profitable between 1785 and 1795 that thousands of farmers in the interior tried growing the short-staple variety; by the early 1790s southern farmers were growing 2 to 3 million pounds of it each year, despite their inability to remove the seeds. Some of this cotton was meant for domestic use, but most was grown in the hope that some innovation would make the crop salable to the English. In such circumstances the invention of a cotton gin was almost inevitable, and Eli Whitney, an inventor from Connecticut, responded

New Orleans, the South's largest city and a major port, was a wealthy hub of the cotton trade. This view from 1860 shows hundreds of cotton bales and dozens of steamboats waiting to receive them.   Chicago Historical Society.

in 1793 with a simple machine that removed the seeds from the fibers. By 1800 cotton was spreading rapidly westward from the seaboard states.

The voracious appetite of English mills caused a meteoric rise in cotton production (see maps, page 289). From 1800 until the Civil War, British demand for cotton multiplied rapidly, and southern planters rushed to increase their acreage. Despite occasional periods of low prices, the demand for cotton surged ahead every decade. Southerners with capital bought more land and more slaves and planted ever more cotton. Cotton growers boosted production so successfully that by 1825 the South was the world's dominant supplier of cotton; by the 1850s the South was the source of over 70 percent of all the cotton that Britain imported.

Thus the antebellum South—the Old South before the Civil War—became primarily a cotton South. Large amounts of tobacco and hemp continued to be grown in the Upper South, and rice and sugar were important crops in certain coastal areas, especially in South Carolina, Georgia, and Louisiana. Thousands of southerners grew only food crops, but cotton was the largest and most widespread cash crop, and the wealth it generated shaped the society and fueled the South's hunger for new territory.

Small slaveowners and wealthier planters (those who owned twenty or more slaves) sought out alluvial bottomland and other fertile soils, eager to grasp the opportunity for wealth the cotton boom offered. A Virginian who visited Vicksburg, Mississippi, in 1836 marveled at the atmosphere: "They do business in a kind of frenzy," he wrote. That frenzy produced many brand-new aristocrats. Some old Virginia and South Carolina families were represented among the proud new "cotton snobs," but most of the wealthy were newly rich.

The desire to plant more cotton and buy more slaves often caused men with new wealth to postpone the enjoyment of luxuries. Many first-generation planters lived for decades in their original log cabins, improved only by clapboards or a frame addition. "If you wish to see people worth millions living as [if] they were not worth hundreds," a Mississippi gentleman remarked, "come down here." Yet the planters' wealth put ease and refinement within their grasp, and riches and high social status arrived quickly for some.

A case in point is the family of Jefferson Davis, who later became president of the Confederacy. Like Abraham Lincoln, Davis was born in Kentucky

One-Generation Aristocrats

amid humble circumstances. His father was one of the thousands of American farmers on the western frontier who moved frequently, seeking but never finding his fortune. Luckily for Jefferson Davis, his older brother migrated to Mississippi and made good. Settling on rich bottom-

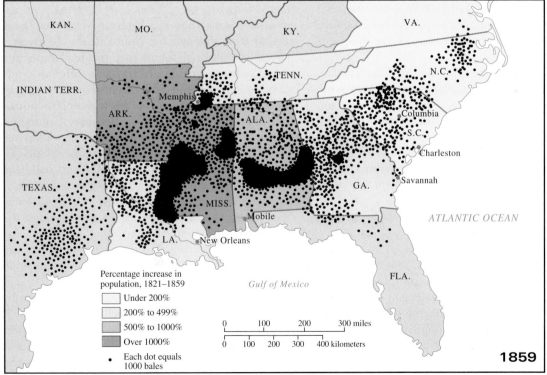

Cotton Production in the South   *These two maps reveal the rapid westward expansion of cotton production and its importance to the antebellum South.*

lands next to the Mississippi River, Joseph Davis expanded his holdings of land and slaves and grew rich. Soon he was an established figure in society, and he used his influence to arrange an education at West Point for his younger brother. A large plantation awaited Jefferson's resignation from the army. The Davis family had become aristocrats in one generation.

The rise of new aristocrats in the Gulf and the migration of thousands of aspiring slaveholders across the Appalachians meant another kind of migration—involuntary—for black southerners. Since Congress had closed the international slave trade in 1808, slaves for new cotton regions had to come from the Upper South, where the slave population was growing through natural increase while tobacco prices fell. Worried by soil exhaustion and low prices, planters in Virginia and North Carolina were shifting toward wheat and corn, crops that were less labor-intensive, and they were glad to sell excess slaves to fertile regions in the cotton South.

Between 1810 and 1820 alone, 137,000 slaves were forced to move from North Carolina and the Chesapeake states to Alabama, Mississippi, and other western regions. Interregional sales and transfers continued thereafter: an estimated 2 million people were sold between 1820 and 1860 to satisfy the need for slave labor. Thousands of black families, like Eliza's, were disrupted every year to serve the needs of the cotton economy.

To white southerners the period from 1800 to 1860 was a time of great change and progress, no less than in the North. The South was growing and expanding, driven by excitement over new lands and energies related to the cotton boom. But the South's growth was different from the North's: its distinguishing features were those of an agricultural and a slave society.

 An Agrarian Society

The South did exhibit some of the diversity of the bustling, urbanizing, commercial North. There were merchants, artisans, and craftsmen in the larger cities, as well as men of commerce who promoted railways and transportation improvements. Immigrants from Ireland and other parts of Europe arrived in Savannah, New Orleans, and other southern ports in dramatically increasing numbers during the 1840s and 1850s. But these developments were only faint shadows of their northern counterparts and had relatively little impact. Southern development was dominated by agriculture and slavery and by the prominence of rural slaves, slaveholders, and yeoman farmers in the population.

Population distribution remained thin. Cotton growers spread out over as large an area as possible to maximize production and income. Farms were set far apart, rather than clustered around villages, and southern society remained predominantly rural. Because most immigrants to the United States sought urban locations, population growth fell behind the North's. Population density was low in the older plantation states and extremely low in the frontier areas. In 1860 there were only 2.3 people per square mile in vast and largely unsettled Texas, 15.6 in Louisiana, and 18.0 in Georgia. By contrast, population density in the non-slaveholding states east of the Mississippi River was almost three times higher. The Northeast had an average of 65.4 people per square mile. Massachusetts had 153.1 people per square mile, and New York City, where overcrowding reached epic proportions, compressed 86,400 people into each square mile.

Population Distribution

Even in the 1850s, much of the South seemed a virtual wilderness. Frederick Law Olmsted, a northerner later renowned as a landscape architect, made several trips through the South in the 1850s as a journalist. Olmsted found that the few trains and stagecoaches available to travelers offered crude accommodations and kept their schedules poorly. Indeed, he had to do most of his traveling on horseback along primitive trails. Between Columbus, Georgia, and Montgomery, Alabama, Olmsted found "a hilly wilderness, with a few dreary villages, and many isolated cotton farms." Alabama had been frontier as recently as 1800, but Olmsted encountered similar conditions in parts of eastern Virginia: "For hours and hours one has to ride through the unlimited, continual, all-shadowing, all-embracing forest. . . . [F]or days and days he may sometimes travel and see never two dwellings of mankind within sight of each other."

Society in such rural areas was characterized by relatively weak institutions outside the family, for it takes a concentration of people to create and support organized activity. Where people were scarce, it was difficult to finance and operate schools, churches, libraries, or even inns, restaurants, and other amenities. Southerners were strongly committed to their

This painting of the Alabama River at Selma (c. 1853–1855), attributed to William Frye, suggests the South's rural nature and the small size of its urban centers.   Selma-Dallas County Library and Birmingham Museum of Art.

churches, and some believed in the importance of universities, but all such institutions were far less fully developed than those in the North.

The South's cities were likewise smaller and less developed. Confined to the region's perimeter, the largest urban areas functioned as ports rather than centers of a vigorous internal commerce. They exported mainly staple crops, such as cotton or tobacco, and imported only a few necessary manufactured goods and luxuries. Factories—stimulus to urban growth in the North—were rare because planters invested most of their capital in slaves. A few southerners did invest in iron or textiles on a small scale. But the largest southern "industry" was lumbering, and the largest factories used slave labor to make cigars.

Weak Urban Sector

More decisively, the South was slower than the North to develop a unified market economy and a regional transportation network. Because planters were eager to invest in land and slaves and often could use waterways for transportation, far less money was spent on canals, turnpikes, or railroads. The South had only 26 percent of the nation's railroad mileage in 1850 and, despite concerted efforts, only 35 percent in 1860. As a result, urban growth after 1820 was far less vigorous than in the North, and metropolitan centers were almost nonexistent. In 1860 only 49,000 out of 704,000 South Carolinians lived in towns with 2,500 or more residents, and less than 3 percent of Mississippi's population lived in places of comparable size. In the same year, the population of Charleston, South Carolina, was only 41,000, that of Richmond, Virginia, 38,000. New Orleans, Louisiana, by far the largest southern city, had only 169,000 residents and was being left behind because it was not linked to the national railroad network, even though it was a major port.

Thus although the South sold huge amounts of cotton on the international market, its economy at home was semideveloped relative to other sections of the country. Its white people were prospering, but not as rapidly as most residents of the North. There, changes in commerce and industry brought unprecedented advances in productivity, raising the average person's standard of living and widening the range of affordable goods and services (see Chapter 12). In the South, change was quantitative rather than qualitative. Using the same farming techniques, southern planters and farmers sought to grow more, but their region remained rural and its internal market undeveloped.

 ## Free Southerners: Farmers, Planters, and Free Blacks

A large majority of white southern families (three-quarters in 1860) owned no slaves. Some lived in towns and ran stores or businesses, but most were yeoman farmers who owned their own land and grew their own food. They were the typical whites, but the social distance between different groups of whites was great. Still greater was the distance between whites and blacks.

The yeomen were independent, individualistic, and given to hard work and self-reliance. They could be independent thinkers as well, but their status as a numerical majority did not mean that they set the direction of the slave society. Absorbed in the work of their farms, they normally occupied a relatively autonomous position within the slavery-based staple-crop economy expanding around them. By slowly improving their acreage or settling new and better land, yeoman families improved their lot and made steady progress.

But the lives of most southern yeomen, unlike the lives of their northern counterparts, had not been transformed by improvements in transportation. Because few railroads penetrated the southern interior, yeomen generally had little contact with the market or the type of progress it could introduce. Families might raise a small surplus to sell for cash or to trade for needed items, but they were remote from large market networks and therefore not particularly concerned about increasing their cash income. Instead, they valued their self-reliance and freedom from others' control. Living an isolated, demanding rural life, yeomen constituted an important, though often silent, part of southern society. If their rights were threatened, however, they could react strongly.

The yeomen enjoyed a folk culture based on family, church, and neighborhood. They spoke with a drawl, and their inflections were reminiscent of their Scottish and Irish backgrounds. Once a year they flocked to religious revivals called protracted meetings or camp meetings, and in between they enjoyed house-raisings, logrollings, quilting bees, and corn-shuckings. Such occasions combined work with fun, offered food in abundance, and usually included liquor. They also provided fellowship that was especially welcome to isolated rural dwellers.

Folk Culture of the Yeomen

Social conventions imposed uniform roles on yeoman women. A demanding round of work and family responsibilities shaped their lives in the home. At harvest yeoman women frequently helped in the fields, and throughout the year the drying, preserving, and preparing of food consumed much of their time. Household tasks continued during frequent pregnancies and the care of small children. Primary nursing and medical care also fell to the mother, who might have a book of remedies to aid her but often relied on family and folk wisdom. In some evangelical churches women played respected roles on certain committees, but overwhelmingly the busy life of the yeoman woman was tied to the home.

Among the men there were many who aspired to wealth, eager to join the race for slaves, land, and profits from cotton. Such an individual was a North Carolinian named John F. Flintoff, whose diary reveals that the road to wealth was not always easy. At age eighteen in 1841, Flintoff went to Mississippi to seek his fortune. Like other aspiring yeomen, he worked as an overseer of slaves but often found it impossible to please his employers. At one point he gave up and returned to North Carolina, where he married and lived for a while in his parents' house. But Flintoff was "impatient to get along in the world," so he tried Louisiana next and then Mississippi again.

For Flintoff, the fertile Gulf region had its disadvantages. "My health has been very bad here," he wrote. "Chills and fever occasionally has hold of me." Routinely, "first rate employment" alternated with "very low wages." Moreover, as a young man working on isolated plantations, Flintoff often felt lonely. Even a revival meeting in 1844 proved "an extremely cold time" with "little warm feeling." His uncle and other employers found fault with his

How do historians know about the values and ways of life of nonslaveholders in the South? Letters, diaries, and family papers of these people, who generally were not rich or famous, have not been preserved as frequently as the records of the slaveholding elite. Thus historians have turned to various other sources—including travelers' accounts, folklore, and United States census records—to learn more about them. This page from the manuscript "Population Schedules" of the census of 1860 supplies information on family structure and a variety of personal characteristics. The "Census of Agriculture" contains much additional information about the size of each family's farm and the crops grown there.   Photo: North Carolina Division of Archives and History.

Most white southerners were not wealthy slaveowners but yeoman farmers. Artist John Bunyan Bristol called this painting of a farmer's home in northern Florida On the St. Johns River.   Collection of Samuel H. and Roberta Vickers/The Florida Collection.

work, and in 1846 Flintoff concluded in despair that "managing negroes and large farms is soul destroying."

A desire to succeed kept him going. At twenty-six, even before he owned any land, Flintoff bought his first slave, "a negro boy 7 years old." Soon he had purchased two more children, the cheapest slaves available. Conscious of his status as a slaveowner, Flintoff resented the low wages he was paid and complained that his uncle offered him *"hand pay,"* wages suitable for a day laborer rather than a slave-owner and manager. In 1853, with nine young slaves and a growing family, Flintoff faced "the most unhappy time of my life." Fired by his uncle, he returned to North Carolina, sold some of his slaves, and purchased 124 acres with help from his in-laws. Flintoff grew corn, wheat, and tobacco and earned extra cash hauling wood in his wagon. By 1860 he owned three horses, twenty-six hogs, ten head of cattle, and several slaves and was paying off his debts. As the Civil War approached, he looked forward to acquiring more land and slaves, freeing his wife from much of the labor of yeoman women, and possibly sending his sons to college. Although

Flintoff eventually achieved success, his path had not been easy, and he never became the cotton planter he had aspired to be.

Probably more typical of the southern yeoman was Ferdinand L. Steel, who as a young man moved from North Carolina to Tennessee to work as a hatter and river boatman but eventually took up farming in Mississippi. Steel rose every day at five and worked until sundown. With the help of his family he raised corn, wheat, pork, and vegetables for the family table. Cotton was his cash crop: he sold five or six bales (about 2,000 pounds) a year to obtain money for sugar, coffee, salt, calico, gunpowder, and a few other store-bought goods.

Steel picked his cotton himself (never exceeding 120 pounds per day, less than many slaves averaged) and complained that cotton cultivation was arduous and time-consuming. The market fluctuated, and if cotton prices fell, a small grower like Steel could be driven into debt and lose his farm. In fact, he wanted to grow less cotton. "We are too weak handed" to manage it, he noted in his diary. "We had better . . . raise corn and keep out of debt and we will have no necessity of raising cotton."

Steel's life in Mississippi in the 1840s retained much of the flavor of the frontier. He made all the family's shoes; his wife and sister sewed dresses, shirts, and "pantiloons." The Steel women also rendered their own soap and spun and wove cotton into cloth; the men hunted game. House-raisings and corn-shuckings provided entertainment, and Steel doctored his illnesses with boneset tea and other herbs.

The focus of Steel's life was family and religion. Family members prayed together every morning and night, and he prayed and studied Scripture for an hour after lunch. Steel joined a temperance society and looked forward to church and camp meetings. "My Faith increases, & I enjoy much of that peace which the world cannot give," he wrote in 1841. Seeking to improve himself and be ready for Judgment Day, Steel borrowed histories, Latin and Greek grammars, and religious books from his church. Eventually he became a traveling Methodist minister. "My life is one of toil," he reflected, "but blessed be God that it is as well with me as it is."

Toil with even less security was the lot of two other groups of free southerners: landless whites and free blacks. A sizable minority of white southern workers—from 25 to 40 percent, depending on the state—were unskilled laborers who owned no land and worked for others in the countryside and towns. Their property consisted of a few household items and some animals—usually pigs—that could feed themselves on the open range. The landless included some immigrants, especially Irish, who did heavy and dangerous work such as building railroads and digging ditches. By 1860 immigrants were becoming numerous in Savannah, New Orleans, and a few other port cities.

Landless Whites

In the countryside, white farm laborers struggled to become yeomen in the face of low wages or, if they rented, unpredictable market prices for their crops. The shortage of well-paying jobs and competition from speculators made it difficult for them to buy land. Some fell into debt and were frequently sued. By scrimping and saving and finding odd jobs, others managed to climb into the ranks of yeomen. When James and Nancy Bennitt of North Carolina succeeded in their ten-year struggle to buy land, they decided to avoid the unstable market in cotton; thereafter they raised extra corn and wheat as sources of cash. People like the Bennitts viewed pigs and livestock as a major economic asset; good steady employment was uncertain in a region whose large producers relied on slave labor.

For the nearly quarter-million free blacks in the South in 1860, conditions were generally worse than the yeoman's and often little better than the slave's.

Free Blacks

The free blacks of the Upper South were usually descendants of men and women emancipated by their owners in the 1780s and 1790s. Some made substantial progress in towns or cities, but most lived in rural areas and had few material advantages. They usually did not own land and had to labor in someone else's fields, often beside slaves. By law free blacks could not own a gun, buy liquor, violate curfew, assemble except in church, testify in court, or (throughout the South after 1835) vote. Despite these obstacles, a minority bought land, and others found jobs as artisans, draymen, boatmen, and fishermen. A few prospered and bought slave laborers, but most who owned slaves had purchased their own wives and children (whom they could not free, since laws required newly emancipated blacks to leave their state).

Farther south, in the cotton and Gulf regions, a large proportion of free blacks were mulattos, the privileged offspring of wealthy planters. Not all planters freed their mixed-race offspring, but those who did often recognized a moral obligation and gave their children good educations and financial backing. In a few cities like New Orleans and Mobile, extensive interracial sex had produced a mulatto population that was recognized as a distinct class. These people formed a society of their own and sought a status above slaves and other freedmen, if not equal to that of planters. But outside New Orleans, Mobile, and Charleston, such groups were rare, and most mulattos experienced more disadvantages than benefits from their light skin. (For a more detailed discussion of free blacks during this period, see Chapter 12.)

At the opposite end of the social spectrum from free blacks were slaveholders. As a group they lived well, on incomes that enabled them to enjoy superior housing, food, clothing, and luxuries. But most lived in comfortable farmhouses, not on the opulent scale that legend suggests. A few statistics tell the story: 50 percent of southern slaveholders had fewer than five slaves; 72 percent had fewer than ten; 88 percent had fewer than twenty. Thus the average slaveholder was not a wealthy aristocrat but an aspiring farmer, usually a person of

Planters

Most slaveowners lived in comfortable country homes rather than in stately mansions. This rare daguerreotype, dating from about 1853, shows a family in front of their home. Notice the presence of a male slave in the left background.   The J. Paul Getty Museum, Los Angeles, California.

humble origins, with little formal education and many rough edges to his manner. In fact, he probably had little to distinguish him from a nonslaveholder beyond a degree of wealth and greater ambition.

Consider the Louisiana cotton planter Bennet Barrow, who was neither polished nor unusually coarse. His considerable wealth was new, and he was preoccupied with moneymaking: he worried constantly over his cotton crop, filling his diary with tedious weather reports and gloomy predictions of his yields. Yet Barrow also strove to appear above such worries, and in boom times he grandly cosigned loans for men who later defaulted and left him saddled with debt.

Barrow hunted frequently and had a passion for racing horses and raising hounds. He could report the loss of a slave without feeling, but emotion broke through his laconic manner when illness afflicted his sporting animals. "Never was a person more unlucky than I am," he mourned. "My favorite pup never lives." His strongest feelings surfaced when his horse

Jos Bell—equal to "the best Horse in the South"— "broke down running a mile . . . ruined for Ever." The same day the distraught Barrow gave his field hands a "general Whipping." Barrow was rich but not a cultured or gentle man.

The richest planters used their wealth to model genteel sophistication. Rather than eating abundant country food in a spacious, comfortable farmhouse, they served to guests in their mansions a choice of gourmet foods: "gumbo, ducks and olives, *supreme de volaille*, chickens in jelly, oysters, lettuce salad, chocolate cream, jelly cake, claret cup, etc." A traveler in Mississippi saw gentlemen on county court day dressed in "black cloth coats, black cravats and satin or embroidered silk waistcoats; all, too, sleek as if just from a barber's hands, and redolent of perfumes." Extended visits, parties, and balls to which women wore the latest fashions provided opportunities for friendship, courtship, and display.

Slaveholding men dominated society and, especially among the wealthiest and oldest families, justified their dominance through a paternalistic ideology. Instead of stressing the profitable aspects of commercial agriculture, they focused on noblesse oblige, seeing themselves as custodians of the welfare of society as a whole and of the black families who depended on them in particular. The paternalistic planter viewed himself not as an oppressor but as the benevolent guardian of an inferior race. He developed affectionate feelings toward his slaves (as long as they knew their place) and was genuinely shocked at criticism of his behavior.

Southern Paternalism

The letters of Paul Carrington Cameron, North Carolina's largest slaveholder, illustrate this mentality. After a period of sickness among his one thousand North Carolina slaves (he had hundreds more in Alabama and Mississippi), Cameron wrote, "I fear the Negroes have suffered much from the want of proper attention and kindness under this late distemper . . . no love of lucre shall ever induce me to be cruel, or even to make or permit to be made any great exposure of their persons at inclement seasons." On another occasion he described to his sister the sense of responsibility he felt: "Do you remember a cold & frosty morning, during [our mother's] illness, when she said to me 'Paul my son the people ought to be shod' this is ever in my ears, whenever I see any ones shoes in bad order; and in my ears it will be, so long as I am master."

It was comforting to the richest southern planters to see themselves in this way, and slaves—accommodating to the realities of power—encouraged their masters to think their benevolence was appreciated. Paternalism also served as a defense against abolitionist criticism. Still, paternalism affected the manner and not the substance of most planters' behavior. Its softness and warmth were a matter of style, covering harsher assumptions: blacks were inferior, and planters should make money. As talk of paternalistic duties increased, theories about the complete and permanent inferiority of blacks also multiplied.

Even Paul Cameron's benevolence vanished with changed circumstances. After the Civil War, he bristled at African-Americans' efforts to be free and made sweeping economic decisions without regard to their welfare. Writing on Christmas Day 1865, Cameron showed little Christian charity (but a healthy profit motive) when he declared, "I am convinced that the people who gets rid of the free negro first will be the first to advance in improved agriculture. Have made no effort to retain any of mine [and] will not attempt a crop beyond the capacity of 30 hands." With that he turned off his land nearly a thousand black agriculturalists, rented his fields to several white farmers, and invested in industry, which he considered more promising economically.

Relations between men and women in the planter class were similarly paternalistic. The life of an upper-class southern woman was bound by the household, and she was raised and educated to be a wife, mother, and subordinate companion to men. South Carolina's Mary Boykin Chesnut wrote of her husband, "He is master of the house. To hear is to obey. . . . All the comfort of my life depends upon his being in a good humor." In a social system based on the coercion of an entire race, women were not allowed to challenge society's rules on sexual or racial relations. If a woman defied or questioned the status quo, she risked universal condemnation.

Elite Women's Role

After spending her early years within the family circle, a planter's daughter usually attended one of the South's rapidly multiplying academies or boarding schools. There she formed friendships with other girls and received an education that emphasized grammar, composition, penmanship, geography, literature, and languages, but little science and mathematics. Typically the young woman maintained dutiful and affectionate ties with her parents and entertained suitors whom they approved. But very soon she had to choose a husband and commit herself for life to a man whom she generally had known for only a brief time.

Upon marriage, she ceded to her husband most of her legal rights, became part of his family, and was expected to get along with numerous in-laws during extended visits. Most of the year she was isolated on a large plantation, where she had to oversee the cooking and preserving of food, manage the house, supervise care of the children, and attend sick slaves. She was forbidden to travel unless accompanied by a man. All these realities were more rigid and confining on the frontier, where isolation was greater and opportunities for social interaction were fewer.

It is not surprising that an intelligent and perceptive young woman sometimes approached marriage with anxiety, for her future depended on the man she chose. Lucy Breckinridge, a wealthy Virginia girl of twenty, sensed how much autonomy she would have to surrender on her wedding day. In her diary she recorded this unvarnished observation on

Miss Mattie G. Shorter, the daughter of a governor of Alabama, was among the southern women who enjoyed greater opportunities for education. She is shown here with her diploma from Union Female College.   Shorter Mansion and Birmingham Museum of Art.

marriage: "If [husbands] care for their wives at all it is only as a sort of servant, a being made to attend to their comforts and to keep the children out of the way. . . . A woman's life after she is married, unless there is an immense amount of love, is nothing but suffering and hard work."

Lucy loved young children but knew that childbearing often involved grief, poor health, and death. In 1840 the birth rate for white southern women in their childbearing years was almost 30 percent higher than the national average. The average southern white woman could expect to bear eight children in 1800; by 1860 the figure had decreased only to six, with one or more miscarriages likely. For those women who wanted to plan their families, methods of contraception were uncertain, and doctors had few remedies for infection or irritation of the reproductive tract. Complications of childbirth were a major cause of death, occurring twice as often in the hot, moist South as in the Northeast. Moreover, a mother had to endure the loss of many of the infants she bore. Infant mortality in the first year of life exceeded 10 percent and remained high during early childhood. In the South in 1860 almost five out of ten

children died before age five, and in South Carolina more than six in ten failed to reach age twenty.

Slavery was another source of problems that white women had to endure but were not supposed to notice. "Violations of the moral law . . . made mulattoes as common as blackberries," protested a woman in Georgia, but wives had to play "the ostrich game." "A magnate who runs a hideous black harem," wrote Mrs. Chesnut, ". . . poses as the model of all human virtues to these poor women whom God and the laws have given him. From the height of his awful majesty, he scolds and thunders at them, as if he never did wrong in his life."

In the early 1800s, some southern women, especially Quakers, had spoken out against slavery. Although most white women did not criticize the "peculiar institution," they often viewed it less as a system and more as a series of relationships among individuals. Perhaps sensing this, southern men tolerated no discussion by women of the slavery issue. In the 1840s and 1850s, as northern and international criticism of slavery increased, southern men published a barrage of articles stressing that women should restrict their concerns to the home. A writer in the *Southern Literary Messenger* bemoaned "these days of Women's Rights," and the *Southern Quarterly Review* declared, "The proper place for a woman is at home. One of her highest privileges, to be politically merged in the existence of her husband."

But some southern women were beginning to seek a larger role. A study of women in Petersburg, Virginia, a large tobacco-manufacturing town, has revealed behavior that valued financial autonomy. Over several decades before 1860, the proportion of women who never married, or did not remarry after the death of a spouse, grew to exceed 33 percent. Likewise the number of women who worked for wages, controlled their own property, and ran millinery or dressmaking businesses increased. In managing property, these and other women benefited from legal changes—beginning with Mississippi's Married Women's Property Act of 1839—that had not been intended to increase female independence. To protect families from the husband's indebtedness during business panics and recessions, legal reforms gave married women some property rights.

For a large category of southern men and women, rights were nil, freedom was wholly denied, and education in any form was not allowed. Male and female, slaves were expected to accept bondage and ignorance as their condition.

 ## Slaves and Their Status in Bondage

For African-Americans, slavery was a curse that brought no blessings other than the strengths they developed to survive it. Slaves knew a life of poverty, coercion, toil, heartbreak, and resentment. They had few hopes that were not denied; often they had to bear separation from their loved ones; and they were despised as an inferior race. That they endured and found loyalty and strength among themselves is a tribute to their courage, but it could not make up for a life without freedom, dignity, or opportunity.

Southern slaves enjoyed few material comforts beyond the bare necessities. Although they generally had enough to eat, their diet was plain and monotonous. The basic ration was corn-meal, fat pork, molasses, and occasionally coffee. Many masters allowed slaves to tend gardens, which provided the variety and extra nutrition of greens and

Slaves' Diet, Clothing, and Housing

sweet potatoes, and some could fish and hunt. "It was nothin' fine," recalled one woman, "but it was good plain eatin' what filled you up."* Most slave-owners did not starve their slaves, but there is considerable evidence that slaves often suffered the effects of beriberi, pellagra, and other dietary-deficiency diseases.

Clothing too was plain, coarse, and inexpensive. Few slaves received more than one or two changes of clothing for hot and cold seasons and one blanket each winter. Children of both sexes ran naked in hot weather and wore long cotton shirts in winter. When big enough to go to the fields, boys received a work shirt and a pair of breeches, and girls a simple dress. On many plantations slave women made their own clothing of osnaburg, a coarse cotton fabric that whites called "nigger cloth." The minority who were allowed to earn a little money by doing extra work often bought additional clothing. Many slaves had to go without shoes until December, even as far north as Virginia. The shoes they received were frequent objects of complaint—uncomfortable brass-toed brogans or stiff wraparounds made from leather tanned on the plantation.

Summer and winter, slaves typically lived in small one-room cabins, possibly with a window opening but no glass. Some of the richer plantations provided more substantial houses, some of which survive today, but the average slave lived in crude accommodations. Logs chinked with mud formed the walls; dirt was the only floor; and a wattle-and-daub or stone chimney vented the fireplace, which provided both heat and light. Bedding consisted of heaps of straw, straw mattresses, or wooden bed-frames lashed to the walls with rope. A few crude pieces of furniture and cooking utensils completed the furnishings. The gravest drawback of slave cabins, however, was not lack of comfort but their unhealthfulness. Each small cabin housed one or two entire families. Crowding and lack of sanitation fostered the spread of infection and contagious diseases. Many slaves (and whites) carried worms and intestinal parasites picked up from feces or soil. Lice were widespread in both races, and flies and other

---

*Accounts by ex-slaves are quoted from *The American Slave: A Composite Autobiography*, edited by George P. Rawick (Westport, Conn.: Greenwood Press, First Reprint Edition 1972, Second Reprint Edition 1974), from materials gathered by the Federal Writers' Project and originally published in 1941. The spelling in these accounts has been standardized.

George Fuller, an itinerant painter from Massachusetts, worked from 1856 to 1858 in Alabama, where he made this sketch in ink and pencil of a slave and her mistress at work on washday.   Pocumtuck Valley Memorial Association.

insects spread virulent diseases such as typhoid fever, malaria, and dysentery.

Hard work was the central fact of slaves' existence. The long hours and large work gangs that characterized Gulf Coast cotton districts seemed like factories in the field compared to the small clusters of slaves who had worked in the eighteenth-century Chesapeake. Overseers rang the morning bell before dawn—so early that some slaves remembered being "afraid to start work for fear that they would cover the cotton plants with dirt because they couldn't see clearly." And, as one woman recalled when interviewed by workers in the Federal Writers' Project of the 1930s, "it was way after sundown 'fore they could stop that field work. Then they had to hustle to finish their night work [such as watering livestock or cleaning cotton] in time for supper, or go to bed without it."

Except in urban settings and on some rice plantations, where slaves were assigned daily tasks to complete at their own pace, working "from sun to sun" became universal in the South. Long hours and hard work were at the heart of the advantage that

Slaves' Work Routines

slave labor gave slaveowners. As one planter put it, slaves were the best labor because "you could command them and *make* them do what was right." White workers, by contrast, could not be driven: "they wouldn't stand it." Slaves who cultivated tobacco in the Upper South worked long hours picking the sticky, sometimes noxious, tobacco leaves under harsh discipline. The slaves had to "sucker" the plants—pinch off secondary shoots to increase the size of the leaves—and remove tobacco worms by hand. According to many former slaves, workers who overlooked worms were forced to eat them. No free laborers in the South endured such treatment.

Profit also took precedence over paternalistic "protection" of women: slave women did heavy fieldwork, often as much as the men and even during pregnancy. Old people—of whom there were few—were kept busy caring for young children, doing light chores, or carding, ginning, and spinning cotton. Children had to gather kindling, carry water to the fields, or sweep the yard.

Slaves had a variety of ways to keep from being worked to death. It was impossible to supervise every slave every minute, and slaves slacked off when they were not being watched. Thus travelers saw slaves "go through the motions of labor without putting strength into them," and owners complained that slaves "never would lay out their strength freely. . . . It was impossible to make them do it." Stubborn misunderstanding and literal-mindedness were another defense. One exasperated Virginia planter voiced his irritation (and the racism nurtured by slavery) when he said, "You can make a nigger work, *but you cannot make him think.*"

Slaves could not slow their pace too much, of course, because the owner enjoyed a monopoly on force and violence. Whites throughout the South believed that slaves "can't be governed except with the whip."

Physical and Mental Abuse of Slaves

One South Carolinian frankly explained to a northern journalist that he had whipped his slaves occasionally, "say once a fortnight; . . . the fear of the lash kept them in good order." Evidence suggests that whippings were less frequent on small farms than on large plantations, but even most small farmers plied the lash. These beatings symbolized authority to the master and tyranny to the slaves, who made them a benchmark for evaluating a master. In the words of former slaves, a good owner was one who did not "whip too much," whereas a bad owner "whipped till he's bloodied you and blistered you."

As these reports suggest, terrible abuses could and did occur. The master wielded virtually absolute authority on his plantation, and courts did not recognize the word of chattel. Pregnant women were whipped, and there were burnings, mutilations, tortures, and murders. Yet physical cruelty may have been less prevalent in the United States than in other slaveholding parts of the New World. In sugar-growing and mining regions of the Western Hemisphere in the 1800s, slaves were regarded as an expendable resource to be replaced after seven years. Treatment was so poor that death rates were high and the heavily male slave population rapidly shrank in size. In the United States, by contrast, the slave population experienced a steady natural increase as births exceeded deaths and each generation grew larger.

The worst evil of American slavery was not its physical cruelty but the nature of slavery itself: coercion, lack of freedom, belonging to another person, virtually no hope for change. Recalling their days in bondage, some former slaves emphasized the physical abuse—those were "bullwhip days" to one woman. Another woman complained that the black slave "got [his] back cut in slavery time, didn't he?" But their comments focused on the tyranny of whipping as much as the pain. A woman named Delia Garlic made the essential point when she said, "It's bad to belong to folks that own you soul an' body. I could tell you 'bout it all day, but even then you couldn't guess the awfulness of it." A man named Thomas Lewis put it this way: "There was no such thing as being good to slaves. Many people were better than others, but a slave belonged to his master and there was no way to get out of it."

As these comments reveal, the great majority of American slaves retained their mental independence and self-respect despite their bondage. They hated their oppression and, contrary to whites' stereotype of slaves as docile Sambos, were not grateful to their oppressors. They had to be subservient and speak honeyed words to their masters, but they talked quite differently among themselves. The evidence of their resistant attitudes comes from their actions and their own life stories.

Former slaves reported some warm feelings between masters and slaves, but the prevailing picture was one of antagonism and resistance. Slaves mistrusted kindness from whites and saw the self-interest in it.

Slaves' Attitudes Toward Whites

One woman called her mistress "a mighty good somebody to belong to" but explained that the woman was kind "'cause she was raisin' us to work for her." A man recalled that his owners took good care of their slaves, "and Grandma Maria say, 'Why shouldn't they—it was their money.'" Christmas presents of clothing from the master did not mean anything, observed another, "'cause he was going to [buy] that anyhow."

Slaves also saw their owners as people who used human beings as beasts of burden. One man observed that his master "fed us reg'lar on good, 'stantial food, just like you'd tend to your horse, if you had a real good one." Another recalled his master eyeing the slave children and saying, "'That one will be worth a thousand dollars.' . . . You see, it was just like raisin' young mules."

Slaves were alert to the thousand daily signs of their degraded status. One man recalled the general rule that slaves ate cornbread and owners ate biscuits. If blacks did get biscuits, "the flour that we made the biscuits out of was the third-grade shorts." A former slave recalled, "Us catch lots of 'possums," but "the white folks ate 'em. Our mouths would water for some of that 'possum, but it wasn't often they let us have none." If the owner took his slaves' garden produce to town and sold it for them, the slaves suspected him of pocketing part of the profits.

Suspicion and resentment often grew into hatred. According to a former slave from Virginia, white people treated blacks "so mean that all the slaves prayed God to punish their cruel masters." When a yellow-fever epidemic struck in 1852, many slaves saw it as God's retribution. As late as the 1930s an elderly ex-slave named Minnie Fulkes cherished the conviction that God was going to punish white people for their cruelty to blacks. She described the whippings that her mother had had to endure, and then she exclaimed, "Lord, Lord, I hate white people and the flood waters goin' to drown some more."

On the plantation, of course, slaves had to keep such thoughts to themselves. Often they expressed one feeling to whites, another within their own race and culture.

 ## Slave Culture and Everyday Life

The resource that enabled slaves to maintain such defiance was their culture: a body of beliefs and values born of their past and their present and of fellowship in their own community. It was not possible for slaves to change their world, but by drawing strength from their culture they could resist their condition and struggle on against it.

Slave culture changed significantly after the turn of the century. For a few years South Carolina reopened the international slave trade. After 1808, however, when Congress banned further importations, the proportion of native-born blacks rose steadily, reaching 96 percent in 1840 and almost 100 percent in 1860 (see figure, page 303). (For this reason many blacks can trace their American ancestry back farther than many white Americans can.) Meanwhile, more and more slaves adopted Christianity as African culture gave way to a maturing African-American culture.

African influences remained strong, for African practices and beliefs reminded slaves that they were and ought to be different from their oppressors. The

Influence of African Culture

most visible features of African culture were slaves' appearance and forms of recreation. Some slave men plaited their hair into rows and fancy designs; slave

women often wore their hair "in string"—tied in small bunches secured by a string or piece of cloth. A few men and many women wrapped their heads in kerchiefs of the styles and colors of West Africa.

For entertainment slaves made musical instruments with carved motifs that resembled African stringed instruments. Their drumming and dancing clearly followed African patterns; whites marveled at them. One visitor to Georgia in the 1860s described a ritual dance of African origin: "A ring of singers is formed. . . . They then utter a kind of melodious chant, which gradually increases in strength, and in noise, until it fairly shakes the house, and it can be heard for a long distance." This observer also noted the agility of the dancers and the African call-and-response pattern in their chanting.

Many slaves continued to see and believe in spirits. Whites, too, believed in ghosts, but the slaves' belief resembled the African concept of the living dead—the idea that deceased relatives visit the earth for many years until the process of dying is complete. Slaves also practiced conjuration, voodoo, and quasi-magical root medicine. By 1860 the most notable conjurers and root doctors were reputed to live in South Carolina, Georgia, Louisiana, and other isolated coastal areas of heavy slave importation.

These cultural survivals provided slaves with a sense of their separate past. Black achievement in music and dance was so exceptional that some whites became aware that the slave community was a different world and that they did not "know" their slaves. Conjuration and folklore also directly fed resistance; slaves could cast a spell or direct the power of a hand (a bag of articles belonging to the person to be conjured) against the master. Not all masters felt confident enough to dismiss such a threat.

Slaves fashioned Christianity into an instrument of support and resistance. Theirs was a religion of justice, quite unlike the religious propaganda their masters pushed at them.

Slaves' Religion

"You ought to have heard that preachin'," said one man. "'Obey your master and mistress, don't steal chickens and eggs and meat,' but nary a word about havin' a soul to save." Slaves believed that Jesus cared about their souls and their plight. They rejected the idea that in heaven whites would have "the colored folks . . . there to wait on 'em." Instead, slaveholders would be "broilin' in hell for their sin" when God's justice came.

For slaves, Christianity was a religion of personal and group salvation. Devout men and women worshiped and prayed every day, "in the field or by the side of the road," or in special "prayer grounds" such as a "twisted thick-rooted muscadine bush" that afforded privacy. Beyond seeking personal guidance, slaves prayed for deliverance. Some held fervent secret prayer meetings that lasted far into the night. Many slaves nurtured an unshakable belief that God would end their bondage. "It was the plans of God to free us," one man asserted. This faith—and the joy and emotional release that accompanied worship—sustained blacks.

Enslaved African-Americans also developed a sense of racial identity. Their experience taught them that whites despised their race. As one ex-slave put it, white people "have been and are now and always will be against the Negro." Even "the best white woman that ever broke bread wasn't much," said another, "'cause they all hated [us]." Blacks naturally drew together, helping each other in danger, need, and resistance. "We never told on each other," one woman declared. Although some slaves did betray others, former slaves were virtually unanimous in denouncing those who were disloyal to the group or sought personal gain through allegiance to whites.

Of course, different jobs, talents, and circumstances created variations in status among slaves. But most slaves did not encounter a class system within the black community. Only one-quarter of all slaves lived on plantations of fifty or more blacks, so few sensed a wide chasm separating house servants and lowly field hands. Many slaves did both housework and fieldwork, depending on their age and the season, and this arrangement helped create unity rather than division.

The main source of support for individuals was the family. Slave families faced severe dangers. At any moment the master could sell a husband or wife, give a slave child away as a wedding present, or die in debt, forcing a division of his property. Many families were broken up in such ways. Others were separated in the trans-Appalachian expansion of the South, which caused the forced migration and sale of Eliza and her children and hundreds of thousands of other slaves. When the Union Army registered thousands of black marriages in Mississippi and Louisiana in 1864 and 1865, fully 25 percent of the men over forty reported that they had been forcibly separated from a previous wife. A similar proportion of former slaves later recalled that slavery had destroyed one of their marriages.

Slaves' Family Life

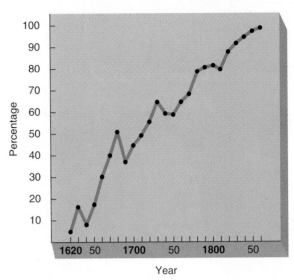

Percentage of African-Americans Born in the Colonies or the United States

Percentage of African-Americans Born in the Colonies or the United States   The North American slave population increased through natural reproduction. That fact, plus Congress's closing of the international slave trade in 1808, ensured that by 1860 virtually all African-Americans had been born in the United States.

But this did not mean that slave families could not exist. American slaves clung tenaciously to the personal relationships that gave meaning to life. Although American law did not protect slave families, masters permitted them; in fact, slaveowners expected slaves to form families and have children. As a result, even along the rapidly expanding edge of the cotton kingdom, where the effects of the slave trade would have been most visible, there was a normal ratio of men to women, young to old.

Following African kinship taboos, African-Americans avoided marriage between cousins (commonplace among aristocratic slaveowners). Adapting the West African custom of polygyny to American circumstances, they did not condemn unwed mothers but did expect a young woman to enter a monogamous relationship after one pregnancy, if not before. By naming their children after relatives of past generations, African-Americans emphasized their family histories. If they chose to bear the surname of a slaveowner, it was often the name not of their current master but of the owner under whom their family had begun in America.

Slaves hated interference in their family lives. Some of their strongest protests sought to prevent

This photograph of five generations of a slave family, taken in Beaufort, South Carolina, in 1862, is silent but powerful testimony to the importance that enslaved African-Americans placed on their ever-threatened family ties.   Library of Congress.

the breakup of a family. Indeed, some individuals refused to accept such separations and struggled for years to maintain or reestablish contact. Rape was a horror for both men and women. Some husbands faced death rather than permit their wives to be sexually abused, and the women sometimes fought back. In other cases slaves seethed with anger at the injustice but could do nothing except soothe each other and condemn the guilty party.

Slave men and women followed gender roles familiar to whites and similar to West African customs. After work in the fields was done, men's

Gender Roles in Slavery

activities focused on "outdoor" tasks and women did "indoor" work. Men hunted and fished for the family stewpot, made furniture, and repaired implements; women cooked, mended, and cleaned house. Slave families resembled white families in that African-American men held a respected

place in their homes. Since slave marriages were not legal, husbands did not have legal power over their wives and did not dominate them in a manner similar to that of free husbands. It would be misleading, however, to say that slave women enjoyed equality in gender roles and family life. Under the pressures of bondage men and women had to share parental and household responsibilities. At any time, each might have to stand in for the other and assume extra duties. Similarly, uncles, aunts, and grandparents sometimes raised the children of those who had been sold away.

Work routines frequently promoted among slave women close associations that heightened their sense of sisterhood. On plantations young girls worked together as house servants. Nursing mothers got together to feed and care for their children, and adults worked together at tasks like soap making and stitching quilts like the one shown on page 305, prepared for the annual visit of a Texas bishop. Old women gathered to spin thread or supervise a nursery. Female slaves thus spent significant portions of their lives as participants in a group of women, an experience that strengthened their ties to each other.

Slave marriage ceremonies were usually brief, often involving jumping over a broomstick in the master's presence. But partners "stuck lots closer then," in one woman's words. "[When] they marries they stay married," said another. When husbands and wives lived on neighboring plantations, visits on Wednesday and Saturday nights included big dinners of welcome and celebration. Christmas was a similarly joyous time "'cause husbands is coming home and families is getting united again."

Slaves brought to their efforts at resistance the same common sense, determination, and practicality that characterized their family lives. American slavery produced some fearless and implacable revolutionaries. Gabriel's conspiracy apparently was known to more than a thousand slaves when it was discovered in 1800, just before it was put into action (see pages 221–222). A similar conspiracy in Charleston in 1822, led by a free black named Denmark Vesey, involved many of the prominent whites' most trusted slaves. And the most famous rebel of all, Nat Turner, rose in violence in Southampton County, Virginia, in 1831.

Resistance to Slavery

The son of an African woman who passionately hated her enslavement, Nat Turner was a precocious child who learned to read when he was very young. Encouraged by his first owner to study the Bible, he enjoyed certain privileges but also endured hard work and changes of masters. His father, who successfully escaped to freedom, inspired him as an example of defiance. Eventually young Nat became a preacher with a reputation for eloquence among whites as well as blacks. He also developed a tendency toward mysticism and became increasingly withdrawn. After nurturing his plan for several years, Turner led a band of rebels from farm to farm in the predawn

Nat Turner Rebellion

In addition to the heavy labor required on southern plantations, slaves also performed work of fine craftsmanship in furniture making, needlework, and other areas. This dining-room corner cupboard is walnut veneer on pine and cedar and was built around 1840. The quilt, emblazoned with chalice cups to celebrate the annual visit of an Anglican bishop, was made around 1860. Both are from Texas. Cupboard: Courtesy of the Witte Museum and the San Antonio Museum Association, San Antonio, Texas. Quilt: The American Museum in Britain, photo courtesy of The Museum of the Confederacy.

darkness of August 22, 1831. The group severed limbs and crushed skulls with axes or killed their victims with guns. Before alarmed planters stopped them, Nat Turner and his followers had slaughtered sixty whites of both sexes and all ages. The rebellion was soon put down, and in retaliation, whites killed slaves at random all over the country. Turner was eventually caught and then hanged. As many as two hundred African-Americans, including innocent victims of marauding whites, lost their lives as a result of the rebellion.

Most slave resistance, however, was not violent, for the odds against revolution were especially poor in North America, compared to South America and the Caribbean islands, where some successful revolts did occur. Among slaveholding societies, the South had the highest ratio of whites to blacks in the hemisphere and, because most plantations were small, whites could thoroughly supervise the slaves' activities. There was thus literal truth to one slave's remark that "the white man was the slave's jail." In addition, the South lacked the geographic and demographic features of South America and the Caribbean that made revolt more possible. The South offered no jungles and few mountain fastnesses to which rebels could flee. Furthermore, compared with slave importations in South America, southern slave importations were neither large nor prolonged. The South therefore lacked a preponderance of young male slaves who might be more likely and able to rebel. Nor were its military forces weak and overtaxed like those of many Latin American nations and colonies. In the South, slave patrols and militias were always ready to suppress rebellion, and federal troops were also available under the Constitution.

The scales weighed heavily against revolution, and the slaves knew it. Consequently they directed their energies toward creating the means of survival and resistance within slavery. Many individual slaves attempted to run away to the North, and some received assistance from a loose network of sympathetic citizens, known collectively as the Underground Railroad. But it was more common for slaves to run off temporarily to hide in the woods. There they were close to friends and allies who could help them escape capture in an area they knew well. Every day that a slave "lay out" in this way, the master lost a day's labor. Most owners chose not to mount an exhaustive search and instead sent word that the slave's grievances would be redressed. The

runaway would then return to bargain with the master, who often was glad to have his property back.

Other modes of resistance had the same object: to resist but survive under bondage. Appropriating food (stealing, in the master's eyes) was so common that even whites sang humorous songs about it. Blacks also learned to ingratiate themselves and play off one white person against another. Field hands frequently tested a new overseer to intimidate him or win more favorable working conditions. Some blacks fought with patrollers, and others argued with overseers and even resorted to physical violence to deter or resist beatings.

 ## Harmony and Tension in a Slave Society

As the 1800s advanced, slavery impinged on laws and customs, individual values, and—increasingly—every aspect of southern politics. Legal restrictions on slaves, in effect since the seventeenth century, steadily increased. In all things, from their workaday movements to Sunday worship, slaves fell under the supervision of whites. State courts held that a slave "has no civil right" and could not even hold property "except at the will and pleasure of his master." In response to revolts, legislators tightened the legal straitjacket: after the Nat Turner insurrection of 1831, for example, they prohibited owners from teaching their slaves to read. As political conflicts between North and South deepened, fears of slave revolt grew, and restrictions on slaves increased accordingly.

State and federal laws aided the capture of fugitive slaves and required nonslaveholders to support the slave system. All white male citizens had a legal duty to ride in patrols to discourage slave movements at night. Ship captains, harbor masters, and other whites in strategic positions were required to scrutinize the papers of African-Americans who might be attempting to escape bondage. Urban residents who did not supervise their domestic slaves as closely as planters did were subject to criticism for endangering the community. And the South's few manufacturers, instead of receiving encouragement to expand their enterprises, often felt pressure to substitute slave for free labor.

Slavery had a deep effect on southern values precisely because it was the main determinant of wealth in the South. Ownership of slaves guaranteed

Slavery as the Basis of Wealth and Social Standing

the labor to produce cotton and other crops on a large scale—labor otherwise unavailable in rural society. Slaves were therefore vital to the acquisition of a fortune. Beyond that, they were a commodity and an investment, much like gold; people bought them on speculation, hoping for a steady rise in their value. In fact, throughout southern society, slaveholding indicated overall wealth with remarkable precision. Variations in wealth from county to county corresponded very closely to variations in slaveholding; important economic enterprises not based on slavery were too rare to have an effect on the pattern.

Wealth in slaves also translated into political power: a solid majority of political officeholders were slaveholders, and the most powerful were usually large-scale slaveholders. Lawyers and newspaper editors were sometimes influential, but they did not hold independent positions in the economy or society. Dependent on planters for business and support, they served planters' interests and reflected their outlook.

Slavery's influence spread throughout the social system until even the values and mores of nonslaveholders bore its imprint. The availability of slave labor tended to devalue free labor: where strenuous work under another's supervision was reserved for an enslaved race, few free people relished working like a slave. Nonslaveholders preferred to work for themselves, and those who had to sell their labor tended to resent or reject tasks that seemed degrading. This kind of thinking engendered an aristocratic value system ill suited to a newly established democracy.

The values of the aristocrat—lineage, privilege, pride, and refinement of person and manner—gained considerable respect among the masses. Many

Aristocratic Values and Frontier Individualism

of those qualities were in short supply, however, in the recently settled portions of the cotton kingdom, where frontier values of courage and self-reliance modified the aristocratic ideal. Thus independence and defense of one's honor became highly valued traits for planter and frontier farmer alike.

Fights and even duels over personal slights were not uncommon in southern communities. Instead of gradually disappearing as it did in the North,

A bill of sale documents that this slave woman, Louisa, was owned by the young child whom she holds on her lap. In the future Louisa's life would be subject to his wishes and decisions. Missouri Historical Society.

the *code duello*, which required men to defend their honor through violence, hung on in the South and gained acceptance throughout the society. In North Carolina in 1851 a wealthy planter named Samuel Fleming responded to a series of disputes with the lawyer William Waightstill Avery by "cowhiding" (whipping) him on a public street. According to the code, Avery had two choices: to redeem his honor violently or to brand himself a coward through inaction. Three weeks later Avery shot Fleming dead at point-blank range during a session of Burke County Superior Court, with Judge William Battle and numerous spectators looking on. A jury later took only ten minutes to find Avery not guilty, and the spectators gave him a standing ovation. Though some, including Judge Battle, were troubled by this outcome, most white males seemed satisfied.

Other aristocratic values of the planter class were less acceptable to the average voter. Planters believed they were better than other people. In their pride, they expected not only to wield power but to receive special treatment. By the 1850s, some planters openly rejected the democratic creed, vilifying Thomas Jefferson for his statement that all men were equal.

Such beliefs were never acceptable to the individualistic members of the yeoman class. Independent and proud, yeomen resisted any infringement of their rights. They believed they were as good as anyone, and many belonged to evangelical faiths that exalted values of simplicity and otherworldliness that were alien to the planters' love of wealth. They were conscious, too, that they lived in a nation in which democratic ideals were gaining strength. Thus occasional conflicts erupted between aristocratic pretensions and democratic zeal. Mary Boykin Chesnut described a South Carolina aristocrat who refused to make the necessary gestures of respect toward the average voter—mingling with the crowd, exchanging jokes and compliments. Such haughtiness doomed this man's hopes for political leadership. The voters would not accept him.

Class tensions emerged in the western parts of the seaboard states during the 1820s and 1830s. There yeoman farmers and other citizens resented their underrepresentation in state legislatures, the corruption in government, and the undemocratic control over local government. After vigorous debate, the reformers won most of their battles. Voters in more recently settled areas—Alabama, Mississippi, Tennessee, Arkansas, and Texas—adopted white manhood suffrage and other electoral reforms, including popular election of governors, legislative apportionment based on white population only, and locally chosen county government. Kentucky enacted all these measures except for elected county governments. Georgia, Florida, and Louisiana were not far behind, and reformers won significant concessions in Maryland and made some headway in North Carolina. Only South Carolina and Virginia effectively defended property qualifications for office, legislative malapportionment, appointment of county officials, and selection of the governor by lawmakers. The formal structure of government thus became more democratic than many planters wished.

Movements for Electoral Reform

Slaveowners knew that a more open government structure could permit troubling issues to arise. In Virginia, nonslaveholding westerners raised a basic challenge to the slave system in 1832, a year after the Nat Turner Rebellion. Advocates of gradual abolition forced a two-week legislative debate on slavery, arguing that it was injurious to the state and inherently dangerous. When the House of Delegates finally voted, the motion favoring abolition lost by just 73 to 58. This was the last public debate on slavery in the antebellum South.

Given such tensions, it was perhaps remarkable that slaveholders and nonslaveholders did not experience more overt conflict. Why were class confrontations among whites so infrequent? Historians have given several answers. One of the most important factors was race. The South's racial ideology stressed the superiority of all whites to blacks. Thus slavery became the basis of equality among whites, and racism inflated the status of poor whites and gave them a common interest with the rich. Moreover, family ties linked some nonslaveholders to wealthy planters. The experience of frontier living, in which all were starting out together, also created a relatively informal, egalitarian atmosphere.

Relations Between the Classes

The cotton boom itself relieved tension by bringing opportunity to thousands of whites. The "Old South" was a new and mobile society in which many people rose in status by acquiring land or slaves and far more moved about geographically. Even in cotton-rich Alabama in the 1850s, fewer than half of the richest families in a typical county belonged to its elite ten years later. Most did not die or lose their wealth; they merely moved on to some new state. This constant mobility meant that southern society did not settle into a rigid, unchanging pattern.

Most importantly, in their daily lives yeomen and slaveholders were seldom in conflict. Before the Civil War most yeomen were able to pursue unhindered their independent lifestyle. Marginally involved in the market economy, they worked their farms, avoided debt, and marked progress for their families that was unrelated to slaveholding. More over, yeomen lived in a rural and uncrowded region: travel was difficult, and daily life usually took place within the family unit. Consequently, they lived their lives with little reference to, or interference from, slaveholders. As long as they could follow their values and aspirations, yeomen had no grievance.

Likewise, slaveholders pursued their goals quite independently of yeomen. Planters farmed for the market but also for themselves. The complementary growing patterns of corn and cotton allowed them to raise food for their animals and laborers without reducing cotton production: from spring to December slaves could work first in the cotton fields, then move to fields of corn, and cultivate both. Thus the planter did not depend on the nonslaveholder as a producer of food crops. In politics, too, national economic issues, such as the tariff, that affected planters rarely had much meaning to yeomen because they were not enmeshed in the market economy.

Suppression of dissent also played a significant and increasing role. After 1830 white southerners who criticized the slave system out of moral conviction or class resentment were intimidated, attacked, or legally prosecuted. (Some, like James Birney, went north and joined the antislavery movement. Two sisters from Charleston, Angelina and Sarah Grimké, became leading advocates of both abolition and women's rights—see page 357.) Southern cities impounded abolitionist literature and sought to bar antislavery influences. Intellectuals developed elaborate justifications for slavery as newspapers railed at northern antislavery agitation. By the 1850s the defense of slavery's interests dominated public discussion, and politicians vied with each other in an aggressive defense of the South's peculiar institution. The slavery issue exerted an ever-more-powerful influence on southern politics and society.

Still, there were signs that the relative lack of conflict between slaveholders and nonslaveholders was coming to an end. As cotton lands filled up, nonslaveholders saw their opportunities beginning to narrow; meanwhile, wealthy planters enjoyed expanding profits. The risks of entering cotton production were becoming too great and the cost of slaves too high for many yeomen to rise in society. From 1830 to 1860 the percentage of white southern families holding slaves declined steadily from 36 to 25 percent. At the same time, the monetary gap be-

Hardening of Class Lines

tween the classes was widening. Although nonslaveholders were becoming more prosperous, slaveowners' wealth was increasing much faster. And although slaveowners accounted for a smaller portion of the population in 1860 than in 1830, their share of the South's agricultural wealth remained at between 90 and 95 percent. In fact, the average slaveholder was almost fourteen times as rich as the average nonslaveholder.

Urban artisans and mechanics felt the pinch acutely. Their numbers were few, their place in society was hardly recognized, and in bad times they were often the first to lose work. Moreover, they faced stiff competition from urban slaves, whose masters wanted to hire them out to practice trades. White workers in Charleston, Wilmington, and elsewhere staged protests demanding that economic competition from slaves be forbidden, but they were ignored. The powerful slaveowners would not tolerate interference with their property and their income. The angry protests of white workers, however, resulted in harsh restrictions on *free* African-American workers and craftsmen, who had no powerful allies to defend their interests. On the eve of the Civil War, many successful free blacks actually felt compelled to leave Charleston for fear of being reenslaved.

Pre–Civil War politics reflected these tensions. Anticipating the prospect of a war to defend slavery, slaveowners expressed growing fear about the loyalty of nonslaveholders. Schemes to widen the ownership of slaves were discussed, including reopening the African slave trade. In North Carolina, a prolonged and increasingly bitter controversy over the combination of high taxes on land and low taxes on slaves erupted, and a class-conscious nonslaveholder named Hinton R. Helper denounced the slave system. Convinced that slavery had impoverished many whites and retarded the whole region, Helper attacked the institution in *The Impending Crisis*, published in New York in 1857. Discerning planters knew that such fiery controversies could easily erupt in every southern state.

But for the moment slaveowners stood secure. They occupied from 50 to 85 percent of the seats in state legislatures and a similarly high percentage of the South's congressional seats. In addition to their near monopoly on political office, they had established their point of view in all the other major social institutions. Professors who criticized slavery had been dismissed from colleges and universities;

schoolbooks that contained "unsound" ideas had been replaced. And almost all the Methodist and Baptist clergy, some of whom had criticized slavery in the 1790s, had given up preaching against it. In fact, except for a few obscure persons of conscience, southern clergy had become slavery's most vocal defenders.

 Conclusion

The South of the early to mid-1800s was a diverse society that embraced a variety of elements and differing viewpoints, but the coercive influence of slavery was increasingly pressing the region into a single mold. The reality of the South's rapid growth and mobility contrasted with its increasing ideological emphasis on conservatism and stability. The values of democratic yeomen and aristocratic planters clashed, despite the rhetoric of white supremacy. Simmering resentments generated by slavery's oppression gave the lie to the benevolent image of bondage put forth in paternalist ideology. Yet leading southerners ignored evidence of diversity, preferring to submerge these contradictions in visions of a stable, slaveholding social order.

Slavery's extent and influence in the South grew markedly after 1800. Powerful groups dependent on slavery worked tirelessly to promote unity and eradicate dissent. The potential for conflict persisted, but few southerners saw it. As the influence of the peculiar institution spread through the region, the evolving South took on the aspect of a conservative and traditional society wedded to slavery. The social order as southerners knew it seemed to be stable, with threats to the status quo under control.

Outside the South, however, society was anything but stable. Market forces and the rise of industry were producing an increasingly diverse population in the North. Social and economic changes were transforming the North, and the currents of change eventually would affect the South as well.

Suggestions for Further Reading

Southern Society

Edward L. Ayers, *Vengeance and Justice* (1984); Bradley G. Bond, *Political Culture in the Nineteenth-Century South* (1995); William J. Cooper, *The South and the Politics of Slavery, 1828–1856* (1978); Clement Eaton, *The Growth of Southern Civilization, 1790–1860* (1961); Clement Eaton, *Freedom of Thought in the Old South* (1940); William W. Freehling, *Prelude to Civil War* (1965); Eugene D. Genovese, *The Political Economy of Slavery* (1965); Peter Kolchin, *Unfree Labor: American Slavery and Russian Serfdom* (1987); Donald G. Mathews, *Religion in the Old South* (1977); Robert McColley, *Slavery and Jeffersonian Virginia* (1964); James Hebron Moore, *The Emergence of the Cotton Kingdom in the Old Southwest: Mississippi, 1770–1860* (1987); Frederick Law Olmsted, *The Slave States*, ed. Harvey Wish (1959); Charles S. Sydnor, *The Development of Southern Sectionalism, 1819–1848* (1948); Larry E. Tise, *Proslavery* (1987); Ralph A. Wooster, *Politicians, Planters, and Plain Folk* (1975); Ralph A. Wooster, *The People in Power* (1969); Gavin Wright, *The Political Economy of the Cotton South* (1978); Bertram Wyatt-Brown, *Southern Honor* (1982).

Slaveholders and Nonslaveholders

Edward L. Ayers and John C. Willis, eds., *The Edge of the South* (1991); Bennet H. Barrow, *Plantation Life in the Florida Parishes of Louisiana, as Reflected in the Diary of Bennet H. Barrow*, ed. Edwin Adams Davis (1943); Ira Berlin, *Slaves Without Masters* (1974); Joan E. Cashin, *A Family Venture* (1991); Bill Cecil-Fronsman, *The Common Whites* (1992); Charles B. Dew, *Bond of Iron* (1995); Everett Dick, *The Dixie Frontier* (1948); Clement Eaton, *The Mind of the Old South* (1967); Paul D. Escott, ed., *North Carolina Yeoman* (1996); Drew Faust, *James Henry Hammond and the Old South* (1982); Drew Faust, *A Sacred Circle: The Dilemma of the Intellectual in the Old South* (1977); John Hope Franklin, *The Militant South, 1800–1861* (1956); John Inscoe, *Mountain Masters* (1989); Michael P. Johnson and James L. Roark, *Black Masters* (1984); Robert E. May, *John A. Quitman* (1985); Stephanie McCurry, *Masters of Small Worlds* (1995); Robert Manson Myers, ed., *The Children of Pride* (1972); James Oakes, *The Ruling Race* (1982); Frank L. Owsley, *Plain Folk of the Old South* (1949); Loren Schweninger, *Black Property Owners in the South, 1790–1915* (1990); J. Mills Thornton III, *Politics and Power in a Slave Society: Alabama, 1800–1860* (1978).

Southern Women

Carol Bleser, *In Joy and in Sorrow* (1990); Carol Bleser, ed., *Tokens of Affection* (1995); Victoria Bynum, *Unruly Women* (1992); Jane Turner Censer, *North Carolina Planters and Their Children, 1800–1860* (1984); Catherine Clinton, *The Plantation Mistress* (1982); Elizabeth Fox-Genovese, *Within the Plantation Household* (1988); Jean E. Friedman, *The Enclosed Garden* (1985); Harriet Jacobs, *Incidents in the Life of a Slave Girl*, ed. Jean Fagan Yellin (1987); Jacqueline Jones, *Labor of Love, Labor of Sorrow* (1985); Frances Anne Kemble, *Journal of a Residence on a Georgia Plantation in 1838–1839* (1863); Suzanne Lebsock, *Free Women of Petersburg* (1984); Sally McMillen, *Motherhood in the Old South* (1990); Patricia Morton, ed., *Discovering the Women in Slavery* (1995); Elisabeth Muhlenfeld, *Mary Boykin Chesnut* (1981); Mary D. Robertson, ed., *Lucy Breckinridge of Grove Hill* (1979); Ann Firor Scott, *The Southern Lady* (1970); Deborah G. White, *Ar'n't I a Woman?* (1985); Virginia Ingraham Burr, ed., *The Secret Eye* (1990).

Conditions of Slavery

Kenneth F. Kiple and Virginia H. Kiple, "Black Tongue and Black Men," *Journal of Southern History* 43 (August 1977): 411–428; Peter Kolcin, *American Slavery, 1619–1877* (1993); Ronald L.

Lewis, *Coal, Iron, and Slaves* (1979); Richard G. Lowe and Randolph B. Campbell, "The Slave Breeding Hypothesis," *Journal of Southern History* 42 (August 1976): 400–412; Willie Lee Rose, ed., *A Documentary History of Slavery in North America* (1976); Todd L. Savitt, *Medicine and Slavery* (1978); Kenneth M. Stampp, *The Peculiar Institution* (1956); Robert S. Starobin, *Industrial Slavery in the Old South* (1970); Michael Tadman, *Speculators and Slaves* (1989).

Slave Culture and Resistance

Herbert Aptheker, *American Negro Slave Revolts* (1943); John W. Blassingame, *The Slave Community* (1979); Judith Wragg Chase, *Afro-American Art and Craft* (1971); Douglas Egerton, *Gabriel's Rebellion* (1993); Dena J. Epstein, *Sinful Tunes and Spirituals* (1977); Paul D. Escott, *Slavery Remembered: A Record of Twentieth-Century Slave Narratives* (1979); Eric Foner, ed., *Nat Turner* (1971); Eugene D. Genovese, *From Rebellion to Revolution* (1979); Eugene D. Genovese, *Roll, Jordan, Roll* (1974); Herbert G. Gutman, *The Black Family in Slavery and Freedom, 1750–1925* (1976); Vincent Harding, *There Is a River* (1981); Charles Joyner, *Down by the Riverside* (1984); Lawrence W. Levine, *Black Culture and Black Consciousness* (1977); Stephen B. Oates, *The Fires of Jubilee* (1975); Albert J. Raboteau, *Slave Religion* (1978); Robert S. Starobin, *Denmark Vesey* (1970); Sterling Stuckey, *Slave Culture* (1987).

CHAPTER

12

The American Social Landscape

1800–1860

I hope that things will get better," Anna Maria Klinger wrote from New York to her family in Württemberg, Germany, in March 1849. "For it's always like that, no one really likes it at first, and especially if you are so lonely and forlorn in a foreign land like I am, no friends or relatives around." Twenty-eight-year-old Anna Maria had crossed the Atlantic among strangers. Her religious faith kept her going. "The dear Lord is my shield and refuge," she wrote home.

It had taken 105 days to reach America, including seven weeks docked in Plymouth, England, while the ship was fitted. Three other young women migrants to America proved unsuitable as traveling companions. They "started behaving so badly" with young men, Anna Maria wrote her parents, that "I got annoyed because I couldn't stand such loose behavior."

Her luck improved in New York. She quickly found a job at $4 a month as a domestic servant with a German family. New York was so large, she wrote her parents, that she could not walk around it in one day. She counted nearly two hundred churches and reported that there were "about 4,000 German residents alone." There were actually fifty-six thousand Germans in the city at the time.

Anna Maria Klinger had left Germany during the political and economic crises of 1848. She was the first in her immediate family to emigrate, though two cousins had come to America some years before. Soon after arriving in New York, she met her future husband, Franz Schano, a deserter from the Bavarian army. Over the next decade she and Schano brought five of her siblings to New York: Babett, Gottlieb, Katharina, Daniel, and finally in 1858 the youngest, Rosina.

Moving Day in Philadelphia (c. 1850) commonly was May Day. On that day, literally, the life of the city was in the streets. The density, competition, and even violence of urban life was becoming common to Americans.
Courtesy of Mr. and Mrs. Screvan Lorillard.

313

Finding work could be difficult—Franz, a stone-cutter, was unemployed for a time—but teenagers like Babett and Katharina could always get jobs as servants. Babett, who now called herself Barbara, came in 1852 and adjusted quickly. "Here you don't go out of the house without a hat or a bonnet," she wrote her parents, "you don't go out on the *Striet* [street] with your head bare, they all look at you and you'd be laughed at. If I were to run into you, none of you would recognize me with my hat on." Barbara was a servant, first for an English family then for a French family, and quickly repaid her sister for her fare to America.

Within a year of Barbara's arrival, Franz wrote home that she had taken up with a young man whom "we could see from the start would not be to her advantage." They "tried everything to dissuade her, but to no use." She soon gave birth to a baby son, "for whom she has a father all right but no husband, and when we noticed that she was expecting, we urged him to marry her but then he said he had never promised to marry her and he wouldn't ever marry her." He did provide a cash settlement of $80 to Barbara.

Anna Maria, assisted by Franz, guided the family, keeping them together by sheer force of will. But the siblings' lives eventually diverged. In 1855 Anna Maria and Franz moved to Albany, New York, where Franz opened his own business and they bought a house for $1,000.

When the Schanos moved to Albany, Barbara went west, leaving her son with Anna Maria and Franz. Within a year she wrote that she was in Indiana, married and living in a log cabin on forty acres of land. She wanted her son at first but said that the distance between Albany and Indiana prevented her from fetching him. She complained that living in rural Indiana was boring. In 1861 she finally got her son from Anna Maria. In the 1860s, a widow, she remarried and raised seven "Christian children" on her Indiana farm.

In 1860 Franz Schano died of consumption. Thirteen months later Anna Maria married Adam Plantz, a Prussian-born blacksmith; he too died of consumption, only five weeks after the wedding. Anna Maria now had a son, a nephew, and a stepson to support. She feared losing her home, but she had been left enough money to prosper. As Anna Maria became more preoccupied with providing for her son and stepson, her brother Gottlieb took over the role of head of the family.

Through Gottlieb, the Klinger siblings stayed in touch for most of their lives. Gottlieb and his brother, Daniel, settled in Albany near Anna Maria and rode the roller coaster of the economy, prospering in good times, unemployed in hard times. Gottlieb ran a saloon, lost it, then worked in a piano factory and later as a wood carver. Daniel worked as a teamster. Eventually, they lost touch with two of their sisters. After Katharina, a widow, married a prosperous New York grocer, they no longer heard from her. They also lost contact with Rosina, who had moved to Canada. Years later they heard she was living again in New York and had "a whole brood of children" with her tinsmith husband.

Despite jealousies and conflicts, the Klingers remained close, helped each other, and regularly sent money to their parents. They represented both the old values of traditional culture and the new values of the market system. Anna Maria worked hard, saved money, and found success in Albany even though widowhood twice threatened her security. Barbara lived a hard-scrabble life and was an unwed mother. She reestablished her life 700 miles from New York, eventually finding peace in a German-American rural community. Katharina worked hard but spent most of her income on herself, saving very little; her siblings complained of her selfishness. Even after years in the United States, the Klinger siblings were only partially Americanized. They always lived in German neighborhoods, and they socialized almost exclusively with family and fellow immigrants from Württemberg.

The Klinger family's experiences were similar to those of millions of other Americans. From the 1830s through the 1850s, millions of immigrants arrived on America's shores, and hundreds of thousands of native-born Americans moved from farm to town and from town to city. The American population grew so much—largely through natural increase in the first two decades of the century, then through immigration—that most Americans were newcomers in their neighborhoods and on the job. The populations of the largest cities numbered in the hundreds of thousands and were highly diverse ethnically, religiously, and racially. Within large cities and in the countryside, whole districts became enclaves of ethnic groups.

What it meant to be an American changed. The Revolution and early nation building diminished as sources of American identity. European immigrants, slaves, free people of color, and Native Americans

• *Important Events* •

1810	New York City surpasses Philadelphia in population	**1835**	Arkansas passes first women's property law
1821	Horse racing legalized in New York State	**1835–42**	Seminoles resist removal in Second Seminole War
1823	Catharine and Mary Beecher establish Hartford Female Seminary	**1837**	Boston employs paid policemen Ralph Waldo Emerson's *Nature* appears
1824	President Monroe proposes removal of Indians west of the Mississippi	**1837–48**	Horace Mann heads the Massachusetts Board of Education
1827	*Freedom's Journal*, first African-American newspaper, appears	**1841–47**	Brook Farm combines spirituality, work, and play in a utopian rural community
1830	Joseph Smith founds Mormon Church Congress passes Indian Removal Act	**1842**	Knickerbocker baseball club formed
1830s–50s	Urban riots commonplace	**1844**	Nativist riots peak in Philadelphia
1831	Cherokees turn to courts to defend treaty rights in *Cherokee Nation* v. *Georgia*	**1845**	Start of the Irish potato famine
		1846–47	Mormon trek to the Great Salt Lake
1831–32	Alexis de Tocqueville travels across America: his observations form the basis for *Democracy in America*	**1847–57**	Peak period of immigration before the Civil War
1831–38	Indian tribes resettled in the West	**1848**	Abortive revolutions in German states
1832	Chief Justice Marshall declares the Cherokee nation to be a distinct political community in *Worcester* v. *Georgia*, but the ruling is never enforced		

had cultural traditions different than those of the American colonial past. New cultural patterns flourished. Economic opportunity, the market economy, and expansionism energized Americans. In the nation's cities, opulent mansions rose within sight of notorious slums, and both wealth and poverty reached extremes unknown in agrarian America. As in the past, Americans sought community in their neighborhoods, not in the nation, but ethnic, racial, and religious differences were greater than ever before. Farm families attempted to maintain cohesive, rural villages while utopians and groups like the Mormons sought to create self-governing communal havens.

Family life was changing too. With the growth of commerce and industry, the home began to lose its function as a workplace and center of leisure. Cities took over some of the traditional family's educational role, and consumer items and leisure became commodities to be purchased. Families shrank in size, and more people lived outside family units.

Free people of color and Native Americans were at a particular disadvantage in a society that considered their very presence disturbing. Native Americans struggled to maintain their traditional lands but were forced to resettle beyond the Mississippi River. Free people of color fought against their second-class status. They founded the institutions and communities that would be the basis of modern African-American life.

Many Americans were uncomfortable with the new direction of American life. Antipathy toward immigrants was common among native-born Americans, who feared competition for jobs. Riots and violence became commonplace in cities. In a society growing ever more diverse and complex, conflict became common.

The United States remained a predominantly agricultural country, but economic and social traditions were yielding to the influence of the market economy, urban growth, and immigration. Although this change intensified in the final three decades of the century, an industrializing, urbanizing, and pluralist society was emerging before the Civil War.

 ## Country Life

Rural life changed significantly in the first half of the nineteenth century. Within a generation many western settlements became sources rather than destinations of migrants. The villages of western New York State had lured the sons and daughters of New England in the first two decades of the century; after the mid-1820s when the Erie Canal opened, New York sent its young people to new lands in the Midwest. Later, Ohio and Michigan towns and farms would watch their young people move farther west. Their counterparts in the Upper South went to Illinois and Ohio, and those farther south settled the Gulf states.

For all the romance of moving westward, many longed for a sense of community. In *Domestic Manners of the Americans* (1832) Frances Trollope, an English writer, described her visit to a farm family near Cincinnati. The family produced all their necessities except coffee, tea, and whiskey, which they acquired by sending butter and chickens to market. But until other settlers moved near them, they lacked the human contact that a community provides. For their inexpensive land and self-sufficiency they paid the price of isolation and loneliness. "'Tis strange to us to see company," observed the mother. "I expect the sun may rise and set a hundred times before I shall see another human that does not belong to the family."

Government policy fostered farm life. Farming was associated with virtue, productivity, and independence—essential values in the new republic. The acquisition of Louisiana in 1803 and later annexations of Florida, Texas, and Oregon all increased available agricultural land. The internal improvements—harbors, roads, canals, and railroads—following the War of 1812 were a boost to agriculture. Indian removal opened additional land for farmers, and the inexpensive sale of public lands facilitated new farm settlements. State governments promoted agricultural education through schools and county and state fairs.

The farm village, with its churches, post office, general store, and tavern, was the center of rural life—the farmers' link with religion, politics, and the

Farm Communities

outside world. But rural social life was not limited to trips to the village; families gathered on one another's farms to accomplish as a community what they could not manage individually. Barn-raisings regularly brought people together. A farmer and an itinerant carpenter prepared the site before the neighbors arrived by buggy and wagon to help on the appointed day. After the walls were put together and raised into position, they attached a roof. Then everyone celebrated with a communal meal and sang, danced, and played games. They might compete in foot races, wrestling, or marksmanship, and on occasion they raced horses. Similar gatherings took place at harvest time and on special occasions.

Men and women had active, social lives. Men met frequently at general stores, weekly markets, and taverns, and they hunted and fished together. Some women also attended market, especially those engaged in dairy farming. More typically they met at after-church dinners, prayer and Bible-study groups, sewing and corn-husking bees, and quilting parties. These were occasions to exchange experiences, thoughts, and spiritual support, and to swap letters, books, and news.

Irene Hardy, who grew up in rural southwestern Ohio in the 1840s, left a memoir of the gatherings she had attended as a girl. Fifty years later she recalled apple bees at which neighbors gathered to make apple butter or preserves. Typical of rural society, bees combined leisure and work activities. A dinner feast followed, Hardy recalled. After cleaning up, "the old folks went home to send their young ones for their share of work and fun." The elders gossiped; the youngsters joked and teased each other and flirted. "Then came supper, apple and pumpkin pies, cider, doughnuts, cakes, cold chicken and turkey," Hardy wrote, "after which games, 'Forfeits,' 'Building a Bridge,' 'Snatchability,' even 'Blind Man's Bluff' and 'Pussy Wants a Corner.'"

Traditional country bees had their town counterparts. Fredrika Bremer, a Swedish visitor to the United States, described a sewing bee in Cambridge, Massachusetts, in 1849, at which neighborhood women made clothes for "a family who had lost all their clothing by fire." Yet town bees were not the all-day family affairs of the countryside, and when the Hardy family moved to the town of Eaton, Ohio, Irene missed the country gatherings. Life was changing: the families of Eaton seldom held bees, and they purchased most of their goods at the store. They were wage earners and consumers, and the market economy shaped their daily lives. Many felt a loss of autonomy.

Americans were increasingly conscious of such changes. Some turned to rural utopian experiments in an effort to find an antidote to the market economy and the untamed growth of large urban communities and an opportunity to restore tradition and social cohesion. In the religious ferment of the Second Great Awakening (see pages 219–220), many people reacted favorably to new religious communities, whatever their philosophy. Utopian experiments offered to restore order and regularity to daily life and to provide a cooperative rather than competitive environment. Virtually all of the utopian experiments offered communal living and nontraditional work, family, and gender roles.

The Shakers, named for the way they danced at worship services, undertook one of the earliest utopian experiments. Founder Ann Lee imported

Shakers

this offshoot of the Quakers to America in 1774. While living in England, she had experienced a vision foretelling Jesus's second coming in America and urging her to go there. The Shakers believed that the end of the world was near and that sin entered the world through sexual intercourse. They considered existing churches too worldly and viewed the Shaker community as the instrument of salvation.

After the death of Mother Ann Lee in 1784, the Shakers turned to communal living to fulfill their mission. In 1787 they "gathered in" at New Lebanon, New York, to live and work communally. At its peak, between 1820 and 1860, the sect had recruited about six thousand members in twenty settlements in eight states; it was the largest and most permanent of the utopian experiments. Shaker communities emphasized agriculture and handcrafts; most managed to become self-sufficient and profitable enterprises. Shaker furniture became famous for its simplicity, excellent construction, and beauty of design.

Though economically conservative, the Shakers were social radicals. They abolished individual families; each colony was one large family. They also gave women new prospects for spiritual leadership. During its period of greatest growth, the Shaker ministry was headed by a woman, Lucy Wright. The sect's practice of celibacy, however, led inevitably to its demise. Because Shakers have been unable to perpetuate themselves naturally, only one Shaker colony remains in the late twentieth century.

The most successful communitarian group was the Church of Jesus Christ of Latter-day Saints, known as the Mormons. Joseph Smith, a young

Mormon Community of Saints

farmer in western New York, reported in 1827—a time of religious ferment in the Northeast—that he had been visited by the angel Moroni, who gave him a set of gold plates engraved with divine revelation. Smith published his revelations as the *Book of Mormon* and organized a church in western New York in 1830. Violence stalked the Mormons; angry mobs drove them from Ohio, Illinois, and Missouri. People objected most to the Mormon belief in continuous revelation and the practice of allowing men to have several wives at once. Finally in 1846 and 1847 the Mormons found a home in the Great Salt Lake valley. There, under Brigham Young, head of the Twelve Apostles (the Mormons' governing body), they established a patriarchal community of Saints based on communal republicanism. They achieved not only religious freedom but also political self-government.

Religious conviction fortified the Latter-day Saints to withstand persecution and economic hardship. The Mormon Church offered success and community in this world and salvation in the next to anyone who would join. Indeed, many recruits were poor and uneducated. The Mormons also held out a hand of fellowship to those who rejected existing churches. Mormonism offered religious certainty within a tight-knit society.

In Utah the Mormons distributed agricultural land according to family size. An extensive irrigation system, constructed by men who contributed their labor in proportion to the quantity of land they received and the amount of water they expected to use, transformed the arid valley into a rich oasis. As the colony developed, the church elders gained control of water, trade, industry, and even the territorial government of Utah.

Not all utopian communities were founded by religious sects. In 1825 Robert Owen, a wealthy Scottish industrialist, attempted to establish a socialist utopia in New Harmony, Indiana. According to his plan, its nine hundred members were to exchange their labor for goods at a communal store. Handicrafts (hat and boot making) flourished at New Harmony, but a textile mill—which was to have been the economic base of the community—failed after Owen gave it to the community to run. The turnover in membership at New Harmony was so great that the community never developed cohesion, and by 1827 Owen's experiment had ended.

The impact of the Brook Farm cooperative in West Roxbury, Massachusetts, was longer lasting, although its achievements were more artistic than economic. Inspired by transcen-

Brook Farm

dentalism—the belief that the physical world is secondary to the spiritual realm, which human beings can know by ignoring custom and experience and relying instead on intuition—Brook Farm's members rejected materialism in favor of rural communalism, combining spirituality, manual labor, intellectual life, and play. Founded in 1841 by the Unitarian minister George Ripley, a literary critic and friend of transcendentalist lecturer and essayist Ralph Waldo Emerson, Brook Farm attracted farmers, craftsmen, and writers, among them the novelist Nathaniel Hawthorne. Indeed, the fame of Brook Farm rested on the intellectual achievements of its members. Its school drew students from outside the community, and its residents contributed regularly to the *Dial*, the leading transcendentalist journal. In 1845 Brook Farm's hundred members organized themselves into model phalanxes (working-living units) in keeping with the philosophy of the French utopian Charles Fourier. Rigid regimentation replaced individualism, and membership dropped. After a disastrous fire in 1846, the experiment collapsed in 1847.

Though short-lived, Brook Farm played a significant role in the flowering of a national literature. During these years Hawthorne, Emerson, and Margaret Fuller, the *Dial*'s editor, joined Henry David Thoreau, James Fenimore Cooper, Herman Melville, and others in creating what is known today as the American Renaissance. In its philosophical intensity and moral idealism, their work was both distinctively American and an outgrowth of the European romantic movement. Their themes were universal, their settings and character American. Cooper, for instance, used the frontier as a backdrop, and Melville wrote of great spiritual quests as seafaring adventures.

The essayist Ralph Waldo Emerson was the prime mover of the American Renaissance and a pillar of the transcendental movement. Emerson had followed his father and grandfather into the ministry but quit his Boston Unitarian pulpit in 1831. After a two-year sojourn in Europe, he returned to lecture and write, preaching individualism and self-reliance. "We live in succession, in division, in parts, in particles," Emerson wrote. "We see the world piece by piece, as the sun, the moon, the animal, the tree; but the whole, of which these are the shining parts, is the soul." Intuitive experience of God is attainable, insisted Emerson, because "the Highest dwells" within every individual in the form of the "Over-soul." What gave Emerson's writings force was his simple, direct prose. In his first book, *Nature* (1836), and in "The American Scholar" (1837), a Phi Beta Kappa address at Harvard, Emerson explored human nature and American culture. Widely admired, he influenced Thoreau, Fuller, Hawthorne, and other members of Brook Farm.

Utopian communities can be seen as attempts to recapture the cohesiveness of traditional agricultural and artisan life in reaction to the competitive pressures of the market economy and urbanization. Utopians resembled Puritan perfectionists; like the Separatists of seventeenth-century New England (see page 50), they sought to begin anew in their own colonies.

 ## City Life

The transportation revolution and the expansion of commerce and manufacturing enabled the urban population to grow geometrically between 1800 and 1860, especially in the North. The nation's population increased during this period from 5 million to 31 million. Meanwhile, settlement spread westward, and small rural settlements became towns. In 1800 the nation had only 33 towns with 2,500 or more people and only 3 with more than 25,000. By 1860, 392 towns exceeded 2,500 residents, 35 had more than 25,000, and 9 exceeded 100,000 (see maps, page 319). In the Northeast, the percentage of people living in urban areas grew from 9 to 35 percent between 1800 and 1860.

Some cities became great metropolitan centers. By 1810, New York City passed Philadelphia as the nation's most populous city and major commercial center. By 1860, Baltimore and New Orleans dominated the South, and San Francisco was the leading West Coast city. In the Midwest, the new lake cities (Chicago, Detroit, and Cleveland) began to overtake the frontier river cities (Cincinnati, Louisville, and Pittsburgh) founded a generation earlier. The largest cities of the North belonged to a nationwide

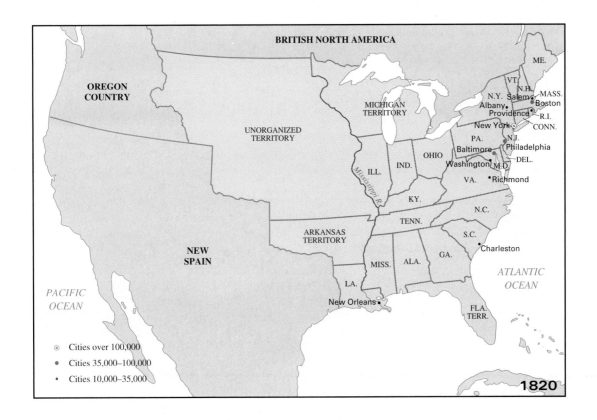

1820

Cities over 100,000
Cities 35,000–100,000
Cities 10,000–35,000

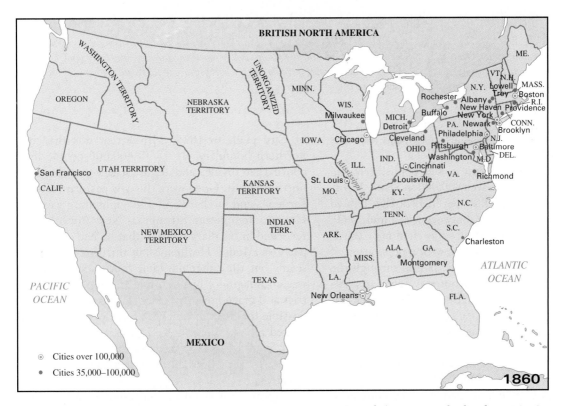

1860

Cities over 100,000
Cities 35,000–100,000

Major American Cities in 1820 and 1860   *The number of Americans who lived in cities increased rapidly between 1820 and 1860, and the number of large cities grew as well. In 1820, only New York had a population exceeding one hundred thousand; forty years later, eight more cities had surpassed that level.*

The Lackawanna Valley *(1855) by George Inness. Hired by the Lackawanna Railroad to paint a picture showing the company's new roundhouse at Scranton, in northeastern Pennsylvania, Inness combined landscape and locomotive technology into an organic whole. Industrialism, Inness seemed to say, belonged to the American landscape; it would neither overpower nor obliterate the land.*   Gift of Mrs. Huttleston Rogers, © National Gallery of Art, Washington, D.C.

urban network linked by canals, roads, and railroads (see Chapter 10).

New York City became a metropolis, growing from 60,500 in 1800 to over 800,000 in 1860. Across the East River, Brooklyn tripled in size between 1850 and 1860, becoming the nation's third-largest city, with a population of over 260,000. Many people just passed through the two cities; the majority did not stay ten years. Although contemporary depictions of New York appear almost pastoral, the city's energy and aromas of sweat, horse dung, and garbage would make twentieth-century cities seem sanitized in comparison. An immigrant port city, mostly Irish and German by the 1850s, New York City teemed with people.

New York City

New York City literally had burst its boundaries in the 1820s. Up to that time New Yorkers regarded the city of 150,000 as a village because they could walk from one end to the other in an hour. Until the 1820s nearly all New Yorkers lived within two miles of City Hall. In 1825, 14th Street was the city's northern boundary. By 1860, 400,000 people lived above that divide, and 42nd Street was the city's northern limit. Gone were the cow pastures, kitchen gardens, and orchards of the eighteenth century. George Templeton Strong, a New York lawyer, recorded in his diary in 1856 that he had attended a party at a Judge Hoffman's "in thirty-seventh!!!—it seems but the other day that thirty-seventh Street was an imaginary line running through a rural district and grazed over by cows." Mass transit made it possible for cities to expand. Horse-drawn buses appeared in New York in 1827, and the Harlem Railroad, completed in 1832, ran the length of Manhattan. By the 1850s all big cities had horse-drawn streetcars.

By modern standards early-nineteenth-century cities were disorderly, unsafe, and unhealthy. Expansion occurred so rapidly that few cities could handle the problems it brought. For example, migrants from rural areas were accustomed to relieving themselves outside and throwing refuse in any vacant area. In the city, such waste smelled, spread disease, and polluted water. New York City partially solved the problem in the 1840s by abandoning wells in favor of reservoir water piped into buildings and outdoor fountains. In some districts, scavengers and refuse collectors carted away garbage and human waste, but in much of the city it just rotted on the ground. Only one-quarter of New York City's streets had sewers by 1857.

New York and other cities lacked adequate taxing power to provide services for all. The best the city could do was to assess the adjoining property for the cost of sewers, street paving, and water mains. Thus the spread of new services and basic sanitation depended on residents' ability to pay. As a result, those most in need of services typically got them last. Another solution was to charter private companies to sell basic services. This plan worked well with gas service. Baltimore first chartered a private gas company in 1816; New York did so in 1842. By mid-century every major city was lit by a private gas supplier. The private sector, however, failed to supply the water the cities needed. Private firms lacked the capital to build adequate systems, and they laid pipe only in commercial and well-to-do residential areas, ignoring the poor. As population grew, city governments had to take over.

A singular urban innovation was the creation of public education. In 1800 there were no public schools outside New England; by 1860 every state offered some public education.

Horace Mann and Public Schools

Massachusetts, which had taken the lead in education since Puritan times, again led in expansion of schooling under Horace Mann, secretary of the state board of education from 1837 to 1848. Massachusetts established a minimum school term of six months, formalized the training of teachers, and emphasized secular subjects and applied skills rather than religious training. In the process, schoolteaching became a woman's profession. "Females govern with less resort to physical force," Mann asserted, "and exert a more kindly, humanizing and refining influence upon the dispositions and manners of their pupils."

Horace Mann was an evangelist for public education and school reform; his preaching on behalf of free, state-sponsored education changed schooling throughout the nation. "If we do not prepare children to become good citizens, if we do not develop their capacities, . . . imbue their hearts with the love of truth and duty, and a reverence for all things sacred and holy, then our republic must go down to destruction." The abolition of ignorance, according to Mann, would end misery, crime, and suffering. He advocated educating all children. Mann and others were responding to the changes wrought by the market economy, urbanization, and immigration. The typical city dweller was a newcomer, whether from abroad or from the country. Public schools would take the children of strangers and give them shared values.

Free public schools altered the scope of education. Schooling previously had focused on literacy, religious training, and discipline. Under Mann's leadership, the school curriculum became more secular and appropriate for the future clerks, farmers, and workers of America. Students studied geography, American history, arithmetic, and science. Moral education was retained, but direct religious indoctrination was dropped. However, the basic texts—*McGuffey's Eclectic Readers*—used Protestant Scripture to teach children to accept their position in society. A good child, McGuffey taught, does not envy the rich: "It is God who makes some poor and others rich." McGuffey further preached that "the rich have troubles which we know nothing of; and . . . the poor, if they are good, may be very happy."

Catholics, immigrants, blacks, and working-class people sought to have local control over their own schools, but the state legislatures established secular statewide standards under Protestant educators. Catholics in New York responded by building their own educational system over the next half-century. When Los Angeles became a city in 1850, it attempted to establish bilingual Spanish-English instruction. Trained bilingual teachers could not be found, however, and when the schools opened, only English was permitted.

Urban population concentration, growth in commerce, and shifts in work altered patterns of leisure. In rural society, as Irene Hardy recalled,

Leisure

both leisure activities and work often took place at home. But in cities, new dedicated spaces—streets, theaters, sports fields—constituted a social sphere where people could come together away from home. Through the sale of admission tickets or membership in various types of associations, leisure became a commodity to be purchased. As the population became more diverse, leisure associations reflected ethnic, racial, and class divisions.

Traditional colonial leisure pursuits continued in the city. Men frequented taverns and spent spare time drinking and playing tavern games of skill and strength—arm wrestling, ninepins, and pitching coins. Though city dwellers had less opportunity than their rural counterparts to ride and hunt, fishing remained popular among both men and women. Churches continued to remain centers for leisure, especially for women interested in religious activities and in clubs that combined socializing with good works.

Americans read more. Thanks to the expansion of public education, the vast majority of native-born white Americans were literate by the 1850s. Power printing presses and better transportation made possible wide distribution of books and periodicals. The religious press—of both traditional sects and dissenters—produced pamphlets, hymnbooks, Bibles, and religious newspapers. Americans also read secular publications. Newspapers and magazines—political organs, literary journals, and the voices of specialized groups like millworkers—abounded in the 1830s and after. In Brookfield, Massachusetts, in 1798, the mails brought one weekly newspaper; fifty years later, in 1848, fifty different newspapers and another fifty-five monthly magazines arrived on subscribers' doorsteps every week.

Fiction and autobiographies competed with religious tracts as popular literature. Newspapers and magazines printed fiction, and bookstores and stationers in large cities sold book-length novels and autobiographies. Susanna Rowson's 1794 novel *Charlotte Temple*, which offered a critique of women's dependence on men, and the powerful attack on slavery in the *Narrative of the Life of Frederick Douglass, an American Slave, Written by Himself* (1845) were widely read. Many popular novels, written by women, often for women, were set in the home and upheld Christian values. They reflected growing gender differences in American society in their exploration of the divisions between home and work, between emotion and authority, and between sentimentality and power. Yet in their support of traditional female moral roles, they also can be read as a challenge to prevailing values. Rowson's *Charlotte Temple*, for instance, never depicts the heroine performing domestic chores. And, although Susan Warners' *The Wide, Wide, Wide World* (1850), Nathaniel Hawthorne's *The House of the Seven Gables* (1851), and Fanny Fern's *Ruth Hall* (1855) did not challenge women's traditional domestic roles, they gave women a special moral bearing. In describing in positive terms community and republican virtue, they implicitly criticized the growing market economy.

Theater was a central institution in American life and provided a social sphere in which both men and women could gather. A theater was often the second public building constructed in a town—after a church. Large cities boasted two or more theaters catering to different classes. In New York City the Park Theater enjoyed the patronage of the carriage trade, the Bowery drew the middle class, and the Chatham attracted workers. Some plays cut across class lines. Shakespeare was performed so often and appreciated so widely that even illiterate theatergoers knew passages of his blank verse well. In the 1840s, musical and dramatic presentations took on a more professional tone; like the Hutchinson Family (see pages 253–254), newly popular minstrel shows and traveling circuses offered carefully rehearsed routines. Dancing and music remained popular.

Sports, like theater, increasingly involved city dwellers as spectators. Horseracing, boxing, walking races, and, in the 1850s, baseball began to attract large urban male crowds. More and more people purchased leisure by buying a ticket.

After New York State legalized horseracing in 1821, a track opened in Queens County across the East River from New York City. Two years later a single race drew fifty thousand people, and the newspapers reported a massive traffic jam of carriages from the ferry to the racecourse. Many spectators found betting as compelling as the sport. From 1831, enthusiasts could follow sports in a sports newspaper, *Spirit of the Times*. By 1849 boxing was so popular that a round-by-round account of a Maryland boxing match was telegraphed throughout the East.

Sports

Increasingly, urban sports and recreation became more formal and a commodity to be purchased. They had become less spontaneous and relied increasingly on formal rules. A group of Wall Street office workers formed the Knickerbocker Club in 1842, and in 1845 they drew up rules for the game of baseball. Their rules were widely adopted and continue to serve as the basis for the game. Entertainment became a commodity: one had to buy a ticket to go to the theater, the circus, P. T. Barnum's American Museum in New York City, the racetrack, or the ballpark.

Ironically, public leisure soon developed a private dimension. Exclusive private associations arose to provide space and occasions for leisure. Some

Nicholino Calyo's watercolor Soap-Locks, or Bowery Boys *(c. 1847) captured the bold body language and showy dress of the youths who controlled the sidewalks of the Bowery.*   New-York Historical Society.

represented class divisions as the growing middle and upper classes distanced themselves from the crowds and rowdiness of public events. In 1829 a group of Ohio merchants organized the Cincinnati Angling Club, which had a formal constitution and bylaws and limited membership to twenty-five. Ethnic, racial, religious groups seeking to socialize and share and preserve similar traditions formed clubs and societies. The Irish formed the Hibernian Society and the Sons of Erin; Germans brought Turnvereine physical-cultural clubs from across the Atlantic; Jews founded B'nai B'rith as a men's club; and African-Americans had chapters of the Prince Hall Masons in nearly every community. Women too organized their own associations, ranging from social organizations to benevolent societies.

As cities grew, their populations seemed increasingly fragmented. Finding people similar to oneself required more of a conscious effort. The new associations served as a bulwark against the cultures of other groups—immigrants, migrants, blacks, and artisans. Middle- and upper-class New Yorkers who felt alienated in the city of their birth founded exclusive clubs. Some joined the Masonic order, which offered everything

City Culture

the bustling city did not: an elaborate hierarchy, an orderly code of deference between ranks, harmony, and shared values. Members knew each other. The Masonic order played a political role as well: Masons recruited officeholders and marched in the parades that were a regular feature of the city's political life. Americans of all sorts—native- and foreign-born, black and white—also formed churches and church-associated clubs. Associations brought together like people, but they also formalized divisions between different groups.

Divisions seemed to occur naturally on city streets. A youth culture developed on the Bowery in the 1840s. In the evenings the broad street—lined with theaters, dance halls, ice-cream shops, and cafés—became an urban midway. Older New Yorkers feared the "Bowery boys and gals," whose ostentatious dress and behavior seemed threatening to them. Around 1847, artist Nicholino Calyo depicted three Bowery boys in a watercolor painting. A Bowery boy had long hair, often greased into a roll. He wore a broad-brimmed black hat, an open shirt collar, a black frock coat that reached below the knee, and as much jewelry as he could afford. His swaggering gait, especially when he had a girlfriend on his arm, frightened many in the middle class. Equally disturbing to old New Yorkers were the young working women who promenaded on the Bowery. They came in groups to enjoy each other's company and to meet Bowery boys. Unlike more genteel ladies who wore modest veils or bonnets, Bowery "gals" drew attention to themselves with bright, outlandish clothes and ornate hats.

Cities offered diversity and anonymity. People interested in same-sex liaisons, though often publicly ostracized, could find each other in the city and live together in urban boarding houses.

Most working people spent much of their lives outdoors; they worked in the streets as laborers, shopped in open markets, and paraded on special occasions. Young people courted, neighbors argued, and ethnic groups defended their turf on the streets. Increasingly, urban streets served as a political arena as crowds formed to listen to speakers, to parade, and sometimes to form mobs.

Economic, political, social, and ethnic conflict erupted on city streets. In the 1830s riots became commonplace as professionals and merchants, craftsmen, and laborers vented their rage against political and economic rivals. "Gentlemen of property and standing," unnerved by antislavery proponents, sacked abolitionist and antislavery organizations, even murdering newspaper editor Elijah Lovejoy in Alton, Illinois, in 1837. In the 1840s, "respectable" citizens drove the Mormons out of Illinois and Missouri. In Philadelphia native-born workers attacked Irish weavers in 1828, and whites and blacks fought on the docks in 1834 and 1835. Residents of North Philadelphia took to the streets continuously from 1840 to 1842 until the construction of a railroad through their neighborhood was abandoned. These disturbances came to a head in the Philadelphia riots of 1844, in which mostly Protestant skilled workers attacked Irish Catholics. Smaller cities, too, became battlegrounds as nativist riots peaked in the 1850s; Louisville, for instance, witnessed an anti-German riot in 1855. By 1840 more than 125 people had died in urban riots, and by 1860 fatalities exceeded 1,000.

Urban Riots

As public disorder spread, Boston hired uniformed policemen in 1837 to supplement its part-time watchmen and constables, and New York in 1845 established an entirely uniformed force. Nonetheless, middle-class men and women did not venture out alone at night, and even during the day they avoided certain districts. The police tried to control and suppress street activity, as did local ordinances that licensed and regulated street vendors and banned bells and horns. Local laws against vagrancy and disturbing the peace often were used against free blacks and immigrants. The continuing inflow of immigrants to the cities worsened social tensions by pitting people of dissimilar backgrounds against each other in the contest for jobs and housing. In the midst of so much noise, crime, and conflict, the lavish residences of the very rich rose like a deliberate affront to those struggling to survive.

Extremes of Wealth

The French nobleman Alexis de Tocqueville and other observers characterized the United States before the Civil War as primarily a place of equality and opportunity. Tocqueville and his companion Gustave de Beaumont traveled 4,000 miles and visited all twenty-four states over a nine-month period in 1831 and 1832. Tocqueville opened *Democracy in America*, his classic analysis of the American people and nation, with this statement: "No novelty in the United States struck me more vividly during my stay there than the equality of conditions."

Tocqueville attributed American equality—the relative fluidity of the social order—to Americans' mobility and restlessness. Geographic mobility offered people a chance to start anew regardless of where they came from or who they were. Wealth and family mattered little; a person could be known by deeds alone. Indeed, Americans seemed driven by restlessness and ambition. "An American will build a house in which to pass his old age," Tocqueville wrote, "and sell it before the roof is on; he will plant a garden and rent it just as the trees are coming into bearing; he will clear a field and leave others to reap the harvest; he will take up a profession and leave it, settle in one place and soon go off elsewhere with his changing desires."

Most Americans believed that hard work reaped rewards. This belief was supported by traditional religious values and a deeply rooted work ethic. According to the conventional wisdom, anyone could advance by working hard and saving money. A local legend from Newburyport, Massachusetts, illustrated this theme. Tristram Dalton, a Federalist lawyer, wanted his carriage repaired. Moses Brown, an ambitious mechanic, refused to wait for Dalton's servants to tow the carriage to his shop; he sought out the vehicle and fixed it on the spot. After Dalton's death his heirs squandered the family fortune, but Brown's industriousness paid off. Through hard work the humble carriage craftsman became one of Massachusetts's richest men, eventually buying the Dalton homestead and living out his life there. The moral was clear: "Men succeed or fail . . . not from accident or external surroundings," as the *Newburyport Herald* put it in 1856, but from "possessing or wanting the elements of success in themselves."

Others disagreed with this egalitarian view of American life. Among those who traced the rise of a new aristocracy based on wealth and power was *New*

"If Not an Aristocracy"

York Sun publisher Moses Yale Beach. Author of twelve editions of *Wealth and Biography of the Wealthy Citizens of New York City*, Beach listed 750 New Yorkers with assets of $100,000 or more in 1845. John Jacob Astor led the list of nineteen millionaires with a fortune of $25 million. Ten years later, Beach reported more than a thousand New Yorkers worth $100,000, among them twenty-eight millionaires. Combining gossip-column items with wild guesses at people's wealth, Beach's publications suggest the enormous wealth of New York's upper class. Tocqueville himself, sensitive to conflicting trends in American life, had described the new industrial wealth. The rich and well educated "come forward to exploit industries," Tocqueville wrote, and become "more and more like the administrators of a huge empire. . . . What is this if not an aristocracy?"

Wealth throughout the United States was becoming concentrated in the hands of a relatively small number of people. In New York City between 1828 and 1845, the richest 4 percent of the city's population increased their holdings from an estimated 63 percent to 80 percent of all individual wealth. Meanwhile, the holdings of many ordinary people virtually disappeared. In Brooklyn between 1810 and 1841, the share of wealth held by the bottom two-thirds of families decreased from 10 percent to almost nothing. By 1860 the top 5 percent of American families owned more than half of the nation's wealth, and the top 10 percent owned more than 70 percent.

Meanwhile, a cloud of uncertainty hovered over working men and women. Many feared hard times and resented the competition of immigrant and slave labor. They dreaded the insecurities and indignities of poverty, chronic illness, disability, old age, widowhood, and desertion. Women feared having to raise a family without a

Urban Poverty

spouse. And they had good reason: few women could find a job that paid sufficient money to support a family. Fear of poverty prompted the Klinger sisters, for instance, to marry again and again.

Poverty dogged the urban working class. Newly arrived immigrants, indigent free blacks, the working poor, and thieves, beggars, and prostitutes eked out a living in urban slums. New York City's Five Points, a few blocks from City Hall, was notorious for its squalor. Dominated by the Old Brewery, which had been converted to housing for hundreds of adults and children in 1837, the neighborhood was predominantly Irish and black. Lacking running water and sewers, Five Points exemplified the worst of urban life. Contemporaries estimated that more than a thousand people lived in its rooms, cellars, and subcellars. Throughout the city, workers' housing was at a premium. Houses built for two families often held four; tenements built for six families held twelve. Many families took in lodgers to help pay the rent.

New York and other large cities harbored "street rats," boys without families, who earned their living on the streets by petty thievery. They slept on boats, in haylofts, or in warehouses. Charles Loring Brace, a founder of the Children's Aid Society (1853), described them in *Dangerous Classes of New York* (1872): "Like the rats, they were too quick and cunning to be often caught in their petty plunderings, so they gnawed away at the foundations of society undisturbed." Brace and others considered such rootlessness a threat to American society more serious than Shays's Rebellion or Burr's conspiracies. "They will vote—they will have the same rights as we ourselves," warned the first report of the Children's Aid Society in 1854, "though they have grown up ignorant of moral principle, as any savage or Indian. . . . They will perhaps be embittered at the wealth and luxuries they never share. Then let society beware, when the vicious, reckless multitude of New York boys, swarming now in every foul alley and low street, come to know their power and use it!"

A world apart from Five Points and the people of the streets, though only a short walk away, lived the upper-class elite society of Philip Hone, onetime mayor of New York. Hone's

The Urban Elite

diary, meticulously kept from 1826 until his death in 1851, records the activities of an American aristocrat. On February 28, 1840, for instance, Hone attended a masked ball at the Fifth Avenue mansion of Henry Breevoort, Jr.,

This view of the Five Points section of New York City's Sixth Ward, around 1829, depicts life in what was probably the worst slum in pre–Civil War America. Immodestly dressed prostitutes cruise the streets, attracting the attention of well-dressed men in top hats while a pig runs loose in their midst.   Courtesy of Mr. and Mrs. Screven Lorillard.

and Laura Carson Breevoort. The ball began at the fashionable hour of 10 P.M., and the five hundred ladies and gentlemen who filled the mansion wore costumes adorned with ermine and gold. For more than a week, Hone believed, the affair "occupied the minds of people of all stations, ranks, and employments." At one time or another similar parties were held in Boston, Philadelphia, Baltimore, and Charleston.

Hone regularly attended elegant dinner parties graced by fine cuisine and imported wines. The New York elite who filled the pages of Hone's diary—the 1 percent of the population who owned 50 percent of the city's wealth—lived in mansions attended by a corps of servants. In the summer, country estates, ocean resorts, mineral spas, and grand tours of Europe offered relief from the strenuous winter and spring social seasons and escape from the heat and smell of the city.

Much of this new wealth was inherited. For every John Jacob Astor who made millions in the western fur trade or George Law who left a farm to become a millionaire contractor and investor, ten others used money they had inherited or married as a steppingstone to additional wealth. Andrew H. Mickle, a poor Irish immigrant who became a millionaire and mayor of New York City, derived his fortune from marrying the daughter of his employer. Many of the wealthiest New Yorkers bore the names of the colonial commercial elite: Beekman, Breevoort, Roosevelt, Van Rensselaer, and Whitney. These rich New Yorkers were not idle; they worked at increasing their fortunes and power. Urban capitalists like Philip Hone and the fashionable elite profited enormously from the transportation, commercial, and manufacturing revolutions. Wealth begat wealth, and marriage cemented family ties.

Meanwhile, a distinct middle class became part of the urban scene, and the growth and specialization of trade rapidly increased its numbers. The

The Middle Class

men were businessmen or professionals, the women homemakers and volunteers. Middleclass families enjoyed the new consumer items: wool carpeting, fine wallpaper, and rooms full of furniture replaced the bare floors, whitewashed walls, and relative sparseness of eighteenth-century homes. Houses were large, often having from four to six rooms. Middle-class children slept one to a bed, and by the 1840s and 1850s middle-class families used indoor toilets. When Philadelphia publishing agent Joseph Engles died in 1861, an inventory of his estate indicated that his parlor contained two sofas, thirteen chairs, three card tables, a fancy table, a piano, a mirror, and a fine carpet. Other rooms were similarly furnished.

Middle-class families formed the backbone of the rich associational life that Tocqueville had observed in America. They filled the family pews in church on Sundays; their children pursued whatever educational opportunities were available. They were as distant from Philip Hone's world as they were from the working class and the poor. Increasingly they looked to the family and home as the core of middle-class life.

Women, Families, and the Domestic Ideal

Distinctions among families grew in the nineteenth century. Once primarily an economic unit, nonfarm families lost their role as producers (see Chapter 10). And as manufacturing left the home, so did wage workers. One result was specialization of roles by gender and by life stage.

The family was dominated by the husband and father. English common law gave husbands control over the family. The men owned their wives' personal property; they were legal guardians of the children; and they owned whatever family members produced or earned. A father still had the legal authority to oppose his daughter's choice of husband. Nonetheless, most American women, with their parents' blessing, were choosing their own marriage partners.

Marriage and family life were the central adult experiences of most women. Although married women still had limited legal rights and standing, they made modest gains in property and spousal rights from the 1830s on. Arkansas in 1835 passed the first women's property law, and by 1860 sixteen more states had followed suit. In those states, women, including wives, could own and convey property: when a wife inherited, earned, or acquired property, it was hers, not her husband's; and she could write a will. In the 1830s states began to liberalize divorce,

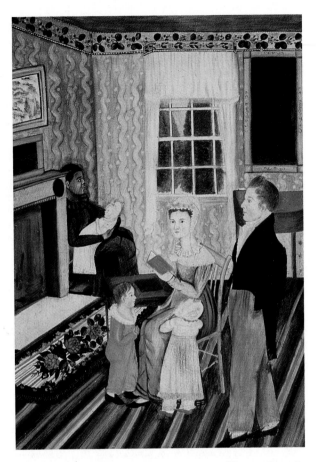

The homes of middle-class citizens were a world apart from the slums of New York City. This 1828 oil painting (by an unknown artist) shows the luxurious domestic furnishings, tailored clothing, and African-American servant of a family in York, Pennsylvania.   The Saint Louis Art Museum, Bequest of Edgar William and Bernice Chrysler Garbisch.

adding cruelty and desertion as grounds for divorce. Women who had the financial means could leave unhappy marriages.

As the urban workplace and home became separate, men worked for wages outside the home. Rural sons worked on their family farms, worked for hire on other people's farms, or sought wage work in towns. New England daughters left farms to work in textile mills. In the 1840s the new urban department stores hired young women as clerks and cash runners. Many women worked for a time as teachers, usually for two to five years. Paid employment typically represented a brief stage in women's lives before they left their parental households and entered their marital households.

Supporting Families

Rebecca Lukens pioneered in an unusual role for a woman in early-nineteenth-century America: she ran the Lukens Steel Company in eastern Pennsylvania from 1825 until she died in 1854. The deaths of her father in 1823 and of her husband in 1825 left her with the mill and large debts. She revived the steel company and soon was shipping iron plates as far away as Europe. Lukens Steel Company.

Working-class women—the poor, widows, and free blacks—worked to support themselves and their families. Leaving their parental homes as early as age twelve, they earned wages most of their lives, with only short respites for bearing and rearing children. But unlike men and New England farm daughters, most of these women did not work in the new shops and factories. Instead, they sold their domestic skills for wages outside their own households. Unmarried girls and women worked as domestic servants in other women's homes; married and widowed women worked as laundresses, seamstresses, and cooks. Some hawked food and wares on city streets; others did piecework sewing; and some became prostitutes. Few of these occupations enabled them to support themselves or a family at a respectable level.

Most women's work continued to be unpaid labor in the home. As the urban family lost its role in the production of goods, household upkeep and child rearing claimed women's full-time attention. Religion, morality, domestic arts, and music and literature filled the void left by the decline in the economic functions of the family; these realms came to be known as woman's sphere. A woman who achieved mastery in these areas lived up to the middle-class ideal of the cult of domesticity.

Middle-class Americans idealized the family as a moral institution characterized by selflessness and cooperation. Many viewed the family as a utopian retreat. Women were idealized in turn as the embodiment of self-sacrificing republicanism. The role of the mother was to strengthen the nation by rearing her children in a spiritual and virtuous environment unlike the world outside the home. The world of work—the market economy—was seen as an arena of conflict increasingly identified with men and dominated by base self-interest. In a rapidly changing world, the family represented stability and traditional values. But the family, no less than other American institutions, was also in flux.

The domestic ideal restricted the range of paying jobs available to middle-class women. Most paid work was viewed with disapproval, but one occupation was considered consonant with the genteel female role: teaching. In 1823 the Beecher sisters, Catharine and Mary, established the Hartford Female Seminary and offered history and science in addition to the traditional women's curriculum of domestic arts and religion. A decade later Catharine Beecher successfully campaigned for teacher-training schools for women. By the 1850s teaching was regarded as a woman's vocation, and most urban teachers were women, nearly all unmarried. Men teachers, few in number, were often paid twice as much as women teachers. For society, the services of talented, educated women were a bargain.

Meanwhile, family size was shrinking. In 1800 American women bore an average of six to seven children. By 1860 the figure had dropped to five, by 1900 to four. This decline occurred even though many immigrants with large-family traditions were settling in the United States; thus the birth rate among native-born women declined even more steeply. Although rural families remained larger than their urban counterparts, birth rates among both groups declined comparably.

Decline in Family Size

A number of factors reduced family size. Small families were viewed as increasingly desirable in an economy in which the family was a unit of consumption rather than production. Children in smaller families would have greater opportunities: parents could give them more attention, better education, and more financial help. Also, contemporary marriage manuals stressed that too many births had a harmful effect on a woman's health, weakening her physically and overworking her as a mother. Thus, evidence suggests, many wives and husbands made deliberate decisions to limit the size of families. In places where farmland was relatively expensive, for instance, family size was smaller than in cheaper agricultural districts. In urban areas, children tended to become an economic burden rather than an asset as the family lost its role as a producer of goods.

How did men and women limit their families in the early nineteenth century? Average age at marriage rose, thus shortening the period of potential childbearing. Women also bore their last child at a younger age, dropping from around forty in the mid-eighteenth century to around thirty-five in the mid-nineteenth. This change suggests that family planning was becoming more common. Many couples used traditional forms of birth control, such as coitus interruptus (withdrawal of the male before completion of the sexual act) and breast-feeding, which makes some women temporarily infertile. Medical devices, however, were beginning to compete with these ancient and imperfect practices. Although animal-skin condoms imported from France were too expensive for popular use, cheap rubber condoms became available in the 1850s. Some couples used the rhythm method—attempting to confine intercourse to a woman's infertile periods. Awareness of the "safe period," however, was uncertain, even among physicians.

Limiting Families

If all else failed, abortion was available, especially after 1830. Ineffective folk methods of self-induced abortion had been around for centuries, but in the 1830s abortionists, mostly women, advertised surgical services in large cities. To protect women from unqualified abortionists, and in response to reformers opposed to abortion, states began to regulate abortions. Between 1821 and 1841, ten states and one territory either restricted late-term abortions or prohibited abortion altogether; by 1860, twenty states had adopted such restrictions. Only three of those twenty states punished the women who chose to end a pregnancy; the abortionists were considered to be the criminals. Such laws, however, were rarely enforced.

Significantly, the birth-control methods that women themselves controlled—the rhythm method, abstinence, and abortion—became increasingly common. The new emphasis on domesticity encouraged women's autonomy in the home and by extension gave them greater control over their own bodies. Women ruled the household, including the bedroom, with refinement and purity. As one woman put it, "woman's duty was to subdue male passions, not to kindle them."

Smaller families and fewer births changed women's lives. At one time birth and infant care had occupied virtually the entire span of women's adult lives, and few mothers had lived to see their youngest child reach maturity. After the 1830s many women found time for other activities. Smaller families also allowed women to devote more time to their older children, and childhood gradually came to be perceived as a distinct period in the life span. The expansion of public education in the 1830s and the policy of grouping schoolchildren by age reinforced this trend.

Urban life always offered a place for men outside families. Rooming and boarding houses provided them with places to live. The expansion of cities and the market economy offered independence for women outside families as well. Single women departed from the centuries-old pattern in which a woman moved from her father's household to the household of her husband. Louisa May Alcott (1832–1888), the author of *Little Women* (1868), sought independence and financial security for herself. Her father, the philosopher Bronson Alcott, never adequately supported his family. Not even the family's participation in a utopian cooperative put enough food on the table. Alcott worked as a seamstress, governess, teacher, and housemaid before her writing brought her success. "I think I shall come out right, and prove that though an *Alcott*, I *can* support myself," she wrote her father in 1856. "I like the independent feeling; and though not an easy life, it is a free one, and I enjoy it. I can't do much with my hands; so I will make a battering-ram of my head and make a way through this rough-and-tumble world."

Single Men and Women

Louisa May Alcott foreswore marriage. She and other unmarried women pursued careers and lives defined by female relationships. Given the difficulty women had finding work that would allow them to be self-supporting, they undertook independence at great risk. Nonetheless, the proportion of single women in the population increased significantly in the first three quarters of the nineteenth century. In Massachusetts in 1850, 17 percent of native-born women never married—a far larger percentage than in colonial days. Independent white women, in sum, were taking advantage of new opportunities offered by the market economy and urban expansion.

 ## Immigrant Lives in America

The United States continued to be a nation of newcomers; the 5 million immigrants who came to the United States between 1820 and 1860 outnumbered the entire population of the country recorded in the first census in 1790. They came from every continent, though the vast majority were European (see figure, page 331). During the peak period of pre–Civil War immigration, from 1847 through 1857, 3.3 million immigrants entered the United States; 1.3 million were from Ireland and 1.1 million from the German states. By 1860, 15 percent of the white population was foreign-born.

This massive migration had been set in motion decades earlier. At the turn of the nineteenth century, the Napoleonic wars had given rise to one of the greatest population shifts in history; it was ultimately to last more than a century. War, revolution, famine, religious persecution, and the lure of industrialization led many Europeans to leave home. Most Asian immigrants came from southern China to work in heavy construction. The United States beckoned, offering economic opportunity and religious freedom.

Both private firms and governments recruited European immigrants. Midwestern and western states lured potential settlers to promote economic growth. Two transplanted New Yorkers, Augustus and Joe Kirby Allen, for instance, in 1836 set themselves up in what became Houston, Texas, and advertised in newspapers for settlers. In the 1850s, Wisconsin appointed a commissioner of emigration, who advertised the state's advantages in European newspapers. Wisconsin also opened an office in New York and hired European agents to compete with other

Promotion of Immigration

states and with firms like the Illinois Central Railroad in recruiting immigrants.

Large construction projects and mines needed strong young laborers. Textile mills and cities attracted young women workers. Europeans' awareness of the United States grew as employers, states, and shipping companies advertised opportunities across the Atlantic. Often the message was stark: work and prosper in America or starve in Europe. The price of a ticket on the regularly scheduled sailing ships crossing the ocean after 1848 was within easy reach of millions of Europeans.

Success in America stimulated further emigration. "I wish, and do often say that we wish you were all in this happy land," wrote shoemaker John West of Germantown, Pennsylvania, to his kin in Corsley, England, in 1831, adding: "A man nor woman need not stay out of employment one hour here." John Down, a weaver from Frome, England, who emigrated to New York without his family, wrote to his wife in 1830 to describe the bountiful meal he had shared with a farmer's family: "They had on the table puddings, pyes, and fruit of all kind that was in season, and preserves, pickles, vegetables, meats, and everything that a person would wish, and the servants [farm hands] set down at the same table with their masters." Though Down sorely missed his family, he wrote, "I do not repent of coming, for you know that there was nothing but poverty before me, and to see you and the dear children want was what I could not bear. *I would rather cross the Atlantic ten times than hear my children cry for victuals once.*" Such testimonials to the success of pauper immigrants in America were widely circulated in Europe.

So they came, enduring the hardships of travel and of living in a strange land. The average trans-Atlantic crossing took six weeks; in bad weather it could take three months. Joseph Gear made sketches during his crowded, unpleasant journey to the United States aboard the *Acasta* in 1824. Disease spread unchecked among people packed together like cattle in steerage. More than seventeen thousand immigrants, mostly Irish, died from "ship fever" in 1847. On arrival, immigrants became fair game for the con artists and swindlers who worked the docks. Boarding-house and employment agents tried to lure them from their chosen destinations. In response, New York State established Castle Garden as an immigrant center in 1855. There, at the tip of Manhattan Island, the major port for European entry, immigrants were somewhat sheltered from fraud. Authorized transportation companies main-

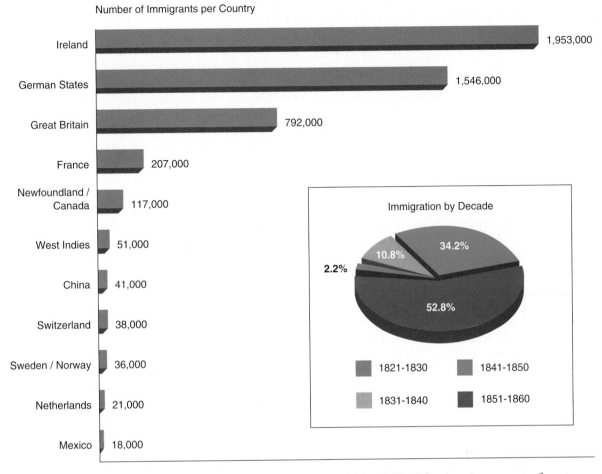

Major Sources of Immigration to the United States, 1821–1860

Number of Immigrants per Country

Country	Number
Ireland	1,953,000
German States	1,546,000
Great Britain	792,000
France	207,000
Newfoundland / Canada	117,000
West Indies	51,000
China	41,000
Switzerland	38,000
Sweden / Norway	36,000
Netherlands	21,000
Mexico	18,000

Immigration by Decade

- 34.2%
- 10.8%
- 2.2%
- 52.8%

1821–1830 1841–1850
1831–1840 1851–1860

Major Sources of Immigration to the United States, 1821–1860 *Most immigrants came from two areas: Great Britain, of which Ireland was a part, and the German states. These two areas sent more immigrants between 1820 and 1860 than the inhabitants of the United States enumerated at the first census in 1790. By 1860, 15 percent of the white population was of foreign birth.* Source: U.S. Bureau of the Census, *Historical Statistics of the United States, Colonial Times to 1970*, 2 parts (Washington, D.C., 1975), Part 1, pp. 206, 208.

tained offices in the large rotunda and assisted new arrivals with their travel plans.

Most immigrants gravitated toward cities, since only a minority had farming experience or the means to purchase land and equipment. Many stayed in New York City itself. By 1855 52 percent of its 623,000 inhabitants were immigrants, 28 percent from Ireland and 16 percent from the German states. Boston, another major entry port for the Irish, took on a European tone; throughout the 1850s the city was about 35 percent foreign-born, of whom more than two-thirds were Irish. Southern cities also had sizable immigrant populations. In 1860 New Orleans was 44

percent foreign-born, Savannah 33 percent, and the western city of St. Louis 61 percent. On the West Coast, San Francisco had a foreign-born majority.

Some immigrants settled in rural areas. German, Dutch, and Scandinavian farmers, in particular, gravitated toward the Midwest. Greater percentages of Scandinavians and Netherlanders took up farming than did other nationalities; both groups came mostly as religious dissenters and migrated in family units. The Dutch who founded colonies in Michigan and Wisconsin, for instance, had seceded from the official Reformed Church of the Netherlands, fleeing persecution in their native land to establish new and more pious communities such as Holland and Zeeland in Michigan.

Not all immigrants found success in the United States; hundreds of thousands returned to their homelands disappointed. Before the potato blight hit Ireland, American recruiters had lured many Irish to swing picks and shovels on American canals and railroads and to work in construction. Among them was Michael Gaugin, who for thirteen years had been an assistant engineer in the construction of a Dublin canal. Gaugin was attracted to the United States by the promise that "he should soon become a wealthy man." The Dublin agent for a New York firm convinced him to quit his job, which included a house and an acre of ground, and emigrate. Gaugin had the misfortune to land in New York City during the financial panic of 1837, and within two months of arriving he was a pauper. Gaugin told an Irish investigation that he was "now without means for the support of himself and his family, and has no employment, and has already suffered great deprivation since he arrived in this country; and is now soliciting means to enable him to return with his family home to Ireland."

Immigrant Disenchantment

Such experiences did not deter other Irish men and women from coming to the United States. Ireland was the most densely populated place in Europe and among the most impoverished. From 1815 on, small harvests prompted a steady stream of Irish to emigrate to America. Then in 1845 and 1846 potatoes—Ireland's staple food—rotted in the fields. From 1845 to 1849, death from starvation, malnutrition, and typhus spread. In all, 1 million died and about 1.5 million fled, two-thirds of them to the United States. Ireland's major export was its people. At the peak of Irish immigration, from 1847 to 1854, 1.2 million Irish men and women entered the United States. Each year between 1820 and 1854, with only two exceptions, the Irish constituted the largest group of immigrants. By the end of the nineteenth century there would be more Irish in the United States than in Ireland.

Irish Immigrants

The new Irish immigrants differed greatly from those who had left Ireland to settle in the American colonies. The Protestant Scots-Irish who predominated in the eighteenth century (see page 94) had journeyed from one part of the British Empire to another. The nineteenth-century Irish immigrants to America, however, were mostly Roman Catholic, and they moved from a British colony to an independent republic. Most of the new immigrants from Ireland were young, female, and from rural counties. Eldest sons, who expected to inherit family farms, stayed home, and eldest daughters stayed home to care for their parents. Younger children were expendable in Ireland's declining economy. Farmers' daughters could find work only as domestic servants, and poverty-stricken Ireland could not absorb all of them. In American cities, however, they found work in factories and households. If they wed, they married late, as did their sisters in Ireland. They supported their families in Ireland, built Catholic churches and schools, and established a network of charitable and social organizations in American cities.

In American cities Irish immigrants met anti-Catholic sentiment. "No Irish Need Apply" signs were common. During the colonial period, white Protestants had feared "popery" as a system of tyranny and had discriminated against the few Catholics in America. After the Revolution anti-Catholicism receded, but in the 1830s it reappeared wherever the Irish did. Anti-Catholicism was most overt and nastiest in Boston but could be found everywhere. Anti-Catholic riots were almost commonplace. In Charlestown, Massachusetts, a mob burned a convent (1834); in Philadelphia a crowd attacked priests and nuns and vandalized churches (1844); and in Lawrence, Massachusetts, a mob leveled the Irish neighborhood (1854).

Anti-Catholicism

The native-born who embraced anti-Catholicism were motivated largely by anxiety. They feared the Roman Catholic Church, unskilled Irish workers, and the urban slums inhabited by the Irish (among others). They blamed every social problem—from immorality and alcoholism to poverty and economic upheaval—on immigrant Irish Catholics. Impoverished native-born workers complained to the Massachusetts legislature in 1845 that the Irish displaced "the honest and respectable laborers of the State . . . and from their manner of living . . . work for much less per day . . . being satisfied with food to support the animal existence alone." American workers, they claimed, "not only labor for the body but for the mind, the soul, and the State." The new public schools, with their Protestant bias, represented another form of attack on Irish Catholics. Friction increased as Irish-American men fought back by entering politics.

In 1854, Germans replaced the Irish as the largest group of new arrivals. The Klinger family was part of this migration. Potato blight also had

German Immigrants

prompted emigration from the German states in the 1840s; other hardships added to the steady stream. Many people came from regions where small landholdings made it hard to eke out a living. Others were craftsmen displaced by the industrial revolution. These refugees were joined by middle-class Germans—a whole generation of liberals and freethinkers, some of whom were socialists, communists, and anarchists—who emigrated to the United States after the abortive revolutions of 1848.

It is not easy to characterize German-Americans. There was not a single German culture. Though New York had a sizable German population, making it the world's third great German-speaking city—after Vienna and Berlin—Germans settled everywhere in the United States. In the South they were peddlers and merchants; in the North and West they worked as farmers, urban laborers, and businessmen. Their tendency to migrate as families and groups helped them maintain German culture and institutions. Many settled in small towns and rural areas where they could preserve their local and regional identities. In larger cities immigrants from the same German states tended to cluster together. Their presence transformed the tone and culture of cities like Cincinnati and Milwaukee.

Native-born Americans accepted German immigrants more readily than they accepted the Irish, stereotyping Germans as hard working, self-reliant, and intelligent. Many believed that Germans would "harmonize" better with American culture. Nevertheless, Germans, too, encountered hostility. A significant number of German immigrants were Jewish, and they experienced anti-Semitism. Many German immigrants were Catholic, and their Sabbath traditions differed from those of Protestants. On Sundays urban German families customarily gathered at beer gardens to eat and drink beer, to dance, sing, and listen to band music, and sometimes to play cards. Protestants were outraged by this behavior, which they believed to be a violation of the Lord's day. The Germans' persistent use of their native language also set them apart. Even German Protestants, mostly Lutherans, founded their own churches and German-language schools.

Some Hispanic groups became "immigrants" to the United States without actually moving. Mexican

This painting (c. 1840) of Saint Isadore of Madrid, patron saint of farmers, is attributed to Rafael Aragon. Hispanic farmers in the Southwest sought the aid of Saint Isadore as they struggled to raise crops and preserve their culture.   Courtesy of Dr. and Mrs. Ward Alan Minge.

inhabitants of northern Mexico—present-day New Mexico and California—were unhappy because under the Mexican constitution of 1824 they lived in

Hispanics

Mexican territory, not states. Similarly Texas was part of the Mexican state of Coahuila. Lack of political autonomy made Mexicans in these areas unhappy, and many welcomed the events that brought them into the United States: the independence and later annexation of Texas, the Mexican War, and the Gadsden Purchase (see pages 369, 376).

In Texas, Anglos and European immigrants seized economic and political power. Tejanos retained their language, Roman Catholic religion, and community affiliations by means of newspapers, mutual-aid societies, schools, and the church, but they lost power and status to Anglos. In Nueces County, Texas, at the time of the Texas Revolution (1836), Mexicans held all the land; twenty years later, they had lost it all. Commerce eclipsed their agricultural and ranching economy; rancheros and vaqueros—cowboys—became obsolete. Although many Tejanos had fought for Texas's independence, arriving Anglo settlers tended to treat them as inferiors. They became second-class citizens on land where they had lived for generations.

Nonetheless, Tejanos retained their culture. They held fast to Roman Catholic and Hispanic traditions. San Antonio, Mexican from 1821 to 1836 and thereafter a Texas city, illustrates the persistence of Hispanic culture. The church, free public schools (established in 1827), life-cycle events from baptism to marriage to funerals, and public holidays and celebrations all supported Hispanic Roman Catholic traditions. Thus during the period of Texas independence, from 1836 to 1845, and after Texas statehood in 1845, Hispanic identity continued even in the face of a loss of political power.

In California—unlike Texas, New Mexico, and Arizona—Hispanic culture as well as political power quickly gave way to American and European culture. Californios, the Mexican population, numbered 10,000 in 1848, or two-thirds of the non-Indian population. By the end of the century the Hispanic population was 15,000 out of 1.5 million, and Hispanic culture was only a remnant, though it would be reestablished by Mexican immigrants in the twentieth century.

For immigrants, becoming part of American society involved conflict, but once in the United States they claimed their right to a fair economic and political share. Native Americans, however, like the Hispanics in the Southwest, had to defend what they regarded as prior rights. Their lands, their religions, and their ways of life came under constant attack because Americans viewed them as obstacles to expansion and economic growth.

 ## Native American Resistance and Removal

The Constitution gave the United States government responsibility for dealing with Native Americans. For better or worse, there had to be a federal Indian policy. From the Indians' point of view, it usually was for the worse. United States territorial expansion took place at the Indians' expense. The result was removal of the great Native American nations to lands west of the Mississippi. While the population of other groups was increasing by leaps and bounds, the Indian population was shrinking.

Alexis de Tocqueville noticed the contrast. "Not only have these wild tribes receded, but they are destroyed," Tocqueville concluded, after personally observing the tragedy of forced removal, "and as they give way or perish, an immense and increasing people fill their place. There is no instance upon record of so prodigious a growth or so rapid a destruction." War, forced removal, disease—especially smallpox—and malnutrition reduced many Indian nations by half. More than half of the Pawnees, Omahas, Otoes, Missouris, and Kansas died in the 1830s alone.

Like the colonial powers in North America, the United States government treated Native American groups as sovereign nations, until Congress ended the practice in 1871. In its relations with Indian leaders, the government followed international protocol. Indian delegations to Washington were received with the appropriate pomp and ceremony. Native American and United States leaders exchanged presents as tokens of friendship, and commemorative flags and silver medals with presidents' likenesses became prized possessions among Indian chiefs. Agreements between a given Indian nation and the United States were signed, sealed, and ratified like any other international pact.

In practice, however, Native American sovereignty was a fiction. Protocol appeared to signify mutual respect and independence, but treaty negotiations exposed the sham. Treaty making was essentially a tactic that the American government used to acquire Indian land. Instead of bargains struck by two equal nations, treaties often were agreements imposed by the victor on the vanquished. Old treaties gave way to new ones requiring Native Americans to cede their traditional holdings in exchange for other land in the West. Beginning with President Jefferson, the federal government withheld payments for land cessions to pressure Native Americans to sign new treaties.

The War of 1812 snuffed out whatever realistic hopes eastern Indian leaders had of resisting American expansion by warfare. After the war, armed resistance by the Indians persisted, and blood was shed on both sides, as in the Seminole Wars (see pages 247, 338). But it only delayed the inevitable. The Shawnee chiefs Prophet and Tecumseh led the most significant movement against the United States (see pages 238–239), but Prophet failed to sustain the movement after Tecumseh's death.

The experiences of Prophet and other Shawnees were typical of the wanderings of an uprooted people. Until the 1870s only the Delawares and Kickapoos moved more. After

Shawnees

giving up 17 million acres in Ohio in the 1795 Treaty of Greenville (see pages 189–190), the Shawnees scattered to Indiana and eastern Missouri. After the War of 1812, Prophet's Indiana group withdrew to Canada under British protection. In 1822 other Shawnees sought Mexican protection and moved from Missouri to present-day eastern Texas. As the United States government began promoting removal to Kansas, Prophet returned from Canada to lead a group to the new Shawnee lands in eastern Kansas in 1825. When Missouri achieved statehood in 1821, Shawnees living there were also forced to move to Kansas, where they were joined in the 1830s by Shawnees removed from Ohio and others expelled from Texas. By 1854 Kansas was open to white settlement, and the Shawnees had to cede back seven-eighths of their land there—1.4 million acres.

Removal had a profound impact on all Shawnees. The men had to give up their traditional role as providers; their methods of hunting and their knowledge of woodland animals were useless on the prairies of Kansas. As grain became the tribe's dietary staple, Shawnee women played a greater role as providers, supplemented by government aid under treaty provisions. (Typically, treaties required annual distributions of grain, blankets, and cash payments.) Remarkably, the Shawnees preserved their language and culture in the face of these drastic changes. Although resistance proved incapable of protecting their lands, it did help maintain their culture.

In the 1820s Native Americans in Ohio, southern Indiana and Illinois, southwestern Michigan, most of Missouri, central Alabama, and southern

Federal Indian Policy

Mississippi were pressured to cede their lands. They gave up nearly 200 million acres for pennies an acre. The appetite of the United States for land was insatiable. The federal Indian agency system, which monopolized trade with Native Americans and paid out the rations, supplies, and annuities they received in exchange for abandoning their land, made Indians dependent on government payments. Dependency made them pliant in treaty negotiations and furthered assimilation by bringing them into the market system.

Ever since the early days of European colonization, the assimilation of Native Americans through education and Christianity had been an explicit goal

of whites (see page 54). It took on renewed urgency as the United States expanded westward. "Put into the hand of [Indian] children the primer and the hoe," the House Committee on Indian Affairs recommended in 1818, "and they will naturally, in time, take hold of the plough; and, as their minds become enlightened and expand, the Bible will be their book, and they will grow up in habits of morality and industry . . . and become useful members of society." In 1819, in response to missionary lobbying, Congress appropriated $10,000 annually for "civilization of the tribes adjoining the frontier settlements." Protestant missionaries administered the "civilizing fund" and established mission schools.

Within five years thirty-two such schools were in operation. These new boarding schools substituted English for Native American languages and taught agriculture alongside the Christian Gospel. The emphasis on agriculture was intended to demonstrate the value of private property and hard work and to lay the basis for stable Christian communities. But to settlers eyeing Native American land, assimilation through education seemed too slow a process. At any given time there were never more than fifteen hundred students in all the schools; at that rate it would take centuries to assimilate all the Indians. Thus wherever Native Americans lived, illegal settlers disrupted their lives. Though obligated to protect the integrity of treaty lands, the federal government did so only halfheartedly. With government supporting westward expansion, legitimate Indian claims had to give way to the advance of white civilization.

In the 1820s it became apparent that neither economic dependency, education, nor Christianity could persuade Native Americans to cede enough land to satisfy the expansionists. Attention focused on southeastern tribes—Cherokees, Creeks, Choctaws, Chickasaws, and Seminoles—because much of their land remained intact after the War of 1812 and because they aggressively resisted white encroachment. Possessing some formal political institutions, they were better organized than the northern tribes to resist.

In his last annual message to Congress in late 1824, President James Monroe suggested that all Indians be moved beyond the Mississippi River. Three

Indian Removal to the West

days later he sent a special message to Congress proposing removal. Monroe described his proposal as an "honorable" one that would protect Indians from invasion and provide them with independence for "improvement and civilization." Force would be unnecessary, he believed; the promise of a home free from white encroachment would be sufficient to win Indian acceptance.

The proposal was aimed at the Cherokees, Creeks, Choctaws, and Chickasaws, and they unanimously rejected it. Between 1789 and 1825 they had negotiated thirty treaties with the United States. They had reached the limits of their tolerance. They wished to remain on what was left of their ancestral land.

Pressure from Georgia had prompted Monroe's policy. Cherokees and Creeks lived in northwestern Georgia, and in the 1820s the state accused the federal government of not fulfilling its 1802 promise to remove the Indians in return for the state's renunciation of its claim to western lands. Georgia was satisfied neither by Monroe's removal messages nor by further cessions by the Creeks. In 1826, under federal pressure, the Creek nation ceded all but a small strip of its Georgia acreage. But Georgia still was not satisfied. Only the removal of the Georgia Creeks to the West could resolve the conflict between Georgia and the federal government.

For the Creeks the outcome was a devastating blow. In an ultimately unsuccessful attempt to hold fast to the remainder of their traditional lands, which were in Alabama, they radically altered their political structure. In 1829, at the expense of traditional village autonomy, they centralized tribal authority and forbade any chief from ceding land. So in the end, they lost not only their land but their traditional forms of social and political organization.

If civilizing Indians was the American goal, no tribe met that test better than the Cherokees. Between 1819 and 1829 the tribe became economically self-sufficient and politically self-governing: during this Cherokee renaissance the twelve to fifteen thousand adult Cherokees came to think of themselves as a nation, not a collection of villages. In 1821 and 1822 Sequoyah, a self-educated Cherokee, devised an eighty-six-character phonetic alphabet that made possible a Cherokee-language Bible and a bilingual tribal newspaper, *Cherokee Phoenix* (1828). Between 1820 and 1823 the Cherokees created a formal government with a bicameral legislature, a court system, and a salaried bureaucracy. In 1827 they adopted a written constitution, modeled after that of the United States. Cherokee land laws, however, differed from United

Cherokees

States law. The tribe as a whole owned all Cherokee land, and complex provisions covered land sales (forbidden to outsiders) and the proximity of farms (minimum distance apart was one-quarter mile). Nonetheless, the Cherokees assimilated American cultural patterns. By 1833 they held fifteen hundred black slaves whose legal status was the same as that of slaves held by southern whites. Moreover, missionaries had been so successful that the Cherokees could be considered a Christian community.

Although the Cherokees developed a political system similar to that of an American state, they failed to win respect or acceptance from southerners. Georgia pressed them to sell the 7,200 square miles of land they held in the state. Congress appropriated $30,000 in 1822 to buy the Cherokee land in Georgia, but the Cherokees preferred to stay where they were. Impatient with their refusals to negotiate cession, Georgia annulled the Cherokee's constitution, extended the state's sovereignty over them, and ordered their lands seized.

Backed by sympathetic whites but not by the new president, Andrew Jackson, the Cherokees under Chief John Ross turned to the federal courts to defend their treaty with the United States and prevent Georgia's seizure of their land. Their legal strategy reflected their growing political sophistication.

**Cherokee
Nation
v. Georgia**

In *Cherokee Nation* v. *Georgia* (1831), Chief Justice John Marshall ruled that under the federal Constitution an Indian tribe was neither a foreign nation nor a state and therefore had no standing in federal courts. Nonetheless, said Marshall, the Indians had an unquestionable right to their lands; they could lose title only by voluntarily giving it up. A year later, in *Worcester* v. *Georgia*, Marshall defined the Cherokee position more clearly. The Indian nation was, he declared, a distinct political community in which "the laws of Georgia can have no force" and into which Georgians could not enter without permission or treaty privilege. Georgia refused to comply.

President Andrew Jackson, whose reputation had been built as an Indian fighter, refused to interfere because the case involved a state action. It was widely reported that Jackson had said, "John Marshall has made his decision: now let him enforce it." Keen to open up new lands for settlement, Jackson was determined to remove the Cherokees. In the Removal Act of 1830 Congress provided Jackson with the funds he needed to negotiate new treaties

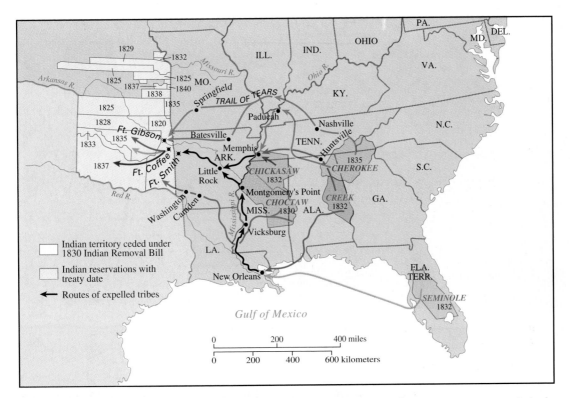

Removal of Native Americans from the South, 1820–1840   *Over a twenty-year period, the federal government and southern states forced Native Americans to exchange their traditional homes for western land. Some tribal groups remained in the South, but most settled in the alien western environment.*   Source: Acknowledgment is due to Martin Gilbert and George Weidenfeld and Nicholson Limited for permission to reproduce this map taken from *American History Atlas*.

and resettle the resistant tribes west of the Mississippi (see map).

The Choctaws were the first to go; they made the forced journey from Mississippi and Alabama to the West in the winter of 1831 and 1832. Alexis de Tocqueville was visiting Memphis when they arrived there:

Trail of Tears

"The wounded, the sick, newborn babies, and the old men on the point of death. . . . I saw them embark to cross the great river," he wrote, "and the sight will never fade from my memory. Neither sob nor complaint rose from that silent assembly. Their afflictions were of long standing, and they felt them to be irremediable." Other tribes soon joined the forced march. The Creeks in Alabama resisted removal until 1836, when the army pushed them westward. A year later the Chickasaws followed.

Having fought removal in the courts, the Cherokees were divided. Some believed that further resistance was hopeless and accepted removal as the only

chance to preserve their civilization. The leaders of this minority agreed in 1835 to exchange their southern home for western land in the Treaty of New Echota. John Ross, with petitions signed by fifteen thousand Cherokees, lobbied Congress against ratification. They lost. But when the time for evacuation came in 1838, most Cherokees refused to move. President Martin Van Buren sent federal troops to round them up. About twenty thousand Cherokees were evicted, held in detention camps, and marched to Indian Territory in present-day Oklahoma under military escort. Nearly one-quarter of them died of disease and exhaustion on what came to be known as the Trail of Tears.

When the forced march to the West ended, the Indians had traded about 100 million acres east of the Mississippi for 32 million acres west of the river plus $68 million. Only a few scattered remnants, among them the Seminoles in Florida and the Cherokees in the southern Appalachian Mountains, remained in the East and South.

The Trail of Tears *by contemporary Cherokee artist Brummet Echohawk. About twenty thousand Cherokees were evicted in 1838–1839, and about one quarter of them died on the forced march to present-day Oklahoma.*   Thomas Gilcrease Institute of American History and Art.

The impact of the forced removal on Native American life was disastrous. In the West they encountered an alien environment, and, lacking traditional ties with the new land, few felt at peace with it. The animals and plants they found were unfamiliar. No longer able to live off the land, many Native Americans became dependent on government payments for survival. Removal also brought new internal conflicts. The Cherokees in particular struggled over their tribal government. In 1839 followers of John Ross assassinated the leaders of the protreaty faction. Violence continued sporadically until a new treaty in 1846 imposed a temporary truce. In 1861 the American Civil War renewed the factionalism, forever shattering Cherokee unity.

Conflicts also arose among migrating Native American groups from the South and East and Indians already living in the West, as they were forced to share land and scarce resources. Nearly one hundred thousand newcomers settled west of the Mississippi, and the existing game could not support them all. The Osages and Pawnees fought the newcomers who were invading their land and homes. The story was repeated among the Apaches and Comanches in the Southwest, as the pressure of white settlement led to treaties, cession, and removal and then to new treaties, further cession, and removal.

In the Southeast a small band of Seminoles successfully resisted removal and remained in Florida.

They had resisted Andrew Jackson's 1818 campaign against the Seminoles in Florida. Some Seminole leaders agreed in the 1832 Treaty of Payne's Landing to relocate to the West within three years. Others opposed the treaty, and some probably did not know it existed. A minority under Osceola, a charismatic leader, refused to vacate their homes and fought the protreaty group. When federal troops were sent to impose removal in 1835, Osceola waged a fierce guerrilla war against them.

Second Seminole War

The Florida Indians were a varied group that included many Creeks and mixed Indian–African Americans (ex-slaves or descendants of runaway slaves). The American army, however, considered them all Seminoles, subject to removal. General Thomas Jesup believed that the runaway-slave population was the key to the war. "This, you may be assured, is a Negro, not an Indian war," he wrote a friend in 1836, "and if it be not speedily put down, the South will feel the effects of it on their slave population before the end of the next season."

Osceola was captured under a white flag of truce and died in an army prison in 1838, but the Seminoles fought on under Chief Coacoochee (Wild Cat) and other leaders. In 1842 the United States abandoned the removal effort. Most of Osceola's followers agreed to move west to Indian Territory in 1858, but many Seminoles remained in the Florida Everglades, proud of having resisted conquest.

Native Americans in the West found themselves pressured to cede land. To facilitate white settlement, Commissioner of Indian Affairs William Medill in 1848 proposed gathering the western Indians onto two

Indian Removal in the West

great reservations, one northern and one southern, separated by a wide corridor for white settlers to use on their way westward. In 1853 and 1854, however, the federal government took back most of the northern reservation lands in a new round of treaties, and Kansas and Nebraska were opened to white settlement.

A complex set of attitudes drove whites to remove Native Americans forcibly. Most wanted land and had little or no respect for the Indians' rights or culture. Others were aware of the injustice but believed that Indians inevitably had to give way to white settlement. Some, like John Quincy Adams, believed the only way to preserve Indian civilization was to separate Indians and white settlers physically. Others hoped to "civilize" Indians and assimilate them gradually into American culture. Whatever the source of white attitudes, it resulted in the devastation of Native American cultures.

 # Free People of Color

Free people of color also struggled for recognition and legal rights. Like Native Americans, they were involuntary participants in American society. Unlike Indians, however, they wished to partake fully in American life. During this period, African-Americans fought for equal rights, formed cohesive communities, and maintained their cultural heritage. Most whites, however, treated African-Americans as outsiders in the land of their birth.

On the surface, the Bill of Rights seemed to protect free African-Americans. The Fifth Amendment specified that "no person shall . . . be deprived of life, liberty, or property, without due process of law." But eighteenth-century political theory had defined the republic as being for whites only (see page 181), and early federal legislation reflected this exclusionist thinking: naturalization, for example, was limited to white aliens in 1790. After the admission of Missouri in 1821, every new state admitted until the Civil War banned blacks from voting. When the Oregon

and New Mexico Territories were organized, public land grants were reserved for whites.

African-Americans in the North were second-class citizens. Newly admitted states barred free blacks or required them to post bonds ranging from $500 to $1,000 to guarantee their good conduct, as did Ohio (1804), Illinois (1819), and Oregon (1857). Only in Massachusetts, New Hampshire, Vermont, and Maine could blacks vote on an equal basis with whites throughout the pre–Civil War period. In 1842 African-Americans gained the right to vote in Rhode Island (where all voters faced restrictive property qualifications), but they had lost it earlier in Pennsylvania and Connecticut. Only Massachusetts permitted blacks to serve on juries. Four midwestern states and California did not allow African-Americans to testify against whites. In Oregon, blacks could not own real estate, make contracts, or sue in court. The laws were meant to render African-Americans powerless.

Throughout the North white social custom excluded or segregated free people of color. Hotels and restaurants barred them, as did most theaters and white churches. Abolitionist

Exclusion and Segregation of African-Americans

Frederick Douglass was repeatedly turned away from public facilities during a speaking tour of the North in 1844.

African-Americans encountered discrimination in hiring everywhere. Countinghouses, retail stores, and factories refused to hire black men except as janitors and handymen. New England mills hired only whites. Except for a small professional and skilled elite, free black men in the North found steady work elusive; most toiled as unskilled daily laborers. African-American women found jobs more easily because their domestic skills were in great demand in the cities; they worked as servants, cooks, laundresses, and seamstresses. Unlike their white counterparts, these women did not view paid employment as a temporary phase in their lives; around 40 percent of black women worked for wages during their child-rearing years.

Free people of color faced severe legal and social barriers in the southern slave states. Whites viewed their presence as subversive. Fearing free African-Americans, southern states restricted their presence. In 1806,

Southern Free Blacks

Virginia required newly freed blacks to leave the state. After the Nat Turner Rebellion in 1831,

This watercolor of Augustus Jones was painted in 1852 when Jones was forty-nine. A leader in the Philadelphia community of free people of color, Jones was the grandson of Absalom Jones, a founder of the African Free Society and the African Episcopal Church in Philadelphia.   Private collection. Photo courtesy of David A. Schorsch.

almost 500,000 in 1860. Nearly half lived in the North, some in rural settlements but far more in cities like Philadelphia, New York, and Cincinnati. Baltimore had the largest community, but sizable free black populations formed in New Orleans, Charleston, and Mobile. Although differences in occupation, wealth, education, religion, and social status divided free people of color, the common necessity of self-defense promoted solidarity among them.

The ranks of free people of color were constantly increased by ex-slaves. Some, like Frederick Douglass and Harriet Tubman, were fugitives. Douglass, a Baltimore ship caulker, escaped by bluffing his way to Philadelphia and freedom. Tubman, a slave in Maryland, escaped to Philadelphia in 1849 when it was rumored that she would be sold out of the state. Within the next two years she returned twice to free her two children, her sister, her mother, and her brother and his family. Some slaves received freedom in owners' wills when masters sought, at death, to rid themselves of the stain of owning slaves. Some owners freed elderly slaves after a lifetime of service rather than support them in old age.

Free people of color forged cohesive communities and created autonomous institutions within them. Churches became the center of community life, and pastors became political leaders. Church buildings functioned as town halls, and they housed schools, political forums and conventions, protest meetings, and benevolent and self-help associations as well as prayer meetings.

African-American Communities

Like European immigrants, free people of color sought to assist members of their own community. But they had a greater burden. Although their taxes supported white schools, for instance, they had to raise additional funds to establish African-American schools because their children were excluded from the new public schools. A network of voluntary associations—self-help societies, female benevolent societies, and literary and social clubs—became the hallmark of their communities. Most of these organizations were political as well as social.

In the majority of states where free blacks were excluded from the ballot, they formed protest organizations to fight for equal rights. Among the early efforts to organize for self-defense was the Negro Convention movement. From 1830 to 1835, and irregularly thereafter, free blacks held national conventions with delegates drawn from city and state organizations. Under the leadership of the small

the position of free blacks deteriorated throughout the South. Within five years nearly every southern state prohibited the freeing of slaves without legislative or court approval, and by the 1850s Texas, Mississippi, and Georgia had banned manumission altogether.

In essence, the legal status of southern free people of color was somewhere between slave and free. Southern states adopted elaborate "black codes" to curtail the activities and opportunities of African-Americans, who provided most of the South's skilled labor. They were barred from a number of occupations. Virginia and Georgia, for instance, denied work to black riverboat captains and pilots. Some states forbade blacks to assemble without a license. Some prohibited them from learning to read and write. In the late 1830s, the codes were tightened, and free people of color moved northward even though northern states discouraged the migration.

In spite of these obstacles, the free African-American population rose from 108,000 in 1800 to

How do historians know about African-American political thought and activity in the early nineteenth century? One important source is the published minutes of black conventions, first held in 1830. Free people of color held at least eleven national conventions and about forty state conventions prior to the Civil War. The first national convention, a special meeting in Philadelphia in September 1830, was presided over by Bishop Richard Allen, founder of the African Methodist Episcopal Church. The delegates agreed to explore a settlement in Canada as a haven for free people of color and fugitive slaves. They also called for pursuing "all legal means for the speedy elevation of ourselves and brethren to the scale and standing of men." Less than a year later, delegates to the "First Annual Meeting of the People of Colour" condemned the persecution of African-Americans, appealed for funds to support their work, called for the establish-

ment of a college for poor blacks, and stressed the importance of education. They also were consciously building a movement of annual conventions. The report of this convention, and subsequent convention minutes and addresses, demonstrate the involvement of African-Americans in the reforms of the times and the importance they placed on education and equality of opportunity. At conventions held in the 1850s nationalism took hold among African-Americans.

The convention movement was democratic. Most communities elected their delegates to the national conventions at public meetings or at local and state conventions. Although the minutes reveal a wide range of opinion within black communities, there was agreement about the abolition of slavery, immediate emancipation, and equal rights for free people of color. Minutes of the Proceedings of the National Negro Convention, 1831.

CONSTITUTION

OF THE

AMERICAN SOCIETY

OF

FREE PERSONS OF COLOUR,

FOR IMPROVING THEIR CONDITION IN THE UNITED STATES;
FOR PURCHASING LANDS; AND FOR THE ESTABLISH-
MENT OF A SETTLEMENT IN UPPER CANADA,

ALSO

THE PROCEEDINGS OF THE CONVENTION,

WITH THEIR

ADDRESS

TO

THE FREE PERSONS OF COLOUR

IN THE

UNITED STATES.

PHILADELPHIA:
PRINTED BY J. W. ALLEN, NO 26, STRAWBERRY-ST.
1831.

black middle class, which included the Philadelphia sail manufacturer James Forten and the orator Reverend Henry Highland Garnet, the convention movement served as a forum to attack slavery and agitate for equal rights. Militant new black newspapers joined the struggle. *Freedom's Journal*, the first black weekly, appeared in 1827; in 1837 the *Weekly Advocate* began publication in New York City. Both papers circulated throughout the North, disseminating African-American political analysis and promoting activism.

The mood of free blacks began to shift in the late 1840s and 1850s. Many were frustrated by the failure of the abolitionist movement and angered by

Black Nationalism

the passage of the Fugitive Slave Act of 1850 (see page 383). Some fled to Canada, others became more militant, and a few joined John Brown in his plans for a slave uprising (see page 395). Many more were swept up in a wave of black nationalism that stressed racial solidarity, self-help, and a growing interest in Africa. Before this time, efforts to send African-Americans "back to Africa" had originated with whites seeking to rid the United States of blacks. But in the 1850s blacks held emigrationist conventions of their own under the leadership of abolitionists Henry Bibb and Martin Delany. Delany led an exploration party to the Niger valley as the emissary of a black convention, there signing a treaty with Yoruba rulers allowing him to settle American blacks in their African kingdom.

Nothing illustrates the position of free blacks in the United States better than the flight of black Americans to Canada and Africa in search of freedom while millions of European migrants were coming to the United States for liberty and opportunity. With the coming of the Civil War, the status of blacks would move onto the national political agenda, and African-Americans would focus on their position at home.

 Conclusion

The American people and communities were far more diverse and turbulent in 1860 than they had been in 1800. The market economy, immigration, and the growth of cities had altered the way people lived and worked. Inequality increased everywhere, and competition and insecurity produced resentment and conflict. Cities housed both ostentatious

wealth and abject poverty, and disorder became commonplace. Many Americans felt as if they were strangers to each other.

In the midst of these changes, middle-class families sought to insulate their homes from the competition of the market economy. Many women found fulfillment in the domestic ideal; others found it confining. Middle-class urban women became associated with nurturing roles, first in homes and schools, then in churches and reform societies. Working-class women had more modest goals: escaping poverty and winning respect. Most Americans found some comfort in religion.

Famine and religious and political oppression in Europe propelled millions of people across the Atlantic. They were drawn to the United States by the promise of jobs and tolerance. Although conditions usually were better than in their native lands, most found the going rough. In the process of adapting, immigrants changed the profile of the American people: Americans differed from each other more and shared fewer traditions and experiences. Competition and diversity in turn bred intolerance. Native Americans, free African-Americans, and Hispanics were made to feel like aliens in their own land. Indians, forced off their traditional lands, found themselves uprooted and deprived of much that had given their lives meaning. African-Americans sought acceptance as citizens, but without much success. A small number attempted to return to Africa. Hispanics saw economic and political power shift to English-speaking settlers.

Conflict became increasingly commonplace in the public arena. The manifestations of division in America were many: utopian communities, conflicts over public space, backlash against immigrants, urban riots, black protest, and Indian resistance. Conflict also took the form of reform movements, which came to characterize American life from the 1820s through the 1850s. Through reform and political action, many Americans sought to harness and control the forces of change. Spurred on by religious revival and individualism, they turned to politics as a collective means of restoring harmony and order. In the process, divisions became even sharper.

Suggestions for Further Reading

Rural and Utopian Communities

Leonard J. Arrington and Davis Bitton, *The Mormon Experience: A History of the Latterday Saints* (1979); Priscilla J. Brewer, *Shaker*

Communities, Shaker Lives (1986); David B. Danbom, *Born in the Country: A History of Rural America* (1995); Don H. Doyle, *The Social Order of a Frontier Community: Jacksonville, Illinois, 1825–1870* (1978); John Mack Faragher, *Sugar Creek: Life on the Illinois Prairie* (1986); Laurence Foster, *Religion and Sexuality: Three American Communal Experiments of the Nineteenth Century* (1981); Steven Hahn and Jonathan Prude, eds., *The Countryside in the Age of Capitalist Transformation* (1985); Joan M. Jensen, *Loosening the Bonds: Mid-Atlantic Farm Women, 1750–1850* (1986); Sally McMurry, *Families and Farmhouses in Nineteenth Century America: Vernacular Design and Social Change* (1988); Anthony F. C. Wallace, *Rockdale: The Growth of an American Village in the Early Industrial Revolution* (1978); Kenneth H. Winn, *Exiles in a Land of Liberty: Mormons in America, 1830–1846* (1989).

Urban Communities

Melvin A. Adelman, *A Sporting Time: New York City and the Rise of Modern Athletics, 1820–1870* (1986); Stuart M. Blumin, *The Emergence of the Middle Class: Social Experience in the American City, 1760–1900* (1989); Susan G. Davis, *Parades and Power: Street Theater in Nineteenth-Century Philadelphia* (1986); Timothy J. Gilfoyle, *City of Eros: New York City, Prostitution, and the Commercialization of Sex, 1790–1920* (1992); Karen V. Hansen, *A Very Social Time: Crafting Community in Antebellum New England* (1994); Carl Kaestle, *Pillars of the Republic: Common Schools and American Society, 1780–1860* (1982); Jack Larkin, *The Reshaping of Everyday Life, 1790–1840* (1988); Scott Martin, *Killing Time: Leisure and Culture in Southwestern Pennsylvania, 1800–1850* (1995); Edward Pessen, *Riches, Class and Power Before the Civil War* (1973); Christine Stansell, *City of Women: Sex and Class in New York, 1789–1860* (1986); Richard B. Stott, *Workers in the Metropolis: Class, Ethnicity, and Youth in Antebellum New York City* (1990); Stephan Thernstrom, *Poverty and Progress: Social Mobility in a Nineteenth Century City* (1964); Alexis de Tocqueville, *Democracy in America*, 2 vols. (1835, 1840).

American Families

Virginia K. Bartlett, *Keeping House: Women's Lives in Western Pennsylvania, 1790–1850* (1994); Janet Farrell Brodie, *Contraception and Abortion in Nineteenth-Century America* (1994); Lee Virginia Chambers-Schiller, *Liberty, A Better Husband: Single Women in America: The Generations of 1780–1840* (1984); Clifford Edward Clark, Jr., *The American Family Home, 1800–1960* (1986); Nancy F. Cott, *The Bonds of Womanhood: "Woman's Sphere" in New England, 1780–1835* (1977); Carl N. Degler, *At Odds: Women and the Family in America from the Revolution to the Present* (1980); Linda Gordon, *Woman's Body, Woman's Right: A Social History of Birth Control in America* (1976); Joan Hoff, *Law, Gender and Injustice: A Legal History of U.S. Women* (1991); Suzanne Lebsock, *The Free Women of Petersburg: Status and Culture in a Southern Town, 1784–1860* (1984); Glenda Riley, *Divorce: An American Tradition* (1991); Mary P. Ryan, *Women in Public: Between Banners and Ballots, 1825–1880* (1990); Mary P. Ryan, *Cradle of the Middle Class: The Family in Oneida County, New York, 1790–1865* (1981); Kathryn Kish Sklar, *Catharine Beecher: A Study in American Domesticity* (1973); Maris A. Vinovskis, *Fertility in Massachusetts from the Revolution to the Civil War* (1981); Robert V. Wells, *Revolutions in Americans' Lives* (1982); Barbara Welter, "The Cult of True Womanhood, 1820–1860," *American Quarterly* 18 (Summer 1966): 151–174.

Immigrants and Hispanics

Gunther Barth, *Bitter Strength: A History of Chinese in the United States, 1850–1870* (1964); Kathleen Neils Conzen, *Immigrant Milwaukee: 1836–1860* (1976); Arnoldo De León, *The Tejano Community, 1836–1900* (1982); Hasia R. Diner, *Erin's Daughters in America: Irish Immigrant Women in the Nineteenth Century* (1983); Jay P. Dolan, *The Immigrant Church: New York's Irish and German Catholics, 1815–1865* (1975); Charlotte Erickson, *Invisible Immigrants* (1972); David A. Gerber, *The Making of an American Pluralism: Buffalo, New York, 1825–60* (1989); Walter D. Kamphoefner, *The Westfalians: From Germany to Missouri* (1987); Walter D. Kamphoefner et al., eds., *News from the Land of Freedom: German Immigrants Write Home* (1991); Dale T. Knobel, *Paddy and the Republic: Ethnicity and Nationality in Antebellum America* (1986); Timothy M. Matovina, *Tejano Religion and Ethnicity: San Antonio, 1821–1860* (1995); Kerby A. Miller, *Emigrants and Exiles: Ireland and the Irish Exodus to North America* (1985); Stanley Nadel, *Little Germany: Ethnicity, Religion, and Class in New York City, 1845–80* (1990); Philip Taylor, *The Distant Magnet: European Emigration to the United States of America* (1971); Mark Wyman, *Immigrants in the Valley: Irish, Germans, and Americans in the Upper Mississippi, 1830–1860* (1984).

Native Americans

Robert F. Berkhofer, Jr., *The White Man's Indian* (1978); James W. Covington, *The Seminoles of Florida* (1993); Grant Foreman, *Indian Removal: The Emigration of the Five Civilized Tribes of Indians*, rev. ed. (1953); Michael D. Green, *The Politics of Indian Removal: Creek Government and Society in Crisis* (1982); William G. McLoughlin, *Cherokee Renascence in the New Republic* (1986); Theda Perdue, *Slavery and the Evolution of Cherokee Society, 1540–1866* (1979); Francis P. Prucha, *American Indian Policy in the Formative Years* (1967); Ronald N. Satz, *American Indian Policy in the Jacksonian Era* (1975); Anthony F. C. Wallace, *The Long, Bitter Trail: Andrew Jackson and the Indians* (1993); Richard White, *The Roots of Dependency: Subsistence, Environment, and Social Change Among the Choctaws, Pawnees, and Navajos* (1983); J. Leitch Wright, Jr., *Creeks and Seminoles: The Destruction and Regeneration of the Muscogulge People* (1986).

Free People of Color

Ira Berlin, *Slaves Without Masters: The Free Negro in the Antebellum South* (1974); Leonard P. Curry, *The Free Black in Urban America, 1800–1850* (1981); James Horton, *Free People of Color: Inside the African American Community* (1993); James O. Horton and Lois E. Horton, *In Hope of Liberty: Culture, Community and Protest Among Northern Free Blacks, 1700–1860* (1996); Luther Porter Jackson, *Free Negro Labor and Property Holding in Virginia, 1830–1860* (1942); David M. Katzman, *Before the Ghetto: Black Detroit in the Nineteenth Century* (1973); Rudolph M. Lapp, *Blacks in Gold Rush California* (1977); Leon Litwack, *North of Slavery: The Negro in the Free States, 1790–1860* (1961); Floyd J. Miller, *The Search for a Black Nationality: Black Colonization and Emigration, 1787–1863* (1975); Gary B. Nash, *Forging Freedom: The Formation of Philadelphia's Black Community, 1720–1840* (1988); Harry Reed, *Platform for Change: The Foundations of the Northern Free Black Community, 1775–1865* (1994); Julie Winch, *Philadelphia's Black Elite: Activism, Accommodation, and the Struggle for Autonomy, 1787–1848* (1988); Arthur Zilversmit, *The First Emancipation: The Abolition of Slavery in the North* (1967).

13

Reform, Politics, and Expansion

1824–1844

I proceed, Gentlemen, briefly to call your attention to the *present* state of Insane persons confined within this Commonwealth," Dorothea Dix petitioned the Massachusetts legislature in 1843, "in *cages, closets, stalls, pens! Chained, naked, beaten with rods and lashed into obedience*."

Dix described the nether world she had uncovered in her investigations of the treatment of the insane in the previous two years. She reported appalling conditions in Massachusetts towns: men and women in cages, chained to walls, in dark dungeons, brutalized and held in solitary confinement. In a surprise visit to a Newburyport almshouse in the summer of 1842, Dix expressed her surprise at the comfortable conditions for the "one idiotic" and seven insane inhabitants. On the grounds she discovered, however, one man residing in a shed whose door opened to the local "dead room" or morgue; the man's only companions were corpses. Shocked, she heard from an attendant about another insane inmate whom no one spoke of: "a woman in a *cellar*."

She asked to see the woman. The superintendent tried to dissuade her, warning Dix that the *woman "was dangerous to be approached*; that 'she had lately attacked his wife,' *and was often naked*." Dix pressed on: "if you will not go with me," she said, "give me the keys and I will go alone." They unlocked the doors and entered an underground cell. Beneath the staircase was a tiny door. In the shadows Dix saw "a female apparently wasted to a skeleton, partially wrapped in blankets." She was withered, wrote Dix, "not by age, but by suffering." When the inmate saw the visitors, she wailed with despair: "Why am I consigned to hell? dark—dark—I used to pray, I used to read the Bible—I have done no crime in my heart; I had friends, why have all forsaken me!—my God! my God! why hast *those* forsaken me?"

Dorothea Dix's powerful personal descriptions of the brutal treatment of the mentally ill propelled her from reform to politics. This early photograph of Dix portrays both her austere demeanor and her crusading spirit.
Boston Athenaeum.

Dix described in the most personal and vivid terms her visits to jails, almshouses, and private homes, and the brutal treatment of the insane. Her petition to the General Court of Massachusetts was so graphic and shocking that the legislature voted to reprint it as a government pamphlet: *"Memorial to the Massachustts Legislature* (1843).

The first-person narrative—*"I tell what I have seen"*—gave Dix's message power. She seemed, however, to be an unlikely herald. Reared in Massachusetts, she began teaching in Worcester at age fourteen in 1816. She wrote an elementary science text and published children's devotional verse and poetry. She dressed in a somber manner; she wore dark dresses with starched white collars and pulled her hair back tightly, making her face look more angular and austere. She never married and seemed aloof and remote to other Bostonians.

She became obsessed with exploring the ill treatment of the insane. What drove her was not only a sense of outrage but also a belief in human perfectibility and in the corollary idea that the insane could be treated and cured. Proper humane treatment, Dix argued, could bring them back to the community; they could be healed if they were treated as ill rather than as criminal.

Dix became a one-issue reformer. From teacher and Boston lady, she became a crusader for asylum reform, advocating hospitals for the mentally ill. In the 1840s she traveled more than 40,000 miles, investigating the treatment of the insane and petitioning state legislatures. From 1848 through 1856 she lobbied Congress annually to set aside 5 million acres to fund insane asylums. In 1854 President Franklin Pierce vetoed the bill, which finally had passed Congress. During the Civil War she recruited and supervised nurses for the federal government; afterward she resumed her crusade on behalf of the mentally ill. She died in 1887 in a hospital she had founded.

Dix epitomized so much of early- to mid-nineteenth-century reform. She started with a belief in individual self-improvement that led her to advocate collective responsibility, especially on behalf of those dependent on the kindness of others. She became so personally absorbed in reform that it became her career. She was single-minded, expressing little concern for abolition or women's rights. Unlike Susan B. Anthony, Lucretia Mott, or Elizabeth Cady Stanton, Dix never joined the early feminists in agitating for women's political equality. Nonetheless, her obsession with reform took her into politics. In investigating asylums, in petitioning the Massachusetts General Court in 1843, and in lobbying other state legislatures and Congress, she joined other women in moving from reform to politics, and she helped create a new public role for women.

The reform fervor of the 1820s to the 1850s, which stirred interest in asylum reform, arose in part as a response to the enormous transformation that the United States experienced after the War of 1812. Immigration, internal migration, urbanization, the spread of a market economy, growing inequality, loosening family and community ties, the westward advance of settlement, and territorial expansion all contributed to the remaking of the United States. Many Americans felt they were no longer masters of their own fate. People had difficulty keeping up with the rapid pace of change. And social institutions did not always keep up with change.

Americans had fought the Revolution to make themselves independent, but poverty and wage work made many of them dependent again. Other changes were equally disturbing. Respectable citizens felt threatened by urban mobs and paupers, and the Protestant majority feared the growing Catholic minority. Protestants had waged the Revolution to preserve the rights they claimed as Englishmen, not to protect alien cultures and religions. To many, all these changes seemed to be undermining traditional values.

Religious reformers sought to reimpose order on a society in which economic change and discord had reached a crescendo. Prompted by the evangelical spirit of the Second Great Awakening and convinced of their moral rectitude, they crusaded for individual self-improvement. Many renounced alcohol and gambling. Gradually the personal impulse to reform oneself led to the creation of benevolent and reform societies. Religious ardor drew men and women to reform, in time broadening the political base. Reform soon eclipsed benevolent work and became an instrument for restoring discipline and order in a changing society. "Americans love their country not as it is but as it will be," the English visitor Francis Grund observed in the 1830s. Women became prominent in reform, first to improve life for others, then to secure rights and freedom for themselves.

Members of reform organizations eventually turned to politics, viewing it as an instrument of change; that perception is what led Dorothea Dix to

• *Important Events* •

1790s–1840s	Second Great Awakening spreads religious fervor	**1837**	*Caroline* affair sparks Anglo-U.S.-Canadian hostility Financial panic ends boom of the 1830s
1820s	Reformers in New York and Pennsylvania establish model penitentiaries	**1838–39**	United States and Canada mobilize their militias over Maine–New Brunswick border dispute
1824	No presidential candidate wins a majority in the electoral college	**1839–43**	Hard times spread unemployment and deflation
1825	House of Representatives elects John Quincy Adams president	**1840**	Whigs win presidency under William Henry Harrison
1826	American Society for the Promotion of Temperance founded Morgan affair is catalyst for Antimasonry movement	**1841**	John Tyler assumes the presidency after Harrison's death "Oregon fever" attracts settlers to the Northwest and intensifies expansionism
1828	Protectionist Tariff stirs nullification Andrew Jackson elected president	**1843**	Dorothea Dix petitions Massachusetts legislative regarding deplorable condition of insane asylums
1830	Webster-Hayne debate explores the nature of the Union	**1844**	James K. Polk elected president
1830s–40s	Democratic-Whig competition gels in second party system	**1845**	Texas admitted to the Union
1831	Abolitionist newspaper *The Liberator* begins publication First national Antimason convention	**1848**	Woman's Rights Convention at Seneca Falls, New York, calls for women's suffrage
1832	Jackson vetoes rechartering of the Second Bank of the United States Jackson reelected president	**1851**	Maine adopts prohibition
1832–33	South Carolina nullifies the Tariff of 1832, prompting nullification crisis		
1836	Republic of Texas established after breaking from Mexico Specie Circular ends credit purchase of public lands Martin Van Buren elected president		

political lobbying. The line between social reform and politics was not always clear, however. Temperance, institutional reform, and, most notably, Antimasonry and abolition lured new voters into politics. But opponents of reform were just as concerned with social problems and just as interested in political solutions. What distinguished them from reformers was their skepticism about human perfectibility and their distrust of institutions and the exercise of power, both public and private. To them, government coercion was the greater evil. They sought to reverse, not shape, change.

Two issues in particular served as bridges between reform and politics: the short-lived Antimasonry frenzy and the intense, uncompromising crusade for immediate emancipation. Though Antimasons organized the first third-party movement, abolition eventually overrode all other concerns. No single issue evoked the passion that slavery did. It pitted neighbor against neighbor, settler against settler, section against section. Politicians had long recognized that slavery was a political powder keg, and they had adopted the Missouri Compromise of 1820 to avoid igniting it. Territorial expansion in the 1840s and 1850s, however, made slavery politically explosive. Abolitionism influenced the woman's movement as well.

Opponents of religious reform found a champion in Andrew Jackson and a home in the Democratic Party in the late 1820s. Yet the Jacksonians, too, saw themselves as reformers; they sought to foster individualism and restore restraint in the federal government. They opposed special privileges and the Second Bank of the United States with the same vigor with which reformers opposed sin. President Jackson believed that a strong federal government restricted individual freedom by favoring one group over another. In response, social reformers rallied around the new Whig Party, which became the vehicle of humanitarian reform. Democrats and Whigs constituted a new party system, characterized by strong organizations, intensely loyal followings, and energetic religious and ethnic competition.

Both parties eagerly promoted expansionism during the prosperous 1840s. Democrats saw the agrarian West as an antidote to urbanization and industrialization; Whigs focused on the new commercial opportunities it offered. Expansion from coast to coast seemed to Americans to be the manifest destiny of the United States. Texas, California, and Oregon, unknown to most Americans at the turn of the century, had become familiar places by the 1830s and 1840s, and the United States was on the road to war with Mexico. Then race was added to the brew as the politics of territorial expansion and the antislavery movement boiled over in the 1850s and 1860s.

 ## From Revival to Reform

Religion was probably the prime motivating force behind organized benevolence and reform. Religious revival stimulated by the Second Great Awakening galvanized Protestants, especially women, from the late 1790s to the 1840s. Under its influence, the role of churches and ministers in community life began to change, and Christians in all parts of the country tried to right the wrongs of the world.

Before the Second Great Awakening, churches found themselves diminishing in influence and having to compete with other voluntary societies for members. A new generation of seminary-trained ministers successfully introduced revivals and advocacy of benevolent works—aid to the poor, education of the young, and temperance campaigns—to attract new members, especially women. But while

churches grew, their authority continued to erode. They stimulated people emotionally, but less and less they controlled people's behavior.

Revivals—the lifeblood of evangelical Christianity—won converts to a religion of the heart rather than the head. In 1821 New York lawyer Charles G. Finney, the father of modern revivalism, experienced a soul-shaking conversion that he interpreted as "a retainer from the Lord Jesus Christ to plead his cause." Finney abandoned the law to convert souls, taking revival services and three- to four-day camp meetings to towns in western New York. Social reformer Elizabeth Cady Stanton attended a Finney revival and was converted.

Second Great Awakening

Salvation could be achieved, Finney preached, through spontaneous conversion or spiritual rebirth like his own. He evoked emotional responses. Using everyday language, Finney preached that "God has made man a moral free agent." In other words, evil was avoidable: Christians were not doomed by original sin, and anyone could achieve salvation. Finney's brand of revivalism transcended sects, class, and race but had a particularly strong base among Baptists and Methodists. These sects grew the most because their structure maximized democratic participation and they drew their ministers from ordinary folk.

The Second Great Awakening raised people's hopes for the Second Coming of the Christian messiah and establishment of the Kingdom of God on earth. Revivalists resolved to speed the Second Coming by creating a heaven on earth, marshaling the forces of good and light—reform—to combat the forces of evil and darkness. Some revivalists even believed that the United States had a special mission in God's design and therefore a special role in eliminating evil.

Regardless of theology, all revivalists shared a belief in individual self-improvement. Thus the Second Great Awakening bred reform, and evangelical Protestants became missionaries for both religious and secular salvation. Wherever they preached, evangelists generated new religious groups and voluntary reform societies. New sects like the Mormons arose out of this ferment. Evangelical reformers organized associations to address pressing issues: temperance, education, Sabbath observance, dueling, and later antislavery. Collectively these groups constituted a national web of benevolent and moral-reform societies. Finney's doctrine of perfectibility demanded that Christians actively work with other people. By organizing and converting others, and by renouncing their own personal corruptions and dependency, the converted confirmed their status as Christians. They also moved toward reform and ultimately toward public action.

Women's involvement grew remarkably during the Second Great Awakening and invigorated local churches. In Andover, Massachusetts, revivalism gave rise in 1814 to a men's society dedicated to uplifting morality, banishing swearing, observing the Sabbath, and discouraging drunkenness. The next year local women formed the Female Charitable Society, and a year later youth joined the Juvenile Bible Society. During the 1820s, without any revivals in Andover, the benevolent societies brought in new church members, of whom 70 to 80 percent were women.

Role of Women

Women were the earliest converts to evangelism, and they tended to sustain the Second Great Awakening. Pious middle-class women in Rochester, New York, for instance, responded to Finney's prayer meetings by spreading the word to other women during the day while their husbands were at work. Gradually women brought their families and husbands into church and reform. Although many businessmen recruited their employees to revivalism and benevolent work, women more than men tended to feel personally responsible for counteracting the increasingly secular orientation of the expanding market economy. Many women felt guilty for neglecting their religious duties, and the emotionally charged conversion experience returned them to what they believed was the right path.

Beyond conversion, the great influence of the Second Great Awakening was the spread of women's participation in benevolent societies to ameliorate social ills. The prayer groups and female missionary societies gave rise to organized religious and benevolent activity on an unprecedented scale. In cities women responded both to their inner voices and to the growing inequality, turbulence, and wretched conditions around them. The poverty and vice that accompanied urbanization touched the hearts of women, especially those caught up in the fervor of revival. By 1800 most cities had women's benevolent societies to help needy women and orphans.

Religion and Reform

Both female and male reformers sometimes opposed traditional political leaders. An exposé of prostitution in New York City illustrates the gulf between reform-minded men and women and the political establishment. John R. McDowall, a divinity student, published a report in 1830 documenting the prevalence of prostitution in New York City. Philip Hone, a prominent civic leader (see pages 325–326), denounced McDowall's report as "a disgraceful document," and he and other New York businessmen and politicians united to defend the city's good name against "those base slanders." Reform-minded women, however, moved by the plight of "fallen women" and the calls for reform from McDowall and others, organized to fight prostitution. While male reformers made the prostitutes the target of their zeal, the newly organized Female Moral Reform Society focused on the men who victimized young women, publicizing the names of men who entered brothels in New York City.

The New York–based Female Moral Reform Society led the crusade against prostitution. During the 1830s, the organization expanded its activities and geographical scope, calling itself the American Female Moral Reform Society. By 1840 it had 555 affiliated female societies across the nation. They combated prostitution by focusing on men and by assisting poor women whose economic desperation might lead them to turn to prostitution. They also entered the political sphere. In New York State in the 1840s the movement successfully crusaded for criminal sanctions against the men who seduced women into prostitution and against the prostitutes themselves.

As the pace of social change quickened in the 1830s and 1840s, so did religious fervor and reform. In western New York and Ohio, Finney's preaching acted as a catalyst to reform. Western New York experienced such continuous and heated waves of revivalism that it became known as "the burned-over district." The westward migration of New Englanders along the newly opened Erie Canal carried religious ferment to Ohio. There, revivalist institutions—notably Ohio's Lane Seminary and Oberlin College—sent committed graduates out into the world to spread the gospel of reform. The efforts of these early reformers stirred nonevangelical Protestants, Catholics, and Jews, as well as evangelical Christians, and they became involved in new grassroots political movements. In the late 1830s and 1840s they rallied around the Whig Party in hopes of using government as an instrument of reform.

One of the most successful reform efforts was the campaign against alcohol. Drinking was more widespread in the early nineteenth century than it is

Temperance

today. American men gathered in public houses, saloons, and rural inns to gossip, talk politics, play cards, escape work and home, and drink whiskey, rum, and hard cider. Contracts were sealed, celebrations commemorated, and harvests toasted with liquor. Respectable women did not drink in public, but many regularly tippled alcohol-based patent medicines promoted as cure-alls. Why then did temperance become such a vital issue? And why were women especially active in the movement? Like all nineteenth-century reform, temperance had a strong religious foundation.

Evangelicals considered drinking a sin, and forsaking alcohol was part of conversion. The sale of whiskey often involved a Sabbath violation, for workers commonly labored six days a week and spent Sunday at the public house drinking and socializing. Equally important, alcoholism destroyed families. In the early 1840s thousands of ordinary women formed Martha Washington societies to protect families by reforming alcohols, raising children as teetotalers, and spreading temperance. Contemporary imagery was laced with domestic images—abandoned wives, prodigal sons, drunken fathers. Timothy Shay Arthur dramatized all these evils in *Ten Nights in a Barroom* (1853), a classic American melodrama, as did Deacon Robert Peckham in his temperance paintings. Employers complained that drinkers took "St. Monday" as a holiday to recover from Sunday. In the new world of the factory, drinking was unacceptable.

Demon rum became a prime target of reformers. As the temperance movement gained momentum, its goal shifted from moderate use of alcohol to voluntary abstinence and finally to prohibition. The American Society for the Promotion of Temperance, organized in 1826 to sign drinkers to a pledge of abstinence, became a pressure group for state prohibition legislation. By the mid-1830s there were five thousand state and local temperance societies, and more than a million people had taken the pledge. Several hundred thousand children, for instance, enlisted in the Cold Water Army. Thousands of wives and mothers joined the Martha Washingtons in the 1840s.

Temperance Societies

The temperance movement's success was reflected in a sharp decline in alcohol consumption. Per capita consumption fell from five gallons in 1800 to below two gallons in the 1840s. Success bred more victories. Maine prohibited the manufacture and sale of alcohol except for medicinal purposes in 1851, and by 1855 similar laws had been enacted throughout New England, in New York, Pennsylvania, and the Midwest.

Though consumption was declining, opposition to alcohol grew. From the 1820s on, many reformers expressed their prejudices by regarding alcohol as an evil introduced by Catholic immigrants. The Irish and Germans, the *American Protestant Magazine* complained in 1849, "bring the grog shops like the frogs of Egypt upon us." Rum and immigrants defiled the Sabbath; rum and immigrants brought poverty; rum and immigrants supported the feared papacy. Some Catholics took the pledge of abstinence and formed their own organizations, such as the St. Mary's Mutual Benevolent Total Abstinence Society in Boston. Even some nondrinking Catholics tended to oppose state regulation of drinking, however; temperance seemed to them a question of individual choice. They favored self-control, not state coercion.

Another aspect of the temperance movement was opposition to gambling. People gambled in taverns, and reformers believed that both drinking and gambling undermined independence and self-reliance. Of special concern in the nineteenth century was the spread of lotteries.

Lotteries

Lotteries were common in colonial times. The Continental Congress tried to raise $1.5 million from a lottery to wage revolutionary war against England but fell short of that amount. In the early nineteenth century, state and local governments seeking to ease the tax burden used lotteries to raise money for capital improvements. Lotteries, however, became a target of reform, and between 1830 and 1860 every state banned them.

Reformers compared lotteries to slavery and alcohol. Others objected to the abuses inherent in the states' practice of delegating their lottery powers to private sponsors. An 1831 Pennsylvania investigation, for instance, revealed that a state-authorized lottery to raise $27,000 a year for internal improvements, specifically for the Union Canal Company, had generated enormous profits for the lottery company. From annual sales of $5 million, the state received its $27,000, and the sponsors received $800,000. At the urging of Protestant reformers

The evils of drinking and the bliss of temperance were a major theme in popular culture. Deacon Robert Peckham illustrated the contrast in two paintings from the 1840s: The Woes of Liquor (Intemperance) *and* The Happy Abstemious Family (Temperance).   Worcester Historical Museum.

who condemned all forms of gambling, Pennsylvania prohibited lotteries. (When some states revived lotteries in the twentieth century, they learned from the previous century's experiences and chose to run their own contests.)

The age of reform also brought about the construction of asylums and other institutions to house prisoners, the mentally ill, orphans, delinquent children, and the poor. Such institutions were needed, reformers believed, to shelter victims of society's instability and turbulence and of the lack of discipline in families. In an environment of order, stability, and discipline, inmates would have an opportunity to become self-reliant and responsible.

Penitentiaries and Asylums

The penitentiary movement exemplified this outlook. In the 1820s New York and Pennsylvania developed competing models for reforming criminals. Both rejected incarceration simply to punish criminals or remove them from society, believing instead that disciplined regimens would rehabilitate them. New York's Auburn (1819–1823) and Sing-Sing (1825) prisons isolated prisoners in individual cells but brought them together in common workshops. Pennsylvania's Pittsburgh (1826) and Philadelphia (1829) prisons isolated prisoners completely, forcing them to eat, sleep, and work in their individual cells and allowing them contact only with guards and visitors. Both systems sought to separate criminals from evil societal and individual influences and to expose them to a regimen of order and discipline. It was widely believed that criminals came from unstable families whose lack of discipline and restraint led to vice and drink. Idleness was believed to be both a symptom and a cause of individual corruption and crime; thus the clock governed a prisoner's day, and idleness was banished.

Similar approaches were employed in insane asylums, hospitals, and orphanages. By exposing the inhumane treatment of the mentally ill, Dorothea Dix built a national movement. Formerly the prescribed treatment had been to remove disturbed individuals from their families and society and isolate them among strangers; many were incarcerated with criminals. The new asylums removed them from society but attempted to impose discipline and order in a humane fashion. In response to Dix's crusade and reform societies, twenty-eight of the thirty-three states had public institutions for the mentally ill by 1860.

Antimasonry

More intense than the asylum movement but of shorter duration was the crusade against Freemasonry, a secret middle- and upper-class fraternity that had come to the United States from England in the eighteenth century. Sons of the Enlightenment such as Benjamin Franklin and George Washington were attracted to Masonry, with its emphasis on individual belief in a deity (as opposed to organized religion) and on brotherhood (as opposed to one church). In the early nineteenth century Freemasonry spread, attracting men prominent in commerce and civic affairs. For ambitious young men, the Masons offered access to and fellowship with the leading lights of the community.

Opponents of Masonry charged that the order's secrecy was antidemocratic and antirepublican, as were its elite membership and its use of uniforms. Publications such as the *Anti Masonic Almanac* attacked Masonic initiation rites. Evangelicals labeled the order satanic. Antimasons argued that Masonry threatened the family because it excluded women and encouraged men to neglect their families for alcohol and ribald entertainments at Masonic lodges.

The Antimasonry movement arose overnight in the burned-over district of western New York in 1826 and virtually disappeared in the 1830s. Foreshadowing abolitionism, it quickly became a political movement. Antimasonry created the first third-party movement and drew new white voters into politics at a time when male suffrage was being extended. As the temperance movement sought to liberate individuals from drink, Antimasons sought to liberate society from the grip of what they considered a powerful and antirepublican secret fraternity. Just as asylums would restore individual discipline and harmony, the Antimasons believed, the abolition of Masonry would reestablish communal moral discipline and harmony. The political arena quickly absorbed Antimasonry, and its short life illustrates the close association of politics and reform between the 1820s and the 1840s.

Morgan Affair

The catalyst for Antimasonry as an organized movement was the Morgan affair. In 1826 William Morgan, a disillusioned Mason, published an exposé, *The Illustration of Masonry, By One of the Fraternity Who Has Devoted Thirty Years to the Subject*, to which his printer David Miller added a scathing attack on the order. Just prior to the book's appearance, a group of Masons abducted Morgan in Canandaigua, New York. It was widely believed that they murdered him, though his body was never found.

Events seemed to confirm the Antimasonry crusade's depiction of Masonry as a secret conspiracy. Many officeholders in western New York, especially prosecutors, were Masons, and they appeared to obstruct the investigation of Morgan's abduction. The public pressed for justice, and the series of notorious trials that ensued from 1827 through 1831 led many to suspect a conspiracy. The cover-up became as much of an issue as Masonry itself, and the movement spread from the burned-over district to other states.

As a moral crusade, Antimasonry spilled over into the political arena almost immediately. The issue itself was political, because of the perceived obstruction of justice. Furthermore, Antimasonry attracted the lower and middle classes, pitting them against higher-status Masons and exploiting the general public's distrust and envy of local political leaders.

Unwittingly, the Masons stoked the fires of Antimasonry. By their silence they seemed to condone the murder of Morgan, and by their construction of monumental lodges in Boston and elsewhere they called attention to their affluence and prominence. The conflict aroused a high level of public interest in politics. Wherever religious fervor flared and wherever families were entering the market economy for the first time, Antimasonry flourished.

As Antimasonry won a popular following, it introduced the convention system in place of caucuses for choosing political candidates. Invoking public morality and republican principles, the Antimasons held conventions in 1827 to select candidates to oppose Masons. The next year the conventions supported the National Republican candidate, John Quincy Adams, and opposed Andrew Jackson because he was a Mason. The Antimasons held the first national political convention in Baltimore in 1831, and a year later they nominated William Wirt as their presidential candidate. Thus the Antimasons became a rallying point for those opposed to President Andrew Jackson. Their electoral strength lay in New England and New York. In Vermont the Antimasons became the dominant party for a brief time in 1833; in Massachusetts Antimasons replaced the Democrats as the second major party. Antimasonry found little support, however, in the South.

Convention System

No. IV.
ANTI MASONIC ALMANAC,
FOR THE YEAR
1831:
BY EDWARD GIDDINS.

Antimasonic publications, such as this 1831 almanac, made much of the allegedly sinister initiation rites that bound a new member "to keep all Masonic secrets, under the penalty of having his throat cut, his tongue torn out, and his body buried in the ocean." Print collection, Miriam and Ira D. Wallach Division of Art, Prints, and Photographs, New York Public Library.

By the mid-1830s, Antimasonry had lost momentum as a moral and political movement. A single-issue party, the Antimasons declined along with Freemasonry. Yet the movement left its mark on the politics of the era. As a moral crusade focused on public officeholders, it inspired broad participation in the political process. The Antimasons also changed party organization by pioneering the convention system and stimulating grassroots involvement.

Antimasonry also had much in common with abolitionism. Indeed, as Antimasonry waned, the antislavery movement gathered momentum. Abolitionist William Lloyd Garrison at first ignored the frenzy over the Morgan affair but in 1832 he joined the ranks of Antimasons. Echoing his stand on emancipation, Garrison wrote: "I go for the immediate, unconditional and total abolition of Freemasonry." In his eyes, both slavery and Masonry undermined republican values.

Abolitionism and the Women's Movement

The issue of slavery eventually became so compelling that it consumed all other reforms. Passions became so heated that they threatened the nation itself. Those who advocated immediate emancipation saw slavery as, above all, a moral issue—evidence of the sinfulness of the American nation. When territorial expansion forced the issue of slavery to center stage in the 1850s, the abolitionist forces were well prepared (see Chapter 14).

Before the 1830s few whites advocated the abolition of slavery. Quakers had shown the way, freeing their slaves and preaching that bondage was a sin. But in the North, where most states had begun to abolish slavery by 1800, whites took little interest in the issue. Antislavery sentiment appeared strongest in the Upper South, though northern involvement grew with the expansion of benevolent societies after the War of 1812. The American Colonization Society, founded in 1816, advocated gradual, voluntary emancipation and resettlement of former slaves in Africa, and it attracted evangelicals, Quakers, some blacks (briefly), and some slaveholders. The gradualist antislavery movement remained strong, but in the 1830s the immediatists—those who demanded immediate, complete, and uncompensated emancipation—surpassed the gradualists as the dominant strand of abolitionism.

At first only African-Americans demanded an immediate end to slavery. By 1830 there were more than fifty black abolitionist societies. They as-

Black Abolitionists sisted fugitive slaves, lobbied for emancipation, exposed the evils of slavery, and reminded the nation that its mission as defined in the Declaration of Independence remained unfulfilled. A free black press helped to spread the word. Black abolitionists Frederick Douglass, Sojourner Truth, and Harriet Tubman joined forces in the 1840s with white reformers in the American Anti-Slavery Society. Their militant and unrelenting campaign also won European support. "Brethren, arise, arise, arise!" Henry Highland Garnet commanded the 1843 National Colored Convention. "Strike for your lives and liberties. Now is the day and hour. Let every slave in the land do this and the days of slavery are numbered. Rather die freemen than live to be slaves."

In the 1830s a small number of white reformers, driven by moral urgency, crusaded for immediate emancipation. The most prominent and uncompromising immediatist, though far from the most representative,

William Lloyd Garrison was William Lloyd Garrison, who demanded "immediate and complete emancipation." Garrison, a talented journalist, broke with moderate abolitionists in 1831. That year he published the first issue of *The Liberator*, which was to be his major weapon against slavery for thirty-five years. As he declared in the first issue, "I am in earnest—I will not equivocate—I will not excuse—I will not retreat a single inch—*and I will be heard.*"

Garrison's staunch refusal to work with anyone who tolerated the delay of emancipation isolated him from other opponents of slavery. He even forswore political action on the grounds that it was government that permitted slavery. (Garrison burned a copy of the Constitution on July 4, 1854, proclaiming, "So perish all compromises with tyranny.") Through sheer rhetorical power, Garrison helped to make antislavery a national issue. His brand of immediatism consisted of a refusal to tolerate delay in ending slavery; he had no specific plan for abolishing it. In essence, what Garrison called for was *conversion* of those who held slaves or cooperated with institutions that supported slavery; they should cast off their sins, repent, and do battle against evil.

It is difficult to differentiate between those who became immediatists and those who did not. But immediatists like Garrison, Elizabeth Chandler, Amos Phelps, and Theodore

Immediatists Weld had much in common. They were young evangelicals active in benevolent societies in the 1820s; many became ordained ministers or flirted with the ministry as a career; and they had personal contact with free blacks and were sympathetic to African-American rights. They were convinced that slaveholding was a sin. Their immediatism made them more concerned about sin in the United States than about converting "heathens across the seas," and their concern in turn made them more political: to abolish sin, they sought to change institutions at home. Finally, they shared

How do historians know how the abolitionists, especially women and African-Americans, built their movement? Abolitionists lived open lives. They used newspapers, pamphlets, speeches, and sermons to expose the evils of slavery, to mount a crusade for emancipation, and to build a network of like-minded people. Much of their correspondence and most of their speeches were printed in abolitionist newspapers, such as The Liberator, *published by William Lloyd Garrison.*

Here, twentieth-century African-American artist Jacob Lawrence depicts abolitionist Frederick Douglass lecturing in eastern Massachusetts, describing his life as a slave and telling of the cruelty of the system. In 1841 Douglass became a supporter of Garrison and a contributor to The Liberator, *which appeared from 1831 to 1866. The newspaper printed passionate attacks on slavery, reported on meetings of antislavery societies, and published letters, especially from women and African-American abolitionists. Under the banners "No Union with Slaveholders" and "The United States Constitution is a 'convenant with death, and an agreement with hell,'"* The Liberator *circulated to abolitionists advocating immediate emancipation. The subscription lists that have survived indicate that a majority of its subscribers probably were African-Americans.* Hampton University Museum, Hampton, Virginia.

great moral intensity. They were unwilling to compromise their beliefs, and their zeal made them activists. Their main organizational vehicle was the American Anti-Slavery Society, founded in 1833.

Most benevolent workers and reformers kept their distance from the immediatists. Many regarded the intensity of the immediatist approach as unchristian. They shared with immediatists the view that slavery was a sin but believed in gradual emancipation. They feared that if they moved too fast, attacked sinners too harshly, or interfered too aggressively in time-honored customs and beliefs, they would destroy the harmony and order they sought to bring about through benevolent and reform work.

Immediatists' greatest recruitment successes resulted from their defense of their own constitutional and natural rights, not the rights of slaves. Wherever they went, immediatists found their civil rights, especially free speech at risk. Hostile crowds threatened abolitionist speakers and presses. Mobs violently defended what they considered to be American traditions. At Utica, New York, merchants and professionals broke up the state Anti-Slavery Convention in 1835. Abolitionist conventions provoked hostility by welcoming blacks and women. Fear and hatred moved proslavery proponents to take to the streets. In 1837 a mob in Alton, Illinois, murdered abolitionist editor Elijah P. Lovejoy, who had been driven out of slaveholding Missouri. Before killing Lovejoy, rioters sacked his office with the cooperation of local authorities. Public outrage at Lovejoy's murder broadened the base of antislavery support in the North.

Opposition to Abolitionists

In the South, mobs blocked distribution of antislavery pamphlets. Using high-speed printing presses, the American Anti-Slavery Society increased its distribution of antislavery propaganda tenfold in the 1830s by sending out 1.1 million pieces. But southern mobs frequently seized and destroyed the mailings, and South Carolina intercepted and burned abolitionist literature that entered the state. President Andrew Jackson even proposed a law prohibiting the mailing of antislavery tracts.

The opposition saw danger in abolitionism. At a rally in Boston's Faneuil Hall in 1835 former Federalist Harrison Gray Otis portrayed abolitionists as subversives. He attacked Garrison's American Anti-Slavery Society as a "revolutionary society" that not only recruited all men to its "holy crusade" but also asked women to "turn their sewing parties into abolition clubs." If it prevailed, Otis charged, school primers would teach "that A stands for abolition." The abolitionists, he predicted, would soon turn to politics, causing unforeseeable calamity. "What will become of the nation?" Otis asked. "What will become of the union?" Others believed that the immediatists' opposition to sending black people back to Africa undermined the best solution. Keeping blacks in America, they believed, eventually would lead to slave rebellions and racial amalgamation.

Another confrontation focused on the House of Representatives. Abolitionists, exercising their con-

Gag Rule

stitutional right to petition Congress, campaigned to abolish slavery and the slave trade in the District of Columbia. (Because the district was under federal rule, states' rights arguments against interfering with slavery did not apply there.) The House responded in 1836 by adopting the "gag rule," which automatically tabled abolitionist petitions, effectively preventing debate on them. Immediatists flooded Congress with nearly seven hundred thousand petitions. In a dramatic defense of the right of petition, former president John Quincy Adams, a Massachusetts representative, took to the floor repeatedly to defy the gag rule and in 1844 succeeded in getting it repealed.

Frustration with the federal government also fed northern support for antislavery. Generally speaking, politicians and government officials sought to avoid the question of slavery. The Missouri Compromise of 1820 had been an effort to quarantine the issue by adopting a formula—prohibition of slavery north of 36°30', Missouri's southern boundary—that would make debate on the slave or free status of new states unnecessary (see map, page 368). Censorship of the mails and the gag rule also represented attempts to keep the issue out of the political arena. Yet the more intensely national leaders, especially Democrats, worked to avoid the matter, the more they hardened the resolve of the antislavery forces.

The unlawful and violent tactics used by opponents of abolition unified the movement by forcing the various factions to work together for mutual defense. Antislavery was not at the outset a unified movement. It was factionalized, and its adherents fought each other as doggedly and as often as they fought the defenders of slavery. They were divided over Garrison's emphasis on "moral suasion" versus the more practical political approach of James G. Birney, the Liberty Party's candidate for president in 1844 (see page 371). They were split over support for other reforms, especially the rights of women. And they disagreed about the place of free people of color in American society.

Many women joined local female antislavery societies through churches as part of the network of reform societies. Some opposed extending benevolent work into the political arena, and this issue led to the disbanding of the seven-year-old Boston Female Anti-Slavery Society in 1840. Especially in abo-

Women Abolitionists

lition issues and in women's rights, however, women became more politically involved and took an equal role with men. Lydia Maria Child, Maria Chapman, and Lucretia Mott all joined the American Anti-Slavery Society's executive committee; Child edited its official organ, the *National Anti-Slavery Standard*, from 1841 to 1843, and Chapman coedited it from 1844 until 1848. Garrison's *moral* suasion attracted many women because it gave them a platform from which to oppose slavery. Where *political* power was stressed, women were often excluded because they could not vote.

Opposition to women's prominent public roles in reform movements led some women to reexamine their position in society. In the 1830s Angelina and Sarah Grimké challenged slavery and women's right to speak out. Born into a slaveholding family in Charleston, South Carolina, both sisters experienced conversion and independently became Quakers. In 1834 both aspired to be more politically involved in reform, especially in abolitionism. They found in Garrison's immediatism a home. Yet they were soon attacked for speaking before mixed groups of men and women. Some New England Congregationalists and even abolitionists joined in the criticism; as one pastoral letter put it, women should obey, not lecture, men. This reaction turned the Grimkés' attention from slavery to the women's condition. The two attacked the concept of "subordination to man," insisting that men and women had the "same rights and same duties." Sarah Grimké's *Letters on the Condition of Women and the Equality of the Sexes* (1838) and her sister's *Letters to Catharine E. Beecher*, published the same year, were the opening volleys in the long war over the legal and social inequality of women.

Women involved with abolitionism crossed the path from pious and moral opposition against slavery to political engagement. Like the Grimké sisters, other women abolitionists encountered restrictions because they were women. Elizabeth Cady Stanton and Lucretia Mott had traveled to London in 1840 for the World Anti-Slavery Convention and had to sit in a balcony, denied participation, because they were women. But women active in abolitionism had developed the experience to do something about their limited rights: they could organize on their own behalf.

Women's Rights

In July 1848 three hundred women and men reformers gathered at the Woman's Rights Conven-

Women played an activist role in reform, especially in abolitionism. A rare daguerreotype from August 1850 shows women and men, including Frederick Douglass, on the podium at an abolitionist rally in Cazenovia, New York. Collection of J. Paul Getty Museum, Los Angeles, California.

tion at Seneca Falls, New York, to demand political, social, and economic equality for women. Led by Stanton, Mott, and Lucy Stone, they protested women's legal disabilities—inability to vote, limited property rights—and their social restrictions—exclusion from advanced schooling and from most occupations. Their Declaration of Sentiments, modeled after the Declaration of Independence, was an indictment of the injustices suffered by women, and it launched the women's rights movement. "All men and women are created equal," the declaration proclaimed. If women had the vote, participants argued, they could protect themselves and realize their full potential as moral and spiritual leaders.

Advocates of women's rights were slow to garner support, especially from men, who held most of the political and legal power. In the 1840s the question of women's rights split the antislavery movement; the majority declared themselves opposed. Some

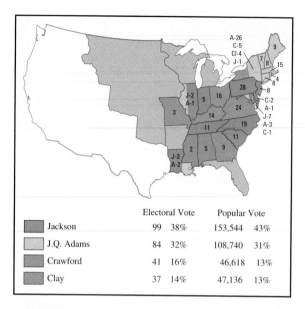

	Electoral Vote		Popular Vote	
Jackson	99	38%	153,544	43%
J.Q. Adams	84	32%	108,740	31%
Crawford	41	16%	46,618	13%
Clay	37	14%	47,136	13%

Presidential Election, 1824 Andrew Jackson led in both electoral and popular votes but failed to win a majority of electoral college votes. The House elected John Quincy Adams president.

men joined the ranks, notably Garrison and Frederick Douglass, but most men actively opposed. Not everyone at Seneca Falls signed the resolution on women's suffrage. Of the one hundred who did, only two would live to see the passage of the Nineteenth Amendment to the Constitution seventy-two years later.

Jacksonianism and Party Politics

In the 1820s the distinction between reform and politics began to erode as reform pushed its way into politics. No less than reformers, politicians sought to control the direction of change in the expanding nation. After a brief flirtation with single-party politics after the War of 1812, the United States entered a period of intense political competition. As the age of Virginia presidents came to an end in 1825, the Republican Party was split by hard times, sectional disputes, abolitionism, and reform. The 1824 presidential election ignited a political barn fire that reformers, abolitionists, and expansionists would continuously stoke. By the 1830s, politics had become the great nineteenth-century American pastime.

The election of 1824, in which John Quincy Adams and Andrew Jackson faced off for the first time, heralded a new, more open political system.

End of the Caucus System

From 1800 through 1820 the system in which a congressional caucus chose Jefferson, Madison, and Monroe as the Republican nominees had worked well. Such a system limited voters' involvement in choosing candidates but at first was not an anomaly because in 1800 only five of the sixteen states selected presidential electors by popular vote. (In most cases, state legislatures selected the electors who voted for president.) By 1816, however, ten out of nineteen states chose electors by popular vote, and by 1824 eighteen out of twenty-four did so. With the voters choosing electors, Congress could no longer sustain its control over the nomination system.

The Republican caucus in 1824 chose William H. Crawford, secretary of the treasury, as its presidential candidate. But other Republicans, emboldened by the chance to appeal directly to voters, put themselves forward as sectional candidates. Secretary of State John Quincy Adams drew support from New England, and westerners backed Speaker of the House Henry Clay of Kentucky. Secretary of War John C. Calhoun looked to the South for support and hoped to win Pennsylvania as well. The Tennessee legislature nominated Andrew Jackson, a popular military hero whose political views were unknown. Jackson had the most widespread support, but Crawford led in the party caucus. By boycotting the caucus and by attacking it as undemocratic, the four other candidates and their supporters ended the role of Congress in nominating presidential candidates.

In the four-way presidential election of 1824, Andrew Jackson led in both electoral and popular votes, but no candidate received a majority in the electoral college (see map).

Election of 1824

Adams finished second, and Crawford and Clay trailed far behind. (Calhoun had dropped out of the race before the election.) As required by the Twelfth Amendment to the Constitution, the House of Representatives, voting by state delegation, one vote to a state, selected the next president from among the leaders in electoral votes. Clay, who had received the fewest votes, was dropped. Crawford, a stroke victim, never received serious consideration. The influential Clay—Speaker of the House and leader of the Ohio valley states—

backed Adams, who received the votes of thirteen of the twenty-four state delegations. Clay then became secretary of state in the Adams administration, the traditional steppingstone to the presidency.

Angry Jacksonians denounced the outcome of the election as a "corrupt bargain" that had stolen the office from the front runner. Congressional intrigue had thwarted the will of the people, Jacksonians believed, and Jackson's bitterness reinforced his opposition to elitism and fueled his later emphasis on the people's will. The Republican Party split. The Adams wing emerged as the National Republicans, and the Jacksonians became the Democratic-Republicans (shortened to Democrats). The Jacksonians immediately began planning for 1828.

After taking the oath of office, Adams (the sixth president) proposed a strong nationalist policy incorporating Henry Clay's program of protective tariffs, a national bank, and internal improvements (see page 245). Adams believed the federal government should take an activist role not only in the economy but also in education, science, and the arts. He accordingly proposed the establishment of a national university in Washington, D.C. Brilliant as a diplomat and secretary of state, Adams was an inept president. The political skills he had demonstrated in winning the office eluded him as chief executive. He underestimated the lingering effects of the Panic of 1819 and the resulting bitter opposition to a national bank and protective tariffs. Meanwhile, supporters of Andrew Jackson sabotaged Adams's administration at every opportunity.

The 1828 campaign pitted Adams against Jackson in an intensely personal conflict. Principles gave way to mudslinging by both sides. Jackson's supporters renewed their claim that Adams had stolen the 1824 election. In his diary Adams declared Jackson "incompetent both by his ignorance and by the fury of his passions." The two camps traded charges of adultery and procuring prostitutes. When Rachel Jackson died a month after the election, the president-elect attributed his wife's death to the abuse heaped on him in the campaign. He never forgave her "murderers."

Election of 1828

Adams won the states he had won in 1824, but this time the opposition was unified, and Jackson swamped him (see map). Jackson polled 56 percent of the popular vote and won in the electoral college by 178 to 83 votes. He and his supporters believed

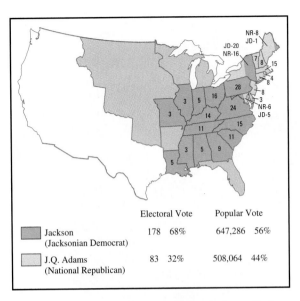

	Electoral Vote		Popular Vote	
Jackson (Jacksonian Democrat)	178	68%	647,286	56%
J.Q. Adams (National Republican)	83	32%	508,064	44%

Presidential Election, 1828 *Andrew Jackson avenged his 1824 loss of the presidency, sweeping the election in 1828.*

that the will of the people had finally been served. Many voters displayed their enthusiasm for Jackson with badges, medals, and other campaign paraphernalia, which were mass-produced for the first time.

Through a lavishly financed coalition of state parties, political leaders, and newspaper editors, a popular movement had elected the president, and an era had ended. The Democratic Party became the first well-organized national political party in the United States. Tightly organized parties would become the hallmark of nineteenth-century American politics.

Nicknamed "Old Hickory" after the toughest of American hardwoods, Andrew Jackson was a rough-and-tumble, ambitious man. Born in South Carolina in 1767, he rose from humble beginnings to become a wealthy Tennessee planter and slaveholder. Jackson was the first American president from the West and the first born in a log cabin; he was a self-made man at ease among both frontiersmen and southern planters. Though vindictive and given to violent displays of temper, he could charm away the suspicions of those opposed to him. A natural leader, Jackson inspired immense loyalty. He had an instinct

Andrew Jackson

President Andrew Jackson is portrayed here on a snuff box, an example of the campaign paraphernalia that were widely sold to partisan Jackson supporters.   Collection of David J. and Janice L. Frent.

for politics and picked both issues and supporters shrewdly.

Few Americans have been as celebrated as Jackson. Having fought in the Revolution as a boy, he bore scars from a redcoat attack. In the Tennessee militia General Jackson led the campaign to remove Creeks from the Alabama and Georgia frontier (see page 243). He burst onto the national scene as the great hero of the War of 1812, and in 1818 enhanced his glory in an expedition against Seminoles in Spanish Florida. Jackson also served as a congressman and senator from Tennessee, and as the first territorial governor of Florida (1821), before running for president in 1824.

Jackson and his Democratic supporters offered a distinct alternative to the strong federal government advocated by John Quincy Adams. The Democrats

Democrats

represented a wide range of views but shared a fundamental commitment to the Jeffersonian concept of an agrarian society. They harkened back to the belief that a strong central government is the enemy of individual liberty, a tyranny to be feared. The 1824 "corrupt bargain" had strengthened their suspicion of Washington

politics. Jackson himself, symbol of the backwoodsman and the farmer, affirmed the familiar old values that predated the new party politics and the new market system.

Jacksonians feared the concentration of economic and political power. They believed that government intervention in the economy benefited special-interest groups and created corporate monopolies; they rejected an activist economic program as favoring the rich. They sought to restore the independence of the individual—the artisan and the yeoman farmer—by ending federal support of banks and corporations and restricting the use of paper currency, which they distrusted. Their definition of the proper role of government tended to be negative, and Jackson's political power was largely expressed in negative acts. He exercised the veto more than all previous presidents combined.

Jackson and his supporters also opposed reform as a movement. Reformers eager to turn their programs into legislation were calling for a more activist and interventionist government. But Democrats tended to oppose programs like educational reform and the establishment of public education. They believed, for instance, that public schools restricted individual liberty by interfering with parental responsibility and undermined freedom of religion by replacing church schools. Nor did Jackson share reformers' humanitarian concerns. He showed little sympathy for Native Americans, initiating the removal of the Cherokees along the Trail of Tears (see page 337).

Jackson and the Jacksonians considered themselves reformers in a different way. By restraining government and emphasizing individualism, they

Jacksonians as Reformers

sought to restore old republican virtues, such as prudence and economy. No less zealous than reformers, Jackson sought to encourage self-discipline and self-reliance and to restore the harmony and unity that he saw disrupted by economic and social change. In doing so, Jackson looked to Jefferson and the generation of the founders as models of traditional values. "My political creed," Jackson wrote to Tennessee congressman James K. Polk in 1826, "was formed in the old republican school."

Like Jefferson, Jackson strengthened the executive branch of government even as he weakened the federal role. Given his popularity and the strength of his personality, this concentration of power in the presidency was perhaps inevitable, but in combining the roles of party leader and chief of state, he increased the centralization of power in the White House. Jackson relied on political friends, his "Kitchen Cabinet," for advice; he rarely consulted his official cabinet. Enamored of power, Jackson never hesitated to confront his opponents with all the weapons at his disposal. He commanded enormous loyalty, and he rewarded his followers handsomely. Invoking the principle that rotating officeholders would make government more responsive to the public will, Jackson used the spoils system to appoint loyal Democrats to office. He removed fewer than one-quarter of the federal officeholders he inherited, but he used patronage to strengthen party organization and loyalty.

Jackson stressed rejection of elitism and special favors, rotation of officeholders, and belief in popular government. Time and again he declared that sovereignty resided with the people, not with the states or the courts. In this respect Jackson was a reformer; he returned government to majority rule. Yet it is hard to distinguish between Jackson's belief in himself as the instrument of the people and simple egotism and demagogic arrogance. After all, his opponents, too, claimed to represent the people.

Animosity grew year by year among President Jackson's supporters and opponents. Massachusetts senator Daniel Webster feared the men around the president; Henry Clay most feared Jackson himself. Rotation in office, they contended, corrupted government. Opponents mocked Jackson as "King Andrew I," charging him with abusing his presidential powers by ignoring the Supreme Court's ruling on Cherokee rights (see page 336), by his use of the spoils system, and by his dependence on the Kitchen Cabinet. Critics rejected his claim of restoring republican virtue. They charged him with recklessly and impulsively destroying the economy.

Jackson injected new vigor into the philosophy of limited government. In 1830 he vetoed the Maysville Road bill—which would have funded construction of a 60-mile turnpike from Maysville to Lexington, Kentucky. A federally subsidized internal improvement confined to one state was unconstitutional, he charged; such projects were properly a state responsibility. The veto undermined Henry Clay's nationalist program and personally embarrassed Clay because the project was in his home district. Such federal-state issues were to loom even larger in the nullification crisis.

Federalism at Issue: The Nullification and Bank Controversies

Soon Jackson had to face the question of the proper division of sovereignty between state and central government more directly. The slave South feared federal power, no state more so than South Carolina, where the planter class was strongest and slavery most concentrated. Southerners, hard hit by the Panic of 1819, from which they never fully recovered, also resented protectionist tariffs.

To protect their interests, South Carolinian political leaders articulated the doctrine of *nullification*, according to which a state had the right to overrule, or nullify, federal legislation that conflicted with its own. Nullification was based on the idea expressed in the Virginia and Kentucky Resolutions of 1798 (see page 215)—that the states, representing the people, have a right to judge the constitutionality of federal actions. Jackson's vice president, John C. Calhoun of South Carolina, argued in his unsigned *Exposition and Protest* that, in any disagreement between the federal government and a state, a special state convention—like the conventions called to ratify the Constitution—should decide the conflict by either nullifying or affirming the federal law. Only the power of nullification, Calhoun asserted, could protect the minority against the tyranny of the majority.

In public, Calhoun let others take the lead in advancing nullification. As Jackson's running mate in 1828, he had avoided publicly endorsing nullification and thus embarrassing the Democratic ticket; he hoped to win Jackson's support as the Democratic presidential heir-apparent. Thus Calhoun presided silently over the Senate and its packed galleries when Senator Daniel Webster of Massachusetts and Senator Robert Y. Hayne of South Carolina debated nullification in early 1830. The debate explored North-South frictions and the nature of the Union. With Vice President Calhoun nodding in agreement, Hayne charged that the North was threatening to bring disunity, as it had done before at the Hartford Convention (see page 245). Hayne accused reformers in "the spirit of false philanthropy" of wanting to destroy the South.

For two days Webster eloquently defended the New England states and the republic, as he kept

Webster-Hayne Debate

nullification on the defense. Though debating Hayne, he really aimed his remarks at Calhoun, depicting the nation as a compact of people, not merely of states. At the climax of the debate, Webster invoked two powerful images. One was the outcome of nullification: "states dissevered, discordant, belligerent; on a land rent with civil feuds, or drenched . . . in fraternal blood!" The other was a patriotic vision of a great nation flourishing under the motto "Liberty *and* Union, now and forever, one and inseparable."

Though sympathetic to states' rights and distrustful of the federal government, Jackson rejected the idea of state sovereignty. He strongly believed that sovereignty rested with the people. Deeply loyal to the Union, he shared Webster's dread of nullification. Soon after the Webster-Hayne debate, the president made his position clear at a Jefferson Day dinner with the toast "Our Federal Union, it *must* and *shall be* preserved." Vice President Calhoun, when his turn came, toasted: "The Federal Union—next to our liberty the most dear." Torn between devotion to the Union and loyalty to his state, Calhoun had revealed his preference for states' rights. Politically and personally, Calhoun and Jackson grew apart, and it soon became apparent that Jackson favored Secretary of State Martin Van Buren, not Calhoun, as his successor.

South Carolina invoked the theory of nullification against the Tariff of 1832, which reduced some duties but retained high taxes on imported iron, cottons, and woolens. Though a majority of southern representatives supported the new tariff, South Carolinians refused to go along. In their eyes, the constitutional right to control their own destiny had been sacrificed to the demands of northern industrialists. More than the tariff, they feared the consequences of accepting such an act, because it could set a precedent for congressional legislation on slavery. In November 1832 a South Carolina state convention nullified the tariff, making it unlawful for federal officials to collect duties in the state. Recruiters immediately began to organize a volunteer army to ensure nonenforcement of the tariff.

Old Hickory responded with toughness. Privately he threatened to invade South Carolina and hang Vice President Calhoun; publicly he sought to avoid the use of force. In December Jackson issued a presidential proclamation nullifying nullification. He moved troops to federal forts in South Carolina

Nullification Crisis

and prepared United States marshals to collect the required duties. At Jackson's request, Congress passed the Force Act, which gave the president renewed authority to call up troops but also offered a way to avoid using force by collecting duties before foreign ships reached Charleston Harbor in South Carolina. At the same time, Jackson extended an olive branch by recommending tariff reductions.

Calhoun, disturbed by South Carolina's drift toward separatism, resigned as vice president and soon won election to represent South Carolina in the United States Senate. There he worked with Henry Clay to draw up the compromise Tariff of 1833. Quickly passed by Congress and signed by the president, the new tariff lengthened the list of duty-free items and reduced duties over nine years. Satisfied, South Carolina's convention repealed its nullification law. In a final salvo, it also nullified Jackson's Force Act. Jackson ignored the gesture.

Nullification offered a genuine debate on the nature and principles of the republic. Each side believed it was upholding the Constitution. Both sides felt they were opposing special privilege and subversion of republican values. South Carolina was fighting the tyranny of the federal government and manufacturers who sought tariff protection. Jackson was fighting the tyranny of South Carolina, whose refusal to bow to federal authority threatened to split the republic. Neither side won a clear victory, though both claimed to have done so. It took another crisis, over a central bank, to define the powers of the federal government more clearly.

At stake was survival of the Second Bank of the United States, whose twenty-year charter was scheduled to expire in 1836. Like its predecessor, the bank served as a depository for federal funds and was an important source of credit for business people. Its bank notes circulated as currency throughout the country; they could be readily exchanged for gold, and the federal government accepted them as payment in all transactions. Through its twenty-five branch offices, the Second Bank acted as a clearing-house for state banks, keeping them honest by refusing to accept in transactions state bank notes from any state bank that had insufficient gold in reserve.

Western farmers, urban workers, and many other Americans were suspicious of bank notes, regarding only specie—gold and silver coins—as real money. Coins—hard money—had intrinsic value (the value of the gold or silver contained in the coin).

Second Bank of the United States

Bank notes, by contrast, represented only a promise to pay specie on demand; the paper itself had no value. But as long as people had faith in the issuing institutions, bank notes circulated freely. The growing, market-oriented society needed more currency than the nation's supply of gold and silver could accommodate. Manufacturers, wholesalers, and retailers needed capital for investment and cash for transactions and thus were supporters of the Second Bank.

Enemies of the Second Bank made the redemption of bank notes for specie an issue. Most state banks resented the central bank's police role: by presenting a state bank's notes for redemption all at once, the Second Bank could easily ruin a state bank. Moreover, with less money in reserve, state banks found themselves unable to compete on an equal footing with the Second Bank. Many state governments also regarded the national bank, with its headquarters in Philadelphia, as unresponsive to local needs. Westerners and urban workers remembered with bitterness the bank's conservative credit policies during the Panic of 1819 (see page 248). Although the Second Bank served some of the functions of a central bank, it was a private, profit-making institution, and its policies reflected the interest of its owners. Its president, Nicholas Biddle, controlled the bank completely. An eastern patrician, Biddle symbolized all that westerners found wrong with the bank.

Rechartering was a volatile issue in the 1832 presidential campaign. The bank's charter was valid until 1836, but Henry Clay, the National Republican presidential candidate, persuaded Biddle to ask Congress to approve an early rechartering. This strategy was designed to marshal public pressure to force Jackson to sign the rechartering bill or to override his veto of it. The plan backfired, however. The president vetoed the bill, and the Senate failed to override. Jackson's veto message was an emotional attack on the undemocratic nature of the bank. "It is to be regretted," he wrote, "that the rich and powerful too often bend the acts of government to their selfish purposes."

The bank thus became the prime issue in the presidential campaign of 1832. Jackson led the way by denouncing special privilege and economic power. Operating in a system in which every state but South Carolina now chose electors by popular vote, the Jacksonians used their party organization to mobilize voters by advertising the presidential election as the focal point of the political system. When the Antimasons adopted a party platform, the first in the nation's history, the Democrats and the National Republicans quickly followed suit. Jackson and Martin Van Buren, Jackson's first secretary of state and then American minister to Great Britain, were nominated at the Democratic convention; Clay and John Sergeant, at the National Republican convention. South Carolina had its own candidate, John Floyd. Jackson was reelected easily in a Democratic party triumph.

Jackson's Second Term

After his sweeping victory and second inauguration, Jackson moved in 1833 to dismantle the Second Bank of the United States and to kill it forever. He deposited federal funds in state-chartered banks (critics called them his "pet banks"). Without federal money, the Second Bank shriveled. When its federal charter expired in 1836, it became just another Pennsylvania-chartered private bank. Five years later it closed its doors.

In conjunction with this coup de grâce to the Bank of the United States, Congress passed the Deposit Act of 1836 with Jackson's support. The act authorized the secretary of the treasury to designate one bank in each state and territory to provide the services formerly performed by the Bank of the United States. The act provided that the federal surplus in excess of $5 million be distributed to the states as interest-free loans beginning in 1837. These loans were never repaid—a fitting Jacksonian restraint on the federal purse.

Specie Circular

Jackson was worried about more than just restraining the government. The surplus had derived from wholesale speculation in public lands: speculators bought public land on credit, used the land as collateral to borrow more money to buy additional acreage, and repeated the cycle. Between 1834 and 1836 federal receipts from land sales rose from $5 million to $25 million. The state banks providing the loans issued bank notes. Jackson, an opponent of paper money, feared that the speculative craze threatened the stability of state banks and undermined the interests of settlers, who could not compete with speculators in bidding for the best land.

In keeping with his hard-money instincts and opposition to paper currency, the president ordered Treasury Secretary Levi Woodbury to issue the Specie Circular. It provided that after August 1836 only specie or Virginia scrip would be accepted as payment for federal lands. The circular sought to end "the monopoly of the public lands in the hands of speculators and capitalists" and the "ruinous extension" of bank notes and credit. By ending credit sales, it significantly reduced purchases of public land and the federal budget surplus. As a result the government suspended its loan payments to the states soon after they began.

The policy was a disaster. Although federal land sales were sharply reduced, speculation continued as available land for sale became scarce. The ensuing increased demand for specie squeezed banks, and many suspended the redemption of bank notes for specie. Credit contracted further as banks issued fewer notes and gave less credit. Equally damaging was the way Jackson attacked the problem. He instinctively pursued a tight money policy and remained indifferent to its impact. More important, the Specie Circular was similar to a bill defeated in the Senate just three months earlier. Jackson's opponents thus saw King Andrew at work. In the waning days of Jackson's administration, Congress voted to repeal the circular, but the president pocket-vetoed the bill. Finally in mid-1838, a joint resolution of Congress overturned the circular. Restrictions on land sales ended, but the speculative fervor was over. The federal government did not revive loans to states.

From George Washington to John Quincy Adams, presidents had vetoed nine bills; Jackson vetoed twelve. Previous presidents believed that vetoes were justified only on constitutional grounds, but Jackson, as in

Use of the Veto

the veto of the bill rechartering the Second Bank of the United States, considered policy disagreement legitimate grounds as well. He made the veto an effective weapon for controlling Congress, since representatives and senators had to consider the possibility of a presidential veto in their deliberations on any bill. In effect, Jackson made the executive for the first time a rival branch of government, equal in power to Congress.

The Whig Challenge and the Second Party System

Historians used to call the 1830s and 1840s the Age of Jackson, and the personalities of leading political figures dominated their accounts of the era. Most historians now view these years as an age of reform and popularly based political parties. Only when the passionate concerns of reformers and abolitionists spilled over into politics did party differences become paramount and party loyalties solidify. For the first time in American history, grassroots political groups, organized from the bottom up, set the tone of political life.

Opponents of the Democrats, including remnants of the National Republican Party, found shelter under a common umbrella, the Whig Party, in the 1830s. Resentful of Jackson's domination of Congress, the Whigs borrowed the name of the British party that had opposed the tyranny of Hanoverian monarchs in the eighteenth century. From 1834 through the 1840s, the Whigs and the Democrats competed on a nearly equal footing. They fought at the city, county, state, and national levels and achieved a stability previously unknown in American politics. The political competition of this period—known as the second party system—was more intense and well organized than that of the first party system of Republicans and Federalists (see page 235).

The two parties were responsive to their supporters, reflecting important changes in the electoral process. Only a handful of states significantly restricted adult white male suffrage by the 1830s. Some even allowed immigrants who had taken out first citizenship papers to vote. Moreover, hotly contested elections stimulated public interest in politics. The net effect of these changes was a sharp increase in the number of votes cast in presidential elections. Between 1824 and 1828 that number increased threefold, from 360,000 to over 1.1 million. In 1840, 2.4 million men cast votes. The proportion of eligible voters who cast ballots also increased, from about 27 percent in 1824 to more than 80 percent in 1840.

Increasingly the parties differed in their approaches. Whigs favored economic expansion through an activist government, Democrats through limited central government. Whigs sup-

Whigs

ported corporate charters, a national bank, and paper currency; Democrats were opposed. Whigs also favored more humanitarian reforms than did Democrats, including public schools, abolition of capital punishment, prison and asylum reform, and temperance.

Whigs were more optimistic than Democrats, generally speaking, and more enterprising. They did not object to helping a specific group if doing so would promote the general welfare. The chartering of corporations, they argued, expanded economic opportunity for everyone by providing work for laborers and increasing demand for food from farmers. Democrats, distrustful of concentrated economic power and of moral and economic coercion, held fast to the Jeffersonian principle of limited government.

Neither economics nor class was a key determinant of party affiliation. Instead, religion and ethnicity most influenced party membership. The Whigs' support for energetic government and humanitarian and moral reform won the favor of evangelical Protestants in the North, especially those involved in religious revival. Methodists and Baptists were overwhelmingly Whigs, as were the small number of free black voters. Democrats, by contrast, tended to be foreign-born Catholics and nonevangelical Protestants, both of whom preferred to keep religious and secular affairs separate.

The Whig Party was the vehicle of revivalist Protestantism. In many locales the membership rolls of reform societies overlapped those of the party.

Whigs and Reformers

Indeed, Whigs practiced a kind of political revivalism. Their rallies resembled camp meetings; in their speeches they employed evangelical rhetoric; their programs embodied the perfectionist beliefs of reformers. This potent blend of religion and politics— "intimately united" in America, according to Tocqueville—greatly intensified political loyalties.

In their appeal to evangelicals, Whigs alienated members of other faiths. In the evangelicals' ideal Christian state there was no room for Catholics, Mormons, Unitarians, Universalists, or religious freethinkers. Those groups opposed Sabbath laws and temperance legislation in particular and state interference in moral and religious questions in general. As a result, more than 95 percent of Irish Catholics, 90 percent of Reformed Dutch, and 80 percent of German Catholics voted Democratic.

Vice President Martin Van Buren, handpicked by Jackson, headed the Democratic ticket in the presidential election of 1836. Van Buren was a

Election of 1836

shrewd politician who had built a political machine—the Albany Regency—in New York and had left that state's government to join Jackson's cabinet in 1829. Having helped found the Democratic Party, Van Bu-

ren was one member of a new generation of men who made their careers in party politics.

The Whigs in 1836 had not yet coalesced into a national party. They entered three sectional candidates: Daniel Webster of New England, Hugh White of the South, and William Henry Harrison of the West. By splintering the vote, they hoped to throw the election into the House of Representatives. Van Buren, however, comfortably captured the electoral college even though he had only a 25,000-vote edge out of a total of 1.5 million votes cast. No vice-presidential candidate received a majority of electoral votes, and for the only time in American history the Senate decided a vice-presidential race, selecting Democratic candidate Richard M. Johnson of Kentucky.

Van Buren took office just weeks before the American credit system collapsed. In response to the impact of the Specie Circular, New York banks stopped redeeming paper currency with gold in mid-1837.

President Martin Van Buren and Hard Times

Soon all banks suspended payments in hard coin. Thus began a cycle that led to curtailment of bank loans and reduced business confidence. The credit contraction only made things worse; after a brief recovery, hard times persisted from 1839 until 1843.

Ill advisedly, Van Buren followed Jackson's hard-money policies. He cut federal spending, which caused prices to drop further, and he opposed a national bank, which would have expanded credit. Even worse, the president proposed a new regional treasury system for government deposits. The proposed treasury branches would accept and pay out only gold and silver coin; they would not accept paper currency or checks drawn on state banks. Van Buren's independent treasury bill became law in 1840. By creating a constant demand for hard coin, it deprived banks of gold and further accelerated the deflation of prices.

Whigs and Democrats faced off at the state level over these issues. Whigs favored new banks, more paper currency, and more corporations. As the party of hard money, Democrats favored eliminating paper currency altogether. Increasingly the Democrats became distrustful even of state banks, and by the mid-1840s a majority favored eliminating all bank corporations. The Whigs, riding the wave of economic distress into office, made banking and corporate charters more readily available.

Using techniques that look familiar to twentieth-century politicians, General William Henry Harrison in 1840 ran a "log cabin and hard cider" campaign against Jackson's heir, President Martin Van Buren. The campaign handkerchief shows Harrison welcoming two of his comrades to his log cabin, with a barrel of cider outside. The Log Cabin, *a newspaper edited by Horace Greeley, was the voice of the Harrison campaign, and it reached eighty thousand partisans.* Handkerchief: New-York Historical Society. Newspaper: Division of Political History, Smithsonian Institution, Washington, D.C.

With the nation again in the grip of hard times, the Whigs prepared confidently for the election of 1840. Their strategy was simple: hold on to loyal supporters and win over independents distressed by the economic downturn. The Democrats renominated President Van Buren at a somber convention. The Whigs rallied behind a military hero, General William Henry Harrison, conqueror of the Shawnees at Tippecanoe Creek in 1811 (see page 243).

William Henry Harrison Wins Election of 1840

Harrison, or "Old Tippecanoe," and his running mate, John Tyler of Virginia, ran a "log cabin and hard cider" campaign—a people's crusade—against the aristocratic president in "the Palace." Harrison presented himself as an ordinary farmer, though he was descended from a Virginia plantation family. The Whigs wooed supporters and independents alike with huge rallies, parades, songs, posters, campaign mementos, and a campaign newspaper, *The*

Log Cabin. Harrison took a position above the issues, earning himself the nickname "General Mum," but party hacks bluntly blamed the hard times on the Democrats. In a huge turnout, 80 percent of eligible voters cast ballots. Harrison won the popular vote by a narrow margin but swept the electoral college by 234 to 60.

Immediately after taking office in 1841, President Harrison convened a special session of Congress to pass the Whig economic program: repeal of the independent treasury system, a new national bank, and a higher protective tariff. But the sixty-eight-year-old Harrison caught pneumonia and died within a month of his inauguration. His successor, John Tyler, was a former Democrat who had left the party to protest Jackson's nullification proclamation.

In office, Tyler turned out to be more of a Democrat than a Whig. As critical of the Whigs' economic nationalism as he had been of Jackson's use of executive power, Tyler consistently opposed the Whig congressional program. He repeatedly vetoed

Henry Clay's protective tariffs, internal improvements, and bills aimed at reviving the Bank of the United States. The only important measures that became law during his term were repeal of the independent treasury system and passage of a higher tariff. Two days after Tyler's second veto of a bank bill, the entire cabinet except Secretary of State Daniel Webster resigned; Webster, busy negotiating a new treaty with Great Britain, left shortly thereafter. Tyler thus became a president without a party, and the Whigs lost the presidency without losing an election. Whigs referred to Tyler as "His Accidency."

Hard times in the late 1830s and early 1840s deflected attention from a renewal of Anglo-American tensions that had multiple sources: northern commercial rivalry with Britain, the default of state governments and corporations on British-held debts during the Panic of 1837, rebellion in Canada, boundary disputes, southern alarm over West Indian emancipation, and American expansionism.

Anglo-American Tensions

One of the most troublesome disputes arose from the *Caroline* affair. A United States citizen, Amos Durfee, had been killed when Canadian militia set afire the privately owned steamer *Caroline* in the Niagara River. (The *Caroline* had supported an unsuccessful uprising against Great Britain in 1837.) Britain refused to apologize, and American newspapers called for revenge. Fearing that popular support for the Canadian rebels would ignite war, President Van Buren posted troops at the border to discourage border raids. Tensions subsided in late 1840 when Alexander McLeod, a Canadian deputy sheriff, was arrested in New York for the murder of Durfee. McLeod eventually was acquitted. If he had been found guilty and executed, Lord Palmerston, the British foreign minister, might have sought war.

At almost the same time a border dispute disrupted Anglo-American relations. The Treaty of Ghent, ending the War of 1812, had not resolved the boundary dispute between Maine and New Brunswick. Great Britain had accepted an 1831 arbitration decision fixing a new boundary, but the United States Senate rejected it. Thus when Canadian lumbermen cut trees in the disputed region in the winter of 1838–1839, the citizens of Maine attempted to expel them. The lumbermen captured the Maine land agent and posse, both sides mobilized their militias, and Congress authorized a call-up of fifty thousand men. Ultimately, no blood was spilled. General Winfield Scott, who had patrolled the border during the *Caroline* affair, was dispatched to Aroostook, Maine, where he arranged a truce. The two sides compromised on their conflicting claims in the Webster-Ashburton Treaty (1842).

These border disputes with Great Britain prefigured the conflicts that were to erupt in the 1840s over the expansion of the United States. With Tyler's succession to power in 1841 and a Democratic victory in the presidential election of 1844, federal activism in the domestic sphere ended for the rest of the decade, and attention turned to the debate over territorial expansion. Reform, however, was not dead. Its passions would resurface in the 1850s in the debate over slavery in the territories.

 ## Manifest Destiny and Expansionism

The belief that American expansion westward and southward was inevitable, just, and divinely ordained was first labeled *manifest destiny* by John L. O'Sullivan, editor of the *United States Magazine and Domestic Review*. The annexation of Texas, O'Sullivan wrote in 1845, was "the fulfillment of our manifest destiny to overspread the continent allotted by Providence for the free development of our yearly multiplying millions." In the 1840s expansionism reached a new fervor.

Since colonial days Americans had hungered for more land. Acquisition of the Louisiana Territory (1803) and Florida (1819) had set the process in motion (see map, page 368). As the proportion of Americans living west of the Appalachians grew from one-quarter to one-half between 1830 and 1860, both national parties joined the popular clamor for expansion. Agrarian Democrats saw the West as an antidote to urbanization and industrialization. Enterprising Whigs looked to the new commercial opportunities the West offered. Southerners envisioned the extension of slavery and more slave states.

Fierce national pride spurred the quest for land. Subdued during hard times, it reasserted itself in the boom times of the 1840s. Americans were convinced that theirs was the greatest country on earth, with a special role to play in the world. As reform sought to perfect American society, so too expansionism promised to improve foreign lands. The acquisition of new territory, many Americans reasoned, would extend the benefits of America's republican system of government to the less fortunate and the inferior.

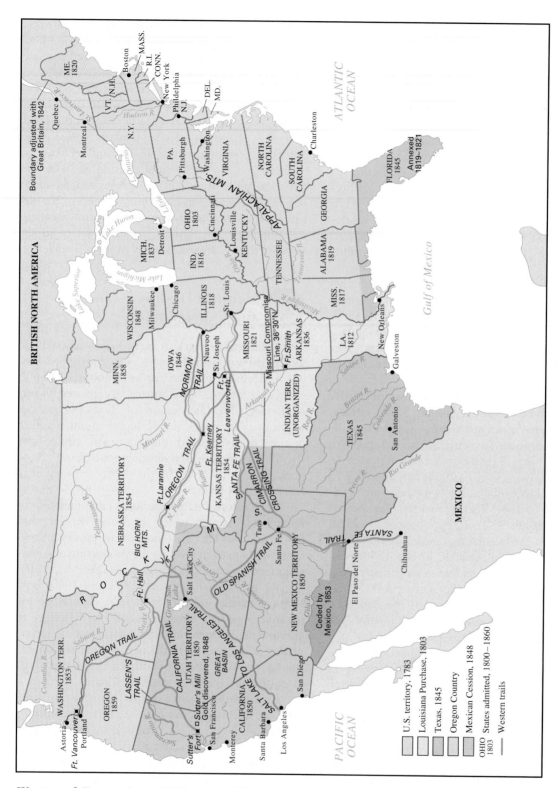

Westward Expansion, 1800–1860 *Through exploration, purchase, war, and treaty, the United States became a continental nation, stretching from the Atlantic to the Pacific.*

In part, racism drove the belief in manifest destiny. Native Americans were perceived as savages best confined to small areas in the West. Hispanics were seen as inferior peoples, best controlled or conquered. Thus the same racism that justified slavery in the South and discrimination in the North supported expansion in the West. For some, expansion also offered a solution to the American race problem: free people of color, unwanted in the North and the South, could find refuge in distant territories. But racism also could limit expansion, for Americans did not look on Mexicans—whether Indian, European, African, or mestizo—with favor.

The desire to secure the nation from perceived external threats also fed expansionist fever. The internal enemies of the 1830s—a monster bank, corporations, paper currency, alcohol, Sabbath violation—seemed pale in comparison to the opportunities Americans saw along their borders in the 1840s. Expansion, some believed, was necessary to preserve American independence.

The establishment of an independent Texas and its annexation by the United States were major events. With the acquisition of Louisiana and California, they were critical steps in the United States's domination of the continent. Among the long-standing objectives of expansionists was the Republic of Texas, which in addition to Texas included parts of present-day Oklahoma, Kansas, Colorado, Wyoming, and New Mexico (see map, page 368). After winning its independence from Spain in 1821, Mexico encouraged the development of its rich but remote northern province, offering large tracts of land virtually free to settlers called *empresarios*. The settlers in turn agreed to become Mexican citizens, adopt the Catholic religion, and bring two hundred or more families into the area. Americans Moses and Stephen Austin, who had helped to formulate the policy, responded eagerly.

Republic of Texas

By 1835, thirty-five thousand Americans, including many slaveholders, lived in Texas. The new settlers' power grew. The dictatorship of General Antonio López de Santa Anna tightened control over the region. In response, Anglos and Tejanos rebelled. At the Alamo mission in San Antonio in 1836, fewer than two hundred Texans made a heroic but unsuccessful stand against three thousand Mexicans under General Santa Anna. "Remember the Alamo" became the Texans' rallying cry. By the end of the year the Texans had won independence, delighting most Americans. Some saw the victory as a triumph of Protestants over Catholic Mexico; others cheered that proslavery Texans had defeated antislavery Mexicans.

Texas established the independent Lone Star Republic but soon sought annexation to the United States. Sam Houston, president of the Texas republic, opened negotiations with Washington, but the issue quickly became politically explosive. Southerners favored annexing proslavery Texas; abolitionists, many northerners, and most Whigs opposed annexation. In recognition of the political dangers, President Jackson reneged on his promise to recognize Texas, and President Van Buren ignored annexation.

Rebuffed by the United States, Texans talked about closer ties with the British and extending their republic all the way to the Pacific coast. With British colonies already entrenched in Canada, the prospect of a rival republic to the south caused some Americans to fear encirclement. If Texas reached the ocean and became an English ally, would not American independence be threatened?

President Tyler, committed to expansion and eager to build political support in the South, pushed for annexation. Tyler was hoping to build a political base in the South to gain the 1844 Democratic nomination. Southerners also pressed for annexation; they lobbied former president Jackson, who responded that the United States must have Texas, "peacefully if we can, forcibly if we must." But the opposition was too strong, and the Senate rejected annexation in 1844. A letter from Secretary of State Calhoun to the British minister, justifying annexation as a step in protecting slavery, so outraged senators that the treaty was defeated 16 to 35.

Like southerners who sought expansion to the Southwest, northerners looked to the Northwest. "Oregon fever" struck thousands in 1841. Lured by the glowing reports of missionaries who seemed as enthusiastic about the Northwest's riches and beauty as about conversion of Indians, migrants in wagon trains took to the Oregon Trail. "Ho for California," Helen Carpenter wrote in her diary, "We are off to the Promised Land." Others' enthusiasm was tempered by apprehension. Lavinia Porter had to face the sober realization that her husband did not have "the training to make a living on the plains of the West or the crossing of the continent in an ox team a successful

Oregon Fever

Texans believed that their war for independence paralleled the Revolutionary War. The lady of liberty on this banner, carried by Texans in 1836, brings to mind similar images that stirred patriots during the American Revolution.   Archives Division, Texas State Library.

venture." The 2,000-mile journey took six months or more, but within a few years five thousand settlers had arrived in the fertile Willamette valley south of the Columbia River.

Britain and the United States had jointly occupied the disputed Oregon Territory since the Anglo-American Convention of 1818 (see pages 246–247). Beginning with the administration of President John Quincy Adams, the United States had tried to fix the boundary at the 49th parallel, but Britain was determined to maintain access to Puget Sound and the Columbia River. Time only increased the American appetite. In 1843 a Cincinnati convention of expansionists demanded the entire Oregon Country for the United States, up to its northernmost border at latitude 54°40'. Soon "Fifty-four Forty or Fight" became the rallying cry of American expansionists.

Expansion into Oregon and rejection of the annexation of Texas, both favored by antislavery forces, worried southern leaders. Anxious about their diminishing ability to control the debate over slavery, they persuaded the 1844 Democratic convention to adopt a rule requiring the presidential nominee to receive two-thirds of the convention votes. In effect, the southern states acquired a veto, and they blocked Van Buren as the nominee; most southerners objected to his antislavery stance and opposition to Texas annexation. Instead, the party chose "Young Hickory," House Speaker James K. Polk, a hard-money Jacksonian, avid expansionist, and slaveholding cotton planter from Tennessee. The Whig leader Henry Clay, who opposed annexation, won his party's nomination unanimously. The Democratic platform called for occupation of the entire Oregon Territory and annexation of Texas. The Whigs, though favoring expansion, argued that

James K. Polk Wins Election of 1844

the Democrats' belligerent nationalism would lead the nation into war with Great Britain or Mexico or both. Clay favored expansion through negotiation.

With a well-organized campaign, Polk and the Democrats won the election by 170 electoral votes to 105. (They won the popular vote by just 38,000 out of 2.7 million votes cast.) Polk won New York's 36 electoral votes by just 6,000 popular votes. Abolitionist James G. Birney, the Liberty Party candidate, had drawn almost 16,000 votes away from Clay, handing New York and the election to Polk. Abolitionist forces thus unwittingly brought about the choice of a slaveholder as president, but they viewed Polk as more moderate than Clay on slavery and the lesser of two evils.

Interpreting Polk's victory as a mandate for annexation, President Tyler proposed in his final days in office that Texas be admitted by joint resolution of Congress. (The usual method of annexation, by treaty negotiation, required a two-thirds vote in the Senate—which expansionists clearly did not have. Joint resolution required only a simple majority in each house.) Congressmen debated the extension of slavery into the territory, and the resolution passed in the House by 120 to 98 and in the Senate by 27 to 25. Three days before leaving office, Tyler signed the measure. Mexico immediately broke relations with the United States; war was inevitable. In October, the citizens of Texas ratified annexation, and Texas joined the Union in December 1845.

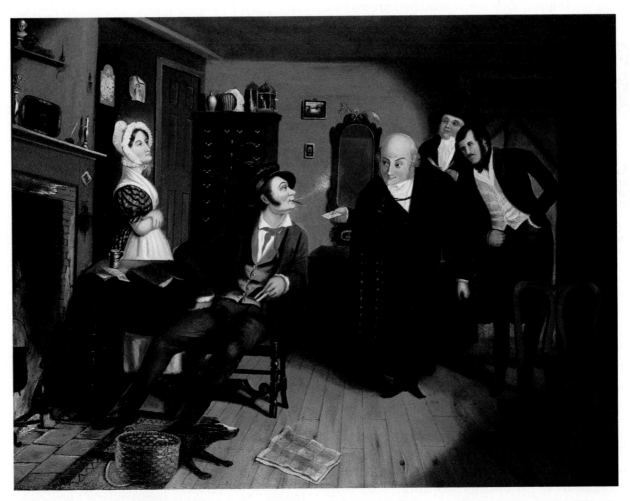

An unknown artist depicted, in rich detail, the election campaign of 1844. A team of Polk supporters offers a campaign handbill to the seated voter. Passions were so high and party organization was so extensive that door-to-door politicking became the norm. Courtesy, Nathan Liverant & Son.

Conclusion

Religion, reform, and expansionism colored politics in the 1830s and 1840s. As the Second Great Awakening spread through villages and towns, the converts, especially women, changed American religion and organized to reform a rapidly changing society. Religion imbued men and women with zeal to right the wrongs of American society and the world. Reformers pursued perfectionism and republican virtue by doing battle with the evils of the growing cities, seeking to ban alcohol and gambling, and expanding education. Two issues elicited particular intensity: Antimasonry flared only briefly; abolitionism smoldered over time. The passions that both aroused were so potent, and success was so elusive, that Antimasons and abolitionists transformed their moral crusades into political movements. But reformers had no monopoly on claims of republican virtue; their opponents laid claim to a heritage of revolutionary values that held individual liberty particularly dear.

Once reform forced itself into politics, it generated a broader-based interest in politics that would remake the political system. The ensuing conflicts, and the highly organized parties that arose during the era, stimulated even greater interest in campaigns and political issues. The Democrats, who rallied around Andrew Jackson, and Jackson's opponents, who found shelter under the Whig tent, competed almost equally for the loyalty of voters. Both parties built strong organizations that faced off in national and local elections. And both parties favored economic expansion. Their world-views, however, were fundamentally different. Whigs were more optimistic and favored greater centralized government initiative. Democrats harbored a deep-seated belief in limited government.

Territorial expansion would provide the kindling for the firestorm that would overtake the United States in 1861. Manifest destiny, the admission of Texas, and debates over territorial expansion awaited a spark. Ultimately, one issue would rivet the attention of nearly all Americans and ignite the fire that would threaten to sever the Union: slavery.

Suggestions for Further Reading

Religion, Revivalism, and Reform

Robert H. Abzug, *Cosmos Crumbling: American Reform and the Religious Imagination* (1994); Michael Barkun, *Crucible of the Millennium: The Burned-over District of New York in the 1840s* (1986); Terry Bilhartz, *Urban Religion and the Second Great Awakening: Church and Society in Early National Baltimore* (1986); Clifford S. Griffen, *Their Brother's Keepers: Moral Stewardship in the United States, 1800–1865* (1960); Keith J. Hardman, *Charles Grandison Finney, 1792–1875: Revivalist and Reformer* (1987); Nathan O. Hatch, *The Democratization of American Christianity* (1989); Curtis D. Johnson, *Islands of Holiness: Rural Religion in Upstate New York, 1790–1860* (1989); Paul E. Johnson, *A Shopkeeper's Millennium: Society and Revivals in Rochester, New York, 1815–1837* (1978); Steven Mintz, *Moralists and Modernizers: America's Pre-Civil War Reformers* (1995); Richard D. Shiels, "The Scope of the Second Great Awakening: Andover, Massachusetts, as a Case Study," *Journal of the Early Republic* 5 (Summer 1985): 223–246; Timothy L. Smith, *Revivalism and Social Reform in Mid–Nineteenth Century America* (1957); Alice Felt Tyler, *Freedom's Ferment* (1944); Ronald G. Walters, *American Reformers, 1815–1860*, 2nd ed. (1997).

Temperance, Asylums, and Antimasonry

David Gollaher, *Voice for the Mad: The Life of Dorothea Dix* (1995); Paul Goodman, *Towards a Christian Republic: Antimasonry and the Great Transition in New England, 1826–1836* (1988); Gerald N. Grob, *Mental Institutions in America: Social Policy to 1875* (1973); Kathleen Smith Kutolowski, "Antimasonry Reexamined: Social Bases of the Grass-Roots Party," *Journal of American History* 71 (September 1984): 269–293; W. J. Rorabaugh, *The Alcoholic Republic: An American Tradition* (1979); David J. Rothman, *The Discovery of the Asylum: Social Order and Disorder in the New Republic* (1971); Ian R. Tyrrell, *Sobering Up: From Temperance to Prohibition in Antebellum America, 1800–1860* (1979); William Preston Vaughn, *The Antimasonic Party in the United States, 1826–1843* (1983).

Women and Reform

Barbara J. Berg, *The Remembered Gate: Origins of American Feminism: The Woman and the City, 1800–1860* (1977); Ellen C. Du Bois, *Feminism and Suffrage: The Emergence of an Independent Woman's Movement in America, 1848–1869* (1978); Barbara Leslie Epstein, *The Politics of Domesticity: Women, Evangelism, and Temperance in Nineteenth-Century America* (1981); Lori D. Ginzberg, *Women and the Work of Benevolence: Morality, Politics, and Class in the Nineteenth-Century United States* (1990); Debra Gold Hansen, *Strained Sisterhood: Gender and Class in the Boston Female Anti-Slavery Society* (1993); Nancy A. Hewitt, *Women's Activism and Social Change: Rochester, New York, 1822–1872* (1984); Sylvia D. Hoffert, *When Hens Crow: The Woman's Rights Movement in Antebellum America* (1995); Gerda Lerner, *The Grimké Sisters of South Carolina* (1967); Mary P. Ryan, *Cradle of the Middle Class: The Family in Oneida County, New York, 1790–1865* (1981); Shirley J. Yee, *Black Women Abolitionists: A Study in Activism, 1828–1860* (1992); Jean Fagan Yellin, *Women & Sisters: The Antislavery Feminists in American Culture* (1989).

Antislavery and Abolitionism

David Brion Davis, *Slavery and Human Progress* (1984); Frederick Douglass, *Life and Times of Frederick Douglass* (1881); George M. Fredrickson, *The Black Image in the White Mind: The Debate on Afro-American Character and Destiny, 1817–1914* (1971); Lawrence J. Friedman, *Gregarious Saints: Self and Community in American Abolitionism, 1830–1870* (1982); Aileen S. Kraditor, *Means and Ends* in *American Abolitionism: Garrison and His Critics on Strategy and Tactics* (1967); William Lee Miller, *Arguing About Slavery: The Great Battle in the United States Congress* (1995); William H. Pease and Jane H. Pease, *They Who Would Be Free: Blacks' Search for Freedom, 1830–1861* (1974); Benjamin Quarles, *Black Abolitionists* (1969); Leonard L. Richards, *"Gentlemen of Property and Standing": Anti-Abolition Mobs in Jacksonian America* (1970); John L. Thomas, *The Liberator: William Lloyd Garrison* (1963); Ronald G. Walters, *The Antislavery Appeal: American Abolitionism After 1830* (1976).

Andrew Jackson and the Jacksonians

Donald B. Cole, *Martin Van Buren and the American Political System* (1984); Daniel Feller, *The Jacksonian Promise: America, 1815–1840* (1995); Mary W. M. Hargreaves, *The Presidency of John Quincy Adams* (1985); Michael F. Holt, *Political Parties and American Political Development from the Age of Jackson to the Age of Lincoln* (1992); Richard B. Latner, *The Presidency of Andrew Jackson* (1979); Marvin Meyers, *The Jacksonian Persuasion* (1960); John Niven, *Martin Van Buren* (1983); Edward Pessen, *Jacksonian America: Society, Personality, and Politics*, rev. ed. (1979); Robert V. Remini, *The Legacy of Andrew Jackson: Essays on Democracy, Indian Removal, and Slavery* (1988); Robert V. Remini, *The Life of Andrew Jackson* (1988); Charles Sellers, *The Market Revolution: Jacksonian America, 1815–1846* (1991); Harry L. Watson, *Liberty and Power: The Politics of Jacksonian America* (1990).

Democrats and Whigs

William J. Cooper, *The South and the Politics of Slavery, 1828–1856* (1978); Ronald P. Formisano, *The Transformation of Political Culture: Massachusetts Parties, 1790s–1840s* (1983); William W. Freehling, *Prelude to Civil War: The Nullification Controversy in South Carolina* (1966); Daniel Walker Howe, *The Political Culture of the American Whigs* (1979); Lawrence Frederick Kohl, *The Politics of Individualism: Parties and the American Character in the Jacksonian Era* (1989); Richard P. McCormick, *The Second American Party System: Party Formation in the Jacksonian Era* (1966); Merrill D. Peterson, *The Great Triumvirate: Webster, Clay, and Calhoun* (1987); Norman Lois Peterson, *The Presidencies of William Henry Harrison and John Tyler* (1989); Robert V. Remini, *Henry Clay: Statesman for the Union* (1991); James Roger Sharp, *The Jacksonians Versus the Banks: Politics in the States After the Panic of 1837* (1970).

Manifest Destiny and Foreign Policy

John M. Belohlavek, *"Let the Eagle Soar!" The Foreign Policy of Andrew Jackson* (1985); T. R. Fehrenbach, *Lone Star: A History of Texas and the Texans* (1968); Norman B. Graebner, ed., *Manifest Destiny* (1968); Thomas R. Hietala, *Manifest Destiny: Anxious Aggrandizement in Late Jacksonian America* (1985); Reginald Horsman, *Race and Manifest Destiny* (1981); Michael Hunt, *Ideology and U.S. Foreign Policy* (1987); Bradford Perkins, *The Creation of a Republican Empire, 1776–1865* (1993); David M. Pletcher, *The Diplomacy of Annexation: Texas, Oregon, and the Mexican War* (1973); Charles G. Sellers, Jr., *James K. Polk: Continentalist, 1843–1846* (1966); Anders Stephanson, *Manifest Destiny: American Expansionism and the Empire of Right* (1995); Paul A. Varg, *United States Foreign Relations, 1820–1860* (1979); Albert K. Weinberg, *Manifest Destiny* (1935).

CHAPTER

14

Slavery and America's Future: The Road to War
1845–1861

A s the nation expanded, so did slavery, bringing with it a chain of consequences. On the frontier, slavery proved a source of wealth and financial progress for many white slaveowners, but for slaves it brought suffering, pain, and injustice. With slavery also came violence and controversy. Such was the case in Missouri, where Robert Newsom purchased Celia, a female slave, in 1850.

Almost sixty and a widower, Newsom lived with his two adult daughters and four of his grandchildren. Five male slaves worked the family's land. Celia, who was only fourteen, probably assumed that Newsom wanted her to cook and clean for the family. But he had more in mind for Celia. Almost immediately he raped her and made it clear that he would continue to demand her sexual services. He installed her in a small house only fifty yards behind his home. Over the next five years he visited her often, fathering two children. Newsom's adult daughters and his neighbors knew what he was doing to Celia but said nothing. They respected him and knew that slavery spawned such arrangements.

In 1855, Celia began a relationship with George, another of the Newsom slaves, and resolved to end the relationship with her master. She appealed first to Newsom's daughters, but they said they could do nothing to stop their father's behavior. Celia then begged her master to leave her alone, pleading that she was again pregnant and ill. One evening in June 1855, Robert Newsom read until his family was asleep and then walked to Celia's door. When he brushed aside her objections to sex, she grabbed a club and struck him on the skull. As he sank to the floor, she struck him again. He never arose. Panicked at having killed her master, Celia proceeded to burn his body all through the night in her large fireplace.

Thomas S. Noble's painting *The Last Sale of Slaves* in Saint Louis stimulated a lengthy debate in the former border state between the liberal *St. Louis Guardian* and the conservative *St. Louis Times* over the painting's abolitionist message. Interestingly, the *Dred Scott* case moved through this courthouse on its way to the Supreme Court. *Missouri Historical Society, St. Louis.*

Physical evidence of Newsom's murder soon came to light, and Celia was arrested. Her trial received only local publicity, but in that district of Missouri it stirred conflicting passions. News of the murder made some slaveowners fear for their safety, but Celia's attorneys sympathized with her plight enough to argue, unsuccessfully, that laws against rape entitled her to defend herself. After a jury of twelve white men convicted her, Celia went to the gallows four days before Christmas.

By the time Celia was hanged, her drama had been overshadowed by a larger drama of violence in the neighboring territory of Kansas. Open warfare had broken out there between advocates and foes of slavery. Proslavery men, intent on spreading the peculiar institution and preserving a balance of free and slave states in the United States Senate, rode across the border from Missouri, stole elections by voting illegally, and physically attacked those who wanted Kansas to be free soil. Antislavery activists organized the New England Emigrant Aid Company to send opponents of slavery to Kansas. Before long the New Englanders were arming their settlers with Sharps rifles, nicknamed "Beecher's Bibles" after the well-known antislavery minister Henry Ward Beecher of New York. On the proslavery side a United States senator, Missouri's David Atchison, publicly advocated violence and pledged his readiness "to shoot, burn and hang." Expansion and slavery proved an incendiary combination, arousing passions in national politics as on the Newsom farm. As the 1850s advanced, slavery pulled Americans deeper and deeper into a maelstrom of conflict and violence.

Between 1845 and 1853 the United States added Texas, the West Coast, and the Southwest to its domain and launched the settlement of the Great Plains. Each time the nation expanded, it confronted a thorny issue: should new territories and states be slave or free? This question stirred disagreements too extreme for compromise. Sensing the danger of conflict, Senator John C. Calhoun of South Carolina called Mexico "the forbidden fruit; the penalty of eating it would be to subject our institutions to political death." A host of political leaders, including Henry Clay, Lewis Cass, Stephen A. Douglas, and Presidents Jackson and Van Buren, tried to postpone or resolve disagreements about slavery in the territories. Repeatedly, though, these disputes injected into national politics the bitterness surrounding slavery. If slavery was the sore spot in the body politic, territorial disputes rubbed salt into the wound.

The United States had always been a diverse, heterogeneous society, not a cohesive unit. Now, however, diverse interests that used to balance each other became linked to a divisive issue. The second party system disintegrated, and a realigned system that emphasized sectional conflict took its place. Sectional parties emphasizing conflict replaced nationwide organizations that had promoted compromise. The ensuing political storms gave rise to a feeling in both North and South that America's future was at stake. The new Republican Party charged that southerners were taking over the federal government and planning to make slavery legal throughout the Union. Republicans believed that America's future depended on the free labor of free men, whose rights were protected by a government devoted to liberty. Southern leaders defended slavery and charged the North with lawless behavior in violation of the Constitution. To these southerners enslavement of blacks was the foundation of equality and republicanism among whites, and a government that failed to protect slavery was un-American and unworthy of their loyalty.

Not all citizens were obsessed with these conflicts. In fact, the results of the 1860 presidential election indicated that most voters wanted neither disunion nor civil war. Within six months, however, they had both, for slavery aroused passions that could be neither contained nor resolved. What had begun as a dark cloud over the territories became a storm engulfing the nation.

 ## Conflict Begins: The Mexican War

Territorial expansion surged forward under the leadership of President James K. Polk. The annexation of Texas (see page 371) just before his inauguration did not weaken Polk's determination to acquire California and the Southwest, and he desired Oregon as well. Polk achieved his goals but was unaware of the price in domestic harmony that expansion would exact. Territorial conquest divided the Whig Party, drove southern Whigs into a full embrace of slavery, and brought into the open an aggressive new southern theory about slavery's position in the territories. Expansion also sparked protests and proposals from the North that angered southerners.

During the 1844 campaign Polk's supporters had threatened war with Great Britain to gain all of Oregon. As president, however, Polk turned first to diplomacy. Not wanting to fight Mexico and

• *Important Events* •

1846	War with Mexico begins Oregon Treaty negotiated Wilmot Proviso inflames sectional divisions
1847	Lewis Cass proposes idea of popular sovereignty
1848	Treaty of Guadalupe Hidalgo gives United States new territory in the Southwest Free-Soil Party formed Zachary Taylor elected president
1849	California applies for admission to Union as free state
1850	Compromise of 1850 passed in separate bills
1852	Publication of *Uncle Tom's Cabin*, by Harriet Beecher Stowe Franklin Pierce elected president
1854	Publication of "Appeal of the Independent Democrats" Kansas-Nebraska Act wins approval and ignites controversy Republican Party formed Democrats lose ground in congressional elections

1856	"Bleeding Kansas" troubles nation Preston Brooks attacks Charles Sumner in Senate chamber James Buchanan elected president
1857	*Dred Scott* v. *Sandford* endorses southern views on race and territories Lecompton Constitution proposed; President Buchanan supports it
1858	Kansas voters reject Lecompton Constitution Lincoln-Douglas debates attract attention Stephen A. Douglas proposes Freeport Doctrine
1859	John Brown raids Harpers Ferry
1860	Democratic Party splits in two Abraham Lincoln elected president Crittenden Compromise fails South Carolina secedes from Union
1861	Six more Deep South states secede Confederacy established at Montgomery, Alabama Attack on Fort Sumter begins Civil War Four states in the Upper South join the Confederacy

Great Britain at the same time, he tried to avoid bloodshed in the Northwest, where America and Britain had jointly occupied disputed territory since 1818. Dropping the demand for a boundary at latitude 54°40', he pressured the British to accept the 49th parallel. In 1846 Great Britain agreed. The Oregon Treaty gave the United States all of present-day Oregon, Washington, and Idaho and parts of Wyoming and Montana (see map, page 378).

Toward Mexico, Polk was more aggressive. He ordered American troops to defend the border claimed by Texas but contested by Mexico (see map, page 379), and he attempted to buy from the angry Mexicans a huge tract of land in the Southwest. When that effort failed, Polk resolved to ask Congress for a declaration of war. As he was drawing up a list of grievances, word arrived that Mexican forces had engaged American troops on disputed territory and American blood had been shed. Eagerly, Polk declared that "war exists by the act of Mexico itself" and summoned the nation to arms.

Congress recognized a state of war between Mexico and the United States in May 1846, and soon American forces made significant gains. The troops—as in previous wars, mainly volunteers furnished by the states—proved unruly and undisciplined, and their politically ambitious commanders often quarreled among themselves. Nevertheless, progress was steady. General Zachary Taylor's forces attacked and occupied Monterrey, securing northeastern Mexico (see map, page 379). Polk then ordered Colonel Stephen Kearny and a small detachment to invade the remote and thinly populated provinces of New Mexico and California. Taking Santa Fe without opposition, Kearny pushed into California, where he joined forces with rebellious American settlers led by Captain John C. Frémont and with a couple of United States naval units. A quick victory was followed by reverses, but American soldiers soon reestablished their dominance in distant California.

Because losses on the periphery had not broken Mexican resistance, General Winfield Scott carried the war to the enemy's heartland. From Veracruz on the Gulf of Mexico, he led fourteen thousand men toward Mexico City. This daring invasion was the

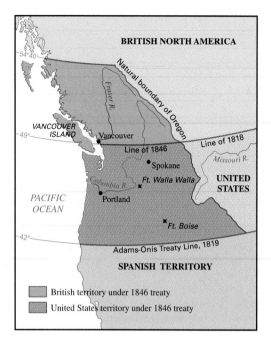

American Expansion in Oregon *The slogan of Polk's supporters had been "Fifty-four forty or fight," but negotiation of a boundary at the 49th parallel avoided the danger of war with Great Britain.*

decisive campaign of the war. Scott's men, outnumbered and threatened by yellow fever, encountered a series of formidable Mexican defenses, but engineers repeatedly discovered flanking routes around the enemy. After a series of hard-fought battles, United States troops captured the Mexican capital and brought the war to an end.

Representatives of both countries signed the Treaty of Guadalupe Hidalgo in February 1848. The United States gained California and New Mexico

Treaty of Guadalupe Hidalgo

(including present-day Nevada, Utah, and Arizona) and recognition of the Rio Grande as the southern boundary of Texas. In return, the American government agreed to settle the claims of its citizens against Mexico and to pay Mexico a mere $15 million.

The costs of the war included the deaths of thirteen thousand Americans (mostly from disease) and fifty thousand Mexicans, plus Mexican-American enmity that endured into the twentieth century. The

domestic cost to the United States was even higher. Public opinion was sharply divided, despite widespread hostility toward Mexicans. Southwesterners were enthusiastic about the war; New Englanders strenuously opposed it. Whigs in Congress charged that Polk, a Democrat, had "literally provoked" an unnecessary war (which they called "Mr. Polk's war") and "usurped the power of Congress." The aged John Quincy Adams denounced the war; and a tall, young, Illinois Whig named Abraham Lincoln questioned its justification. Abolitionists and a small minority of antislavery Whigs charged that the war was no less than a plot to extend slavery. Congressman Joshua Giddings of Ohio charged that Polk's purpose was "to render slavery secure in Texas" and to extend slavery's domain to vast expanses of new territory.

These charges fed northern fear of the so-called Slave Power. Abolitionists had long warned of a Slave Power—a slaveholding oligarchy that controlled the South and intended to dominate the nation. These dangerous aristocrats had gained power in their region by persecuting critics of slavery and suppressing dissent. The Slave Power's assault on northern liberties, abolitionists argued, had begun in 1836, when Congress passed the gag rule (see page 356). Many white northerners, even those who saw nothing wrong with slavery, had opposed restrictions on free speech and the right of petition. It was the battle over free speech that first made the idea of a Slave Power credible. The Mexican War deepened fears about this sinister power. Why, asked antislavery northerners, had claims to part of Oregon been abandoned and a questionable war begun for slave territory?

Idea of a Slave Power

Northern opinion began to shift, but the impact of events on southern opinion and southern leaders was even more dramatic. At first many southern leaders criticized the war with Mexico. Southern Whigs attacked the Democratic president for causing the war, and few southern congressmen saw defense of slavery as the paramount issue. In 1845 Alexander H. Stephens of Georgia had declared, "I am no defender of slavery in the abstract," and even John C. Calhoun—despite his earlier schemes to annex Texas for slavery—strongly opposed the seizure of large amounts of land from Mexico. A Whig editor in Georgia argued that "we have territory enough, especially if every province, like Texas, is to bring in its train war and debt and death."

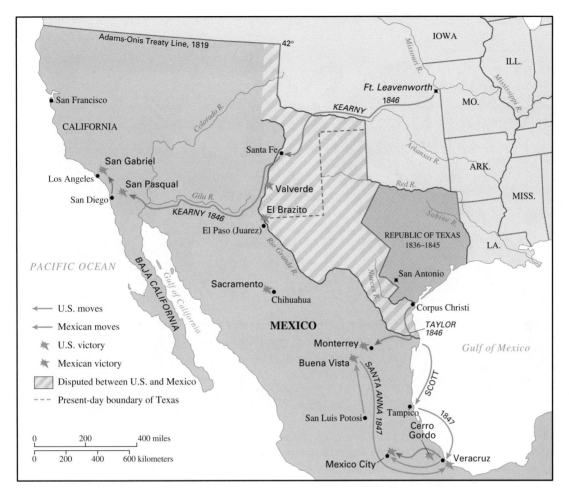

The Mexican War   *This map shows the territory disputed between the United States and Mexico. After United States gains in northeastern Mexico and in New Mexico and California, General Winfield Scott captured Mexico City in the decisive campaign of the war.*

But the Mexican War proved generally popular with southern voters, and no southern Whig could oppose it once slavery became the central issue. That happened in August 1846, when David Wilmot, a Pennsylvania Democrat, proposed an amendment, or proviso, to a military appropriations bill: that "neither slavery nor involuntary servitude shall ever exist" in any territory gained from Mexico. His proviso did not pass both houses of Congress, but it immediately transformed the debate.

Wilmot Proviso

Alexander H. Stephens, only recently "no defender of slavery," now declared that slavery was based on the Bible and above moral criticism, and John C. Calhoun asserted a radical new southern position. The territories, Calhoun insisted, belonged to all the states, and the federal government could do nothing to limit the spread of slavery there. Southern slaveholders had a constitutional *right*, Calhoun claimed, to take their slaves anywhere in the territories. This position, which quickly became orthodox for every southern politician, was a radical reversal of history. In 1787 the Confederation Congress had excluded slavery from the Northwest Territory (see pages 187–188); Article IV of the federal Constitution had authorized Congress to make "all needful rules and regulations" for the territories; and the

Enthusiastic publishers vied to furnish the American public with up-to-date news of the Mexican War. This is one of three litho-graphs issued by Currier and Ives in 1846 to celebrate United States forces' capture of Mexico's General La Vega during the Battle of Resaca, fought near the border of Texas and Mexico.   Amon Carter Museum, Fort Worth, Texas.

Missouri Compromise had barred slavery from most of the Louisiana Purchase. Now, however, southern leaders demanded protection for slavery.

In the North, the Wilmot Proviso became a rallying cry for abolitionists. Eventually the legislatures of fourteen northern states endorsed it—and not because all its supporters were abolitionists. David Wilmot, significantly, was neither an abolitionist nor an antislavery Whig. He denied having any "squeamish sensitiveness upon the subject of slavery" or "morbid sympathy for the slave." Instead, his goal was to defend "the rights of white freemen" and to obtain California "for free white labor." Wilmot sought opportunity for "the sons of toil, of my own race and own color." His involvement in antislavery controversy is a measure of the remarkable ability of the territorial issue to alarm northerners of many viewpoints.

Like Wilmot, most white northerners were racists, not abolitionists. It was possible, however, to be both a racist *and* an opponent of slavery. Fear of the Slave Power was building a potent antislavery movement that united abolitionists *and* antiblack voters. The latter's concern was to protect themselves, not southern blacks, from the Slave Power. Abolition had few followers, but opposition to slavery's extension and fear of the Slave Power was growing. And as northerners became increasingly antislavery, southern slaveholders felt deep alarm.

The slavery question divided northerners and southerners in both parties and could not be kept out of national politics. After Polk renounced a second term as president, the Democrats nominated Senator Lewis Cass of Michigan for president and General William Butler of Kentucky for vice president. Cass, a party loyalist who had served in Jackson's cabinet, in 1847 had devised the idea of "popular sover-

Election of 1848 and Popular Sovereignty

eignty" for the territories—letting residents in the territories decide the question of slavery for themselves. His party's platform declared that Congress lacked the power to interfere with slavery and criticized those who pressed the question. The Whigs nominated General Zachary Taylor, a southern slaveholder and the conqueror of Monterrey; Congressman Millard Fillmore of New York was his running mate. The Whig convention similarly refused to assert that Congress had power over slavery in the territories.

But the issue would not stay in the background. Many southern Democrats distrusted Cass and eventually voted for Taylor because he was a slaveholder. Among northerners, concern over slavery led to the formation of a new party. New York Democrats committed to the Wilmot Proviso rebelled against Cass and nominated former president Van Buren. Antislavery Whigs and former supporters of the Liberty Party then joined them to organize the Free-Soil Party, with Van Buren as its candidate (see table). This party, whose slogan was "Free Soil, Free Speech, Free Labor, and Free Men," won almost 300,000 northern votes. Taylor polled 1.4 million votes to Cass's 1.2 million and won the White House, but the results were more ominous than decisive. In both public opinion and the political parties, a North-South division was deepening.

The conflicts of 1848 would dominate politics throughout the 1850s, as slavery in the territories colored every other national issue. The nation's uncertain attempts to deal with economic and social change gave way to more pressing questions about the nature of the Union itself. Soon the second party system succumbed to the crisis over slavery and the future.

Territorial Problems Are Compromised but Reemerge

The first sectional battle of the decade involved California. More than eighty thousand Americans flooded into California during the gold rush of 1849. With Congress unable to agree on a formula to govern the territories, President Taylor urged these settlers to apply directly for admission to the Union. They promptly did so, proposing a state constitution that did not allow for slavery. Because California's admission as a free state would upset the sectional balance of power in the Senate, southern politicians wanted to postpone admission and make California a slave territory, or at least to extend the Missouri Compromise line west to the Pacific. Representatives from nine southern states, meeting in Nashville, asserted the South's right to part of the territory.

Henry Clay, the venerable Whig leader, sensed that the Union was in peril. Twice before—in 1820 and 1833—Clay, the "Great Pacificator," had taken the lead in shaping sectional compromise; now he struggled one last time to preserve the nation. To hushed Senate galleries Clay presented a series of compromise measures. Over the weeks that followed, he and Senator Stephen A. Douglas of Illinois, the

New Political Parties

Party	Period of Influence	Area of Influence	Outcome
Liberty Party	1839–1848	North	Merged with other antislavery groups to form Free-Soil Party
Free-Soil Party	1848–1854	North	Merged with Republican Party
Know-Nothings (American Party)	1853–1856	Nationwide	Disappeared, freeing some northern voters to join Republican Party
Republican Party	1854–present	North (later nationwide)	Became rival of Democratic Party in third party system

"Little Giant," steered their omnibus bill, or compromise package, through debate and amendment.

The problems to be solved were numerous and difficult. Would California, or part of it, become a free state? How should the territory acquired from Mexico be organized? Texas, which allowed slavery, claimed large portions of the new land as far west as Santa Fe, so that claim, too, had to be settled. Southerners complained that fugitive slaves were not being returned as the Constitution required, and northerners objected to the sale of human beings in the nation's capital. But most troublesome of all was the status of slavery in the territories.

Clay and Douglas hoped to avoid a specific formula, for Lewis Cass's idea of popular sovereignty possessed a vagueness that appealed to practical politicians. Like many others, Cass wanted Congress to stay out of the territorial wrangle. Ultimately Congress would have to approve statehood for a territory, but "in the meantime," he said, it should allow the people living there "to regulate their own concerns in their own way."

Those simple words proved highly ambiguous. When could settlers prohibit slavery? To avoid dissension within their party, northern and southern Democrats explained Cass's statement to their constituents in two incompatible ways. Southerners claimed that neither Congress nor a territorial legislature could bar slavery. Only when settlers assumed sovereignty under a state constitution could they take that step. Northerners insisted that Americans living in a territory were entitled to local self-government and thus could outlaw slavery at any time. Northern and southern Whigs, too, were divided over the issue.

The cause of compromise gained a powerful supporter when Senator Daniel Webster committed his prestige and eloquence to Clay's bill. "I wish to speak today," Webster declaimed, "not as a Massachusetts man, nor as a Northern man, but as an American. I speak today for the preservation of the Union. Hear me for my cause." Abandoning his earlier support for the Wilmot Proviso, Webster urged northerners not to "taunt or reproach" the South with antislavery measures. To southern firebrands he issued a warning that disunion inevitably would cause great convulsion and destruction.

Yet even Webster's influence was not enough. After months of labor, Clay and Douglas finally brought their legislative package to a vote, and lost. But the determined Douglas would not give up. With Clay sick and absent from Washington, Douglas reintroduced the compromise measures one at a time. Though there was no majority for compromise, Douglas shrewdly realized that different majorities might be created for the separate measures. Because southerners favored some bills and northerners the rest, the small bloc for compromise could vote first with one section and then with the other. The strategy worked, and Douglas's resourcefulness salvaged a positive result from more than eight months of congressional effort. The Compromise of 1850 became law.

Under its various measures, California became a free state, and the Texas boundary was set at its present limits (see map, page 383). The United States paid Texas $10 million in consideration of the boundary agreement. The territories of New Mexico and Utah were organized with power to legislate on "all rightful subjects . . . consistent with the Constitution." A stronger fugitive slave law and an act to suppress the slave trade in the District of Columbia completed the compromise.

Compromise of 1850

Jubilation greeted passage of the compromise; crowds in Washington celebrated the happy news. "On one glorious night," records a modern historian, "the word went abroad that it was the duty of every patriot to get drunk. Before the next morning many a citizen had proved his patriotism," and several prominent senators "were reported stricken with a variety of implausible maladies—headaches, heat prostration, or overindulgence in fruit."

In reality, there was less cause for celebration than people hoped. Fundamentally, the Compromise of 1850 was not a settlement of sectional disputes; at best, it was an artful evasion. Douglas had found a way to pass his proposals without convincing northerners and southerners to come together and agree. This compromise bought time for the nation, but it did not create guidelines for the settlement of future territorial questions. It merely put them off. Furthermore, the compromise had two basic flaws. The first concerned the ambiguity of territorial legislation: what were "rightful subjects of legislation, consistent with the Constitution"? During debate, southerners said these words meant that there would be no prohibition of slavery during the territorial stage, and northerners declared that settlers could bar slavery whenever they wished. The compromise even acknowledged this disagreement by providing for the appeal of a territorial legislature's action to

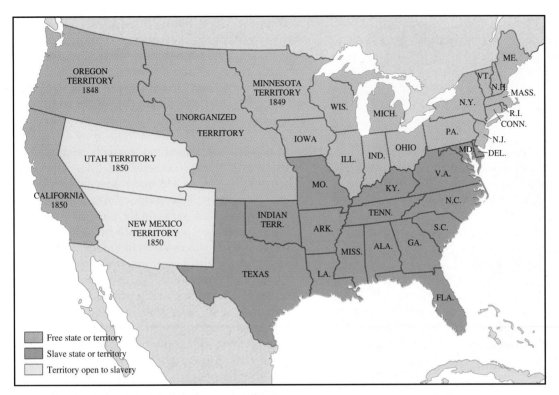

The Compromise of 1850   *The territorial provisions of the Compromise of 1850 made California a free state and set Texas's western boundary. The Utah and New Mexico Territories were opened to slavery, but northerners and southerners disagreed over when settlers could legally decide to prohibit slavery.*

the Supreme Court, but no such case ever arose. One witty politician remarked that the legislators had enacted a lawsuit instead of a law.

The second flaw lay in the Fugitive Slave Act, which gave added—and controversial—protection to slavery. The new law empowered slaveowners to

Fugitive Slave Act

go into court in their own states to present evidence that a slave who owed them service had escaped. The resulting transcript and a description of the fugitive would then serve as legal proof of a person's slave status, even in free states and territories. Court officials would decide only whether the person brought before them was the person described, not whether he or she was indeed a slave. Penalties discouraged citizens from harboring fugitives, and the fees paid to United States marshals seemed to favor slaveholders. (Authorities were paid $10 if the alleged fugitive was turned over to the slaveowner, $5 if not.)

Abolitionist newspapers quickly attacked the Fugitive Slave Act as a violation of fundamental American rights. Why, in a land of freedom, were alleged fugitives denied a trial by jury? Why were they given no chance to present evidence or cross-examine witnesses? Why did the law give authorities a financial incentive to send suspected fugitives into bondage? These arguments convinced some northerners that free blacks could be sent into slavery, mistakenly or otherwise, with no means to defend themselves. Protest meetings were held in Massachusetts, New York, Pennsylvania, northern Ohio, northern Illinois, and elsewhere. In 1851 a mob in Boston grabbed a runaway slave from a federal marshal and sent him to safety in Canada.

At this point a novel portrayed the humanity and suffering of slaves in a way that touched millions of northerners. Harriet Beecher Stowe, whose New

Uncle Tom's Cabin

England family had produced many prominent ministers, wrote *Uncle Tom's Cabin* out of deep moral conviction. Her story, serialized in 1851 and published as a book in 1852, conveyed the agonies faced by slave families and described a mother's dash to freedom

The Webb Family toured the North, presenting dramatic readings of Uncle Tom's Cabin. *Performances by the Webbs and others deepened the already powerful impact of Harriet Beecher Stowe's novel.* Harriet Beecher Stowe Center, Hartford, CT.

with her child across the frozen Ohio River. Stowe also portrayed slavery's evil effects on slaveholders, indicting the institution itself more harshly than she indicted the southerners caught in its web. In nine months the book sold over three hundred thousand copies; by mid-1853, over a million. Countless people saw *Uncle Tom's Cabin* performed as a stage play or heard the story in dramatic readings or read similar novels inspired by it. Stowe brought home the evil of slavery to many who had never given it much thought.

The popularity of *Uncle Tom's Cabin* alarmed and appalled anxious southern whites. In the territorial controversies and now in popular literature they saw threats to their way of life. Behind the South's aggressive claims about territorial rights lay fear—fear that if nearby areas became free soil, they would be used as bases from which to spread abolitionism into the slave states. Jefferson Davis of Mississippi, President Franklin Pierce's secretary of war, wrote in 1855 that "abolitionism would gain but little in excluding slavery from the territories, if it were never

to disturb that institution in the States." To defend slavery against political threats, southern leaders relied on Calhoun's territorial theories and the dogmas of states' rights and strict construction.

To protect slavery in the arena of ideas, southerners needed to counter indictments of the institution as a moral wrong. Accordingly, proslavery theorists elaborated numerous arguments based on partially scientific or pseudoscientific data. They discussed anthropological evidence suggesting separate origins of the races and physicians' views on the physical infirmities of blacks. Other proslavery spokesmen expounded the new "science" of phrenology, citing measurements of skulls to "prove" that blacks were an inferior race.

Proslavery Theories

One southern sociologist, a Virginian named George Fitzhugh, focused on relations between management and labor and declared that slavery was morally superior to free labor. Wage labor in northern industry was inhumane, Fitzhugh charged, because factory owners turned workers out when they grew old or sick. Paternalistic slaveowners, he claimed, took care of aged slaves. From these points he drew a startling conclusion: slavery ought to be practiced in all societies, whatever their racial composition. His notions, extreme even for the South, reveal why southern defenses deepened northern fears of the Slave Power.

In private and in their hearts, most southern leaders fell back on two rationales for slavery: their belief that blacks were inferior and biblical accounts of slaveholding. Like many whites, Jefferson Davis believed that whites and blacks could not coexist as equals in freedom and that slavery therefore was unavoidable. Among friends Davis reverted to the eighteenth-century argument that southerners were doing the best they could with a situation they had inherited. "Is it well to denounce an evil for which there is no cure?" he asked.

The 1852 election gave Davis and other southerners hope that slavery would be secure under the administration of a new president. Franklin Pierce, a Democrat from New Hampshire, won an easy victory over the Whig presidential nominee, General Winfield Scott. Pierce believed that the defense of each section's rights was essential to the nation's unity, and southerners hoped that his firm support for the Compromise of 1850 might end sectional divi-

Election of 1852

sions. Because Scott's views on the compromise had been unknown and the Free-Soil candidate, John P. Hale of New Hampshire, had openly rejected it, Pierce's victory suggested strong support for the compromise.

That interpretation of the election, however, was erroneous. Pierce's victory derived less from his strengths than from the Whig Party's weakness. The Whigs were a congressional and state-based party that never had achieved much success in presidential politics. Sectional discord was splitting the party in two, further undermining its national competitiveness, and the deaths of President Taylor, Daniel Webster, and Henry Clay had deprived Whigs of the few dominant personalities they had. In 1852 the Whig Party ran on little but its past reputation, and many observers predicted its demise.

When President Pierce actively supported the compromise, the results appalled many northerners. His vigorous enforcement of the fugitive slave law provoked outrage and fear of the Slave Power. In 1854 Pierce learned that a fugitive slave named Anthony Burns was in custody in Boston. Burns had fled from Virginia by stowing away on a ship. Thinking he was safe in a city known for its abolitionists, Burns wrote to an enslaved relative in Virginia. His letter was intercepted, and federal marshals placed him under guard in Boston's federal courthouse. Abolitionists attacked the courthouse, protesting for Burns's freedom.

Pierce moved decisively to enforce the Fugitive Slave Act. He telegraphed local officials to "incur any expense to insure the execution of the law" and sent marines, cavalry, and artillery to Boston. When Burns's owner seemed willing to sell his property, the United States attorney blocked the sale and won a decision that Anthony Burns must return to slavery. United States troops marched Burns to Boston harbor through streets draped in black and hung with American flags at half mast. At a cost of $100,000, equivalent to roughly $2 million today, a single black man was returned to slavery through the power of federal law.

This demonstration of federal support for slavery radicalized opinion, even among many conservatives. "I put my face in my hands and wept," wrote one man. Textile manufacturer Amos A. Lawrence observed that "we went to bed one night old fashioned, conservative, Compromise Union Whigs & waked up stark mad Abolitionists." Juries refused to convict the abolitionists who had stormed the court-

house, and New England states passed personal-liberty laws designed to impede or block federal enforcement. But where northerners saw evidence that the Slave Power was dominating American government, outraged slaveholders saw northern "faithlessness" to the law.

Pierce seemed unable to avoid sectional conflict in other arenas as well. His proposal for a transcontinental railroad derailed when congressmen fought over its location, North or South. His attempts to acquire foreign territory stirred more trouble. An annexation treaty with Hawai'i failed because southern senators would not vote for another free state, and efforts to acquire slaveholding Cuba angered antislavery northerners. After he tried to purchase Cuba from Spain in 1854, publication of a government document, the Ostend Manifesto, revealed that three administration officials had rashly talked of "wresting" Cuba from Spain. Some northerners concluded that Pierce was determined to acquire more slave territory. Then another territorial bill threw Congress and the nation into a bitter conflict that was to have significant results.

 ## Territorial Problems Shatter the Party System

The new controversy began in a surprising way. Stephen A. Douglas, one of the architects of the Compromise of 1850, introduced a bill to establish the Kansas and Nebraska Territories. A talented and ambitious man, Douglas was known for compromise, not sectional quarreling. But he did not view slavery as a fundamental problem, and he was willing to risk some controversy to win economic benefits for Illinois, his home state. A transcontinental railroad would encourage settlement of the Great Plains and stimulate the economy of Illinois; but no company would build such a railroad before Congress organized the territories it would cross. Thus it was probably for the sake of promoting the construction of a railroad that Douglas introduced a bill that inflamed sectional passions and thwarted his own ambitions for national office. The Kansas-Nebraska bill also finished off the Whig Party, damaged the northern Democrats, and gave birth to a new Republican Party.

The Kansas-Nebraska bill exposed the first flaw of the Compromise of 1850—the conflicting interpretations of popular sovereignty. Douglas's bill

PEOPLE'S MEETING!!

CITIZENS OF CHESTER COUNTY:—The time has arrived when it is necessary to make preparations for the next general election. In view of existing circumstances, it is proper that the citizens of this County

WITHOUT RESPECT TO PARTY,

Should meet for the purpose of Conferring together, and forming such an organization as will give effect to their views on important public questions. A fixed and resolute determination has recently been manifested on the part of the

SLAVE POWER,

To extend its dominion—to carry its blighting influence to territory now free—to control the government of the nation, and make it subservient to its wicked designs. Compacts entered into, under circumstances the most solemn, have been violated; an extended territory, dedicated by the MISSOURI COMPROMISE to Freedom, in violation of faith and honor, has been thrown open to the traffickers in human flesh, who in disregard of law and order, have seized upon its fertile plains with a view of adding

OTHER SLAVE STATES TO THE UNION

And giving to the Slave Power an ascendency over freedom in the Nation. Experience has satisfied the people that while the emigration to this country of the peaceable industrious foreigner, should be regarded with favor, the facility with which persons reared abroad, under systems of government radically different from our own, approach the ballot box, and influence our elections, is an evil dangerous alike to the adopted and native citizen. A change in the

NATURALIZATION LAWS

Extending the probative period of the alien—the separation of Church and State in practice as well as in theory—the freedom of the government from all improper foreign influence—and the protection of the

AMERICAN LABORER

Are believed to be essential to the welfare of all classes of the people. All persons who are willing to co-operate upon the principles here indicated and which we believe to be those of a true democracy, are earnestly invited to meet at the

COURT HOUSE IN THE BOROUGH OF WEST CHESTER

On Saturday the 18th instant at ten o'clock A. M.   *August 1855.*

U. V. Pennypacker,	Francis James,	Joseph Painter,	Samuel Way,	James Sweney,
Hickman James,	William Hoopes,	Wm. Sweney,	N. Mendenhall,	Isaac Thomas,
Jonathan T. Marshall,	Jesse C. Green,	Mordecai T. Ruth,	Wm. Darlington,	J. B. Wood,
Joshua Darlington,	J.B. Jeffris,	Benj. J. Passmore,	Samuel S. Heed,	Reuben White,
Geo. F. Worrall,	C. P. Sweney,	Whiddin M. Foster,	William Hoopes,	Wm. Windle,
Thos. W. Parker,	Wm. Whitehead,	C. M. Valentine,	Sam. J. Parker,	Thos. H. Hall

☞ Other names omitted for want of room.

Independent Herald Steam Press, Market Street, West Chester Pa.

Throughout the North the Kansas-Nebraska Act kindled fires of alarm over the Slave Power's "determination to extend its dominion" and "control the government of the nation." Public meetings like the one announced here, held in West Chester, Pennsylvania, aided the new Republican Party. American Antiquarian Society.

Kansas-Nebraska Bill

left "all questions pertaining to slavery in the Territories . . . to the people residing therein." Northerners and southerners, however, still disagreed violently over what territorial settlers could constitutionally do. Moreover, the Kansas and Nebraska Territories lay within the Louisiana Purchase, and the Missouri Compromise prohibited slavery in all that land from latitude 36°30' north to the Canadian border. If popular sovereignty were to mean anything in Kansas and Nebraska, it had to mean that the Missouri Compromise was no longer in effect and that settlers could establish slavery there.

Southern congressmen, anxious to establish slaveholders' right to take slaves into any territory, pressed Douglas to concede this point. They de-

manded an explicit repeal of the 36°30' limitation as the price of their support. During a carriage ride with Senator Archibald Dixon of Kentucky, Douglas debated the point at length. Finally he made an impulsive decision: "By God, Sir, you are right. I will incorporate it in my bill, though I know it will raise a hell of a storm."

Perhaps Douglas underestimated the storm because he believed that conditions of climate and soil would keep slavery out of Kansas and Nebraska. Nevertheless, his bill threw open to slavery land from which it had been prohibited for thirty-four years. Opposition from Free-Soilers and antislavery forces was immediate and enduring (see broadside). The titanic struggle in Congress lasted three-and-a-half months. Douglas won the support of President Pierce and eventually prevailed: the bill became law in May 1854 (see map, page 387).

Unfortunately, the storm was just beginning. Abolitionists charged sinister aggression by the Slave Power, and northern fears of slavery's influence deepened. Opposition to the Fugitive Slave Act grew dramatically; between 1855 and 1859 Connecticut, Rhode Island, Massachusetts, Michigan, Maine, Ohio, and Wisconsin passed personal-liberty laws. These laws interfered with the Fugitive Slave Act— and enraged southern leaders—by providing counsel for alleged fugitives and requiring trial by jury. More important was the devastating impact of the Kansas-Nebraska Act on political parties. The weakened Whig Party broke apart into northern and southern wings that could no longer cooperate nationally. One of the two foundations of the second party system was now gone. The Democrats survived, but their support in the North fell drastically in the 1854 elections. Northern Democrats lost sixty-six of their ninety-one congressional seats and lost control of all but two free-state legislatures.

The beneficiary of northern voters' wrath was a new political party. During debate on the Kansas-Nebraska bill, six congressmen had published an "Appeal of the Independent Democrats." Joshua Giddings, Salmon Chase, and Charles Sumner—the principal authors of this protest—attacked Douglas's legislation as a "gross violation of a sacred pledge" (the Missouri Compromise) and a "criminal betrayal of precious rights" that would make free territory a "dreary region of despotism." Their appeal tapped a reservoir of deep

The New Republican Party

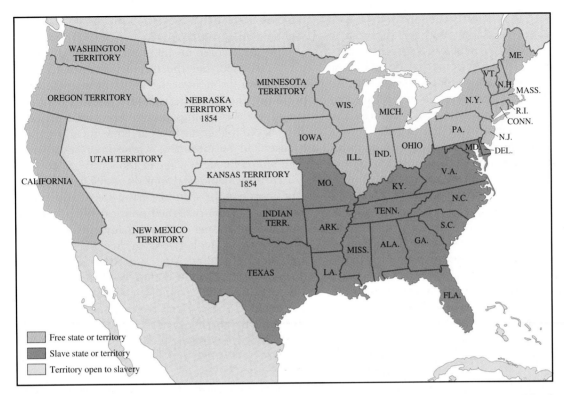

The Kansas-Nebraska Act, 1854 *Stephen Douglas's bill raised a storm of opposition in the North because it repealed the Missouri Compromise's limitation on slavery. In Kansas and Nebraska, land was opened to slavery where it had been prohibited before.*

concerns in the North—concerns that Illinois's Abraham Lincoln cogently expressed.

Although Lincoln did not condemn southerners—"They are just what we would be in their situation"—he exposed the moral bankruptcy and historic significance of the Kansas-Nebraska Act. Denying "that there can be moral right in the enslaving of one man by another," Lincoln argued that the founders, from love of liberty, had banned slavery from the Northwest Territory, kept the word *slavery* out of the Constitution, and treated it overall as a "cancer" that eventually had to be removed. Rather than encouraging liberty, the Kansas-Nebraska Act put slavery "on the high road to extension and perpetuity," and that constituted a "moral wrong and injustice." America's future, Lincoln warned, was being mortgaged to slavery. The nation should "readopt the Declaration of Independence" and commit itself to freedom.

Thousands agreed. During the summer and fall of 1854, antislavery Whigs and Democrats, Free-Soilers, and other reformers throughout the Old Northwest met to form the new Republican Party, dedicated to keeping slavery out of the territories. The influence of the Republicans rapidly spread to the East, and they won a stunning victory in the 1854 elections. In their first appearance on the ballot, Republicans captured a majority of northern House seats. Antislavery sentiment had created a new party and caused roughly a quarter of northern Democrats to desert their party.

For the first time, too, a sectional party had gained significant power in the political system. Previously, every major party was a national organization whose leaders patched up sectional differences to achieve partisan goals. Now the Whigs were gone, and only the Democrats struggled to maintain a national following. The sectional Republican Party, which absorbed the Free-Soil Party, grew rapidly in the North by raising moral issues that angered many southerners.

Nor were Republicans the only new party. For a brief period, an anti-immigrant organization, the American Party, seemed likely to replace the Whigs.

This party, popularly known as the Know-Nothings (because its first members kept their purposes secret, answering "I know nothing" to all questions), exploited nativist fear of foreigners. Between 1848 and 1860, nearly 3.5 million immigrants entered the United States—proportionally the heaviest inflow of foreigners ever in American history (see pages 330–334). Democrats courted these new citizens and relied on their votes, but many native-born Americans harbored serious misgivings about them. In 1854 anti-immigrant fears gave the Know-Nothings more supporters in some northern states than either the Republicans or the Free-Soilers. The temperance movement also gained new strength early in the 1850s with its promises to stamp out the evils associated with liquor and immigrants. In this context the Know-Nothings campaigned to reinforce Protestant morality and restrict voting and officeholding to the native-born.

By the mid-1850s the American Party was powerful and growing. But like the Whigs, the Know-Nothings could not keep their northern and southern wings together, and they melted away after 1856. That left the field to the Republicans, who wooed the nativists and in several states passed temperance ordinances and laws postponing suffrage for naturalized citizens (see table, page 381).

Republicans, Know-Nothings, and Democrats were all scrambling to attract former Whig voters. The demise of that party ensured a major realignment of the political system, with nearly half of the old electorate up for grabs. To woo these homeless Whigs, the remaining parties made appeals to various segments of the electorate. Immigration, temperance, homestead bills, the tariff, internal improvements—all played important roles in attracting voters during the 1850s.

The Republicans appealed strongly to those interested in the economic development of the West. Commercial agriculture was booming in the Ohio–Mississippi–Great Lakes area, but residents of that region desired more canals, roads, and river and harbor improvements to reap the full benefit of their labors. Because credit was scarce, there was also widespread interest in a homestead program: its pro-

ponents argued that western land should be made available free to those who would farm it. The Whigs had favored all these measures before their party collapsed, but the Democrats resolutely opposed them throughout the 1850s. Seizing their opportunity, the Republicans added internal improvements and land-grant planks to their platform. They also backed higher tariffs as an enticement to industrialists and businessmen, whose interest in tariffs grew after a financial panic in 1857.

Partisan ideological appeals, which had a significant impact on the sectional crisis, were another major feature of the realigned political system. In the North, Republicans attracted many voters through effective use of ideology. When they preached "Free Soil, Free Labor, Free Men," they captured an image that northerners had of themselves and their future. These phrases resonated with traditional ideals of equality, liberty, and opportunity under self-government—the heritage of republicanism. Use of that heritage also undercut charges that the Republican Party was radical and unreliable.

"Free Soil, Free Labor, Free Men" seemed an appropriate motto for a northern economy that was energetic, expanding, and prosperous. Thousands of farmers had moved west to establish productive farms and growing communities. Midwesterners were using new machines, such as disk harrows and mechanical reapers, which multiplied their yields. Railroads were carrying their crops to urban markets. And industry was beginning to perform wonders of production, making available goods that had been beyond the reach of the average person. As northerners surveyed the general growth and prosperity, they thought they saw a reason for it.

The key to progress appeared, to many people, to be free labor. People believed in the dignity of labor and the incentive of opportunity. Any hardworking and virtuous man, it was thought, could improve his condition and achieve economic independence by seizing opportunities that the country had to offer. Republicans argued that the South, which relied on slave labor and had little industry, was backward and retrograde by comparison, and their arguments captured much of the spirit of the age in the North.

Traditional republicanism hailed the virtuous common man as the backbone of the country. In Abraham Lincoln, a man of humble origins who had become a successful lawyer and political leader, Republicans had a symbol of that tradition. They portrayed their party as the guardian of economic opportunity, giving individuals a chance to work, acquire land, and attain success. In the words of an Iowa Republican, the United States was thriving because its "door is thrown open to all, and even the poorest and humblest in the land, may, by industry and application, gain a position which will entitle him to the respect and confidence of his fellow-men."

The Republican Party thus attracted support from a variety of sources. Opposition to the extension of slavery had brought the party into being, but party members carefully broadened their appeal by adopting the causes of other groups. They were wise to do so. As the New York newspaper editor Horace Greeley wrote in 1856, "It is beaten into my bones that the American people are not yet anti-slavery." Four years later, Greeley again observed that "an Anti-Slavery man *per se* cannot be elected." But, he added, "a Tariff, River-and-Harbor, Pacific Railroad, Free Homestead man, *may* succeed *although* he is Anti-Slavery." As these elements joined the Republican Party, they also learned more about the dangers of slavery. Thus the process of party building deepened the sectional conflict.

A similar process was under way in the South. The disintegration of the Whig Party had left many southerners at loose ends politically; they included a good number of wealthy planters, smaller slaveholders, and urban businessmen. Some gravitated to the American Party, but not for long. In the increasingly tense atmosphere of sectional crisis, these people were highly susceptible to strong states' rights positions and defense of slavery. Democratic leaders emphasized such appeals during the 1850s and managed to convert most of the formerly Whig slaveholders, who responded to their class interests.

Southern Democrats

Most Democrats south of the Mason-Dixon line, however, were not slaveholders. Since Andrew Jackson's day, small farmers had been the heart of the Democratic Party. Democratic politicians, though often slaveowners themselves, lauded the common man and argued that their policies advanced his interests. According to the southern version of republicanism, white citizens in a slave society enjoyed liberty and social equality *because* black people were enslaved. Slavery supposedly prevented the evil of aristocracy by making all white men

equal. As Jefferson Davis put it in 1851, in other societies distinctions were drawn "by property, between the rich and the poor." But in the South, slavery elevated every white person's status and allowed the nonslaveholder to *"stand upon the broad level of equality with the rich man."* To retain the support of ordinary whites, southern Democrats emphasized this appeal to racism. The issue in the sectional crisis, they warned, was "shall negroes govern white men, or white men govern negroes?"

Southern leaders also portrayed sectional controversies as matters of injustice and insult to the South. The rights of all southern whites were in jeopardy, they argued, because antislavery and Free-Soil forces were attacking an institution protected in the Constitution. The stable, well-ordered South was the true defender of constitutional principles; the rapidly changing North did not respect constitutional principles.

Those arguments had their effect. Racial fears and traditional political loyalties helped keep the political alliance between yeoman farmers and planters intact through the 1850s. Potential conflicts of interest between slaveholders and nonslaveholders were not discussed, and no viable party emerged to replace the Whigs. The result was a one-party system that emphasized sectional issues. In the South as in the North, political realignment sharpened sectional divisions.

Political leaders of both sections argued that racial change threatened opportunity, but northerners and southerners saw different futures. The *Montgomery* (Alabama) *Mail* warned southern whites in 1860 that the Republicans intended "to free the negroes and force amalgamation between them and the children of the poor men of the South. The rich will be able to keep out of the way of the contamination." Republicans warned northern workers that if slavery entered the territories, the great reservoir of opportunity for ordinary citizens would be poisoned. Republicans claimed that free labor had to be extended to the territories if coming generations were to prosper.

In the territory of Kansas a succession of events, like hammer blows, deepened the conflict. The Kansas-Nebraska Act spawned hatred and violence as land-hungry claim jumpers and partisans in the sectional struggle clashed repeatedly in Kansas Territory. Abolitionists and religious groups sent in armed Free-Soil settlers; southerners sent in their reinforcements to establish slavery and prevent "northern hordes" from stealing Kansas away. Conflicts led

The Border Ruffians, depicted in this pen-and-ink drawing, were proslavery Missourians who periodically invaded Kansas to vote and help establish slavery there. Conflicts over land claims further complicated the violence in Bleeding Kansas.   Yale University Art Gallery, Mabel Brady Garvan Collection.

to bloodshed, and soon the whole nation was talking about "Bleeding Kansas."

Politics in the territory resembled war more than democracy. During elections for a territorial legislature in 1855, thousands of proslavery Missourians—known as Border Ruffians—invaded the polls and ran up a large but fraudulent majority for slavery candidates.

Bleeding Kansas

The resulting legislature legalized slavery, and in response Free-Soilers held an unauthorized convention at which they created their own government and constitution. A proslavery posse sent to arrest the Free-Soil leaders sacked the town of Lawrence. In revenge John Brown, an antislavery zealot who saw himself as God's instrument to destroy slavery, murdered five proslavery settlers. Soon, armed bands of guerrillas roamed the state, battling over land claims as well as slavery.

These passions brought violence to the United States Senate in May 1856, when Charles Sumner of Massachusetts denounced "the Crime against Kansas." Radical in his antislavery views, Sumner bitterly assailed the president, the South, and Senator Andrew P. Butler of South Carolina. Soon thereafter Butler's cousin, Representative Preston Brooks, approached Sumner at the latter's Senate desk, raised his cane, and began to beat Sumner on the head. Trapped behind his desk, which was bolted in place, Sumner tried to rise, eventually wrenching the desk free before he collapsed, bleeding, on the floor. Shocked northerners recoiled from what they saw as another southern assault on free speech and the South's readiness to use violence to have its way. William Cullen Bryant, editor of the *New York Evening Post,* asked, "Has it come to this, that we must speak with bated breath in the presence of our southern masters?" As if in reply, the *Richmond En-*

quirer denounced "vulgar Abolitionists in the Senate" who "have been suffered to run too long without collars. They must be lashed into submission." Popular opinion in Massachusetts strongly supported Sumner; South Carolina voters reelected Brooks and sent him dozens of new canes. The country was becoming polarized.

The election of 1856 showed how extreme that polarization had become. When Democrats met to select a nominee, they shied away from prominent leaders whose views on the territories were well known. Instead, they chose James Buchanan of Pennsylvania, whose chief virtue was that for the past four years he had been ambassador to Britain, uninvolved in territorial controversies. This anonymity and superior party organization helped Buchanan win 1.8 million votes and the election, but he owed his victory to southern support. Eleven of sixteen free states voted against him, and Democrats did not regain ascendancy in those states for decades. The Republican candidate, John C. Frémont, won those eleven free states and 1.3 million votes; Republicans had become the dominant party in the North. The Know-Nothing candidate, Millard Fillmore, won almost 1 million votes, but this election was to be his party's last hurrah. The coming battle would be between a sectional Republican Party and an increasingly divided Democratic Party.

The earliest known photograph of John Brown, probably taken in 1846 in Massachusetts, shows him pledging his devotion to an unidentified flag, possibly an abolitionist banner. Already Brown was aiding runaway slaves and pondering ways to strike at slavery.   Ohio Historical Society.

 ## Slavery and the Nation's Future

For years the issue of slavery in the territories had convulsed Congress, and for years Congress had tried to settle the issue with vague formulas. In 1857 a different branch of government stepped onto the scene. The Supreme Court took up this emotionally charged subject and attempted to silence controversy with a definitive verdict.

A Missouri slave named Dred Scott had sued his owner for his freedom. Scott based his claim on the fact that his former owner, an army surgeon, had taken him for several years into Illinois, a free state, and into the Wisconsin Territory, from which slavery had been barred by the Missouri Compromise. Scott first won and then lost his case as it moved on appeal through the state courts, into the federal system, and finally after eleven years to the Supreme Court.

Dred Scott Case

Normally Supreme Court justices were reluctant to inject themselves into political issues, and it seemed likely that the Court would stay out of this one. An 1851 decision had declared that state courts determined the status of Negroes who lived within their jurisdiction. The Supreme Court had only to follow this precedent to avoid ruling on substantive, and very controversial, issues: Was a black person like Dred Scott a citizen of the United States and thus eligible to sue in federal court? Had residence in a free state or free territory made him free? Did Congress have the power to prohibit slavery in a territory or to delegate that power to a territorial legislature?

Initially the Supreme Court seemed ready to dispose of *Dred Scott* v. *Sandford* by following the 1851 precedent. The chief justice even assigned one justice the task of writing such an opinion. Then, for a number of reasons, the Court decided to rule on the Missouri Compromise after all. Two northern justices indicated that they would dissent from the assigned

Dred Scott, a slave who brought suit in Missouri for his freedom, and Chief Justice Roger Taney, a descendant of Maryland's slave-holding elite, were principal figures in the most controversial Supreme Court decision of the nineteenth century. Dred Scott: Missouri Historical Society; Roger Taney: Maryland Historical Society.

opinion and argue for Scott's freedom and the constitutionality of the Missouri Compromise. Their decision emboldened southerners on the Court, who were growing eager to declare the 1820 compromise unconstitutional. Southern sympathizers in Washington were pressing for a proslavery verdict, and several justices simply felt they should try to resolve an issue whose uncertainties had caused so much strife.

In March 1857, Chief Justice Roger B. Taney of Maryland delivered the majority opinion of a divided Court. Taney declared that Scott was not a citizen of either the United States or Missouri; that residence in free territory did not make Scott free; and that Congress had no power to bar slavery from a territory, as it had done in the Missouri Compromise. The decision not only overturned a sectional compromise that had been honored for years; it also invalidated the basic ideas of the Wilmot Proviso and probably popular sovereignty as well.

The Slave Power seemed to have won a major constitutional victory. African-Americans were especially dismayed, for Taney's decision asserted that the founders had never intended for black people to be citizens. At the nation's founding, the chief justice wrote, blacks had been regarded "as beings of an inferior order" with "no rights which the white man was bound to respect." Taney was mistaken, however. African-Americans had been citizens in several of the original states. Nevertheless, the *Dred Scott* decision seemed to shut the door permanently on their hopes for justice and equal rights.

Northern whites who rejected the decision's content were suspicious of the circumstances that produced it. Five of the nine justices were southerners; three of the northern justices actively dissented or refused to concur in crucial parts of the decision. The only northerner who supported Taney's opinion, Justice Robert Grier of Pennsylvania, was known to be close to President Buchanan. In fact, Buchanan had secretly brought to bear improper but effective influence.

A storm of angry reaction broke in the North. The decision alarmed a wide variety of northerners

How do historians know what motivated Abraham Lincoln to oppose the extension of slavery? Lincoln, of course, was a public man who made many addresses and public statements. His words as a politician and leader of the Republican Party show his reverence for the Declaration of Independence and America's heritage of freedom. But Lincoln also produced many private writings. The page reproduced below comes from a notebook in which he recorded his reactions to a proslavery book, Slavery Ordained of God, *by Rev. Fred A. Ross. Criticizing Ross, Lincoln revealed his dislike of privilege and exposed the self-interest of those who would exploit others: "Dr. Ross sits in the shade, with gloves on his hands, and subsists on the bread that Sambo is earning in the burning sun" rather than "delv[ing] for his own bread."* Illinois State Historical Society and Library.

and seemed to confirm every charge against the aggressive Slave Power. "There is such a thing as the slave power," warned the *Cincinnati Daily Commercial*. "It has marched over and annihilated the boundaries of the states. We are now one great homogenous slaveholding community." The *Cincinnati Freeman* asked, "What security have the Germans and the Irish that their children will not, within a hundred years, be reduced to slavery in this land of their adoption?" "Where will it end?" asked the *Atlantic Monthly*. "Is the success of this conspiracy to be final and eternal?" The poet James Russell

Lowell expressed the anxieties of poor northern whites when he had his Yankee character Ezekiel Biglow say:

> Wy, it's just ez clear ez figgers,
> Clear ez one an' one make two,
> Chaps thet make black slaves o' niggers,
> Want to make wite slaves o' you.

Republican politicians used these fears to strengthen their coalition of abolitionists and other northerners, including racists who feared that slavery jeopardized their interests.

Abraham Lincoln on the Slave Power

Abraham Lincoln stressed that the territorial question affected every citizen. "The whole nation," he declared as early as 1854, "is interested that the best use shall be made of these Territories. We want them for homes of free white people. This they cannot be, to any considerable extent, if slavery shall be planted within them." The territories must be reserved, he insisted, "as an outlet for *free white people everywhere*" so that immigrants could come to America and "find new homes and better their condition in life."

More importantly, Lincoln warned of slavery's increasing control over the nation. The founders had created a government dedicated to freedom, Lincoln insisted. Admittedly they had recognized slavery's existence, but "this Government has endured eighty-two years because," he argued in 1858, "during all that time, until the introduction of the Nebraska Bill, the public mind did rest . . . in the belief that slavery was in course of ultimate extinction." After the *Dred Scott* decision, he charged, it was clear that slavery's advocates, including highly placed government officials, were trying to "push it forward, till it shall become lawful in *all* the states . . . *North* as well as *South*."

The next step in the unfolding Slave Power conspiracy, Lincoln alleged, would be a Supreme Court decision "declaring that the Constitution does not permit a State to exclude slavery from its limits. . . . We shall lie down pleasantly, dreaming that the people of Missouri are on the verge of making their State free; and we shall awake to the reality instead, that the Supreme Court has made Illinois a slave State." This charge was not pure hyperbole, for lawsuits soon challenged state laws that freed slaves brought within their borders.

Lincoln's most eloquent statement against the Slave Power was his famous "House Divided" speech, in which he declared:

> I do not expect the Union to be dissolved—I do not expect the House to fall—but I do expect it to cease to be divided. It will become all one thing or all the other. Either the opponents of slavery will arrest the further spread of it, and place it where the public mind shall rest in the belief that it is in the course of ultimate extinction; or its advocates will push it forward, till it shall become alike lawful in all the States, old as well as new, North as well as South.

Lincoln warned repeatedly that the latter possibility was real, and events convinced countless northerners that slaveholders were nearing their goal of making slavery a national institution.

Politically, these forceful Republican arguments offset the difficulties that the *Dred Scott* decision posed. By endorsing Calhoun's theories, the Court had in effect declared that the central position of the Republican Party—no extension of slavery—was unconstitutional. Republicans could only repudiate the decision, appealing to a "higher law," or hope to change the personnel of the Court. They did both and probably gained politically as fear of the Slave Power grew.

For northern Democrats like Stephen Douglas, the Court's decision posed an awful dilemma. Northern voters were alarmed by the prospect that the territories would be opened to slavery. To retain their support, Douglas had to find some way to reassure them. Yet, given his ambitions to lead the national Democratic Party and become president, Douglas could not afford to alienate southern Democrats. His task was problematic at best; given the emotions of the era, it proved impossible.

Douglas chose to stand by his principle of popular sovereignty, even if the result angered southerners. In 1857 Kansans voted on a proslavery constitution that had been drafted at Lecompton. It was defeated by more than ten thousand votes. The evidence was overwhelming that Kansans did not want slavery, yet President Buchanan tried to force the Lecompton Constitution through Congress.

Never had the Slave Power's influence over the government seemed more blatant; the Buchanan administration and southerners were demanding a proslavery outcome, contrary to the desires of the majority in Kansas. Breaking with the administration, Douglas threw his weight against the Lecompton Constitution. He gauged opinion in Kansas correctly, for in 1858 voters there rejected the constitution again. But his action infuriated southern

Democrats. After the *Dred Scott* decision, southerners like Senator Albert G. Brown of Mississippi believed that slavery was *protected* in the territories: "The Constitution as expounded by the Supreme Court awards it. We demand it; we mean to have it."

Douglas further alienated the southern wing of his party in his well-publicized debates with Abraham Lincoln, who challenged him for the Illinois Senate seat in 1858. Speaking at Freeport, Illinois, Douglas attempted to revive the concept of popular sovereignty with some tortured arguments. Asserting that the Supreme Court had ruled only on the powers of Congress, not on the powers of a *territorial* legislature, Douglas claimed that the latter could bar slavery either by passing a law against it or by doing nothing. Without the patrol laws and police regulations that supported slavery, he reasoned, the institution could not exist. This argument, called the Freeport Doctrine, temporarily shored up Douglas's crumbling position in the North. But it gave southern Democrats further evidence that Douglas was unreliable, and many turned viciously against him. Some, like Representative William L. Yancey of Alabama, studied the trend in northern opinion and concluded that southern rights and slavery would be safe only in a separate nation.

Stephen Douglas Proposes the Freeport Doctrine

Such feelings were not new. As early as 1838, the Louisiana planter Bennet Barrow had written in his diary, "Northern States meddling with slavery . . . openly speaking of the sin of Slavery in the southern states . . . must eventually cause a separation of the Union." In 1856, a calmer, more polished Georgian named Charles Colcock Jones, Jr., rejoiced at James Buchanan's defeat of Republican John C. Frémont for the presidency. The result guaranteed four more years of peace and prosperity, wrote Jones, but "beyond that period . . . we scarce dare expect a continuance of our present relations." Increasingly, slaveowners agreed with Jones and Barrow.

The immediate consequence for politics, however, was the likelihood of a split in the Democratic Party. Northern Democrats could not support the territorial protection for slavery that southern Democrats insisted was theirs as a constitutional right. Thus the issue of slavery in the territories continued to generate wider conflict, even though it had little immediate, practical significance. In territories outside Kansas the number of settlers was small, and

in all territories the number of African-Americans was negligible—less than 1 percent of the populations of Kansas and New Mexico. By 1858 even Jefferson Davis had abandoned hopes of agricultural development in the Southwest and admitted that slavery might not succeed in Kansas. Nevertheless, men like Davis and Douglas spent many hours in bitter, alarming debate. The situation had become explosive.

 ## Breakup of the Union

One year before the 1860 presidential election, John Brown, who had slain proslavery settlers in Kansas, led a small band of whites and blacks in an attack on the federal arsenal at Harpers Ferry, Virginia. Hoping to trigger a slave rebellion, Brown failed miserably and was quickly captured, tried, and executed. Yet his attempted insurrection struck fear into the South. Then it became known that Brown had received financial backing from several prominent abolitionists. When northern intellectuals such as Emerson and Thoreau praised Brown as a hero and a martyr, white southerners' fears and anger multiplied many times over.

Many believed that the election of 1860 would decide the fate of the Union. Only the Democratic Party remained as an organization that was truly national in scope. Even religious denominations had split into northern and southern wings during the 1840s and 1850s. "One after another," wrote a Mississippi newspaper editor, "the links which have bound the North and South together, have been severed . . . [but] the Democratic party looms gradually up, its nationality intact, and waves the olive branch over the troubled waters of politics." At its 1860 convention, however, the Democratic Party broke in two.

Stephen A. Douglas wanted his party's presidential nomination, but he could not afford to alienate northern voters by accepting the southern position on the territories. Southern Democrats like William L. Yancey, however, insisted on recognition of their rights—as Chief Justice Roger Taney had defined them—and they moved to block Douglas's nomination. When Douglas obtained a majority for his version of the platform, delegates from the five Gulf states plus

Splintering of the Democratic Party

THE NATIONAL GAME. THREE "OUTS" AND ONE "RUN".
ABRAHAM WINNING THE BALL.

The 1860 presidential campaign, like great political contests today, rapidly entered popular culture. This cartoon by Currier and Ives was one of the first to apply the terminology of baseball to that other national game: politics. From left to right, the presidential candidates are Breckinridge, Douglas, Bell, and the victorious Lincoln. Museum of American Political Life, University of Hartford.

South Carolina, Georgia, and Arkansas walked out of the party convention in Charleston. After efforts at compromise failed, the Democrats presented two nominees: Douglas for the northern wing, and Vice President John C. Breckinridge of Kentucky for the southern. The Republicans nominated Abraham Lincoln. A Constitutional Union Party, formed to preserve the nation but strong only in the Upper South, nominated John Bell of Tennessee.

Three of the candidates stressed their support for the Union in the ensuing campaign. Bell's only issue was the urgency of preserving the Union, and Douglas desperately wanted to hold his northern and southern supporters together. Even Breckinridge quickly backed away from the appearance of extremism, and his supporters in several states de-

clared that he was not a threat to the Union. Then the *New Orleans Bee* charged that every disunionist in the land applauded Breckinridge, and a Texas paper challenged his association with radicals: "Mr. Breckinridge claims that he isn't a disunionist. An animal not willing to pass for a pig shouldn't stay in the stye." Reacting to such criticism, Breckinridge reversed his decision to give no speeches and delivered one address in which he flatly denied that his aim was secession. Thereafter his supporters stressed his loyalty and even ridiculed the possibility of secession in case of a Republican victory. Although Lincoln and the Republicans denied any intent to interfere with slavery in the states where it existed, they stood firm against the extension of slavery into the territories.

The results of the balloting were sectional in character. Lincoln won, but Douglas, Breckinridge, and Bell together received most of the votes (see cartoon, page 396). Douglas had broad-based support but won few states. Breckinridge, whose strength was concentrated in the Deep South, carried nine southern states. Bell won pluralities in Virginia, Kentucky, and Tennessee. Lincoln prevailed in the North, but in the states that ultimately remained loyal to the Union he gained only a plurality, not a majority (see table). Lincoln's victory was won in the electoral college.

Election of 1860

Given the heterogeneous nature of Republican voters, it is likely that many of them did not view the issue of slavery in the territories as paramount. But opposition to slavery's extension was the core issue of the Republican Party, and Lincoln's alarm over slavery's growing political power was genuine. Moreover, abolitionists and supporters of free soil in the North worked to keep the Republicans from compromising on their territorial stand. Meanwhile in the South, proslavery advocates and secessionists whipped up public opinion and demanded that state conventions assemble to consider secession.

Lincoln made the crucial decision not to soften his party's position on the territories. He wrote of the necessity of maintaining the bond of faith between voter and candidate and of declining to set "the minority over the majority." But Lincoln's party had not won a majority of votes. His refusal to compromise probably derived both from conviction and from concern for the unity of the Republican Party. Although many conservative Republicans—eastern businessmen and former Whigs who did not feel strongly about slavery—hoped for a compromise, the original and most committed Republicans—antislavery voters and "conscience Whigs"—were adamant for free soil. Lincoln chose to preserve party unity by standing firm against slavery's extension.

Southern leaders in the Senate were willing, conditionally, to accept a compromise drawn up by Senator John J. Crittenden of Kentucky. Hoping to don the mantle of Henry Clay and avert disunion, Crittenden proposed that the two sections divide the territories between them at latitude 36°30'. But the southerners would agree to this *only* if the Republicans did, too, for they wanted no less and knew that extremists in the South would demand much more. When Lincoln ruled out concessions on the territorial issue, Crittenden's peacemaking effort

collapsed. Virginians called for a special convention in Washington, to which several states sent representatives. But this gathering, too, failed to find a solution.

Though political leaders in North and South had communicated clearly with each other about the Crittenden proposal, misjudgment also played a role in the coming of war. As the historian David Potter has shown, Lincoln and other prominent Republicans believed that southerners were bluffing when they threatened secession; Republicans expected a pro-Union majority in the South to assert itself. Therefore Lincoln determined not to yield to threats but to call the southerners' bluff. On their side, southern leaders had become convinced, more accurately, that northern leaders were not taking them seriously and that a posture of strength was necessary to win respect for their demands. "To rally the men of the North, who would preserve the government as our fathers found it, we . . . should offer no doubtful or divided front," wrote Jefferson Davis. With such attitudes shaping leaders' actions, confrontation was more likely than compromise.

Meanwhile, the Union was being destroyed. On December 20, 1860, South Carolina passed an ordinance of secession amid jubilation and cheering.

Presidential Vote in 1860

	Lincoln	Other Candidates
Entire United States	1,866,452	2,815,617
North plus border and southern states that rejected secession prior to war[1]	1,866,452	2,421,752
North plus border states that fought for the Union[2]	1,864,523	1,960,842

Source: From David Potter, *Lincoln and His Party in the Secession Crisis.* Copyright 1942, 1967 by Yale University Press. Reprinted by permission.

[1]Kentucky, Missouri, Maryland, Delaware, Virginia, North Carolina, Tennessee, Arkansas

[2]Kentucky, Missouri, Maryland, Delaware

On February 18, 1861, in Montgomery, Alabama, Jefferson Davis took an oath as president of the Confederate States of America. Davis later recalled that he foresaw "troubles innumerable" but was committed to seek independence as his paramount goal.   Boston Athenaeum.

Secession of South Carolina

This step marked the inauguration of a strategy favored by secessionists: separate-state secession. Recognizing the difficulty of persuading all the southern states to challenge the federal government simultaneously, secessionists concentrated their efforts on the most extreme proslavery state. They hoped South Carolina's secession would induce other states to follow, with each decision building momentum for disunion.

The strategy proved effective. By reclaiming its independence, South Carolina raised the stakes in the sectional confrontation. No longer was secession an unthinkable step; the Union was broken. Extremists now argued that other states should secede to support South Carolina and that those who favored

compromise could make a better deal outside the Union than in it. Moderates found it difficult to dismiss such arguments, since most of them—even those who felt deep affection for the Union—were committed to defending southern rights and the southern way of life.

Southern extremists soon got their way in the Deep South. Overwhelming their opposition, they called separate state conventions and passed secession ordinances in Mississippi, Florida, Alabama, Georgia, Louisiana, and Texas. By February 1861 these states had joined South Carolina to form a new government in Montgomery, Alabama: the Confederate States of America. The delegates at Montgomery chose Jefferson Davis as their president, and the Confederacy began to function independently of the United States.

Confederate States of America

This apparent unanimity of action was deceiving. Confused and dissatisfied with the alternatives, many southerners who in 1860 had voted in the United States presidential election stayed home a few months later rather than vote for delegates who would decide on secession. Even so, in some state conventions the vote to secede was close, with secession decided by overrepresentation of plantation districts. Furthermore, the conventions were noticeably unwilling to let voters ratify their acts. Four states in the Upper South—Virginia, North Carolina, Tennessee, and Arkansas—flatly rejected secession and did not join the Confederacy until after fighting had begun. In the border states, popular sentiment was deeply divided; minorities in Kentucky and Missouri tried to secede, but these slave states ultimately came under Union control, along with Maryland and Delaware (see map, page 399).

Such misgivings were not surprising. Secession posed new and troubling issues for southerners, especially the possibility of war and the question of who would die. Analysis of election returns from 1860 and 1861 indicates that slaveholders and nonslaveholders were beginning to part company politically. Heavily slaveholding counties strongly supported secession. But nonslaveholding areas that had favored Breckinridge in the United States presidential election proved far less willing to support secession: most counties with few slaves took an antisecession position or were staunchly Unionist (see figure, page 400). Large numbers of yeomen also sat out the election. With war on the horizon, nonslave-

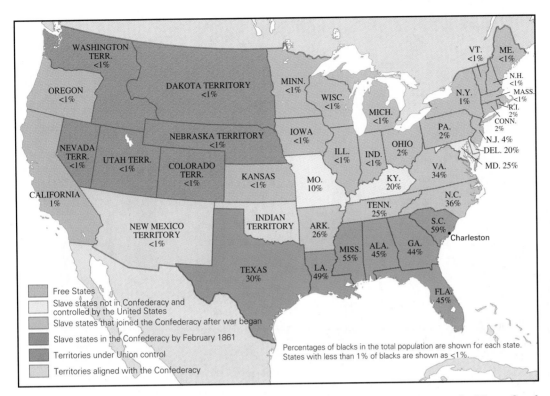

WASHINGTON TERR. <1%
OREGON <1%
DAKOTA TERRITORY <1%
MINN. <1%
WISC. <1%
MICH. <1%
VT. <1%
ME. <1%
N.H. <1%
MASS. <1%
N.Y. 1%
R.I. 2%
CONN. 2%
PA. 2%
N.J. 4%
DEL. 20%
MD. 25%
NEVADA TERR. <1%
UTAH TERR. <1%
NEBRASKA TERRITORY <1%
IOWA <1%
ILL. <1%
IND. <1%
OHIO 2%
COLORADO TERR. <1%
KANSAS <1%
MO. 10%
KY. 20%
VA. 34%
CALIFORNIA 1%
NEW MEXICO TERRITORY <1%
INDIAN TERRITORY
ARK. 26%
TENN. 25%
N.C. 36%
S.C. 59%
Charleston
MISS. 55%
ALA. 45%
GA. 44%
TEXAS 30%
LA. 49%
FLA. 45%

Free States
Slave states not in Confederacy and controlled by the United States
Slave states that joined the Confederacy after war began
Slave states in the Confederacy by February 1861
Territories under Union control
Territories aligned with the Confederacy

Percentages of blacks in the total population are shown for each state. States with less than 1% of blacks are shown as <1%.

The Divided Nation—Slave and Free Areas, 1861   *After fighting began, the Upper South joined the Deep South in the Confederacy. How does the nation's pattern of division correspond to the distribution of slavery and the percentage of blacks in the population?*

holders were beginning to consider their class interests and to ask how far they would go to support slavery and slaveowners.

Some opponents of secession was fervently pro-Union. After Alabama's convention approved secession, one delegate wrote: "Here I set & from my window see the nasty little thing flaunting in the breeze which has taken the place of that glorious banner which has been the pride of millions of Americans and the boast of freemen the wide world over." Although such sentiments presented problems for the Confederacy, they were not sufficiently developed to prevent secession.

The dilemma facing President Lincoln on inauguration day in March 1861 was how to maintain the authority of the federal government without provoking war. Proceeding cautiously, he sought only to hold on to forts in the states that had left the Union, reasoning that in this way he could assert federal sovereignty while waiting for a restoration of rela-

Attack on Fort Sumter

tions. But Jefferson Davis, who could not claim to lead a sovereign nation if the Confederate ports were under foreign (that is, United States) control, was unwilling to be so patient. A collision was inevitable.

It arrived in the early morning hours of April 12, 1861, at Fort Sumter in Charleston harbor. A federal garrison there ran low on food, and Lincoln notified the South Carolinians that he was sending a ship to resupply the fort. For the Montgomery government, the alternatives were to attack the fort or to acquiesce to Lincoln's authority. After the Confederate cabinet met, the Secretary of War ordered local commanders to obtain a surrender or attack the fort. After two days of heavy bombardment, the federal garrison finally surrendered. No one died in battle, though an accident during postbattle ceremonies killed one Union soldier. Confederates permitted the United States troops to sail away on unarmed vessels while Charlestonians celebrated wildly. The Civil War—the bloodiest war in America's history—had begun.

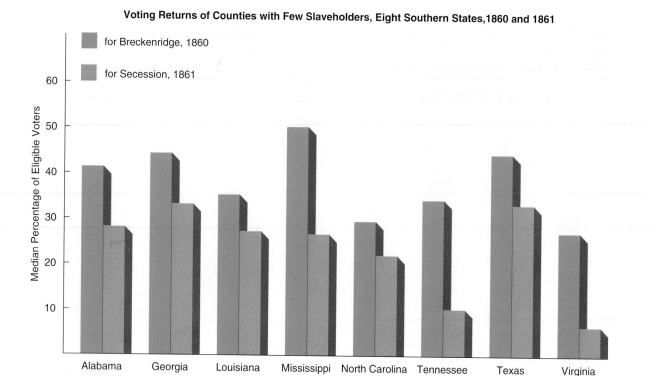

Voting Returns of Counties with Few Slaveholders, Eight Southern States,1860 and 1861

Voting Returns of Counties with Few Slaveholders, Eight Southern States, 1860 and 1861 This *graph depicts voting in counties whose percentage of slaveholders ranked them among the lower half of the counties in their state. How does voters' support for secession in 1861 compare with support for John Breckinridge, the southern Democratic candidate in 1860? Why was their support for secession so weak? At this time counties with many slaveholders were giving increased support to secession.*

 ## Conclusion

Throughout the 1840s and 1850s many able leaders had worked diligently to avert this outcome. Most people, North and South, had hoped to keep the nation together. As late as 1858 even Jefferson Davis had declared, "This great country will continue united," saying that "to the innermost fibers of my heart I love it all, and every part." Secession dismayed northern editors and voters, and it also plunged some planters into depression. Paul Cameron, the largest slaveowner in North Carolina, confessed that he was "very unhappy. I love the Union." Why, then, had war broken out? Why had all efforts to prevent it failed?

Slavery was an issue on which compromise was impossible. The conflict it generated was fundamental and beyond adjustment. The emotions bound up in attacking and defending it were too powerful, and the motives it affected too vital, for compromise. Because it was deeply entwined with major policy questions of the present and the foreseeable future, each

section ultimately regarded slavery as too important to be put aside.

Even if one excludes extreme views, North and South had fundamentally different attitudes toward the institution. The logic of Republican ideology tended in the direction of abolishing slavery, even though Republicans denied any such intention. The logic of southern leaders' arguments led toward establishing slavery everywhere, though southern leaders denied that they sought to do any such thing. Lincoln put these facts succinctly. In a postelection letter to his old friend Alexander Stephens of Georgia, Lincoln offered assurance that Republicans would not attack slavery in the states where it existed. But Lincoln continued, "You think slavery is *right* and ought to be expanded; while we think it is *wrong* and ought to be restricted. That I suppose is the rub."

Fundamental disagreements have not always led to war. A nation may face unresolvable issues yet manage to get past them. New events can capture people's attention; time can alter interests and attitudes, if in the intervening years conflict is contained or restricted. That is precisely what the advocates of compromise sought to achieve. They tried to contain conflict and buy time for the nation, to avoid issues that could not be settled, and to preserve the many areas of consensus among Americans. Their efforts were well intentioned and patriotic but doomed to failure.

The issue of slavery in the territories made conflict impossible to avoid. Territorial expansion generated disputes so frequently that the nation never enjoyed a breathing space. As the conflict recurred, its influence on policy and effect on the government deepened. Every southern victory increased fear of the Slave Power, and each new expression of Free-Soil sentiment made alarmed slaveholders more insistent in their demands. Eventually even those opposed to war could see no way to avoid it.

In the profoundest sense, slavery was tied up with the war. Concern over slavery had driven all the other conflicts. But as the fighting began, this, the war's central issue, was shrouded in confusion. How would the Civil War affect slavery, its place in the law, and African-Americans' place in society? The answers to those questions, and the degree to which answers were sought, would be of fateful import.

Suggestions for Further Reading

Politics: General

Thomas B. Alexander, *Sectional Stress and Party Strength* (1967); Tyler Anbinder, *Nativism and Slavery* (1992); Maurice G. Baxter, *One and Inseparable: Daniel Webster and the Union* (1984); Paul Bergeron, *The Presidency of James K. Polk* (1987); Ray Allen Billington, *The Protestant Crusade, 1800–1860* (1938 and 1964); Frederick J. Blue, *The Free Soilers: Third Party Politics, 1848–1854* (1973); Stanley W. Campbell, *The Slave Catchers* (1968); Don E. Fehrenbacher, *The Dred Scott Case* (1978); George M. Fredrickson, *The Black Image in the White Mind* (1971); Holman Hamilton, *Prologue to Conflict: The Crisis and Compromise of 1850* (1964); Michael F. Holt, *Political Parties and American Political Development* (1992); Michael F. Holt, *The Political Crisis of the 1850s* (1978); Stephen E. Maizlish and John J. Kushma, eds., *Essays on American Antebellum Politics, 1840–1860* (1982); William Lee Miller, *Arguing About Slavery* (1996); Chaplain W. Morrison, *Democratic Politics and Sectionalism: The Wilmot Proviso Controversy* (1967); Paul D. Nagle, *One Nation Indivisible* (1964); Russell B. Nye, *Fettered Freedom* (1949); Merrill D. Peterson, *The Great Triumvirate: Webster, Clay, and Calhoun* (1987); David M. Potter, *The Impending Crisis, 1848–1861* (1976); James A. Rawley, *Race and Politics* (1969); Joel H. Silbey, *The Transformation of American Politics, 1840–1960* (1967); Elbert B. Smith, *The Presidency of James Buchanan* (1975); Kenneth M. Stampp, *America in 1857*

(1991); Kenneth M. Stampp, *And the War Came* (1950); Gerald W. Wolff, *The Kansas-Nebraska Bill* (1977).

The South and Slavery

William L. Barney, *The Secessionist Impulse* (1974); Steven A. Channing, *A Crisis of Fear: Secession in South Carolina* (1970); William J. Cooper, Jr., *The South and the Politics of Slavery, 1828–1856* (1978); Avery O. Craven, *The Growth of Southern Nationalism, 1848–1861* (1953); Daniel W. Crofts, *Reluctant Confederates: Upper South Unionists in the Secession Crisis* (1989); Merton L. Dillon, *Slavery Attacked* (1991); Drew G. Faust, *The Ideology of Slavery* (1981); Drew G. Faust, *A Sacred Circle: The Dilemma of the Intellectual in the Old South* (1978); Lacy K. Ford, Jr., *Origins of Southern Radicalism* (1988); William W. Freehling, *The Road to Disunion* (1990); Eugene D. Genovese, *The World the Slaveholders Made* (1969); Eugene D. Genovese, *The Political Economy of Slavery* (1967); Michael P. Johnson, *Toward a Patriarchal Republic: The Secession of Georgia* (1977); John Niven, *John C. Calhoun and the Price of Union* (1988); David M. Potter, *The South and the Sectional Conflict* (1968); Thomas E. Schott, *Alexander H. Stephens of Georgia* (1988); William R. Stanton, *The Leopard's Spots* (1960); J. Mills Thornton III, *Politics and Power in a Slave Society* (1978); Larry E. Tise, *Proslavery* (1987); Ralph Wooster, *The Secession Conventions of the South* (1962).

The North and Antislavery

Dale Baum, *The Civil War Party System* (1984); Eugene H. Berwanger, *The Frontier Against Slavery* (1967); Frederick J. Blue, *Salmon P. Chase* (1987); David Donald, *Charles Sumner and the Coming of the Civil War* (1960); Louis Filler, *The Crusade Against Slavery, 1830–1860* (1960); Eric Foner, *Free Soil, Free Labor, Free Men* (1970); Louis S. Gerteis, *Morality and Utility in American Antislavery Reform* (1987); William E. Gienapp, *The Origins of the Republican Party, 1852–1856* (1986); Henry V. Jaffa, *Crisis of the House Divided* (1959); Robert W. Johannsen, *Lincoln, the South, and Slavery* (1991); Robert W. Johannsen, *Stephen A. Douglas* (1973); Aileen S. Kraditor, *Means and Ends in American Abolitionism* (1969); Stephen B. Oates, *To Purge This Land with Blood*, 2d ed. (1984); Lewis Perry and Michael Fellman, eds., *Antislavery Reconsidered* (1979); Jeffrey Rossbach, *Ambivalent Conspirators* (1982); Richard Sewell, *Ballots for Freedom: Antislavery Politics in the United States, 1837–1860* (1976); Alice Felt Tyler, *Freedom's Ferment* (1944).

The Mexican War and Foreign Policy

K. Jack Bauer, *Zachary Taylor* (1985); Gene M. Brack, *Mexico Views Manifest Destiny, 1821–1846* (1976); Richard Griswold del Castillo, *The Treaty of Guadalupe Hidalgo* (1990); Neal Harlow, *California Conquered* (1982); Reginald Horsman, *Race and Manifest Destiny* (1981); Robert W. Johannsen, *To the Halls of the Montezumas: The Mexican War and the American Imagination* (1985); Ernest M. Lander, Jr., *Reluctant Imperialists: Calhoun, the South Carolinians, and the Mexican War* (1980); Robert E. May, *The Southern Dream of a Caribbean Empire, 1854–1861* (1973); Frederick Merk, *The Monroe Doctrine and American Expansion, 1843–1849* (1966); Frederick Merk, *Manifest Destiny and Mission in American History* (1963); David M. Pletcher, *The Diplomacy of Annexation: Texas, Oregon, and the Mexican War* (1973); Dirk Raat, *Mexico and the United States* (1992); John H. Schroeder, *Mr. Polk's War: American Opposition and Dissent* (1973); Otis A. Singletary, *The Mexican War* (1960); Anders Stephanson, *Manifest Destiny* (1995); David J. Weber, *The Mexican Frontier, 1821–1846* (1982).

CHAPTER

15

Transforming Fire: The Civil War
1861–1865

He was a living legend. A frontiersman who fought with Andrew Jackson at the Battle of Horseshoe Bend, he had a distinguished career as lawyer, congressman, and governor of Tennessee. But in 1829 he abruptly resigned his governorship and spent the next three years living among the Cherokees. In 1836 he reemerged as commander-in-chief of the armies winning Texan independence. Then he became president of the new Republic of Texas, holding that office twice. After Texas joined the Union, he served fourteen years as United States senator. In 1859 voters in Texas elected him governor. No one in Texas rivaled the reputation or prestige of Sam Houston, yet in March 1861 he was deposed. Why? Houston opposed secession, warned of defeat, refused to take an oath of allegiance to the Confederacy, and challenged the authority of the secession convention. Its members ended his career by declaring his office vacant.

A similar reversal of fortune befell Nathaniel Banks in Texas. Banks had built a distinguished public career in Massachusetts. Hard-working and self-educated, he had risen from bobbin boy in a cotton mill to lawyer, state legislator, congressman, Speaker of the United States House of Representatives, and governor of Massachusetts. When the Civil War began, Banks promptly volunteered to fight and was commissioned a major general. His troops met defeat in Virginia, however, and his reputation was slipping when he arrived on Texas's coast to try to capture the Rio Grande valley. After some success in 1863, a failed offensive along the Red River in 1864 led to scathing criticism and his departure from the military.

War drastically altered the lives of millions of Americans. Winslow Homer gave the ironic title *Home, Sweet, Home* to this painting of Union soldiers in camp about 1863.
Private Collection, photograph courtesy of Hirschl and Adler Galleries, New York.

The Civil War brought astonishing, unexpected changes not only to Sam Houston and Nathaniel Banks but everywhere in both North and South. For some, wealth changed to poverty and hope to despair; for others, the suffering of war spelled opportunity. Contrasts abounded, between noble and crass motives and between individuals seeking different goals. Even the South's slaves, who hoped that they were witnessing God's "Holy War for liberation," encountered unsympathetic liberators. When a Yankee soldier ransacked a slave woman's cabin, stealing her best quilts, she denounced him as a "nasty, stinkin' rascal" who had betrayed his cause of freedom. Angrily the soldier contradicted her, saying, "I'm fightin' for $14 a month and the Union."

Northern troops were not the only ones to feel anger over their sacrifice. Impoverished by the war, one southern farmer had endured inflation, taxes, and shortages to support the Confederacy. Then an impressment agent arrived to take still more from him—grain and meat, horses and mules, and wagons. In return, the agent offered only a certificate promising repayment sometime in the future. Bitter and disgusted, the farmer declared, "The sooner this damned Government falls to pieces, the better it will be for us."

Many northern businessmen, however, viewed the economic effects of the war with optimism and anticipation. The conflict ensured vast government expenditures, a heavy demand for goods, and lucrative federal contracts. *Harper's Monthly* reported that an eminent financier expected a long war—the kind of war that would mean huge purchases, paper money, active speculation, and rising prices. "The battle of Bull Run," predicted the financier, "makes the fortune of every man in Wall Street who is not a natural idiot."

For these people and millions of others, the Civil War was a life-changing event. It obliterated the normal patterns and circumstances of life. Millions of men were swept away into training camps and battle units. Armies numbering in the hundreds of thousands marched over the South, devastating once-peaceful countrysides. Families struggled to survive without their men; businesses tried to cope with the loss of workers. Women in both North and South took on extra responsibilities in the home and moved into new jobs in the work force. No sphere of life was untouched.

Change was most drastic in the South, where the leaders of the secession movement had launched a revolution for the purpose of keeping things unchanged. Never were men more mistaken: their revolutionary means were fundamentally incompatible with their conservative purpose. Southern whites had feared that a peacetime government of Republicans would interfere with slavery and upset the routine of plantation life. Instead their own actions led to a war that turned southern life upside down and imperiled the very existence of slavery. Jefferson Davis, president of the Confederate States of America, devised policies more objectionable to the elite than any proposed by President-elect Lincoln. Life in the Confederacy proved to be a shockingly unsouthern experience.

War altered the North as well, but less deeply. Because most of the fighting took place on southern soil, northern farms and factories remained virtually unscathed. The drafting of workers and the changing need for products slowed the pace of industrialization somewhat, but factories and businesses remained busy. Workers lost ground to inflation, but the economy hummed. A new probusiness atmosphere dominated Congress, where the seats of southern representatives were empty. To the alarm of many, the powers of the federal government and of the president increased during the war.

The war created social strains in both North and South. Disaffection was strongest in the Confederacy, where poverty and class resentment fed a lower-class antagonism to the war that threatened the Confederacy from within as federal armies assailed it from without. In the North, dissent also flourished, and antiwar sentiment occasionally erupted into violence.

Ultimately, the Civil War forced on the nation new social and racial arrangements. Its greatest effect was to compel leaders and citizens to deal directly with the issue they had debated and argued over but had been unable to resolve: slavery. This issue, in complex and indirect ways, had given rise to the war. Now the scope and demands of the war forced reluctant Americans to confront it.

"Fighting Means Killing": The War in 1861 and 1862

Few Americans understood what they were getting into when the war began. The onset of hostilities sparked patriotic sentiments, optimistic speeches, and joyous ceremonies in both North and South. Northern communities, large and small, raised companies of volunteers eager to save the Union and sent them off with fanfare (a scene captured in the

• *Important Events* •

1861	Battle of Bull Run takes place
	General George McClellan organizes Union Army
	Union blockade begins
	United States Congress passes first confiscation act
	Trent affair
1862	Union captures Fort Henry and Fort Donelson
	United States Navy captures New Orleans
	Battle of Shiloh shows the war's destructiveness
	Confederacy enacts conscription
	General Robert E. Lee thwarts McClellan's offensive on Richmond
	United States Congress passes second confiscation act
	Confederacy mounts offensive in Maryland and Kentucky
	Battle of Antietam ends Lee's drive into Maryland
1863	Emancipation Proclamation takes effect
	United States Congress passes National Banking Act
	Union enacts conscription
	African-American soldiers join Union Army
	Food riots occur in southern cities
	Battle of Chancellorsville ends in Confederate victory but General "Stonewall" Jackson's death
	Union wins key victories at Gettysburg and Vicksburg
	Draft riots take place in New York City
	Battle of Chattanooga leaves South vulnerable to General William T. Sherman's march
1864	Battles of the Wilderness and Spotsylvania produce heavy casualties on both sides in the effort to capture and defend Richmond
	Battle of Cold Harbor continues carnage in Virginia
	Abraham Lincoln requests Republican Party plank abolishing slavery
	General Sherman captures Atlanta
	Lincoln wins reelection
	Jefferson Davis proposes emancipation within the Confederacy
	Sherman marches through Georgia
1865	Sherman marches through Carolinas
	United States Congress approves Thirteenth Amendment
	Hampton Roads Conference
	Lee abandons Richmond and Petersburg
	Lee surrenders at Appomattox Courthouse
	Lincoln assassinated

painting *Departure of the Seventh Regiment*). In the South, confident recruits boasted of whipping the Yankees and returning home in time for dinner, and southern women sewed dashing uniforms for men who soon would be lucky to wear drab gray or butternut homespun.

Through the spring of 1861 both sides scrambled to organize and train their inexperienced, undisciplined armies. On July 21, 1861, the first

Battle of Bull Run

battle took place outside Manassas Junction, Virginia, near a stream called Bull Run. General Irvin McDowell and 30,000 Union troops attacked General P. G. T. Beauregard's 22,000 southerners (see map, page 407). As raw recruits struggled amid the confusion of their first battle, federal forces began to gain ground. Then they ran into a line of Virginia troops under General Thomas Jackson. "There is Jackson standing like a stone wall," shouted one Confederate. "Stonewall" Jackson's line held, and the arrival of 9,000 Confederate reinforcements won the day for the South. Union troops fled back to Washington and shocked northern congressmen and spectators, who had watched the battle from a point two miles away, suddenly feared their capital would be taken.

The unexpected rout at Bull Run gave northerners their first hint of the nature of the war to come.

In Departure of the Seventh Regiment *(1861), flags and the spectacle of thousands of young men from New York marching off to battle give a deceptively gay appearance to the beginning of the Civil War.*   Museum of Fine Arts, Boston; M. and M. Karolik Collection.

Victory would not be easy, even though the United States enjoyed an enormous advantage in resources. Pro-Union feeling was growing in western Virginia, and loyalties were divided in the four border slave states—Missouri, Kentucky, Maryland, and Delaware. But the rest of the Upper South had joined the Confederacy. Moved by an outpouring of regional loyalty, half a million southerners volunteered to fight; there were so many would-be soldiers that the Confederate government could not arm them all. The United States therefore undertook a massive buildup of troops in northern Virginia.

Lincoln gave command of the army to General George B. McClellan, an officer who proved to be better at organization and training than at fighting. McClellan devoted the fall and winter of 1861 to readying a formidable force of a quarter-million men whose mission would be to destroy southern forces guarding Richmond, the new Confederate capital.

"The vast preparation of the enemy," wrote one southern soldier, produced a "feeling of despondency" in the South for the first time.

While McClellan prepared, the Union began to implement other parts of its overall strategy, which called for a blockade of southern ports and eventual capture of the Mississippi River. Like a constricting snake, this "Anaconda plan" would strangle the Confederacy (see map, page 409). At first the Union Navy had too few ships to patrol 3,550 miles of coastline and block the Confederacy's avenues of commerce and supply. Gradually, however, the navy increased the blockade's effectiveness, though it never bottled up southern commerce completely.

Confederate strategy was essentially defensive. A defensive posture not only was consistent with the South's claim that it merely wanted to be left alone, but also took into account the North's advantage in resources (see figure, page 410). Furthermore, communities all across the South demanded to be defended. Jefferson Davis, however, wisely rejected a static or wholly defensive strategy. The South would pursue an "offensive defensive," taking advantage of opportunities to attack and using its interior lines of transportation to concentrate troops at crucial points.

Strategic thinking on both sides slighted the importance of "the West," that vast expanse of territory between Virginia and the Mississippi River. When the war began, both sides were unprepared for large-scale and sustained operations in the West, but before the end of the war it would prove to be a crucial theater. North and South also shared a fondness for "turning movements," in which an army marched around its opponent to force a withdrawal or unleashed a flank attack in battle. In the Far West, beyond the Mississippi River, the Confederacy hoped to gain an advantage by negotiating treaties with the Creeks, Choctaws, Chickasaws, Cherokees, Seminoles, and smaller tribes of Plains Indians.

The last half of 1861 brought no major land battles, but the North made gains by sea. Late in the summer Union naval forces captured Cape Hatteras and then seized Hilton Head, one

Union Naval Campaign

of the Sea Islands off Port Royal, South Carolina. A few months later, similar operations secured vital coastal points in North Carolina, as well as Fort Pulaski, which defended Savannah. Federal naval operations were biting into the Confederate coastline (see map, page 409).

The coastal victories off South Carolina foreshadowed major changes in slave society. At the federal gunboats' approach, frightened planters abandoned their lands and fled. Their slaves greeted what they hoped to be freedom with rejoicing and broke the hated cotton gins. Their jubilation and the constantly growing stream of runaways who poured into the Union lines eliminated any doubt about which side slaves would support, given the opportunity. Unwilling at first to wage a war against slavery, the federal government did not acknowledge the slaves' freedom—though it began to use their labor in the Union cause.

The coastal incursions worried southerners, but the spring of 1862 brought even stronger evidence of the war's seriousness. In March two ironclad ships—the *Monitor* (a Union warship) and the *Merrimack* (a Union ship recycled by the Confederacy)— fought each other for the first time; their battle, though indecisive, ushered in a new era in naval de-

McClellan's Campaign *The water route chosen by McClellan to threaten Richmond during the peninsular campaign.*

sign. In April Union ships commanded by Admiral David Farragut smashed through log booms blocking the Mississippi River and fought their way upstream to capture New Orleans. Farther west a Union victory at Elkhorn Tavern, Arkansas, shattered Confederate control of Indian Territory. (Thereafter, dissension within Native American groups and a Union victory the following year at Honey Springs, Arkansas, reduced Confederate operations in Indian Territory to guerrilla raids.)

In February 1862 land and river forces in northern Tennessee won significant victories for the Union. A hard-drinking, hitherto unsuccessful general named Ulysses S. Grant saw

Grant's Campaign in Tennessee

the strategic importance of Fort Henry and Fort Donelson, the Confederate outposts guarding the Tennessee and Cumberland Rivers. If federal troops could capture these forts, Grant realized, two prime routes into the heartland of the Confederacy would lie open. In just ten days he seized the forts, using his forces so well that he was in a position to demand unconditional surrender of Fort Donelson's defenders. A path into Tennessee, Alabama, and Mississippi now lay open before the Union Army.

Grant moved on into southern Tennessee and the first of the war's shockingly bloody encounters, the Battle of Shiloh. On April 6, Confederate General Albert Sidney Johnston caught federal troops in an undesirable position on the Tennessee River. With their backs to the water, Grant's men were awaiting reinforcements. The Confederates attacked early in the morning and inflicted heavy damage all day. Close to victory, General Johnston was struck and killed by a ball that severed an artery in his thigh. Southern forces almost achieved a breakthrough, but Union reinforcements arrived that night. The next day the tide of

Battle of Shiloh

battle turned, and after ten hours of heavy combat, Grant's men forced the Confederates to withdraw. Neither side won a victory, yet the losses were staggering. Northern troops lost 13,000 men (killed, wounded, or captured) out of 63,000; southerners sacrificed 11,000 out of 40,000. Total casualties in this single battle exceeded those in all three of America's previous wars combined. Now both sides were beginning to sense the true nature of the war. Shiloh utterly changed Grant's thinking about it. He had hoped that southerners soon would be "heartily tired" of the conflict. After Shiloh, he recalled, "I gave up all idea of saving the Union except by complete conquest."

Meanwhile, on the Virginia front, President Lincoln had a different problem. Conquest was impossible without battles, but General McClellan seemed

Both armies experienced religious revivals during the war. This photograph shows members of a largely Irish regiment from New York celebrating Mass at the beginning of the war. Notice the presence of some female visitors in the left foreground.   Library of Congress.

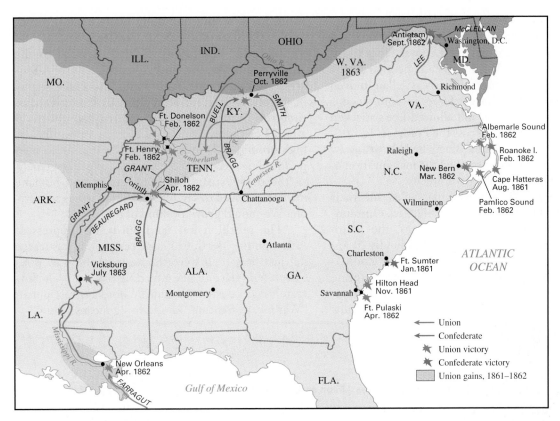

Anaconda Plan   *An overview of the Union's "Anaconda Plan" and key battles on the coast and in the West, 1861–1863.*

unwilling to fight. Only thirty-six, McClellan had already achieved notable success as an army officer and railroad president. Keenly aware of his historic role, he did not want to fail and insisted on having everything in order before he attacked. Habitually overestimating the size of enemy forces, McClellan called repeatedly for reinforcements and ignored Lincoln's directions to advance. Finally McClellan chose to move by a roundabout water route, sailing his troops around the York peninsula and advancing on Richmond from the east (see map, page 407).

By June the sheer size of the federal armies outside the Confederacy's capital was highly threatening. But southern leaders foiled McClellan's legions. First, Stonewall Jackson moved north into the Shenandoah valley behind Union forces and threatened Washington, D.C., drawing some of the federal troops away from Richmond to protect their own capital. Then, in a series of engagements known as the Seven Days Battles, Confederate general Robert E. Lee struck at McClellan's army. Lee never managed to close his pincers around the retreating Union forces, but on August 3 McClellan withdrew to the Potomac. Richmond remained safe for almost two more years.

Buoyed by these results, Jefferson Davis conceived an ambitious plan to turn the tide of the war and gain recognition of the Confederacy by European nations. He ordered a general offensive, sending Lee north into Maryland and Generals Kirby Smith and Braxton Bragg into Kentucky. Calling on residents of Maryland and Kentucky to make a separate peace with his government, Davis also invited northwestern states like Indiana, which sent much of their trade down the Mississippi to New Orleans, to leave the Union.

Confederate Offensive in Maryland and Kentucky

The plan was promising, but every part of the offensive failed. In the bloodiest day of the entire war, September 17, 1862, McClellan turned Lee back from Sharpsburg, Maryland. In the Battle of Antietam 5,000 men died (3,500 had died at Shiloh), and another 18,000 were wounded. Lee was lucky to escape destruction, for McClellan had obtained a copy of Lee's marching orders. But McClellan moved slowly, failed to use his larger forces in simultaneous attacks all along the line, and allowed Lee's stricken army to retreat to safety across the Potomac. In Kentucky Generals Smith and Bragg had to withdraw just one day after Bragg attended the inauguration of a provisional Confederate governor.

Confederate leaders had marshaled all their strength for a breakthrough but had failed. Outnumbered and disadvantaged in resources, the South could not continue the offensive. Profoundly disappointed, Davis admitted to a committee of Confederate representatives that southerners were entering "the darkest and most dangerous period we have yet had." Tenacious defense and stoic endurance now

seemed the South's only long-range hope. Perceptive southerners shared their president's despair.

But 1862 also brought painful lessons to the North. Confederate General James E. B. (Jeb) Stuart executed a daring cavalry raid into Pennsylvania in October. Then on December 13 Union general Ambrose Burnside unwisely ordered his soldiers to attack Lee's army, which held fortified positions on high ground at Fredericksburg, Virginia. Lee's men performed so coolly and controlled the engagement so thoroughly that Lee, a restrained and humane man, was moved to say, "It is well that war is so terrible. We should grow too fond of it."

The rebellion was far from being suppressed. Although the North had large reserves, it was learning just how high were the costs of the war. Both sides would have to pay a terrible price. As Confederate cavalry leader Nathan Bedford Forrest put it, "War means fighting. And fighting means killing."

Comparative Resources, Union and Confederate States, 1861

Union States   Confederate States

Total Population, 2.5 to 1

Free Men 18-60 Yrs., 4.4 to 1

Free Men in Military Service, 1864 — 44% / 90%

Wealth Produced, 3 to 1

Railroad Mileage, 2.4 to 1

Merchant Ship Tonnage, 9 to 1

Naval Ship Tonage, 25 to 1

Factory Production Value, 10 to 1

Textile Goods Production, 14 to 1

Iron Production, 15 to 1

Coal Production, 38 to 1

Firearms Production, 32 to 1

Farm Acerage, 3 to 1

Draft Animals, 1.8 to 1

Livestock, 1.5 to 1

Wheat Productrion, 4.2 to 1

Corn Production, 2 to 1

Cotton Production, 1 to 24

Comparative Resources, Union and Confederate States, 1861 *The North had vastly superior resources. Although the North's advantages in manpower and industrial capacity proved very important, the South could not really be conquered until it chose to give up the fight.* Source: From *The Times Atlas of World History.* Time Books, London, 1978. Used with permission.

In October 1862 in New York City, photographer Matthew Brady opened an exhibition of photographs from the Battle of Antietam. The camera, whose modern form had been invented only in 1826, made war's carnage hideously real. Although few knew it, Brady's vision was very poor, and this photograph of Confederate dead was actually made by his assistants, Alexander Gardner and James F. Gibson. Confederate dead: Library of Congress; camera: George Eastman House Collection.

 ## War Transforms the South

Even more than the fighting itself, disruptions in civilian life robbed southerners of their gaiety and nonchalance. The war altered southern society beyond all expectations and with astonishing speed. One of the first traditions to fall was the southern preference for local government. The South had been characterized by limited government. States' rights had been its motto, but by modern standards even the state governments were weak and sketchy affairs. The average citizen, on whom the hand of government had rested lightly, probably knew county authorities best. To withstand the massive power of the North, however, the South needed to centralize;

like the colonial revolutionaries, southerners faced a choice of join or die. No one saw the necessity of centralization more clearly than Jefferson Davis. If the states of the Confederacy insisted on fighting separately, said Davis, "we had better make terms as soon as we can."

Promptly Davis moved to bring all arms, supplies, and troops under his control. But by early 1862 the scope and duration of the conflict required

Confederacy Resorts to a Draft

something more. Tens of thousands of Confederate soldiers had volunteered for just one year's service, planning to return home in the spring to plant their crops. To keep southern armies in the field, the War Department encouraged reenlistments and called for new volunteers. However, as one official admitted, "the spirit of volunteering had died out." Three states threatened or instituted a draft. Finally, faced with a critical shortage of troops, in April 1862 the Confederate government enacted the first national conscription (draft) law in American history. Thus the war forced unprecedented change on states that had seceded out of fear of change.

Though Jefferson Davis was careful to observe the Confederate constitution, he was a strong chief executive. He adopted a firm leadership role toward the Confederate Congress, which raised taxes and later passed a tax-in-kind—a tax paid in farm products. Almost three thousand agents dispersed to collect the tax, assisted by almost fifteen hundred appraisers. Where opposition arose, the government suspended the writ of habeas corpus (which prevented individuals from being held without trial) and imposed martial law. In the face of political opposition that cherished states' rights, Davis proved unyielding.

Centralization of Power

To replace the food that men in uniform would have grown, Davis exhorted farmers to switch from cash crops to food crops; he encouraged the states to require them to do so. But the army remained short of food and labor. In emergencies the War Department resorted to impressing slaves to work on fortifications, and after 1861 the government relied heavily on confiscation of food to feed the troops. Officers swooped down on farms in the line of march and carted away grain, meat, wagons, and draft animals.

Soon the Confederate administration in Richmond was exercising virtually complete control over the southern economy. Because it controlled the supply of labor through conscription, the administration could compel industry to work on government contracts and supply the military's needs. The Confederate Congress also gave the central government almost complete control of the railroads; in 1864 shipping, too, came under extensive regulation. New statutes even limited corporate profits and dividends. A large bureaucracy sprang up to administer these operations: over seventy thousand civilians staffed the Confederate administration. By the war's end, the southern bureaucracy was larger in proportion to population than its northern counterpart.

Clerks and subordinate officials crowded the towns and cities where Confederate departments had their offices. The sudden population booms that resulted overwhelmed the housing supply and stimulated new construction. The pressure was especially great in Richmond, whose population increased 250 percent. Before the war's end, Confederate officials were planning the relocation of entire departments to lessen crowding in Richmond. Mobile's population jumped from 29,000 to 41,000; Atlanta began to grow; and 10,000 people poured into war-related industries in little Selma, Alabama.

Effects of War on Southern Cities and Industry

Another prime cause of urban growth in the South was industrialization. The Union blockade disrupted imports of manufactured products and caused the traditionally agricultural South to become interested in industry. Davis exulted that manufacturing was making the South "more and more independent of the rest of the world." Many planters shared his hope that industrialization would bring "deliverance, full and unrestricted, from all commercial dependence" on the North. Indeed, beginning almost from scratch, the Confederacy achieved tremendous feats of industrial development. Chief of Ordnance Josiah Gorgas increased the capacity of Richmond's Tredegar Iron Works and other factories to the point that by 1865 his Ordnance Bureau was supplying all Confederate small arms and ammunition. Meanwhile, the government constructed new railroad lines to improve the efficiency of the South's transportation system.

Southerners adopted new ways in response to these changes. Women, restricted to narrow roles in antebellum society, gained substantial new responsibilities. The wives and mothers of soldiers now headed households and performed men's work, adding to their traditional chores the tasks of raising crops and tending animals. Women in non-slaveowning families cultivated fields themselves, while wealthier women suddenly had to manage field hands unaccustomed to female overseers. Only the very rich had enough servants to allow a woman's routine to continue undisturbed. In the cities, white women—who had been virtually excluded from the labor force—found a limited number of respectable new paying jobs. Clerks had always been males, but the war changed that, too. "Government girls" staffed the Confederate bureaucracy, and female schoolteachers became commonplace in the South for the first time.

Change in the Role of Southern Women

Some women gained confidence from their new responsibilities. Among these was Janie Smith, a young North Carolinian. Raised in a rural area by prosperous parents, she had faced few challenges or grim realities before the war reached her farm and troops turned her home into a hospital. "It makes me shudder when I think of the awful sights I witnessed that morning," she wrote to a friend. "Ambulance after ambulance drove up with our wounded. . . . Under every shed and tree, the tables were carried for amputating the limbs. . . . The blood lay in puddles in the grove; the groans of the dying and complaints of those undergoing amputation were horrible." But Janie Smith learned to cope with crisis. She ended her account with the proud words, "I can dress amputated limbs now and do most anything in the way of nursing wounded soldiers."

Patriotic sacrifice appealed to some women, but others resented their new burdens. Many among the wealthy found their new tasks difficult and their changed situation distasteful. North Carolina diarist Catherine Devereux Edmondston was enthusiastic for the southern cause but wanted her husband to remain at home. A Texas woman who had struggled to discipline slaves pronounced herself "sick of trying to do a man's business." Others grew angry over shortages and resented cooking and unfamiliar contact with lower-class women.

Yet the Confederate experience produced some new values. Legislative bodies yielded power to the executive branch of government, which could act more decisively in time of war. Achievement and bravery under fire began to take precedence over aristocratic lineage. Men such as Josiah Gorgas, Stonewall Jackson, and Nathan Bedford Forrest gained renown by distinguishing themselves in industry and on the battlefield.

For millions of ordinary southerners, however, change brought privation and suffering. Mass poverty descended for the first time on a large minority of the white population. Many yeoman families had lost their breadwinners to the army. As a South Carolina newspaper put it, "The duties of war have called away from home the sole supports of many, many families. . . . Help must be given, or the poor will suffer." The poor sought help from relatives, neighbors, friends, anyone. Sometimes they pleaded their cases to the Confederate government. "In the name of humanity," begged one woman, "discharge my husband he is not able to do your government much

Human Suffering

This Confederate soldier, like thousands of his comrades, took advantage of an opportunity to pose with his wife and brother. As the death toll mounted and suffering increased, southern women grew less willing to urge their men into battle. Collection of Larry Williford.

good and he might do his children some good . . . my poor children have no home nor no Father."

Other factors aggravated the effect of the labor shortage. The South was in many places so sparsely populated that the conscription of one skilled craftsman could work a hardship on the people of an entire county. Often they begged in unison for the exemption or discharge of the local miller or the neighborhood tanner, wheelwright, or potter. Physicians also were in short supply. Most serious, however, was the loss of a blacksmith. As a petition from Alabama explained, "our Section of County [is] left entirely Destitute of any man that is able to keep in order any kind of Farming Tules."

The blockade of Confederate shipping created shortages of common but important items—salt, sugar, coffee, nails—and speculation and hoarding made the shortages worse. Greedy businessmen cornered the supply of some commodities; prosperous citizens stocked up on food. The *Richmond Enquirer* criticized one man for hoarding

Hoarding and Runaway Inflation

seven hundred barrels of flour; another man, a planter, purchased so many wagonloads of supplies that his "lawn and paths looked like a wharf covered with a ship's loads." "This disposition to speculate upon the yeomanry of the country," lamented the *Richmond Examiner*, "is the most mortifying feature of the war." North Carolina's Governor Zebulon Vance worried about "the cry of distress . . . from the poor wives and children of our soldiers. . . . What will become of them?"

Inflation raged out of control, fueled by the Confederate government's heavy borrowing and inadequate taxes, until prices had increased almost 7,000 percent. Inflation particularly imperiled urban dwellers and the many who could no longer provide for themselves. As early as 1861 and 1862, newspapers reported that "want and starvation are staring thousands in the face," and troubled officials predicted that "women and children are bound to come to suffering if not starvation." Some concerned citizens tried to help. "Free markets," which disbursed goods as charity, sprang up in various cities. Some families came to the aid of their neighbors. But other people would not cooperate: "It is folly for a poor mother to call on the rich people about here," raged one woman. "Their hearts are of steel they would sooner throw what they have to spare to the dogs than give it to a starving child." The need was so vast that it overwhelmed private charity. A rudimentary relief program organized by the Confederacy offered hope but was soon curtailed to supply the armies. Thus southern yeomen sank into poverty and suffering.

As their fortunes declined, people of once-modest means looked around and found abundant evidence that all classes were not sacrificing equally.

Inequities of the Confederate Draft

They saw that the wealthy gave up only their luxuries, while many poor families went without necessities. And they noted that the Confederate government contributed to these inequities through policies that favored the upper class. Until the last year of the war, for example, prosperous southerners could avoid military service by hiring substitutes. Prices for substitutes skyrocketed until it cost a man $5,000 or $6,000 to send someone to the front in his place. Well over 50,000 upper-class southerners purchased such substitutes. South Carolina's Mary Boykin Chesnut knew of one young aristocrat who "spent a fortune in substitutes. Two have been taken from him [when *they* were conscripted], and two he paid to change with him when he was ordered to the front. He is at the end of his row now, for all able-bodied men are ordered to the front. I hear he is going as some general's courier." As Chesnut's last remark indicates, the rich also traded on their social connections to avoid danger. "It is a notorious fact," complained an angry Georgian, that "if a man has influential friends—or a little money to spare he will never be enrolled." A Confederate senator from Mississippi, James Phelan, informed Jefferson Davis that apparently "nine tenths of the youngsters of the land whose relatives are conspicuous in society, wealthy, or influential obtain some safe perch where they can doze with their heads under their wings."

Anger at such discrimination exploded in October 1862 when the Confederate Congress exempted from military duty anyone who was supervising at least twenty slaves. "Never did a law meet with more universal odium," observed one representative. "Its influence upon the poor is most calamitous." Protests poured in from every corner of the Confederacy, and North Carolina's legislators formally condemned the law. Its defenders argued, however, that the exemption preserved order and aided food production, and the statute remained on the books.

Dissension spread as growing numbers of citizens concluded that the struggle was "a rich man's war and a poor man's fight." Alert politicians and newspaper editors warned that class resentment was building to a dangerous level. The bitterness of letters to Confederate officials during this period suggests the depth of the people's anger. "If I and my little children suffer [and] die while there Father is in service," threatened one woman, "I invoke God Almighty that our blood rest upon the South." Another woman swore to the secretary of war that unless help was provided to poverty-stricken wives and mothers "an allwise god . . . will send down his fury and judgment in a very grate manar . . .[on] those that are in power." War was magnifying social tensions in the Confederacy.

 ## The Northern Economy Copes with War

With the onset of war, a tidal wave of change rolled over the North as well. Factories and citizens' associations geared up to support the war, and the federal government and its executive branch gained new powers. The energies of an industrializing, cap-

Despite initial problems, the task of supplying a vast war machine kept the northern economy humming. This photograph shows businesses on the west side of Hudson Street in New York City in 1865.   New-York Historical Society.

italist society were harnessed to serve the cause of the Union. Idealism and greed flourished together, and the northern economy proved its awesome productivity. Northern factories ran overtime, and unemployment was low. The war did not destroy the North's prosperity. Northern farms and factories came through the war unharmed, whereas most of the South suffered extensive damage. To Union soldiers on the battlefield, sacrifice was a grim reality, but northern civilians experienced only the bustle and energy of wartime production.

At first the war was a shock to business. Northern firms lost their southern markets, and many companies had to change their products and find new customers in order to remain open. Southern debts became uncollectible, jeopardizing not only northern merchants but also many western banks. In farming regions, families struggled with an aggravated shortage of labor. A few enterprises never pulled out of the tailspin caused by the war.

Initial Slump in Northern Business

Cotton mills lacked cotton; construction declined; shoe manufacturers sold few of the cheap shoes that planters had bought for their slaves.

Overall the war slowed the pace of industrialization in the North, but its economic impact was not all negative. Certain entrepreneurs, such as wool producers, benefited from shortages of competing products, and soaring demand for war-related goods swept some businesses to new heights of production. To feed the hungry war machine, the federal government pumped unprecedented sums into the economy. The Treasury issued $3.2 billion in bonds and paper money called greenbacks, and the War Department spent over $360 million in revenues from new taxes (including a broad excise tax and the nation's first income tax). Government contracts soon totaled more than $1 billion.

Secretary of War Edwin M. Stanton's list of the supplies needed by the Ordnance Department indicates the scope of government demand: "7,892 cannon, 11,787 artillery carriages, 4,022,130 small-arms, . . . 1,022,176,474 cartridges for small-arms,

1,220,555,435 percussion caps, . . . 26,440,054 pounds of gunpowder, 6,395,152 pounds of niter, and 90,416,295 pounds of lead." Stanton's list covered only weapons; the government also purchased huge quantities of uniforms, boots, food, camp equipment, saddles, ships, and other necessities. War-related spending revived business in many northern states. In 1863, a merchants' magazine examined the effects of the war in Massachusetts: "Seldom, if ever, has the business of Massachusetts been more active or profitable than during the past year. . . . In every department of labor the government has been, directly or indirectly, the chief employer and paymaster." Government contracts had a particularly beneficial impact on the state's wool, metal, and shipbuilding industries, and also saved Massachusetts shoe manufacturers from ruin.

Nothing illustrated the wartime partnership between business and government better than the work of Jay Cooke, a wealthy New York financier. Cooke threw himself into the marketing of government bonds to finance the war effort. With great imagination and energy, he convinced both large investors and ordinary citizens to invest enormous sums in the war effort, in the process earning hefty commissions for himself. But the financier's profit served the Union cause, as the interests of capitalism and government, finance and patriotism, merged. The booming economy, the Republican alliance with business, and the frantic wartime activity combined to create a new atmosphere in Washington. The notion spread that government should aid businessmen and not interfere with them. Noting the favorable atmosphere, railroad builders and industrialists—men such as Leland Stanford, Collis P. Huntington, John D. Rockefeller, John M. Forbes, and Jay Gould—took advantage of it. Their enterprises grew with the aid of government loans, grants, and tariffs.

War production aided some heavy industries in the North. Coal output rose substantially. Iron makers improved the quality of their product while

Effects of War on Northern Industry and Agriculture

boosting the production of pig iron from 920,000 tons in 1860 to 1.1 million tons in 1864. Foundries developed new and less expensive ways to make steel. Although new railroad construction slowed, repairs helped the manufacture of rails to increase. Of considerable significance for the future was the railroad industry's adoption of a standard gauge (width) for track, which eliminated the unloading and reloading of boxcars and created a unified transportation system.

Another strength of the northern economy was the complementary relationship between agriculture and industry. Mechanization of agriculture had begun before the war. Wartime recruitment and conscription, however, gave western farmers an added incentive to purchase labor-saving machinery. The shift from human labor to machines created new markets for industry and expanded the food supply for the urban industrial work force. The boom in the sale of agricultural tools was tremendous. Cyrus and William McCormick built an industrial empire in Chicago from the sale of their reapers. Between 1862 and 1864 the manufacture of mowers and reapers doubled to 70,000 yearly; even so, manufacturers could not satisfy the demand. By the end of the war, 375,000 reapers were in use, triple the number in 1861. Large-scale commercial agriculture had become a reality. As a result, northern farm families whose breadwinners went to war did not suffer as their counterparts did in the South. "We have seen," one magazine observed, "a stout matron whose sons are in the army, cutting hay with her team . . . and she cut seven acres with ease in a day, riding leisurely upon her cutter."

Northern industrial and urban workers did not fare as well. After the initial slump, jobs became plentiful, but inflation ate up much of a worker's paycheck. By 1863 9-cent-a-pound beef cost 18 cents. The price of coffee had tripled; rice and sugar had doubled; and clothing, fuel, and rent had all climbed. Between 1860 and 1864 consumer prices rose at least 76 percent, while daily wages rose only 42 percent. Workers' families consequently suffered a substantial decline in their standard of living.

As their real wages shrank, industrial workers lost job security. To increase production, some employers were replacing workers with labor-saving machines. Other employers urged

New Militancy Among Northern Workers

the government to promote immigration so they could import cheap labor. Workers responded by forming unions and sometimes by striking. Skilled craftsmen organized to combat the loss of their jobs and status to machines; women and unskilled workers, excluded by the craftsmen, formed their own unions. In recognition of the increasingly national scope of business activity, thirteen occupational groups—including tailors, coal miners, and railway engineers—formed national unions during the Civil War. Because of the tight labor market, unions won many of their demands without striking, but the number of strikes also rose steadily.

Employers reacted with hostility to this new spirit among workers—a spirit that William H. Sylvis, leader of the iron molders, called a "feeling of manly independence." Manufacturers viewed labor activism as a threat to their property rights and freedom of action, and accordingly formed statewide or craft-based associations to cooperate and pool information. These employers shared blacklists of union members and required new workers to sign "yellow dog" contracts (promises not to join a union). To put down strikes, they hired strikebreakers from the ranks of the poor and desperate—blacks, immigrants, and women—and sometimes received additional help from federal troops.

Troublesome as unions were, they did not prevent many employers from making a profit. The highest profits were made from profiteering on government contracts. Unscrupulous businessmen took advantage of the suddenly immense demand for army supplies by selling clothing and blankets made of "shoddy"—wool fibers reclaimed from rags or worn cloth. Shoddy goods often came apart in the rain; most of the shoes purchased in the early months of the war were worthless, too. Contractors sold inferior guns for double the usual price and passed off tainted meat as good. Corruption was so widespread that it led to a year-long investigation by the House of Representatives. A group of contractors that had demanded $50 million for their products dropped their claims to $17 million as a result of the findings of the investigation.

Legitimate enterprises also made healthy profits. The output of woolen mills increased so dramatically that dividends in the industry nearly tripled.

Wartime Benefits to Northern Business

Some cotton mills made record profits on what they sold, even though they reduced their output. Brokerage houses worked until midnight and earned unheard-of commissions. Railroads carried immense quantities of freight and passengers, increasing their business to the point that railroad stocks doubled or even tripled in value. The price of Erie Railroad stock rose from $17 to $126 a share during the war.

Railroads also were a leading beneficiary of government largesse. Congress had failed in the 1850s to resolve the question of a northern versus a southern route for the first transcontinental railroad. With the South absent from Congress, the northern route quickly prevailed. In 1862 and 1864 Congress chartered two corporations, the Union Pacific Railroad and the Central Pacific Railroad, and assisted them financially in connecting Omaha, Nebraska, with Sacramento, California. For each mile of track laid, the railroads received a loan of from $16,000 to $48,000 in government bonds plus 20 square miles of land along a free 400-foot-wide right of way. Overall, the two corporations gained approximately 20 million acres of land and nearly $60 million in loans.

Other businessmen benefited handsomely from the Morrill Land Grant Act (1862). To promote public education in agriculture, engineering, and military

Morrill Land Grant Act

science, Congress granted each state 30,000 acres of federal land for each of its congressional districts. The states could sell the land, as long as they used the income for the purposes Congress had intended. The law eventually fostered sixty-nine colleges and universities, but one of its immediate effects was to enrich a few prominent speculators. Hard-pressed to meet wartime expenses, some states sold their land cheaply to wealthy entrepreneurs. For example, Ezra Cornell, a leader in the telegraph industry, invested in 500,000 acres in the Midwest.

Higher tariffs also pleased many businessmen. Northern businesses did not uniformly favor high import duties; some manufacturers desired cheap imported raw materials more than they feared foreign competition. But northeastern congressmen traditionally supported higher tariffs, and after southern lawmakers left Washington, they had their way: the Tariff Act of 1864 raised tariffs generously. According to one scholar, manufacturers had only to mention the rate they considered necessary and that rate was declared. Some healthy industries earned artificially high profits by raising their prices to a level just below that of the foreign competition. By the end of the war, tariff increases averaged 47 percent, and rates were more than double those of 1857.

 Wartime Society in the North

The outbreak of war stimulated patriotism in the North just as it initially had done in the South. Northern society, which had suffered the stresses associated with industrialization, immigration, and widespread social change, found a unifying cause in the preservation of the nation and the American form of government. In thousands of self-governing towns and communities, northern citizens felt a personal connection to representative government. Secession threatened to destroy their system, and northerners rallied to its defense. Secular and church leaders supported the cause, and even ministers who preferred to separate politics and pulpit denounced "the iniquity of causeless rebellion."

Such enthusiasm proved useful as northerners encountered a multitude of wartime changes. The powers of the federal government and the president grew steadily during the crisis. Abraham Lincoln, like Jefferson Davis, found that war required active presidential leadership. At the beginning of the conflict, Lincoln launched a major shipbuilding program without waiting for Congress to assemble. The lawmakers later approved his decision, and Lincoln continued to act in advance of Congress when he deemed such action necessary. In one striking exercise of executive power, Lincoln suspended the writ of habeas corpus for everyone living between Washington D.C., and Philadelphia. There was scant legal justification for this act, but the president's motive was practical: to ensure the loyalty of Maryland. Later in the war, with congressional approval, Lincoln repeatedly suspended habeas corpus and invoked martial law, mainly in the border states but elsewhere as well. Between fifteen and twenty thousand United States citizens were arrested on suspicion of disloyal acts.

Expanded Powers of the United States President

On occasion Lincoln used his wartime authority to bolster his own political fortunes. He and his generals proved adept at furloughing soldiers so they could vote in close elections; those whom Lincoln furloughed, of course, usually voted Republican. He also came to the aid of other officeholders in his party. When the Republican governor of Indiana, who was battling propeace Democrats in his legislature, ran short of funds, Lincoln had the War Department supply $250,000. This procedure lacked constitutional sanction, but it advanced the Union cause.

Among the clearest examples of the wartime expansion of federal authority were the National Banking Acts of 1863, 1864, and 1865. Before the Civil War, the nation lacked a uniform currency, for the federal government had never exercised its authority in this area. Banks operating under state charters issued no fewer than seven thousand different kinds of notes, which were difficult to distinguish from a variety of forgeries. On the recommendation of Secretary of the Treasury Salmon Chase, Congress established a national banking system empowered to issue national bank notes. At the close of the war in 1865, Congress imposed a prohibitive tax on state bank notes and forced most state institutions to join the national system. This process created a sounder currency and a simpler monetary system—but also inflexibility in the money supply and an eastern-oriented financial structure.

Social attitudes on the home front evolved in directions that would have shocked the soldiers in the field. In the excitement of moneymaking, an eagerness to display one's wealth flourished in the largest cities. A visitor to Chicago commented that "so far as lavish display is concerned, the South Side in some portions has no rival in Chicago, and perhaps not outside New York." *Harper's Monthly* reported that "the suddenly enriched contractors, speculators, and stock-jobbers . . . are spending money with a profusion never before witnessed in our country, at no time remarkable for its frugality. . . . The men button their waistcoats with diamonds . . . and the women powder their hair with gold and silver dust." The *New York Herald* summarized that city's atmosphere: "The richest silks, laces and jewelry are the soonest sold. . . . Not to keep a carriage, not to wear diamonds, . . . is now equivalent to being a nobody. This war has entirely changed the American character. . . . The individual who makes the most money—no matter how—and spends the most—no matter for what—is considered the greatest man."

Extravagance Amid War

Yet idealism coexisted with ostentation. Many churches endorsed the Union cause as God's cause. One Methodist newspaper described the war as a contest between "equalizing, humanizing Christianity" and "disunion, war, selfishness, [and] slavery." Abolitionists, after initial uncertainty over whether to let the South go, campaigned to turn the war into a crusade against slavery. Free black communities and churches both black and white responded to the needs of slaves who flocked to the Union lines, sending clothing, ministers, and teachers to aid the runaways.

Northern women, like their southern counterparts, took on new roles. Those who stayed home organized over ten thousand soldiers' aid societies, rolled innumerable bandages, and raised $3 million to aid injured troops. Thousands served as nurses in front-line hospitals, where they pressed for better care of the wounded. Yet women were only a small minority of all nurses, and they had to fight for a chance to serve at all. The professionalization of medicine since the Revolution had created a medical system dominated by men, and many male physicians did not want women's aid. Female nurses proved their worth, but only the wounded welcomed them. Even Clara Barton, the most famous female nurse, was ousted from her post in 1863.

The poet Walt Whitman left a record of his experiences as a volunteer nurse in Washington, D.C. As he dressed wounds and tried to comfort suffering

Walt Whitman

and lonely men, Whitman found "the marrow of the tragedy concentrated in those Army Hospitals." But despite "indescribably horrid wounds," he also found in the hospitals inspiration and a deepening faith in American democracy. Whitman celebrated the "incredible dauntlessness" and sacrifice of the common soldier who fought for the Union. As he had written in the preface to his great work *Leaves of Grass* (1855), "The genius of the United States is not best or most in its executives or legislatures, but always most in the common people." Whitman worked this idealization of the common man into his poetry, which also explored homoerotic themes and rejected the lofty meter and rhyme of European verse to strive for a "genuineness" that would appeal to the masses.

Thus northern society embraced strangely contradictory tendencies. Materialism and greed flourished alongside idealism, religious conviction, and self-sacrifice. While some soldiers risked their lives willingly out of a desire to preserve the Union or extend freedom, many others openly sought to avoid service. Under the law, a draftee could stay at home by providing a substitute or paying a $300 commutation fee. Many wealthy men chose these options, and in response to popular demand, clubs, cities, and states provided the money for others. In all, 118,000 substitutes were provided and 87,000 commutations paid before Congress ended the commutation system in 1864.

The Strange Advent of Emancipation

At the highest levels of government in the United States and in the Confederacy there was a similar lack of clarity about the purpose of the war. Throughout the first several months of the struggle, both Davis and Lincoln studiously avoided references to slavery. Davis realized that emphasis on the issue could increase class conflict in the South. To avoid identifying the Confederacy only with the interests of slaveholders, he articulated a broader, traditional ideology. Davis told southerners that they were fighting for constitutional liberty: northerners had betrayed the founders legacy, and southerners had seceded to preserve it. As long as Lincoln also avoided making slavery an issue, Davis's line seemed to work.

Lincoln had his own reasons for not mentioning slavery. It was crucial at first not to antagonize the Union's border slave states, whose loyalty was tenuous. Also for many months Lincoln hoped that a pro-Union majority would assert itself in the South. It might be possible, he thought, to coax the South back into the Union and stop the fighting. Raising the slavery issue would severely undermine both goals. Powerful political considerations also dictated that Lincoln remain silent. The Republican Party was a young and unwieldy coalition. Some Republicans burned with moral outrage over slavery; others were frankly racist, dedicated to protecting free whites from the Slave Power and the competition of cheap slave labor; still others saw the tariff or immigration or some other issue as paramount. A forthright stand by Lincoln on the subject of slavery could split the party, gratifying some groups and alienating others. Until a consensus developed or Lincoln found a way to appeal to all the elements of the party, silence was the best approach.

The president's hesitancy ran counter to some of his personal feelings. Lincoln was a sensitive and compassionate man whose humility and moral anguish during the war were evident in his speeches and writings. But as a politician, Lincoln distinguished between his own moral convictions and his official acts. His political positions were studied and complex, calculated for maximum advantage. Frederick Douglass, the astute and courageous black protest leader, sensed that Lincoln was without prejudice toward black people. Yet Douglass judged him "pre-eminently the white man's president."

Lincoln first broached the subject of slavery in a substantive way in March 1862, when he proposed that the states consider emancipation on their own. He

Lincoln's Plan for Gradual Emancipation

asked Congress to promise aid to any state that decided to emancipate, and he appealed to border-state representatives to consider this course seriously. What Lincoln proposed was gradual emancipation, with compensation for slaveholders and colonization of the freed slaves outside the United States. To a delegation of free blacks he explained that "it is better for us both . . . to be separated." Until well into 1864 Lincoln steadfastly promoted an unpromising and wholly impractical scheme to colonize blacks in some region like Central America. Despite Secretary of State William H. Seward's care to insert phrases such as "with their consent," the word *deportation* crept into one of Lincoln's speeches in place of *colonization*. Thus his was as conservative a scheme as could be devised. Moreover, since the states would make the decision voluntarily, no responsibility for it would attach to Lincoln.

Others wanted to go much further. A group of Republicans in Congress, known as the Radicals and led by men such as George Julian, Charles Sumner, and Thaddeus Stevens, dedicated themselves to seeing that the war was prosecuted vigorously. They were instrumental in creating a special House-Senate committee on the conduct of the war, which investigated Union reverses, sought to make the war effort more efficient, and prodded the president to take stronger measures. Early in the war these Radicals, with support from other representatives, turned their attention to slavery.

In August 1861, at the Radicals' instigation, Congress passed its first confiscation act. Designed to punish the Confederate rebels, the law confiscated all property used for "insurrectionary purposes." Thus if the South used slaves in a hostile action, those slaves were declared seized and liberated. A second confiscation act (July 1862) was much more drastic: it confiscated the property of all those who supported the rebellion, even those who merely resided in the South and paid Confederate taxes. Their slaves were declared "forever free of their servitude, and not again [to be] held as slaves." The logic behind these acts was that the insurrection—as Lincoln always termed it—was a serious revolution requiring strong measures. Let the government use its full powers, free the slaves, and crush the revolution, urged the Radicals.

Confiscation Acts

Lincoln refused to adopt that view. He stood by his proposal of voluntary gradual emancipation by the states and made no effort to enforce the second confiscation act. His stance provoked a public protest from Horace Greeley, editor of the powerful *New York Tribune*. In an open letter to the president entitled "The Prayer of Twenty Millions," Greeley pleaded with Lincoln to "execute the laws" and declared, "On the face of this wide earth, Mr. President, there is not one disinterested, determined, intelligent champion of the Union cause who does not feel that all attempts to put down the Rebellion and at the same time uphold its inciting cause are preposterous and futile."

Lincoln's reply was an explicit statement of his complex and calculated approach to the question. He disagreed, he said, with all those who would make the maintenance or destruction of slavery the paramount issue of the war. "I would save the Union," announced Lincoln. "If I could save the Union without freeing *any* slave I would do it, and if I could save it by freeing *all* the slaves I would do it; and if I could save it by freeing some and leaving others alone I would also do that. What I do about slavery, and the colored race, I do because I believe it helps to save the Union." Lincoln closed with a personal disclaimer: "I have here stated my purpose according to my view of *official* duty; and I intend no modification of my oft-expressed *personal* wish that all men everywhere could be free."

When he wrote those words, Lincoln had already decided on a new step: issuance of the Emancipation Proclamation. On the advice of the cabinet, however, he was waiting for a Union victory before announcing the proclamation, so that it would not appear to be an act of desperation. Yet the letter to Greeley was not simply an effort to stall; it was an integral part of Lincoln's approach to the future of slavery, as the text of the Emancipation Proclamation would show.

On September 22, 1862, shortly after the Battle of Antietam, Lincoln issued the first part of his two-part proclamation. Invoking his powers as commander-in-chief of the armed forces, he announced that on January 1, 1863, he would emancipate the slaves in states whose people "shall then be in rebellion against the United States." Lincoln made plain that he would judge a state to be in rebellion in January if it lacked bona fide representatives in the United States Congress. Thus his September proclamation was less a declaration of the right of slaves to be free than a threat to southerners: unless they stopped fighting and returned to Congress, they would lose their slaves. "Knowing the value that was set on the slaves by the rebels," said Garrison Frazier, a black Georgian, "the President thought that his proclamation would stimulate them to lay down their arms . . . and their not

Emancipation Proclamations

doing so has now made the freedom of the slaves a part of the war." Lincoln may not actually have expected southerners to give up their effort, but he was careful to offer them the option, thus putting the onus of emancipation on them.

When Lincoln designated the areas in rebellion on January 1, his proclamation excepted every Confederate county or city that had fallen under Union control. Those areas, he declared, "are, for the present, left precisely as if this proclamation were not issued." Nor did Lincoln liberate slaves in the border slave states that remained in the Union. "The President has purposely made the proclamation inoperative in all places where . . . the slaves [are] accessible," charged the anti-administration *New York World*. "He has proclaimed emancipation only where he has notoriously no power to execute it." Partisanship aside, even Secretary of State Seward, a moderate Republican, said sarcastically, "We show our sympathy with slavery by emancipating slaves where we cannot reach them and holding them in bondage where we can set them free." A British official, Lord Russell, commented on the "very strange nature" of the document, noting that it did not declare "a principle adverse to slavery."

By making the liberation of the slaves "a fit and necessary war measure," furthermore, Lincoln raised a variety of legal questions. How long did a war measure remain in force? Did it expire with the suppression of a rebellion? The proclamation did little to clarify the status or citizenship of the freed slaves. And a reference to garrison duty in one of the closing paragraphs suggested that former slaves would have inferior duties and rank in the army. For many months, in fact, their pay and treatment were inferior.

Thus the Emancipation Proclamation was a puzzling and ambiguous document that said less than it seemed to say. It freed no slaves, and serious limitations were embedded in its language. But if as a moral and legal document it was wanting, as a political document it was nearly flawless. Because the proclamation defined the war as a war against slavery, radicals could applaud it, even if the president had not gone as far as Congress. Yet at the same time it protected Lincoln's position with conservatives, leaving him room to retreat if he chose and forcing no immediate changes on the border slave states.

The need for men soon convinced the administration to recruit northern and southern blacks for the Union Army. By the spring of 1863, African-American troops were proving their value. Lincoln came to see them as "the great *available* and yet *un-*availed *of* force for restoring the Union." African-American leaders hoped that military service would secure equal rights for their people. Once the black soldier had fought for the Union, wrote Frederick Douglass, "there is no power on earth which can deny that he has earned the right of citizenship in the United States." If black soldiers turned the tide, asked another man, "would the nation refuse us our rights?"

In June 1864, Lincoln gave his support to a constitutional ban on slavery. Reformers such as Elizabeth Cady Stanton and Susan B. Anthony were pressing for an amendment that would write emancipation into the Constitution. On the eve of the Republican national convention, Lincoln called the party's chairman to the White House and instructed him to have the party "put into the platform as the keystone, the amendment of the Constitution abolishing and prohibiting slavery forever." The party promptly called for a new amendment, the Thirteenth. Republican delegates probably would have adopted such a plank without his urging, but Lincoln demonstrated his commitment by lobbying Congress for quick approval of the measure. The proposed amendment passed in 1865 and was sent to the states for ratification or rejection. Lincoln's strong support for the Thirteenth Amendment—an unequivocal prohibition of slavery—constitutes his best claim to the title "Great Emancipator."

Yet Lincoln soon clouded that clear stand, for in 1865 the newly reelected president considered allowing the defeated southern states to reenter the Union and delay or defeat the amendment. In February he and Secretary of State Seward met with three Confederate commissioners at Hampton Roads, Virginia. The end of the war was clearly in sight, and southern representatives angled vainly for an armistice that would allow the South to remain a separate nation. But Lincoln was doing some political maneuvering of his own, apparently contemplating the creation of a new national party based on a postwar alliance with southern Whigs and moderate and conservative Republicans. The cement for the coalition would be concessions to planter interests.

Hampton Roads Conference

Pointing out that the Emancipation Proclamation was only a war measure, Lincoln predicted that the courts would decide whether it had granted all, some, or none of the slaves their freedom. Seward observed that the Thirteenth Amendment, which would be definitive, was not yet ratified and that reentry into the Union would allow the southern states to defeat it. Lincoln did not contradict Seward but spoke in favor of "prospective" ratification: approval with the effective date postponed for five years. He also promised to seek $400 million in compensation for slaveholders and to consider their views on related questions such as confiscation. Such financial aid would provide an economic incentive for planters to rejoin the Union and capital to cushion the economic blow of emancipation.

These were startling propositions from a president on the verge of military victory. Most northerners opposed them, and only the opposition of Jefferson Davis, who set himself against anything short of independence, prevented discussion of the proposals in the South. Even at the end of the war, Lincoln was keeping his options open and maintaining the distinction he had drawn between "*official* duty" and "*personal* wish." Lincoln did not attempt to mold public opinion on race, as did advocates of equality in one direction and racist Democrats in the other. Instead, he moved cautiously, constructing complex and ambiguous positions and avoiding the risks inherent in challenging, educating, or inspiring the nation's conscience.

Before the war was over, the Confederacy, too, addressed the issue of emancipation. Jefferson Davis himself offered a strong proposal in favor of libera-

Davis's Plan for Emancipation

tion. Though emancipation was less popular in the South than in the North, Davis did not flinch or conceal his purpose. He was dedicated to independence, and he was willing to sacrifice slavery to achieve that goal. After considering the alternatives for some time, Davis concluded late in 1864 that the military status of the Confederacy was desperate and that independence with emancipation was preferable to defeat with emancipation. He proposed that the Confederate government purchase forty thousand slaves to work for the army as laborers, with a promise of freedom at the end of their service. Soon Davis upgraded his proposal, calling for the recruitment and arming of slaves as soldiers, who likewise would gain their freedom at the end of the war. The wives and children of these soldiers, he made plain, must also receive freedom from the states. Davis and his advisers did not favor full equality—they envisioned "an intermediate state of serfage or peonage." Thus they shared with Lincoln and their entire generation racial attitudes that blinded them to the massive changes taking place around them.

Still, Davis had proposed a radical change for the slaveholding South. Bitter debate resounded through the Confederacy, but Davis stood his ground. When the Confederate Congress approved slave enlistments without the promise of freedom, Davis insisted on more. He issued an executive order to guarantee that owners would emancipate slave soldiers, and his allies in the states started to work for emancipation of the soldiers' families. Some black troops had started to drill as the end of the war approached.

Confederate emancipation began too late to revive southern armies or win diplomatic advantages with antislavery Europeans. By contrast, Lincoln's Emancipation Proclamation stimulated a vital infusion of forces into the Union armies. Beginning in 1863 slaves from the Confederacy and the border states shouldered arms for the North. Before the war was over, 134,000 slaves (and 52,000 free African-Americans) had fought for freedom and the Union. Their participation aided northern victory while it discouraged recognition of the Confederacy by foreign governments. Lincoln's policy, whatever its limitations and lack of clarity, had profound practical effects.

 ## The Soldier's War

The intricacies of policymaking were far from the minds of ordinary soldiers. Military service completely altered their lives. Enlistment took young men from their homes and submerged them in large organizations whose military discipline ignored their individuality. Army life meant tedium, physical hardship, and separation from loved ones even in the best of times. Soldiers in battle confronted fear and danger, and the risk of death from wounds or disease was very high. Yet the military experience had powerful attractions as well. It molded men on both sides so thoroughly that they came to resemble each other far more than they resembled civilians back home. Many soldiers forged amid war a bond with their fellows and a connection to a noble purpose that they cherished for years afterward.

Union soldiers may have sensed most clearly the massive scale of modern war. Most were young; eighteen was the most common age, followed by twenty-one. Many went straight from small towns and farms into large armies supplied by extensive bureaucracies. By late 1861 there were 640,000 volunteers in arms, a stupendous increase over the regular

How do historians know what the average soldier thought and felt? A vast number of diaries and letters written by soldiers have been preserved in archives and libraries and reveal a wide range of experiences. Many soldiers acted on noble ideals, but others did not. Papers at the University of Michigan document one Union soldier's worry that "If this experiment in self-government by the people shall fail, where are the oppressed and the downtrodden millions of the earth to look for hope of better days?" They also contain letters from Private Robert Sherry of New York, shown here. Sherry cared little for the Republican Party. The enlisted men and officers in his regiment rarely got along, and after twenty soldiers were sent to Dry Tortugas, in the Gulf of Mexico, as punishment for a mutiny, Sherry wrote bitterly that he hoped "to see the day when we will get into some battle that will be the means of getting a great portion of our Officers killed or wounded." A rough man in a rough regiment, Sherry enjoyed looting and fighting. Clements Library, University of Michigan.

army of 20,000 men. The increase occurred so rapidly that it is remarkable the troops were supplied and organized as well as they were. Yet many soldiers' first experiences with a large military organization were unfortunate.

Soldiers benefited from certain new products, such as canned condensed milk, but blankets, clothing, and arms were often of poor quality. Vermin abounded. Hospitals were badly managed at first. Rules of hygiene in large camps were badly written or unenforced; latrines were poorly made or carelessly used. One investigation turned up "an area of over three acres, encircling the camp as a broad belt, on which is deposited an almost perfect layer of human excrement." Water supplies were unsafe and typhoid epidemics common. About 57,000 army men died from dysentery and diarrhea. The situation would have been much worse but for the United States Sanitary Commission. A voluntary civilian organization, the commission worked to improve conditions in camps and to aid sick and wounded soldiers. Even so, 224,000 Union troops died from disease or accidents, far more than the 140,000 who died as a result of battle. Confederate troops were less well supplied, especially in the latter part of the war, and they had no sanitary commission. Still, an extensive network of hospitals, aided by many female volunteers, sprang up to aid the sick and wounded.

On both sides troops quickly learned that soldiering was far from glorious. "The dirt of a camp life knocks all its poetry into a cocked hat," wrote

Realities of a Soldier's Life

a North Carolina volunteer in 1862. One year later he marveled at his earlier innocence. Fighting had taught him "the realities of a soldier's life. We had no tents after the 6th of August, but slept on the ground, in the woods or open fields, without regard to the weather. . . . I learned to eat fat bacon raw, and to like it. . . . Without time to wash our clothes or our persons, and sleeping on the ground all huddled together, the whole army became lousy more or less with body lice." Union troops "skirmished" against lice by boiling their clothes or holding them over a hot fire, but, reported one soldier, "I find some on me in spite of all I can do."

Few had seen violent death before, but war soon exposed them to the blasted bodies of their friends and comrades. "Any one who goes over a battlefield after a battle," wrote one Confederate, "never cares to go over another. . . . It is a sad sight to see the dead and if possible more sad to see the wounded—shot in every possible way you can imagine." Many men died gallantly; there were innumerable striking displays of courage. But far more often soldiers gave up their lives in the mass, as part of a commonplace sacrifice. "They mowed us down like grass," recalled one survivor of a Union assault.

Advances in technology made the Civil War particularly deadly. By far the most important were the rifle and the "minie ball." Bullets fired from a smoothbore musket tumbled and wobbled as they flew through the air and thus were not accurate at distances over eighty yards. Cutting spiraled grooves inside the barrel gave the projectile a spin and much greater accuracy, but rifles remained difficult to load and use until the Frenchman Claude Minie and the American James Burton developed a new kind of bullet.

Civil War bullets were sizable lead slugs with a cavity at the bottom that expanded upon firing so that the bullet "took" the rifling and flew accurately. With these bullets, rifles were accurate at four hundred yards and useful up to one thousand yards.

This meant, of course, that soldiers assaulting a position defended by riflemen were in greater peril than ever before. Even though Civil War rifles were

Impact of the Rifle

cumbersome to load (relatively few of the new, untried, breech-loading and repeating rifles were ordered), the defense gained a significant advantage. While artillery now fired from a safe distance, there was no substitute for the infantry assault or the popular turning movements aimed at an enemy's flank. Thus advancing soldiers had to expose themselves repeatedly to accurate rifle fire. Large lead bullets shattered bones and destroyed flesh, and, because medical knowledge was rudimentary, even minor wounds often led to death through infection. Thus the toll from Civil War battles was very high. Never before in Europe or America had such massive forces pummeled each other with weapons of such destructive power. Yet the armies in the Civil War seemed virtually indestructible. Even in the bloodiest engagements, in which thousands of men died, the losing army was never destroyed. As losses mounted, many citizens wondered at what Union soldier (and future Supreme Court justice) Oliver Wendell Holmes called "the butcher's bill."

Still, Civil War soldiers developed deep commitments to each other and to their task. As campaigns dragged on, fighting and dying with their comrades became their reality, and most soldiers who did not desert grew determined to see the struggle through. "We now, like true Soldiers go determined not to yield one inch," wrote a New York corporal. When at last the war was over, "it seemed like breaking up a family to separate," one man observed. Another admitted, "We shook hands all around, and laughed and seemed to make merry, while our hearts were heavy and our eyes ready to shed tears."

The bonding may have been most dramatic among officers and men in the northern black regiments, for there white and black troops took their

Black Soldiers Fight for Acceptance

first steps toward bridging a deep racial divide. Racism in the Union Army was strong. Most white soldiers wanted nothing to do with black people and regarded them as inferior. "I never came out here for to free the black devils," wrote one soldier, and another objected to fighting beside African-Americans because, "We are a too superior race for that." For many, acceptance of black troops grew only because they could do heavy labor and "stop Bullets as well as white people." A popular song celebrated "Sambo's Right to Be Kilt" as the only justification for black enlistments.

But among some a change occurred. White officers who volunteered for black units only to gain promotion found that experience altered their opinions. After just one month with black troops, a white captain informed his wife, "I have a more elevated opinion of their abilities than I ever had before. I *know* that many of them are vastly the *superiors* of those (many of those) who would condemn them all to a life of brutal degradation." One general reported that his "colored regiments" possessed "remarkable apti-

tude for military training," and another observer said, "They fight like fiends."

Black troops created this change through their dedication. They had a mission to destroy slavery and demonstrate their equality. "When Rebellion is crushed," wrote a black volunteer from Connecticut, "who will be more proud than *I* to say, 'I was one of the first of the despised race to leave the free North with a rifle on my shoulder, and give the lie to the old story that the black man will not fight.'" Corporal James Henry Gooding of Massachusetts's black 54th Regiment explained that his unit intended "to live down all prejudice against its color, by a determination to do well in any position it is put." After an engagement he was proud that "a regiment of white men gave us three cheers as we were passing them," because "it shows that we did our duty as men should." Through such experience under fire the blacks and

Black enlistments were vital to the Union Army, and military service made a major impact on those who had been slaves. These photographs, taken by a photographer accompanying the Union troops, show Hubbard Pryor before and after he enlisted in 1864 in Tennessee. Pryor survived the war. He married a former slave, and he and his wife worked as farmers and raised four children. National Archives.

whites of the 54th Massachusetts forged deep bonds. Just before the regiment launched its costly assault on Fort Wagner, in Charleston harbor, a black soldier called out to abolitionist Colonel Robert Gould Shaw, "Colonel, I will stay by you till I die." "And he kept his word," noted a survivor of the attack. "He has never been seen since."

Such valor emerged despite persistent discrimination. Off-duty black soldiers were sometimes attacked by northern mobs; on duty, they did most of the "fatigue duty," or heavy labor. The Union government, moreover, paid white privates $13 per month plus a clothing allowance of $3.50, whereas black privates earned only $10 per month less $3 deducted for clothing. Outraged by this injustice, the men of the 54th and 55th Massachusetts refused to accept any pay whatever, and Congress eventually remedied the inequity. In this instance, at least, the majority of legislators agreed with a white private that black troops had "proved their title to *manhood* on many a bloody field fighting freedom's battles."

 ## The Tide of Battle Begins to Turn

The fighting in the spring and summer of 1863 did not settle the war, but it began to place clear limits on the outcome. The campaigns began in a deceptively positive way for Confederates, as their Army of Northern Virginia performed brilliantly in the Battle of Chancellorsville. For once a large Civil War army was not slow and cumbersome but executed tactics with speed and precision. On May 2 and 3, some 130,000 members of the Union Army of the Potomac bore down on fewer than 60,000 Confederates (see map, page 427). Boldly, as if they enjoyed being outnumbered, Lee and Stonewall Jackson divided their forces, ordering 30,000 men under Jackson on a day-long march westward to gain position for a flank attack. This classic turning movement was boldly carried out in the face of great numerical disadvantage. Arriving at their position late in the afternoon, Jackson's seasoned "foot cavalry" found unprepared Union troops laughing, smoking, and playing cards. The Union soldiers had no idea they were under attack until frightened deer and rabbits bounded out of the forest, followed by gray-clad troops. The Confederate attack drove the entire right side of the Union Army back in confusion. Eager to press his advantage, Jackson rode forward with

Battle of Chancellorsville

a few officers to study the ground. As they returned, southern troops mistook them for federals in the fading light and fired, fatally wounding their commander. The next day Union forces left in defeat. Chancellorsville was a remarkable southern victory but costly because of the loss of Stonewall Jackson.

July brought crushing defeats for the Confederacy in two critical battles—Vicksburg and Gettysburg—that effectively circumscribed Confederate hopes for independence. Vicksburg was a vital western citadel, the last major fortification on the Mississippi River in southern hands (see map, page 409). After months of searching through swamps and bayous, General Ulysses S. Grant found an advantageous approach to the city. He laid siege to Vicksburg in May, bottling up the defending army of General John Pemberton. If Vicksburg fell, Union forces would control the river, cutting the Confederacy in half and gaining an open path into its interior. To stave off such a result, Jefferson Davis gave command of all other forces in the area to General Joseph E. Johnston and beseeched him to go to Pemberton's aid. Meanwhile, at a council of war in Richmond, General Robert E. Lee proposed a Confederate invasion of the North. Although such an offensive would not relieve Vicksburg directly, it could stun and dismay the North and, if successful, possibly even lead to peace.

Battle of Vicksburg

Lee's troops streamed through western Maryland and into Pennsylvania, threatening both Washington and Baltimore. As his superb army advanced, the possibility of a major victory near the Union capital became more and more likely. Confederate prospects along the Mississippi, however, darkened. Davis repeatedly wired General Johnston, urging him to concentrate his forces and attack Grant's army. Johnston, however, did nothing effective and telegraphed at one point, "I consider saving Vicksburg hopeless." Grant's men, meanwhile, were supplying themselves from the abundant crops of the Mississippi River valley and could continue their siege indefinitely. Their rich meat-and-vegetables diet became so tiresome, in fact, that one day, as Grant rode by, a private looked up and muttered, "Hardtack" (dry biscuits). Soon a line of soldiers was shouting "Hardtack! Hardtack!" demanding respite from turkey and sweet potatoes.

In such circumstances the fall of Vicksburg was inevitable, and on July 4, 1863, its commander surrendered. The same day a battle that had been rag-

The Battle of Chancellorsville, May 2–3, 1863 *At Chancellorsville on the first day, Jackson and Lee successfully carried out a daring flanking movement to the west, around the Union forces' right. Although federal forces were driven back in confusion, the victory was costly to the Confederacy, for Jackson suffered a fatal wound.*

Battle of Gettysburg

ing for three days concluded at Gettysburg, Pennsylvania. On July 1 Confederate forces hunting for a supply of shoes had collided with part of the Union Army. Heavy fighting on the second day left federal forces in possession of high ground along Cemetery Ridge. There they enjoyed the protection of a stone wall and a clear view of their foe across almost a mile of open field. Undaunted, Lee believed his splendid troops could break the Union line, and on July 3 he ordered a direct assault. Full of foreboding, General James Longstreet warned Lee that "no 15,000 men ever arrayed for battle can take that position." But Lee stuck to his plan. Brave troops under General George E. Pickett methodically marched up the slope in a doomed assault known as Pickett's Charge. For a moment a hundred Confederates breached the enemy's line, but most fell in heavy slaughter. On

July 4 Lee had to withdraw, having suffered almost 4,000 dead and about 24,000 missing and wounded. The Confederate general reported to President Davis that "I am alone to blame" and offered to resign. Davis replied that to find a more capable commander was "an impossibility."

Southern troops displayed unforgettable courage and dedication at Gettysburg, but the results there and at Vicksburg were disastrous. The Confederacy was split in two; west of the Mississippi General E. Kirby Smith had to operate on his own, virtually independent of Richmond. Moreover, the heartland of the Confederacy lay exposed to invasion, and Lee's defeat spelled the end of major southern offensive actions. Too weak to prevail in attack, the Confederacy henceforth would have to conserve its limited resources and rely on a prolonged defense. By refusing to be beaten, the South might yet win, but its prospects were darker than ever before.

These "children of the battlefield" aroused great interest in the North after a burial detail at Gettysburg found this ambrotype clutched in the hand of a fallen Union soldier. After thousands of copies of the picture were circulated, the wife of Sergeant Amos Humiston of the 154th New York Infantry (above) recognized her children and knew that she was a widow. The C. Craig Caba Gettysburg Collection, from *Gettysburg*. Larry Sherer © 1991 Time-Life Books, Inc.

The Disintegration of Confederate Unity

Both northern and southern governments waged the final two years of the war in the face of increasing opposition at home. Dissatisfactions that had surfaced earlier grew more intense and sometimes violent. The gigantic costs of a war that neither side seemed able to win fed the unrest. But protest also arose from fundamental stresses in the social structures of North and South.

The Confederacy's problems were both more serious and more deeply rooted than the North's. Vastly disadvantaged in industrial capacity, natural resources, and labor, southerners felt the cost of the war more quickly, more directly, and more painfully than northerners. But even more fundamental were the Confederacy's internal problems; crises that were integrally connected with the southern class system threatened the Confederate cause.

One ominous development was the planters' increasing opposition to their own government, whose actions often had a negative effect on them. Not only did the Richmond government impose new taxes and the tax-in-kind, but Confederate military authorities also impressed slaves to build fortifications. And when Union forces advanced on plantation areas, Confederate commanders burned stores of cotton that lay in the enemy's path. Such interference with plantation routines and financial interests was not what planters had expected of their government, and they complained bitterly.

Nor were the centralizing policies of the Davis administration popular. The increasing size and power of the Richmond administration startled and alarmed planters who had condemned federal usurpations. In fact, the Confederate constitution had granted substantial powers to the central government, especially in time of war. But many planters assumed with R. B. Rhett, editor of the *Charleston Mercury*, that the Confederate constitution "leaves the States untouched in their Sovereignty, and commits to the Confederate Government only a few simple objects, and a few simple powers to enforce them." Governor Joseph E.

Brown of Georgia took a similarly inflated view of the importance of the states. During the brief interval between Georgia's secession from the Union and its admission to the Confederacy, Brown sent an ambassador to Europe to seek recognition for the sovereign republic of Georgia from Queen Victoria, Napoleon III, and the king of Belgium.

Years of opposition to the federal government within the Union had frozen southerners in a defensive posture. Now they erected the barrier of states' rights as a defense against change, hiding behind it while their capacity for creative statesmanship atrophied. Planters sought, above all, a guarantee that their plantations and their lives would remain untouched; they were not deeply committed either to building a southern nation or to winning independence. If the Confederacy had been allowed to depart from the Union in peace and continue as a semideveloped cotton-growing region, they would have been content. When secession revolutionized their world, they could not or would not adjust.

Confused and embittered planters struck out at Jefferson Davis. Conscription, thundered Governor Brown, was "subversive of [Georgia's] sovereignty, and at war with all the principles for the support of which Georgia entered into this revolution." Searching for ways to frustrate the law, Brown bickered over draft exemptions and ordered local enrollment officials not to cooperate with the Confederacy. The *Charleston Mercury* told readers that "conscription . . . is . . . the very embodiment of Lincolnism, which our gallant armies are today fighting." In a gesture of stubborn selfishness, Robert Toombs of Georgia, a former United States senator, refused to switch from cotton to food crops, defying the wishes of the government, the newspapers, and his neighbors' petitions. His action bespoke the inflexibility and frustration of the southern elite at a crucial point in the Confederacy's struggle to survive.

The southern courts ultimately upheld Davis's power to conscript. He continued to provide strong leadership and steered through Congress measures that gave the Confederacy a fighting chance. Despite his cold formality and inability to disarm critics, Davis possessed two important virtues: iron determination and total dedication to independence. These qualities kept the Confederacy afloat, for he implemented his measures and enforced them. But his actions earned him the hatred of most influential and elite citizens.

Meanwhile, for ordinary southerners, the dire predictions of hunger and suffering were becoming a

The impoverishment of nonslaveholding white families was a critical problem for the Confederacy. The sale of this sheet music was intended not only to boost morale but also to raise money that could be used to aid the hungry and needy. This effort and larger government initiatives, however, failed to solve the problem. Chicago Historical Society.

reality. Food riots occurred in the spring of 1863 in Atlanta, Macon, Columbus, and Augusta, Georgia, and in Salisbury and High Point, North Carolina. On April 2, a crowd assembled in Richmond, the Confederate capital, to demand relief. A passerby, noticing the excitement, asked a young girl, "Is there some celebration?" "We celebrate our right to live," replied the girl. "We are starving. As soon as enough of us get together we are going to the bakeries and each of us will take a loaf of bread." Soon they did just that, sparking a riot that Davis himself had to quell at gunpoint. Later that year, another group of angry rioters looking for food ransacked a street in Mobile, Alabama.

Food Riots in Southern Cities

Throughout the rural South, ordinary people resisted more quietly—by refusing to cooperate with conscription, tax collection, and impressments of food. "In all the States impressments are evaded by every means which ingenuity can suggest, and in some openly resisted," wrote a high-ranking commissary officer. Farmers who did provide food for the army refused to accept payment in certificates of credit or government bonds, as required by law. Conscription officers increasingly found no one to draft—men of draft age were hiding out in the forests. "The disposition to avoid military service is general," observed one of Georgia's senators in 1864. In some areas tax agents were killed in the line of duty.

Jefferson Davis was ill equipped to deal with such discontent. Austere and private by nature, he failed to communicate with the masses. Often he buried himself in military affairs or administrative details, until a crisis forced him to rush off on a speaking tour to revive the spirit of resistance. His class perspective also distanced him from the sufferings of the common people. While his social circle in Richmond dined on duck and oysters, ordinary southerners recovered salt from the drippings on their smokehouse floors and went hungry. State governors who responded to people's needs won the public's loyalty, but Davis failed to reach out to the plain folk and thus lost their support.

Such discontent was certain to affect the Confederate armies. "What man is there that would stay in the army and no that his family is sufring at home?" an angry citizen wrote anonymously to the secretary of war. Worried about their loved ones and resentful of what they saw as a rich man's war, large numbers of men did indeed leave the armies. Their friends and neighbors gave them support. Mary Boykin Chesnut observed a man being dragged back to the army as his wife looked on. "Desert agin, Jake!" she cried openly. "You desert agin, quick as you kin. Come back to your wife and children."

Desertions from the Confederate Army

Desertion did not become a serious problem for the Confederacy until mid-1862, and stiffer policing solved the problem that year. But from 1863 on, the number of men on duty fell rapidly as desertions soared. By mid-1863, John A. Campbell, the South's assistant secretary of war, wondered whether "so general a habit" as desertion could be considered a crime. Campbell estimated that 40,000 to 50,000 troops were absent without leave and that 100,000 were evading duty in some way. Furloughs, amnesty proclamations, and appeals to return had little effect; by November 1863, Secretary of War James Seddon admitted that one-third of the army could not be accounted for. The situation was to worsen.

The defeats at Gettysburg and Vicksburg dealt a body blow to Confederate morale. When the news reached Josiah Gorgas, the genius of Confederate

ordnance operations, he confided to his diary, "Today absolute ruin seems our portion. The Confederacy totters to its destruction." In desperation President Davis and several state governors resorted to threats and racial scare tactics to drive southern whites to further sacrifice. Defeat, Davis warned, would mean "extermination of yourselves, your wives, and children." Governor Charles Clark of Mississippi predicted "elevation of the black race to a position of equality—aye, of superiority, that will make them your masters and rulers." Abroad, British officials held back the delivery of badly needed warships, and recognition of the Confederate state became even more unlikely (see page 433).

From this point on, the internal disintegration of the Confederacy quickened. A few newspapers began to call openly for peace. "We are for peace," admitted the *Raleigh* (North Carolina) *Daily Progress*, "because there has been enough of blood and carnage, enough of widows and orphans." A neighboring journal, the *North Carolina Standard*, tacitly admitted that defeat was inevitable and called for negotiations. Similar proposals were made in several state legislatures, though they were presented as plans for independence on honorable terms. Confederate leaders began to realize that they were losing the support of the common people. Governor Zebulon Vance of North Carolina wrote privately that independence would require more "blood and misery . . . and our people will not pay this price I am satisfied for their independence. . . . The great popular heart is not now & never has been in this war."

In North Carolina a peace movement grew under the leadership of William W. Holden, a popular Democratic politician and editor. Over one hundred public meetings took place in the summer of 1863 in support of peace negotiations, and many seasoned political observers believed that Holden had the majority of the people behind him. In Georgia early in 1864, Governor Brown and Alexander H. Stephens, vice president of the Confederacy, led a similar effort. Ultimately, however, these movements came to naught. The lack of a two-party system threw into question the legitimacy of any criticism of the government; even Holden and Brown could not entirely escape the taint of dishonor and disloyalty. That the movement existed at all demonstrates deep disaffection.

Southern Peace Movements

The results of the 1863 congressional elections strengthened dissent in the Confederacy. Everywhere secessionists and supporters of the administration lost seats to men not identified with the government. Many of the new representatives were former Whigs who opposed the Davis administration or publicly favored peace. In the last years of the war, much of Davis's support in the Confederate Congress came from Union-occupied districts, whose people would share no burdens of the war effort until success was achieved.

Having previously secured the legislation he needed, Davis used the government bureaucracy and the army to enforce his unpopular policies. Ironically, as the Confederacy's prospects grew desperate, former critics such as the *Charleston Mercury* became supporters of the administration. They and a core of courageous, determined soldiers kept the Confederacy alive in spite of disintegrating popular support.

By 1864 much of the opposition to the war had moved entirely outside the political sphere. Southerners were simply giving up the struggle and withdrawing their cooperation from the government. Deserters dominated whole towns and counties. Secret societies favoring reunion, such as the Heroes of America and the Red Strings, sprang up. Active dissent spread everywhere and was particularly common in upland and mountain regions. "The condition of things in the mountain districts of North Carolina, South Carolina, Georgia, and Alabama," admitted Assistant Secretary of War John A. Campbell, "menaces the existence of the Confederacy as fatally as either of the armies of the United States." Confederate officials tried using the army to round up deserters and compel obedience, but this approach was only temporarily effective. The government was losing the support of its citizens.

 ## Antiwar Sentiment in the North

In the North opposition to the war was similar but less severe. Alarm intensified over the growing centralization of government, and war-weariness was widespread. Resentment of the draft sparked protest, especially among poor citizens, and the Union Army struggled with a desertion rate as high as the Confederates'. But the Union was so much richer than the South in human resources that none of these problems ever threatened the effectiveness of the government. Fresh recruits were always available, and there were no shortages of food and other necessities.

Also, Lincoln possessed a talent that Davis lacked: he knew how to stay in touch with the ordinary citizen. Through letters to newspapers and to soldiers' families, he reached the common people and demonstrated that he had not forgotten them. The daily carnage, the tortuous political problems, and the ceaseless criticism weighed heavily on him. But this president—a self-educated man of humble origins—was able to communicate his suffering. His moving words helped to contain northern discontent, though they could not remove it.

Much of the wartime protest in the North was political in origin. The Democratic Party fought to regain power by blaming Lincoln for the war's carnage, the expansion of federal powers, inflation and the high tariff, and the emancipation of blacks. Appealing to tradition, its leaders called for an end to the war and reunion on the basis of "the Constitution as it is and the Union as it was." The Democrats denounced conscription and martial law and defended states' rights and the interests of agriculture. They charged repeatedly that Republican policies were designed to flood the North with blacks, depriving white males of their status, their jobs, and their women. These claims appealed to southerners who had settled north of the Ohio River, to conservatives, to many poor people, and to some eastern merchants who had lost profitable southern trade. In the 1862 congressional elections, the Democrats made a strong comeback, and peace Democrats—who would go much farther than others in their party to end the war—had influence in New York State and majorities in the legislatures of Illinois and Indiana.

Peace Democrats

Led by outspoken men like Representative Clement L. Vallandigham of Ohio, the peace Democrats made themselves highly visible. Vallandigham criticized Lincoln as a dictator who had suspended the writ of habeas corpus without congressional authority and had arrested thousands of innocent citizens. Like other Democrats, he condemned both conscription and emancipation and urged voters to use their power at the polling place to depose "King Abraham." Vallandigham stayed carefully within legal bounds, but his attacks seemed so damaging to the war effort that military authorities arrested him for treason after Lincoln suspended habeas corpus. Lincoln wisely decided against punishment—and martyr's status—for the senator and exiled him to the Confederacy, thus ridding himself of a troublesome critic and saddling puzzled Confederates with a man who insisted on talking about "our country." (Eventually Vallandigham returned to the North through Canada.)

Mobs in the New York City draft riots directed much of their anger at African-Americans. Rioters burned an orphanage for black children and killed scores of blacks. This wood engraving, which appeared in the Illustrated London News *on August 8, 1863, depicts a lynching in Clarkson Street.*   Chicago Historical Society.

Lincoln believed that antiwar Democrats were linked to secret organizations that harbored traitorous ideas, such as the Knights of the Golden Circle and the Order of American Knights. These societies, he feared, encouraged draft resistance, discouraged enlistment, sabotaged communications, and plotted to aid the Confederacy. Likening such groups to a poisonous snake, Republicans sometimes branded them—and by extension the peace Democrats—as Copperheads. Though Democrats were connected with these organizations, most engaged in politics rather than treason. And though some saboteurs and Confederate agents were active in the North, they never brought about any major demonstration of support for the Confederacy.

More violent opposition to the government arose from ordinary citizens facing the draft, which became law in 1863. The urban poor and immigrants in strongly Democratic areas were especially hostile to conscription. Federal enrolling officers made up the lists of eligibles, a procedure open to personal favoritism and prejudice. Many men, including some of modest means, managed to avoid the army by hiring a substitute or paying commutation, but the poor viewed the commutation fee as discriminatory, and many immigrants suspected (wrongly, on the whole) that they were called in disproportionate numbers. (Approximately 200,000 men born in Germany and 150,000 born in Ireland served in the Union Army.)

As a result, there were scores of disturbances and melees. Enrolling officers received rough treatment in many parts of the North, and riots occurred in New Jersey, Ohio, Indiana, Pennsylvania, Illinois, and Wisconsin. By far the most serious outbreak of violence occurred in New York City in July 1863. The war was unpopular in that Democratic stronghold, and racial, ethnic, and class tensions ran high. Shippers had recently broken a longshoremen's strike by hiring black strikebreakers to work under police protection. Working-class New Yorkers feared an inflow of black labor from the South and regarded blacks as the cause of the bloody war. Irish workers, many recently arrived and poor, resented being forced to serve in the place of others who could afford to avoid the draft.

New York City Draft Riot

Military police officers came under attack first; then mobs crying "Down with the rich" looted wealthy homes and stores. But blacks became the special target. Those who happened to be in the rioters' path were beaten; soon the mob rampaged through African-American neighborhoods, destroying an orphans' asylum. At least seventy-four people died in the violence, which raged out of control for three days. Only the dispatch of army units fresh from Gettysburg ended the episode.

Discouragement and war-weariness reached a peak in the summer of 1864, when the Democratic Party nominated the popular General George B. McClellan for president and inserted a peace plank into its platform. The plank, written by Vallandigham, condemned "four years of failure to restore the Union by the experiment of war," called clearly for an armistice, and spoke vaguely about preserving the Union. Lincoln, running with Tennessee's Andrew Johnson on a "National Union" ticket, concluded that it was "exceedingly probable that this Administration will not be reelected." During a publicized interchange with Confederate officials sent to Canada, Lincoln insisted that the terms for peace include reunion and "the abandonment of slavery." A wave of protest arose in the North from voters who were weary of war and dedicated only to reunion. Lincoln quickly backtracked, denying that his offer meant "that nothing *else* or *less* would be considered, if offered." He would insist on freedom only for those slaves (about 134,000) who had joined the Union Army under his promise of emancipation. Lincoln's action showed his political weakness, but the fortunes of war soon changed the electoral situation.

Northern Pressure and Southern Will

The success of the North's long-term diplomatic strategy was sealed in 1864. From the outset, the North had pursued one paramount goal: to prevent recognition of the Confederacy by European nations. Foreign recognition would belie Lincoln's claim that the United States was fighting an illegal rebellion and would open the way to the financial and military aid that could ensure Confederate independence. The British elite, however, felt considerable sympathy for southern planters, whose aristocratic values were similar to their own. And both England and France stood to benefit from a divided and weakened America. Thus to achieve their goal, Lincoln and Secretary of State Seward needed to avoid both serious military defeats and unnecessary controversies with the European powers.

Northern Diplomatic Strategy

Aware that the textile industry employed one-fifth of the British population directly or indirectly, southerners assumed that British leaders would have to recognize the Confederacy. But at the beginning of the war, British mills had a 50 percent surplus of cotton on hand; later on, new sources of supply in India, Egypt, and Brazil helped to meet Britain's needs; and throughout the war, some southern cotton continued to reach Europe, despite the Confederacy's recommendation that southerners plant and ship no cotton. Refusing to be stampeded into recognition of the Confederacy, the British government kept its eye on the battlefield. France, though sympathetic to the South, was unwilling to act independently of Britain. Confederate agents were able to purchase valuable arms and supplies in Europe and obtained loans from European financiers, but they never achieved a diplomatic breakthrough.

More than once the Union strategy nearly broke down. An acute crisis occurred in 1861 when the overzealous commander of an American frigate stopped the British steamer *Trent* and removed two Confederate ambassadors sailing to Britain. They were imprisoned after being brought ashore. This action was cheered in the North, but the British protested this violation of freedom of the seas and demanded the prisoners' release. Lincoln and Seward waited until northern public opinion cooled and then released the two southerners. Then the sale to the Confederacy of warships constructed in England sparked vigorous protest from United States ambassador Charles Francis Adams. A few English-built ships, notably the *Alabama*, reached open water to serve the South. Over a period of twenty-two months, without entering a southern port (because of the Union blockade), the *Alabama* destroyed or captured more than sixty northern ships. But the British government, as a neutral power, soon barred delivery of warships such as the Laird rams, formidable vessels whose pointed prows were designed to end the blockade by battering the Union ships.

On the battlefield, the northern victory was far from won in 1864. General Nathaniel Banks's Red River campaign, designed to capture more of Louisiana and Texas, quickly fell apart, and the capture of Mobile Bay in August did not cause the fall of Mobile. Union general William Tecumseh Sherman commented that the North had to "keep the war South until they are not only ruined, exhausted, but humbled in pride and spirit."

Military authorities throughout history have agreed that deep invasion is very risky: the farther an army penetrates enemy territory, the more vulnerable its own communications and support become.

Both General Grant (left) and General Lee (right) were West Point graduates and had served in the United States Army during the Mexican War. Their bloody battles against each other in 1864 stirred northern revulsion to the war even as they brought its end in sight. National Archives.

Moreover, observed the Prussian expert Karl von Clausewitz, if the invader encountered a "truly national" resistance, his troops would be "everywhere exposed to attacks by an insurgent population." Thus if southerners were determined enough to mount a "truly national" resistance, their defiance and the South's vast size could make a northern victory virtually impossible.

General Grant, by now in command of all the federal armies, decided to test these conditions—and southern will—with a strategic innovation of his own: raids on a massive scale. Grant proposed to use whole armies, not just cavalry, to destroy Confederate railroads, thus ruining the enemy's transportation and damaging the South's economy. Abandoning their lines of support, Union troops would live off the land while laying to waste all resources useful to the military and to the civilian population of the Confederacy. After General George H. Thomas's troops won the Battle of Chattanooga in November 1863 by ignoring orders and charging up Missionary Ridge, the heartland of the South lay open. Moving to Virginia, Grant entrusted General Sherman with 100,000 men for a raid deep into the South, toward Atlanta.

Jefferson Davis countered by positioning the army of General Joseph E. Johnston in Sherman's path. Davis's entire political strategy for 1864 was based on demonstrating Confederate military strength and successfully defending Atlanta. The United States presidential election of 1864 was approaching, and Davis hoped that southern resolve would lead to the defeat of Lincoln and the election of a president who would sue for peace. When General Johnston slowly but steadily fell back toward Atlanta, Davis grew anxious and sought assurances that Atlanta would be held. From a purely military point of view, Johnston maneuvered skillfully, but the president of the Confederacy could not take a purely military point of view. When Johnston provided no information and continued to drop back, Davis replaced him with the one-legged General John Hood, who knew his job was to fight. "Our all depends on that army at Atlanta," wrote Mary Boykin Chesnut. "If that fails us, the game is up."

For southern morale, the game was up. Hood attacked but was beaten, and Sherman's army occupied Atlanta on September 2, 1864. The victory buoyed northern spirits and ensured Lincoln's reelection. "There is no hope," Mary Chesnut acknowledged, and a government clerk in Richmond wrote, "Our fondly-cherished visions of peace have vanished like a mirage of the desert." Davis exhorted southerners to fight on and win new victories before the federal elections, but he had to admit that "two-thirds of our men are absent . . . most of them absent without leave." Hood's army marched north to cut Sherman's supply lines and force him to retreat, but Sherman began to march sixty thousand of his men straight to the sea, planning to live off the land and destroying Confederate resources as he went (see map).

Sherman's army was an unusually formidable force, composed almost entirely of battle-tested veterans and officers who had risen through the ranks.

The March to the Sea

Before the march began, army doctors weeded out any men who were weak or sick. Tanned, bearded, tough, and unkempt, the remaining veterans were determined, as one put it, "to Conquer this Rebelien or Die." They believed "the South are to blame for this war" and were ready to make the South pay. Although many harbored racist attitudes, most had come to support emancipation because, as one said,

"Slavery stands in the way of putting down the rebellion." Confederate General Johnston later commented, "There has been no such army since the days of Julius Caesar."

As Sherman's men moved across Georgia, they cut a path 50 to 60 miles wide and more than 200 miles long. The totality of the destruction they caused was awesome. A Georgia woman described the "Burnt Country" this way: "The fields were trampled down and the road was lined with carcasses of horses, hogs, and cattle that the invaders, unable either to consume or to carry with them, had wantonly shot down to starve our people and prevent them from making their crops. The stench in some places was unbearable." Such devastation diminished the South's material resources and sapped its will to resist.

After reaching Savannah in December, Sherman marched his armies north into the Carolinas. To his soldiers, South Carolina was "the root of secession." They burned and destroyed as they moved through, encountering little resistance. The opposing army of General Johnston was small, but Sherman's men should have been prime targets for guerrilla raids and harassing attacks by local defense units. The absence

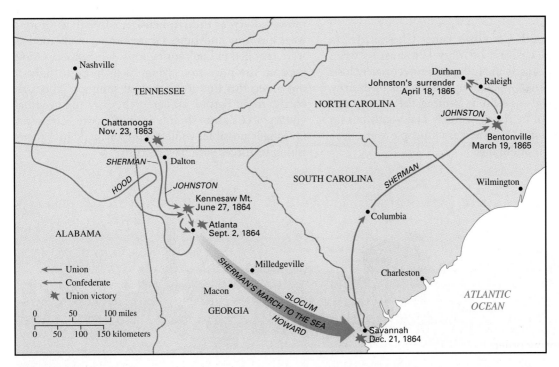

Sherman's March to the Sea   *The West proved a decisive theater at the end of the war. From Chattanooga, Union forces drove into Georgia, capturing Atlanta. Then General Sherman embarked on his march of destruction through Georgia to the coast and then northward through the Carolinas.*

The War in Virginia, 1864–1865 *At great cost, Grant hammered away at Lee's army until the weakened southern forces finally surrendered at Appomattox Courthouse.*

Sherman's march drew additional human resources to the Union cause. In Georgia alone as many as nineteen thousand slaves gladly took the opportunity to escape bondage and join the Union troops as they passed through the countryside. Others remained on the plantations to await the end of the war, either from an ingrained wariness of whites or negative experiences with federal soldiers. The destruction of food harmed slaves as well as white rebels, and many blacks lost blankets, shoes, and other valuables to their liberators. In fact, the brutality of Sherman's troops shocked these veterans of the whip. "I've seen them cut the hams off of a live pig or ox and go off leavin' the animal groanin'," recalled one man. "The master had 'em kilt then, but it was awful."

It was awful, too, in Virginia, where the preliminaries to victory proved protracted and ghastly. Throughout the spring and summer of 1864, intent on capturing Richmond, Grant hurled his troops at Lee's army in Virginia and suffered appalling losses: almost 18,000 casualties in the Battle of the Wilderness, where skeletons poked out of the shallow graves dug one year before; more than 8,000 at Spotsylvania; and 12,000 in the space of a few hours at Cold Harbor (see map). Before the last battle, Union troops pinned scraps of paper bearing their names and addresses to their backs, certain they would be mowed down as they rushed Lee's trenches. In four weeks in May and June, Grant lost as many men as were enrolled in Lee's entire army. Undaunted, Grant kept up the pressure, saying, "I propose to fight it out along this line if it takes all summer." Though costly, these battles prepared the way for eventual victory: Lee's army shrank until offensive action was no longer possible, while Grant's army kept replenishing its forces with new recruits.

of both led South Carolina's James Chesnut, Jr., (a politician and husband of Mary Chesnut) to write that his state "was shamefully and unnecessarily lost. . . . We had time, opportunity and means to destroy him. But there was wholly wanting the energy and ability required by the occasion." The South put up no "truly national" resistance; its people were near the end of their endurance.

At the war's end, the United States flag flew over the state capitol in Richmond, Virginia, which bore many marks of destruction. National Archives.

The death of President Lincoln caused a vast outpouring of grief in the North. As this Currier and Ives print shows, on its way to Illinois, his funeral train stopped at several cities to allow local services to be held. Anne S. K. Brown Military Collection, John Hay Library, Brown University.

The end finally came in the spring of 1865. Grant kept battering Lee, who tried but failed to break through the Union line. With the numerical superiority of Grant's army now greater than two to one, Confederate defeat was inevitable. On April 2 Lee abandoned Richmond and Petersburg. On April 9, hemmed in by Union troops, short of rations, and having fewer than thirty thousand men left, Lee surrendered at Appomattox Courthouse. Grant treated his rival with respect and paroled the defeated troops, allowing cavalrymen to keep their horses and take them home. Within weeks, Davis, who had wanted the war to continue, was captured in Georgia, and the remaining Confederate forces laid down their arms and surrendered. The war was over at last.

Heavy Losses Force Lee's Surrender

With Lee's surrender, Lincoln knew that the Union had been preserved, yet he did not live to see the war's end. On the evening of Good Friday, April 14, he accompanied his wife to Ford's Theatre in Washington to enjoy a popular comedy. There John Wilkes Booth, an embittered southern sympathizer, shot the president in the head at point-blank range. Lincoln died the next day. Twelve days later, troops tracked down and killed Booth. The Union had lost its wartime leader, and millions publicly mourned the martyred chief executive along the route of the funeral train that took his body home to Illinois. Relief at the war's end mingled uncomfortably with a renewed sense of loss and uncertainty about the future.

 ## Costs and Effects

The human costs of the Civil War were enormous (see figure, page 438). The total number of military casualties on both sides exceeded 1 million— a frightful toll for a nation of 31 million people. Approximately 360,000 Union soldiers died, 110,000 of them from wounds suffered in battle. Another 275,175 Union soldiers were wounded but survived. On the Confederate side, an estimated 260,000 lost their lives, and almost as many suffered wounds. More men died in the Civil War than in all other American wars combined until Vietnam. Fundamental disagreements that would continue to trouble the Reconstruction era had caused unprecedented loss of life.

Casualties

Although precise figures on enlistments are impossible to obtain, it appears that 700,000 to 800,000 men served in the Confederate armies. Far more, possibly 2.3 million, served in the Union armies. All

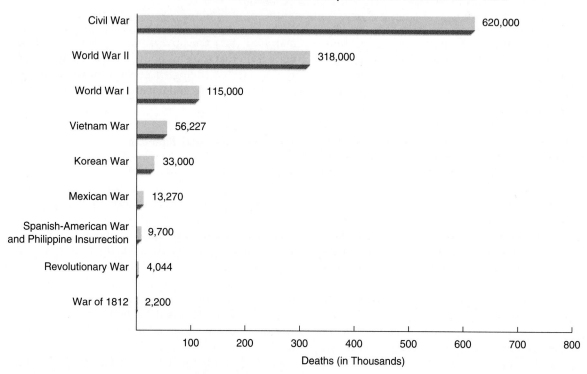

The Unprecedented Human Losses of the Civil War *Month after month newspapers in every community published the names of men who had become casualties. As this graph implies, the newspapers' lists were long.* Source: Shelby Foote, *The Civil War, a Narrative,* 3 vols. (1958–1974); Richard B. Morris, *Encyclopedia of American History* (1982); Archer Jones, *Civil War Command and Strategy* (1992).

these men were taken from home, family, and personal goals and had their lives disrupted in ways that were not easily repaired.

Property damage and financial costs were also enormous, though difficult to tally. United States loans and taxes during the conflict totaled almost $3 billion, and interest on the war debt was $2.8 billion. The Confederacy borrowed over $2 billion but lost far more in the destruction of homes, crops, livestock, and other property. As an example of the wreckage that attended four years of conflict on southern soil, the number of hogs in South Carolina plummeted from 965,000 in 1860 to approximately 150,000 in 1865, leaving many families without their primary source of meat. Scholars have noted that small farmers lost just as much, proportionally, as planters whose slaves were emancipated.

Financial Cost of the War

In southern war zones the landscape was desolated. Soldiers seeking fuel or shelter had cut down many large stands of trees, and artillery shells had blasted many others. Over wide regions fences and crops were destroyed, houses and bridges burned, and fields abandoned and left to erode. Union troops had looted factories and put two-thirds of the South's railroad system out of service. Levees and roads had deteriorated. Visitors to the countryside were struck by how empty and impoverished it looked. Nature would repair much of the damage in time, but large investments of human skill and energy were gone.

Estimates of the total cost of the war exceed $20 billion—five times the total expenditures of the federal government from its creation to 1861. The northern government increased its spending by 700 percent in the first full year of the war; by the last year its spending had soared to twenty times the prewar level. By 1865 the federal government accounted for over 26 percent of the gross national product.

Many of these changes were more or less permanent. In the 1880s, interest on the war debt still accounted for approximately 40 percent of the federal budget and Union soldiers' pensions for as much as 20 percent. The federal government had used its power to support manufacturing and business interests by means of tariffs, loans, and subsidies, and wartime measures left the federal government more deeply involved in the banking and transportation systems. Thus although many southerners had hoped to remove government from the economy, the war made such separation an impossibility. After the war, federal expenditures shrank but stabilized at twice the prewar level, or at 4 percent of the gross national product.

 Conclusion

The Civil War altered American society in many ways. During the war, in both North and South, women had taken on new roles, which could grow or stagnate. Industrialization and large economic enterprises played a larger role than ever before. Ordinary citizens found that their futures were increasingly tied to great organizations. Politically, the defense of national unity brought far-reaching changes in government and policy. Under Republican leadership, the federal government had expanded its power not only to preserve the Union but also to extend freedom. In a sweeping expropriation of what had been considered property, the government emancipated the slaves, and Lincoln had called for "a new birth of freedom" in America. It was unclear, however, whether the nation would use its power to protect the rights of individuals. Would the government guarantee the rights of the former slaves, whose humanity was now recognized? Extreme forms of states' rights dogma clearly were dead, but would Americans continue to favor a state-centered federalism? How would white southerners, embittered and impoverished by the war, respond to efforts to reconstruct the nation?

Closely related to these issues was a question of central importance: what would be the place of black men and women in American life? The Union victory provided a partial answer: slavery as it had existed before the war could not persist. But whether full citizenship and equal rights would take slavery's place remained unclear. Black veterans and former slaves eagerly sought an answer. They would find it during Reconstruction.

Suggestions for Further Reading

The War and the South

Thomas B. Alexander and Richard E. Beringer, *The Anatomy of the Confederate Congress* (1972); Stephen Ash, *When the Yankees Came* (1995); Richard E. Beringer et al., *Why the South Lost the Civil War* (1986); Gabor S. Boritt, *Why the Confederacy Lost* (1992); Richard N. Current, *Lincoln's Loyalists* (1992); William C. Davis, *Jefferson Davis* (1991); Robert F. Durden, *The Gray and the Black: The Confederate Debate on Emancipation* (1972); Paul D. Escott, *Many Excellent People* (1985); Paul D. Escott, *After Secession: Jefferson Davis and the Failure of Confederate Nationalism* (1978); Eli N. Evans, *Judah P. Benjamin* (1987); Mark Grimsley, *The Hard Hand* of War (1995); J. B. Jones, *A Rebel War Clerk's Diary*, 2 vols., ed. Howard Swiggett (1935); Ella Lonn, *Desertion During the Civil War* (1928); Mary Elizabeth Massey, *Refugee Life in the Confederacy* (1964); Larry E. Nelson, *Bullets, Ballots, and Rhetoric: Confederate Policy for the United States Presidential Contest of 1864* (1980); Alan T. Nolan, *Lee Considered* (1991); Harry P. Owens and James J. Cooke, eds., *The Old South in the Crucible of War* (1983); James L. Roark, *Masters Without Slaves* (1977); Daniel Sutherland, *Seasons of War* (1995); Georgia Lee Tatum, *Disloyalty in the Confederacy* (1934); Emory M. Thomas, *The Confederate Nation* (1979); Emory M. Thomas, *The Confederacy as a Revolutionary Experience* (1971); William A. Tidwell, *April '65* (1995); Bell Irvin Wiley, *The Life of Johnny Reb* (1943); Bell Irvin Wiley, *The Plain People of the Confederacy* (1943); W. Buck Yearns, ed., *The Confederate Governors* (1985).

The War and the North

Ralph Andreano, ed., *The Economic Impact of the American Civil War* (1962); Robert Cruden, *The War That Never Ended* (1973); David Donald, ed., *Why the North Won the Civil War* (1960); James W. Geary, *We Need Men* (1991); Wood Gray, *The Hidden Civil War* (1942); Randall C. Jimerson, *The Private Civil War* (1988); Frank L. Klement, *The Copperheads in the Middle West* (1960); Susan Previant Lee and Peter Passell, *A New Economic View of American History* (1979); James M. McPherson, *Battle Cry of Freedom* (1988); James H. Moorhead, *American Apocalypse* (1978); Phillip S. Paludan, *"A People's Contest": The Union and the Civil War, 1861–1865* (1989); Robert Hunt Rhodes, ed., *All for the Union: The Civil War Diary and Letters of Elisha Hunt Rhodes* (1991); George Winston Smith and Charles Burnet Judah, *Life in the North During the Civil War* (1966); George Templeton Strong, *Diary*, 4 vols., ed. Allan Nevins and Milton Hasley Thomas (1952); Paul Studenski, *Financial History of the United States* (1952); Bell Irvin Wiley, *The Life of Billy Yank* (1952).

Women

John R. Brumgardt, ed., *Civil War Nurse: The Diary and Letters of Hannah Ropes* (1980); Beth Gilbert Crabtree and James W. Patton, eds., *"Journal of a Secesh Lady": The Diary of Catherine Ann Devereux Edmondston, 1860–1866* (1979); Jacqueline Jones, *Labor of Love, Labor of Sorrow* (1985); Mary Elizabeth Massey, *Bonnet Brigades* (1966); George C. Rable, *Civil Wars: Women and the Crisis of Southern Nationalism* (1989); Mary D. Robertson, ed., *Lucy Breckinridge of Grove Hill: The Journal of a Virginia Girl, 1862–1864* (1979); C. Vann Woodward and Elisabeth Muhlenfeld, eds., *Mary Chesnut's Civil War* (1981); Agatha Young, *Women and the Crisis* (1959).

African-Americans

Virginia M. Adams, ed., *On the Altar of Freedom: A Black Soldier's Civil War Letters from the Front* (1991); Ira Berlin, ed., *Freedom: A Documentary History of Emancipation, 1861–1867*, Series I, *The Destruction of Slavery* (1979), and Series II, *The Black Military Experience* (1982); David W. Blight, *Frederick Douglass' Civil War* (1989); Dudley Cornish, *The Sable Arm* (1956); Barbara Jeanne Fields, *Slavery and Freedom on the Middle Ground* (1985); Joseph T. Glatthaar, *Forged in Battle* (1990); Leon Litwack, *Been in the Storm So Long* (1979); James M. McPherson, *The Negro's Civil War* (1965); James M. McPherson, *The Struggle for Equality* (1964); Clarence L. Mohr, *On the Threshold of Freedom* (1986); Benjamin Quarles, *The Negro in the Civil War* (1953).

Military History

Nancy Scott Anderson and Dwight Anderson, *The Generals: Ulysses S. Grant and Robert E. Lee* (1987); Albert Castel, *Decision in the West* (1992); Bruce Catton, *Grant Takes Command* (1969); Bruce Catton, *Grant Moves South* (1960); Benjamin Franklin Cooling, *Forts Henry and Donelson* (1988); Peter Cozzens, *This Terrible Sound* (1992); William C. Davis, ed., *The Image of War*, multivolume (1983–1985); Michael Fellman, *Citizen Sherman* (1995); Shelby Foote, *The Civil War, a Narrative*, 3 vols. (1958–1974); Douglas Southall Freeman, *Lee's Lieutenants*, 3 vols. (1942–1944); Douglas Southall Freeman, *R. E. Lee*, 4 vols. (1934–1935); Joseph T. Glatthaar, *The March to the Sea and Beyond* (1985); Herman Hattaway and Archer Jones, *How the North Won* (1983); Laurence M. Hauptman, *Between Two Fires: American Indians in the Civil War* (1995); Archer Jones, *Civil War Command and Strategy* (1992); Alvin M. Josephy, Jr., *The Civil War in the American West* (1991); Gerald F. Linderman, *Embattled Courage* (1989); Thomas L. Livermore, *Numbers and Losses in the Civil War in America* (1957); Grady McWhiney and Perry D. Jamieson, *Attack and Die* (1982); J. B. Mitchell, *Decisive Battles of the Civil War* (1955); Reid Mitchell, *Civil War Soldiers* (1988); Roy Morris, Jr., *Sheridan* (1992); Charles Royster, *The Destructive War* (1991); Stephen W. Sears, *To the Gates of Richmond* (1992); Stephen W. Sears, *George B. McClellan* (1988); Emory M. Thomas, *Robert E. Lee* (1995); Emory M. Thomas, *Bold Dragoon: The Life of J. E. B. Stuart* (1987); Noah Andre Trudeau, *The Last Citadel* (1991); Steven E. Woodworth, *Jefferson Davis and His Generals* (1990).

Foreign Relations

Stuart L. Bernath, *Squall Across the Atlantic: American Civil War Prize Cases and Diplomacy* (1970); Kinley J. Brauer, "The Slavery Problem in the Diplomacy of the American Civil War," *Pacific Historical Review* 46, no. 3 (1977): 439–469; David P. Crook, *The North, the South, and the Powers, 1861–1865* (1974); Charles P. Cullop, *Confederate Propaganda in Europe* (1969); Norman B. Ferris, *The Trent Affair* (1977); Howard Jones, *Union in Peril* (1992); Frank J. Merli, *Great Britain and the Confederate Navy* (1970); Frank L. Owsley and Harriet Owsley, *King Cotton Diplomacy* (1959); Gordon H. Warren, *Fountain of Discontent: The Trent Affair and Freedom of the Seas* (1981).

Abraham Lincoln and the Union Government

Allan G. Bogue, *The Earnest Men: Republicans of the Civil War Senate* (1981); Gabor S. Borit, ed., *The Historian's Lincoln* (1989); Fawn Brodie, *Thaddeus Stevens* (1959); Richard N. Current, *The Lincoln Nobody Knows* (1958); Leonard P. Curry, *Blueprint for Modern America: Non-Military Legislation of the First Civil War Congress* (1968); Christopher Dell, *Lincoln and the War Democrats* (1975); David Donald, *Charles Sumner and the Rights of Man* (1970); Ludwell H. Johnson, "Lincoln's Solution to the Problem of Peace Terms, 1864–1865," *Journal of Southern History* 34 (November 1968): 441–447; Peyton McCrary, *Abraham Lincoln and Reconstruction: The Louisiana Experiment* (1978); James M. McPherson, *Abraham Lincoln and the Second American Revolution* (1990); Mark Neely, *The Fate of Liberty* (1991); Joel Silbey, *A Respectable Minority: The Democratic Party in the Civil War Era* (1977); Benjamin P. Thomas, *Abraham Lincoln* (1952); Hans L. Trefousse, *The Radical Republicans* (1969); Glyndon G. Van Deusen, *William Henry Seward* (1967); T. Harry Williams, *Lincoln and His Generals* (1952); T. Harry Williams, *Lincoln and the Radicals* (1941).

16

Reconstruction:
A Partial Revolution
1865–1877

For both men, war and Reconstruction brought stunning changes and swift reversals of fortune. In 1861 Robert Smalls was a slave in South Carolina, while Wade Hampton was a South Carolina legislator and one of the richest planters in the South. The events of the next fifteen years turned each man's world upside down more than once.

Robert Smalls became a Union hero when he stole a Confederate ship from Charleston harbor and piloted it to the blockading federal fleet. Thereafter, Smalls guided Union gunboats and toured the North recruiting black troops. Though he enjoyed celebrity status, Smalls encountered racial discrimination in the North and found in 1865 that neither his heroism nor his freedom entitled him to vote. But by 1868 that, too, had changed, and he began a career in politics. Robert Smalls helped write his state's constitution, served in the legislature, and won election to Congress. There he denounced white violence and worked for educational and economic opportunity for his people. But Smalls was helpless to prevent the end of Reconstruction or delay the return of white control in South Carolina.

Wade Hampton joined the Confederate Army in 1861 and soon became a lieutenant-general. The South's defeat profoundly shocked him; and as Union forces closed in, he spoke wildly of "forc[ing] my way across the Mississippi" with "a devoted band of Cavalry" and continuing to fight. The postwar years brought further painful and unexpected changes, including forced bankruptcy. In 1867 Hampton surprised other privileged whites by supporting suffrage for a few educated and propertied former slaves. By 1876 Hampton's fortunes were again on the rise: Democrats nominated him for governor, promising that he would "redeem"

On January 6, 1874, Congressman Robert B. Elliott of South Carolina made an eloquent defense of the proposed civil rights bill. After a review of legal issues, he called on Congress to ignore the opposition of southerners, who had tried to destroy the nation, and deal justly with the Negro race, which had faithfully defended the Union.

Chicago Historical Society.

443

South Carolina from Republican misrule. While Hampton spoke misleadingly of respect for blacks' rights, each member of the paramilitary Red Shirts who supported him pledged to "control the vote of at least one Negro, by intimidation, purchase," or other means. Hampton won the governor's chair and then a seat in the United States Senate.

As the careers of Smalls and Hampton suggest, Reconstruction's change was extensive but not lasting. Robert Smalls rose from bondage to experience glory, emancipation, political power, and, ultimately, disappointment. Wade Hampton fell from privilege to endure failure, bankruptcy, powerlessness, and, eventually, a return to power. Similarly, American society experienced both extraordinary change and fundamental continuity. Unprecedented social, political, and constitutional changes took place, but the underlying realities of economic power, racial prejudice, and judicial conservatism limited Reconstruction's revolutionary potential.

Nowhere was the turmoil of Reconstruction more evident than in national politics. Lincoln's successor, Andrew Johnson, and Congress fought bitterly over the shaping of a plan for Reconstruction. Though a southerner, Johnson had always been a foe of the South's wealthy planters, and his first acts as president suggested that he would be tough on traitors. Before the end of 1865, however, Johnson's policies changed direction, and southern aristocrats soon came to view Johnson as their friend and protector. Jefferson Davis stayed in prison for two years, but Johnson pardoned other rebel leaders and allowed them to occupy high offices. He also ordered tax officials to return plantations to their original owners, including abandoned coastal lands on which forty thousand freed men and women had settled by order of General William Tecumseh Sherman early in 1865.

This turn of events alarmed northern voters. Republican congressmen began to discuss plans to keep rebels from regaining control of the South or of Congress. Northern legislators produced a new Reconstruction program, embodied in the Fourteenth Amendment. But southern intransigence blocked that plan and forced a more radical step, the Reconstruction Act of 1867. When Congress put the act into effect, Johnson tried to subvert it, and by 1868 the president and Congress were bitterly antagonistic.

Before these struggles were over, Congress had impeached the president, enfranchised the freedmen, and given them a role in reconstructing the South. The nation also adopted the Fourteenth and Fifteenth Amendments. Yet some underlying realities never changed. Little was done to open the doors of economic opportunity to black southerners. Judicially, the Supreme Court adopted interpretations of the Thirteenth, Fourteenth, and Fifteenth Amendments that crippled their power for decades. Throughout this period of upheaval, few saw equal rights for African-Americans as the central aim of Reconstruction.

By 1869 the Ku Klux Klan was employing extensive violence to thwart Reconstruction and undermine black freedom. As white Democrats in the South recaptured state governments, undoing the political revolution, they encountered little opposition from the North. Voters had grown weary and suspicious of the use of federal power to prop up failing Republican governments. Moreover, as the 1870s advanced, other issues drew attention away from Reconstruction. Industrial growth accelerated, creating new opportunities and raising new problems. Interest in territorial expansion revived. Political corruption became a nationwide scandal, bribery a way of doing business. "Money has become the God of this country," wrote one disgusted observer, "and men, otherwise good men, are almost compelled to worship at her shrine." Eventually these other forces triumphed. As politics moved on to new concerns, the courts turned their attention away from civil rights, and even northern Republicans abandoned racial reforms in 1877.

Thus only limited change emerged from a period of tremendous upheaval. Congress asserted the principle of equality before the law for African-Americans and gave black men the right to vote. But more far-reaching measures to advance black freedom never had much support in Congress, and when suffrage alone proved insufficient to remake the South, the nation soon lost interest. Reconstruction proclaimed anew the American principle of human equality but failed to secure it in reality.

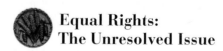 **Equal Rights: The Unresolved Issue**

For America's former slaves, Reconstruction had one paramount meaning: a chance to explore freedom. A southern white woman admitted in her diary that the black people "showed a natural and exultant joy at being free." Former slaves remembered singing far

• *Important Events* •

1865	President Andrew Johnson begins Reconstruction	1870	Congress passes first Enforcement Act
	Confederate leaders regain power	1871	Congress passes second Enforcement Act and Ku Klux Klan Act
	White southern governments pass restrictive black codes		Treaty with England settles *Alabama* claims
	Congress refuses to seat southern representatives	1872	Amnesty Act frees almost all remaining Confederates from restrictions on holding office
	Thirteenth Amendment ratified		Liberal Republicans organize

1865
President Andrew Johnson begins Reconstruction
Confederate leaders regain power
White southern governments pass restrictive black codes
Congress refuses to seat southern representatives
Thirteenth Amendment ratified

1866
Congress passes Civil Rights Act and renewal of Freedmen's Bureau over Johnson's veto
Congress approves Fourteenth Amendment
Most southern states reject Fourteenth Amendment
In *Ex parte Milligan* the Supreme Court reasserts its influence

1867
Congress passes Reconstruction Act and Tenure of Office Act
Secretary of State William Seward arranges purchase of Alaska
Constitutional conventions called in southern states

1868
House impeaches Johnson; Senate acquits him
Most southern states gain readmission to the Union
Fourteenth Amendment ratified
Ulysses S. Grant elected president

1869
Congress approves Fifteenth Amendment (ratified in 1870)

1870
Congress passes first Enforcement Act

1871
Congress passes second Enforcement Act and Ku Klux Klan Act
Treaty with England settles *Alabama* claims

1872
Amnesty Act frees almost all remaining Confederates from restrictions on holding office
Liberal Republicans organize
Debtors urge government to keep greenbacks in circulation
Grant reelected

1873
Slaughter-House cases limit power of Fourteenth Amendment
Panic of 1873 damages economy

1874
Grant vetoes increase in supply of paper money
Democrats win majority in House of Representatives

1875
Several Grant appointees indicted for corruption
Congress passes weak Civil Rights Act
Congress requires that after 1878 greenbacks be convertible into gold

1876
U.S. v. *Cruikshank* and *U.S.* v. *Reese* further weaken Fourteenth Amendment
Presidential election disputed

1877
Congress elects Rutherford B. Hayes president
Exodusters migrate to Kansas

---

into the night after federal troops, who confirmed rumors of their emancipation, reached their plantations. The slaves on a Texas plantation jumped up and down and clapped their hands as one man shouted, "We is free—no more whippings and beatings." A few people gave in to the natural desire to do what had been impossible before. One grandmother who had long resented her treatment dropped her hoe and ran to confront the mistress. "I'm free!" she yelled. "Yes, I'm free! Ain't got to work for you no more! You can't put me in your pocket [sell me] now!" Another man recalled that he and others "started on the move," either to search for family members or just to exercise their newfound freedom of movement.

Most freed men and women reacted more cautiously and shrewdly, taking care to test the boundaries of their new condition. "After the war was over," explained one man, "we was afraid to move. Just like terrapins or turtles after emancipation. Just stick our heads out to see how the land lay." As slaves they had learned to expect hostility from white people, and they did not presume it would instantly disappear. Life in freedom might still be a matter of what was allowed, not what was right. "You got to say master?" asked a freedman in Georgia. "Naw," answered his fellows, but "they said it all the same. They said it for a long time." One sign of this shrewd caution was the way freed people evaluated potential employers. "Most all the Negroes that had good owners stayed with 'em, but the others left. Some of 'em come back and some didn't," explained one man. If a white person had been relatively considerate to blacks in bondage, they reasoned that he might prove a desirable employer in freedom. Others left their plantations all at once, for, as one put it, "that master am sure mean and if we doesn't have to stay we shouldn't, not with that master."

In addition to a fair employer, freed men and women wanted opportunity through education and, especially, through landownership. Land represented their chance to farm for themselves, to enjoy the independence that generations of American farmers valued. It represented compensation for generations of travail in bondage. A northern observer noted that slaves freed in the Sea Islands of South Carolina and Georgia made "plain, straight-forward" inquiries as they settled the land set aside for them by Sherman. They wanted to be sure the land "would be theirs after they had improved it." Everywhere, blacks young and old thirsted for homes of their own.

African-Americans' Desire for Land

But how much of a chance would whites, who were in power in 1865, give to blacks? Northerners' racial attitudes were evolving but remained generally unfavorable. Abolitionists and many Republicans helped African-Americans fight for equal rights, and they won some victories. In 1864 the federal courts accepted black testimony, and the next year the Thirteenth Amendment became law. New York City and the District of Columbia desegregated their streetcars, and Massachusetts enacted a comprehensive public accommodations law. Nevertheless, signs of resistance to racial equality abounded. The Democratic Party fought hard against equality, charging that Republicans favored race-mixing and were undermining the status of white workers. Voters in three states—Connecticut, Minnesota, and Wisconsin—rejected black suffrage in 1865.

Even northern reformers who with Lincoln's encouragement had administered the Sea Islands during the war showed little sympathy for black aspirations. The former Sea Island slaves wanted to establish small, self-sufficient farms. Northern soldiers, officials, and missionaries of both races brought education and aid to the freedmen but also insisted that they grow cotton. They emphasized profit and the values of competitive capitalism. It would be "most unwise and injurious," wrote one worker in the Sea Islands, to give former slaves free land.

"The Yankees preach nothing but cotton, cotton!" complained one Sea Island black. "We wants land," wrote another, but tax officials "make the lots too big, and cut we out." Indeed, the United States government sold thousands of acres in the Sea Islands for nonpayment of taxes, but 90 percent of the land went to wealthy investors from the North. Even after blacks pooled their earnings, they were able to buy fewer than two thousand of nearly seventeen thousand acres sold in March 1863. Thus even from their strongest northern supporters the former slaves received only partial support. How much opportunity would freedom bring? That was a vital question, whose answer depended on the evolution of policy in Washington.

 ## Johnson's Reconstruction Plan

When Reconstruction began under President Andrew Johnson, many expected his policies to be harsh. Throughout his career in Tennessee he had criticized the wealthy planters and championed the small farmers. When an assassin's bullet thrust Johnson into the presidency, many former slaveowners shared the dismay of a North Carolina woman who wrote, "Think of Andy Johnson [as] the president! What will become of us—'the aristocrats of the South' as we are termed?" Northern Radicals also had reason to believe that Johnson would deal sternly with the South. When one of them suggested the exile or execution of ten or twelve leading rebels to set an example, Johnson replied, "How are you going to pick out so small a number? . . . *Treason* is a crime; and *crime* must be punished."

Through 1865 Johnson alone controlled Reconstruction policy, for Congress recessed shortly before he became president and did not reconvene until December. In the following eight months, Johnson devised and put into operation his own plan, forming new state governments in the South by using his power to grant pardons.

Wartime proposals for Reconstruction had produced much controversy but no consensus. In December 1863 Lincoln had proposed a "10 percent" plan for a government being organized in captured parts of Louisiana. Under this plan, a state government could be established as soon as 10 percent of those who had voted in 1860 took an oath of future loyalty to the Union. Only high-ranking Confederate officials would be denied

Lincoln's Reconstruction Plan

a chance to take the oath, and Lincoln urged that at least a few well-qualified blacks be given the ballot. Radicals bristled, however, at such a mild plan, and Congress backed the much stiffer Wade-Davis bill, which required 50 percent of the voters to swear an "iron-clad" oath that they had never voluntarily supported the rebellion. Lincoln pocket-vetoed this measure.

Later, in 1865, Lincoln suggested but then abandoned even more lenient terms. At the Hampton Roads Conference, he raised questions about the extent of emancipation and discussed compensation and restoration to the Union, with full rights, of the very state governments that had tried to leave it. In April he considered allowing the Virginia legislature to convene in order to withdraw its support from the Confederate war effort. Faced with strong opposition in his cabinet, Lincoln reversed himself, denying that he had intended to confer legitimacy on a rebel government. At the time of his death, he had given tentative approval to a plan, drafted by Secretary of War Edwin Stanton, to impose military authority and appoint provisional governors as steps toward the creation of new state governments. Beyond these general outlines, it is impossible to say what Lincoln would have done had he survived.

Johnson began with Stanton's plan. New governments would be created in the South, but which southerners would be allowed to vote? At a cabinet meeting in May 1865, Johnson's advisers split evenly on the question of giving voting rights to black men in the South. Johnson claimed that he favored black suffrage, but *only* if the southern states adopted it voluntarily. A champion of states' rights and no friend of African-Americans, he regarded this decision as too important to be taken out of the hands of the states.

This racial conservatism had an enduring effect on Johnson's policies. Where whites were concerned, however, Johnson seemed to be pursuing radical changes in class relations. He proposed rules that would keep the wealthy planter class out of power. Southerners were required to swear an oath of loyalty as a condition of gaining amnesty or pardon, but Johnson barred several categories of people from taking the oath. Former federal officials who had violated their oaths to support the United States and had aided the Confederacy could not take the oath. Nor

Oaths of Amnesty and New State Governments

Combative and inflexible, President Andrew Johnson contributed greatly to the failure of his own reconstruction program. Library of Congress.

could high-ranking Confederate officers and political leaders or graduates of West Point or Annapolis who had resigned their commissions to fight for the South. To this list Johnson added another important group: all southerners who aided the rebellion and whose taxable property was worth more than $20,000. All such individuals had to apply personally to the president for pardon and restoration of their political rights; otherwise, they risked legal penalties, which included confiscation of their land.

Thus it appeared that the leadership class of the Old South would be removed from power, for virtually all the rich and powerful whites of prewar days needed Johnson's special pardon. Many observers in both South and North sensed that the president meant to take revenge on the haughty aristocrats whom he had always resented and to raise up a new leadership of deserving yeomen.

Johnson appointed provisional governors who began the Reconstruction process by calling constitutional conventions. The delegates chosen for these conventions had to draft new constitutions that eliminated slavery and invalidated secession. After ratification of these constitutions, new governments could be elected, and the states would be restored to the Union with full congressional representation. But only those southerners who had taken the oath of amnesty and been eligible to vote on the day the state seceded could participate in this process. Thus unpardoned whites and former slaves were not eligible.

If Johnson intended to strip the old elite of its power, his plan did not work as he hoped. The old white leadership proved resilient and influential; prominent Confederates (a few with pardons but many without) won elections and turned up in various appointive offices. Then, surprisingly, Johnson helped to subvert his own plan: he started pardoning aristocrats and leading rebels who should not have been in office. He hired additional clerks to write out the necessary documents and then began to issue pardons to large categories of people. These pardons, plus the return of planters' abandoned lands, restored the old elite to power.

Why did Johnson allow the planters to regain power? Perhaps vanity betrayed his judgment. Wealthy men of the type who previously had scorned him now waited for appointments with him. Too long a lonely outsider, Johnson may have succumbed to the attention and flattery of the pardon seekers. But he also ran out of time. It took months for the constitutional conventions and elections to take place; by the time the process had restored Confederate leaders to powerful positions, the reconvening of Congress was imminent. To scrap his plan and remove the planters would be to admit failure. Since Johnson believed in white supremacy and wanted southern support in the 1866 elections, he decided to endorse the new governments and declare Reconstruction complete. Thus in December 1865 many Confederate congressmen traveled to Washington to claim seats in the United States Congress. Even Alexander Stephens, vice president of the Confederacy, returned to the capital as a senator-elect.

The election of such prominent rebels troubled many northerners. So did other results of Johnson's program. Some of the state conventions were slow to repudiate secession; others admitted only grudgingly that slavery was dead. Two refused to take any action to repudiate the large Confederate debt, which northerners felt should not be paid. Even

Johnson admitted that these acts showed "something like defiance, which is all out of place at this time."

Furthermore, to define the status of freed men and women and control their labor, some legislatures merely revised large sections of the slave codes by substituting the word *freedmen* for *slave*. The new black

Black Codes

codes compelled the former slaves, now supposedly free, to carry passes, observe a curfew, live in housing provided by a landowner, and give up hope of entering many desirable occupations. Stiff vagrancy laws and restrictive labor contracts bound supposedly free laborers to plantations, and "anti-enticement" laws punished anyone who tried to lure these workers to other employment. State-supported institutions in the South, such as schools and orphanages, excluded blacks entirely.

It seemed to northerners that the South was intent on returning African-Americans to a position of servility. Thus the Republican majority in Congress decided to take a closer look at the results of Johnson's plan. On reconvening, the House and Senate considered the credentials of the newly elected southern representatives and decided not to admit them. Instead, they established a joint committee to study Reconstruction and consider new policies. Reconstruction thus entered a second phase, one in which Congress would play the decisive role.

 ## The Congressional Reconstruction Plan

Northern congressmen disagreed about what to do, but they did not doubt their right to shape Reconstruction policy. The Constitution mentioned neither secession nor reunion, but it gave Congress an important role in the federal government. Moreover, the Constitution declared that the United States shall guarantee to each state a republican government. This provision, legislators believed, gave them the right to devise policies for Reconstruction.

They soon found that other constitutional questions affected their policies. What, for example, had rebellion done to the relationship between southern states and the Union? Lincoln had always insisted that states could not secede and that the Union remained intact. Not even Andrew Johnson, however, accepted the southern position that state governments of the Confederacy could simply reenter the nation. Johnson argued that the Union had endured, though individuals had erred—thus the use of his power to grant or withhold pardons. Congressmen who favored vigorous Reconstruction measures argued that the war *had* broken the Union. They maintained that the southern states had committed legal suicide and reverted to the status of territories, or that the South was a conquered nation subject to the victor's will. Moderate congressmen held that the states had forfeited their rights through rebellion and thus had come under congressional supervision.

These diverse theories mirrored the diversity of Congress itself. Northern Democrats denounced any idea of racial equality and supported Johnson's policies. Conservative Republicans, despite their party loyalty, favored a limited federal role in Reconstruction. The Radical Republicans, led by Thaddeus Stevens, Charles Sumner, and George Julian, wanted to transform the South. Although they were a minority within their party, they had the advantage of a clearly defined goal. They believed it was essential to democratize the South, establish public education, and ensure the rights of freed people. They favored black suffrage, often supported land confiscation and redistribution, and were willing to exclude the South from the Union for several years if necessary to achieve their goals. A large group of moderate Republicans did not want to go as far as the Radicals but believed some change in Johnson's policies was necessary.

The Radicals

One overwhelming political reality faced all four groups: the 1866 elections were approaching in the fall. Having questioned Johnson's program, Congress needed to develop an alternative plan and avoid going before the voters empty-handed. Thus these politicians had to forge a majority coalition composed either of Democrats and Republicans or of various elements of the Republican Party. The nature of the coalition would determine the kind of plan that Congress developed.

Ironically, Johnson and the Democrats sabotaged the possibility of a conservative coalition. They refused to cooperate with conservative or moderate Republicans and stubbornly insisted that Reconstruction was over, that the new state governments were legitimate, and that southern representatives should be admitted to Congress. These intransigent positions eliminated the Democrats' potential influence and blasted any possibility of bipartisan compromise. To devise a Republican program, conservative and moderate elements in the party had to work with the Radicals. This development and subsequent

events enhanced the Radicals' influence. In 1865, however, Republican congressmen were still reluctant to break with the president, who was, for better or for worse, the titular head of their party.

Trying to work with Johnson, Republicans thought a compromise had been reached in the spring of 1866. Under its terms Johnson would agree to two modifications of his program: extension of the life of the Freedmen's Bureau, which Congress had established in 1865 to feed the hungry, negotiate labor contracts, and start schools; and passage of a civil rights bill to counteract the black codes. This bill would force southern courts to practice equality before the law by allowing federal judges to remove from state courts cases in which blacks were treated unfairly. Its provisions applied to discrimination by private individuals as well as by government officials. This was the first major bill to enforce the Thirteenth Amendment's abolition of slavery, and it was to become very important in the twentieth century.

Congress Struggles for a Compromise

Johnson destroyed the compromise, however, by vetoing both bills (they later became law when Congress overrode the president's veto). Denouncing any change in his program, the president condemned Congress's action, questioned its right to make policy, and revealed his own racism. Because the civil rights bill defined United States citizens as native-born persons who were taxed, Johnson claimed it discriminated against "large numbers of intelligent, worthy, and patriotic foreigners . . . in favor of the negro." The bill, he said, operated "in favor of the colored and against the white race."

All hope of working with the president was now dead. But northern Republicans sensed that their constituents remained dissatisfied with Reconstruction. Newspapers reported daily violations of blacks' rights in the South and carried troubling accounts of antiblack violence—notably in Memphis and New Orleans, where police aided brutal mobs in their attacks. Such violence convinced Republicans, and the northern public, that more needed to be done. The various factions of Republican lawmakers therefore continued bargaining among themselves until a plan emerged. It took the form of a proposed amendment to the Constitution, and it represented a compromise between radical and conservative elements of the party. The Fourteenth Amendment was Congress's alternative to Johnson's program of Reconstruction.

In 1866, as Congress reviewed the progress of Reconstruction, news from the South had a considerable impact. Violence against black people, like the riot in Memphis depicted here, helped convince northern legislators that they had to modify President Johnson's policies.   Library of Congress.

Of the four points in the amendment, there was near-universal agreement on one: the Confederate debt was declared null and void, and the war debt of the United States was guaranteed. Northerners rejected the notion of paying taxes to reimburse those who had financed a rebellion, and business groups agreed on the necessity of upholding the credit of the United States government. There was also general support for prohibiting prominent Confederates from holding political office. The amendment therefore barred Confederate leaders from state and federal office. Only Congress, by a two-thirds vote of each house, could remove the penalty.

Fourteenth Amendment

The first section of the Fourteenth Amendment, which would have the greatest legal significance in later years, conferred citizenship on freedmen and prohibited states from abridging their constitutional "privileges and immunities" (see the Appendix). It also barred any state from taking a person's life, liberty, or property "without due process of law" and from denying "equal protection of the laws." These broad phrases became powerful guarantees of African-Americans' civil rights—indeed, of the rights of all citizens—in the twentieth century. They also took on added meaning with court rulings that corporations were legally "persons" (see page 530).

The second section of the amendment dealt with representation and embodied the compromises and political motives that had produced the amendment. Northerners disagreed about whether black citizens should have the right to vote. As a citizen of Indiana wrote to a southern relative, there was strong feeling in favor of "humane and liberal laws for the government and protection of the colored population." But there was prejudice, too. "Although there is a great deal [of] profession among us for the relief of the darkey yet I think much of it is far from being cincere. I guess we want to compell you to do right by them while we are not willing ourselves to do so."

Republican congressmen shied away from confronting this ambivalence, but political reality required them to do something. Representation in Congress depended on population, and each slave had counted as three-fifths of a person. Emancipation made every former slave five-fifths of a person, a fact that would increase southern representation. Thus the postwar South stood to *gain* power in Congress, and if white southerners did not allow blacks to vote, former secessionists would derive all the political benefit from emancipation. What a strange result that would seem to most northerners! They had never planned to reward the South for rebellion, and Republicans in Congress were determined not to hand over power to their political enemies. So they offered the South a choice. According to the second section of the Fourteenth Amendment, states did not have to grant black men the right to vote. But if they did not do so, their representation would be reduced proportionally. If they did enfranchise black men, their representation would be increased proportionally—but, of course, Republicans could seek the support of the new black voters. This compromise protected northern interests and gave Republicans a chance to compete if freedmen gained the ballot.

The Fourteenth Amendment raised the possibility of suffrage for black men but ignored female citizens, black and white. For this reason it provoked a strong reaction from the women's rights movement. Advocates of equal rights for women had worked with abolitionists for decades, often subordinating their cause to that of the slaves. During the drafting of the Fourteenth Amendment, however, female activists demanded to be heard. When legislators defined women as nonvoting citizens, prominent leaders such as Elizabeth Cady Stanton and Susan B. Anthony decided that it was time to end their alliance with abolitionists and fight more determinedly for themselves. Thus the amendment infused new determination into the independent women's rights movement.

In 1866, however, the major question in Reconstruction politics was how the public would respond to the amendment. Johnson did his best to block the Fourteenth Amendment in both North and South. Condemning Congress for its refusal to seat southern representatives, the president urged state legislatures in the South to vote against ratification. Every southern legislature except Tennessee's rejected the amendment by a wide margin. Its best showing was in Alabama,

Southern Rejection of the Fourteenth Amendment

where it failed by a vote of 69 to 8 in the assembly and 27 to 2 in the senate. In three other states the amendment received no support at all.

To present his case to northerners, Johnson organized a National Union Convention and took to the stump himself. In an age when active personal campaigning was rare for a president, Johnson boarded a special train for a "swing around the circle" that carried his message deep into the Midwest and then back to Washington. In cities such as Cleveland and St. Louis, he criticized the Republicans in a ranting, undignified style. Increasingly, audiences rejected his views and hooted and jeered at him.

The elections of 1866 were a resounding victory for Republicans in Congress. Radical and moderate Republicans whom Johnson had denounced won reelection by large margins, and the Republican majority grew as new candidates defeated incumbent Democrats. The North had spoken clearly: Johnson's policies were giving the advantage to rebels and traitors. Although reformers who hoped to eliminate prejudice were only a minority, most northerners feared for "the future peace and safety of the Union." Thus Republican congressional leaders won a mandate to pursue their Reconstruction plan. But, thanks to Johnson and southern intransigence, that plan had reached an impasse. All but one of the southern state governments created by the president had rejected the Fourteenth Amendment and remained adamant. Nothing could be accomplished as long as those governments existed and the southern electorate was constituted as it was. To honor their constituents' wishes, Republicans had little choice but to form new state governments in the South and enfranchise the freedmen. They therefore decided to do both. The unavoidable logic of the situation forced the majority to accept part of the Radical plan.

The Reconstruction Act of 1867 incorporated only a small part of the Radical program. Until new state governments could be set up, Union generals assumed control in five military districts in the South (see map, page 459). Confederate leaders designated in the Fourteenth Amendment were barred from voting until new state constitutions were ratified. The act guaranteed freedmen the right to vote in elections for state constitutional conventions and in subsequent elections under the new constitutions. In addition, each southern state was required to ratify the Fourteenth Amendment and to ratify its new

Reconstruction Act of 1867

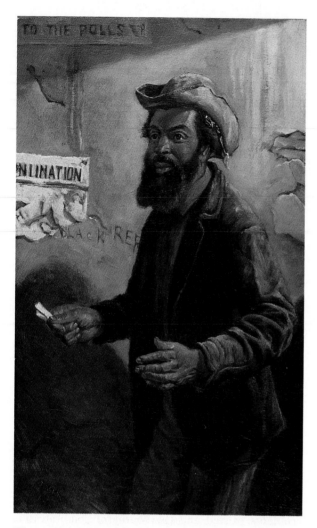

Thomas Waterman Wood, who had painted portraits of society figures in Nashville before the war, sensed the importance of Congress's decision in 1867 to enfranchise the freedmen. This oil painting, one of a series on suffrage, emphasizes the significance of the ballot for the black voter. Cheekwood Museum of Art, Nashville, Tennessee.

constitution and submit it to Congress for approval. Thus African-Americans gained an opportunity to fight for a better life through the political process.

The Radicals had hoped Congress would do much more. Thaddeus Stevens, for example, argued that economic opportunity was essential to the freedmen. "If we do not furnish them with homesteads from forfeited and rebel property," Stevens declared, "and hedge them around with protective laws . . . we had better left them in bondage." Stevens therefore drew up a plan for extensive confiscation and redistribution of land. Only one-tenth

of the land affected by his plan was earmarked for freedmen, in forty-acre plots. The rest was to be sold to generate money for veterans' pensions, compensation to loyal citizens for damaged property, and payment of the federal debt. By these means Stevens hoped to win support for a basically unpopular measure. But he failed, and in general the Radicals were not able to generate public support. Northerners were accustomed to a limited role for government, and the business community staunchly opposed any interference with private property rights. Thus black farmers were forced to seek work in a hostile environment in which landowners opposed their acquisition of land, even as renters.

Congress's role as the architect of Reconstruction was not quite over, for its quarrels with Andrew Johnson were growing more bitter. To restrict Johnson's influence and safeguard its plan, Congress passed a number of controversial laws. First, it set the date for its own reconvening—an unprecedented act, for the president traditionally summoned legislators to Washington. Then it limited Johnson's power over the army by requiring the president to issue military orders through the General of the Army, Ulysses S. Grant, who could not be sent from Washington without the Senate's consent. Finally, Congress passed the Tenure of Office Act, which gave the Senate power to interfere with changes in the president's cabinet. Designed to protect Secretary of War Stanton, who sympathized with the Radicals, this law violated the tradition that a president controlled his own cabinet.

Johnson took several belligerent steps of his own. He issued orders to military commanders in the South limiting their powers and increasing the powers of the civil governments he had created in 1865. Then he removed officers who were conscientiously enforcing Congress's new law, preferring commanders who allowed disqualified Confederates to vote. Finally, he tried to remove Secretary of War Stanton. With that attempt the confrontation reached its climax.

Twice before, the House Judiciary Committee had considered impeachment of Johnson, rejecting the idea once and then recommending it by only a 5-to-4 vote. That recommendation was decisively defeated by the House. After Johnson's last action, however, a third attempt to impeach the president carried easily. In fact, the House was so determined to indict Johnson in 1868 that it voted

Impeachment of President Johnson

Plans for Reconstruction Compared

	Johnson's Plan	Radicals' Plan	Fourteenth Amendment	Reconstruction Act of 1867
Voting	Whites only; Confederate leaders must seek pardons	Give vote to black males	Southern whites may decide but can lose representation	Black men gain vote; whites barred from office by Fourteenth Amendment cannot vote while new state governments are being formed
Officeholding	Many prominent Confederates regain power	Only loyal white and black males eligible	Confederate leaders barred until Congress votes amnesty	Fourteenth Amendment in effect
Time out of Union	Brief	Years; until South is thoroughly democratized	Brief	Brief
Other change in southern society	Little; gain of power by yeomen not realized	Expand public education; confiscate land and provide farms for freedmen	Probably slight	Depends on action of new state governments

before drawing up specific charges. The indictment concentrated on his violation of the Tenure of Office Act, though modern scholars regard his efforts to impede enforcement of the Reconstruction Act of 1867 as a far more serious offense.

Johnson's trial in the Senate began promptly and lasted more than three months. The prosecution, led by Radicals such as Thaddeus Stevens and Benjamin Butler, attempted to prove that Johnson was guilty of "high crimes and misdemeanors." But they also argued that the trial was a means to judge Johnson's performance, not a judicial determination of guilt or innocence. The Senate ultimately rejected such reasoning, which could have made removal from office a political weapon against any chief executive who disagreed with Congress. Although a majority of senators voted to convict Johnson, the prosecution fell one vote short of the necessary two-thirds majority. Johnson remained in office, politically weakened and with only a few months left in his term. His acquittal established a precedent that only serious misdeeds merited removal from office.

In 1869, in an effort to write democratic principles and colorblindness into the Constitution, the Radicals succeeded in presenting the Fifteenth

Fifteenth Amendment

Amendment for ratification. This measure forbade states to deny the right to vote "on account of race, color, or previous condition of servitude." Such wording did not guarantee the right to vote. It deliberately left states free to restrict suffrage on other grounds so that northern states could continue to deny suffrage to women and certain groups of men—Chinese immigrants, illiterates, and those too poor to pay taxes. Ironically, the votes of four uncooperative southern states—compelled by Congress to approve the amendment as an added condition to rejoining the Union—proved necessary to impose even this language on parts of the North. Although several states outside the South refused to ratify, the Fifteenth Amendment became law in 1870.

 ## Reconstruction Politics in the South

From the start, Reconstruction encountered the resistance of white southerners. In the black codes and in private attitudes, many whites stubbornly opposed

Thomas Nast, in this 1868 cartoon, pictured the combination of forces that threatened the success of Reconstruction: southern opposition and the greed, partisanship, and racism of northern interests.   Library of Congress.

White Resistance

emancipation, and the former planter class proved especially unbending. In 1866 a Georgia newspaper frankly observed that "most of the white citizens believe that the institution of slavery was right, and . . . they will believe that the condition, which comes nearest to slavery, that can now be established will be the best." Andrew Johnson's encouragement of southern whites to resist Congress only intensified such opposition to change.

Fearing loss of control over their slaves, some planters attempted to postpone freedom by denying or misrepresenting events. Former slaves reported that their owners "didn't tell them it was freedom" or "wouldn't let [them] go." Agents of the Freedmen's Bureau reported that "the old system of slavery [is] working with even more rigor than formerly at a few miles distant from any point where U.S. troops are stationed." To hold onto their workers, some landowners claimed control over black children and used guardianship and apprentice laws to bind black families to the plantation.

Whites also blocked blacks from acquiring land. A few planters divided up plots among their slaves, but most condemned the idea of making blacks landowners. One planter in South Carolina refused to sell as little as 1.5 acres to each family. Even a Georgia woman whose family was known for its support of religious education for slaves was outraged that two property owners planned to "rent their lands to the Negroes!" Such action was, she declared, "injurious to the best interest of the community."

Adamant resistance by propertied whites soon manifested itself in other ways, including violence. In one North Carolina town a local magistrate clubbed a black man on a public street, and bands of "Regulators" terrorized blacks in parts of that state and Kentucky. Such incidents were predictable in a society in which many planters believed, as a South Carolinian put it, that blacks "can't be governed except with the whip."

After President Johnson encouraged the South to resist congressional Reconstruction, white conservatives worked hard to capture the new state governments. Many whites also boycotted the polls in an attempt to defeat Congress's plans; by sitting out the elections, whites might block the new constitutions, which had to be approved by a majority of registered voters. This tactic was tried in North Carolina and succeeded in Alabama, forcing Congress to base ratification on a majority of those voting.

Very few black men stayed away from the polls. Enthusiastically and hopefully, they voted Republican. Most agreed with one man who felt he should "stick to the end with the party that freed me." Illiteracy did not prohibit blacks (or uneducated whites) from making intelligent choices. Although Mississippi's William Henry could read only "a little," he testified that he and his friends had no difficulty selecting the Republican ballot. "We stood around and watched," he explained. "We saw D. Sledge vote; he owned half the county. We knowed he voted Democratic so we voted the other ticket so it would be Republican." Women, who could not vote, encouraged their husbands and sons, and preachers exhorted their congregations to use the franchise. Such community spirit helped to counter white pressure tactics, and zeal for voting spread through the entire black community.

Thanks to a large black turnout and the restrictions on prominent Confederates, a new southern Republican Party came to power in the constitutional conventions. Republican delegates consisted of a sizable contingent of blacks (265 out of the total of just over 1,000 delegates throughout the South), some northerners who had moved to the South, and native southern whites who favored change. Together these Republicans brought the South into line with progressive reforms that had been adopted in the rest of the nation. The new constitutions were more democratic. They eliminated property qualifications for voting and holding office, and they turned many appointed offices into elective posts. They provided for public schools and institutions to care for the mentally ill, the blind, the deaf, the destitute, and the orphaned. They also put an end to imprisonment for debt and punishments such as branding.

The conventions broadened women's rights in property holding and divorce. Usually, the goal was not to make women equal with men but to provide relief to thousands of suffering debtors. In families left poverty-stricken by the war and weighed down by debt, it was usually the husband who had contracted the debts. Thus giving women legal control over their own property provided some protection to their families. The goal of some delegates, however, was to elevate women. Blacks in particular called for laws to provide for women's suffrage, but they were ignored by their white colleagues.

Under these new constitutions the southern states elected new governments. Again the Republican Party triumphed, putting new men in positions of power. For the first time, the

Triumph of Republican Governments

ranks of state legislators in 1868 included some black southerners. Congress's second plan for Reconstruction was well under way. It remained to be seen what these new governments would do and how much social change they would bring about.

One way to achieve radical change would have been to disfranchise substantial numbers of Confederate leaders. Barring many whites from politics as punishment for rebellion would have given the Republicans a solid electoral majority based on black

voters and their white allies. Land reform and the assurance of racial equality would have been possible. None of the Republican governments, however, did this or even gave it serious consideration. Why did the new legislators reject this course of action?

First, they appreciated the realities of power and the depth of racial enmity. In most states, whites were in the majority and former slaveowners controlled the best land and other sources of economic power. James Lynch, a leading black politician from Mississippi, explained why African-Americans shunned the "folly" of disfranchisement. Unlike northerners who "can leave when it becomes too uncomfortable," landless former slaves "must be in friendly relations with the great body of the whites in the state. Otherwise . . . peace can be maintained only by a standing army." Despised and lacking economic or social power, southern Republicans saw mere acceptance and legitimacy as ambitious goals.

Second, blacks believed in the principle of universal suffrage and the Christian goal of reconciliation. Far from being vindictive toward the race that had enslaved them, they treated leading rebels with generosity and appealed to white southerners to adopt a spirit of fairness and cooperation. Henry McNeil Turner, like other black ministers, urged his fellow Georgians to "love whites . . . soon their prejudice would melt away, and with God for our father, we will all be brothers." (Years later Turner criticized his own naiveté, saying that in the constitutional convention his motto had been "Anything to please the white folks.") Therefore southern Republicans quickly (in some cases immediately) restored the voting rights of former Confederates, as Congress steadily released more individuals from the penalties of the Fourteenth Amendment.

The South's Republican Party committed itself to a strategy of winning white support. To put the matter another way, the Republican Party condemned itself to defeat if white voters would not cooperate. Within a few years Republicans were reduced to the embarrassment of making futile appeals to whites while ignoring the claims of their strongest supporters, blacks. But for a time both Republicans and their opponents, who called themselves Conservatives or Democrats, moved to the center and appealed for support from a broad range of groups. Some propertied whites accepted congressional Reconstruction as a reality and declared themselves willing to compete under the new rules. While these Democrats angled for some black votes, Republicans

One notable success in Reconstruction efforts to stimulate industry was Birmingham, Alabama. Here workers cast molten iron into blocks called pigs.   Birmingham Public Library.

sought to attract more white voters. Both parties found an area of agreement in economic policies.

The Reconstruction governments enthusiastically promoted industry. This policy reflected northern ideals, but it also sprang from a growing southern eagerness to build up the region.

Industrialization

Confederates had seen how industry aided the North during the war. Accordingly, Reconstruction legislatures encouraged investment with loans, subsidies, and exemptions from taxation for periods up to ten years. The southern railroad system was rebuilt and expanded, and coal and iron mining made possible Birmingham's steel plants. Between 1860 and 1880, the number of manufacturing establishments in the South nearly doubled. This emphasis on big business, however, produced higher state debts and taxes, drew money away from schools and other programs, and multiplied possibilities for corruption. It also locked Republicans into a conservative strategy. In appealing to elite whites who never joined the Republican Party, they lost the opportunity of building support among poorer whites.

Policies appealing to African-American voters never went beyond equality before the law. In fact, the whites who controlled the southern Republican Party were reluctant to allow blacks a share of offices proportionate to their electoral strength. Aware of their weakness, black leaders did not push for revolutionary economic or social change. In every southern state, they led ef-

Other Republican Policies

forts to establish public schools but usually did not press for integrated facilities. Having a school to attend was the most important thing at the time, for the Johnson governments had excluded blacks from schools and other state-supported institutions. As a result, virtually every public school organized during Reconstruction was racially segregated, and these separate schools established a precedent. By the 1870s segregation was becoming a common though not universal practice in theaters, trains, and other public accommodations in the South.

A few African-American politicians did fight for civil rights and integration. Most were mulattos from cities such as New Orleans or Mobile, where large populations of light-skinned free blacks had existed before the war. Their experience in such communities had made them sensitive to issues of status, and they spoke out for open and equal public accommodations. Laws requiring equal accommodations won passage throughout the Deep South, but they often went unenforced or required an injured party to bring legal action for enforcement.

Economic progress was uppermost in the minds of most freed people and black representatives from rural districts. Black southerners needed land, but only a few promoted confiscation. Some hoped that high taxes would force portions of large estates onto the market (small farmers' lands were protected by homestead exemptions). In fact, much land did fall into state hands for nonpayment of taxes and was offered for sale in small lots. But most freedmen had too little cash to bid against investors or speculators, and few acquired land in this way. South Carolina established a land commission, but it could help only those with money to buy. Any widespread redistribution of land had to arise from Congress, which never supported such action.

Within a few years, as centrists in both parties met with failure, white hostility to congressional Reconstruction began to dominate. Some conservatives had always desired to fight Reconstruction through pressure and racist propaganda. They put economic and social pressure on blacks: one black Republican reported that "my neighbors will not employ me, nor sell me a farthing's worth of anything." Charging that the South had been turned over to ignorant blacks, conservatives deplored "black domination" and "Negro rule."

Such attacks were inflammatory but inaccurate. African-Americans participated in politics but did not dominate or control events. They were a major-ity in only two out of ten state conventions (transplanted northerners were a majority in one). In the state legislatures, only in the lower house in South Carolina did blacks ever constitute a majority; among officeholders, their numbers generally were far inferior to their proportion in the population. Sixteen blacks won seats in Congress before Reconstruction was over, but none was ever elected governor. Only eighteen served in a high state office such as lieutenant governor, treasurer, superintendent of education, or secretary of state.

Conservatives also assailed the allies of black Republicans. Their propaganda denounced whites from the North as "carpetbaggers," greedy crooks planning to pour stolen tax revenues into their sturdy luggage made of carpet material. Immigrants from the North, who held the largest share of Republican offices, were all tarred with this brush.

Carpetbaggers and Scalawags

In fact, most northerners who settled in the South had come seeking business opportunities or a warmer climate and never entered politics. Those who did enter politics generally wanted to democratize the South and to introduce northern ways, such as industry, public education, and the spirit of enterprise. Their ideals were tested by hard times and ostracism by white southerners. Although carpetbaggers supported black suffrage and educational opportunities, most opposed social equality and integration.

Conservatives invented the term *scalawag* to discredit any native white southerner who cooperated with the Republicans. A substantial number of southerners did so, including some wealthy and prominent men. Most scalawags, however, were yeoman farmers, men from mountain areas and non-slaveholding districts who had been restive under the Confederacy. They saw that they could benefit from the education and opportunities promoted by Republicans. Banding together with freedmen, they pursued common class interests and hoped to make headway against the power of long-dominant planters. Cooperation even convinced a few scalawags that "there is but little if any difference in the talents of the two races," as one observed, and that all should have "an equal start."

Yet this black-white coalition was vulnerable to the race issue, and most scalawags shied away from support for racial equality. Republican tax policies also cut into upcountry yeoman support because

Members of the Ku Klux Klan devised ghoulish costumes to heighten the terror inspired by their acts. This photograph shows the costume of a Mississippi Klansman from 1871.   Courtesy, Herbert Peck, Jr.

reliance on the property tax hit many small land-holders hard. In addition, poll taxes (whose proceeds often were earmarked for education) endangered the independence of subsistence farmers, pressuring them to participate in the market economy to obtain cash.

Taxation was a major problem for the Reconstruction governments. Republicans wanted to maintain prewar services, repair the war's destruction, stimulate industry, and support important new ventures such as public schools. But the Civil War had destroyed much of the South's tax base. One category of valuable property—slaves—had disappeared entirely. And hundreds of thousands of citizens had lost much of the rest of their property—money, livestock,

fences, and buildings—to the war. Thus an increase in taxes was necessary even to maintain traditional services, and new ventures required still higher taxes. Inevitably, Republican tax policies aroused strong opposition.

Corruption was another serious charge levied against the Republicans. Unfortunately, it often was true. Many carpetbaggers and black politicians engaged in fraudulent schemes, sold their votes, or padded expenses, taking part in what scholars recognize was a nationwide surge of corruption (see page 459). Many white Democrats shared in corruption, and some Republicans fought it, but the Democrats successfully pinned the blame on unqualified blacks and greedy carpetbaggers.

All these problems hurt the Republicans, whose leaders also allowed factionalism along racial and class lines to undermine party unity. But in many southern states the deathblow came through violence. The Ku Klux Klan, a secret veterans' club that began in Tennessee, spread through the South and rapidly evolved into a terrorist organization. Violence against African-Americans occurred from the first days of Reconstruction but became far more organized and purposeful after 1867. Klansmen rode to frustrate Reconstruction and keep the freedmen in subjection. Nighttime harassment, whippings, beatings, and murder became common, and terrorism dominated some areas.

Ku Klux Klan

Although the Klan persecuted blacks who stood up for their rights as laborers or individuals, its main purpose was political. Lawless nightriders made active Republicans the target of their attacks. Leading white and black Republicans were killed in several states. After freedmen who worked for a South Carolina scalawag started voting, terrorists visited the plantation and, in the words of one victim, "whipped every nigger man they could lay their hands on." Klansmen also attacked Union League Clubs—Republican organizations that mobilized the black vote—and schoolteachers who were aiding the freedmen.

Klan violence was not a spontaneous outburst of racism; very specific social forces shaped and directed it. In North Carolina, for example, Alamance and Caswell Counties were the sites of the worst Klan violence. Slim Republican majorities there rested on cooperation between black voters and white yeomen, particularly those whose Unionism or discontent with the Confederacy had turned them against local Democratic officials. Together, these black and white Republicans had ousted officials long entrenched in power. The wealthy and powerful men in Alamance and Caswell who had lost their accustomed political control were the Klan's county officers and local chieftains. They organized a deliberate campaign of terror, recruiting members and planning atrocities. By whipping up racism or intimidating enough Republicans, the Ku Klux Klan weakened the Republican coalition and restored a Democratic majority.

Klan violence injured Republicans across the South. No fewer than one-tenth of the black leaders who had been delegates to the 1867–1868 state constitutional conventions were attacked, seven fatally. In one judicial district of North Carolina the Ku Klux Klan was responsible for twelve murders, over seven hundred beatings, and other acts of violence, including rape and arson. A single attack on Alabama Republicans in the town of Eutaw left four blacks dead and fifty-four wounded. In South Carolina five hundred masked Klansmen lynched eight black prisoners at the Union County jail, and in nearby York County the Klan committed at least eleven murders and hundreds of whippings. According to historian Eric Foner, the Klan "made it virtually impossible for Republicans to campaign or vote in large parts of Georgia."

Thus a combination of difficult fiscal problems, Republican mistakes, racial hostility, and terror brought down the Republican regimes. In most

Failure of Reconstruction

southern states so-called Radical Reconstruction lasted only a few years (see map). The most enduring failure of Reconstruction, however, was not political; it was social and economic. Reconstruction failed to alter

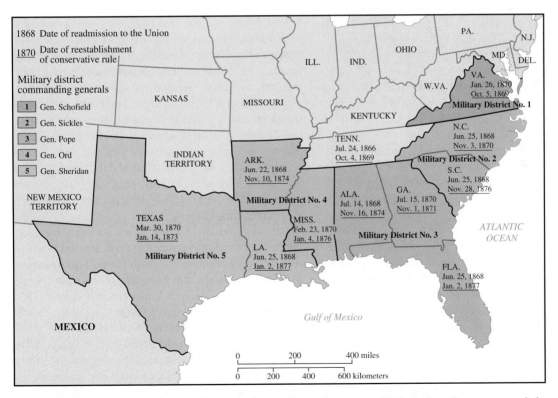

1868 Date of readmission to the Union

1870 Date of reestablishment of conservative rule

Military district commanding generals

1 Gen. Schofield
2 Gen. Sickles
3 Gen. Pope
4 Gen. Ord
5 Gen. Sheridan

The Reconstruction   *This map shows the five military districts established when Congress passed the Reconstruction Act of 1867. As the dates within each state indicate, conservative Democratic forces quickly regained control of government in four southern states. So-called Radical Reconstruction was curtailed in most of the others as factions within the weakened Republican Party began to cooperate with conservative Democrats.*

the South's social structure or its distribution of wealth and power. Exploited as slaves, freed men and women remained vulnerable to exploitation during Reconstruction. Without land of their own, they were dependent on white landowners who could and did use their economic power to compromise blacks' political freedom. Armed only with the ballot, freed men in the South had little chance to effect major changes.

To reform the southern social order, Congress would have had to redistribute land, but most lawmakers opposed an attack on private property. Radical Republicans like Albion Tourgée condemned Congress's timidity. Turning the freedman out on his own without protection, said Tourgée, constituted "cheap philanthropy." Indeed, African-Americans who had to live with the consequences of Reconstruction considered it a failure, for the North "threw all the Negroes on the world without any way of getting along." Moreover, without careful supervision by Congress, the situation of the freed men and women was sure to deteriorate. Whenever the North lost interest, Reconstruction would collapse.

 The Social and Economic Meaning of Freedom

Black southerners entered into life after slavery hopefully but not naively. They had had too much experience with white people to assume that all would be easy. A Texas man recalled his father telling him, even before the war was over, "Our forever was going to be spent living among the Southerners, after they got licked." Expecting hostility, freed men and women tried to gain as much as they could from their new circumstances. Often the changes they valued the most were personal—alterations in location, employer, or living arrangements that could make an enormous difference to individuals or families.

One of the first decisions was whether to leave the old plantation. This choice meant making a judgment about where opportunities for liberty and progress were likely to be greatest. Many cruel slaveholders saw their former property walk off en masse, as former slaves used their experience in bondage to assess the whites with whom they had to deal. Throughout Reconstruction as many as one-third changed employers at the end of a crop year.

After choosing an employer, ex-slaves reached out for valuable things in life that had been denied

them. One of these was education. Blacks of all ages hungered for the knowledge in books that had been permitted only to whites. With freedom, they started schools and filled classrooms both day and night. On log seats and dirt floors, freed men and women studied their letters in old almanacs, discarded dictionaries, or whatever was available. Young children brought infants to school with them, and adults attended at night or after "the crops were laid by." Many a teacher had "to make herself heard over three other classes reciting in concert" in a small room, but the students kept coming. The desire to escape slavery's ignorance was so great that, despite their poverty, many blacks paid tuition, typically $1 or $1.50 a month. These small amounts constituted one-tenth of many people's agricultural wages and added up to more than $1 million by 1870.

Education for African-Americans

The federal government and northern reformers of both races assisted this pursuit of education. In its brief life the Freedmen's Bureau founded over four thousand schools, and idealistic men and women from the North established and staffed others. The Yankee schoolmarm—dedicated, selfless, and religious—became an agent of progress in many southern communities. Thus with the aid of religious and charitable organizations throughout the North, African-Americans in the South began the nation's first assault on the problems created by slavery. The results included the beginnings of a public school system in each southern state and the enrollment of over 600,000 African-Americans in elementary school by 1877.

Blacks and their white allies also saw the need for colleges and universities to train teachers, ministers, and professionals for leadership. The American Missionary Association founded seven colleges, including Fisk and Atlanta Universities, between 1866 and 1869. The Freedmen's Bureau helped to establish Howard University in Washington, D.C., and northern religious groups such as the Methodists, Baptists, and Congregationalists supported dozens of seminaries, colleges, and teachers' colleges. By the late 1870s black churches had joined in the effort, founding numerous colleges despite limited resources.

Even during Reconstruction, African-American leaders often were highly educated individuals; many of them came from the prewar elite of free people of color. This group had benefited from its association

African-Americans of all ages eagerly pursued the opportunity in freedom to gain an education. This young woman in Mt. Meigs, Alabama, is helping her mother learn to read. Smithsonian Institute, photo by Rudolf Eickmeyer.

with wealthy whites, many of whom were blood relatives; some planters had given their mulatto children outstanding educations. Francis Cardozo, who held various offices in South Carolina, had attended universities in Scotland and England. P. B. S. Pinchback, who became lieutenant governor of Louisiana, was the son of a planter who had sent him to school in Cincinnati. Both of the two black senators from Mississippi, Blanche K. Bruce and Hiram Revels, had had privileged educations. Bruce was the son of a planter who had provided tutoring at home; Revels was the son of free North Carolina mulattos who had sent him to Knox College in Illinois. These men and many self-educated former slaves brought to politi-

cal office their experience as artisans, businessmen, lawyers, teachers, and preachers.

Meanwhile, millions of former slaves concentrated on improving life on their farms and in their neighborhoods. Surrounded by an unfriendly white population, black men and women sought to insulate themselves from white interference and to strengthen the bonds of their own community. Throughout the South they devoted themselves to reuniting their families, moving away from the slave quarters, and founding black churches. Given the eventual failure of Reconstruction, the gains that African-Americans made in their daily lives often proved the most enduring.

How do historians know about the relationships between former slaves and former slaveholders during Reconstruction? The records of the federal Bureau of Refugees, Freedmen, and Abandoned Lands contain a wealth of information on daily conflicts and confrontations. They reveal that one strategy used by planters to retain the labor of their former slaves was to control the slaves' children. The entry shown here, from a Bureau record book in Texas, recounts the complaint of Amanda Hayes. In 1866, her former owner, Captain William Hayes, took her son "to help him drive his cattle." In July 1867, "Mr. Hayes has not returned the boy yet," and Amanda Hayes "wishes the Bureau to compel" his return, with pay.   National Archives.

Churches became a center of African-American life, for social and political purposes as well as for worship. This engraving, which appeared in Harper's Weekly *in 1874, shows the minister of the First African Baptist Church of Richmond, Virginia, preaching to the congregation from an elevated pulpit.* The Valentine Museum, Richmond, Virginia.

The search for family members who had been sold away during slavery was awe inspiring. With only shreds of information to guide them, thousands of freed people embarked on odysseys in search of a husband, wife, child, or parent. By relying on the black community for help and information, many succeeded in their quest, sometimes almost miraculously. Others walked through several states and never found loved ones.

Reunification of African-American Families

Husbands and wives who had belonged to different masters established homes together for the first time, and parents asserted the right to raise their own children. A mother bristled when her old master claimed a right to whip her children. She informed him that "he warn't goin' to brush none of her chilluns no more." The freed men and women were too much at risk to act recklessly, but, as one man put it, they were tired of punishment and "sure didn't take no more foolishment off of white folks."

Many black people wanted to minimize contact with whites because, as Reverend Garrison Frazier told General Sherman in January 1865, "There is a prejudice against us . . . that will take years to get over." To avoid contact with overbearing whites who were used to supervising and controlling them, blacks abandoned the slave quarters and fanned out to distant corners of the land they worked. "After the war my stepfather come," recalled Annie Young, "and got my mother and we moved out in the piney woods." Others described moving "across the creek to [themselves]" or building a "saplin house . . . back in the woods." Some rural dwellers established small all-black settlements that still exist today along the backroads of the South.

Even once-privileged slaves shared this desire for independence and social separation. One man turned down the master's offer of the overseer's house and moved instead to a shack in "Freetown." He also declined to let the former owner grind his grain for free, because it "make him feel like a free man to pay for things just like anyone else." One couple, a carriage driver and trusted house servant during slavery, passed up the fine cooking of the "big house" to move "in the colored settlement."

The other side of movement away from whites was closer communion within the black community. Freed from the restrictions and regulations of slavery, blacks could build their own institutions as they saw fit. The secret churches of slavery came into the open; in countless communities throughout the South, ex-slaves "started a brush arbor." A brush arbor was

Founding of Black Churches

Sharecropping became an oppressive system in the postwar South. At plantation stores like this one, photographed in Mississippi in 1868, merchants recorded in their ledger books debts that few sharecroppers were able to repay.   Recordbook: Smithsonian Institute, Division of Community Life; Plantation store: Amistad Foundation Collection at the Wadsworth Athenaeum, Hartford, Connecticut.

merely "a sort of . . . shelter with leaves for a roof," but the freed men and women worshiped in it enthusiastically. "Preachin' and shouting sometimes lasted all day," they recalled, for the opportunity to worship together freely meant "glorious times." Within a few years independent branches of the Methodist and Baptist denominations had attracted the great majority of black Christians in the South.

The desire to gain as much independence as possible also shaped the former slaves' economic arrangements. Since most of them lacked money to buy land, they preferred the next best thing: renting the land they worked. But few whites would consider renting land to blacks, and most blacks had no means to get cash before the harvest. Thus other alternatives had to be tried.

Northerners and officials of the Freedmen's Bureau favored contracts between owners and laborers. To northerners who believed in "Free Soil, Free Labor, Free Men," contracts and wages seemed the key to progress. For a few years the Freedmen's Bureau helped draw up and enforce such contracts, but they proved unpopular with both races. Owners often filled the contracts with detailed requirements that led to close supervision and reminded blacks of their

circumscribed lives under slavery. Besides, cash for wages was not readily available in the early years of Reconstruction. Times were hard, and the failure of Confederate banks had left the South with a shortage of credit facilities.

Black farmers and white landowners therefore turned to sharecropping, a system in which farmers kept part of their crop and gave the rest to the landowner while living on his property. The landlord or a merchant "furnished" food and supplies needed before the harvest, and he received payment from the crop. Republican laws gave laborers the first lien, or legal claim, on the crop, enhancing their sense of ownership. Although

Rise of the Sharecropping System

landowners tried to set the laborers' share at a low level, black farmers had some bargaining power. By holding out and refusing to sign contracts at the end of the year, sharecroppers succeeded in keeping the owners' share at around one-half during Reconstruction.

The sharecropping system originated as a desirable compromise. It eased landowners' problems with cash and credit; blacks accepted it because it gave them more freedom from daily supervision. Instead of working under a white overseer, as in slavery, they farmed a plot of land on their own in family groups. But sharecropping later proved to be a disaster for all concerned. When the Democrats returned to power, they often changed the lien laws to favor landlords; when crop prices were low, landlords received their payment first, even if there was no money left over for the laborer. And in a discriminatory society whites had many opportunities to cheat sharecroppers. Owners and merchants frequently underpaid or overcharged them and manipulated records so that they were always in debt (see page 498).

The fundamental problem, however, was that southern farmers were concentrating on cotton, a crop with a bright past and a dim future. During the Civil War, India, Brazil, and Egypt had begun to supply cotton to Britain, and this loss of markets reduced per capita income, as did a decline in the amount of labor invested by the average southern farmer. In freedom, black women, like their white counterparts, often stayed away from the fields. Black families placed greater value on human dignity than on the reaching the levels of production that they had achieved under the lash. By 1878, the South had recovered its prewar share of British cotton purchases. But even as southerners grew more cotton, eventually surpassing prewar totals, their reward diminished. Cotton prices began a long decline whose causes by chance coincided with the Civil War. From 1820 to 1860, world demand for cotton had grown at a rate of 5 percent per year, but from 1866 to 1895 the rate of growth slowed to only 1.3 percent per year. By 1860 the English textile industry, the world leader in production, had penetrated all the major new markets, and from that point on increases in demand were slight. As a result, when southern farmers planted more cotton, they tended to depress the price.

Over-dependence on Cotton

In these circumstances overspecialization in cotton was a mistake, but for most southern farmers there was no alternative. Landowners required sharecroppers to grow the prime cash crop, whose salability was certain. Because of the shortage of banks and credit in the South, white farmers often had to borrow from a local merchant, who insisted on cotton production to secure his loan. Thus southern agriculture slipped deeper and deeper into depression. Black sharecroppers struggled under a growing burden of debt that reduced their independence and bound them to landowners almost as oppressively as slavery had bound them to their masters. Many white farmers became debtors, too, and gradually lost their land. These were serious problems, but few people in the North were paying attention.

Reconstruction's Decline and Fall

Northerners had always been far more interested in suppressing rebellion than in aiding southern blacks, and by the early 1870s the North's partial commitment to bringing about change in the South was weakening. Criticism of the southern governments grew, new issues captured people's attention, and soon voters began to look favorably on reconciliation with southern whites. In one southern state after another, Democrats regained control, and they threatened to defeat Republicans in the North as well. Before long the situation had returned to "normal" in the eyes of southern whites.

Antagonism between Unionists and rebels was still very strong in 1868. That year Ulysses S. Grant, running as a Republican, defeated Horatio Seymour, a New York Democrat, for president. Grant was not a Radical, but his platform supported congressional Reconstruction and endorsed black suffrage in the South. (Significantly, Republicans stopped short of endorsing it in the North.) The Democrats, meanwhile, vigorously denounced Reconstruction and thus renewed the sectional conflict. By associating themselves with rebellion and with Johnson's repudiated program, the Democrats went down to defeat in all but eight states, though the popular vote was fairly close.

Election of 1868

In office Grant acted as an administrator of Reconstruction but not as its enthusiastic advocate. He vacillated in his dealings with the southern states, sometimes defending Republican regimes and sometimes currying favor with Democrats. On occasion Grant called out federal troops to stop violence or enforce acts of Congress, but only when he had to do so. Neither Andrew Johnson nor he imposed anything approaching a military occupation on the South. Rapid demobilization had reduced a federal army of more than 1 million to 57,000 within a year of the surrender at Appomattox. Thereafter the number of troops in the South continued to fall, until in 1874 there were only 4,000 in the southern states outside Texas. Throughout Reconstruction, the strongest federal units were in Texas and the West, fighting Indians, not white southerners.

In 1870 and 1871 the violent campaigns of the Ku Klux Klan forced Congress to pass two Enforcement Acts and an anti-Klan law. These laws made actions by *individuals* against the civil and political rights of others a federal criminal offense for the first time. They also provided for election supervisors and permitted martial law and suspension of the writ of habeas corpus to combat murders, beatings, and threats by the Klan. Federal prosecutors used the laws rather selectively. In 1872 and 1873 Mississippi and the Carolinas saw many prosecutions; but in other states where violence flourished, the laws were virtually ignored. (Meanwhile, the Republican Party vigorously used the laws in northern cities to combat Democratic election fraud.) Southern juries sometimes refused to convict Klansmen; out of a total of 3,310 cases, only 1,143 ended in convictions. Though many Klansmen (roughly two thousand in South Carolina alone) fled their states to avoid prosecution, and the Klan officially disbanded, the threat of violence did not end. Paramilitary organizations known as Rifle Clubs and Red Shirts often took the Klan's place.

Klan terrorism defied Congress in an especially clear-cut way, yet even on this issue there were ominous signs that the North's commitment to racial justice was fading. Some conservative but influential Republicans opposed the anti-Klan laws. Rejecting other Republicans' arguments that the Thirteenth, Fourteenth, and Fifteenth Amendments had made the federal government the protector of the rights of citizens, these dissenters echoed an old Democratic charge that Congress was infringing on states' rights. Senator Lyman Trumbull of Illinois declared that the states remained "the depositories of the rights of the individual." If Congress could punish

crimes like assault or murder, he asked, "what is the need of the State governments?" For years Democrats had complained of "centralization and consolidation"; now some Republicans seemed to agree with them. This opposition foreshadowed a more general revolt within Republican ranks in 1872.

Disenchanted with Reconstruction, a group calling itself the Liberal Republicans bolted the party in 1872 and nominated Horace Greeley, the well-known editor of the *New York Tribune*, for president. The Liberal Republicans were a varied group, including civil service reformers, foes of corruption, and advocates of a lower tariff. Normally such disparate elements would not cooperate with each other, but two popular and widespread attitudes united them: distaste for federal intervention in the South and a desire to let market forces and the "best men" determine events there.

Liberal Republicans Revolt

The Democrats also gave their nomination to Greeley in 1872. The combination was not enough to defeat Grant, who won reelection, but it reinforced Grant's desire to avoid confrontation with white southerners. He continued to use military force sparingly and in 1875 refused a desperate request for troops from the governor of Mississippi.

Dissatisfaction with Grant's administration grew during his second term. Strong-willed but politically naive, Grant made a series of poor appointments. His secretary of war, his private secretary, and officials in the Treasury and Navy Departments were involved in bribery or tax-cheating scandals. Instead of exposing the corruption, Grant defended some of the culprits. In 1874, as Grant's popularity and his party's prestige declined, the Democrats recaptured the House of Representatives. The Republican Party faced more unfavorable publicity in 1875, when several of Grant's appointees were indicted.

The effect of Democratic gains in Congress was to weaken the legislature's resolve on southern issues. Congress had already lifted the political disabilities of the Fourteenth Amendment from many former Confederates. In 1872 it had adopted a sweeping Amnesty Act, which pardoned most of the remaining rebels and left only five hundred barred from political officeholding. In 1875 Congress passed a Civil Rights Act purporting to guarantee black people equal accommodations in public places, such as inns and theaters, but the bill was

Amnesty Act

watered down and contained no effective provisions for enforcement. (The Supreme Court later struck down this law; see page 501.)

Democrats regained power in the South rather quickly, winning control of state government in four states before 1872 and in a total of eight by January 1876 (see map, page 469). In the North Democrats successfully stressed the failure and scandals of Reconstruction governments. As opinion shifted, historian Brooks Adams, the grandson and great-grandson of presidents, published an article condemning the enfranchisement of blacks as "a wholesale creation of the most ignorant mass of voters to be found in the civilized world." Many Republicans sensed that their constituents were tiring of southern issues.

In fact, new concerns were capturing the public's attention. Both industrialization and immigration were surging, hastening the pace of change in national life. Within only eight years, postwar industrial production increased by an impressive 75 percent. For the first time, nonagricultural workers outnumbered farmers, and only Britain's industrial output was greater than that of the United States. Government financial policies did much to bring about this rapid growth. Soon after the war Congress used a portion of tax revenues to pay off the interest-bearing war debt: the debt fell from $2.33 billion in 1866 to only $587 million in 1893, and every dollar repaid was a dollar injected into the economy for potential reinvestment. Approximately 1 percent of the gross national product was pumped back into the economy from 1866 to 1872, and only slightly less than that during the rest of the 1870s. Low taxes on investment and high tariffs on manufactured goods also aided industrialists. With such help, the northern economy quickly recovered its prewar rate of growth.

Between 1865 and 1873 3 million new immigrants entered the country, most of them joining the labor force of industrial cities in the North and West. As the number of immigrants rose, there was a corresponding revival of ingrained suspicion and hostility among native-born Americans. Also prominent was the question of how Utah's growing Mormon community, which practiced polygamy, could be reconciled to American law.

Then the Panic of 1873 ushered in over five years of economic contraction. Three million people lost their jobs, and the clash between labor and capital became the major issue of the day (see Chapter 18). Class attitudes diverged, especially in the large cities. Debtors and the unemployed sought easy money policies to spur economic expansion. Businessmen, disturbed by the strikes and industrial violence that accompanied the panic, became increasingly concerned about the defense of property.

Class conflict fueled a monetary issue: whether paper money—the Civil War greenbacks—should be kept in circulation. In 1872, Democratic farmers and debtors urged this policy to expand the money supply and raise prices, but businessmen, bankers, and creditors overruled them. Now hard times swelled the ranks of the "greenbackers"—voters who favored greenbacks and easy money. Congress voted in 1874 to increase the number of greenbacks in circulation, but Grant vetoed the bill in deference to the opinions of financial leaders. The next year, "sound money" interests prevailed in Congress, winning passage of a law requiring that greenbacks be convertible into gold after 1878. This law limited the inflationary impact of the greenbacks and aided creditors rather than debtors (such as the hard-pressed and angry farmers).

Greenbacks Versus Sound Money

In international affairs, there was renewed pressure for, and controversy about, expansion (see Chapter 22). In 1867 Secretary of State William H. Seward arranged a vast addition of territory to the national domain through the purchase of Alaska from the Russian government for $7.2 million. Opponents ridiculed Seward's venture, calling Alaska Frigidia, the Polar Bear Garden, and Walrussia. But Seward convinced important congressmen of Alaska's economic potential, and other lawmakers favored the dawning of friendship with Russia. Also in 1867, the United States took control of the Midway Islands, a thousand miles from Hawai'i. And in 1870, President Grant tried to annex the Dominican Republic, but Senator Charles Sumner blocked the attempt. Seward and his successor, Hamilton Fish, also resolved troubling Civil War grievances against Great Britain. Through diplomacy they arranged a financial settlement of claims on Britain for damage done by the *Alabama* and other cruisers built in England and sold to the Confederacy (see page 639).

Meanwhile, the Supreme Court was participating in the northern retreat from Reconstruction. During the Civil War the Court, which in 1857 declared that black people could not be citizens, had been cautious and reluctant to assert itself. Reaction to the *Dred Scott* decision (1857) had been so violent, and the Union's wartime emergency so great, that the Court avoided interference with government actions. The justices breathed a collective sigh of relief, for example, when legal technicalities prevented them from reviewing the case of Clement Vallandigham, a Democratic opponent of Lincoln's war effort, who had been convicted by a military tribunal of aiding the enemy. But in 1866 a similar case, *Ex parte Milligan*, reached the Court through proper channels.

Lambdin P. Milligan of Indiana had plotted to free Confederate prisoners of war and overthrow state governments. For these acts a military court sentenced Milligan, a civilian, to death. Milligan challenged the authority of the military tribunal, claiming that he had a right to a civil trial. The Supreme Court declared that military trials were illegal when civil courts were open and functioning, and its language indicated that the Court intended to reassert itself as a major force in national affairs. This case could have led to a direct clash with Congress, which established military districts and military courts in the 1867 Reconstruction Act. But Congress altered part of the Court's jurisdiction, removing such matters from its purview. (Congress was constitutionally empowered to do so but never had taken such action before and has not done so since.)

In the 1870s the Court successfully renewed its challenge to Congress's actions when it narrowed the meaning and effectiveness of the Fourteenth Amendment. The *Slaughter-House* cases (1873) began in 1869, when the Louisiana legislature granted one company a monopoly on the slaughtering of livestock in New Orleans. Rival butchers in the city promptly sued. Their attorney, former Supreme Court justice John A. Campbell, argued that Louisiana had violated the rights of some of its citizens in favor of others. The Fourteenth Amendment, Campbell contended, had revolutionized the constitutional system by bringing individual rights under federal protection. Campbell thus articulated an original goal of the Republican Party: to nationalize civil rights and guard them from state interference. Over the years his argument would win acceptance, sheltering corporate "persons" from government regulation in the nineteenth century and protecting blacks and other minorities in the twentieth.

Supreme Court Decisions on Reconstruction

But in the *Slaughter-House* decision, the Supreme Court dealt a stunning blow to the scope and vitality of the Fourteenth Amendment. Refusing to accept Campbell's argument, it interpreted the "privileges and immunities" of citizens so narrowly that it reduced them almost to trivialities. State citizenship and national citizenship were separate, the Court declared. National citizenship involved only matters such as the right to travel freely from state to state and to use the navigable waters of the nation, and only these narrow rights were protected by the Fourteenth Amendment. With this interpretation, the words "No state shall make or enforce any law which shall abridge the privileges or immunities of citizens of the United States" disappeared, from that day until now, as a meaningful and effective part of the Constitution.

The Supreme Court also concluded that the butchers who sued had not been deprived of their rights or property in violation of the due-process clause of the amendment. Shrinking from a role as "perpetual censor upon all legislation of the States, on the civil rights of their own citizens," the Court's majority declared that the framers of the recent amendments had not intended to "destroy" the federal system, in which the states exercised "powers for domestic and local government, including the regulation of civil rights." Thus the justices dismissed Campbell's central contention and severely limited the amendment's potential for securing and protecting the rights of black citizens.

The next day the Court decided *Bradwell v. Illinois*, a case in which Myra Bradwell, a female attorney, had been denied the right to practice law in Illinois on account of her gender. Pointing to the Fourteenth Amendment, Bradwell's attorneys contended that the state had unconstitutionally abridged her "privileges and immunities" as a citizen. The Supreme Court rejected her claim, alluding to women's traditional role in the home.

In 1876 the Court weakened the Reconstruction-era amendments even further by emasculating the enforcement clause of the Fourteenth Amendment and revealing deficiencies inherent in the Fifteenth Amendment. In *U.S. v. Cruikshank* the Court overruled the conviction under the 1870 Enforcement Act of Louisiana whites who had attacked a meeting of blacks and conspired to deprive them of their rights. The justices ruled that the Fourteenth Amendment did not give the federal government power to act against these whites. The duty of protecting citizens' equal rights "was originally assumed by the States; and it still remains there." As for the protection of "unalienable rights," the Court said that "Sovereignty, for this purpose, rests alone with the States." In *U.S.* v. *Reese* the Court noted that the Fifteenth Amendment did not guarantee a citizen's right to vote but merely listed certain impermissible grounds for denying suffrage. Thus a path lay open for southern states to disfranchise blacks for supposedly nonracial reasons—lack of education or property or descent from a grandfather qualified to vote before the Reconstruction Act of 1867. These "grandfather clauses" became a means to give the vote to illiterate whites while excluding blacks (see page 500).

As the 1876 elections approached, most political observers saw that the North was no longer willing to pursue the goals of Reconstruction. The results

Election of 1876

of a disputed presidential election confirmed this fact. Samuel J. Tilden, the Democratic governor of New York, ran strongly in the South and needed only one more electoral vote to triumph over Rutherford B. Hayes, the Republican nominee. Nineteen votes from Louisiana, South Carolina, and Florida were disputed; both Democrats and Republicans claimed to have won in those states despite fraud committed by their opponents. One vote from Oregon was undecided because of a technicality (see map).

To resolve this unprecedented situation, on which the Constitution gave no guidance, Congress established a fifteen-member electoral commission. In the interest of impartiality, membership on the commission was to be balanced between Democrats and Republicans. But one independent Republican, Supreme Court Justice David Davis, refused appointment in order to accept his election as a senator. A regular Republican took his place, and the Republican Party prevailed 8 to 7 on every decision, along strict party lines. Hayes would become president if Congress accepted the commission's findings.

Congressional acceptance was not certain. Democrats controlled the House and could filibuster to block action on the vote. Many citizens worried that the nation had entered a major constitutional crisis and would slip once again into civil war. The crisis was resolved when Democrats acquiesced in the election of Hayes. Scholars have found evidence of negotiations between Hayes's supporters and southerners who wanted federal aid to railroads, internal

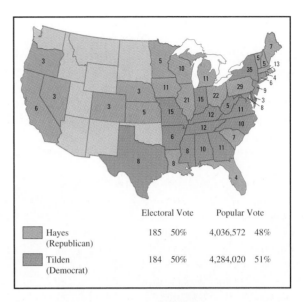

	Electoral Vote		Popular Vote	
Hayes (Republican)	185	50%	4,036,572	48%
Tilden (Democrat)	184	50%	4,284,020	51%

Presidential Election, 1876   *In 1876 a combination of solid southern support and Democratic gains in the North gave Samuel Tilden the majority of popular votes, but Rutherford B. Hayes won the disputed election in the electoral college.*

improvements, federal patronage, and removal of troops from southern states. But studies of Congress conclude that these negotiations did not have a deciding effect on the outcome: neither party was well enough organized to implement and enforce a bargain between the sections. Northern and southern Democrats simply decided they could not win and did not contest the election of a Republican who was not going to continue Reconstruction. Thus Hayes became president, and Reconstruction was unmistakably over.

Southern Democrats rejoiced, but African-Americans grieved over the betrayal of their hopes for equality. Tens of thousands considered leaving the South, where real freedom

Exodusters Move West

was no longer a possibility. "[We asked] whether it was possible we could stay under a people who had held us in bondage," said Henry Adams, who led a migration to Kansas. In South Carolina, Louisiana, Mississippi, and other southern states, thousands gathered up their possessions and migrated to Kansas. They were known as Exodusters, disappointed people still searching for

THE "STRONG" GOVERNMENT 1869–1877.   THE "WEAK" GOVERNMENT 1877–1881.

These cartoons reveal the North's readiness to give up on a strong Reconstruction policy. According to the images on the left, only federal bayonets could support the "rule or ruin" carpetbag regimes that oppressed the South. What do the background and foreground of the cartoon on the right suggest will be the results of President Hayes's "Let 'Em Alone Policy"? Library of Congress.

their share in the American dream. Even in Kansas they met disillusionment, as the welcome extended by the state's governor soon gave way to hostile public reactions.

 Conclusion

The nation ended over fifteen years of bloody Civil War and controversial Reconstruction without establishing full freedom for African-Americans. This contradictory record typified the results of Reconstruction in many other ways. A tumultuous period brought tremendous change, yet many things remained the same. Because extraordinary situations required revolutionary changes, the North acted

strongly for a time. The Union victory brought about an increase in federal power, stronger nationalism, unprecedented federal intervention in the southern states, and landmark amendments to the Constitution. But there was no commitment to make these changes endure, so the revolution remained partial.

The North embraced emancipation, black suffrage, and constitutional amendments strengthening the central government. But it did so to defeat the rebellion, secure the peace, and prevent rebellion from reemerging. As the pressure of these crises declined, strong underlying continuities emerged and placed their mark on Reconstruction. The American people and the courts maintained a preference for state authority and a distrust of federal power. The ideology of free labor dictated that property should be respected and that individuals should take care of themselves without much help from government. Racism endured, and the black minority struggled to gain the attention of the white majority. Concern for the human rights of African-Americans was strongest when their plight threatened to undermine the interests of whites, and reform frequently had less appeal than moneymaking in a diverse, individualistic, and enterprising society. Thus the status of African-Americans would continue to be a major social and political issue.

A host of other issues would arise from industrialization. How would the country develop its immense resources in a growing and increasingly interconnected national economy? How would farmers, industrial workers, immigrants, and capitalists fit into the new social system? Industrialization promised not just a higher standard of living but also a different lifestyle in both urban and rural areas. Moreover, industry increased the nation's power and laid the foundation for an enlarged American role in international affairs. Americans' thoughts again turned to expansion and the conquest of new frontiers. As the United States entered its second hundred years of existence, it confronted these challenging issues. The experiences of the 1860s and 1870s suggested that solutions, if any, might be neither clear nor complete.

Suggestions for Further Reading

National Policy, Politics, and Constitutional Law

Richard H. Abbott, *The Republican Party and the South, 1855–1877* (1986); Herman Belz, *Emancipation and Equal Rights* (1978); Herman Belz, *A New Birth of Freedom* (1976); Michael Les Benedict, *A Compromise of Principle: Congressional Republicans and Reconstruction, 1863–1869* (1974); Michael Les Benedict, *The Impeachment and Trial of Andrew Johnson* (1973); Charles S. Campbell, *The Transformation of American Foreign Relations, 1865–1900* (1976); Adrian Cook, *The Alabama Claims* (1975); Michael Kent Curtis, *No State Shall Abridge* (1987); David Donald, *Charles Sumner and the Rights of Man* (1970); Harold M. Hyman, *A More Perfect Union* (1973); Ronald J. Jensen, *The Alaska Purchase and Russian-American Relations* (1975); William S. McFeely, *Grant* (1981); William S. McFeely, *Yankee Stepfather: General O. O. Howard and the Freedmen* (1968); Eric L. McKitrick, *Andrew Johnson and Reconstruction* (1966); James M. McPherson, *The Abolitionist Legacy* (1975); Brooks D. Simpson, *Let Us Have Peace* (1991); Kenneth M. Stampp, *The Era of Reconstruction* (1965); Hans L. Trefousse, *Andrew Johnson* (1989).

The Freed Slaves

Roberta Sue Alexander, *North Carolina Faces the Freedmen* (1985); Ira Berlin, ed., *Freedom: A Documentary History of Emancipation,* *1861–1867* (1984); Elizabeth R. Bethel, *Promiseland* (1981); Orville Vernon Burton, *In My Father's House Are Many Mansions* (1985); Edmund L. Drago, *Black Politicians and Reconstruction in Georgia* (1982); Paul D. Escott, *Slavery Remembered* (1979); Eric Foner, "Reconstruction and the Crisis of Free Labor," in *Politics and Ideology in the Age of the Civil War,* ed. Eric Foner (1980); Gerald Jaynes, *Branches Without Roots: The Genesis of the Black Working Class in the American South, 1862–1882* (1986); Leon Litwack, *Been in the Storm So Long* (1979); Edward Magdol, *A Right to the Land* (1977); Robert Morris, *Reading, 'Riting and Reconstruction* (1981); Howard Rabinowitz, ed., *Southern Black Leaders in Reconstruction* (1982); Emma Lou Thornbrough, ed., *Black Reconstructionists* (1972); Okon Uya, *From Slavery to Public Service* (1971); Clarence Walker, *A Rock in a Weary Land* (1982).

Politics and Reconstruction in the South

Robert W. Coakley, *The Role of Federal Military Forces in Domestic Disorders, 1789–1878* (1988); Richard N. Current, *Those Terrible Carpetbaggers* (1988); Jonathan Daniels, *Prince of Carpetbaggers* (1958); W. E. B. Du Bois, *Black Reconstruction* (1935); Paul D. Escott, *Many Excellent People: Power and Privilege in North Carolina, 1850–1900* (1985); W. McKee Evans, *Ballots and Fence Rails: Reconstruction on the Lower Cape Fear* (1966); Michael W. Fitzgerald, *The Union League Movement in the Deep South* (1989); Eric Foner, *Reconstruction: America's Unfinished Revolution, 1863–1877* (1988); Eric Foner, *Nothing but Freedom* (1983); William C. Harris, *The Day of the Carpetbagger* (1979); Thomas Holt, *Black over White: Negro Political Leadership in South Carolina During Reconstruction* (1977); J. Morgan Kousser and James M. McPherson, eds., *Region, Race and Reconstruction* (1982); Elizabeth Studley Nathans, *Losing the Peace* (1968); Michael Perman, *The Road to Redemption* (1984); Michael Perman, *Reunion Without Compromise* (1973); Lawrence N. Powell, *New Masters* (1980); George C. Rable, *But There Was No Peace* (1984); James Roark, *Masters Without Slaves* (1977); James Sefton, *The United States Army and Reconstruction, 1865–1877* (1967); Mark W. Summers, *Railroads, Reconstruction, and the Gospel of Prosperity* (1984); Allen Trelease, *White Terror* (1967); Ted Tunnell, *Carpetbagger from Vermont* (1989); Ted Tunnell, *Crucible of Reconstruction* (1984); Michael Wayne, *The Reshaping of Plantation Society* (1983); Sarah Woolfolk Wiggins, *The Scalawag in Alabama Politics, 1865–1881* (1977).

Women, Family, and Social History

Virginia I. Burr, ed., *The Secret Eye* (1990); Ellen Carol Dubois, *Feminism and Suffrage* (1978); Herbert G. Gutman, *The Black Family in Slavery and Freedom, 1750–1925* (1976); Elizabeth Jacoway, *Yankee Missionaries in the South* (1979); Jacqueline Jones, *Labor of Love, Labor of Sorrow* (1985); Jacqueline Jones, *Soldiers of Light and Love* (1980); Robert C. Kenzer, *Kinship and Neighborhood in a Southern Community* (1987); Mary P. Ryan, *Women in Public* (1990); Rebecca Scott, "The Battle over the Child," *Prologue* 10 (Summer 1978): 101–113.

The End of Reconstruction

Michael Les Benedict, "Southern Democrats in the Crisis of 1876–1877," *Journal of Southern History* 66 (November 1980): 489–524; William Gillette, *Retreat from Reconstruction, 1869–1879*

(1980); William Gillette, *The Right to Vote* (1969); Keith Ian Polakoff, *The Politics of Inertia* (1973); John G. Sproat, *"The Best Men": Liberal Reformers in the Gilded Age* (1968); C. Vann Woodward, *Reunion and Reaction* (1951).

Reconstruction's Legacy for the South

Robert G. Athearn, *In Search of Canaan* (1978); Edward L. Ayers, *The Promise of the New South* (1992); Norman L. Crockett, *The Black Towns* (1979); Stephen J. DeCanio, *Agriculture in the Postbellum South* (1974); Steven Hahn, *The Roots of Southern Populism* (1983); Jay R. Mandle, *The Roots of Black Poverty* (1978); Nell Irvin Painter, *Exodusters* (1976); Howard Rabinowitz, *Race Relations in the Urban South, 1865–1890* (1978); Roger L. Ransom and Richard Sutch, *One Kind of Freedom* (1977); Laurence Shore, *Southern Capitalists* (1986); Peter Wallenstein, *From Slave South to New South* (1987); Jonathan M. Wiener, *Social Origins of the New South* (1978); C. Vann Woodward, *Origins of the New South* (1951).

Historical Reference Books by Subject:
Encyclopedias, Dictionaries, Atlases, Chronologies, and Statistics

American History: General

Gorton Carruth, ed., *The Encyclopedia of American Facts and Dates* (1993); *Dictionary of American History* (1976) and Joan Hoff and Robert H. Ferrell, eds., *Supplement* (1996); Eric Foner and John A. Garraty, eds., *The Reader's Companion to American History* (1991); Bernard Grun, *The Timetables of History* (1991); *International Encyclopedia of the Social Sciences* (1968–); Richard B. Morris and Jeffrey B. Morris, eds., *Encyclopedia of American History* (1996); Harry Ritter, *Dictionary of Concepts in History* (1986); Arthur M. Schlesinger, Jr., ed., *The Almanac of American History* (1983); Lawrence Urdang, ed., *The Timetables of American History* (1996); U.S. Bureau of the Census, *Historical Statistics of the United States* (1975).

American History: General, Twentieth Century

John D. Buenker and Edward R. Kantowicz, eds., *Historical Dictionary of the Progressive Era, 1890–1920* (1988); Robert H. Ferrell and John S. Bowman, eds., *The Twentieth Century: An Almanac* (1984); George H. Gallup, *The Gallup Poll: Public Opinion, 1935–1971* (1972), *1972–1977* (1978), and annual reports (1979–); Stanley Hochman and Eleanor Hochman, *A Dictionary of Contemporary American History* (1993); Stanley I. Kutler, ed., *Encyclopedia of the United States in the Twentieth Century* (1995); Peter B. Levy, *Encyclopedia of the Reagan-Bush Years* (1996); James S. Olson, *Historical Dictionary of the 1920s* (1988); Thomas Parker and Douglas Nelson, *Day by Day: The Sixties* (1983).

American History: General Atlases and Gazetteers

Geoffrey Barraclough, ed., *The Times Atlas of World History* (1994); Rodger Doyle, *Atlas of Contemporary America* (1994); Robert H. Ferrell and Richard Natkiel, *Atlas of American History* (1987); Edward W. Fox, *Atlas of American History* (1964); Archie Hobson, *The Cambridge Gazetteer of the United States and Canada* (1996); Eric Homberger, *The Penguin Historical Atlas of North America* (1995); Kenneth T. Jackson and James T. Adams, *Atlas of American History*

(1978); Catherine M. Mattson and Mark T. Mattson, *Contemporary Atlas of the United States* (1990); National Geographic Society, *Historical Atlas of the United States* (1994); U.S. Department of the Interior, *National Atlas of the United States* (1970). Other atlases are listed under specific categories.

American History: General Biographies

Lucian Boia, ed., *Great Historians of the Modern Age* (1991); John S. Bowman, *The Cambridge Dictionary of American Biography* (1995); *Current Biography* (1940–); *Dictionary of American Biography* (1928–); John Garraty and Jerome L. Sternstein, eds., *The Encyclopedia of American Biography* (1996); *National Cyclopedia of American Biography* (1898–). Other biographical works appear under specific categories.

African Americans

Molefi Asante and Mark T. Mattson, *Historical and Cultural Atlas of African-Americans* (1991); John N. Ingham, *African-American Business Leaders* (1993); Bruce Kellner, *The Harlem Renaissance* (1984); Rayford W. Logan and Michael R. Winston, eds., *The Dictionary of American Negro Biography* (1983); W. A. Low and Virgil A. Clift, eds., *Encyclopedia of Black America* (1981); Sharon Harley, *The Timetables of African-American History* (1995); Darlene C. Hine et al., eds., *Black Women in White America* (1994); Charles D. Lowery and John F. Marszalek, eds., *Encyclopedia of African-American Civil Rights* (1992); Randall M. Miller and John D. Smith, eds., *Dictionary of Afro-American Slavery* (1997); Larry G. Murphy et al., eds., *Encyclopedia of African American Religions* (1993); Harry A. Ploski and James Williams, eds., *The Negro Almanac* (1989); Dorothy C. Salem, ed., *African American Women* (1993).

American Revolution and Colonies

Richard Blanco and Paul Sanborn, eds., *The American Revolution* (1993); Lester J. Cappon, ed., *Atlas of Early*

American History: The Revolutionary Era, 1760–1790 (1976); Jacob E. Cooke, ed., *Encyclopedia of the American Colonies* (1993); John M. Faragher, ed., *The Encyclopedia of Colonial and Revolutionary America* (1990); Jack P. Greene and J. R. Pole, eds., *The Blackwell Encyclopedia of the American Revolution* (1991); Douglas W. Marshall and Howard H. Peckham, *Campaigns of the American Revolution* (1976); Gregory Palmer, ed., *Biographical Sketches of Loyalists of the American Revolution* (1984); John W. Raimo, ed., *Biographical Directory of American Colonial and Revolutionary Governors, 1607–1789* (1980); *Rand-McNally Atlas of the American Revolution* (1974); Seymour I. Schwartz, *The French and Indian War, 1754–1763* (1995).

Architecture

William D. Hunt, Jr., ed., *Encyclopedia of American Architecture* (1980).

Business and the Economy

Christine Ammer and Dean S. Ammer, *Dictionary of Business and Economics* (1983); Douglas Auld and Graham Bannock, *The American Dictionary of Economics* (1983); Michael J. Freeman, *Atlas of World Economy* (1991); Douglas Greenwald, *Encyclopedia of Economics* (1982); John N. Ingham, *Biographical Dictionary of American Business Leaders* (1983); John N. Ingham and Lynne B. Feldman, *Contemporary American Business Leaders* (1990); William H. Mulligan, Jr., ed., *A Historical Dictionary of American Industrial Language* (1988); Glenn G. Munn, *Encyclopedia of Banking and Finance* (1973); Glenn Porter, *Encyclopedia of American Economic History* (1980); Richard Robinson, *United States Business History, 1602–1988* (1990). See also "African Americans" and "Transportation."

Cities and Towns

Charles Abrams, *The Language of Cities: A Glossary of Terms* (1971); John L. Androit, ed., *Township Atlas of the United States* (1979); Melvin G. Holli and Peter d'A. Jones, eds., *Biographical Dictionary of American Mayors, 1820–1980: Big City Mayors* (1981); Kenneth T. Jackson, ed., *Encyclopedia of New York City* (1995); Ory M. Nergal, ed., *The Encyclopedia of American Cities* (1980); David D. Van Tassel and John J. Grabowski, eds., *The Dictionary of Cleveland Biography* (1996); David D. Van Tassel and John J. Grabowski, eds., *The Encyclopedia of Cleveland History* (1987). See also "Politics and Government."

Civil War and Reconstruction

Mark M. Boatner III, *The Civil War Dictionary* (1988); Richard N. Current, ed., *Encyclopedia of the Confederacy* (1993); John T. Hubbell and James W. Geary, eds., *Biographical Dictionary of the Union* (1995); Kenneth C. Martis, *The Historical Atlas of the Congresses of the Confederate States of America: 1861–1865* (1994); James M. McPherson, ed., *The Atlas of the Civil War* (1994); Mark E.

Neely, Jr., *The Abraham Lincoln Encyclopedia* (1982); Craig L. Symonds, *A Battlefield Atlas of the Civil War* (1983); Hans L. Trefousse, *Historical Dictionary of Reconstruction* (1991); U.S. War Department, *The Official Atlas of the Civil War* (1958); Jon L. Wakelyn, ed., *Biographical Dictionary of the Confederacy* (1977); Ezra J. Warner and W. Buck Yearns, *Biographical Register of the Confederate Congress* (1975); Steven E. Woodworth, ed., *The American Civil War* (1996). See also "South" and "Politics and Government."

Constitution, Supreme Court, and Judiciary

Congressional Quarterly, *The Supreme Court A to Z* (1994); Kermit L. Hall, ed., *The Oxford Companion to the Supreme Court of the United States* (1992); Richard F. Hixson, *Mass Media and the Constitution* (1989); Robert J. Janosik, ed., *Encyclopedia of the American Judicial System* (1987); John W. Johnson, ed., *Historic U.S. Court Cases, 1690–1990* (1992); Arthur S. Leonard, ed., *Sexuality and the Law* (1993); Leonard W. Levy et al., eds., *Encyclopedia of the American Constitution* (1986); Fred R. Shapiro, *The Oxford Dictionary of American Legal Quotations* (1993); Melvin I. Urofsky, ed., *The Supreme Court Justices* (1994). See also "Politics and Government."

Crime, Violence, Police, and Prisons

William G. Bailey, *Encyclopedia of Police Science* (1994); Sanford H. Kadish, ed., *Encyclopedia of Crime and Justice* (1983); Marilyn D. McShane and Frank P. Williams III, eds., *Encyclopedia of American Prisons* (1995); Michael Newton and Judy Ann Newton, *The FBI Most Wanted* (1989); Michael Newton and Judy Ann Newton, *Racial and Religious Violence in America* (1991); Michael Newton and Judy Newton, *The Ku Klux Klan* (1990); Carl Sifakis, *Encyclopedia of Assassinations* (1990); Carl Sifakis, *The Encyclopedia of American Crime* (1982).

Culture and Folklore

Hennig Cohen and Tristam Potter Coffin, eds., *The Folklore of American Holidays* (1987); Richard M. Dorson, ed., *Handbook of American Folklore* (1983); Robert L. Gale, *A Cultural Encyclopedia of the 1850s in America* (1993); Robert L. Gale, *The Gay Nineties in America* (1992); M. Thomas Inge, ed., *Handbook of American Popular Culture* (1979–1981); Wolfgang Mieder et al., eds., *A Dictionary of American Proverbs* (1992); J. F. Rooney, Jr., et al., eds., *This Remarkable Continent: An Atlas of United States and Canadian Society and Cultures* (1982); Jane Stern and Michael Stern, *Encyclopedia of Pop Culture* (1992); Justin Wintle, ed., *Makers of Nineteenth Century Culture, 1800–1914* (1982). See also "Entertainment," "Mass Media and Journalism," "Music," and "Sports."

Education and Libraries

Lee C. Deighton, ed., *The Encyclopedia of Education* (1971); Joseph C. Kiger, ed., *Research Institutions and Learned*

Societies (1982); John F. Ohles, ed., *Biographical Dictionary of American Educators* (1978); Wayne A. Wiegard and Donald E. Davis, Jr., eds., *Encyclopedia of Library History* (1994).

Entertainment

Tim Brooks and Earle Marsh, *The Complete Directory to Prime Time Network and Cable TV Shows, 1946–Present* (1995); Barbara N. Cohen-Stratyner, *Biographical Dictionary of Dance* (1982); John Dunning, *Tune in Yesterday* (radio) (1967); Larry Langman and Edgar Borg, *Encyclopedia of American War Films* (1989); Larry Langman and David Ebner, *Encyclopedia of American Spy Films* (1990); *Notable Names in the American Theater* (1976); *New York Times Encyclopedia of Television* (1977); Andrew Sarris, *The American Cinema: Directors and Directions, 1929–1968* (1968); Anthony Slide, *The American Film Industry* (1986); Anthony Slide, *The Encyclopedia of Vaudeville* (1994); Evelyn M. Truitt, *Who Was Who on Screen* (1977); Don B. Wilmeth and Tice L. Miller, eds., *The Cambridge Guide to American Theatre* (1993). See also "Culture and Folklore," "Mass Media and Journalism," "Music," and "Sports."

Environment and Conservation

André R. Cooper, ed., *Cooper's Comprehensive Environmental Desk Reference* (1996); Forest History Society, *Encyclopedia of American Forest and Conservation History* (1983); Irene Franck and David Brownstone, *The Green Encyclopedia* (1992); Robert J. Mason and Mark T. Mattson, *Atlas of United States Environmental Issues* (1990); Robert Paehlke, ed., *Conservation and Environmentalism* (1995); World Resources Institute, *Environmental Almanac* (1992).

Exploration: From Columbus to Space

Silvio A. Bedini, ed., *The Christopher Columbus Encyclopedia* (1992); Michael Cassutt, *Who's Who in Space* (1987); W. P. Cumming et al., *The Discovery of North America* (1972); William Goetzmann and Glyndwr Williams, *The Atlas of North American Exploration* (1992); Clive Holland, *Arctic Exploration and Development* (1993); Adrian Johnson, *America Explored* (1974); Kenneth Nebenzahl, *Atlas of Columbus and the Great Discoveries* (1990). See also "Science and Technology."

Foreign Relations

Thomas S. Arms, *Encyclopedia of the Cold War* (1994); Gerard Chaliand and Jean-Pierre Rageau, *Strategic Atlas* (1990); Alexander DeConde, ed., *Encyclopedia of American Foreign Policy* (1978); Margaret B. Denning and J. K. Sweeney, *Handbook of American Diplomacy* (1992); Graham Evans and Jeffrey Newnham, eds., *The Dictionary of World Politics* (1990); John E. Findling, *Dictionary of American Diplomatic History* (1989); Chas. W. Freeman, Jr., *The Diplomat's Dictionary* (1997); Michael Kidron and Ronald Segal, *The State of the World Atlas* (1995); Bruce W.

Jentleson and Thomas G. Paterson, eds., *Encyclopedia of U.S. Foreign Relations* (1997); Warren F. Kuehl, ed., *Biographical Dictionary of Internationalists* (1983); Edward Lawson, *Encyclopedia of Human Rights* (1991); Jack C. Plano and Roy Olton, eds., *The International Relations Dictionary* (1988); Bruce W. Watson et al., eds., *United States Intelligence: An Encyclopedia* (1990). See also "Peace Movements and Pacifism," "Politics and Government," "Military and Wars," and specific wars.

Immigration and Ethnic Groups

James P. Allen and Eugene J. Turner, *We the People: An Atlas of America's Ethnic Diversity* (1988); Gerald Chaliand and Jean-Pierre Rageau, *The Penguin Atlas of Diasporas* (1995); Francesco Cordasco, ed., *Dictionary of American Immigration History* (1990); Nicolás Kanellos, ed., *The Hispanic-American Almanac* (1993); Hyung-Chan Kim, ed., *Dictionary of Asian American History* (1986); Judy B. Litoff and Judith McDonnell, eds., *European Immigrant Women in the United States* (1994); Matt S. Meier, *Mexican American Biographies* (1988); Matt S. Meier and Feliciano Rivera, *Dictionary of Mexican American History* (1981); Sally M. Miller, ed., *The Ethnic Press in the United States* (1987); Stephan Thernstrom, ed., *Harvard Encyclopedia of American Ethnic Groups* (1980). See also "Jewish-Americans."

Jewish-Americans

American Jewish Yearbook (1899–); Jack Fischel and Sanford Pinsker, eds., *Jewish-American History and Culture* (1992); Geoffrey Wigoder, *Dictionary of Jewish Biography* (1991). See also "Immigration and Ethnic Groups."

Labor

Ronald L. Filippelli, *Labor Conflict in the United States* (1990); Gary M. Fink, ed., *Biographical Dictionary of American Labor* (1984); Gary M. Fink, ed., *Labor Unions* (1977); Philip S. Foner, *First Facts of American Labor* (1984).

Literature

James T. Callow and Robert J. Reilly, *Guide to American Literature* (1976–1977); *Dictionary of Literary Biography* (1978–); Eugene Ehrlich and Gorton Carruth, *The Oxford Illustrated Literary Guide to the United States* (1982); Jon Tuska and Vicki Piekarski, *Encyclopedia of Frontier and Western Fiction* (1983). See also "Culture and Folklore," "The South," and "Women."

Mass Media and Journalism

Robert V. Hudson, *Mass Media* (1987); Joseph P. McKerns, ed., *Biographical Dictionary of American Journalism* (1989); William H. Taft, ed., *Encyclopedia of Twentieth-Century Journalists* (1986). See also "Constitution, Supreme Court, and Judiciary," "Entertainment," and "Immigration and Ethnic Groups."

Medicine and Nursing

Rima D. Apple, ed., *Women, Health, and Medicine in America* (1990); Vern L. Bullough et al., eds., *American Nursing: A Biographical Dictionary* (1988); Martin Kaufman et al., eds., *Dictionary of American Nursing Biography* (1988); Martin Kaufman et al., eds., *Dictionary of American Medical Biography* (1984); George L. Maddox, ed., *The Encyclopedia of Aging* (1987).

Military and Wars

William M. Arkin et al., *Encyclopedia of the U.S. Military* (1990); Charles D. Bright, ed., *Historical Dictionary of the U.S. Air Force* (1992); Andre Corvisier, ed., *A Dictionary of Military History* (1994); R. Ernest Dupuy and Trevor N. Dupuy, *The Harper Encyclopedia of Military History* (1993); John E. Jessup, ed., *Encyclopedia of the American Military* (1994); Stanley I. Kutler, ed., *Encyclopedia of the Vietnam War* (1996); Kenneth Macksey and William Woodhouse, *The Penguin Encyclopedia of Modern Warfare* (1992); Franklin D. Margiotta, ed., *Brassey's Encyclopedia of Naval Forces and Warfare* (1996); James I. Matray, ed., *Historical Dictionary of the Korean War* (1991); Trevor Royle, *A Dictionary of Military Quotations* (1990); Stanley Sandler, ed., *The Korean War* (1995); Roger J. Spiller and Joseph G. Dawson III, eds., *Dictionary of American Military Biography* (1984); Jerry K. Sweeney, ed., *A Handbook of American Military History* (1996); Peter G. Tsouras et al., *The United States Army* (1991); U.S. Military Academy, *The West Point Atlas of American Wars, 1689–1953* (1959); Bruce W. Watson et al., eds., *United States Intelligence* (1990); *Webster's American Military Biographies* (1978); Bruce W. Watson and Susan M. Watson, *The United States Air Force* (1992); Bruce W. Watson and Susan M. Watson, *The United States Navy* (1991). See also "American Revolution and Colonies," "Civil War and Reconstruction," "Vietnam War," and "World War II."

Music

John Chilton, *Who's Who of Jazz* (1972); Donald Clarke, ed., *The Penguin Encyclopedia of Popular Music* (1989); Edward Jablonski, *The Encyclopedia of American Music* (1981); Roger Lax and Frederick Smith, *The Great Song Thesaurus* (1984); Philip D. Morehead, *The New International Dictionary of Music* (1993); Austin Sonnier, Jr., *A Guide to the Blues* (1994). See also "Culture and Folklore" and "Entertainment."

Native Americans and Indian Affairs

Gretchen M. Bataille, ed., *Native American Women* (1992); Michael Coe et al., *Atlas of Ancient America* (1986); Mary B. Davis, ed., *Native America in the Twentieth Century* (1994); Frederick J. Dockstader, *Great North American Indians* (1977); *Handbook of North American Indians* (1978–); Sam D. Gill and Irene F. Sullivan, *Dictionary of Native American Mythology* (1992); J. Norman Heard et al., *Handbook of the American Frontier: Four Centuries of Indian-White Relationships* (1987–); Barry Klein, ed., *Reference Encyclopedia of the American Indian* (1993); Francis P. Prucha, *Atlas of American Indian Affairs* (1990); Paul Stuart, *Nation Within a Nation: Historical Statistics of American Indians* (1987); Helen H. Tanner, ed., *Atlas of Great Lakes Indian History* (1987); Carl Waldman, *Encyclopedia of Native American Tribes* (1988); Carl Waldman, *Atlas of the North American Indian* (1985).

The New Deal and Franklin D. Roosevelt

Otis L. Graham, Jr., and Meghan R. Wander, eds., *Franklin D. Roosevelt: His Life and Times* (1985); James S. Olson, ed., *Historical Dictionary of the New Deal* (1985). See also "Politics and Government."

Peace Movements and Pacifism

Harold Josephson et al., eds., *Biographical Dictionary of Modern Peace Leaders* (1985); Ervin Laszlo and Jong Y. Yoo, eds., *World Encyclopedia of Peace* (1986); Robert S. Meyer, *Peace Organizations Past and Present* (1988); Nancy L. Roberts, *American Peace Writers, Editors, and Periodicals* (1991). See also "Military and Wars" and specific wars.

Politics and Government: General

Erik W. Austin and Jerome M. Clubb, *Political Facts of the United States Since 1789* (1986); *The Columbia Dictionary of Political Biography* (1991); Jack P. Greene, ed., *Encyclopedia of American Political History* (1984); Leon Hurwitz, *Historical Dictionary of Censorship in the United States* (1985); Earl R. Kruschke, *Encyclopedia of Third Parties in the United States* (1991); Edwin V. Mitchell, *An Encyclopedia of American Politics* (1968); Philip Rees, *Biographical Dictionary of the Extreme Right Since 1890* (1991); Charles R. Ritter et al., *American Legislative Leaders, 1850–1910* (1989); William Safire, *Safire's Political Dictionary* (1978); Edward L. Schapsmeier and Frederick H. Schapsmeier, eds., *Political Parties and Civic Action Groups* (1981); Robert Scruton, *A Dictionary of Political Thought* (1982); Jay M. Shafritz, *The HarperCollins Dictionary of American Government and Politics* (1992). See also "Cities and Towns," "Constitution, Supreme Court, and Judiciary," "States," and the following sections.

Politics and Government: Congress

Donald C. Brown et al., eds., *The Encyclopedia of the United States Congress* (1995); Stephen G. Christianson, *Facts About the Congress* (1996); Congressional Quarterly, *Biographical Directory of the American Congress, 1774–1996* (1997); Congressional Quarterly, *Congress and the Nation, 1945–1984* (1965–1985); Kenneth C. Martis, *Historical Atlas of Political Parties in the United States Congress, 1789–1989* (1989); Kenneth C. Martis, *Historical Atlas of United States Congressional Districts, 1789–1983* (1982); Joel H. Silbey, ed., *Encyclopedia of the American Legislative System* (1994).

Politics and Government: Election Statistics

Congressional Quarterly, *Guide to U.S. Elections* (1975); L. Sandy Maisel, ed., *Political Parties and Elections in the United States* (1991); Richard M. Scammon et al., eds., *America Votes* (1956–); Harold W. Stanley and Richard G. Niemi, *Vital Statistics on American Politics* (1990); G. Scott Thomas, *The Pursuit of the White House: A Handbook of Presidential Election Statistics and History* (1987).

Politics and Government: Presidency and Executive Branch

Henry F. Graff, *The Presidents* (1996); Bernard S. Katz and C. Daniel Vencill, eds., *Biographical Dictionary of the United States Secretaries of the Treasury, 1789–1995* (1996); Richard S. Kirkendall, ed., *The Harry S Truman Encyclopedia* (1989); Leonard W. Levy and Louis Fisher, eds., *Encyclopedia of the American Presidency* (1993); Merrill D. Peterson, ed., *Thomas Jefferson: A Reference Biography* (1986); Robert A. Rutland, ed., *James Madison and the American Nation* (1994); Robert Sobel, ed., *Biographical Directory of the United States Executive Branch, 1774–1977* (1977). See other categories for various presidents.

Politics and Government: Radicalism and the Left

Mari Jo Buhle et al., eds., *The American Radical* (1994); Mari Jo Buhle et al., eds., *Encyclopedia of the American Left* (1990); David DeLeon, ed., *Leaders of the 1960s* (1994); Bernard K. Johnpoll and Harvey Klehr, eds., *Biographical Dictionary of the American Left* (1986).

Religion and Cults

Henry Bowden, *Dictionary of American Religious Biography* (1993); S. Kent Brown et al., eds., *Historical Atlas of Mormonism* (1995); John T. Ellis and Robert Trisco, *A Guide to American Catholic History* (1982); Edwin S. Gaustad, *Historical Atlas of Religion in America* (1976); Samuel S. Hill, Jr., ed., *Encyclopedia of Religion in the South* (1984); Bill J. Leonard, *Dictionary of Baptists in America* (1994); Donald Lewis, ed., *A Dictionary of Evangelical Biography* (1995); Charles H. Lippy and Peter W. Williams, eds., *Encyclopedia of the American Religious Experience* (1988); J. Gordon Melton, *The Encyclopedia of American Religions* (1987); J. Gordon Melton, *Biographical Dictionary of American Cult and Sect Leaders* (1986); J. Gordon Melton, *The Encyclopedic Handbook of Cults in America* (1992); Mark A. Noll and Nathan O. Hatch, eds., *Eerdmans Handbook to Christianity in America* (1983); Arthur C. Piepkorn, *Profiles in Belief: The Religious Bodies of the United States and Canada* (1977–1979); Paul J. Weber and W. Landis Jones, *U.S. Religious Interest Groups* (1994). See also "African Americans."

Science and Technology

James W. Cortada, *Historical Dictionary of Data Processing* (1987); Clark A. Elliott, *Biographical Index to American Science: The Seventeenth Century to 1920* (1990); Charles C. Gillispie, ed., *Dictionary of Scientific Biography* (1970–); National Academy of Sciences, *Biographical Memoirs* (1877–); Roy Porter, ed., *The Biographical Dictionary of Scientists* (1994). See also "Exploration."

Social History and Reform

Mary K. Cayton et al., eds., *Encyclopedia of American Social History* (1993); Wayne R. Dynes, ed., *Encyclopedia of Homosexuality* (1990); Louis Filler, *Dictionary of American Social Change* (1982); Louis Filler, *A Dictionary of American Social Reform* (1963); Robert S. Fogarty, *Dictionary of American Communal and Utopian History* (1980); Joseph M. Hawes and Elizabeth I. Nybakken, eds., *American Families* (1991); David Hey, ed., *The Oxford Companion to Local and Family History* (1996); Harold M. Keele and Joseph C. Kiger, eds., *Foundations* (1984); Mark E. Lender, *Dictionary of American Temperance Biography* (1984); Patricia M. Melvin, ed., *American Community Organizations* (1986); Randall M. Miller and Paul A. Cimbala, eds., *American Reform and Reformers* (1996); Roger S. Powers and William B. Vogele, eds., *Protest, Power, and Change* (1996); Alvin J. Schmidt, *Fraternal Organizations* (1980); Peter N. Stearns, ed., *Encyclopedia of Social History* (1993); Walter I. Trattner, *Biographical Dictionary of Social Welfare in America* (1986); Alden Whitman, ed., *American Reformers* (1985). See also "Crime, Violence, Police, and Prisons."

South

Edward L. Ayers and Brad Mittendorf, eds., *The Oxford Book of the American South* (1997); Robert Bain et al., eds., *Southern Writers* (1979); Kenneth Coleman and Charles S. Gurr, eds., *Dictionary of Georgia Biography* (1983); William S. Powell, ed., *Dictionary of North Carolina Biography* (1979–1996); David C. Roller and Robert W. Twyman, eds., *The Encyclopedia of Southern History* (1979); Walter P. Webb et al., eds., *The Handbook of Texas* (1952, 1976); Charles R. Wilson and William Ferris, eds., *Encyclopedia of Southern Culture* (1986). See also "Civil War and Reconstruction," "Politics and Government," and "States."

Sports

Peter C. Bjarkman, ed., *Encyclopedia of Major League Baseball Team Histories* (1991); Ralph Hickok, *The Encyclopedia of North American Sports History* (1991); Zander Hollander, *The NBA's Official Encyclopedia of Pro Basketball* (1981); Frank G. Menke and Suzanne Treat, *The Encyclopedia of Sports* (1977); *The NFL's Official Encyclopedic History of Professional Football* (1977); David L. Porter, *Biographical Dictionary of American Sports: Baseball* (1987), *Basketball and Other Indoor Sports* (1989), *Football* (1987), and *Outdoor Sports* (1988); David L. Porter, ed., *Biographical Dictionary of American Sports: 1989–1992 Supplement* (1992) and *1992–1995 Supplement* (1995); Paul

Soderberg et al., *The Big Book of Halls of Fame in the United States and Canada* (1977); David Wallechinsky, *The Complete Book of the Summer Olympics* (1996); David Wallechinsky, *The Complete Book of the Winter Olympics* (1993). See also "Culture and Folklore."

States

Roy R. Glashan, comp., *American Governors and Gubernatorial Elections, 1775–1978* (1979); John Hoffmann, ed., *A Guide to the History of Illinois* (1991); Joseph E. Kallenback and Jessamine S. Kallenback, *American State Governors, 1776–1976* (1977); Joseph N. Kane et al., eds., *Facts About the States* (1994); John E. Kleber et al., eds., *The Kentucky Encyclopedia* (1992); Thomas A. McMullin and Marie Mullaney, *Biographical Directory of the Governors of the United States, 1983–1987* (1988) and *1988–1993* (1994); Marie Mullaney, *Biographical Directory of the Governors of the United States 1988–1994* (1994); Thomas J. Noel, *Historical Atlas of Colorado* (1994); John W. Raimo, ed., *Biographical Directory of the Governors of the United States, 1978–1983* (1985); James W. Scott and Ronald L. De Lorme, *Historical Atlas of Washington* (1988); Benjamin F. Shearer and Barbara S. Shearer, *State Names, Seals, Flags, and Symbols* (1994); Robert Sobel and John W. Raimo, eds., *Biographical Directory of the Governors of the United States, 1789–1978* (1978); Richard W. Wilkie and Jack Tager, eds., *Historical Atlas of Massachusetts* (1991). See also "Politics and Government," "South," and "West and Frontier."

Transportation

Keith L. Bryant, ed., *Railroads in the Age of Regulation, 1900–1980* (1988); Rene De La Pedraja, *A Historical Dictionary of the U.S. Merchant Marine and Shipping Industry* (1994); Robert L. Frey, ed., *Railroads in the Nineteenth Century* (1988). See also "Business and the Economy."

Vietnam War

John S. Bowman, ed., *The Vietnam War: An Almanac* (1986); James S. Olson, ed., *Dictionary of the Vietnam War* (1988); Harry G. Summers, Jr., *Vietnam War Almanac* (1985). Also see "Peace Movements and Pacifism" and "Military and Wars."

West and Frontier

William A. Beck and Ynez D. Haase, *Historical Atlas of the American West* (1989); Doris O. Dawdy, *Artists of the American West* (1974–1984); J. Norman Heard, *Handbook of the American Frontier* (1987); Howard R. Lamar, ed., *The Reader's Encyclopedia of the American West* (1977); Clyde A. Milner III et al., eds., *The Oxford History of the American West* (1994); Jay Robert Nash, *Encyclopedia of Western Lawmen and Outlaws* (1992); Doyce B. Nunis, Jr., and Gloria R. Lothrop, eds., *A Guide to the History of California* (1989); Charles Phillips and Alan Axelrod, eds., *Encyclopedia of the American West* (1996); Dan L. Thrapp, *The Encyclopedia of Frontier Biography* (1988–1994); David Walker, *Biographical Directory of American Territorial Governors* (1984). See also "Literature" and "Native Americans and Indian Affairs."

Women

Anne Gibson and Timothy Fast, *The Women's Atlas of the United States* (1986); Karen Greenspan, *The Timetables of Women's History* (1996); Maggie Humm, *The Dictionary of Feminist Theory* (1990); Edward T. James et al., *Notable American Women, 1607–1950* (1971); Lina Mainiero, ed., *American Women Writers* (1979–1982); Kirstin Olsen, *Chronology of Women's History* (1994); Barbara G. Shortridge, *Atlas of American Women* (1987); Barbara Sicherman and Carol H. Green, eds., *Notable American Women, The Modern Period* (1980); Helen Tierney, ed., *Women's Studies Encyclopedia* (1991); Angela H. Zophy and Frances M. Kavenik, eds., *Handbook of American Women's History* (1990). See also "African Americans," "Immigration and Ethnic Groups," "Medicine and Nursing," and "Native Americans and Indian Affairs."

World War I

Arthur Banks, *A Military History Atlas of the First World War* (1975); Martin Gilbert, *Atlas of World War I* (1994); Holger H. Herwig and Neil M. Heyman, *Biographical Dictionary of World War I* (1982); George T. Kurian, *Encyclopedia of the First World War* (1990); Stephen Pope and Elizabeth-Anne Wheal, *The Dictionary of the First World War* (1995); Anne C. Venzon, *The United States in the First World War* (1995). See also "Military and Wars."

World War II

Marcel Baudot et al., eds., *The Historical Encyclopedia of World War II* (1980); David G. Chandler and James Lawton Collins, Jr., eds., *The D-Day Encyclopedia* (1993); I. C. B. Dear and M. R. D. Foot, eds., *The Oxford Companion to World War II* (1995); Simon Goodenough, *War Maps: Great Land Battles of World War II* (1988); Robert Goralski, *World War II Almanac, 1931–1945* (1981); John Keegan, ed., *The Times Atlas of the Second World War* (1989); George T. Kurian, *Encyclopedia of the Second World War* (1991); Norman Polmer and Thomas B. Allen, *World War II: America at War* (1991); Louis L. Snyder, *Louis L. Snyder's Historical Guide to World War II* (1982); U.S. Military Academy, *Campaign Atlas to the Second World War: Europe and the Mediterranean* (1980); Peter Young, ed., *The World Almanac Book of World War II* (1981). See also "Military and Wars."

Documents

DECLARATION OF INDEPENDENCE IN CONGRESS, JULY 4, 1776

When, in the course of human events, it becomes necessary for one people to dissolve the political bonds which have connected them with another, and to assume, among the powers of the earth, the separate and equal station to which the laws of nature and of nature's God entitle them, a decent respect to the opinions of mankind requires that they should declare the causes which impel them to the separation.

We hold these truths to be self-evident: That all men are created equal; that they are endowed by their Creator with certain unalienable rights; that among these are life, liberty, and the pursuit of happiness; that, to secure these rights, governments are instituted among men, deriving their just powers from the consent of the governed; that whenever any form of government becomes destructive of these ends, it is the right of the people to alter or to abolish it, and to institute new government, laying its foundation on such principles, and organizing its powers in such form, as to them shall seem most likely to effect their safety and happiness. Prudence, indeed, will dictate that governments long established should not be changed for light and transient causes; and accordingly all experience hath shown that mankind are more disposed to suffer, while evils are sufferable, than to right themselves by abolishing the forms to which they are accustomed. But when a long train of abuses and usurpations, pursuing invariably the same object, evinces a design to reduce them under absolute despotism, it is their right, it is their duty, to throw off such government, and to provide new guards for their future security. Such has been the patient sufferance of these colonies; and such is now the necessity which constrains them to alter their former systems of government. The history of the present King of Great Britain is a history of repeated injuries and usurpations, all having in direct object the establishment of an absolute tyranny over these states. To prove this, let facts be submitted to a candid world.

He has refused his assent to laws, the most wholesome and necessary for the public good.

He has forbidden his governors to pass laws of immediate and pressing importance, unless suspended in their operation till his assent should be obtained; and, when so suspended, he has utterly neglected to attend to them.

He has refused to pass other laws for the accommodation of large districts of people, unless those people would relinquish the right of representation in the legislature, a right inestimable to them, and formidable to tyrants only.

He has called together legislative bodies at places unusual, uncomfortable, and distant from the depository of their public records, for the sole purpose of fatiguing them into compliance with his measures.

He has dissolved representative houses repeatedly, for opposing, with manly firmness, his invasions on the rights of the people.

He has refused for a long time, after such dissolutions, to cause others to be elected; whereby the legislative powers, incapable of annihilation, have returned to the people at large for their exercise; the state remaining, in the mean time, exposed to all the dangers of invasions from without and convulsions within.

He has endeavored to prevent the population of these states; for that purpose obstructing the laws for naturalization of foreigners; refusing to pass others to encourage their migration hither, and raising the conditions of new appropriations of lands.

He has obstructed the administration of justice, by refusing his assent to laws for establishing judiciary powers.

He has made judges dependent on his will alone, for the tenure of their offices, and the amount and payment of their salaries.

He has erected a multitude of new offices, and sent hither swarms of officers to harass our people and eat out their substance.

He has kept among us, in times of peace, standing armies, without the consent of our legislatures.

He has affected to render the military independent of, and superior to, the civil power.

He has combined with others to subject us to a jurisdiction foreign to our constitution, and unacknowledged by our laws, giving his assent to their acts of pretended legislation:

For quartering large bodies of armed troops among us;

For protecting them, by a mock trial, from punishment for any murders which they should commit on the inhabitants of these states;

For cutting off our trade with all parts of the world;

For imposing taxes on us without our consent;

For depriving us, in many cases, of the benefits of trial by jury;

For transporting us beyond seas, to be tried for pretended offenses;

For abolishing the free system of English laws in a neighboring province, establishing therein an arbitrary government, and enlarging its boundaries, so as to render it at once an example and fit instrument for introducing the same absolute rule into these colonies;

For taking away our charters, abolishing our most valuable laws, and altering fundamentally the forms of our governments;

For suspending our own legislatures, and declaring themselves invested with power to legislate for us in all cases whatsoever.

He has abdicated government here, by declaring us out of his protection and waging war against us.

He has plundered our seas, ravaged our coasts, burned our towns, and destroyed the lives of our people.

He is at this time transporting large armies of foreign mercenaries to complete the works of death, desolation, and tyranny already begun with circumstances of cruelty and perfidy scarcely paralleled in the most barbarous ages, and totally unworthy the head of a civilized nation.

He has constrained our fellow-citizens, taken captive on the high seas, to bear arms against their country, to become the executioners of their friends and brethren, or to fall themselves by their hands.

He has excited domestic insurrection among us, and has endeavored to bring on the inhabitants of our frontiers the merciless Indian savages, whose known rule of warfare is an undistinguished destruction of all ages, sexes, and conditions.

In every stage of these oppressions we have petitioned for redress in the most humble terms; our repeated petitions have been answered only by repeated injury. A prince, whose character is thus marked by every act which may define a tyrant, is unfit to be the ruler of a free people.

Nor have we been wanting in our attentions to our British brethren. We have warned them, from time to time, of attempts by their legislature to extend an unwarrantable jurisdiction over us. We have reminded them of the circumstances of our emigration and settlement here. We have appealed to their native justice and magnanimity; and we have conjured them, by the ties of our common kindred, to disavow these usurpations, which would inevitably interrupt our connections and correspondence. They, too, have been deaf to the voice of justice and of consanguinity. We must, therefore, acquiesce in the neces-

sity which denounces our separation, and hold them, as we hold the rest of mankind, enemies in war, in peace friends.

We, therefore, the representatives of the United States of America, in General Congress assembled, appealing to the Supreme Judge of the world for the rectitude of our intentions, do, in the name and by the authority of the good people of these colonies, solemnly publish and declare, that these United Colonies are, and of right ought to be, FREE AND INDEPENDENT STATES; that they are absolved from all allegiance to the British crown, and that all political connection between them and the state of Great Britain is, and ought to be, totally dissolved; and that, as free and independent states, they have full power to levy war, conclude peace, contract alliances, establish commerce, and do all other acts and things which independent states may of right do. And for the support of this declaration, with a firm reliance on the protection of Divine Providence, we mutually pledge to each other our lives, our fortunes, and our sacred honor.

JOHN HANCOCK
and fifty-five others

CONSTITUTION OF THE UNITED STATES OF AMERICA AND AMENDMENTS*

Preamble

We the people of the United States, in order to form a more perfect union, establish justice, insure domestic tranquillity, provide for the common defense, promote the general welfare, and secure the blessings of liberty to ourselves and our posterity, do ordain and establish this Constitution for the United States of America.

Article 1

Section 1 All legislative powers herein granted shall be vested in a Congress of the United States, which shall consist of a Senate and a House of Representatives.

Section 2 The House of Representatives shall be composed of members chosen every second year by the people of the several States, and the electors in each State shall have the qualifications requisite for electors of the most numerous branch of the State Legislature.

No person shall be a Representative who shall not have attained to the age of twenty-five years, and been seven years a citizen of the United States, and who shall not, when elected, be an inhabitant of that State in which he shall be chosen.

---

*Passages no longer in effect are printed in italic type.

Representatives and direct taxes shall be apportioned among the several States which may be included within this Union, according to their respective numbers, *which shall be determined by adding to the whole number of free persons, including those bound to service for a term of years and excluding Indians not taxed, three-fifths of all other persons.* The actual enumeration shall be made within three years after the first meeting of the Congress of the United States, and within every subsequent term of ten years, in such manner as they shall by law direct. The number of Representatives shall not exceed one for every thirty thousand, but each State shall have at least one Representative; *and until such enumeration shall be made, the State of New Hampshire shall be entitled to choose three, Massachusetts eight, Rhode Island and Providence Plantations one, Connecticut five, New York six, New Jersey four, Pennsylvania eight, Delaware one, Maryland six, Virginia ten, North Carolina five, South Carolina five, and Georgia three.*

When vacancies happen in the representation from any State, the Executive authority thereof shall issue writs of election to fill such vacancies.

The House of Representatives shall choose their Speaker and other officers; and shall have the sole power of impeachment.

Section 3 The Senate of the United States shall be composed of two Senators from each State, *chosen by the legislature thereof,* for six years; and each Senator shall have one vote.

Immediately after they shall be assembled in consequence of the first election, they shall be divided as equally as may be into three classes. The seats of the Senators of the first class shall be vacated at the expiration of the second year, of the second class at the expiration of the fourth year, and of the third class at the expiration of the sixth year, so that one-third may be chosen every second year; *and if vacancies happen by resignation or otherwise, during the recess of the legislature of any State, the Executive thereof may make temporary appointments until the next meeting of the legislature, which shall then fill such vacancies.*

No person shall be a Senator who shall not have attained to the age of thirty years, and been nine years a citizen of the United States, and who shall not, when elected, be an inhabitant of that State for which he shall be chosen.

The Vice-President of the United States shall be President of the Senate, but shall have no vote, unless they be equally divided.

The Senate shall choose their other officers, and also a President *pro tempore,* in the absence of the Vice-President, or when he shall exercise the office of President of the United States.

The Senate shall have the sole power to try all impeachments. When sitting for that purpose, they shall be on oath or affirmation. When the President of the United States is tried, the Chief Justice shall preside: and no person shall be convicted without the concurrence of two-thirds of the members present.

Judgment in cases of impeachment shall not extend further than to removal from the office, and disqualification to hold and enjoy any office of honor, trust or profit under the United States: but the party convicted shall nevertheless be liable and subject to indictment, trial, judgment and punishment, according to law.

Section 4 The times, places and manner of holding elections for Senators and Representatives shall be prescribed in each State by the legislature thereof; but the Congress may at any time by law make or alter such regulations, except as to the places of choosing Senators.

The Congress shall assemble at least once in every year, and such meeting *shall be on the first Monday in December, unless they shall by law appoint a different day.*

Section 5 Each house shall be the judge of the elections, returns and qualifications of its own members, and a majority of each shall constitute a quorum to do business; but a smaller number may adjourn from day to day, and may be authorized to compel the attendance of absent members, in such manner, and under such penalties, as each house may provide.

Each house may determine the rules of its proceedings, punish its members for disorderly behavior, and with the concurrence of two-thirds, expel a member.

Each house shall keep a journal of its proceedings, and from time to time publish the same, excepting such parts as may in their judgment require secrecy; and the yeas and nays of the members of either house on any question shall, at the desire of one-fifth of those present, be entered on the journal.

Neither house, during the session of Congress, shall, without the consent of the other, adjourn for more than three days, nor to any other place than that in which the two houses shall be sitting.

Section 6 The Senators and Representatives shall receive a compensation for their services, to be ascertained by law and paid out of the treasury of the United States. They shall in all cases except treason, felony and breach of the peace, be privileged from arrest during their attendance at the session of their respective houses, and in going to and returning from the same; and for any speech or debate in either house, they shall not be questioned in any other place.

No Senator or Representative shall, during the time for which he was elected, be appointed to any civil office under the authority of the United States, which shall have been created, or the emoluments whereof shall have been increased, during such time; and no person holding any office under the United States shall be a member of either house during his continuance in office.

Section 7 All bills for raising revenue shall originate in the House of Representatives; but the Senate may propose or concur with amendments as on other bills.

Every bill which shall have passed the House of Representatives and the Senate, shall, before it become a law, be presented to the President of the United States; if he approve he shall sign it, but if not he shall return it with objections to that house in which it originated, who shall enter the objections at large on their journal, and proceed to reconsider it. If after such reconsideration two-thirds of that house shall agree to pass the bill, it shall be sent, together with the objections, to the other house, by which it shall likewise be reconsidered, and, if approved by two-thirds of that house, it shall become a law. But in all such cases the votes of both houses shall be determined by yeas and nays, and the names of the persons voting for and against the bill shall be entered on the journal of each house respectively. If any bill shall not be returned by the President within ten days (Sundays excepted) after it shall have been presented to him, the same shall be a law, in like manner as if he had signed it, unless the Congress by their adjournment prevent its return, in which case it shall not be a law.

Every order, resolution, or vote to which the concurrence of the Senate and House of Representatives may be necessary (except on a question of adjournment) shall be presented to the President of the United States; and before the same shall take effect, shall be approved by him, or being disapproved by him, shall be repassed by two-thirds of the Senate and House of Representatives, according to the rules and limitations prescribed in the case of a bill.

Section 8   The Congress shall have power

To lay and collect taxes, duties, imposts, and excises, to pay the debts and provide for the common defense and general welfare of the United States; but all duties, imposts and excises shall be uniform throughout the United States;

To borrow money on the credit of the United States;

To regulate commerce with foreign nations, and among the several States, and with the Indian tribes;

To establish an uniform rule of naturalization, and uniform laws on the subject of bankruptcies throughout the United States;

To coin money, regulate the value thereof, and of foreign coin, and fix the standard of weights and measures;

To provide for the punishment of counterfeiting the securities and current coin of the United States;

To establish post offices and post roads;

To promote the progress of science and useful arts by securing for limited times to authors and inventors the exclusive right to their respective writings and discoveries;

To constitute tribunals inferior to the Supreme Court;

To define and punish piracies and felonies committed on the high seas and offenses against the law of nations;

To declare war, grant letters of marque and reprisal, and make rules concerning captures on land and water;

To raise and support armies, but no appropriation of money to that use shall be for a longer term than two years;

To provide and maintain a navy;

To make rules for the government and regulation of the land and naval forces;

To provide for calling forth the militia to execute the laws of the Union, suppress insurrections, and repel invasions;

To provide for organizing, arming, and disciplining the militia, and for governing such part of them as may be employed in the service of the United States, reserving to the States respectively the appointment of the officers, and the authority of training the militia according to the discipline prescribed by Congress;

To exercise exclusive legislation in all cases whatsoever, over such district (not exceeding ten miles square) as may, by cession of particular States, and the acceptance of Congress, become the seat of government of the United States, and to exercise like authority over all places purchased by the consent of the legislature of the State, in which the same shall be, for erection of forts, magazines, arsenals, dockyards, and other needful buildings; — and

To make all laws which shall be necessary and proper for carrying into execution the foregoing powers, and all other powers vested by this Constitution in the government of the United States, or in any department or officer thereof.

Section 9   The migration or importation of such persons as any of the States now existing shall think proper to admit shall not be prohibited by the Congress prior to the year 1808; but a tax or duty may be imposed on such importation, not exceeding $10 for each person.

The privilege of the writ of habeas corpus shall not be suspended, unless when in cases of rebellion or invasion the public safety may require it.

No bill of attainder or ex post facto law shall be passed.

No capitation, or other direct, tax shall be laid, unless in proportion to the census or enumeration herein before directed to be taken.

No tax or duty shall be laid on articles exported from any State.

No preference shall be given by any regulation of commerce or revenue to the ports of one State over those of another; nor shall vessels bound to, or from, one State, be obliged to enter, clear, or pay duties in another.

No money shall be drawn from the treasury, but in consequence of appropriations made by law; and a regular statement and account of the receipts and expenditures of all public money shall be published from time to time.

No title of nobility shall be granted by the United States: and no person holding any office of profit or trust under them, shall, without the consent of the Congress, accept of any present, emolument, office, or title, of any kind whatever, from any king, prince, or foreign state.

Section 10   No State shall enter into any treaty, alliance, or confederation; grant letters of marque and reprisal; coin money; emit bills of credit; make anything but gold and silver coin a tender in payment of debts; pass any bill of attainder, ex post facto law, or law impairing the obligation of contracts, or grant any title of nobility.

No State shall, without the consent of Congress, lay any imposts or duties on imports or exports, except what may be absolutely necessary for executing its inspection laws: and the net produce of all duties and imposts, laid by any State on imports or exports, shall be for the use of the treasury of the United States; and all such laws shall be subject to the revision and control of the Congress.

No State shall, without the consent of Congress, lay any duty of tonnage, keep troops or ships of war in time of peace, enter into any agreement or compact with another State, or with a foreign power, or engage in war, unless actually invaded, or in such imminent danger as will not admit of delay.

Article II

Section 1   The executive power shall be vested in a President of the United States of America. He shall hold his office during the term of four years, and, together with the Vice-President, chosen for the same term, be elected as follows:

Each State shall appoint, in such manner as the legislature thereof may direct, a number of electors, equal to the whole number of Senators and Representatives to which the State may be entitled in the Congress; but no Senator or Representative, or person holding an office of trust or profit under the United States, shall be appointed an elector.

The electors shall meet in their respective States, and vote by ballot for two persons, of whom one at least shall not be an inhabitant of the same State with themselves. And they shall make a list of all the persons voted for; and of the number of votes for each; which list they shall sign and certify, and transmit sealed to the seat of government of the United States, directed to the President of the Senate. The President of the Senate shall, in the presence of the Senate and House of Representatives, open all the certificates, and the votes shall then be counted. The person having the greatest number of votes shall be the President, if such number be a majority of the whole number of electors appointed; and if there be more than one who have such majority, and have an equal number of votes, then the House of Representatives shall immediately choose by ballot one of them for President; and if no person have a majority, then from the five highest on the list said house shall in like manner choose the President. But in choosing the President the votes shall be taken by States, the representation from each State having one vote; a quorum for this purpose shall consist of a member or members from two-thirds of the States, and a majority of all the States shall be necessary to a choice. In every case, after the choice of the President, the person having the greatest number of votes of the electors shall be the Vice-President. But if there should remain two or more who have equal votes, the Senate shall choose from them by ballot the Vice-President.

The Congress may determine the time of choosing the electors and the day on which they shall give their votes; which day shall be the same throughout the United States.

No person except a natural-born citizen, *or a citizen of the United States at the time of the adoption of this Constitution,* shall be eligible to the office of President; neither shall any person be eligible to that office who shall not

have attained to the age of thirty-five years, and been fourteen years a resident within the United States.

In cases of the removal of the President from office or of his death, resignation, or inability to discharge the powers and duties of the said office, the same shall devolve on the Vice-President, and the Congress may by law provide for the case of removal, death, resignation, or inability, both of the President and Vice-President, declaring what officer shall then act as President, and such officer shall act accordingly, until the disability be removed, or a President shall be elected.

The President shall, at stated times, receive for his services a compensation, which shall neither be increased nor diminished during the period for which he shall have been elected, and he shall not receive within that period any other emolument from the United States, or any of them.

Before he enter on the execution of his office, he shall take the following oath or affirmation:—"I do solemnly swear (or affirm) that I will faithfully execute the office of the President of the United States, and will to the best of my ability preserve, protect and defend the Constitution of the United States."

Section 2   The President shall be commander in chief of the army and navy of the United States, and of the militia of the several States, when called into the actual service of the United States; he may require the opinion, in writing, of the principal officer in each of the executive departments, upon any subject relating to the duties of their respective offices, and he shall have power to grant reprieves and pardons for offenses against the United States, except in cases of impeachment.

He shall have power, by and with the advice and consent of the Senate, to make treaties, provided two-thirds of the Senators present concur; and he shall nominate, and by and with the advice and consent of the Senate, shall appoint ambassadors, other public ministers and consuls, judges of the Supreme Court, and all other officers of the United States, whose appointments are not herein otherwise provided for, and which shall be established by law: but Congress may by law vest the appointment of such inferior officers, as they think proper, in the President alone, in the courts of law, or in the heads of departments.

The President shall have power to fill up all vacancies that may happen during the recess of the Senate, by granting commissions which shall expire at the end of their next session.

Section 3   He shall from time to time give to the Congress information of the state of the Union, and recommend to their consideration such measures as he shall judge necessary and expedient; he may, on extraordinary occasions, convene both houses, or either of them, and in case of disagreement between them, with respect to the time of adjournment, he may adjourn them to such time as he shall think proper; he shall receive ambassadors and other public ministers; he shall take care that the laws be faithfully executed, and shall commission all the officers of the United States.

Section 4   The President, Vice-President and all civil officers of the United States shall be removed from office on impeachment for, and on conviction of, treason, bribery, or other high crimes and misdemeanors.

Article III

Section 1   The judicial power of the United States shall be vested in one Supreme Court, and in such inferior courts as the Congress may from time to time ordain and establish. The judges, both of the Supreme and inferior courts, shall hold their offices during good behavior, and shall, at stated times, receive for their services a compensation which shall not be diminished during their continuance in office.

Section 2   The judicial power shall extend to all cases, in law and equity, arising under this Constitution, the laws of the United States, and treaties made, or which shall be made, under their authority;—to all cases affecting ambassadors, other public ministers and consuls;—to all cases of admiralty and maritime jurisdiction;—to controversies to which the United States shall be a party;—to controversies between two or more States;—*between a State and citizens of another State;*—between citizens of different States;—between citizens of the same State claiming lands under grants of different States, and between a State, or the citizens thereof, and foreign states, citizens or subjects.

In all cases affecting ambassadors, other public ministers and consuls, and those in which a State shall be party, the Supreme Court shall have original jurisdiction. In all the other cases before mentioned, the Supreme Court shall have appellate jurisdiction, both as to law and fact, with such exceptions, and under such regulations, as the Congress shall make.

The trial of all crimes, except in cases of impeachment, shall be by jury; and such trial shall be held in the State where said crimes shall have been committed; but when not committed within any State, the trial shall be at such place or places as the Congress may by law have directed.

Section 3   Treason against the United States shall consist only in levying war against them, or in adhering to their enemies, giving them aid and comfort. No person shall be convicted of treason unless on the testimony of two witnesses to the same overt act, or on confession in open court.

The Congress shall have power to declare the punishment of treason, but no attainder of treason shall work corruption of blood, or forfeiture except during the life of the person attainted.

Article IV

Section 1   Full faith and credit shall be given in each State to the public acts, records, and judicial proceedings of every other State. And the Congress may by general laws prescribe the manner in which such acts, records, and proceedings shall be proved, and the effect thereof.

Section 2   The citizens of each State shall be entitled to all privileges and immunities of citizens in the several States.

A person charged in any State with treason, felony, or other crime, who shall flee from justice, and be found in another State, shall on demand of the executive authority of the State from which he fled, be delivered up, to be removed to the State having jurisdiction of the crime.

No person held to service or labor in one State, under the laws thereof, escaping into another, shall, in consequence of any law or regulation therein, be discharged from such service or labor, but shall be delivered up on claim of the party to whom such service or labor may be due.

Section 3   New States may be admitted by the Congress into this Union; but no new State shall be formed or erected within the jurisdiction of any other State; nor any State be formed by the junction of two or more States, or parts of States, without the consent of the legislatures of the States concerned as well as of the Congress.

The Congress shall have power to dispose of and make all needful rules and regulations respecting the territory or other property belonging to the United States; and nothing in this Constitution shall be so construed as to prejudice any claims of the United States, or of any particular State.

Section 4   The United States shall guarantee to every State in this Union a republican form of government, and shall protect each of them against invasion; and on application of the legislature, or of the executive (when the legislature cannot be convened), against domestic violence.

Article V

The Congress, whenever two-thirds of both houses shall deem it necessary, shall propose amendments to this Constitution, or, on the application of the legislatures of two-thirds of the several States, shall call a convention for proposing amendments, which, in either case, shall be valid to all intents and purposes, as part of this Constitution, when ratified by the legislatures of three-fourths of the several States, or by conventions in three-fourths thereof, as the one or the other mode of ratification may be proposed by the Congress; provided *that no amendments which may be made prior to the year one thousand eight hundred and eight shall in any manner affect the first and fourth clauses in the ninth section of the first article;* and that no State, without its consent, shall be deprived of its equal suffrage in the Senate.

Article VI

All debts contracted and engagements entered into, before the adoption of this Constitution, shall be as valid against the United States under this Constitution, as under the Confederation.

This Constitution, and the laws of the United States which shall be made in pursuance thereof; and all treaties made, or which shall be made, under the authority of the United States, shall be the supreme law of the land; and the judges in every State shall be bound thereby, anything in the Constitution or laws of any State to the contrary notwithstanding.

The Senators and Representatives before mentioned, and the members of the several State legislatures, and all executive and judicial officers, both of the United States and of the several States, shall be bound by oath or affirmation to support this Constitution; but no religious test shall ever be required as a qualification to any office or public trust under the United States.

Article VII

The ratification of the conventions of nine States shall be sufficient for the establishment of this Constitution between the States so ratifying the same.

Done in Convention by the unanimous consent of the States present, the seventeenth day of September in the year of our Lord one thousand seven hundred and eighty-seven and of the Independence of the United States of America the twelfth. In witness whereof we have hereunto subscribed our names.

GEORGE WASHINGTON
and thirty-seven others

Amendments to the Constitution*

Amendment I

Congress shall make no law respecting an establishment of religion, or prohibiting the free exercise thereof; or abridging the freedom of speech, or of the press; or the right of the people peaceably to assemble, and to petition the government for a redress of grievances.

Amendment II

A well-regulated militia being necessary to the security of a free State, the right of the people to keep and bear arms shall not be infringed.

Amendment III

No soldier shall, in time of peace, be quartered in any house without the consent of the owner, nor in time of war, but in a manner to be prescribed by law.

Amendment IV

The right of the people to be secure in their persons, houses, papers, and effects, against unreasonable searches and seizures, shall not be violated, and no warrants shall issue but upon probable cause, supported by oath or affirmation, and particularly describing the place to be searched, and the persons or things to be seized.

*The first ten Amendments (the Bill of Rights) were adopted in 1791.

Amendment V

No person shall be held to answer for a capital, or otherwise infamous crime, unless on a presentment or indictment of a grand jury, except in cases arising in the land or naval forces, or in the militia, when in actual service in time of war or public danger; nor shall any person be subject for the same offense to be twice put in jeopardy of life or limb; nor shall be compelled in any criminal case to be a witness against himself, nor be deprived of life, liberty, or property, without due process of law; nor shall private property be taken for public use without just compensation.

Amendment VI

In all criminal prosecutions, the accused shall enjoy the right to a speedy and public trial, by an impartial jury of the State and district wherein the crime shall have been committed, which district shall have been previously ascertained by law, and to be informed of the nature and cause of the accusation; to be confronted with the witnesses against him; to have compulsory process for obtaining witnesses in his favor, and to have the assistance of counsel for his defense.

Amendment VII

In suits at common law, where the value in controversy shall exceed twenty dollars, the right of trial by jury shall be preserved, and no fact tried by a jury shall be otherwise reexamined in any court of the United States, than according to the rules of the common law.

Amendment VIII

Excessive bail shall not be required, nor excessive fines imposed, nor cruel and unusual punishments inflicted.

Amendment IX

The enumeration in the Constitution, of certain rights, shall not be construed to deny or disparage others retained by the people.

Amendment X

The powers not delegated to the United States by the Constitution, nor prohibited by it to the States, are reserved to the States respectively, or to the people.

Amendment XI

[Adopted 1798]

The judicial power of the United States shall not be construed to extend to any suit in law or equity, commenced or prosecuted against one of the United States by citizens of another State, or by citizens or subjects of any foreign state.

Amendment XII

[Adopted 1804]

The electors shall meet in their respective States, and vote by ballot for President and Vice-President, one of whom, at least, shall not be an inhabitant of the same State with themselves; they shall name in their ballots the person voted for as President, and in distinct ballots the person voted for as Vice-President, and they shall make distinct lists of all persons voted for as President, and of all persons voted for as Vice-President, and of the number of votes for each, which lists they shall sign and certify, and transmit sealed to the seat of government of the United States, directed to the President of the Senate;—the President of the Senate shall, in the presence of the Senate and House of Representatives, open all the certificates and the votes shall then be counted;—the person having the greatest number of votes for President shall be the President, if such number be a majority of the whole number of electors appointed; and if no person have such majority, then from the persons having the highest numbers not exceeding three on the list of those voted for as President, the House of Representatives shall choose immediately, by ballot, the President. But in choosing the President, the votes shall be taken by States, the representation from each State having one vote; a quorum for this purpose shall consist of a member or members from two-thirds of the States, and a majority of all the States shall be necessary to a choice. And if the House of Representatives shall not choose a President whenever the right of choice shall devolve upon them, before *the fourth day of March* next following, then the Vice-President shall act as President, as in the case of the death or other constitutional disability of the President.

The person having the greatest number of votes as Vice-President shall be the Vice-President, if such number be a majority of the whole number of electors appointed; and if no person have a majority, then from the two highest numbers on the list the Senate shall choose the Vice-President; a quorum for the purpose shall consist of two-thirds of the whole number of Senators, and a majority of the whole number shall be necessary to a choice. But no person constitutionally ineligible to the office of President shall be eligible to that of Vice-President of the United States.

Amendment XIII

[Adopted 1865]

Section 1   Neither slavery nor involuntary servitude, except as a punishment for crime whereof the party shall have been duly convicted, shall exist within the United States, or any place subject to their jurisdiction.

Section 2   Congress shall have power to enforce this article by appropriate legislation.

Amendment XIV

[Adopted 1868]

Section 1   All persons born or naturalized in the United States, and subject to the jurisdiction thereof, are citizens of the United States and of the State wherein they reside. No State shall make or enforce any law which shall abridge the privileges or immunities of citizens of the United States;

nor shall any State deprive any person of life, liberty, or property, without due process of law; nor deny to any person within its jurisdiction the equal protection of the laws.

Section 2   Representatives shall be apportioned among the several States according to their respective numbers, counting the whole number of persons in each State, excluding Indians not taxed. But when the right to vote at any election for the choice of Electors for President and Vice-President of the United States, Representatives in Congress, the executive and judicial officers of a State, or the members of the legislature thereof, is denied to any of the male inhabitants of such State, being twenty-one years of age and citizens of the United States, or in any way abridged, except for participation in rebellion, or other crime, the basis of representation therein shall be reduced in the proportion which the number of such male citizens shall bear to the whole number of male citizens twenty-one years of age in such State.

Section 3   No person shall be a Senator or Representative in Congress, or Elector of President and Vice-President, or hold any office, civil or military, under the United States, or under any State, who, having previously taken an oath, as a member of Congress, or as an officer of the United States, or as a member of any State legislature, or as an executive or judicial officer of any State, to support the Constitution of the United States, shall have engaged in insurrection or rebellion against the same, or given aid or comfort to the enemies thereof. Congress may, by a vote of two-thirds of each house, remove such disability.

Section 4   The validity of the public debt of the United States, authorized by law, including debts incurred for payment of pensions and bounties for services in suppressing insurrection or rebellion, shall not be questioned. But neither the United States nor any State shall assume or pay any debt or obligation incurred in aid of insurrection or rebellion against the United States, or any claim for the loss of emancipation of any slave; but all such debts, obligations, and claims shall be held illegal and void.

Section 5   The Congress shall have power to enforce, by appropriate legislation, the provisions of this article.

Amendment XV

[Adopted 1870]

Section 1   The right of citizens of the United States to vote shall not be denied or abridged by the United States or by any State on account of race, color, or previous condition of servitude.

Section 2   The Congress shall have power to enforce this article by appropriate legislation.

Amendment XVI

[Adopted 1913]

The Congress shall have power to lay and collect taxes on incomes, from whatever source derived, without apportionment among the several States, and without regard to any census or enumeration.

Amendment XVII

[Adopted 1913]

Section 1 The Senate of the United States shall be composed of two Senators from each State, elected by the people thereof, for six years; and each Senator shall have one vote. The electors in each State shall have the qualifications requisite for electors of [voters for]the most numerous branch of the State legislatures.

Section 2 When vacancies happen in the representation of any State in the Senate, the executive authority of such State shall issue writs of election to fill such vacancies: Provided, that the Legislature of any State may empower the executive thereof to make temporary appointments until the people fill the vacancies by election as the Legislature may direct.

Section 3 This amendment shall not be so construed as to affect the election or term of any Senator chosen before it becomes valid as part of the Constitution.

Amendment XVIII

[Adopted 1919; Repealed 1933]

Section 1 After one year from the ratification of this article the manufacture, sale, or transportation of intoxicating liquors within, the importation thereof into, or the exportation thereof from the United States and all territory subject to the jurisdiction thereof, for beverage purposes, is hereby prohibited.

Section 2 The Congress and the several States shall have concurrent power to enforce this article by appropriate legislation.

Section 3 This article shall be inoperative unless it shall have been ratified as an amendment to the Constitution by the legislatures of the several States, as provided by the Constitution, within seven years from the date of the submission thereof to the States by the Congress.

Amendment XIX

[Adopted 1920]

Section 1 The right of citizens of the United States to vote shall not be denied or abridged by the United States or by any State on account of sex.

Section 2 The Congress shall have power to enforce this article by appropriate legislation.

Amendment XX

[Adopted 1933]

Section 1 The terms of the President and Vice-President shall end at noon on the 20th day of January, and the terms of Senators and Representatives at noon on the 3rd day of January, of the years in which such terms would have ended if this article had not been ratified; and the terms of their successors shall then begin.

Section 2 The Congress shall assemble at least once in every year, and such meeting shall begin at noon on the 3d day of January, unless they shall by law appoint a different day.

Section 3 If, at the time fixed for the beginning of the term of the President, the President-elect shall have died, the Vice-President-elect shall become President. If a President shall not have been chosen before the time fixed for the beginning of his term, or if the President-elect shall have failed to qualify, then the Vice-President-elect shall act as President until a President shall have qualified; and the Congress may by law provide for the case wherein neither a President-elect nor a Vice-President-elect shall have qualified, declaring who shall then act as President, or the manner in which one who is to act shall be selected, and such persons shall act accordingly until a President or Vice-President shall have qualified.

Section 4 The Congress may by law provide for the case of the death of any of the persons from whom the House of Representatives may choose a President whenever the right of choice shall have devolved upon them, and for the case of the death of any of the persons from whom the Senate may choose a Vice-President whenever the right of choice shall have devolved upon them.

Section 5 Sections 1 and 2 shall take effect on the 15th day of October following the ratification of this article.

Section 6 This article shall be inoperative unless it shall have been ratified as an amendment to the Constitution by the Legislatures of three-fourths of the several States within seven years from the date of its submission.

Amendment XXI

[Adopted 1933]

Section 1 The eighteenth article of amendment to the Constitution of the United States is hereby repealed.

Section 2 The transportation or importation into any State, Territory, or Possession of the United States for delivery or use therein of intoxicating liquors, in violation of the laws thereof, is hereby prohibited.

Section 3 This article shall be inoperative unless it shall have been ratified as an amendment to the Constitution by conventions in the several States, as provided in the Constitution, within seven years from the date of submission thereof to the States by the Congress.

Amendment XXII

[Adopted 1951]

Section 1 No person shall be elected to the office of President more than twice, and no person who has held the office of President, or acted as President, for more than two years of a term to which some other person was elected

President shall be elected to the office of President more than once. But this article shall not apply to any person holding the office of President when this article was proposed by the Congress, and shall not prevent any person who may be holding the office of President, or acting as President, during the term within which this article becomes operative from holding the office of President or acting as President during the remainder of such term.

Section 2   This article shall be inoperative unless it shall have been ratified as an amendment to the Constitution by the legislatures of three-fourths of the several States within seven years from the date of its submission to the States by the Congress.

Amendment XXIII

[Adopted 1961]

Section 1   The District constituting the seat of Government of the United States shall appoint in such manner as the Congress may direct:

A number of electors of President and Vice-President equal to the whole number of Senators and Representatives in Congress to which the District would be entitled if it were a State, but in no event more than the least populous State; they shall be in addition to those appointed by the States, but they shall be considered for the purposes of the election of President and Vice-President, to be electors appointed by a State; and they shall meet in the District and perform such duties as provided by the twelfth article of amendment.

Section 2   The Congress shall have the power to enforce this article by appropriate legislation.

Amendment XXIV

[Adopted 1964]

Section 1   The right of citizens of the United States to vote in any primary or other election for President or Vice-President, for electors for President or Vice-President, or for Senator or Representative in Congress, shall not be denied or abridged by the United States or any State by reason of failure to pay any poll tax or other tax.

Section 2   The Congress shall have the power to enforce this article by appropriate legislation.

Amendment XXV

[Adopted 1967]

Section 1   In case of the removal of the President from office or of his death or resignation, the Vice-President shall become President.

Section 2   Whenever there is a vacancy in the office of the Vice-President, the President shall nominate a Vice-President who shall take office upon confirmation by a majority vote of both Houses of Congress.

Section 3   Whenever the President transmits to the President pro tempore of the Senate and the Speaker of the House of Representatives his written declaration that he is unable to discharge the powers and duties of his office, and until he transmits to them a written declaration to the contrary, such powers and duties shall be discharged by the Vice-President as Acting President.

Section 4   Whenever the Vice-President and a majority of either the principal officers of the executive departments or of such other body as Congress may by law provide, transmit to the President pro tempore of the Senate and the Speaker of the House of Representatives their written declaration that the President is unable to discharge the powers and duties of his office, the Vice-President shall immediately assume the powers and duties of the office as Acting President.

Thereafter, when the President transmits to the President pro tempore of the Senate and the Speaker of the House of Representatives his written declaration that no inability exists, he shall resume the powers and duties of his office unless the Vice-President and a majority of either the principal officers of the executive department[s] or of such other body as Congress may by law provide, transmit within four days to the President pro tempore of the Senate and the Speaker of the House of Representatives their written declaration that the President is unable to discharge the powers and duties of his office. Thereupon Congress shall decide the issue, assembling within forty-eight hours for that purpose if not in session. If the Congress, within twenty-one days after receipt of the latter written declaration, or, if Congress is not in session, within twenty-one days after Congress is required to assemble, determines by two-thirds vote of both Houses that the President is unable to discharge the powers and duties of his office, the Vice-President shall continue to discharge the same as Acting President; otherwise, the President shall resume the powers and duties of his office.

Amendment XXVI

[Adopted 1971]

Section 1   The right of citizens of the United States, who are eighteen years of age or older, to vote shall not be denied or abridged by the United States or by any State on account of age.

Section 2   The Congress shall have power to enforce this article by appropriate legislation.

Amendment XXVII

[Adopted 1992]

No law, varying the compensation for the services of the Senators and Representatives, shall take effect, until an election of Representatives shall have intervened.

The American People and Nation: A Statistical Profile

Population of the United States

Year	Number of States	Population	Percent Increase	Population Per Square Mile	Percent Urban/ Rural	Percent Male/ Female	Percent White/ Non-white	Persons Per House-hold	Median Age
1790	13	3,929,214		4.5	5.1/94.9	NA/NA	80.7/19.3	5.79	NA
1800	16	5,308,483	35.1	6.1	6.1/93.9	NA/NA	81.1/18.9	NA	NA
1810	17	7,239,881	36.4	4.3	7.3/92.7	NA/NA	81.0/19.0	NA	NA
1820	23	9,638,453	33.1	5.5	7.2/92.8	50.8/49.2	81.6/18.4	NA	16.7
1830	24	12,866,020	33.5	7.4	8.8/91.2	50.8/49.2	81.9/18.1	NA	17.2
1840	26	17,069,453	32.7	9.8	10.8/89.2	50.9/49.1	83.2/16.8	NA	17.8
1850	31	23,191,876	35.9	7.9	15.3/84.7	51.0/49.0	84.3/15.7	5.55	18.9
1860	33	31,443,321	35.6	10.6	19.8/80.2	51.2/48.8	85.6/14.4	5.28	19.4
1870	37	39,818,449	26.6	13.4	25.7/74.3	50.6/49.4	86.2/13.8	5.09	20.2
1880	38	50,155,783	26.0	16.9	28.2/71.8	50.9/49.1	86.5/13.5	5.04	20.9
1890	44	62,947,714	25.5	21.2	35.1/64.9	51.2/48.8	87.5/12.5	4.93	22.0
1900	45	75,994,575	20.7	25.6	39.6/60.4	51.1/48.9	87.9/12.1	4.76	22.9
1910	46	91,972,266	21.0	31.0	45.6/54.4	51.5/48.5	88.9/11.1	4.54	24.1
1920	48	105,710,620	14.9	35.6	51.2/48.8	51.0/49.0	89.7/10.3	4.34	25.3
1930	48	122,775,046	16.1	41.2	56.1/43.9	50.6/49.4	89.8/10.2	4.11	26.4
1940	48	131,669,275	7.2	44.2	56.5/43.5	50.2/49.8	89.8/10.2	3.67	29.0
1950	48	150,697,361	14.5	50.7	64.0/36.0	49.7/50.3	89.5/10.5	3.37	30.2
1960	50	179,323,175	18.5	50.6	69.9/30.1	49.3/50.7	88.6/11.4	3.33	29.5
1970	50	203,302,031	13.4	57.4	73.6/26.4	48.7/51.3	87.6/12.4	3.14	28.0
1980	50	226,542,199	11.4	64.0	73.7/26.3	48.6/51.4	85.9/14.1	2.75	30.0
1990	50	248,718,301	9.8	70.3	75.2/24.8	48.7/51.3	83.9/16.1	2.63	32.8
1995	50	263,034,000	5.1	70.7	NA	48.8/51.2	83.0/17.0	2.65	34.3

NA = Not available.

Vital Statistics

			Life Expectancy in Years						
Year	Birth Rate*	Death Rate*	Total Population	White Females	Nonwhite Females	White Males	Nonwhite Males	Marriage Rate	Divorce Rate
1790	NA	NA	NA	NA	NA	NA	NA	NA	NA
1800	55.0	NA	NA	NA	NA	NA	NA	NA	NA
1810	54.3	NA	NA	NA	NA	NA	NA	NA	NA
1820	55.2	NA	NA	NA	NA	NA	NA	NA	NA
1830	51.4	NA	NA	NA	NA	NA	NA	NA	NA
1840	51.8	NA	NA	NA	NA	NA	NA	NA	NA
1850	43.3	NA	NA	NA	NA	NA	NA	NA	NA
1860	44.3	NA	NA	NA	NA	NA	NA	NA	NA
1870	38.3	NA	NA	NA	NA	NA	NA	NA	NA
1880	39.8	NA	NA	NA	NA	NA	NA	NA	NA
1890	31.5	NA	NA	NA	NA	NA	NA	NA	NA
1900	32.3	17.2	47.3	48.7	33.5	46.6	32.5	NA	NA
1910	30.1	14.7	50.0	52.0	37.5	48.6	33.8	NA	NA
1920	27.7	13.0	54.1	55.6	45.2	54.4	45.5	12.0	1.6
1930	21.3	11.3	59.7	63.5	49.2	59.7	47.3	9.2	1.6
1940	19.4	10.8	62.9	66.6	54.9	62.1	51.5	12.1	2.0
1950	24.1	9.6	68.2	72.2	62.9	66.5	59.1	11.1	2.6
1960	23.7	9.5	69.7	74.1	66.3	67.4	61.1	8.5	2.2
1970	18.4	9.5	70.8	75.6	69.4	68.0	61.3	10.6	3.5
1980	15.9	8.8	73.7	78.1	73.6	70.7	65.3	10.6	5.2
1990	16.6	8.6	75.4	79.4	75.2	72.7	67.0	9.8	4.7
1994	15.3	8.8	75.7	79.6	75.8	73.2	67.5	9.1	4.6

Data per one thousand for Birth, Death, Marriage, and Divorce rates.

NA = Not available. *Data for 1800, 1810, 1830, 1850, 1870, and 1890 for whites only.

Immigrants to the United States

Immigration Totals by Decade			
Years	Number	Years	Number
1820–1830	151,824	1911–1920	5,735,811
1831–1840	599,125	1921–1930	4,107,209
1841–1850	1,713,251	1931–1940	528,431
1851–1860	2,598,214	1941–1950	1,035,039
1861–1870	2,314,824	1951–1960	2,515,479
1871–1880	2,812,191	1961–1970	3,321,677
1881–1890	5,246,613	1971–1980	4,493,314
1891–1900	3,687,546	1981–1990	7,338,062
1901–1910	8,795,386	1991–1994	4,509,852
		Total	61,503,866

Major Sources of Immigrants by Country or Region (in thousands)

Period	Asia[a]	Germany	Mexico	Italy	Great Britain (UK)[b]	Ireland	Canada	Austria and Hungary	Soviet Union (Russia)	Caribbean	Central America and South America	Norway and Sweden
1820–1830	—	8	5	—	27	54	2	—	—	4	—	—
1831–1840	—	152	7	2	76	207	14	—	—	12	—	1
1841–1850	—	435	3	2	267	781	42	—	—	14	4	14
1851–1860	42	952	3	9	424	914	59	—	—	11	2	21
1861–1870	65	787	2	12	607	436	154	8	3	9	1	109
1871–1880	124	718	5	56	548	437	384	73	39	14	1	211
1881–1890	70	1,453	2[c]	307	807	655	393	354	213	29	3	568
1891–1900	75	505	1[c]	652	272	388	3	593	505	33	2	321
1901–1910	324	341	50	2,046	526	339	179	2,145	1,597	108	25	440
1911–1920	247	144	219	1,110	341	146	742	896	921	123	59	161
1921–1930	112	412	459	455	340	211	925	64	62	75	58	166
1931–1940	17	114	22	68	32	11	109	11	1	16	14	9
1941–1950	37	227	61	58	139	20	172	28	—	50	43	21
1951–1960	153	478	300	185	203	48	378	104	—	123	136	45
1961–1970	428	191	454	214	214	33	413	26	2	470	359	33
1971–1980	1,588	74	640	129	137	11	170	16	39	741	430	10
1981–1990	2,738	92	2,336	67	160	32	182	25	58	872	930	15
1991–1994	1,315	43	1,400	49	77	47	88	13	193	333	505	8
Total	7,334	7,126	5,970	5,422	5,196	4,772	4,408	4,356	3,637	3,036	2,575	2,154

Notes: Numbers for periods are rounded. Dash indicates less than one thousand; [a]Includes Middle East;[b]Since 1925, includes England, Scotland, Wales, and Northern Ireland data; [c]No data available for 1886–1894.

The American Worker

Year	Total Number of Workers	Males as Percent of Total Workers	Females as Percent of Total Workers	Married Women as Percent of Female Workers	Female Workers as Percent of Female Population	Percent of Labor Force Unemployed	Percent of Workers in Labor Unions
1870	12,506,000	85	15	NA	NA	NA	NA
1880	17,392,000	85	15	NA	NA	NA	NA
1890	23,318,000	83	17	14	19	4 (1894 = 18)	NA
1900	29,073,000	82	18	15	21	5	3
1910	38,167,000	79	21	25	25	6	6
1920	41,614,000	79	21	23	24	5 (1921 = 12)	12
1930	48,830,000	78	22	29	25	9 (1933 = 25)	11.6
1940	53,011,000	76	24	36	27	15 (1944 = 1)	26.9
1950	62,208,000	72	28	52	31	5.3	31.5
1960	69,628,000	67	33	55	38	5.5	31.4
1970	82,771,000	62	38	59	43	4.9	27.3
1980	106,940,000	58	42	55	52	7.1	21.9
1990	125,840,000	55	45	54	58	5.6	16.1
1995	132,304,000	54	46	55	59	5.6	15.5

NA = Not available.

The American Economy

Year	Gross National Product (GNP) (in $ billions)	Steel Production (in tons)	Automobiles Registered	New Housing Starts	Foreign Trade (in millions of dollars)	
					Exports	Imports
1790	NA	NA	NA	NA	20	23
1800	NA	NA	NA	NA	71	91
1810	NA	NA	NA	NA	67	85
1820	NA	NA	NA	NA	70	74
1830	NA	NA	NA	NA	74	71
1840	NA	NA	NA	NA	132	107
1850	NA	NA	NA	NA	152	178
1860	NA	13,000	NA	NA	400	362
1870	7.4[a]	77,000	NA	NA	451	462
1880	11.2[b]	1,397,000	NA	NA	853	761
1890	13.1	4,779,000	NA	328,000	910	823
1900	18.7	11,227,000	8,000	189,000	1,499	930
1910	35.3	28,330,000	458,300	387,000 (1918 = 118,000)	1,919	1,646
1920	91.5	46,183,000	8,131,500	247,000 (1925 = 937,000)	8,664	5,784
1930	90.7	44,591,000	23,034,700	330,000 (1933 = 93,000)	4,013	3,500
1940	100.0	66,983,000	27,465,800	603,000 (1944 = 142,000)	4,030	7,433
1950	286.5	96,836,000	40,339,000	1,952,000	9,997	8,954
1960	506.5	99,282,000	61,682,300	1,365,000	19,659	15,093
1970	1,016.0	131,514,000	89,279,800	1,434,000	42,681	40,356
1980	2,819.5	111,835,000	121,601,000	1,292,000	220,626	244,871
1990	5,764.9	98,906,000	143,550,000	1,193,000	394,030	485,453
1995	7,237.5	104,930,000	133,930,000[c]	1,354,000	584,742	743,445

[a]Figure is average for 1869–1878.

[b]Figure is average for 1879–1888.

[c]Figure for 1994.

NA = Not available.

Federal Budget Outlays and Debt

Year	Defense[a]	Veterans Benefits[a]	Income Security[a]	Social Security[a]	Health and Medicare[a]	Education[ad]	Net Interest Payments[a]	Federal Debt (dollars)
1790	14.9	4.1[b]	NA	NA	NA	NA	55.0	75,463,000[c]
1800	55.7	.6	NA	NA	NA	NA	31.3	82,976,000
1810	48.4 (1814: 79.7)	1.0	NA	NA	NA	NA	34.9	53,173,000
1820	38.4	17.6	NA	NA	NA	NA	28.1	91,016,000
1830	52.9	9.0	NA	NA	NA	NA	12.6	48,565,000
1840	54.3 (1847: 80.7)	10.7	NA	NA	NA	NA	.7	3,573,000
1850	43.8	4.7	NA	NA	NA	NA	1.0	63,453,000
1860	44.2 (1865: 88.9)	1.7	NA	NA	NA	NA	5.0	64,844,000
1870	25.7	9.2	NA	NA	NA	NA	41.7	2,436,453,000
1880	19.3	21.2	NA	NA	NA	NA	35.8	2,090,909,000
1890	20.9 (1899: 48.6)	33.6	NA	NA	NA	NA	11.4	1,222,397,000
1900	36.6	27.0	NA	NA	NA	NA	7.7	1,263,417,000
1910	45.1 (1919: 59.5)	23.2	NA	NA	NA	NA	3.1	1,146,940,000
1920	37.1	3.4	NA	NA	NA	NA	16.0	24,299,321,000
1930	25.3	6.6	NA	NA	NA	NA	19.9	16,185,310,000
1940	17.5 (1945: 89.4)	6.0	16.0	.3	.5	20.8	9.4	42,967,531,000
1950	32.2	20.3	9.6	1.8	.6	.6	11.3	256,853,000,000
1960	52.2	5.9	8.0	12.6	.9	1.0	7.5	290,525,000,000
1970	41.8	4.4	8.0	15.5	6.2	4.4	7.3	308,921,000,000
1980	22.7	3.6	14.6	20.1	9.4	5.4	8.9	909,050,000,000
1990	23.9	2.3	11.7	19.8	12.4	3.1	14.7	3,206,564,000,000
1995	17.9	2.5	14.5	22.1	18.1	3.6	15.3	5,207,298,000,000[e]

[a]Figures represent percentage of total federal spending for each category. Not included are categories of transportation, commerce, and housing.

[b]1789–1791 figure.

[c]1791 figure.

[d]Includes training, employment, and social services.

[e]1996 figure.

NA = Not available.

The Fifty States, District of Columbia, and Puerto Rico

State	Date of Admission (with Rank)	Capital City	Population (1995) (with Rank)	Racial/Ethnic Distribution (1995)	Per Capita Personal Income (1995) (with Rank)	Total Area in Square Miles (with Rank)
Alabama (AL)	Dec. 14, 1819 (22)	Montgomery	4,253,000 (22)	White: 3,140,000; Black: 1,083,000; Hispanic: 29,000; Asian: 33,000	$18,781 (41)	52,423 (30)
Alaska (AK)	Jan. 3, 1959 (49)	Juneau	604,000 (48)	White: 477,000; Black: 26,000; Hispanic: 22,000; Asian: 29,000; Native American: 102,000	$24,182 (10)	656,424 (1)
Arizona (AZ)	Feb. 14, 1912 (48)	Phoenix	4,218,000 (23)	White: 3,606,000; Black: 123,000; Hispanic: 853,000; Asian: 91,000; Native American: 251,000	$20,421 (35)	114,006 (6)
Arkansas (AR)	June 15, 1836 (25)	Little Rock	2,484,000 (33)	White: 2,047,000; Black: 386,000; Hispanic: 27,000; Asian: 26,000	$17,429 (49)	53,182 (29)
California (CA)	Sept. 9, 1850 (31)	Sacramento	31,589,000 (1)	White: 25,701,000; Black: 2,512,000; Hispanic: 9,143,000; Asian: 3,908,000; Native American: 277,000	$23,699 (12)	163,707 (3)
Colorado (CO)	Aug. 1, 1876 (38)	Denver	3,747,000 (25)	White: 3,431,000; Black: 156,000; Hispanic: 511,000; Asian: 89,000; Native American: 34,000	$23,449 (16)	104,100 (8)
Connecticut (CT)	Jan. 9, 1788 (5)	Hartford	3,275,000 (28)	White: 2,915,000; Black: 293,000; Hispanic: 258,000; Asian: 60,000	$30,303 (1)	5,544 (48)
Delaware (DE)	Dec. 7, 1787 (1)	Dover	717,000 (46)	White: 570,000; Black: 132,000; Hispanic: 22,000; Asian: 14,000	$24,124 (11)	2,489 (49)
District of Columbia (DC)	U.S. Capital, Dec. 1, 1800*	Washington (coextensive with DC)	554,000 (not ranked)	White: 185,000; Black: 384,000; Hispanic: 35,000; Asian: 16,000	$32,274*	68*
Florida (FL)	Mar. 3, 1845 (27)	Tallahassee	14,166,000 (4)	White: 11,867,000; Black: 2,073,000; Hispanic: 1,948,000; Asian: 231,000	$22,916 (20)	65,756 (22)
Georgia (GA)	Jan. 2, 1788 (4)	Atlanta	7,201,000 (10)	White: 5,025,000; Black: 1,955,000; Hispanic: 144,000; Asian: 109,000	$21,278 (28)	59,441 (24)
Hawai'i (HI)	Aug. 21, 1959 (50)	Honolulu	1,187,000 (40)	White: 499,000; Black: 36,000; Hispanic: 106,000; Asian: 679,000	$24,738 (9)	10,932 (43)
Idaho (ID)	July 3, 1890 (43)	Boise	1,163,000 (41)	White: 1,118,000; Black: 5,000; Hispanic: 74,000; Asian: 15,000; Native American: 18,000	$19,264 (38)	83,574 (14)
Illinois (IL)	Dec. 3, 1818 (21)	Springfield	11,830,000 (6)	White: 9,603,000; Black: 1,843,000; Hispanic: 1,086,000; Asian: 383,000	$24,763 (8)	57,918 (25)
Indiana (IN)	Dec. 11, 1816 (19)	Indianapolis	5,803,000 (14)	White: 5,275,000; Black: 476,000; Hispanic: 122,000; Asian: 55,000	$21,273 (29)	36,420 (38)
Iowa (IA)	Dec. 28, 1846 (29)	Des Moines	2,842,000 (30)	White: 2,763,000; Black: 57,000; Hispanic: 45,000; Asian: 33,000	$21,012 (30)	56,276 (26)
Kansas (KS)	Jan. 29, 1861 (34)	Topeka	2,565,000 (32)	White: 2,365,000; Black: 159,000; Hispanic: 116,000; Asian: 50,000	$21,825 (23)	82,282 (15)
Kentucky (KY)	June 1, 1792 (15)	Frankfort	3,860,000 (24)	White: 3,535,000; Black: 286,000; Hispanic: 23,000; Asian: 24,000	$18,612 (43)	40,411 (37)

The Fifty States, District of Columbia, and Puerto Rico, Continued

State	Date of Admission (with Rank)	Capital City	Population (1995) (with Rank)	Racial/Ethnic Distribution (1995)	Per Capita Personal Income (1995) (with Rank)	Total Area in Square Miles (with Rank)
Louisiana (LA)	Apr. 30, 1812 (18)	Baton Rouge	4,342,000 (21)	White: 2,909,000; Black: 1,371,000; Hispanic: 109,000; Asian: 60,000	$18,827 (39)	51,843 (31)
Maine (ME)	Mar. 15, 1820 (23)	Augusta	1,241,000 (39)	White: 1,217,000; Black: 5,000; Hispanic: 9,000; Asian: 8,000; Native American: 6,000	$20,527 (34)	35,387 (39)
Maryland (MD)	Apr. 28, 1788 (7)	Annapolis	5,042,000 (19)	White: 3,500,000; Black: 1,368,000; Hispanic: 158,000; Asian: 196,000	$25,927 (5)	12,407 (42)
Massachusetts (MA)	Feb. 6, 1788 (6)	Boston	6,074,000 (13)	White: 5,445,000; Black: 340,000; Hispanic: 342,000; Asian: 180,000	$26,994 (3)	10,555 (44)
Michigan (MI)	Jan. 26, 1837 (26)	Lansing	9,549,000 (8)	White: 7,958,000; Black: 1,417,000; Hispanic: 242,000; Asian: 140,000; Native American: 61,000	$23,551 (15)	96,705 (11)
Minnesota (MN)	May 11, 1858 (32)	Saint Paul	4,610,000 (20)	White: 4,344,000; Black: 104,000; Hispanic: 68,000; Asian: 113,000; Native American: 58,000	$23,118 (19)	86,943 (12)
Mississippi (MS)	Dec. 10, 1817 (20)	Jackson	2,697,000 (31)	White: 1,688,000; Black: 952,000; Hispanic: 18,000; Asian: 17,000	$16,531 (50)	48,434 (32)
Missouri (MO)	Aug. 10, 1821 (24)	Jefferson City	5,324,000 (16)	White: 4,629,000; Black: 581,000; Hispanic: 71,000; Asian: 56,000	$21,627 (26)	69,709 (21)
Montana (MT)	Nov. 8, 1889 (41)	Helena	870,000 (44)	White: 798,000; Black: 2,000; Hispanic: 15,000; Asian: 6,000; Native American: 55,000	$18,482 (44)	147,046 (4)
Nebraska (NE)	Mar. 1, 1867 (37)	Lincoln	1,637,000 (37)	White: 1,550,000; Black: 64,000; Hispanic: 53,000; Asian: 17,000; Native American: 14,000	$21,703 (25)	77,358 (16)
Nevada (NV)	Oct. 3, 1864 (36)	Carson City	1,530,000 (38)	White: 1,281,000; Black: 100,000; Hispanic: 195,000; Asian: 70,000; Native American: 27,000	$25,013 (7)	110,567 (7)
New Hampshire (NH)	June 21, 1788 (9)	Concord	1,148,000 (42)	White: 1,109,000; Black: 7,000; Hispanic: 13,000; Asian: 14,000	$25,151 (6)	9,351 (46)
New Jersey (NJ)	Dec. 18, 1787 (3)	Trenton	7,945,000 (9)	White: 6,405,000; Black: 1,156,000; Hispanic: 898,000; Asian: 356,000	$28,858 (2)	8,722 (47)
New Mexico (NM)	Jan. 6, 1912 (47)	Santa Fe	1,685,000 (36)	White: 1,460,000; Black: 32,000; Hispanic: 686,000; Asian: 25,000; Native American: 159,000	$18,055 (47)	121,598 (5)
New York (NY)	July 26, 1788 (11)	Albany	18,136,000 (3)	White: 14,025,000; Black: 3,249,000; Hispanic: 2,372,000; Asian: 846,000; Native American: 57,000	$26,782 (4)	54,471 (27)
North Carolina (NC)	Nov. 21, 1789 (12)	Raleigh	7,195,000 (11)	White: 5,378,000; Black: 1,594,000; Hispanic: 100,000; Asian: 88,000; Native American: 90,000	$20,604 (33)	53,821 (28)
North Dakota (ND)	Nov. 2, 1889 (39)	Bismarck	641,000 (47)	White: 600,000; Black: 4,000; Hispanic: 5,000; Asian: 5,000; Native American: 28,000	$18,663 (42)	70,704 (19)
Ohio (OH)	Mar. 1, 1803 (17)	Columbus	11,151,000 (7)	White: 9,806,000; Black: 1,253,000; Hispanic: 170,000; Asian: 122,000	$22,021 (21)	44,828 (34)
Oklahoma (OK)	Nov. 16, 1907 (46)	Oklahoma City	3,278,000 (27)	White: 2,699,000; Black: 244,000; Hispanic: 106,000; Asian: 52,000; Native American: 276,000	$18,152 (46)	69,903 (20)

The Fifty States, District of Columbia, and Puerto Rico, Continued

State	Date of Admission (with Rank)	Capital City	Population (1995) (with Rank)	Racial/Ethnic Distribution (1995)	Per Capita Personal Income (1995) (with Rank)	Total Area in Square Miles (with Rank)
Oregon (OR)	Feb. 14, 1859 (33)	Salem	3,141,000 (29)	White: 2,929,000; Black: 54,000; Hispanic: 151,000; Asian: 111,000; Native American: 47,000	$21,736 (24)	98,386 (9)
Pennsylvania (PA)	Dec. 12, 1787 (2)	Harrisburg	12,072,000 (5)	White: 10,768,000; Black: 1,167,000; Hispanic: 297,000; Asian: 185,000	$23,279 (18)	46,058 (33)
Puerto Rico (PR)	Ascession 1898; Commonwealth Status 1952	San Juan	3,720,000*	White: >1,000; Black: >1,000; Hispanic: 3,621,000; Asian: >1,000	$6,360*	3,427*
Rhode Island (RI)	May 29, 1790 (13)	Providence	990,000 (43)	White: 927,000; Black: 44,000; Hispanic: 58,000; Asian: 25,000	$23,310 (17)	1,545 (50)
South Carolina (SC)	May 23, 1788 (8)	Columbia	3,673,000 (26)	White: 2,561,000; Black: 1,131,000; Hispanic: 40,000; Asian: 31,000	$18,788 (40)	32,008 (40)
South Dakota (SD)	Nov. 2, 1889 (40)	Pierre	729,000 (45)	White: 663,000; Black: 3,000; Hispanic: 7,000; Asian: 5,000; Native American: 62,000	$19,506 (37)	77,121 (17)
Tennessee (TN)	June 1, 1796 (16)	Nashville	5,256,000 (17)	White: 4,327,000; Black: 845,000; Hispanic: 42,000; Asian: 46,000	$20,376 (36)	42,146 (36)
Texas (TX)	Dec. 29, 1845 (28)	Austin	18,724,000 (2)	White: 15,814,000; Black: 2,251,000; Hispanic: 5,260,000; Asian: 461,000	$20,654 (32)	268,601 (2)
Utah (UT)	Jan. 4, 1896 (45)	Salt Lake City	1,951,000 (34)	White: 1,843,000; Black: 14,000; Hispanic: 106,000; Asian: 54,000; Native American: 33,000	$18,223 (45)	84,904 (13)
Vermont (VT)	Mar. 4, 1791 (14)	Montpelier	585,000 (49)	White: 570,000; Black: 2,000; Hispanic: 4,000; Asian: 4,000; Native American: 2,000	$20,927 (31)	9,615 (45)
Virginia (VA)	June 25, 1788 (10)	Richmond	6,618,000 (12)	White: 5,127,000; Black: 1,284,000 Hispanic: 193,000; Asian: 220,000	$25,597 (14)	42,777 (35)
Washington (WA)	Nov. 11, 1889 (42)	Olympia	5,431,000 (15)	White: 4,915,000; Black: 164,000; Hispanic: 291,000; Asian: 318,000; Native American: 101,000	$23,639 (13)	71,302 (18)
West Virginia (WV)	June 20, 1863 (35)	Charleston	1,828,000; (35)	White: 1,756,000; Black: 54,000; Hispanic: 10,000; Asian: 11,000	$17,915 (48)	24,231 (41)
Wisconsin (WI)	May 29, 1848 (30)	Madison	5,123,000 (18)	White: 4,750,000; Black: 288,000; Hispanic: 118,000; Asian: 76,000; Native American: 45,000	$21,839 (22)	65,499 (23)
Wyoming (WY)	July 10, 1890 (44)	Cheyenne	480,000 (50)	White: 467,000; Black: 4,000; Hispanic: 31,000; Asian: 4,000; Native American: 12,000	$21,321 (27)	97,818 (10)

*Not ranked.

Presidential Elections

Year	Number of States	Candidates	Parties	Popular Vote	% of Popular Vote	Electoral Vote	% Voter Participation[b]
1789	11	**George Washington**	No party			69	
		John Adams	designations			34	
		Other candidates				35	
1792	15	**George Washington**	No party			132	
		John Adams	designations			77	
		George Clinton				50	
		Other candidates				5	
1796	16	**John Adams**	Federalist			71	
		Thomas Jefferson	Democratic-Republican			68	
		Thomas Pinckney	Federalist			59	
		Aaron Burr	Democratic-Republican			30	
		Other candidates				48	
1800	16	**Thomas Jefferson**	Democratic-Republican			73	
		Aaron Burr	Democratic-Republican			73	
		John Adams	Federalist			65	
		Charles C. Pinckney	Federalist			64	
		John Jay	Federalist			1	
1804	17	**Thomas Jefferson**	Democratic-Republican			162	
		Charles C. Pinckney	Federalist			14	
1808	17	**James Madison**	Democratic-Republican			122	
		Charles C. Pinckney	Federalist			47	
		George Clinton	Democratic-Republican			6	
1812	18	**James Madison**	Democratic-Republican			128	
		DeWitt Clinton	Federalist			89	
1816	19	**James Monroe**	Democratic-Republican			183	
		Rufus King	Federalist			34	
1820	24	**James Monroe**	Democratic-Republican			231	
		John Quincy Adams	Independent Republican			1	

Presidential Elections, Continued

Year	Number of States	Candidates	Parties	Popular Vote	% of Popular Vote	Electoral Vote	% Voter Participation[b]
1824	24	**John Quincy Adams**	Democratic-Republican	108,740	30.5	84	26.9
		Andrew Jackson	Democratic-Republican	153,544	43.1	99	
		Henry Clay	Democratic-Republican	47,136	13.2	37	
		William H. Crawford	Democratic-Republican	46,618	13.1	41	
1828	24	**Andrew Jackson**	Democratic	647,286	56.0	178	57.6
		John Quincy Adams	National Republican	508,064	44.0	83	
1832	24	**Andrew Jackson**	Democratic	688,242	54.5	219	55.4
		Henry Clay	National Republican	473,462	37.5	49	
		William Wirt	Anti-Masonic	101,051	8.0	7	
		John Floyd	Democratic			11	
1836	26	**Martin Van Buren**	Democratic	765,483	50.9	170	57.8
		William H. Harrison	Whig			73	
		Hugh L. White	Whig	739,795	49.1	26	
		Daniel Webster	Whig			14	
		W. P. Mangum	Whig			11	
1840	26	**William H. Harrison**	Whig	1,274,624	53.1	234	80.2
		Martin Van Buren	Democratic	1,127,781	46.9	60	
1844	26	**James K. Polk**	Democratic	1,338,464	49.6	170	78.9
		Henry Clay	Whig	1,300,097	48.1	105	
		James G. Birney	Liberty	62,300	2.3		
1848	30	**Zachary Taylor**	Whig	1,360,967	47.4	163	72.7
		Lewis Cass	Democratic	1,222,342	42.5	127	
		Martin Van Buren	Free Soil	291,263	10.1		
1852	31	**Franklin Pierce**	Democratic	1,601,117	50.9	254	69.6
		Winfield Scott	Whig	1,385,453	44.1	42	
		John P. Hale	Free Soil	155,825	5.0		
1856	31	**James Buchanan**	Democratic	1,832,955	45.3	174	78.9
		John C. Frémont	Republican	1,339,932	33.1	114	
		Millard Fillmore	American	871,731	21.6	8	
1860	33	**Abraham Lincoln**	Republican	1,865,593	39.8	180	81.2
		Stephen A. Douglas	Democratic	1,382,713	29.5	12	
		John C. Breckinridge	Democratic	848,356	18.1	72	
		John Bell	Constitutional Union	592,906	12.6	39	
1864	36	**Abraham Lincoln**	Republican	2,206,938	55.0	212	73.8
		George B. McClellan	Democratic	1,803,787	45.0	21	
1868	37	**Ulysses S. Grant**	Republican	3,013,421	52.7	214	78.1
		Horatio Seymour	Democratic	2,706,829	47.3	80	
1872	37	**Ulysses S. Grant**	Republican	3,596,745	55.6	286	71.3
		Horace Greeley	Democratic	2,843,446	43.9	[a]	

Presidential Elections, Continued

Year	Number of States	Candidates	Parties	Popular Vote	% of Popular Vote	Electoral Vote	% Voter Participation[b]
1876	38	**Rutherford B. Hayes**	Republican	4,036,572	48.0	185	81.8
		Samuel J. Tilden	Democratic	4,284,020	51.0	184	
1880	38	**James A. Garfield**	Republican	4,453,295	48.5	214	79.4
		Winfield S. Hancock	Democratic	4,414,082	48.1	155	
		James B. Weaver	Greenback-Labor	308,578	3.4		
1884	38	**Grover Cleveland**	Democratic	4,879,507	48.5	219	77.5
		James G. Blaine	Republican	4,850,293	48.2	182	
		Benjamin F. Butler	Greenback-Labor	175,370	1.8		
		John P. St. John	Prohibition	150,369	1.5		
1888	38	**Benjamin Harrison**	Republican	5,477,129	47.9	233	79.3
		Grover Cleveland	Democratic	5,537,857	48.6	168	
		Clinton B. Fisk	Prohibition	249,506	2.2		
		Anson J. Streeter	Union Labor	146,935	1.3		
1892	44	**Grover Cleveland**	Democratic	5,555,426	46.1	277	74.7
		Benjamin Harrison	Republican	5,182,690	43.0	145	
		James B. Weaver	People's	1,029,846	8.5	22	
		John Bidwell	Prohibition	264,133	2.2		
1896	45	**William McKinley**	Republican	7,102,246	51.1	271	79.3
		William J. Bryan	Democratic	6,492,559	47.7	176	
1900	45	**William McKinley**	Republican	7,218,491	51.7	292	73.2
		William J. Bryan	Democratic; Populist	6,356,734	45.5	155	
		John C. Wooley	Prohibition	208,914	1.5		
1904	45	**Theodore Roosevelt**	Republican	7,628,461	57.4	336	65.2
		Alton B. Parker	Democratic	5,084,223	37.6	140	
		Eugene V. Debs	Socialist	402,283	3.0		
		Silas C. Swallow	Prohibition	258,536	1.9		
1908	46	**William H. Taft**	Republican	7,675,320	51.6	321	65.4
		William J. Bryan	Democratic	6,412,294	43.1	162	
		Eugene V. Debs	Socialist	420,793	2.8		
		Eugene W. Chafin	Prohibition	253,840	1.7		
1912	48	**Woodrow Wilson**	Democratic	6,296,547	41.9	435	58.8
		Theodore Roosevelt	Progressive	4,118,571	27.4	88	
		William H. Taft	Republican	3,486,720	23.2	8	
		Eugene V. Debs	Socialist	900,672	6.0		
		Eugene W. Chafin	Prohibition	206,275	1.4		
1916	48	**Woodrow Wilson**	Democratic	9,127,695	49.4	277	61.6
		Charles E. Hughes	Republican	8,533,507	46.2	254	
		A. L. Benson	Socialist	585,113	3.2		
		J. Frank Hanly	Prohibition	220,506	1.2		
1920	48	**Warren G. Harding**	Republican	16,143,407	60.4	404	49.2
		James M. Cox	Democratic	9,130,328	34.2	127	

Presidential Elections, Continued

Year	Number of States	Candidates	Parties	Popular Vote	% of Popular Vote	Electoral Vote	% Voter Participation[b]
		Eugene V. Debs	Socialist	919,799	3.4		
		P. P. Christensen	Farmer-Labor	265,411	1.0		
1924	48	**Calvin Coolidge**	Republican	15,718,211	54.0	382	48.9
		John W. Davis	Democratic	8,385,283	28.8	136	
		Robert M. La Follette	Progressive	4,831,289	16.6	13	
1928	48	**Herbert C. Hoover**	Republican	21,391,993	58.2	444	56.9
		Alfred E. Smith	Democratic	15,016,169	40.9	87	
1932	48	**Franklin D. Roosevelt**	Democratic	22,809,638	57.4	472	56.9
		Herbert C. Hoover	Republican	15,758,901	39.7	59	
		Norman Thomas	Socialist	881,951	2.2		
1936	48	**Franklin D. Roosevelt**	Democratic	27,752,869	60.8	523	61.0
		Alfred M. Landon	Republican	16,674,665	36.5	8	
		William Lemke	Union	882,479	1.9		
1940	48	**Franklin D. Roosevelt**	Democratic	27,307,819	54.8	449	62.5
		Wendell L. Wilkie	Republican	22,321,018	44.8	82	
1944	48	**Franklin D. Roosevelt**	Democratic	25,606,585	53.5	432	55.9
		Thomas E. Dewey	Republican	22,014,745	46.0	99	
1948	48	**Harry S Truman**	Democratic	24,179,345	49.6	303	53.0
		Thomas E. Dewey	Republican	21,991,291	45.1	189	
		J. Strom Thurmond	States' Rights	1,176,125	2.4	39	
		Henry A. Wallace	Progressive	1,157,326	2.4		
1952	48	**Dwight D. Eisenhower**	Republican	33,936,234	55.1	442	63.3
		Adlai E. Stevenson	Democratic	27,314,992	44.4	89	
1956	48	**Dwight D. Eisenhower**	Republican	35,590,472	57.6	457	60.6
		Adlai E. Stevenson	Democratic	26,022,752	42.1	73	
1960	50	**John F. Kennedy**	Democratic	34,226,731	49.7	303	62.8
		Richard M. Nixon	Republican	34,108,157	49.5	219	
1964	50	**Lyndon B. Johnson**	Democratic	43,129,566	61.1	486	61.7
		Barry M. Goldwater	Republican	27,178,188	38.5	52	
1968	50	**Richard M. Nixon**	Republican	31,785,480	43.4	301	60.6
		Hubert H. Humphrey	Democratic	31,275,166	42.7	191	
		George C. Wallace	American Independent	9,906,473	13.5	46	
1972	50	**Richard M. Nixon**	Republican	47,169,911	60.7	520	55.2
		George S. McGovern	Democratic	29,170,383	37.5	17	
		John G. Schmitz	American	1,099,482	1.4		
1976	50	**James E. Carter**	Democratic	40,830,763	50.1	297	53.5
		Gerald R. Ford	Republican	39,147,793	48.0	240	
1980	50	**Ronald W. Reagan**	Republican	43,899,248	50.8	489	52.6
		James E. Carter	Democratic	35,481,432	41.0	49	
		John B. Anderson	Independent	5,719,437	6.6	0	
		Ed Clark	Libertarian	920,859	1.1	0	
1984	50	**Ronald W. Reagan**	Republican	54,455,075	58.8	525	53.1
		Walter F. Mondale	Democratic	37,577,185	40.6	13	

Presidential Elections, Continued

Year	Number of States	Candidates	Parties	Popular Vote	% of Popular Vote	Electoral Vote	% Voter Participation[b]
1988	50	**George H. W. Bush**	Republican	48,901,046	53.4	426	50.2
		Michael S. Dukakis	Democratic	41,809,030	45.6	111[c]	
1992	50	**William J. Clinton**	Democratic	44,908,233	43.0	370	55.0
		George H. W. Bush	Republican	39,102,282	37.4	168	
		H. Ross Perot	Independent	19,741,048	18.9	0	
1996	50	**William J. Clinton**	Democratic	47,401,054	49.2	379	49.0
		Robert J. Dole	Republican	39,197,350	40.7	159	
		H. Ross Perot	Reform	8,085,285	8.4	0	
		Ralph Nader	Green	684,871	0.7	0	

Candidates receiving less than 1 percent of the popular vote have been omitted. Thus the percentage of popular vote given for any election year may not total 100 percent.

Before the passage of the Twelfth Amendment in 1804, the Electoral College voted for two presidential candidates; the runner-up became vice president.

Before 1824, most presidential electors were chosen by state legislatures, not by popular vote.

[a]Greeley died shortly after the election; the electors supporting him then divided their votes among minor candidates.

[b]Percent of voting-age population casting ballots.

[c]One elector from West Virginia cast her Electoral College presidential ballot for Lloyd Bentsen, the Democratic party's vice-presidential candidate.

Presidents, Vice Presidents, and Cabinet Members

Washington Administration, 1789–1797

President	George Washington	1789–1797
Vice President	John Adams	1789–1797
Secretary of State	Thomas Jefferson	1789–1793
	Edmund Randolph	1794–1795
	Timothy Pickering	1795–1797
Secretary of the Treasury	Alexander Hamilton	1789–1795
	Oliver Wolcott, Jr.	1795–1797
Secretary of War	Henry Knox	1789–1795
	Timothy Pickering	1795–1796
	James McHenry	1796–1797
Attorney General	Edmund Randolph	1789–1793
	William Bradford	1794–1795
	Charles Lee	1795–1797
Postmaster General	Samuel Osgood	1789–1791
	Timothy Pickering	1791–1795
	Joseph Habersham	1795–1797

John Adams Administration, 1797–1801

President	John Adams	1797–1801
Vice President	Thomas Jefferson	1797–1801
Secretary of State	Timothy Pickering	1797–1800
	John Marshall	1800–1801
Secretary of the Treasury	Oliver Wolcott, Jr.	1797–1800
Secretary of War	James McHenry	1797–1800
	Samuel Dexter	1800–1801
Attorney General	Charles Lee	1797–1801
Postmaster General	Joseph Habersham	1797–1801
Secretary of Navy	Benjamin Stoddert	1798–1801

Jefferson Administration, 1801–1809

President	Thomas Jefferson	1801–1809
Vice President	Aaron Burr	1801–1805
	George Clinton	1805–1809
Secretary of State	James Madison	1801–1809
Secretary of the Treasury	Samuel Dexter	1801
	Albert Gallatin	1801–1809
Secretary of War	Henry Dearborn	1801–1809
Attorney General	Levi Lincoln	1801–1804
	Robert Smith	1805
	John Breckinridge	1805–1806
	Caesar Rodney	1807–1809
Postmaster General	Joseph Habersham	1801
	Gideon Granger	1801–1809
Secretary of Navy	Benjamin Stoddert	1801
	Robert Smith	1801–1809

Madison Administration, 1809–1817

President	James Madison	1809–1817
Vice President	George Clinton	1809–1813
	Elbridge Gerry	1813–1814
Secretary of State	Robert Smith	1809–1811
	James Monroe	1811–1817
Secretary of the Treasury	Albert Gellatin	1809–1814
	George Campbell	1814
	Alexander Dallas	1814–1816
	William Crawford	1816–1817
Secretary of War	William Eustis	1809–1812
	John Armstrong	1813
	James Monroe	1814–1815
	William Crawford	1815–1816
	George Graham	1816–1817
Attorney General	Caesar Rodney	1809–1811
	William Pinkney	1811–1814
	Richard Rush	1814–1817
Postmaster General	Gideon Granger	1809–1814
	Return Meigs	1814–1817
Secretary of Navy	Paul Hamilton	1809–1813
	William Jones	1813–1814
	Benjamin Crowninshield	1815–1817

Monroe Administration, 1817–1825

President	James Monroe	1817–1825
Vice President	Daniel Tompkins	1817–1825
Secretary of State	John Quincy Adams	1817–1825

Presidents, Vice Presidents, and Cabinet Members, Continued

Secretary of the Treasury	William Crawford	1817–1825
Secretary of War	George Graham	1817
	John C. Calhoun	1817–1825
Attorney General	Richard Rush	1817
	William Wirt	1817–1825
Postmaster General	Return Meigs	1817–1823
	John McLean	1823–1825
Secretary of Navy	Benjamin Crowninshield	1817–1818
	John C. Calhoun	1818–1819
	Smith Thompson	1819–1823
	Samuel L. Southard	1823–1825

John Quincy Adams Administration, 1825–1829

President	John Quincy Adams	1825–1829
Vice President	John C. Calhoun	1825–1829
Secretary of State	Henry Clay	1825–1829
Secretary of the Treasury	Richard Rush	1825–1829
Secretary of War	James Barbour	1825–1828
	Peter Porter	1828–1829
Attorney General	William Wirt	1825–1829
Postmaster General	John McLean	1825–1829
Secretary of Navy	Samuel Southard	1825–1829

Jackson Administration, 1829–1837

President	Andrew Jackson	1829–1837
Vice President	John C. Calhoun	1829–1833
	Martin Van Buren	1833–1837
Secretary of State	Martin Van Buren	1829–1831
	Edward Livingston	1831–1833
	Louis McLane	1833–1834
	John Forsyth	1834–1837
Secretary of the Treasury	Samuel Ingham	1829–1831
	Louis McLane	1831–1833
	William Duane	1833
	Roger B. Taney	1833–1834
	Levi Woodbury	1834–1837
Secretary of War	John H. Eaton	1829–1831
	Lewis Cass	1831–1836
	Benjamin F. Butler	1836–1837
Attorney General	John M. Berrien	1829–1831
	Roger B. Taney	1831–1833
	Benjamin Butler	1833–1837
Postmaster General	William Barry	1829–1835
	Amos Kendall	1835–1837
Secretary of Navy	John Branch	1829–1831
	Levi Woodbury	1831–1834
	Mahlon Dickerson	1834–1837

Van Buren Administration, 1837–1841

President	Martin Van Buren	1837–1841
Vice President	Richard M. Johnson	1837–1841

Secretary of State	John Forsyth	1837–1841
Secretary of the Treasury	Levi Woodbury	1837–1841
Secretary of War	Joel Poinsett	1837–1841
Attorney General	Benjamin Butler	1837–1838
	Felix Grundy	1838–1840
	Henry D. Gilpin	1840–1841
Postmaster General	Amos Kendall	1837–1840
	John M. Niles	1840–1841
Secretary of Navy	Mahlon Dickerson	1837–1838
	James Paulding	1838–1841

William Harrison Administration, 1841

President	William H. Harrison	1841
Vice President	John Tyler	1841
Secretary of State	Daniel Webster	1841
Secretary of the Treasury	Thomas Ewing	1841
Secretary of War	John Bell	1841
Attorney General	John J. Crittenden	1841
Postmaster General	Francis Granger	1841
Secretary of Navy	George E. Badger	1841

Tyler Administration, 1841–1845

President	John Tyler	1841–1845
Vice President	None	
Secretary of State	Daniel Webster	1841–1843
	Abel P. Upshur	1843–1844
	John C. Calhoun	1844–1845
Secretary of the Treasury	Thomas Ewing	1841
	Walter Forward	1841–1843
	John C. Spencer	1843–1844
	George Bibb	1844–1845
Secretary of War	John Bell	1841
	John C. Spencer	1841–1843
	James M. Porter	1843–1844
	William Wilkins	1844–1845
Attorney General	John J. Crittendon	1841
	Hugh S. Legaré	1841–1843
	John Nelson	1843–1845
Postmaster General	Francis Granger	1841
	Charles Wickliffe	1841–1845
Secretary of Navy	George E. Badger	1841
	Abel P. Upshur	1841–1843
	David Henshaw	1843–1844
	Thomas Gilmer	1844
	John Y. Mason	1844–1845

Polk Administration, 1845–1849

President	James K. Polk	1845–1849
Vice President	George M. Dallas	1845–1849

Presidents, Vice Presidents, and Cabinet Members, Continued

Secretary of State	James Buchanan	1845–1849
Secretary of the Treasury	Robert J. Walker	1845–1849
Secretary of War	William L. Marcy	1845–1849
Attorney General	John Y. Mason	1845–1846
	Nathan Clifford	1846–1848
	Isaac Toucey	1848–1849
Postmaster General	Cave Johnson	1845–1849
Secretary of Navy	George Bancroft	1845–1846
	John Y. Mason	1846–1849

Taylor Administration, 1849–1850

President	Zachary Taylor	1849–1850
Vice President	Millard Fillmore	1849–1850
Secretary of State	John M. Clayton	1849–1850
Secretary of the Treasury	William Meredith	1849–1850
Secretary of War	George Crawford	1849–1850
Attorney General	Reverdy Johnson	1849–1850
Postmaster General	Jacob Collamer	1849–1850
Secretary of Navy	William Preston	1849–1850
Secretary of Interior	Thomas Ewing	1849–1850

Fillmore Administration, 1850–1853

President	Millard Fillmore	1850–1853
Vice President	None	
Secretary of State	Daniel Webster	1850–1852
	Edward Everett	1852–1853
Secretary of the Treasury	Thomas Corwin	1850–1853
Secretary of War	Charles Conrad	1850–1853
Attorney General	John J. Crittenden	1850–1853
Postmaster General	Nathan K. Hall	1850–1852
	Samuel D. Hubbard	1852–1853
Secretary of Navy	William A. Graham	1850–1852
	John P. Kennedy	1852–1853
Secretary of Interior	Thomas McKennan	1850
	Alexander Stuart	1850–1853

Pierce Administration, 1853–1857

President	Franklin Pierce	1853–1857
Vice President	William R. King	1853–1857
Secretary of State	William L. Marcy	1853–1857
Secretary of the Treasury	James Guthrie	1853–1857
Secretary of War	Jefferson Davis	1853–1857
Attorney General	Caleb Cushing	1853–1857
Postmaster General	James Campbell	1853–1857
Secretary of Navy	James C. Dobbin	1853–1857
Secretary of Interior	Robert McClelland	1853–1857

Buchanan Administration, 1857–1861

President	James Buchanan	1857–1861
Vice President	John C. Breckinridge	1857–1861
Secretary of State	Lewis Cass	1857–1860
	Jeremiah S. Black	1860–1861
Secretary of the Treasury	Howell Cobb	1857–1860
	Philip Thomas	1860–1861
	John A. Dix	1861
Secretary of War	John B. Floyd	1857–1861
	Joseph Holt	1861
Attorney General	Jeremiah S. Black	1857–1860
	Edwin M. Stanton	1860–1861
Postmaster General	Aaron V. Brown	1857–1859
	Joseph Holt	1859–1861
	Horatio King	1861
Secretary of Navy	Isaac Toucey	1857–1861
Secretary of Interior	Jacob Thompson	1857–1861

Lincoln Administration, 1861–1865

President	Abraham Lincoln	1861–1865
Vice President	Hannibal Hamlin	1861–1865
	Andrew Johnson	1865
Secretary of State	William H. Seward	1861–1865
Secretary of the Treasury	Samuel P. Chase	1861–1864
	William P. Fessenden	1864–1865
	Hugh McCulloch	1865
Secretary of War	Simon Cameron	1861–1862
	Edwin M. Stanton	1862–1865
Attorney General	Edward Bates	1861–1864
	James Speed	1864–1865
Postmaster General	Horatio King	1861
	Montgomery Blair	1861–1864
	William Dennison	1864–1865
Secretary of Navy	Gideon Welles	1861–1865
Secretary of Interior	Caleb B. Smith	1861–1863
	John P. Usher	1863–1865

Andrew Johnson Administration, 1865–1869

President	Andrew Johnson	1865–1869
Vice President	None	
Secretary of State	William H. Seward	1865–1869
Secretary of the Treasury	Hugh McCulloch	1865–1869
Secretary of War	Edwin M. Stanton	1865–1867
	Ulysses S. Grant	1867–1868
	Lorenzo Thomas	1868
	John M. Schofield	1868–1869
Attorney General	James Speed	1865–1866
	Henry Stanbery	1866–1868
	William M. Evarts	1868–1869

Presidents, Vice Presidents, and Cabinet Members, Continued

Postmaster General	William Dennison	1865–1866
	Alexander Randall	1866–1869
Secretary of Navy	Gideon Welles	1865–1869
Secretary of Interior	John P. Usher	1865
	James Harlan	1865–1866
	Orville H. Browning	1866–1869

Grant Administration, 1869–1877

President	Ulysses S. Grant	1869–1877
Vice President	Schuyler Colfax	1869–1873
	Henry Wilson	1873–1877
Secretary of State	Elihu B. Washburne	1869
	Hamilton Fish	1869–1877
Secretary of the Treasury	George S. Boutwell	1869–1873
	William Richardson	1873–1874
	Benjamin Bristow	1874–1876
	Lot M. Morrill	1876–1877
Secretary of War	John A. Rawlins	1869
	William T. Sherman	1869
	William W. Belknap	1869–1876
	Alphonso Taft	1876
	James D. Cameron	1876–1877
Attorney General	Ebenezer R. Hoar	1869–1870
	Amos T. Ackerman	1870–1871
	G. H. Williams	1871–1875
	Edwards Pierrepont	1875–1876
	Alphonso Taft	1876–1877
Postmaster General	John A. J. Creswell	1869–1874
	James W. Marshall	1874
	Marshall Jewell	1874–1876
	James N. Tyner	1876–1877
Secretary of Navy	Adolph E. Borie	1869
	George M. Robeson	1869–1877
Secretary of Interior	Jacob D. Cox	1869–1870
	Columbus Delano	1870–1875
	Zachariah Chandler	1875–1877

Hayes Administration, 1877–1881

President	Rutherford B. Hayes	1877–1881
Vice President	William A. Wheeler	1877–1881
Secretary of State	William B. Evarts	1877–1881
Secretary of the Treasury	John Sherman	1877–1881
Secretary of War	George W. McCrary	1877–1879
	Alex Ramsey	1879–1881
Attorney General	Charles Devens	1877–1881
Postmaster General	David M. Key	1877–1880
	Horace Maynard	1880–1881
Secretary of Navy	Richard W. Thompson	1877–1880
	Nathan Goff, Jr.	1881
Secretary of Interior	Carl Schurz	1877–1881

Garfield Administration, 1881

President	James A. Garfield	1881
Vice President	Chester A. Arthur	1881
Secretary of State	James G. Blaine	1881
Secretary of the Treasury	William Windom	1881
Secretary of War	Robert T. Lincoln	1881
Attorney General	Wayne MacVeagh	1881
Postmaster General	Thomas L. James	1881
Secretary of Navy	William H. Hunt	1881
Secretary of Interior	Samuel J. Kirkwood	1881

Arthur Administration, 1881–1885

President	Chester A. Arthur	1881–1885
Vice President	None	
Secretary of State	F. T. Frelinghuysen	1881–1885
Secretary of the Treasury	Charles J. Folger	1881–1884
	Walter Q. Gresham	1884
	Hugh McCulloch	1884–1885
Secretary of War	Robert T. Lincoln	1881–1885
Attorney General	Benjamin H. Brewster	1881–1885
Postmaster General	Timothy O. Howe	1881–1883
	Walter Q. Gresham	1883–1884
	Frank Hatton	1884–1885
Secretary of Navy	William H. Hunt	1881–1882
	William E. Chandler	1882–1885
Secretary of Interior	Samuel J. Kirkwood	1881–1882
	Henry M. Teller	1882–1885

Cleveland Administration, 1885–1889

President	Grover Cleveland	1885–1889
Vice President	Thomas A. Hendricks	1885–1889
Secretary of State	Thomas F. Bayard	1885–1889
Secretary of the Treasury	Daniel Manning	1885–1887
	Charles S. Fairchild	1887–1889
Secretary of War	William C. Endicott	1885–1889
Attorney General	Augustus H. Garland	1885–1889
Postmaster General	William F. Vilas	1885–1888
	Don M. Dickinson	1888–1889
Secretary of Navy	William C. Whitney	1885–1889
Secretary of Interior	Lucius Q. C. Lamar	1885–1888
	William F. Vilas	1888–1889
Secretary of Agriculture	Norman J. Colman	1889

Benjamin Harrison Administration, 1889–1893

President	Benjamin Harrison	1889–1893
Vice President	Levi P. Morton	1889–1893

Presidents, Vice Presidents, and Cabinet Members, Continued

Secretary of State	James G. Blaine	1889–1892
	John W. Foster	1892–1893
Secretary of the Treasury	William Windom	1889–1891
	Charles Foster	1891–1893
Secretary of War	Redfield Proctor	1889–1891
	Stephen B. Elkins	1891–1893
Attorney General	William H. H. Miller	1889–1891
Postmaster General	John Wanamaker	1889–1893
Secretary of Navy	Benjamin F. Tracy	1889–1893
Secretary of Interior	John W. Noble	1889–1893
Secretary of Agriculture	Jeremiah M. Rusk	1889–1893

Cleveland Administration, 1893–1897

President	Grover Cleveland	1893–1897
Vice President	Adlai E. Stevenson	1893–1897
Secretary of State	Walter Q. Gresham	1893–1895
	Richard Olney	1895–1897
Secretary of the Treasury	John G. Carlisle	1893–1897
Secretary of War	Daniel S. Lamont	1893–1897
Attorney General	Richard Olney	1893–1895
	Judson Harmon	1895–1897
Postmaster General	Wilson S. Bissell	1893–1895
	William L. Wilson	1895–1897
Secretary of Navy	Hilary A. Herbert	1893–1897
Secretary of Interior	Hoke Smith	1893–1896
	David R. Francis	1896–1897
Secretary of Agriculture	Julius S. Morton	1893–1897

McKinley Administration, 1897–1901

President	William McKinley	1897–1901
Vice President	Garret A. Hobart	1897–1901
	Theodore Roosevelt	1901
Secretary of State	John Sherman	1897–1898
	William R. Day	1898
	John Hay	1898–1901
Secretary of the Treasury	Lyman J. Gage	1897–1901
Secretary of War	Russell A. Alger	1897–1899
	Elihu Root	1899–1901
Attorney General	Joseph McKenna	1897–1898
	John W. Griggs	1898–1901
	Philander C. Knox	1901
Postmaster General	James A. Gary	1897–1898
	Charles E. Smith	1898–1901
Secretary of Navy	John D. Long	1897–1901
Secretary of Interior	Cornelius N. Bliss	1897–1899
	Ethan A. Hitchcock	1899–1901
Secretary of Agriculture	James Wilson	1897–1901

Theodore Roosevelt Administration, 1901–1909

President	Theodore Roosevelt	1901–1909
Vice President	Charles Fairbanks	1905–1909
Secretary of State	John Hay	1901–1905
	Elihu Root	1905–1909
	Robert Bacon	1909
Secretary of the Treasury	Lyman J. Gage	1901–1902
	Leslie M. Shaw	1902–1907
	George B. Cortelyou	1907–1909
Secretary of War	Elihu Root	1901–1904
	Willim H. Taft	1904–1908
	Luke E. Wright	1908–1909
Attorney General	Philander C. Knox	1901–1904
	William H. Moody	1904–1906
	Charles J. Bonaparte	1906–1909
Postmaster General	Charles E. Smith	1901–1902
	Henry C. Payne	1902–1904
	Robert J. Wynne	1904–1905
	George B. Cortelyou	1905–1907
	George von L. Meyer	1907–1909
Secretary of Navy	John D. Long	1901–1902
	William H. Moody	1902–1904
	Paul Morton	1904–1905
	Charles J. Bonaparte	1905–1906
	Victor H. Metcalf	1906–1908
	Truman H. Newberry	1908–1909
Secretary of Interior	Ethan A. Hitchcock	1901–1907
	James R. Garfield	1907–1909
Secretary of Agriculture	James Wilson	1901–1909
Secretary of Labor and Commerce	George B. Cortelyou	1903–1904
	Victor H. Metcalf	1904–1906
	Oscar S. Straus	1906–1909

Taft Administration, 1909–1913

President	William H. Taft	1909–1913
Vice President	James S. Sherman	1909–1913
Secretary of State	Philander C. Knox	1909–1913
Secretary of the Treasury	Franklin MacVeagh	1909–1913
Secretary of War	Jacob M. Dickinson	1909–1911
	Henry L. Stimson	1911–1913
Attorney General	George W. Wickersham	1909–1913
Postmaster General	Frank H. Hitchcock	1909–1913
Secretary of Navy	George von L. Meyer	1909–1913
Secretary of Interior	Richard A. Ballinger	1909–1911
	Walter L. Fisher	1911–1913
Secretary of Agriculture	James Wilson	1909–1913
Secretary of Labor and Commerce	Charles Nagel	1909–1913

Presidents, Vice Presidents, and Cabinet Members, Continued

Wilson Administration, 1913–1921

President	Woodrow Wilson	1913–1921
Vice President	Thomas R. Marshall	1913–1921
Secretary of State	William J. Bryan	1913–1915
	Robert Lansing	1915–1920
	Bainbridge Colby	1920–1921
Secretary of the Treasury	William G. McAdoo	1913–1918
	Carter Glass	1918–1920
	David F. Houston	1920–1921
Secretary of War	Lindley M. Garrison	1913–1916
	Newton D. Baker	1916–1921
Attorney General	James C. McReynolds	1913–1914
	Thomas W. Gregory	1914–1919
	A. Mitchell Palmer	1919–1921
Postmaster General	Albert S. Burleson	1913–1921
Secretary of Navy	Josephus Daniels	1913–1921
Secretary of Interior	Franklin K. Lane	1913–1920
	John B. Payne	1920–1921
Secretary of Agriculture	David F. Houston	1913–1920
	Edwin T. Meredith	1920–1921
Secretary of Commerce	William C. Redfield	1913–1919
	Joshua W. Alexander	1919–1921
Secretary of Labor	William B. Wilson	1913–1921

Harding Administration, 1921–1923

President	Warren G. Harding	1921–1923
Vice President	Calvin Coolidge	1921–1923
Secretary of State	Charles E. Hughes	1921–1923
Secretary of the Treasury	Andrew Mellon	1921–1923
Secretary of War	John W. Weeks	1921–1923
Attorney General	Harry M. Daugherty	1921–1923
Postmaster General	Will H. Hays	1921–1922
	Hubert Work	1922–1923
	Harry S. New	1923
Secretary of Navy	Edwin Denby	1921–1923
Secretary of Interior	Albert B. Fall	1921–1923
	Hubert Work	1923
Secretary of Agriculture	Henry C. Wallace	1921–1923
Secretary of Commerce	Herbert C. Hoover	1921–1923
Secretary of Labor	James J. Davis	1921–1923

Coolidge Administration, 1923–1929

President	Calvin Coolidge	1923–1929
Vice President	Charles G. Dawes	1925–1929
Secretary of State	Charles E. Hughes	1923–1925
	Frank B. Kellogg	1925–1929
Secretary of the Treasury	Andrew Mellon	1923–1929
Secretary of War	John W. Weeks	1923–1925
	Dwight F. Davis	1925–1929
Attorney General	Henry M. Daugherty	1923–1924
	Harlan F. Stone	1924–1925
	John G. Sargent	1925–1929
Postmaster General	Harry S. New	1923–1929
Secretary of Navy	Edwin Derby	1923–1924
	Curtis D. Wilbur	1924–1929
Secretary of Interior	Hubert Work	1923–1928
	Roy O. West	1928–1929
Secretary of Agriculture	Henry C. Wallace	1923–1924
	Howard M. Gore	1924–1925
	William M. Jardine	1925–1929
Secretary of Commerce	Herbert C. Hoover	1923–1928
	William F. Whiting	1928–1929
Secretary of Labor	James J. Davis	1923–1929

Hoover Administration, 1929–1933

President	Herbert C. Hoover	1929–1933
Vice President	Charles Curtis	1929–1933
Secretary of State	Henry L. Stimson	1929–1933
Secretary of the Treasury	Andrew Mellon	1929–1932
	Ogden L. Mills	1932–1933
Secretary of War	James W. Good	1929
	Patrick J. Hurley	1929–1933
Attorney General	William D. Mitchell	1929–1933
Postmaster General	Walter F. Brown	1929–1933
Secretary of Navy	Charles F. Adams	1929–1933
Secretary of Interior	Ray L. Wilbur	1929–1933
Secretary of Agriculture	Arthur M. Hyde	1929–1933
Secretary of Commerce	Robert P. Lamont	1929–1932
	Roy D. Chapin	1932–1933
Secretary of Labor	James J. Davis	1929–1930
	William N. Doak	1930–1933

Franklin D. Roosevelt Administration, 1933–1945

President	Franklin D. Roosevelt	1933–1945
Vice President	John Nance Garner	1933–1941
	Henry A. Wallace	1941–1945
	Harry S Truman	1945
Secretary of State	Cordell Hull	1933–1944
	Edward R. Stettinius, Jr.	1944–1945
Secretary of the Treasury	William H. Woodin	1933–1934
	Henry Morgenthau, Jr.	1934–1945
Secretary of War	George H. Dern	1933–1936
	Henry A. Woodring	1936–1940
	Henry L. Stimson	1940–1945
Attorney General	Homer S. Cummings	1933–1939
	Frank Murphy	1939–1940
	Robert H. Jackson	1940–1941
	Francis Biddle	1941–1945

Presidents, Vice Presidents, and Cabinet Members, Continued

Postmaster General	James A. Farley	1933–1940
	Frank C. Walker	1940–1945
Secretary of Navy	Claude A. Swanson	1933–1939
	Charles Edison	1939–1940
	Frank Knox	1940–1944
	James V. Forrestal	1944–1945
Secretary of Interior	Harold L. Ickes	1933–1945
Secretary of Agriculture	Henry A. Wallace	1933–1940
	Claude R. Wickard	1940–1945
Secretary of Commerce	Daniel C. Roper	1933–1938
	Harry L. Hopkins	1938–1940
	Jesse H. Jones	1940–1945
	Henry A. Wallace	1945
Secretary of Labor	Frances Perkins	1933–1945

Truman Administration, 1945–1953

President	Harry S Truman	1945–1953
Vice President	Alben W. Barkley	1949–1953
Secretary of State	Edward R. Stettinius, Jr.	1945
	James F. Byrnes	1945–1947
	George C. Marshall	1947–1949
	Dean G. Acheson	1949–1953
Secretary of the Treasury	Henry Morgenthau, Jr.	1945
	Fred M. Vinson	1945–1946
	John W. Snyder	1946–1953
Secretary of War	Henry L. Stimson	1945
	Robert P. Patterson	1945–1947
	Kenneth C. Royall	1947
Attorney General	Francis Biddle	1945
	Tom C. Clark	1945–1949
	J. Howard McGrath	1949–1952
	James P. McGranery	1952–1953
Postmaster General	Frank C. Walker	1945
	Robert E. Hannegan	1945–1947
	Jesse M. Donaldson	1947–1953
Secretary of Navy	James V. Forrestal	1945–1947
Secretary of Interior	Harold L. Ickes	1945–1946
	Julius A. Krug	1946–1949
	Oscar L. Chapman	1949–1953
Secretary of Agriculture	Claude R. Wickard	1945
	Clinton P. Anderson	1945–1948
	Charles F. Brannan	1948–1953
Secretary of Commerce	Henry A. Wallace	1945–1946
	W. Averell Harriman	1946–1948
	Charles W. Sawyer	1948–1953
Secretary of Labor	Frances Perkins	1945
	Lewis B. Schwellenbach	1945–1948
	Maurice J. Tobin	1948–1953
Secretary of Defense	James V. Forrestal	1947–1949
	Louis A. Johnson	1949–1950
	George C. Marshall	1950–1951
	Robert A. Lovett	1951–1953

Eisenhower Administration, 1953–1961

President	Dwight D. Eisenhower	1953–1961
Vice President	Richard M. Nixon	1953–1961
Secretary of State	John Foster Dulles	1953–1959
	Christian A. Herter	1959–1961
Secretary of the Treasury	George M. Humphrey	1953–1957
	Robert B. Anderson	1957–1961
Attorney General	Herbert Brownell, Jr.	1953–1957
	William P. Rogers	1957–1961
Postmaster General	Arthur E. Summerfield	1953–1961
Secretary of Interior	Douglas McKay	1953–1956
	Fred A. Seaton	1956–1961
Secretary of Agriculture	Ezra T. Benson	1953–1961
Secretary of Commerce	Sinclair Weeks	1953–1958
	Lewis L. Strauss	1958–1959
	Frederick H. Mueller	1959–1961
Secretary of Labor	Martin P. Durkin	1953
	James P. Mitchell	1953–1961
Secretary of Defense	Charles E. Wilson	1953–1957
	Neil H. McElroy	1957–1959
	Thomas S. Gates, Jr.	1959–1961
Secretary of Health, Education, and Welfare	Oveta Culp Hobby	1953–1955
	Marion B. Folsom	1955–1958
	Arthur S. Flemming	1958–1961

Kennedy Administration, 1961–1963

President	John F. Kennedy	1961–1963
Vice President	Lyndon B. Johnson	1961–1963
Secretary of State	Dean Rusk	1961–1963
Secretary of the Treasury	C. Douglas Dillon	1961–1963
Attorney General	Robert F. Kennedy	1961–1963
Postmaster General	J. Edward Day	1961–1963
	John A. Gronouski	1963
Secretary of Interior	Stewart L. Udall	1961–1963
Secretary of Agriculture	Orville L. Freeman	1961–1963
Secretary of Commerce	Luther H. Hodges	1961–1963
Secretary of Labor	Arthur J. Goldberg	1961–1962
	W. Willard Wirtz	1962–1963
Secretary of Defense	Robert S. McNamara	1961–1963
Secretary of Health, Education, and Welfare	Abraham A. Ribicoff	1961–1962
	Anthony J. Celebrezze	1962–1963

Lyndon B. Johnson Administration, 1963–1969

President	Lyndon B. Johnson	1963–1969
Vice President	Hubert H. Humphrey	1965–1969

Presidents, Vice Presidents, and Cabinet Members, Continued

Secretary of State	Dean Rusk	1963–1969		Secretary of Defense	Melvin R. Laird	1969–1973
Secretary of the Treasury	C. Douglas Dillon	1963–1965			Elliot L. Richardson	1973
	Henry H. Fowler	1965–1969			James R. Schlesinger	1973–1974
Attorney General	Robert F. Kennedy	1963–1964		Secretary of Health,	Robert H. Finch	1969–1970
	Nicholas Katzenbach	1965–1966		Education, and	Elliot L. Richardson	1970–1973
	Ramsey Clark	1967–1969		Welfare	Casper W. Weinberger	1973–1974
Postmaster General	John A. Gronouski	1963–1965		Secretary of Housing	George Romney	1969–1973
	Lawrence F. O'Brien	1965–1968		and Urban	James T. Lynn	1973–1974
	Marvin Watson	1968–1969		Development		
Secretary of Interior	Stewart L. Udall	1963–1969		Secretary of	John A. Volpe	1969–1973
Secretary of Agriculture	Orville L. Freeman	1963–1969		Transportation	Claude S. Brinegar	1973–1974

Ford Administration, 1974–1977

Secretary of Commerce	Luther H. Hodges	1963–1964				
	John T. Connor	1964–1967		President	Gerald R. Ford	1974–1977
	Alexander B. Trowbridge	1967–1968		Vice President	Nelson A. Rockefeller	1974–1977
	Cyrus R. Smith	1968–1969		Secretary of State	Henry A. Kissinger	1974–1977
Secretary of Labor	W. Willard Wirtz	1963–1969		Secretary of the Treasury	William E. Simon	1974–1977
Secretary of Defense	Robert F. McNamara	1963–1968		Attorney General	William Saxbe	1974–1975
	Clark Clifford	1968–1969			Edward Levi	1975–1977
Secretary of Health,	Anthony J. Celebrezze	1963–1965		Secretary of Interior	Rogers Morton	1974–1975
Education, and	John W. Gardner	1965–1968			Stanley K. Hathaway	1975
Welfare	Wilbur J. Cohen	1968–1969			Thomas Kleppe	1975–1977
Secretary of Housing	Robert C. Weaver	1966–1969		Secretary of	Earl L. Butz	1974–1976
and Urban	Robert C. Wood	1969		Agriculture	John A. Knebel	1976–1977
Development				Secretary of	Frederick B. Dent	1974–1975
Secretary of	Alan S. Boyd	1967–1969		Commerce	Rogers Morton	1975–1976
Transportation					Elliot L. Richardson	1976–1977

Nixon Administration, 1969–1974

				Secretary of Labor	Peter J. Brennan	1974–1975
President	Richard M. Nixon	1969–1974			John T. Dunlop	1975–1976
Vice President	Spiro T. Agnew	1969–1973			W. J. Usery	1976–1977
	Gerald R. Ford	1973–1974		Secretary of Defense	James R. Schlesinger	1974–1975
Secretary of State	William P. Rogers	1969–1973			Donald Rumsfeld	1975–1977
	Henry A. Kissinger	1973–1974		Secretary of Health,	Casper Weinberger	1974–1975
Secretary of the Treasury	David M. Kennedy	1969–1970		Education, and	Forrest D. Mathews	1975–1977
	John B. Connally	1971–1972		Welfare		
	George P. Shultz	1972–1974		Secretary of Housing	James T. Lynn	1974–1975
	William E. Simon	1974		and Urban	Carla A. Hills	1975–1977
Attorney General	John N. Mitchell	1969–1972		Development		
	Richard G. Kleindienst	1972–1973		Secretary of	Claude Brinegar	1974–1975
	Elliot L. Richardson	1973		Transportation	William T. Coleman	1975–1977
	William B. Saxbe	1973–1974				
Postmaster General	Winton M. Blount	1969–1971				

Carter Administration, 1977–1981

Secretary of Interior	Walter J. Hickel	1969–1970				
	Rogers Morton	1971–1974		President	James E. Carter	1977–1981
Secretary of	Clifford M. Hardin	1969–1971		Vice President	Walter F. Mondale	1977–1981
Agriculture	Earl L. Butz	1971–1974		Secretary of State	Cyrus R. Vance	1977–1980
Secretary of	Maurice H. Stans	1969–1972			Edmund Muskie	1980–1981
Commerce	Peter G. Peterson	1972–1973		Secretary of the Treasury	W. Michael Blumenthal	1977–1979
	Frederick B. Dent	1973–1974			G. William Miller	1979–1981
Secretary of Labor	George P. Shultz	1969–1970		Attorney General	Griffin Bell	1977–1979
	James D. Hodgson	1970–1973			Benjamin R. Civiletti	1979–1981
	Peter J. Brennan	1973–1974		Secretary of Interior	Cecil D. Andrus	1977–1981

Presidents, Vice Presidents, and Cabinet Members, Continued

Secretary of Agriculture	Robert Bergland	1977–1981
Secretary of Commerce	Juanita M. Kreps	1977–1979
	Philip M. Klutznick	1979–1981
Secretary of Labor	F. Ray Marshall	1977–1981
Secretary of Defense	Harold Brown	1977–1981
Secretary of Health, Education, and Welfare	Joseph A. Califano	1977–1979
	Patricia R. Harris	1979
Secretary of Health and Human Services	Patricia R. Harris	1979–1981
Secretary of Education	Shirley M. Hufstedler	1979–1981
Secretary of Housing and Urban Development	Patricia R. Harris	1977–1979
	Moon Landrieu	1979–1981
Secretary of Transportation	Brock Adams	1977–1979
	Neil E. Goldschmidt	1979–1981
Secretary of Energy	James R. Schlesinger	1977–1979
	Charles W. Duncan	1979–1981

Reagan Administration, 1981–1989

President	Ronald W. Reagan	1981–1989
Vice President	George H. W. Bush	1981–1989
Secretary of State	Alexander M. Haig	1981–1982
	George P. Shultz	1982–1989
Secretary of the Treasury	Donald Regan	1981–1985
	James A. Baker III	1985–1988
	Nicholas F. Brady	1988–1989
Attorney General	William F. Smith	1981–1985
	Edwin A. Meese III	1985–1988
	Richard L. Thornburgh	1988–1989
Secretary of Interior	James G. Watt	1981–1983
	William P. Clark, Jr.	1983–1985
	Donald P. Hodel	1985–1989
Secretary of Agriculture	John Block	1981–1986
	Richard E. Lyng	1986–1989
Secretary of Commerce	Malcolm Baldridge	1981–1987
	C. William Verity, Jr.	1987–1989
Secretary of Labor	Raymond J. Donovan	1981–1985
	William E. Brock	1985–1987
	Ann Dore McLaughlin	1987–1989
Secretary of Defense	Casper Weinberger	1981–1987
	Frank C. Carlucci	1987–1989
Secretary of Health and Human Services	Richard S. Schweiker	1981–1983
	Margaret Heckler	1983–1985
	Otis R. Bowen	1985–1989
Secretary of Education	Terrel H. Bell	1981–1984
	William J. Bennett	1985–1988
	Lauro F. Cavazos	1988–1989

Secretary of Housing and Urban Development	Samuel R. Pierce, Jr.	1981–1989
Secretary of Transportation	Drew Lewis	1981–1982
	Elizabeth Hanford Dole	1983–1987
	James H. Burnley IV	1987–1989
Secretary of Energy	James B. Edwards	1981–1982
	Donald P. Hodel	1982–1985
	John S. Herrington	1985–1989

Bush Administration, 1989–1993

President	George H. W. Bush	1989–1993
Vice President	J. Danforth Quayle	1989–1993
Secretary of State	James A. Baker III	1989–1992
	Lawrence Eagleburger	1992–1993
Secretary of the Treasury	Nicholas F. Brady	1989–1993
Attorney General	Richard L. Thornburgh	1989–1991
	William P. Barr	1991–1993
Secretary of Interior	Manuel Lujan, Jr.	1989–1993
Secretary of Agriculture	Clayton K. Yeutter	1989–1991
	Edward Madigan	1991–1993
Secretary of Commerce	Robert A. Mosbacher	1989–1992
	Barbara Hackman Franklin	1992–1993
Secretary of Labor	Elizabeth Hanford Dole	1989–1991
	Lynn Martin	1991–1993
Secretary of Defense	Richard B. Cheney	1989–1993
Secretary of Health and Human Services	Louis W. Sullivan	1989–1993
Secretary of Education	Lauro F. Cavazos	1989–1990
	Lamar Alexander	1991–1993
Secretary of Housing and Urban Development	Jack F. Kemp	1989–1993
Secretary of Transportation	Samuel K. Skinner	1989–1992
	Andrew H. Card	1992–1993
Secretary of Energy	James D. Watkins	1989–1993
Secretary of Veterans Affairs	Edward J. Derwinski	1989–1993

Clinton Administration, 1993–

President	William J. Clinton	1993–
Vice President	Albert Gore	1993–
Secretary of State	Warren M. Christopher	1993–1997
	Madeleine K. Albright	1997–
Secretary of the Treasury	Lloyd Bentsen	1993–1995
	Robert E. Rubin	1995–
Attorney General	Janet Reno	1993–
Secretary of Interior	Bruce Babbitt	1993–

Presidents, Vice Presidents, and Cabinet Members, Continued

Secretary of Agriculture	Mike Espy	1993–1995	Secretary of Education	Richard W. Riley	1993–
	Daniel R. Glickman	1995–			
Secretary of Commerce	Ronald H. Brown	1993–1996	Secretary of Housing and Urban Development	Henry G. Cisneros	1993–1996
	Mickey Kantor	1996–1997		Andrew Cuomo	1997–
	William Daley	1997–			
Secretary of Labor	Robert B. Reich	1993–1997	Secretary of Transportation	Federico F. Peña	1993–1997
	Alexis M. Herman	1997–		Rodney E. Slater	1997–
Secretary of Defense	Les Aspin	1993–1994	Secretary of Energy	Hazel O'Leary	1993–1997
	William J. Perry	1994–1997		Federico F. Peña	1997–
	William S. Cohen	1997–	Secretary of Veterans Affairs	Jesse Brown	1993–
Secretary of Health and Human Services	Donna E. Shalala	1993–			

Party Strength in Congress

Period	Congress	House Majority Party		House Minority Party		Others	Senate Majority Party		Senate Minority Party		Others	Party of President	
1789–91	1st	Ad	38	Op	26		Ad	17	Op	9		F	Washington
1791–93	2nd	F	37	DR	33		F	16	DR	13		F	Washington
1793–95	3rd	DR	57	F	48		F	17	DR	13		F	Washington
1795–97	4th	F	54	DR	52		F	19	DR	13		F	Washington
1797–99	5th	F	58	DR	48		F	20	DR	12		F	J. Adams
1799–1801	6th	F	64	DR	42		F	19	DR	13		F	J. Adams
1801–03	7th	DR	69	F	36		DR	18	F	13		DR	Jefferson
1803–05	8th	DR	102	F	39		DR	25	F	9		DR	Jefferson
1805–07	9th	DR	116	F	25		DR	27	F	7		DR	Jefferson
1807–09	10th	DR	118	F	24		DR	28	F	6		DR	Jefferson
1809–11	11th	DR	94	F	48		DR	28	F	6		DR	Madison
1811–13	12th	DR	108	F	36		DR	30	F	6		DR	Madison
1813–15	13th	DR	112	F	68		DR	27	F	9		DR	Madison
1815–17	14th	DR	117	F	65		DR	25	F	11		DR	Madison
1817–19	15th	DR	141	F	42		DR	34	F	10		DR	Monroe
1819–21	16th	DR	156	F	27		DR	35	F	7		DR	Monroe
1821–23	17th	DR	158	F	25		DR	44	F	4		DR	Monroe
1823–25	18th	DR	187	F	26		DR	44	F	4		DR	Monroe
1825–27	19th	Ad	105	J	97		Ad	26	J	20		C	J. Q. Adams
1827–29	20th	J	119	Ad	94		J	28	Ad	20		C	J. Q. Adams
1829–31	21st	D	139	NR	74		D	26	NR	22		D	Jackson
1831–33	22nd	D	141	NR	58	14	D	25	NR	21	2	D	Jackson
1833–35	23rd	D	147	AM	53	60	D	20	NR	20	8	D	Jackson
1835–37	24th	D	145	W	98		D	27	W	25		D	Jackson
1837–39	25th	D	108	W	107	24	D	30	W	18	4	D	Van Buren
1839–41	26th	D	124	W	118		D	28	W	22		D	Van Buren
1841–43	27th	W	133	D	102	6	W	28	D	22	2	W	W. Harrison
												W	Tyler
1843–45	28th	D	142	W	79	1	W	28	D	25	1	W	Tyler
1845–47	29th	D	143	W	77	6	D	31	W	25		D	Polk
1847–49	30th	W	115	D	108	4	D	36	W	21	1	D	Polk
1849–51	31st	D	112	W	109	9	D	35	W	25	2	W	Taylor
												W	Fillmore
1851–53	32nd	D	140	W	88	5	D	35	W	24	3	W	Fillmore
1853–55	33rd	D	159	W	71	4	D	38	W	22	2	D	Pierce
1855–57	34th	R	108	D	83	43	D	40	R	15	5	D	Pierce
1857–59	35th	D	118	R	92	26	D	36	R	20	8	D	Buchanan

Party Strength in Congress, Continued

		House				Senate				Party of
Period	Congress	Majority Party		Minority Party	Others	Majority Party		Minority Party	Others	President
1859–61	36th	R	114	D	92	31	D	36	R	26	4	D	Buchanan
1861–63	37th	R	105	D	43	30	R	31	D	10	8	R	Lincoln
1863–65	38th	R	102	D	75	9	R	36	D	9	5	R	Lincoln
1865–67	39th	U	149	D	42		U	42	D	10		R	Lincoln
											R	A. Johnson
1867–69	40th	R	143	D	49		R	42	D	11		R	A. Johnson
1869–71	41st	R	149	D	63		R	56	D	11		R	Grant
1871–73	42nd	R	134	D	104	5	R	52	D	17	5	R	Grant
1873–75	43rd	R	194	D	92	14	R	49	D	19	5	R	Grant
1875–77	44th	D	169	R	109	14	R	45	D	29	2	R	Grant
1877–79	45th	D	153	R	140		R	39	D	36	1	R	Hayes
1879–81	46th	D	149	R	130	14	D	42	R	33	1	R	Hayes
1881–83	47th	D	147	R	135	11	R	37	D	37	1	R	Garfield
											R	Arthur
1883–85	48th	D	197	R	118	10	R	38	D	36	2	R	Arthur
1885–87	49th	D	183	R	140	2	R	43	D	34		D	Cleveland
1887–89	50th	D	169	R	152	4	R	39	D	37		D	Cleveland
1889–91	51st	R	166	D	159		R	39	D	37		R	B. Harrison
1891–93	52nd	D	235	R	88	9	R	47	D	39	2	R	B. Harrison
1893–95	53rd	D	218	R	127	11	D	44	R	38	3	D	Cleveland
1895–97	54th	R	244	D	105	7	R	43	D	39	6	D	Cleveland
1897–99	55th	R	204	D	113	40	R	47	D	34	7	R	McKinley
1899–1901	56th	R	185	D	163	9	R	53	D	26	8	R	McKinley
1901–03	57th	R	197	D	151	9	R	55	D	31	4	R	McKinley
											R	T. Roosevelt
1903–05	58th	R	208	D	178		R	57	D	33		R	T. Roosevelt
1905–07	59th	R	250	D	136		R	57	D	33		R	T. Roosevelt
1907–09	60th	R	222	D	164		R	61	D	31		R	T. Roosevelt
1909–11	61st	R	219	D	172		R	61	D	32		R	Taft
1911–13	62nd	D	228	R	161	1	R	51	D	41		R	Taft
1913–15	63rd	D	291	R	127	17	D	51	R	44	1	D	Wilson
1915–17	64th	D	230	R	196	9	D	56	R	40		D	Wilson
1917–19	65th	D	216	R	210	6	D	53	R	42		D	Wilson
1919–21	66th	R	240	D	190	3	R	49	D	47		D	Wilson
1921–23	67th	R	301	D	131	1	R	59	D	37		R	Harding
1923–25	68th	R	225	D	205	5	R	51	D	43	2	R	Coolidge
1925–27	69th	R	247	D	183	4	R	56	D	39	1	R	Coolidge
1927–29	70th	R	237	D	195	3	R	49	D	46	1	R	Coolidge
1929–31	71st	R	267	D	167	1	R	56	D	39	1	R	Hoover
1931–33	72nd	D	220	R	214	1	R	48	D	47	1	R	Hoover
1933–35	73rd	D	310	R	117	5	D	60	R	35	1	D	F. Roosevelt
1935–37	74th	D	319	R	103	10	D	69	R	25	2	D	F. Roosevelt
1937–39	75th	D	331	R	89	13	D	76	R	16	4	D	F. Roosevelt
1939–41	76th	D	261	R	164	4	D	69	R	23	4	D	F. Roosevelt
1941–43	77th	D	268	R	162	5	D	66	R	28	2	D	F. Roosevelt
1943–45	78th	D	218	R	208	4	D	58	R	37	1	D	F. Roosevelt
1945–47	79th	D	242	R	190	2	D	56	R	38	1	D	Truman

Party Strength in Congress, Continued

Period	Congress	House Majority Party		House Minority Party		Others	Senate Majority Party		Senate Minority Party		Others	Party of President	
1947–49	80th	R	245	D	188	1	R	51	D	45		D	Truman
1949–51	81st	D	263	R	171	1	D	54	R	42		D	Truman
1951–53	82nd	D	234	R	199	1	D	49	R	47		D	Truman
1953–55	83rd	R	221	D	211	1	R	48	D	47	1	R	Eisenhower
1955–57	84th	D	232	R	203		D	48	R	47	1	R	Eisenhower
1957–59	85th	D	233	R	200		D	49	R	47		R	Eisenhower
1959–61	86th	D	284	R	153		D	65	R	35		R	Eisenhower
1961–63	87th	D	263	R	174		D	65	R	35		D	Kennedy
1963–65	88th	D	258	R	117		D	67	R	33		D	Kennedy
												D	L. Johnson
1965–67	89th	D	295	R	140		D	68	R	32		D	L. Johnson
1967–69	90th	D	246	R	187		D	64	R	36		D	L. Johnson
1969–71	91st	D	245	R	189		D	57	R	43		R	Nixon
1971–73	92nd	D	254	R	180		D	54	R	44	2	R	Nixon
1973–75	93rd	D	239	R	192	1	D	56	R	42	2	R	Nixon
1975–77	94th	D	291	R	144		D	60	R	37	3	R	Ford
1977–79	95th	D	292	R	143		D	61	R	38	1	D	Carter
1979–81	96th	D	276	R	157		D	58	R	41	1	D	Carter
1981–83	97th	D	243	R	192		R	53	D	46	1	R	Reagan
1983–85	98th	D	267	R	168		R	55	D	45		R	Reagan
1985–87	99th	D	253	R	182		R	53	D	47		R	Reagan
1987–89	100th	D	258	R	177		D	55	R	45		R	Reagan
1989–91	101st	D	259	R	174		D	54	R	46		R	Bush
1991–93	102nd	D	267	R	167	1	D	56	R	44		R	Bush
1993–95	103rd	D	258	R	176	1	D	56	R	44		D	Clinton
1995–97	104th	R	230	D	204	1	R	52	D	48		D	Clinton
1997–99	105th	R	227	D	207	1	R	55	D	45		D	Clinton

AD = Administration; AM = Anti-Masonic; C = Coalition; D = Democratic; DR = Democratic-Republican; F = Federalist; J = Jacksonian; NR = National Republican; Op = Opposition; R = Republican; U = Unionist; W = Whig. Figures are for the beginning of first session of each Congress, except the 93rd, which are for the beginning of the second session.

Justices of the
Supreme Court

	Term of Service	Years of Service	Life Span		Term of Service	Years of Service	Life Span
John Jay	1789–1795	5	1745–1829	*Salmon P. Chase*	1864–1873	8	1808–1873
John Rutledge	1789–1791	1	1739–1800	William Strong	1870–1880	10	1808–1895
William Cushing	1789–1810	20	1732–1810	Joseph P. Bradley	1870–1892	22	1813–1892
James Wilson	1789–1798	8	1742–1798	Ward Hunt	1873–1882	9	1810–1886
John Blair	1789–1796	6	1732–1800	*Morrison R. Waite*	1874–1888	14	1816–1888
Robert H. Harrison	1789–1790	—	1745–1790	John M. Harlan	1877–1911	34	1833–1911
James Iredell	1790–1799	9	1951–1799	William B. Woods	1880–1887	7	1824–1887
Thomas Johnson	1791–1793	1	1732–1819	Stanley Mathews	1881–1889	7	1824–1889
William Paterson	1793–1806	13	1745–1806	Horace Gray	1882–1902	20	1828–1902
*John Rutledge**	1795	—	1739–1800	Samuel Blatchford	1882–1893	11	1820–1893
Samuel Chase	1796–1811	15	1741–1811	Lucius Q. C. Lamar	1888–1893	5	1825–1893
Oliver Ellsworth	1796–1800	4	1745–1807	*Melville W. Fuller*	1888–1910	21	1833–1910
Bushrod Washington	1798–1829	31	1762–1829	David J. Brewer	1890–1910	20	1837–1910
Alfred Moore	1799–1804	4	1755–1810	Henry B. Brown	1890–1906	16	1836–1913
John Marshall	1801–1835	34	1755–1835	George Shiras, Jr.	1892–1903	10	1832–1924
William Johnson	1804–1834	30	1771–1834	Howell E. Jackson	1893–1895	2	1832–1895
H. Brockholst Livingston	1806–1823	16	1757–1823	Edward D. White	1894–1910	16	1845–1921
Thomas Todd	1807–1826	18	1765–1826	Rufus W. Peckham	1895–1909	14	1838–1909
Joseph Story	1811–1845	33	1779–1845	Joseph McKenna	1898–1925	26	1843–1926
Gabriel Duval	1811–1835	24	1752–1844	Oliver W. Holmes	1902–1932	30	1841–1935
Smith Thompson	1823–1843	20	1768–1843	William D. Day	1903–1922	19	1849–1923
Robert Trimble	1826–1828	2	1777–1828	William H. Moody	1906–1910	3	1853–1917
John McLean	1829–1861	32	1785–1861	Horace H. Lurton	1910–1914	4	1844–1914
Henry Baldwin	1830–1844	14	1780–1844	Charles E. Hughes	1910–1916	5	1862–1948
James M. Wayne	1835–1867	32	1790–1867	Willis Van Devanter	1911–1937	26	1859–1941
Roger B. Taney	1836–1864	28	1777–1864	Joseph R. Lamar	1911–1916	5	1857–1916
Philip P. Barbour	1836–1841	4	1783–1841	*Edward D. White*	1910–1921	11	1845–1921
John Catron	1837–1865	28	1786–1865	Mahlon Pitney	1912–1922	10	1858–1924
John McKinley	1837–1852	15	1780–1852	James C. McReynolds	1914–1941	26	1862–1946
Peter V. Daniel	1841–1860	19	1784–1860	Louis D. Brandeis	1916–1939	22	1856–1941
Samuel Nelson	1845–1872	27	1792–1873	John H. Clarke	1916–1922	6	1857–1945
Levi Woodbury	1845–1851	5	1789–1851	*William H. Taft*	1921–1930	8	1857–1930
Robert C. Grier	1846–1870	23	1794–1870	George Sutherland	1922–1938	15	1862–1942
Benjamin R. Curtis	1851–1857	6	1809–1874	Pierce Butler	1922–1939	16	1866–1939
John A. Campbell	1853–1861	8	1811–1889	Edward T. Sanford	1923–1930	7	1865–1930
Nathan Clifford	1858–1881	23	1803–1881	Harlan F. Stone	1925–1941	16	1872–1946
Noah H. Swayne	1862–1881	18	1804–1884	*Charles E. Hughes*	1930–1941	11	1862–1948
Samuel F. Miller	1862–1890	28	1816–1890	Owen J. Roberts	1930–1945	15	1875–1955
David Davis	1862–1877	14	1815–1886	Benjamin N. Cardozo	1932–1938	6	1870–1938
Stephen J. Field	1863–1897	34	1816–1899	Hugo L. Black	1937–1971	34	1886–1971

Justices of the Supreme Court, Continued

	Term of Service	Years of Service	Life Span		Term of Service	Years of Service	Life Span
Stanley F. Reed	1938–1957	19	1884–1980	Byron R. White	1962–1993	31	1917–
Felix Frankfurter	1939–1962	23	1882–1965	Arthur J. Goldberg	1962–1965	3	1908–1990
William O. Douglas	1939–1975	36	1898–1980	Abe Fortas	1965–1969	4	1910–1982
Frank Murphy	1940–1949	9	1890–1949	Thurgood Marshall	1967–1991	24	1908–1993
Harlan F. Stone	1941–1946	5	1872–1946	*Warren C. Burger*	1969–1986	17	1907–1995
James F. Byrnes	1941–1942	1	1879–1972	Harry A. Blackmun	1970–1994	24	1908–
Robert H. Jackson	1941–1954	13	1892–1954	Lewis F. Powell, Jr.	1972–1987	15	1907–
Wiley B. Rutledge	1943–1949	6	1894–1949	*William H. Rehnquist*	1972–	—	1924–
Harold H. Burton	1945–1958	13	1888–1964	John P. Stevens III	1975–	—	1920–
Fred M. Vinson	1946–1953	7	1890–1953	Sandra Day O'Connor	1981–	—	1930–
Tom C. Clark	1949–1967	18	1899–1977	Antonin Scalia	1986–	—	1936–
Sherman Minton	1949–1956	7	1890–1965	Anthony M. Kennedy	1988–	—	1936–
Earl Warren	1953–1969	16	1891–1974	David H. Souter	1990–	—	1939–
John Marshall Harlan	1955–1971	16	1899–1971	Clarence Thomas	1991–	—	1948–
William J. Brennan, Jr.	1956–1990	34	1906–	Ruth Bader Ginsburg	1993–	—	1933–
Charles E. Whittaker	1957–1962	5	1901–1973	Stephen Breyer	1994–	—	1938–
Potter Stewart	1958–1981	23	1915–1985				

*Appointed and served one term, but not confirmed by the Senate.

Note: Chief justices are in italics.

Index